About Integral Research

---

*"The authors Lessem and Schieffer have written this remarkable book on
"Research Methodology" which is responsive to all relevant stakeholders.
Researchers from the North, the South, the East and the West are now able
to draw on their own roots to turn social research into social innovation.
A major achievement!"*

Prof. Dr. Martin Hilb
Managing Director of the Institute for Leadership and Human Resource Management,
University of St. Gallen, Switzerland

---

*"A landmark contribution of social and management research scholarship
conceptually and methodologically. A readable and rigorous book, which is
characterised by comprehensiveness, insights, structure and clarity; and which is
aided by informative executive summaries, figures and illustrations. The book
represents a coherent interpretation and a reliable reference of key and diverse
classical and contemporary schools of research philosophy and methodology. It is a
timely and pioneering book which successfully demonstrates the intellectual and the
practical grounds of 'social innovation' and which convincingly argues for the
beneficial employment of the so long neglected philosophical and conceptual
contributions of South and East in social and management research scholarship. I
strongly believe that the book's provocative, grounded and convincing arguments will
extend the horizons of prevailing research thoughts and practices and would leave a
positive impact on social and management research scholarships and students."*

Prof. Adel Rasheed
Professor of Management, Yarmouk University, Irbid, Jordan

---

*"Ronnie Lessem and Alexander Schieffer have developed a bold new way of
framing transformation processes that crosses the boundaries of several disciplines.
Their 'integral approach' offers a novel analysis that cleverly bridges
research and social innovation. Their way of generating innovation
provides a valuable road map that enables change agents to creatively
synthesize local identities and global context."*

Prof. Dr. Raoul C. D. Nacamulli
Università di Milano-Bicocca, Italy

Integral Research

Integral Research

*A Global Approach towards
Social Science Research
leading to Social Innovation*

Ronnie Lessem & Alexander Schieffer

TRANS ④ M

Four World Center for Social Innovation

Ronnie Lessem, Professor of Transcultural Management at the University of Buckingham, UK, and **Alexander Schieffer**, Lecturer at the University of St. Gallen, Switzerland and an international consultant on leadership and organisational change, have jointly set up the TRANS4M Four World Center for Social Innovation in Geneva. TRANS4M is a research, education and practice based organisation with a specific focus on Social Innovation and Transformation Management, which has developed one of the most innovative (and globally tested) approaches in this field.

© 2008 by TRANS4M Publishing, Geneva

Integral Research: A Global Approach towards
Social Science Research leading to Social Innovation

TRANS4M
Four World Center for Social Innovation
www.trans-4-m.com
Geneva – Switzerland

Cover Design & Layout: Simone Holstein
Production: Books on Demand GmbH, Norderstedt

ISBN 978-3-033-01538-8

CONTENT OVERVIEW

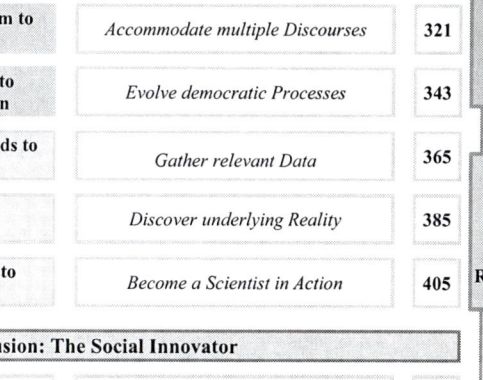

The Southern „Relational Path"

The Eastern „Path of Renewal"

The Northern „Path of Reason"

The Western "Path of Realisation"

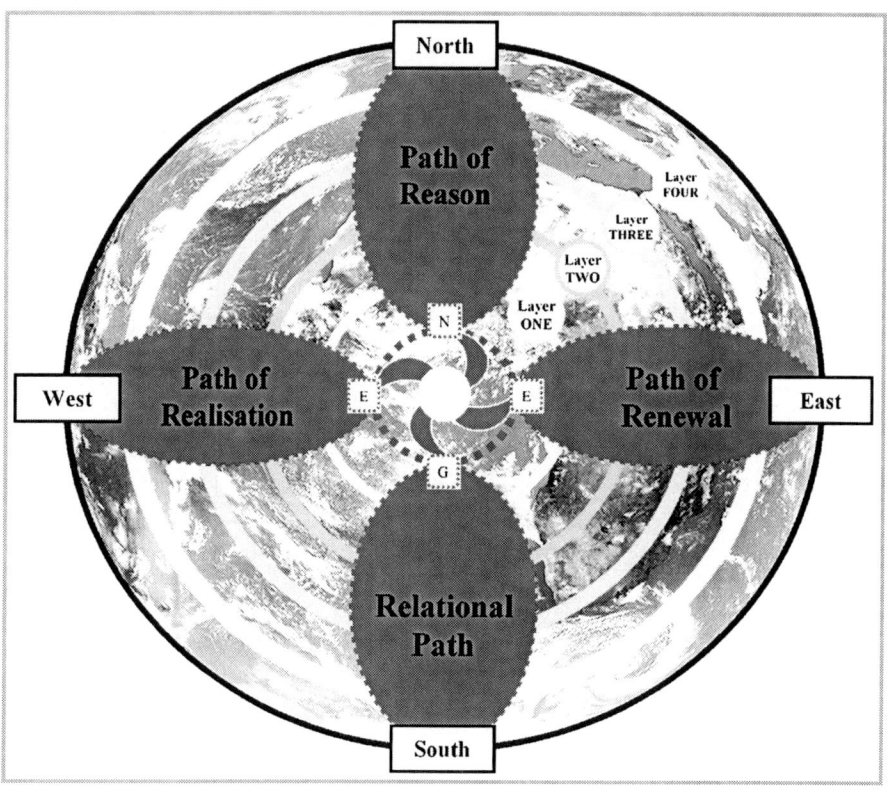

INTEGRAL RESEARCH
Detailed Framework

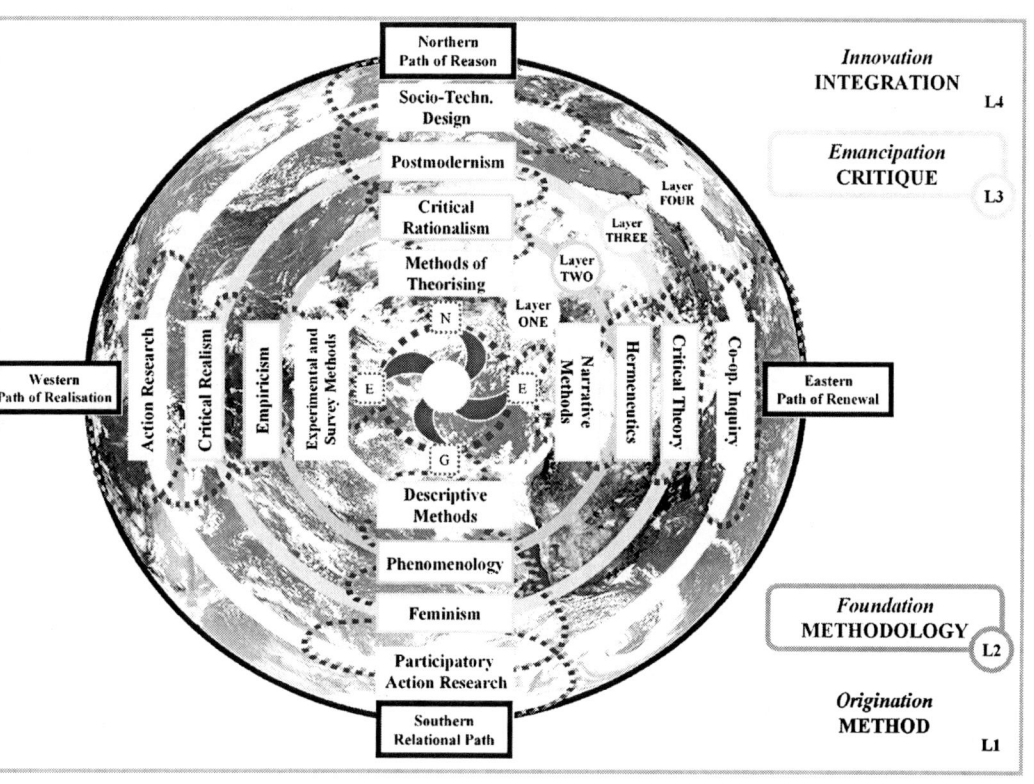

PROLOGUE

HOW CAN RESEARCH
BE TURNED INTO INNOVATION?

**In this book we pursue the following question:
How can research be turned into social innovation?**

Our book is aimed at all of those students and practitioners, individuals together with their institutions, wishing to undertake research leading to innovation in the social sciences. Such research should be transformative, rather than, as it often turns out to be, merely informative!

Most of the research in the social sciences, particularly in business, management and economics, has lost touch with its "social essence": It is guided by rationalism and pragmatism, while humanism and holism have been left out of account. And it does not contribute to the resolution of the burning social issues of our time.

It may seem at first far fetched to link the state of our turbulent world with that of qualitative "research methodology". However, as we shall be revealing in this book, the state of the two is intimately connected. That point of connection, or indeed lack of it, is the bridge or gap between informative and transformative, ultimately innovative research. What links the two is what makes research "integral".

To build up such an integral orientation towards "research as social innovation", the book draws both on a relatively rational and pragmatic perspective from Europe and America, and also upon a more humanistic and holistic one, coming from Africa and the Middle, Near as well as Far East. These latter perspectives tend to be more transformative than the former.

Moreover, "methodology" is "integral" to the approach to research we pursue here, in that it is connected with the whole of the research process: it spans your research question, literature search and fieldwork, rather than being separated off for particular and isolated "methodological" concern. It also becomes not only an educational process, but also a socio-political one, with a strong transformative and ultimately innovative edge.

Our own life stories serve as a backdrop to such an integral approach. One of the authors (Ronnie Lessem) was born and bred in southern Africa, while being educated in economics and management in Europe and America, as well as significantly influenced by the Middle and Near East. He is now active in the Middle East, America and Africa as a social innovator. The other author (Alexander Schieffer) was born, bred and educated in Europe, while also being significantly influenced by the Far East, having run his own business in Singapore. Moreover, he is now active, as a university lecturer and business consultant – and together with Ronnie Lessem also as a social innovator – in Germany and Switzerland as well as in China, more recently also in South Africa and Jordan. So this integral orientation comes naturally to us, combining the informative and analytical orientation of the "north", with the transformative and socio-political orientation of the "south", albeit tempered by "east" and "west". As such, we are together involved with masters and doctoral programmes – all aimed at social innovation – spanning major world regions.

With Integral Research we are now introducing an integral research framework and process leading to Social Innovation

Within this framework we are pursuing four so-called "southern" and "eastern", "northern" and "western" research paths, that we term respectively relational (humanistic), renewal (holistic), reason (rational) and realisation (pragmatic). Each of these paths takes you, the researcher, through four layers (method, methodology, critique and integration), ultimately resulting in social innovation.

Integral Research addresses Social Sciences Researchers from all over the world, who aim to become Social Innovators

Next to general practitioners in social science research, we are in particular addressing the following groups, each with a slightly different focus and a different degree of participation with other researchers as the following graph illustrates:

Integral Research: Main Audience		
Target Audience	**Focus**	**Individual versus Collective Research**
Masters Students (in masters programmes with a transformative edge)	**Focus on the outer Layer:** Focus on the outer layer of Integral Research emphasising Action Research	**Working (project based) alone or in pairs**
Doctoral Researchers (programmes with a clear focus on Social Innovation)	**Focus on all four Layers:** Progressively working through all four layers, as only the complete architecture allows the researcher to fully reach into the cultural depth of his or her own context and besides a practical Social Innovation also flesh out its theoretical knowledge base. **Focus on one particular Path:** Focus on one of the four paths of Integral Research which is most authentic to the researcher	**Working alone or in pairs / Small Research Groups**
Post Doctoral Researchers	**Focus on all four Layers and on crossing Paths:** In addition to doctoral research, in post doctoral research the creative interaction between the different paths should be emphasized	**Cross-Cultural, Interdisciplinary Research Groups**

INTEGRAL RESEARCH

PART A:

The Foundations of Social Innovation

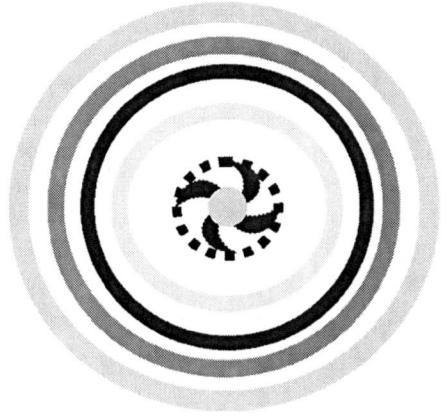

CHAPTER 1

HOW TO BECOME
A SOCIAL INNOVATOR?

"START BY CONNECTING TO YOUR OWN INNOVATIVE ROOTS"

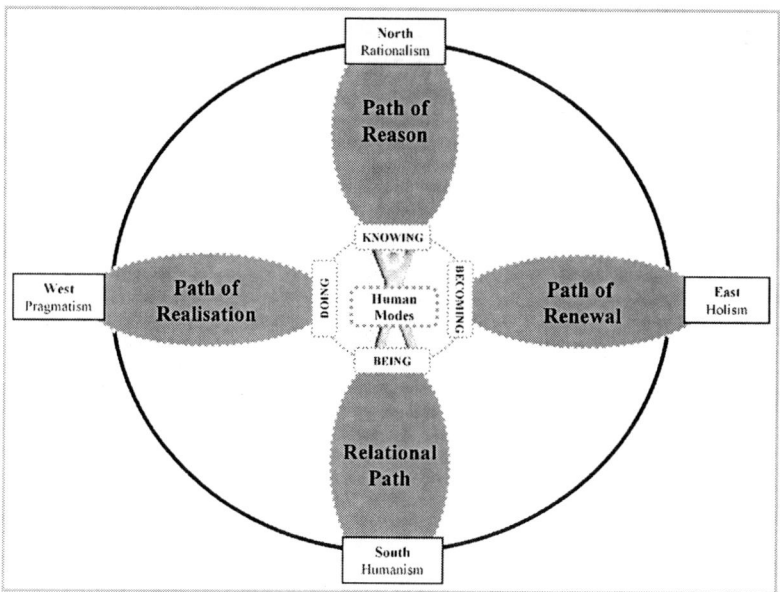

Figure 1.1: Paths of Integral Research

Summary: How to become a Social Innovator?

- The Core Question underlying this book is: "How can Research be turned into social and economic innovation?" We ask this question, because of the distinct lack of social innovation coming out of social research on the one hand, and, of the desperate need for such innovation in most sectors of society, on the other.

- Therefore, this book addresses social scientists, students and practitioners, who want to become social innovators, by applying Integral Research to their research and development work.

- Our claim is that we see innovation in far too one-dimensional terms. There is more to science than technological innovation. There is social innovation, and we shall see why social innovation is equally important and how it can be achieved. We will explore the roots of such and will demonstrate how different cultures have developed over time different ways to generate knowledge and to become socially innovative. We argue that the roots of being socially innovative need to be re-discovered, and, moreover, that such a process can only be undertaken in relation to the particular cultural and societal context.

- In order to achieve true social innovation the social researcher needs to a) connect to the creativity (historic creative achievements) of the culture it is applied to, hence being rooted organically in a specific cultural soil (how else can it be of use for a particular environment and context?) and b) support the further evolution and sustainability of a culture as a whole through fusing indigenous nature and culture (lodged in the local humanities like art, music, architecture etc.), with exogenous social sciences (economics, sociology, psychology etc.).

- We demonstrate with a large number of examples that societies all over the world have, in particular times, developed a perspective about the nature of the diverse elements, which formed their particular cosmos, and how these elements could be held in a dynamic balance. Such modes of being and becoming, knowing and doing found their way into the social design of those societies, and thereby provided an orientation for a particular civilisation.

- In our "tour de world" we shall make another remarkable discovery: While each society embodies the above-mentioned modes, there are regions in the world that have over time developed a particular strength in one particular field as opposed to the others. In research or knowledge generation terms we found that there is a southern "relational path" (linked to the human mode of being), an eastern "path of renewal" (becoming), a northern "path of reason" (knowing) and a western "path of realisation" (doing). Our Four World Model that we rooted in this research suggests that in order to have a dynamic balance on a global level, each world needs to contribute its unique path of knowledge generation into the whole in order to ensure "unity in diversity".

- We recognized that when a society was at its peak, it has managed to keep a kind of dynamic balance between its various parts and modes. It practised "unity in diversity", both internally, through interconnecting its different societal functions, and externally by interacting, on equal terms, with different cultures. This was also a time when there was a relatively free flow of knowledge and innovation in that society.

- Based on these findings, we have developed the integral research design that leads towards social innovation and which simultaneously embodies the four worlds and the centre. You, as the Integral Researcher start by immersing yourself in the very soils of the creative source of your society, before entering a particular research path authentic to you, leading ultimately to Social Innovation.

1.1 The Quest for Social Innovation

1.1.1 Innovation: Buzzword of the Day

Technological innovation is the "buzzword of our day". Each business is concerned with it and claims that it will soon be "out of the market" if it looses its power to innovate. Entire societies, governments and political parties nail their colours to the Innovation mast, and thereby claim to be doing everything in order to promote such technological, as opposed to social, innovation, committing themselves to developing a legal, financial, educational and communicational infrastructure for such, with business being inevitably expected to take the innovative lead. But what do we really mean by innovation?

Invariably the term innovation is used to represent "technical and technological innovation". It reflects advancement in core industries (from automotive to communications, from information technology to chemistry and biotechnology, from solar energy to medical science, from the financial industry to logistics, from airline to space technology). Billions of dollars are pumped into Research and Development to enable technological innovation to take place in those sectors. Of course all of such is important. But, while parts of the world have become highly innovative in technological terms, what we term "social innovation" lags way behind.

So the world increasingly suffers from the downsides of such technological innovation, causing: environmental destruction, sometimes serving to increase the gaps between wealth and poverty, and causing health and security problems, as well as clashes between civilisations. As materialism advances at an outer economic level there is an increasing sense of unrest, insecurity and lack of rootedness, at an inner psychological level. And while we are increasingly aware of this imbalance, we turn again to technology to find the solutions for such problems. We want our industries to become more environmentally friendly, we want our pharmaceutical companies and globally initiated health initiatives to solve our health problems, we want technology to be developed to resolve the digital divide, and so on and technologically on. Moreover, we in the "west" and "north" believe that once the poor countries have equally developed economies, with technology thereby playing a major part, many of the current problems will be solved automatically.

We believe, in fact, otherwise. After all, the might of technology, aligned with economics, has not so far proven to be able to solve these problems on its own, nor to significantly reduce them. Our claim therefore is not that we should abandon innovation, but that we are seeing innovation in far too one-dimensional terms. There is more to life, and work, than technological and economic innovation. There is *social innovation,* and in this book we are going to demonstrate why social innovation is equally important and how it can be achieved, by drawing upon an "integral" research methodology, rooted in the social sciences, and lodged in a particular natural and cultural soils. We will explore the scope of social innovation and will demonstrate how different cultures have developed over time different ways to generate knowledge and to become socially innovative. We argue that the roots as well as the mainstem of being and becoming socially innovative need to be re-discovered, and, moreover, that such a dual process can only be undertaken in relation to the particular cultural context, and overall social science content. Finally, and of greatest significance for us, as social scientists, we will recast research methodology, so called, in the light of such a newly constituted perspective, that of social innovation achieved through an integral research design.

While technological innovation focuses, then, on the Natural Sciences, we focus on the Social Sciences. This book is therefore for Social Scientists, ranging from economists to political scientists, from geographers to historians, from anthropologists to sociologists, from psychologists to students of religious, environmental and of course business studies. But it is particularly for those Social Scientists who aim to become Social Innovators. Our approach to uncovering the roots of Social Innovation, in fact, is not merely an intellectual exercise. It is much more than that. It requires a deep understanding of the roots of Social Innovation in your own specific society. Therefore this is a book for Social Scientists, most specifically those of you undertaking masters, doctoral and post-doctoral studies, and for your sponsoring organisations and societies, with a view to enhancing the ability of each to be socially innovative, through drawing wholeheartedly upon the social sciences within and across a particular cultural and natural context.

But what exactly is Social Innovation? We start by investigating the creative process that underlies it.

1.1.2 Exploring the Nature of Social Innovation

Is creativity the same as innovation?

Creativity comes out of the productive interaction of differences. Be it biological creativity taking place between male and female, be it creativity arising from the interaction between one culture and another, be it through the interplay between tradition and modernity. Social innovation, our point of focus, arises out of the interplay between different social disciplines and a particular culture, ultimately manifested within, and between, public, private and civic enterprise. Let us trace the argument back to its origins.

Differentiation, Variation, Integration

If you assume, firstly, that at the beginning of all times there was chaos (which means there was no particular order), then creation started when at one point in time, at a particular place, some kind of first order established itself (e.g. the amoeba). This new order then allowed other elements that complied with this prior order to join it and would not accept elements that did not concur with its objectives (example: a cell). After that first act of creation there was variation; one could distinguish between the one and the other. Thereafter there is integration, as the new form reconnects with the old.

Over time, as mankind emerged through its first forms of cultural expression, societies differentiated themselves into all kind of distinctive cultural forms, which then evolved further into complex civilisations. Each community or civilisation developed a particular worldview, or form of differentiation and integration, trying to understand the underlying design behind the world and their particular (wo)mankind. At one and the same time, as tradition evolved toward modernity, and onto post and even trans-modernity, a new from of differentiation and integration of scientific disciplines emerged.

At an early stage of human civilisation (wo)man lived in close interaction with nature and derived his or her perspective on the world, and on how it was created, very much out of nature itself (life cycles; seasons). Ever since ancient times (wo)man has tried to understand interactions between opposites, between one and the other: between man and woman, day and night, life and death; our community versus theirs. The earliest forms of cultural expression, then, considered just those phenomena: the relation between him or her, life and death, person and nature, wo(man) and God. (S)he understood that creation came out of the interaction between two poles, and (s)he learned that if the ingredients for creation where out of balance they could become destructive.

Creativity and Innovation: The Quantum Leap

A creative act, secondly, can be merely reproductive (creating something that has been designed at an earlier stage), or it can lead to innovation. Innovation implies a quantum leap or a further evolution, a new variation and a new from of integration. If innovation occurs in nature, it is always a process whereby one organism reaches out to another: together they create something new which ultimately fits better into the environment, thereby contributing to sustaining life as a whole. Innovation in human societies is hence also an expression where one cultural artefact or scientific discipline – as with biochemistry or social ecology – is combined with another; thereby a new form is created that can be applied in the societal context and helps the society as a whole to better adapt to, or co-create with, its environment. The new creation is an innovation, if it has a better "fit" to its context than what has existed before.

1.1.3 The Social Innovator

The task of the social innovator is to root his or her work in the social sciences, and from there to reach out to further evolve that work, ultimately to improve the context from which (s)he has started. In our case such improvement happens through new "social" content. In order to achieve true social innovation (s)he needs to:

a) connect to the creativity (historic creative achievements) of the culture it is applied to, hence being rooted organically in a specific cultural soil
b) support the further evolution and sustainability of a culture as a whole
c) by being grounded in that soil prior to doing such
d) purposefully engage in (fundamental as well as applied) research and development, within and across the social sciences

It is the creative interaction of diverse elements that is needed for innovation. But such innovation can only take place, if the balance between the interacting elements is retained, including the balance between being and becoming, knowing and doing.

All societies have over time developed their own kind of knowledge about the design of their social and material creations and how to maintain a healthy balance with creation itself. Again and again, (wo)man has also tested the limits of this balance, which – in its worst cases – led to wars, to destruction and extinction. Often, those were the times where a particular society became out of touch with its knowledge of how to keep up such a healthy balance. That leads us to the Responsibility of the Social Innovator.

1.1.4 The Responsibility of the Social Innovator

The Agenda of a Social Innovator is to contribute to improving human well-being and livelihood. Such an agenda of innovative social design was strongly influenced by Victor Papanek's idea that social designers and creative professionals have a responsibility and are able to cause real change in the world, through good social design. Papanek coined the term "responsible design". Papanek also alluded to designing for people's needs rather than their wants. Responsible design includes many things and one of these is design for the Third World. Social Innovators have responsibility over the choices they make in the design processes. (1)

According to Victor Margolin a social innovator, through his or her new social designs, has the ability "to envision and give form to ... immaterial products that can address human problems on a large scale and contribute to social well being". (2) Such design should be seen as a professional contribution to development or to enhanced livelihoods. In the context of our integral research design, which we shall introduce in chapter 3, it is innovative concept design with which we are engaged primarily.

Social Design can also be seen as a process that leads to enhancing human capabilities that in turn contribute to their well-being. As Nobel Laureate Amartya Sen writes "poverty is seen as a deprivation of capabilities ... by focussing on developing capabilities, rather than on, for example, income, enhancement of various social aspects of life can contribute to general development. Understanding and using social design processes can contribute to the improvement of livelihood."(3)

Finally, and if you like the innovation presented in this book, is to turn research methodology into a process intrinsically geared towards social innovation. As such, a social design focussing particularly on social improvement needs to bring dynamic balance to the following factors:

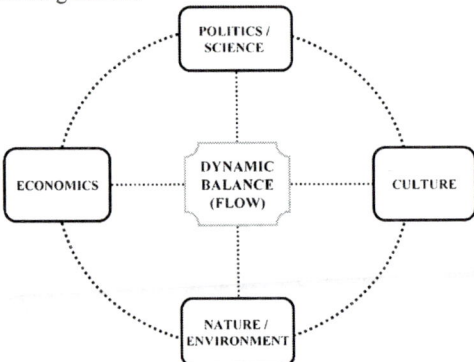

Figure 1.2: The Defining Outer Factors of an Innovative Social Design (generic perspective)

We now turn from our social design to the "four-fold" nature of such an integral approach.

1.2 Archetypal Designs of Social Innovation

The Specific Balance of the Four Fold, the Cycle and the Centre

You may by now have noticed that the model we have presented of social design and social innovation has been presented in a circular way, and contained within, an outer fourfoldness and an inner centre. These serve to express a specifically and dynamically balanced interaction of particularly diverse, worldly factors.

In our intercultural research around the world we have discovered that the core visual design of many cultures is expressed either in fourfolds, cycles or a combination of both. All of them expressed a philosophical and/or spiritual understanding of a balanced order of communities, societies, (wo)man in relation to nature and God. So what does the fourfold and the cycle as "design forms" stand symbolically for:

The Fourfold

According to mythological interpretation, the four is one of the core order-giving principles (four directions, four elements, four seasons, four temperaments, and currently our four research paths). The most elemental visual expressions of the fourfold is the geometric form of the square. On a symbolic level, the square was a symbol for the earth and for the cooperation of the four elements. It stood for absolute beauty (Platonic interpretation); in Islam it represented the heart (as per four sources of inspiration). And in China it stood for the Cosmos as a whole.

The Cycle

In various cultures the cycle was a symbol for the absolute as well as for unity. It has been used as a symbol of the sky (the limitless), again, for absolute beauty (Platonic interpretation) and for emptiness (Hinduism). The cycle embodies harmony of all spiritual forces (Zen), and it is a symbol of time and eternity.

The Process Element

The designs that various cultures created over time often include a process element – in addition to the cycle or the square (or a combination of both of them). While the four-fold cycle could be interpreted as an embodiment of an ongoing process, or dynamic, the form in itself does not express a lot of vitality, but is rather static, or indeed a stabilizing entity.

Such designs were always an expression of a "balanced order" or unity between diverse elements. On a societal level, for us here, the core defining elements can be understood as Nature, Culture, Politics and Economics. On a personal level, such defining elements can be viewed as Being, Becoming, Knowing and Doing. These dimensions can be found in each personality and civilization. And each of these two, in order to survive on a long-term basis, needed then, and needs now, a kind of healthy and dynamically evolving balance between these core elements.

In our studies, we have made another (for us remarkable) discovery. (4) While each society embodies the four worlds of Nature, Culture, Politics and Economics, there are regions in the world that have over time developed a particular strength in one particular field, as opposed to the others. Figure 1.3 illustrates this finding.

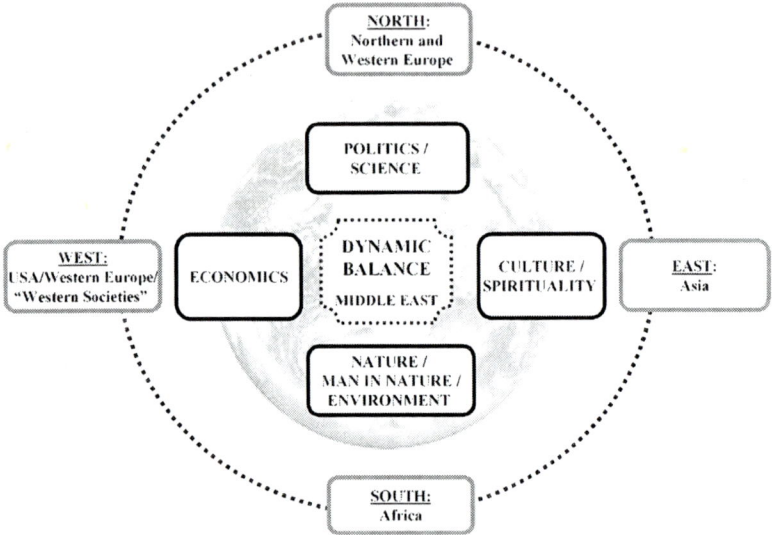

Figure 1.3: The "Archetypal" Social Design of a Four-World Model

This pattern suggests that in order to have a dynamic balance on a global level, each part needs to bring its unique contribution – that is when it is functioning at its "functional" best – into the whole in order to ensure "unity in diversity". Figure 1.4 shows which particular element each world does contribute.

Of course, you find these "archetypal features" in every society, in every organisation, in every individual. We are not saying that, for example, Humanism or Being is only rooted in the South (hence in Africa), or that Holism or Becoming is only rooted in the East (hence in countries like Japan and China). We argue, that each world region has evolved over time one inner dimension (interior design) that seems to be more strongly developed than the others. The East has arguably the longest and deepest tradition in the area of holism, spirituality and non-material aspects, as we shall see for our path of renewal while, for example, the west has developed an enormous capacity for the pragmatic and material self-expression, our path of realisation. And it is the Centre (countries in the Middle East) that has historically been, more so than any other world region, not only a crossroads for the most diverse cultures, but it has also experienced various epochs, most notably in the ninth to fourteenth centuries AD, when a "creative synthesis" between different cultures and religions did prolifically happen. Even Islam itself could be seen as "creative synthesis" and further evolution of Judaism and Christianity – and has in itself been a major social innovation for the region, and ultimately for the world. At its best, the Middle East and Islam have demonstrated an enormous ability to generate a dynamic balance between most diverse parts. That's why we see the integrative ability of "creative synthesis" as the particular contribution of the Centre, including our own ability to "centre" ourselves, when at our integrative best as opposed to dissipative worst.

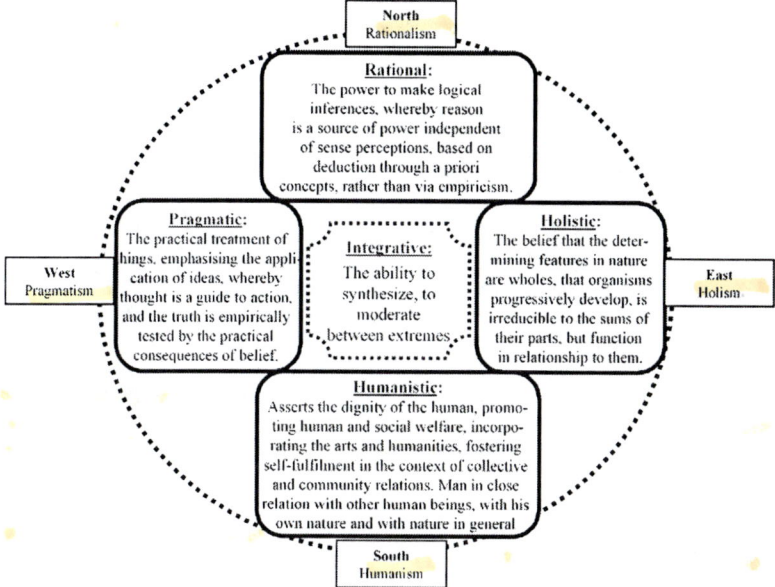

Figure 1.4: Contribution of the Four Worlds and the Centre

You could say that what we can observe on a global level also mirrors the inner archetypes of each individual and society. Each of us has our potential South, its East, its North, its West and Centre. But each of us has developed a particular strength in one or two dimensions, and only a few individuals, organisations and societies "manage" to keep a harmonic, yet dynamic balance between the four elements.

This archetypal social and psychological design is a distillation of our research and observations in different cultures and personalities. It is also a design that resonates with core cultural and artistic artefacts (visual designs) that occur in most societies. We shall demonstrate, that outer design in its more explicit visual expression is implicitly linked with the inner design of a culture or psyche as a whole, whereby such a psychic design can be regarded as the underlying spirit of its material expression. It is hence important to understand this deeper layer, and we shall now explore such and their inner and outer expressions in various cultures.

1.3 Social Innovation through "Creative Synthesis": A Tour of the Four Worlds and the Centre

1.3.1 Paths of Creative Synthesis

We shall start by exploring what kind of "inherently sustainable and dynamically balanced social designs" have been developed over time by different cultures and how that has been expressed inwardly (design) as well as outwardly (symbol). In the case of each of our "four worlds", mediated by our "centre", we shall find an all-encompassing design, in each case with a particular orientation, towards, respectively, a path of realisation (western), renewal (eastern), reason (northern) and a relational path (southern), as well as an ultimately integral one. The outer symbol representing the cosmology of a particular society has an explicit, static outer structure, which is represented, in turn and at a deeper level, an implicit, dynamic inner or process dimension.

When each of our world civilisations were at their peak, the process dimension was at its most active, becoming a field of force if you like, leading to a fruitful exchange amongst its diverse elements. The same of course applies to an individual or an organisation. At such a time, each such entity was able to keep its unity and to orchestrate its diversity in a way that it was fertile for all its parts. Indeed, the great African Muslim philosopher Ali Mazrui defines a civilisation as a "creative synthesis" of diverse parts, related not only to the combination of the rich "interior design" of a society, but also bearing upon the civilisation's interaction with other civilisations, thereby embodying unity-in-diversity. When "creative synthesis" was at its best, so was the inner process of innovation. We well need to bear this in mind when we start to discuss *integral* research methodology and our four research paths: relational, renewal, reason and realisation.

When societies lose their power to socially innovate, through following these research paths as it were, thereby interlinking the explicit structural form (outer design) with the implicit dynamic process (inner design) neither the deeper meaning of the symbol, nor its power to connect, is any longer present. Cultures, as well as individuals and institutions within these, may still use it as a core expression of their civilisation, like the sign of the cross (Christian), or the Star of David (Jewish) but the majority of people and enterprises within it are no longer aware of the deeper meaning (the inner design or implicit process) in the symbol, most particularly the meaning and purpose of its process dimension. For example, in the Arab world, their buildings, both inside and out, are still richly laden with Arabesque forms, but few people know what these structurally symbolize, or indeed the force field, which they dynamically represent.

Many of us, therefore, enjoy visits to museums, where the static artefacts of civilisations are aesthetically displayed for us to get to know. We admire the artefacts that ancient generations of our own and other cultures have been created, from a distance, even how innovative they had been. But we make no conscious connection between material or practical innovations of the past, and the spiritual or mental process that allowed these to come into being, thereby taking into conscious account the current ability of a society to be creative. We shall see later in chapter 17, in the case of Oman, as a powerful case in point, how a deep understanding of a societies deeper grounds can help to reanimate this ability.

We now start with an exploration of Social Design in the West, in fact from the neglected grounds of America's indigenous civilisation. Thereafter we reach out to the other polarities, that is the East, North and South, before we turn toward the Centre.

1.3.2 The West: Creative Synthesis in America or "The Path of Realisation"

Specific Directions: Healer, Visionary, Warrior, Teacher

We identified some astonishing examples of balanced fourfold designs in a number of indigenous (what we term "southern") societies from Northern America. They are, if you like, deep expressions of the original "southern" and also "eastern" dimension of what we now call the "west" or North America. As such we begin with the "original" West, as opposed to the "derivative" western frontier spirit, as exhibited historically, and still to this day, by the American "cowboy" spirit of footloose "get up and go".

The social design of the Native Americans bears a strong relation to mother nature, and introduces balanced ways of portraying how man interacts with nature in general, with his own inner nature, and with the nature of other human beings. Such a rich source of social design has been patently ignored by social researchers in the USA, thereby cutting themselves off from their original cultural and psychic birthright. The cosmos of the Cree and Objiway people (a native American tribe), for example, includes all of the knowledge required to live in harmony with creation; that is the knowledge of body and mind and the ability to disseminate knowledge through communication. All those attributes are, according to this perspective, necessary to form a holistic (nature) and humanistic (culture) worldview. These Native American's recognized particular strengths in specific ethnic groups, who together, once again, constitute a "creative synthesis". It is interesting now to see how they were able to recognize the unique contribution of the "white (wo)man", who, after all, until this day, did not embrace the Native American heritage in his or her own cosmos.

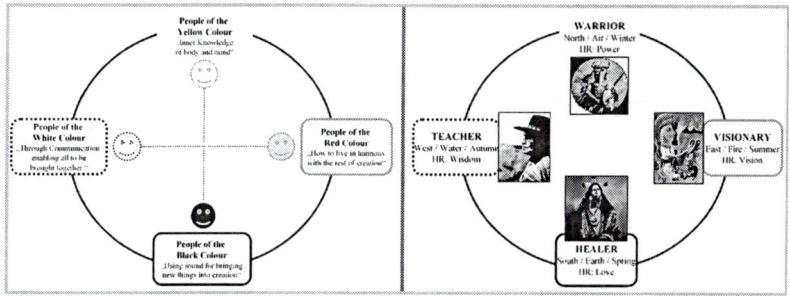

Figure 1.5: Fourfold Design of the Human Cosmos of Cree and Objiway People (left)
Fourfold of an Ancient Medicine Wheel (Native American Origin) (right)

In an ancient medicine wheel, which is also attributed to Native American civilisations (5), it is different personality types that form a fourfold. Each of the four types in the human spectrum, the healer, the visionary, the warrior and the teacher is connected to a specific direction, element, season and human resource (love, vision, power and wisdom). Individuals represent a certain type or a combination of two or more types, and their individual developmental path is influenced by that type. Each type, according to the medicine wheel, is also represented by a particular instrument, emphasizing the strong connection, the "human south" has to music and rhythm. Indeed, music may even be seen as a "way of knowing" and a way to know oneself and the other in a deeper way.

Oriented Toward what is Materially Realisable

North America today is a "melting pot" of all kinds of cultures and personalities, ironically exclusive – rather than inclusive – of the native Indian, who is shut off with a native "reserve". In a most fascinating way, the "United States" has managed to develop out of this enormously diverse cultural amalgam, a society whose economic and technological forces come to the fore. It is active, future oriented and pragmatic like no other country; and it has quite obviously enabled lots of technologically and economically laden "creative synthesis" within the country, focusing on what is materially *realisable*. However, it is also increasingly evident, that the US has lost its ability to engage in such "creative synthesis", both within its own psychic being, and also together with other countries and civilisations. It still interacts most easily with those countries and personalities, which are most comparable to the US – western style economies and democracies, and similar behavioural orientations towards work and life. But it seems to be unable to embrace diversity on a global level, especially when it comes to other religious and cultural, individual and institutional forms and outlooks that do not want to follow the "American Way".

It may be worthwhile to explore to what extent this "out of balance" perspective is also a manifestation of North America's inability to embrace the cultural and spiritual heritage and knowledge that the indigenous Native American cultures had to offer. Such an exploration is such an obvious one, when we recognize that among the greatest of problems that the US faces is its difficulty in engaging with other cultures, including its indigenous own, as well as with nature and environment. America, overall then, is much more at home in exercising reason and in the process realising its material objectives, than at socially relating and spiritually renewing itself.

There are, however, very promising "western" exceptions. There are an increasing number of social scientists who are trying to reconcile the primary focus on economics, politics and natural science, with culture, community and nature. Paul Hawken's, Amory and Hunter Lovins' "Natural Capitalism" (6) and David Peak's "Blackfoot Physics" (7) are just two recent expressions of such.

From Realisable to Relational

These examples of "reflecting back" ("re-ligio") to identify the deep cultural knowledge of a society are becoming more prolific, especially in those countries, where the original indigenous culture has been neglected. Like North America, Australia is a "western" country, in our terms, which has hitherto been disconnected from its indigenous roots, as recently revealed by the Swedish and aboriginal "knowledge management" duo Karl-Erik Sveiby's and Tex Skuthorphe's "Treading Lightly" – Uncovering the Wisdom of the Australian Aborigines. (8)

Yet another strong voice is that of the Israeli peace activist Jesaiah Ben-Aharon who, in outlining "America's Global Responsibility', argues that an evolving Western culture must rather serve to integrate than to isolate or dominate the South, East, North and Centre. He argues that the major destabilising power in the modern era is the modern economy. For Ben-Aharon, globalisation has the capacity to tear away from the state its economic, political and cultural (and natural) assets. Only therefore a clear relational understanding and thereby practical and social implementation of the human interactions and relationships among the various sectors of society will yield the power to replace the pure focus on the economy with more adequate modern social design. (9) We now turn from the south-west, to the "east", and from the path or realisation to that of renewal.

1.3.3 The East: Creative Synthesis in Buddhism/Hinduism or "The Path of Renewal"

Continual Becoming

The quest for knowledge in the East was oriented, more than in other parts of the world, towards a path of ongoing renewal, rooted in dynamic forces within nature, such as, for the ancient Chinese, the forces of yin (feminine-responsive) and yang (masculine-assertive). You could reason things out, or realise the truth, but only if you renewed your connection with the grounds of your being. The truth, moreover, was not what could be seen and touched, but rather somewhere "in between".

Dialogue, as such, means "between the words"; it is about knowledge that is "flowing through" past, present and future, in a process of continual becoming. Hence, it needs to be continuously re-acquired, as the entire cosmos itself underlies continuous change and transformation. The path of renewal is a cyclical one. Two core visualisations of this are the Wheel of Life and the Mandala.

Figure 1.6: Wheel of Life (centre, outer cycle plus a double fourfold) (left) and aTitbetan Mandala (fourfold in a cycle) (right)

The Way of the East

In Buddhism which emerged from ancient India, the wheel of life is a symbol for the Eightfolded Way, aiming for freedom from reincarnation or rebirth. It is also found in Indian Hinduism, Jainism, Sikhism and other related religions.

Mandala (Sanskrit for "circle", "completion") is a term used to refer to various objects. It is of Hindu origin, but is also used in other Dharmic religions, such as Buddhism. In the Tibetan branch of Vajrayana Buddhism, they have been developed into sandpainting, expressing the belief that knowledge can not be fixed, but needs to be regenerated again and again. In practice, mandala has become a generic term for any plan, chart or geometric pattern that represents the cosmos metaphysically or symbolically, a microcosm of the universe from the human perspective.

A mandala, especially its centre, can be used during meditation as an object for focusing attention. The symmetrical geometric shapes tend to draw the attention towards their centre. The Swiss Psychologist Carl Gustav Jung saw the mandala as "a representation of the unconscious self", and believed his paintings of mandalas enabled him to identify emotional disorders and work towards wholeness and integration in personality. (10)

Holistic Design: Existence and Non-Existence

Taoism, for the ancient Chinese, represents the force behind all natural order. Tao can be roughly stated to be the flow of the universe. (11) It is believed to be the influence that keeps the universe balanced and ordered. Tao is associated with nature, due to a belief that nature demonstrates the Tao. (12) The flow of qi, as the essential energy of action and existence, is compared to the universal order of Tao. It is often considered to be the source of both existence and non-existence. And hence, it does not search for knowledge and enhanced awareness through distinction and differentiation (either / or) but embodies the ability of embracing paradox (and holding opposites as equal forces, not valuing them as good or bad).

Taoists believe that man is a microcosm for the universe. (13) The body ties directly into the Chinese five elements. The five organs correlate with the five elements, the five directions (including our four worlds and a centre) and the seasons. (14) Akin to the "neoplatonic maxim" of "as above, so below", Taoism posits that by understanding himself, and in particular his path of becoming, man may gain knowledge of the universe. The "Taijitu" (yin and yang) symbol is a keynote of Taoist symbolism. While almost all Taoist philosophies make use of the yin and yang symbol, one could also call it Confucian, Neo-Confucian or pan-Chinese. (15)

The five directions as conceived by the ancient Chinese (east, south, west, north, centre) can be linked to the yin and yang symbols; each have their own attributes, as follows in the chart below. (16)

Direction	Element	Season	Force
East	Wood	Spring	Yang
South	Fire	Summer	Yang
West	Metal	Autumn	Yin
North	Water	Winter	Yin
Centre	Earth	None	Neutral

Figure 1.7: The cyclical Yin-Yang in relation to the fourfold
(four directions / four seasons) and the centre

We now turn from the underlying force of Realisation in the west, and the perennial flow of Renewal in the east, to the path of Reason in the North, that is within Europe.

1.3.4 The North: Creative Synthesis in Europe or "The Path of Reason"

Europe's civilisation has been influenced mostly by two major sources: the Judaic-Christian influence and its Greek heritage.

The Cross: A Means of Connection

The single strongest symbol in Christianity is the cross and its variations, including the Monogram of Christ. On a superficially explicit level it is a static, structural symbol of a torture instrument, which led to the death of Jesus. However, in its deeper implicit, indeed dynamic meaning the cross could be understood as a symbol that holds opposites together, that incorporates the ability of embracing paradoxes. As such, it is a means of connection not only between earth (matter/mother) and heaven (spirit/father), but also between the past and the future (embracing eternity). These are also implicit aspects of "creative synthesis", here with a stronger emphasis on the metaphysical world. In addition, on such a process-oriented level, the cross stands for the overcoming of death, for eternal life and for the metamorphosis of Christ who goes – so the Christian belief – through this process on behalf of humankind as a whole. If one envisions the cross in the cycle (see below), it is easy to imagine, how it is the "driving force" behind the cycling of a particular civilisation. On the other hand, if taken out of its dynamic context, a cross is simply a static form. Every time an athlete or other performer "crosses him or herself" such a static form is reinforced.

Figure 1.8: Monogram of Christ / Cross / Canterbury Cross (used by Anglian Church)

For a certain period Christianity was indeed the cultural driving force in Western Europe not only in religious and spiritual matters, but also in the arts and the sciences. Especially as a number of Monasteries became true centres of civilisation; they emerged as showcases of social and economic transformation, where communities based on brotherhood, enhanced not only the Christian spiritual tradition, but also fostered the arts and sciences, cultivated the land, and even became economically successful.

However, at a certain stage the church used its enormous influence on politics and economics, on culture and nature, for domination rather than for liberation.

Renaissance Man: Focusing on the Power of Reason

The Enlightenment period, from the fourteenth century onwards, was of particular importance for the birth of a modern society in Europe and it freed the continent from the oppressive medieval form of Christianity. Now man, not god, was in the centre of the universe. Now, so it was believed, it was man who kept the world going (see da Vinci's Vitruvian Man), not Christ. Man could do it with the power of his mind and his own imagination. While in the symbol of the "fourfold" cross the centre is where the two lines meet (many paintings place here the "eye of god"), da Vinci's expression of the Renaissance Man, moves the "centre of power to the mind of the human being". Since then, for Europe (in our archetypal representation: the North), reason and rationalism, or indeed the path of *reason,* becomes the main source of progress.

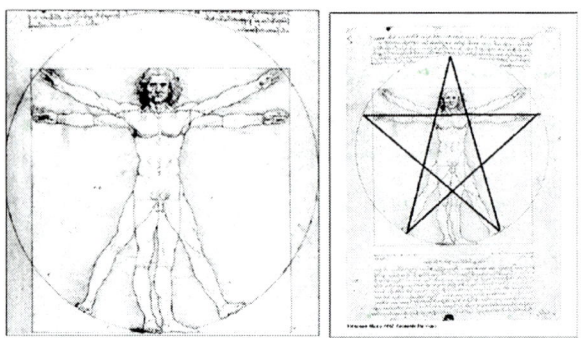

Figure I.9: Leonardo da Vinci's Vitruvian Man (The mind on top of the hierarchy)

In fact, da Vinci himself became the embodiment of imagination, science, and innovation. Some claim, da Vinci was one of the last men in European history embodying universal knowledge, linking science and arts in a most innovative manner.

The period of the Enlightenment, which in arts and design was called "Renaissance" (rebirth), re-animated the second pillar of European civilisation: the Greek tradition. It was the Greek philosophers and their focus on reasoning and democratic interaction of minds who enabled one of the most innovative periods within Europe to take place:

when the Greek civilisation was at its peak, so was their innovative power with regard to politics, arts and science. The Odyssey and the Iliad, as the two core myths of that time, tell stories about the intelligence of man, which helped him, especially in the case of Odysseus, to triumph even over the gods.

Lacking Social Designs for an Integrated Future

However, the sole focus on the power of human reasoning has led to a new kind of distortion. For decades now, Europe has been suffering from a spiritual vacuum. The "more than human" world (17) is evidently missing. Many analysts claim that Christianity has failed to renew itself and to refill this spiritual gap. In contrast, a growing number of Western European (and the US-American) population have taken their spiritual journey in their own hands and are looking for "alternative offerings"; often trying to "re-root" themselves in other belief systems, such as Buddhism and Islam, rather than renew their own "northern" path, as indeed, as we shall see, the "postmodernists" have attempted to do. Furthermore, the sole focus on rationality and mind has increasingly created work and communication processes that are not in synch with nature in general and with human nature specifically. Technology and economics as a single "north-western" world or dimension has taken precedence over all other worlds, and is often out of touch with nature, culture, politics and social sciences. The awareness of this misfit is, however, gradually increasing throughout the globe. Yet we lack social designs for a more integrated future. In effect the "north" (reason) and the "west" (action) dominate over the rest, and, at least for the time being, the "middle" ground has lost its way.

There are however amazing examples of social designers and scientists, from Austrian polymath Rudolf Steiner to Swiss German psychotherapist C.G. Jung, who started to pave the way towards more integrated perspectives of the various dimensions of human psyche and society. In our work, we concertedly build on them. We now turn from the north, the west and the east, to the south, starting with the Yoruba people of West Africa.

1.3.5 The South: Creative Synthesis in Africa or "The Relational Path"

Obtala: Benefactor of Humanity

The spiritual worldview of Nigeria's Yoruba people, for example, influenced a large number of African religious traditions; nowadays these are practiced, aside from Nigeria itself, in a number of American countries. The core cosmology is rooted in an inseparable cosmos, in which the conscious and the unconscious are held together in a kind of creative balance through the life energy called Ashé. There is no polarisation of good and bad.

Within this cosmos, Yoruba religion speaks about a fourfold activation within the human being. This fourfold is represented by Orishas: these divinities are contained not outside the individual but deep within; and the individual possesses the gods and goddesses as a way of repossessing those divine aspects of the self. "Obtala", as such, is creative, compassionate, and patient, one prepared to accept his lot; benefactor of humanity; dedicated to friendship and the maintenance of the social fabric. "Eshu" is the inner guide – that part of ourselves leading us to life-changing and life-sustaining insights and revelations. "Shango" was famous as a king passionately devoted to war and a master magician. He presents us with the tenacious aspect of the human personality – will, determination, commitment. "Ogun", finally, is the dynamic centre of the psyche capable of containing, integrating, synthesizing and even transcending the many opposing forces that operate within us. (18) At the heart of this fourfold system is a cross – uniting a horizontal axis known as the "chief way" with a vertical axis, the "Secondary Way".

Life Emerges from Divinity

For the West African Bambara people, the centre of the cross is symbolically the "kuru" or God Point; here, the Bambara say, life emerges from divinity through birth and merges back into divinity through death, and through this cyclical transformation immortality is achieved. (19)

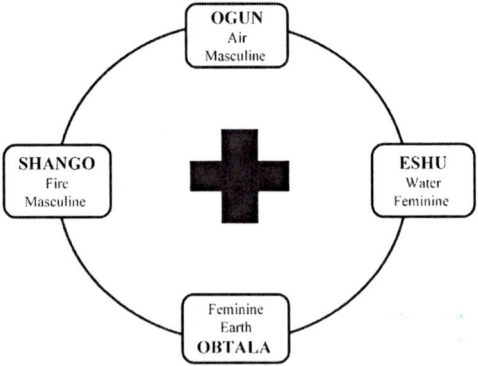

Figure 1.10: Fourfold "Inner World" of the Yoruba (according to Frobenius)

Using Sound for bringing new things into Creation

If you take a second look at the human cosmos introduced earlier for the Cree and Objiway people from Northern America, one notices, that they link sound (music and rhythm) to the "people of black colour" and describe them as people "using sound for bringing new things into creation". Indeed, music, dance and rhythm are until today core expressions of African culture and there is hardly any other form of art that has such an immediate relational power as music and dance. For Africans it is indeed a "way of knowing"; knowing the rhythm of the eternal dance called life. We now turn, finally, to the Centre of the four worlds, represented by the most "synthetic" or integral form of monotheist religion, that is Islam, albeit that voices from both within and without have served to distort such an integral orientation.

1.3.6 The Centre: Creative Synthesis in Islam or "The Integral Research Path"

Infinity, Balance and Architectural Beauty in the Islamic World

The interaction between "self and the other" generally, or between Muslim, Roman, Persian and Byzantine architecture specifically, as an evolutionary catalyst for creation and innovation, is evident in the most important architectural expression of the Islamic world, that is the mosque.

The mosque is the "sacred architecture" of Islam par excellence. It is but a recreation of the harmony, order and peace inherent in nature. The specifically recognisable Islamic architectural style developed soon after the time of the Prophet Mohammed, evolved as a creative synthesis of Roman, Egyptian, Persian/Sassanid and Byzantine models. An early example may be identified as early as 691 with the completion of the Dome of the Rock (Qubbat al Sakkrah) in Jerusalem. It featured a circular dome, and the use of stylised repeating decorative patterns (arabesque). The Hagia Sophia in Istanbul also influenced Islamic architecture. When the Ottomans captured the city from the Byzantines, they converted the Christian basilica to a mosque and incorporated a Byzantine architectural element into their own work.

Distinguishing motifs of Islamic architecture have always been ordered repetition, radiating structures, and rhythmic, metric patterns. In this respect, fractal geometry had been a key feature, especially for mosques and palaces. Many argue that Islamic architecture also borrows heavily from the Persian and in many ways can be called an extension and further evolution of such. Many cities such as Baghdad, for example, were based on precedents such as Firouzabad in Persia. In fact, it is known, that the two designers who were hired by al-Mansur to design the city were Naubakht, a former Persian Zaroastrian, and Mashallah, a former Jew from Khorasan, Iran.

A Meeting of Islamic and Judeo-Christian Cultures

The Moorish architecture (to be found mainly in North Africa and on the Iberian Peninsula) is another example of when a civilisation reaches its peak by predominantly peaceful and constructive interactions with others. The Moorish period in Spain is indeed famous for the atmosphere of peaceful coexistence and creative interaction between Muslims, Christians and Jews. Core examples are the Great Mosque of Cordoba (the Mezquita) and the Alhambra, the magnificent palace-fortress of Granada.

The Alhambra most especially embodies the perfect harmony of manmade architecture and nature, interconnected by the most sophisticated watering and fountain systems that underscore the dynamic, organic and flow-oriented nature of creation. Even after the completion of the so-called "Requoncista", Islamic influence had a lasting impact on the architecture of Spain. In particular, medieval Spaniards used the Mudéjar style, an imitation of Islamic Design. One of the best examples of the Moor's lasting impact is the Alcázar of Seville.

From Egyptian Mamluk to Turkish Ottoman

For many, the Ottomans achieved the highest-level in architecture of Mosque-building. They mastered the technique of building vast inner spaces confined by seemingly weightless yet massive domes, and of achieving perfect harmony between inner and outer spaces, as well as light and shadow. At that stage the mosque was transformed into a sanctuary of aesthetic and technical balance, refined elegance and a hint of heavenly transcendence.

The reign of the Mamluks (1250 to 1517) marked a breathtaking flowering of Islamic art, which is most visible in old Cairo. Mamluk decorative arts were prized around the Mediterranean as well as in Europe, where they had a profound impact on the local production. The influence of Mamluk glassware on the Venetian glass industry is only one such example.

Taj Mahal: Mughal Fusion of Muslim, Persian and Indian

Another distinctive sub-style is the architecture of the Mughal Empire in India in the 16th century: here a fusion of Persian and Hindu elements can be found. The most famous example of Mughal architecture is the Taj Mahal, the "teardrop on eternity", completed in 1648 by the Mughal emperor Shah Jahan. The Taj Mahal is completely symmetrical.

From India we could go on to Sino-Islamic Architecture. The first Chinese mosque was already established in the 7th century. An important feature in Chinese architecture in general is its emphasis on symmetry.

If we take a closer look at most mosques, we immediately find evidence of the interaction of the fourfold (squares, rectangles), the cycle (domes) as well as flow and process oriented designs (arabesque) and natural elements (water, plants).

Distilling the meaning behind the predominant design of most mosques, we conclude that key conceptual and aesthetic elements are those of:

- **Infinity:** Designs with repeating themes suggest infinity and evoke the concept of Allah's infinite power.
- **Balance:** The balance of vast inner spaces confined by seemingly weightless domes, the perfect harmony between inner and outer spaces, as well as light and shadow is a reflection of the perfection of the creation. That also links to balance (justice) as one of the core tenets of Islam.
- **Beauty:** Islam's architecture has been called the "architecture of the veil" because the beauty lies in the inner spaces (courtyards and rooms), which are not visible from the outside.

These three aspects can also be found in the single most prominent ornamental feature in Mosques specifically, but in Islamic design generally: the Arabesque.

The Arabesque: Displaying Unity in Diversity

The Arabesque is an elaborate application of repeating geometric forms. Geometric artwork was not widely used in the Islamic world until the golden age of Islam came into full bloom. During this time, ancient texts were translated from their original Greek and Latin into Arabic at the House of Wisdom, an academic research institution in Baghdad. Like the Renaissance in Europe that followed much later, mathematics, science, literature and history were infused into the Islamic world with mostly positive repercussions. The works of Plato and especially of Euclid became popular among the literate. In fact, it was Euclid's geometry along with the foundations of trigonometry codified by Pythagoras that were expounded on by Al-Jawhari (ca. 800 to 860) whose "Commentary on Euclid's Elements" (20) became the impetus of the art for that was to become the Arabesque. Plato's idea about the existence of a separate reality that was perfect in form and function and crystalline in character also would contribute to the development of the Arabesque.

Hence the Arabesque is a symbol of the particular worldview that Islam developed.

There are two modes to arabesque art: the first reflects the principles that govern the order of the world. These principles included the bare basics of what makes objects structurally sound, and, by extension, beautiful. In this first mode, each repeating geometric form has a built-in symbolism ascribed to it. For example, the square, with its four equilateral sides, is symbolic of the equally important elements of nature: earth, air, fire and water. Without any one of the four, the physical world, represented by a circle that inscribes the square, would collapse and cease to exist. The second mode is based upon the flowing nature of plant forms. This mode recalls the feminine nature of life giving. In addition, upon inspection of many examples of Arabesque art, some would argue that there is in fact a third mode, the mode of Arabic calligraphy.

Figure 1.11: Arabesques (fourfold, circular and process elements, centre)

As figurative art was considered to be idolatrous and was forbidden (haram) in Mosques, calligraphy and abstract figures became the main methods of artistic expression in Islamic cultures. Arabic, Persian and Ottoman Turkish calligraphy is associated with geometric Islamic art on the walls and ceilings of mosques as wells as in books. Contemporary artists in the Islamic world draw on the heritage of calligraphy. The guiding principles of infinity, balance and beauty can also easily be found in Islamic calligrams.

Knowledge (Ilm) as a Historic Driving Force in Muslim Culture

For the Muslim calligraphy is a visible expression of the highest art of all: the art of the spoken word (the transmittal of thoughts and of history) – in short: knowledge. In Islam, the most important document to be transmitted orally is, of course, the Qur'an. Proverbs and complete passages from the Qur'an can be seen in Arabesque art. The coming together of these three forms creates the Arabesque, and this is a reflection of unity arising from diversity, which is another basic tenet of Islam.

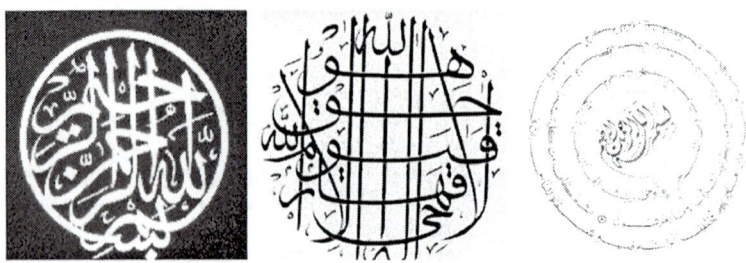

Figure 1.12: Examples of Islamic Calligraphy

Knowledge is indeed the major driving force of Islamic culture. Its Islamic translation "ilm" is one of the most frequently occurring terms in the Qur'an; indeed, only two other words appear more frequently: Allah (God) and Rabb (Creator or Sustainer). One may claim, that without this inner urge to know, without this dedication towards knowledge, an Islamic civilisation would not have been possible. At the same time, if the flow of knowledge is interrupted, e.g. because it is dominated by one societal group, then the civilisation declines. That's, one could argue, what we sadly see in much of the Muslim world today. For seven centuries now, it has been the religious authorities in the Muslim *ummah* that have suppressed the free flow of knowledge.

It is interesting that the written word (expressing knowledge) had such a major influence in the development of the arabesque. The way, in which calligraphy finds its way into this Islamic design form, is always in a flow form. The flow form is beautifully interwoven in the geometric balance that all arabesques display. Hence it is the flow of knowledge that keeps the more static and abstract geometrical forms in a dynamic balance.

This very brief review of Islamic design has served to make it obvious that its development has been continuously furthered and stimulated by the "productive interaction" of various cultural heritages (Arabic, Persian, Turkish and more). At the peak of Muslim civilisation "creative synthesis" worked at its best: knowledge was able to flow. This same flow of knowledge is characteristic of our integral approach to research. We are now ready to review our integral research design.

1.4 An Integral Research Design leading to Social Innovation

In our "tour de world" we have introduced core social designs and the visual manifestations of these, both static (explicit structure) and dynamic (implicit process) of many societies. We have recognized that when a civilisation is at its peak, it has managed to keep a kind of dynamic balance between its various parts. It practises "unity in diversity", both internally, through interconnecting its different functions, and externally by interacting, on equal terms, with different cultures. This was also a time when there was a relatively free flow of knowledge. As such the knowledge creating power of the civilisation was at its height and its artistic expressions (or visual designs) most evolved.

The decline always began, when such a balance was destroyed, usually by the domination of one part over the others, from both within and also without, and all too often in combination. Today we witness such a decline in the "western" world; as the economic realm assumes predominance over the others, and, in the case of America at least, the relationship with nature, embodied within its indigenous peoples, is left far behind. If we choose to live in a knowledge era that embraces the knowledge of all worlds, and that aims for "unity in diversity", we need material and social designs that provide for it. And we need to understand the inner rhythm of such designs that effectively allow for the creative synthesis of its parts.

Social Innovation for us means a purposeful social design (and for us: research design), originating and developing a creative synthesis of the diverse elements within a society's soils (and of a society with other societies). In order to be socially innovative on a sustainable basis, a social organism needs an effective inner process that allows the diverse worlds to interact and to stay in a dynamic balance; such balanced interaction, for us, occurs when each worldview is enabled to fully express itself.

We have demonstrated with a number of examples that societies all over the world have, in particular times, developed a perspective about the nature of the diverse elements, which formed their particular cosmos, and how these elements could be held in a dynamic balance. Such modes of being (relational) and becoming (renewal), knowing (reason) and doing (realisation) found their way into visual designs that embodied such, and thereby provided an orientation for a particular civilisation, which we have now turned into four paths of ultimately integral research. Based on such we have developed an integral research design that leads towards social innovation and which simultaneously embodies our four worlds.

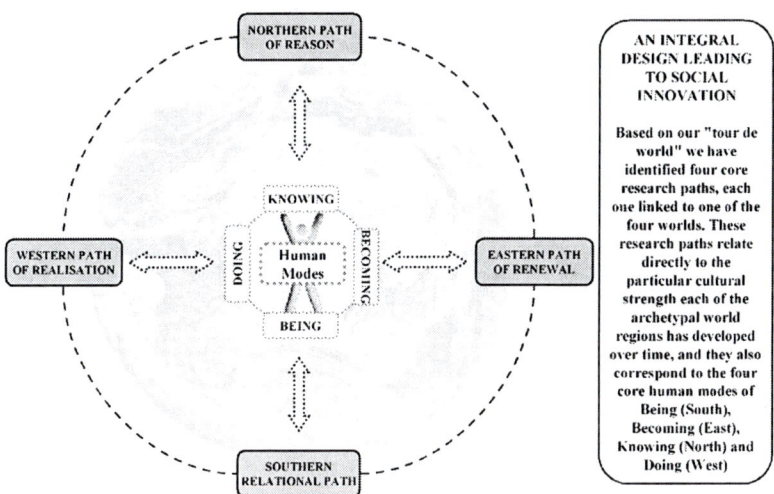

Figure 1.13: Integral Research – The Four Core Research Paths

Integral Research, based on a representation of the four worlds, does not only link the various ways in which knowledge has been generated, it also aims to uncover the inner rhythm of knowledge creation. Thus we seek a coherent link between outer design (social innovation) and inner process (integral research).

As researcher-innovator you start with your own life world, thereby reviewing the history of your society to uncover what structures and processes the society had previously developed, which allowed it to become a dynamic civilisation. From there you take this story forward and work yourself through the integral research process (the inner design), progressively leading towards social innovation (the outer design) that can ultimately have a true impact on your society.

The core defining factors of Integral Research are summarised as follows:

- **Building on Local Roots:** reconnecting the researcher with the innovative power of his or her own civilisation as a starting point for his or her research path; ensuring that the researcher/innovator is true to his own culture

- **Integrating knowledge paths:** integrating and equally valuing different worlds, and hence different approaches to research methodology and knowledge creation

- **Enabling Creative Synthesis:** enabling creative synthesis of diverse dimensions within a social organism (self, organisation, society) and between social organisms (between organisation, between societies) interconnecting different knowledge paths

- **From Local Roots to Global Reach:** through the integration of knowledge paths and the enabling of creative synthesis, *integral research* fosters a gradual evolution from local roots (local identity) to global reach (contributing to an integrated, balanced perspective on a global level), mediated by the social sciences. The connection of the local and global also helps to enable forms of social innovation that, while reaching globally, stay true and authentic to the local context where they are ultimately applied.

The following illustration of a Social Innovation Tree translates our core architecture into an organic picture. While the four-world illustration highlights the cultural morphology of each world, the tree illustration highlights the organic process underlying Social Innovation. Hence we link such cultural and the natural perspectives together, emphasizing the combined significance of culture and nature as a starting point for any social innovation.

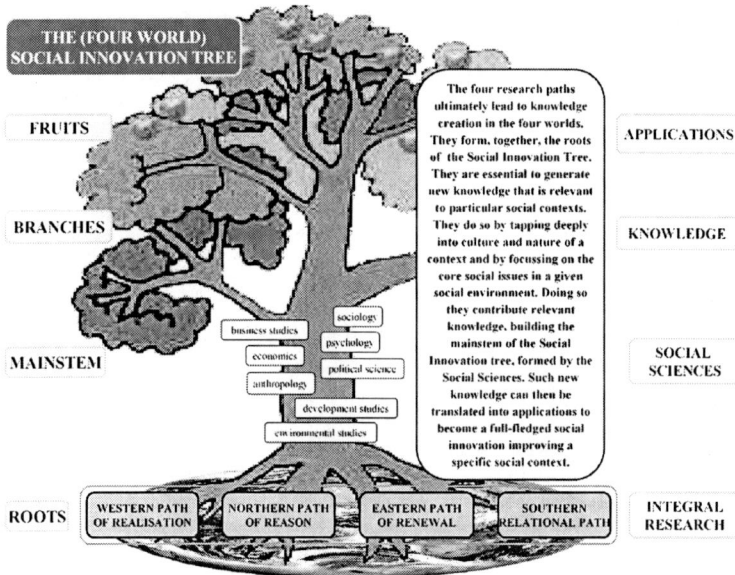

The four research paths ultimately lead to knowledge creation in the four worlds. They form, together, the roots of the Social Innovation Tree. They are essential to generate new knowledge that is relevant to particular social contexts. They do so by tapping deeply into culture and nature of a context and by focussing on the core social issues in a given social environment. Doing so they contribute relevant knowledge, building the mainstem of the Social Innovation tree, formed by the Social Sciences. Such new knowledge can then be translated into applications to become a full-fledged social innovation improving a specific social context.

THE (FOUR WORLD) SOCIAL INNOVATION TREE

FRUITS — APPLICATIONS

BRANCHES — KNOWLEDGE

MAINSTEM — SOCIAL SCIENCES

business studies · sociology · psychology · economics · political science · anthropology · development studies · environmental studies

ROOTS — INTEGRAL RESEARCH

| WESTERN PATH OF REALISATION | NORTHERN PATH OF REASON | EASTERN PATH OF RENEWAL | SOUTHERN RELATIONAL PATH |

Figure 1.14: The Social Innovation Tree

1.5 Conclusion

We have now demonstrated how particular societies and civilisations have developed knowledge about maintaining a healthy and dynamic balance. To the extent that such healthy balance turned to dynamic and creative synthesis, so the society developed its power to innovate. Such a power was born out of the interaction between cultures, as was the case for the Muslim world at its height (in the ninth to fourteenth centuries), and for America in the nineteenth and first half of the twentieth centuries.

We have also illustrated how most civilisations have developed, over time, particular fourfold and circular visuals designs, that represent the totality of the core functions of a culture or path of civilisation. The inner process underlying such a design is responsible for keeping the dynamic balance between such main societal ingredients.

Our "Four Worlds Approach" hence stands for a particular social design that can be found in most cultures. Of course, each culture and indigenous life world have its particular expression, its particular language and metaphors, its particular visual form (pictures and colours), its particular myths and knowledge attached to the social design. However, the resonance between the different expressions is surprisingly high, wherever we tested it.

We have developed in our work a research process that aims for social innovation. We call our research approach "Integral Research". It is an approach that weaves major approaches towards research and knowledge creation that have been developed all over the world, into a coherent framework, or living organism.

We now want to explore how such a design for evolution is specifically applied in our own doctoral and masters programmes in social and economic transformation. We have been studying social designs all over the world. From Jordan to South Africa, from Egypt to the United States, from Eastern to Western Europe, from India to China and Japan. It was surprising to see that we could identify in many life worlds a fourfold rhythm which represented a kind of holistic perspective of (wo)man, of a community, of a society – perspectives that went beyond economics and natural science. In each case, moreover, there is a particular pre-emphasis on either Being (Relational) or Becoming (Renewal), Knowing (Reason) or Doing (Realisation).

As researchers joining our Doctoral and Masters Programmes you are guided through a carefully designed research process with the objective of leading each of you towards Social Innovation, via a path of realisation (western), of renewal (eastern), or reason (northern) or a relational (southern), and ultimately integral (centre) research path.

Each of you grounds your particular research in your own life world, or individual soils, while also reaching out to, and assimilating, other worlds, and the ultimate result of the doctorate or masters is to be applied to your, your institution's, and your society's life world. We believe that enough doctoral and masters theses have been written all over the world with the mere impact of providing the researcher with a post-graduate degree. Most of the resulting theses, in the social sciences, are hardly read, and they live, as we have said, a lonely life on a library shelf, having no social impact whatsoever. In our case, however, the researcher becomes a designer of an integral social innovation, applicable to the particular context in which he or she is embedded.

An innovative Social Design (Social Innovation) is a purposeful process of originating and developing a creative synthesis between the diverse elements of a society, of that particular society in relation to other ones, and also between diverse social disciplines. Such a design enables you, your organisation and society to stay in touch with its inner creative power and to generate a creative synthesis between its own nature and culture, politics and economics, together with those elements in other researchers, researched organisations and societies. Therefore, it is equally important for this inner dynamic, and balance, that each self/world – individually and collectively – engages in "creative synthesis" with others, in our case here represented by "research paths" that connect with four worlds, and through such a process contribute to a dynamic balance of the larger global system of which it itself is a part.

Here's where we see the role that you, the Social Innovator can play. But before we lay out the full architecture of our Integral Research Framework (chapter 3), we need to understand how Social Innovation got stuck.

Bibliography

1) **Papanek**, V. (1984). *Design for the Real World*. Chicago: Academy Chicago Publishers.

2) **Margolin**, V. (2002). *The Politics of the Artificial. Essays on Design and Design Studies*. Chicago and London: The University of Chicago Press.

3) **Sen**, A. (2000). *Development as Freedom*. New York: Anchor Books.

4) **Lessem**, R. & **Palsule**, S. (1996). *Managing in Four Worlds*. Oxford: Blackwell.

5) **Arrien**, A. (1993). *The Four-Fold Way – Walking the Paths of the Warrior, Teacher, Healer and Visionary*. San Francisco: Harper.

6) **Hawken**, P., **Lovins**, A. & **Lovins**, H.L. (1999). *Natural Capitalism – Creating the Next Industrial Revolution*. Boston: Little Brown.

7) **Peak**, F.D. (2005). *Blackfoot Physics. A Journey into the Native American Universe*. York Beach: Red Whell / Weiser.

8) **Sveiby**, K.E. & **Skuthorpe**, T. (2006). Tr*eading Lightly – The Hidden Wisdom of the world's oldest people*. Crows Nest: Allen and Unwin.

9) **Ben-Aharon**, J. (2002). *America's Global Responsibility*. Herdon: Lindisfarne.

10) **Jaffé**, A. (2001). Erinnerung, Träume, Gedanken von C.G. Jung. Zürich: Walter.

11) **Cane**, E.P. (2002). *Harmony: Radical Taoism Gently Applied*. Victoria: Trafford Publishing.

12) **Martinson**, P.V. (1987). *A theology of world religions: Interpreting God, self, and world in Semitic, Indian, and Chinese thought*. Augsburg: Augsburg Publishing House.

13) **Robinet**, I. (1997). *Taoism: Growth of a Religion*. Stanford: Stanford University Press.

14) **Kohn**, L. ed. (2000). *Daoism Handbook*. Leiden: Brill.

15) **Little**, S., **Eichman**, S. et al. (2000). *Taoism and the Arts of China*. Chicago: Art Institute of Chicago.

16) **Little**, S., **Eichman**, S. et al. (2000). *Taoism and the Arts of China*. Chicago: Art Institute of Chicago.

17) **Abram**, D. (1997). *The Spell of the Sensuous*. New York: Random House.

18) **Ford**, C. (2000). *The Hero with an African Face – The Mystic Wisdom of Traditional Africa*. New York: Bantam. (citing: Anthropologist Leo Frobenius)

19) **Ford**, C. (2000). *The Hero with an African Face – The Mystic Wisdom of Traditional Africa.* New York: Bantam.

20) **Al-Jawhari**. *Commentary on Euclid's Elements.*

CHAPTER 2

WHY SOCIAL INNOVATION GETS STUCK

"UNDERSTAND HOW THE WEST AND THE NORTH DOMINATE OVER THE EAST AND THE SOUTH"

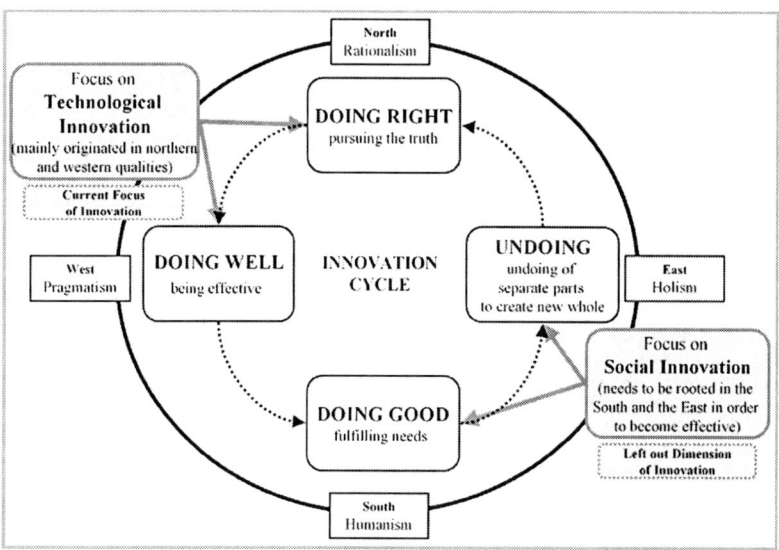

Figure 2.1: Social versus Technological Innovation

+d good

Summary: Why Social Innovation Gets Stuck

- We argue, that most of the research in business, management and economics specifically, if not in social science generally, has lost touch with its "social essence": Most of it is purely guided by rationalism and pragmatism, while humanism and holism have been left out of account. We therefore position research methodologies in a new way, so they form part of an integral framework. This is provided by our Four World Model.

- In the Four World Model the West and the North represent pragmatism and rationalism, while the South and the East represent humanism and holism. This Model is an archetypal model, integrating the four core dimensions of human and of social being and becoming, as well as knowing and doing, equally on the level of the self, the organisation and the society. We are demonstrating in this chapter how the domination of the one world over the other leads ultimately to distortions and to an unhealthy balance for the entire world.

- In research terms, as in "real life", it is the Western and the Northern approach that dominate (with some exceptions), while the Southern and Eastern ones have been left out. That is the reason, so one of our core arguments, why most of research fails to lead to innovation.

- Another negative side effect of the left out Southern World, with the exception of so-called participatory action research and co-operative inquiry, is the resultant absence of co-creative research. Most research in social science is still mainly individually conducted, though, as we will show in this book, the communal dimension of research is a vital ingredient of social innovation.

- In this chapter, we also reconnect with the philosophies, which are the ultimate ground for all research. Philosophies are born out of and also underlie axiology, ontology, epistemology, methodology and method – the founding pillars of all research. We have however all too often failed to recognize the philosophical foundations of research methodologies, which make these in most social science research rather disconnected and indeed boring. Or, in the rare cases, where philosophies are recognized, it is mostly those representing the North and West; while philosophers from the East and South, whose philosophies are not only closer linked to their culture but also to the problematic issues of a particular life world, are usually left out.

- The story of one of us (Ronnie Lessem), which is told in this chapter, may serve as a representative tale of a social researcher delving into the western and northern world, while overseeing (for a while) his own southern (African) home ground, which was in desperate need of social innovation. It is a story of a long journey where in a researcher's lifetime Ronnie embodies the global phenomenon of a left out South and East. The reader understands how the personal experiences of the authors as social researchers in different places of the world was instrumental in looking for ways to bring the South and the East back into the research world – in order to bring true social innovation about.

- We demonstrate in this chapter also, how most universities fail to provide a fruitful ground for Social Innovation. They deliver, however, in the case of the Natural Sciences, and the quality and scope of today's technological innovation is beyond doubt. The problem lies in the lack of social innovation, and we shall illustrate, how the South and the East are instrumental for social innovation. There is a need not only to change the way you undergo research in social sciences; there is also a strong need for reforming the institutions that are supposed to breed social innovators and to foster social innovation.

2.1 Dysfunctional Creative Synthesis: Distorted Social Designs

In chapter 1 we have demonstrated how particular societies and civilisations have developed knowledge about maintaining a healthy and dynamic balance. To the extent that such a dynamic healthy balance turned to creative synthesis, the society developed its power to innovate, socially as well as technologically. We now want to explore those moments, when civilisations lost this specific balance.

The critical moment when this power started to decline occurred, so we argue, when one dimension or sector started to dominate the other, and there was no fertile – that is mutual – interaction. That may have led to particular achievements in one specific area, however, ultimately the entire system got out of balance. Be it that the entire civilisation needed to submit to its military machinery, be it that the religious dimension claimed all power or claimed to be in possession of all knowledge, be it that (as we can see in today's world) entire societies submit purely to economic principles (to the expense of environment and cultural, spiritual meaning). History offers countless examples from Alexander the Great to Caesar, from Communist Ideology to modern day financial Capitalism, when an imbalance or singular pre-emphasis on one particular fact of a society has led to its overall decline.

Disorder may also have been evoked when an outside force challenged the civilisation, but, retracing historical steps, this mostly happened when the civilisation itself was already beyond its peak and vulnerable (example: the defeat of the Aztec empire by the Spaniards in the early 16th century). At such a moment in history the knowledge of keeping a dynamic balance, of staying in the "wheel of social innovation" got lost and a healthy process could not further evolve. The "creative synthesis" between the various parts stopped.

What then happens if the balance gets lost, whereby one part dominates the others, and the creative synthesis is precluded, whereby fertile interaction between cultures is inhibited?

We understand intuitively what happens if the four elements (earth, fire, water and wind) are not "in synch" – which would lead to a hostile environment (examples: flood, tsunami, hurricane, blaze). The same occurs if the four seasons, as well as rainy and dry periods, are out of alignment. We are increasingly experiencing this "disorder", as environmental damage and pollution leads to climate change with a yet unforeseeable chain of consequences.

In terms of the generic social design that we have developed, our Four World Model, the following may happen, if the defining elements (nature, culture, politics and economics) of a society (or between societies) are out of synch. We thereby also include the contribution a particular world region makes, if it is in integral synch with the other three:

Distorted versus Integral Social Designs	
West	An overemphasis on "Western" Pragmatism may lead to Materialism – the belief that material wealth solves all problems (Examples: today's West / Economic Colonialism / Financial Capitalism), as opposed to "*economic opportunity*" for all.
North	An overemphasis of the "Northern" Rationality may lead to Dogmatism / Scienticism – the totalist belief in a technology, science or a particular social system (Examples: an exclusively technocratic approach to global warming: the ex communist, totalitarian regimes in Eastern Europe), as opposed to an" *open society*".
East	An overemphasis of the "Eastern" Holism leads to Fundamentalism – a belief that a particular religion or culture can solve all problems: (Examples: Muslim, Hindu, Tamil, Christian or Jewish Fundamentalism), as opposed to "*peaceful co-evolution*".
South	An overemphasis of the "Southern" Humanism leads to Parochialism – the belief that a total retreat into your own community can solve all problems (Examples: Albania in the 80s / Oman before 1970 / Genocide in Rwanda), as opposed to "*healing societies and the planet*".
Center	A dysfunctional vital center, working towards a dynamic balance of the four dimensions, leads to stagnation of the entire system (Example: continuous conflict within and between the Middle East and the outside world), as opposed to "*integral innovation*".

The US Social Philosopher Francis Fukuyama has declared "The End of History and the Last Man" (1) stating that if all countries would subscribe to the western economic model of free markets and implement western style democracies the problems of the worlds would be overcome. For us, this is another example of a distorted social design, leaving not only the dimension of the south (natural environment) and the east (belief system), but also overlooking the fact that a particular "societal design" needs to be firmly rooted in a specific society's soil and is not be "exported".

Forceful attempts to root foreign systems and approaches in local cultures have always failed, much of the Middle East today being one of the most explosively reactive cases in point. Peaceful assimilation of foreign elements properly linked to indigenous elements, as we will prolifically see in the Omani case in the concluding chapter of this book, have proven much more successful. But let us first have a close look into the deeper nature of the current stuckness, pursuing the question, why social innovation falls so evidently behind technological innovation.

2.2 Why Social Innovation falls behind Technological Innovation

The World on Fire – Autumn 2006

Social innovation has fallen lethally behind technological innovation, and societies in the transition between the two suffer as a result. On the one hand for example, (wo)man can fly to the moon and back, mobile phones can function as sources of global communication, and scientists have cracked the genetic code. On the other hand, local and global terrorism are proliferating, today's weather is wreaking havoc upon our lives, and the gap between the rich and the poor grows bigger every day. In fact, and at the time of writing, for the first time that one if us can remember, a tornado wreaked havoc in northwest London. So, while for the time being, the developed world gains and the developing society loses, sooner rather than later the whole world will be on fire. Indeed, in February 2007 it has been reported by UNESCO that Britain, the free enterprise capital of Europe, has the worst record, of 21 industrialised countries, in the overall wealth and well being of its children.

Whereas technically and economically, the world is an ever more exciting place, socially and communally, as in the run down suburbs of Paris and London, Beirut and Baghdad it is imploding around us. So while the natural sciences have served substantively to advance many a technological cause, the social sciences have proved to be much less successful. Why then is this so? Let us start close to academic home.

Pragmatism and Humanism Fail to Meet

When we ask many of our business or academic colleagues how they are advancing the lot of mankind through their commercial activities or the "research" papers they write, we get incredulous looks. Similarly, when we ask clients in the corporate world how their research and development activities are contributing to resolving our pensions crisis, human poverty around the globe, or the problem of world climate change, we get similarly blank looks. "That's all very well", the academics say, "our students just want to get a degree", or "I have a PhD to complete". Alternately, for business or management practitioners, "I have targets to meet", "We are aiming for a 5 point score in the research assessment exercise", or, indeed "We are addressing these very problems every day; I don't know what you mean by research?" The prospect that one or other may be advancing the lot of mankind, purposefully through social innovations, as opposed to pragmatically and rationally getting on with things, is left way out in the cold. That is why – in Amy Chua's words (2) – the world is on fire!

Three decades ago, then, one of us (Ronnie Lessem) set out on a research journey to re-create "business as an extension of human being", as a would-be social innovation. Having been involved in a large and commercially successful family business in former Rhodesia, he had the nagging feeling that, for all its material benefit, it was failing his people spiritually. For while his company would readily adopt and adapt the latest fashions from Europe, and materials from the Far East, the spirit of Africa seemed to be missing from both the factory floor and from the clothing designs. In other words, the company, of a thousand strong, was technically and economically highly efficient, and was commercially very profitable, but there was no indigenous artistic impulse or overall spiritual uplift to behold.

Moreover, when he first studied "Principles of Economics" at the University of Rhodesia and Nyasaland – as it was called in the early sixties – the "western" free market subject matter was alien to his "southern" soul. Most certainly it was not invented here, in Rhodesia-becoming-Zimbabwe, and the social sciences he studied, ranging from political science to economics theory, political philosophy to economic history had no intrinsic connection with the culture and nature of Africa! Actually, it was just the opposite. "Free market Rhodesia" into Zimbabwe did not altogether go, and many a tragedy was to unfold out of that particular impasse. So Ronnie embarked in the seventies on a journey around what he conceived as a more "Global Business". (3) Soon afterwards, as politics and economics came to blows with each other, Rhodesia in becoming Zimbabwe began to "catch fire", firstly through the liberation war in the seventies, and secondly through the land crisis and Mugabe's response to it, in the eighties and nineties. In fact, Locke's concept of private property, and economically laden free markets in England as Ronnie came to discover, sat uncomfortably with Rousseau's anthropologically oriented "natural man" and the "contrat social" in France. The gap between the two, concepts and countries, the global, propertied rich and the local, landless poor, remains just as great to this day, now spread around the world.

Fiddling Way From Home While the Home Fires Burned

It was in the seventies and eighties, now based in the UK, that Ronnie completed his own PhD, on "Action Learning for Business Development", focused on the development of entrepreneurs in London's inner cities. It feels to him now, looking back, that he was fiddling away from home, while the world of his birth burned. He was not the only one. How many Africans, Indians and others had proceeded onto greener pastures?!

His doctoral research seemed to have no relevance (in the seventies) to his cause: that of linking African as well as Arab, Chinese or Indian spirit to global technique, and there was certainly nothing co-creative about it, as he pursued his individual cause. Indeed no social innovation was in the immediate offing. That having been said, his focus was on "action learning", something he would re-visit later in now "action research" guise (see chapter 16). Moreover, it was the originator of such action learning, the English management philosopher Reg Revans, who proclaimed:

" ... the salvation of individual countries and their enterprises is not to be found by observers scouring the world in the hope of turning up some miracle there. Their salvation rather, their 'Kingdom of God' is to be found within their own shores, and within the wills of their own people. At the level of the individual enterprise, it is not unreasonable to suggest that an essential part of any research and development policy is the study of the human effort, out of which the saleable products of the enterprise are largely created ... Learning as such must demand not only research and analysis. It must demand power to get the knowledge needed to see one's part in what is going on. In particular one needs to know the effect of one's behaviour upon those with whom one works ... best achieved within small action learning groups". (4)

It was indeed in the context of such small action learning groups, together engaged with individual business start-ups in the UK, that Ronnie Lessem pursued his doctoral studies. They were duly inspired by Revans' action learning approach, which also served to underpin the project based masters which he subsequently evolved at City University, in the financial heartlands of London. In fact, as a graduate of the "western" Harvard Business School, he had found its allegedly practical "case study" approach distinctly lacking in genuinely experiential Anglo-Saxon foundations. Whether for a masters or a doctorate, one simply "had to do" research. Further, no distinction was made between method and methodology, not to mention the critical emancipatory or action research orientations Ronnie would discover twenty years later. In fact, it was as far removed at the time from any social innovation, as planet Earth is from Mars. It had no meaning in relation to his personal, professional or societal origins, as Ronnie Lessem, as an economist, or as a Rhodesian/Zimbabwean, and offered his society no potential for innovation.

So when Ronnie returned periodically to a newly independent Zimbabwe, in the eighties, as a management educator and researcher, he tried to make up for lost time, to rediscover the lost spirit of the "south" in a business context. The specific cause he was seeking to advance, of business becoming an extension of human being, only seemed to take off when he assumed authorship of his life through his work as a management researcher and would-be social innovator in the latter part of the 1980's. Unwittingly, he was beginning to uncover an "integral" research methodology that was genuinely "out of this whole world", to be recast thereby as social innovation. Initially it drew upon "global" (5), and subsequently upon African (6) – as well as European, Arab and Chinese – Management. How so?

Uncovering Disconnected European Philosophies and Management

Business enterprise in the European Community, Ronnie wrote in the early nineties – together with his co-author Franz Neubauer (7) – has not emerged in a vacuum. In effect it has evolved in significant part, notwithstanding the ever-increasing influence of America and Japan, out of the European continent's particular set of cultural heritages. These distinctly differentiated and integrated heritages are reflected in art, religion, philosophies and ideologies, duly manifested in its approaches to anthropology and sociology, politics and psychology that have developed over the past three millennia in Europe. At the same time the continent has evolved its diverse people and communities, its multifaceted sciences and institutions, as well as its specific attitudes and behaviours. Yet none of these institutions "speaks for themselves" as its seminal ideas, that is its diverse European philosophies:

"Philosophy brings clarity and meaning into careers of individuals, nations, civilisations. Such is the strength of tradition that men have always tended to accept the particular philosophy or religion prevailing in the group into which they were born. Human beings, primitive or civilised, educated or uneducated, cannot escape from philosophy. Philosophy is everybody's business." (8)

Interestingly enough, a new "action research" (alongside action learning) as a new philosophical fusion of action and knowledge was taking place in the 1970's. Spearheaded by a Columbian Professor of Economics, Orlando Fals Borda, who had become disenchanted with conventional "northern" European academe, "western" (capitalist) and "eastern" (socialist) economics, the new approach came to be called participative action research (PAR). PAR was an intriguing "southern" counterpart to Revans' "western" orientation.

Philosophers like Fals Borda are supposed to be our experts in integration; they form a general staff for coping with the increasing fragmentation of our culture: "They are the liaison officers among the many different and often isolated branches of knowledge; between the civilizations of the past and present; between the great living systems of belief that move the various nations of our day. *Philosophers are always reminding people of the interrelatedness of things, bringing together what has been torn apart and disunited."* (9)

What we did not realise in the nineties, is that philosophy is both born out of and also underlies, as illustrated below, axiology, ontology, epistemology, methodology and method.

Origins and Constituents of Philosophy	
Axiology	the nature of morality
Ontology	the nature of reality
Epistemology	the nature of knowledge
Methodology	our approach to acquiring, and processing knowledge
Method	the technique for processing information in a formalised research context

Altogether, when interconnected, these constitute a basis for integral research, extending from a morally inspired vision to "do good" to a materially based process for "doing it well" (see figure 2.1). Such an integral research process, positioned in the context of a particular set of individuals, organisations and societies, constitutes the basis for social innovation.

Social innovation, moreover, unfolds, from the ground up, and encompasses method and methodology, critique and integrated action research, for each of the four research paths in turn. So the south and the north, the east and the west, each has its own intrinsic path to social innovation. However, the northern and western paths of reason and realisation have taken worldwide precedence over the southern and eastern relational and renewal paths, with very damaging regional effects.

It was indeed such "doing good" that was picked up by "participatory action research" (PAR), already in the 1970's. Until today – now living in the context of the emerging knowledge era – neither socialists nor capitalists have yet purposefully drawn upon PAR. For Bangladesh's Muhammad Anisur Rahman who was formerly based at the ILO and is together with Fals Borda a seminal figure in PAR:

"Historical experience calls for rethinking the meaning of social transformation for people's liberation. The dominant view of such has been preoccupied with the need for changing the oppressive structures of relations in material production – certainly a necessary task. But, and this is the distinctive view of PAR, domination of elites is also rooted in control over social power to determine what is useful knowledge, the one (knowledgeable) then reinforcing the other (material). In fact existence of the gap in knowledge relations can offset the advantages of reducing the gap in relations of physical production ... People then cannot be liberated by a consciousness and knowledge other than their own. It is therefore essential that they develop their own endogenous consciousness-raising and knowledge generation abilities. This requires the social power to assert this vis-à-vis elite consciousness and knowledge." (10)

These participatory action researchers were effective "southern" forerunners of the knowledge revolution, which was to ensue in the "west", "north" and "east" twenty years later. However, they virtually got lost in the process, so that humanistic "doing good" (south) has fallen behind pragmatic "doing well" (west), rational "doing right" (north) and holistic "undoing" of separate parts to create a new whole (east) in the overall knowledge creating process. This falling behind of the "south" – in our integral terms – had led to a predominance of technological, over social, innovation, that is of "doing right" over "doing good", or rationalism (and pragmatism) over humanism (and holism) (see figure 2.1).

Europe and Innovation: Matter and Spirit Apart

As Ronnie Lessem and his German colleague Franz Neubauer – both then based at the IMD Institute for Management Development in Switzerland – wrote in the early 1990's, as Europe develops its knowledge-based economy so the need to replace the materially based factors of production – land, labour and capital – with knowledge based ones becomes paramount. (11) *The four most pervasive sources of knowledge, or philosophies, from our point of view, are pragmatism, rationalism, holism, and humanism.* What would take us long years is to realise that these philosophies (or "ontologies") spawn in turn different "epistemologies", which give rise to the diverse "methodologies" with which Integral Research is concerned. Moreover, and of particular significance for us as researchers and developers, *each of these philosophies have different political and economic implications.*

These generic philosophies have, at a micro level, spawned diverse concepts and applications that at least partly precondition European as well as American business and economic activity. However, at a macro level only one of these, today, that of the pragmatically based market economy (and its derivative business practice of free enterprise) has seen the full light of our economic day. As for the other three philosophies, their time is still to come, both in business theory and in practice. Now that Marxism has suffered its demise, as Fals Borda and Rahman were already recognizing in the 1970's when PAR first began to emerge, we are left with the limiting prospect of only one socio-political ideology – capitalism – dominating the macro economic scene. We hence felt the *need to deepen and extend our business and economic foundations, on the one hand, and our research methodologies, on the other.* In so doing we were following in PAR's emancipatory footsteps, while also recognizing that we needed the altogether integral impetus from the west, north and east, as well as the south. Such an integral approach serves to enliven and transcend both capitalism and socialism, by fusing together pragmatism and rationalism, holism and humanism.

In the course of uncovering "European Management Systems" we probed into the philosophies of Bacon, Locke and Mill in England; Descartes, Diderot and Montesquieu in France; Leibniz, Goethe and Kant in Germany; as well as Vico and Croce in Italy. At that time, in the early nineties, despite having successfully completed his PhD some ten years before, Ronnie was blissfully unaware of the fact that these philosophers had any influence whatsoever on the research method he had deployed in his thesis. In fact, in a subsequent work on "The Light and the Shadow: How Breakthrough Innovation is Shaping European Business" (12), with Japan's Ikijiro Nonaka, as cited in our "Managing in Four Worlds" (13), we still remained completely ignorant of the link. Whereas we were now able to connect Nonaka's knowledge creating cycle of socialisation and externalisation, combination and internalisation with the "four worlds" of humanism (southern) and holism (eastern), rationalism (northern) and pragmatism (western), research methodology remained totally disconnected from such. In effect, John Heron's action research oriented process of co-operative inquiry (see chapter 10), not to mention David Kolb's (14) famous learning cycle (concrete experience – reflective observation – abstract conceptualisation – active experimentation), and indeed Revans' process of action learning (audit – survey – hypothesize – act) are similarly aligned. As a result, altogether lacking in such an integral learning and research process, social innovation was stultified.

Research Method and Social Innovation are a Million Miles Apart

Ronnie's wake up call came when he established a global doctoral programme, through the newly established Trans-cultural Center at the University of Buckingham in the UK. It was then, and only then, that the proverbial penny began to drop. *Not only was research methodology an extension of philosophy, but the philosophers that had spawned such methodologies were all, yes all, social innovators of the day.* This indeed applies as much to Africa and the Middle East today, for example, as it did in the Europe of yesterday.

Even the standard "western" pragmatism, or more specifically the empiricism and "positivism" that characterises such European based research philosophy and methodology, originally emerged in the Enlightenment as a reaction against religious and political dogmatism. It was just that their urge to "do good" as opposed to "do right" (pursue the truth) was implicit rather than explicit (see figure 2.1). Indeed Morton Schlick, a key member of the Vienna Circle of "logical positivists" (15) in the 1920's and 1930's, was shot by the Nazis, because of his anti-fascist beliefs. When Ronnie compared these original philosophies, that he had now systematically begun to absorb from all parts of Europe, with the anodyne way in which they were conventionally described in the academic research texts, he was shocked. In fact, his colleague John Heron from the Center for Human Potential at the University of Surrey put it very well in his seminal work on "co-operative inquiry":

"Research in the human sciences is very much an academic pursuit, based in and originating from universities. They are committed to the intellect as the controlling force in individual and social life, and to the pre-eminence of "propositional" knowledge, a set of intellectual statements published in systematic form. Staff, as such, unilaterally make decisions on behalf of students. They decide what the students should learn, how and when, and assess such according to their own criteria. Academics do not need to acquire the kind of emotional and interpersonal competence to empower students to learn more holistically and participate in educational decisions to enable them to become progressively more self-determining ... Such authoritarian control, moreover, is transferred from teaching to research. While we consider that the 18 year old has the right to vote, he or she has no right to participate in educational decision-making. We consider that a person has the choice whether to take part in a research program, but has no right to have a say in what it is about." (16)

So what we began to realise, firstly, was not only that these quintessentially European philosophies were sources of knowledge creation, but also that they potentially fuelled social innovation. Secondly, such philosophies and derivative methodologies were almost all European – as much as the corresponding research methods were American – so that Asia, the Middle East, Latin America or Africa did not get a look in. Thirdly, the very reason that such methodologies were not explicit sources of social innovation were their lack of global reach. For example, while empirical and experimental research had led to technological innovation in the physical sciences, this was less apparent in the social sciences, where goodness (southern) and truth (northern) needed one another. Similarly, as far as participatory action research was concerned, its social activism all too often has fallen short of social innovation, because doing good (southern) may not have been followed by undoing (eastern), prior to doing right (northern) and doing well (western) (see figure 2.1).

That hurt, because by now we had devoted much time to studying African and Indian, Arab, Chinese and Japanese philosophy as well as their business management, and discovered all these philosophies to be inordinately rich. Why on earth, then had they no local role to play in our global research cause? Needless to say, in our own work, such global philosophies, most specifically from Africa, feature prominently. So what should be the role of a university in relation to such, in order to promote social innovation (process) alongside transformative education (content)?

2.3 Why Universities fail to provide a fruitful base for Social Innovation

2.3.1 The Role of the University in Society

The Liberal Arts Ideal and the University Reality

The American political philosopher Allan Bloom, writing a bestseller in the late eighties on "The Closing of the American Mind", thought profoundly about the university's role in the wider world. (17) Bloom was specifically focusing on the role of the "liberal arts" based university. He controversially maintained (in the 1980's) that the university in America offers no distinctive visage to the young person.

In short, *there is no vision, nor is there a set of competing visions, of what an educated human being is. There is no overall organisation of the sciences, no tree of knowledge.* Better to give up on liberal education he laments and get on with the speciality on which there is at least a prescribed curriculum and a prospective career. *The student gets no intimation in the university of our day that great mysteries might be revealed to him or her, that new and higher motives of action might be discovered within, that a different and more human way of life can be constructed by what he or she is going to learn, that the world extends beyond the shores of America and Europe.*

Disconnect Between Inauthentic Careers and Authentic Learning

Bloom maintains that *no public career these days moreover – not businessman nor doctor nor lawyer nor journalist – has much to do with authentic human learning.* Such an education, purely professional or technical, can even seem to be an impediment to such. Most professors are specialists concerned only with their own fields interested in the advancement of those fields in their own terms, or in their own personal advancement in a world where all rewards are on the side of professional distinction. Such an orientation then forms the "paradigm" for specialised research, with arid research methodologies and methods, which is so very distinct from "integral research" with a view to social innovation with which we are concerned.

For Bloom, academe has been entirely emancipated from the old structure of the university, where it was apparent, at least, that specialists were incomplete, only parts of an undiscovered and unexamined whole. Even the greatest of American universities, which can split the atom, find cures for the most horrible diseases, conduct surveys of whole populations and produce massive dictionaries of lost languages, can not, he maintains, generate a modest programme of general education for undergraduate students. This is a parable, Bloom reckons, of our modern times. Liberal education flourished when it prepared the way for the discussion of a unified view of nature and man's place in it, which the best minds debated on the highest level. It decayed when what lay beyond it were only specialities, like business studies or economic principles, the premises of which do not lead to any such vision.

As we can see, and from his understandably "western" and individualistic perspective, albeit combined with a holistic eastern one, Bloom is somewhat disconnected from the communal orientation that comes from the "participatory" south.

2.3.2 Divide Between the Sciences and the Humanities

Where Natural Science Ends Trouble Begins

How then, for Bloom, do the disciplines – that is the big three disciplines that rule the academic roost and determine what is knowledge: Natural Sciences, Social Sciences and the Humanities – today generally move forward? What foundations are we ourselves in our focus on social innovation able to build upon?

Natural science, to start with, is doing just fine, which is precisely why technological innovation proliferates (design and commercialisation), emerging out of a continuing stream of scientific discoveries (fundamental and applied research). Living alone but happily, running along like a well-wound clock, it is as successful and useful as ever, at least in the developed world. Technological innovation proceeds apace; there have been great things discovered lately. Physicists have uncovered black holes and biologists the genetic code. Its objects and methods are largely agreed upon by the presiding academic community. Our way of life is utterly dependent on natural scientists. Only at the margins are there now questions and doubts as to the use of the results of research, such as is the case for nuclear weapons or genetically modified foods. In general, though, all is well. As a result, technological innovation is all the rage and social innovation falls desperately far behind.

So where natural science ends, trouble begins. It ends at man. To be exact, it ends at that part of man, which is not his body. All that is human lies outside of natural science. The trouble is that for the study of this alternative social theme, pertaining to (wo)man and their activities, there are two great divisions of the university, the humanities (human culture) and social science (human nature), while for bodies there is only one natural science (physical nature). The social sciences and the humanities do not co-operate, though they occupy much of the same ground. Never do the twain meet at university. All our efforts to bring together our social sciences and humanities continually fall on polite but stony ground! The renowned historical social scientist and world systems analyst Immanuel Wallerstein comments as follows:

The modern world system has developed structures of knowledge that are significantly different from previous ones. It is often said that is what is different is the development of scientific thought. However scientific thought long antedates the modern world and is present in all major civilizations. What is specific to Eurocentric structure of knowledge is the separation of "two cultures", science and philosophy/humanities, or the quest for the true and the quest for goodness and beauty. If we are to construct an alternative world-system to the one that is in grievous crisis today, we must treat simultaneously and inextricably the issues of the true and the good. (18)

Moreover, the social sciences are largely disconnected from the worlds of enterprise, reduced by and large to large scale social surveys, or small scale social experiments, rather than fully fledged social innovation.

The social sciences and the humanities, for Bloom, represent the two responses to the crisis caused by the definitive ejection of (hu)man from academe. One route (that of the social sciences) led to valiant efforts to assimilate man into the methodologies of the natural sciences. The science of man became the next rung in the ladder down from biology. Quantitative as well as pseudo-qualitative research methodology follows. In fact, most of the qualitative methodologies to be cited here, while fully recognized within the social sciences at large, are hardly pursued at all in social science faculties around the world. Empirically based, "western" oriented quantitative approaches continue to dominate, thereby inhibiting innovation.

Gap Between African Trading and Place de la Concorde

It was under strong parental influence, that Ronnie selected the economics route, which he originally chose to undertake at the University of Rhodesia and Nyasaland, as an undergraduate, and at the London School of Economics, as a postgraduate. The other route – that of the humanities – he undertook in his spare time. In fact, whereas the study of statistical research method was predominant in Rhodesia at the time (1960's), econometrics was to the fore at the LSE. While, for Bloom, social science humbly tried to find a place at court, and the humanities proudly set up shop next door, there was no junction of these two latter roads, as there is no academic connection between business (social sciences) and culture (humanities) to this day, nor between research and innovation in the social sciences. As Ronnie can remember, his family business drew prolifically upon technical support for the factory from Europe, mainly from France, to the extent that it even changed its name from African Trading to Concorde Clothing, named after Paris' Place de la Concorde.

There was no parallel attempt to draw upon latest development in the social sciences, within Europe, nor from the humanities that surrounded us in Africa. Neither the social sciences nor the humanities, for Bloom as for us, has fully succeeded. *Social science – including management – receives no recognition from natural science.* And the humanities, a Cindarella discipline at our own universities has turned out to be selling diverse and ill-sorted antiques, decaying and even dustier. Social science has proved more robust, more in harmony with a world dominated by natural science. However, it has lost the inspiration and evangelical flavour it had in Europe in the eighteenth and nineteenth centuries, together with the capacity to promote innovation – just witness the birth of capitalism, perhaps the most prolific of contemporary social innovations, via Adam Smith in 1776. Humanities languish, because they don't suit the modern world. Social science comes more out of the school founded by English political philosopher John Locke; humanities out of that founded by the Swiss-French social philosopher, Jean Jacques Rousseau. Let us now delve a little deeper into the social sciences.

2.3.3 Divide and Rule: Locke and Rousseau

The social sciences work largely independently. Each of them makes a claim that the others need to be understood in its terms – economics arguing for the economy or the market, psychology for the individual psyche, sociology for society, anthropology for culture, and political science for the political order.

Each speciality argues that the others are parts of the whole it represents. The social sciences represent a series of perspectives on the human world we see around us, a series that is not harmonious, for there is no agreement on what makes it up altogether. Recent progress with regard to such integration, characteristic of general systems and complexity theory, has not yet made its way into most of the halls of conventional academe. A further disagreement exists on what is to be termed "science". Economics, held to be the most successful social science, is the most mathematized. Many argue though that economic man ("homo oeconomicus") is an abstraction that simply does not exist.

Politics and Economics versus Culture and Nature – Worlds Apart

What students actually see when they first encounter social science are two robust, self-sufficient and self-confident social sciences, economics and cultural anthropology, extremes forming the antipodes, with nothing to say to each other, with the other social sciences falling in between. Locke and Smith, falling on the one side, underpinned the economics. Rousseau, on the other side, was left out in the cold. For management researchers today, Rousseau does not have anywhere near the influence on "corporate culture" or "managing across cultures", as John Locke and Adam Smith have on business and economics.

For Locke, life, liberty and property are the fundamental natural rights, and the "colonial" social contract is made to protect these. These principles agreed upon, economics comes into being as *the* science of man's proper activity, and the "western" free market, currently triumphant in our turbulent world, as the natural and rational order. Rousseau argued that nature is good, and the "white" man far away from it. So the quest for the faraway origins becomes imperative, for Rousseau, champion of "the noble savage", and anthropology is by that very fact founded.

Interestingly enough, anthropology was absent from Ronnie's own, African university heritage as it was for Alexander at his University in Switzerland, Rousseau's home country. It was left to the great Laurens Van der Post to bring the "primitive" to light.

"European man walked into Africa by and large totally incapable of understanding Africa, let alone of appreciating the raw material of mind and spirit with which ... this ancient treasure house of the lost original way of life, was so richly filled. He had, it is true, an insatiable appetite for the riches in the rocks, diamonds and gold ... but not for the precious metal ringing true in the deep toned laughter of indigenous people around him." (19)

Following in Van der Post's footsteps we came to admire those close knit traditional cultures, that channel and sublimate the economic motive and do not permit the emergence of the formalised free market. Anthropologists teach that culture is the fundamental social phenomenon, and its culmination is the sacred. Such is the confrontation, both in academic theory and in colonial practice, between man and woman, the producer of consumption goods, and the producer of culture, the "maximising animal" versus the reverent one. In fact, economics has triumphed over anthropology today, within the social science mainstream, just as Britannia ruled the waves in the eighteenth and nineteenth centuries, America has done in the twentieth century, and China is likely to do, economically at least, in the twenty-first.

2.3.4 Liberal Research and Education

Information versus Transformation

So the glory days, for Bloom, of the liberal education that preceded the formation of business schools are over. Gone are the days when Karl Marx, Sigmund Freud and Max Weber, philosophers and interpreters of the world, were king. Charles Darwin and Albert Einstein would be as relevant to social as to natural science, and modern literature – Fjodor Dostojevski or Franz Kafka in a European context, Kahlil Gibran or Edward Said in an Arab one, Confucius or Lao Tzu in a Chinese one, Leopold Senghor or Chenua Achebe in an African one – would provide insights that social science would systematize or prove. This is the path we are seeking to follow, resurrecting such a "liberal" education past in the light of the present and future.

True liberal education, for Bloom, requires that the student's whole life be radically changed by it, as per the transformation programmes and social innovation projects and processes we run, that what he or she learns may affect their actions, tastes, choices, that no previous attachment be immune to examination and re-evaluation. For us such a "liberal" minded research has the same radical connotation in that now the whole society in which the research is based becomes ripe for social innovation. *Such "liberal" education and research puts everything at risk and requires students and researchers who are willing not only to risk all but to transform all: socially and economically.* Doing so, they stand on the shoulders of the philosophical giants whose derivative research methodologies they follow, and whose original social innovations they seek to renew, albeit in a particular cultural and societal context.

As Natural Science Rises Social Science Falls

For Bloom, philosophy is lost amongst the collection of natural and social science disciplines and the humanities. So we come back full circle to where this chapter began. Such philosophy once proudly proclaimed that it was the best way of life to seek the first causes of things, and not only dictated its rules to the special sciences but constituted and ordered them.

Yet our problems are so great, and their sources so deep, that to understand and resolve them we need philosophy more than ever. That is if we do not despair of the state of our world, and face the challenges it offers; and that is indeed the path we have adopted, as "integral researchers". *Just as in politics the responsibility for the fate of freedom in the world had devolved upon our governments, so the fate of philosophy in the world has devolved upon our universities, and the two are related, as they have never been before.*

The Crisis in the European Sciences

What then about the "south" and "east", so neglected in the literature on management, – of course with the exception of Japan until recently – and in research methodology? We believe, that it is the absence of such a global orientation, which brought about what Edmund Husserl called the "Crisis in the European Sciences" (20) early on in the last century. For him, such a crisis served as a forerunner of the World War II. Today, we would argue, it is one of the factors underlying the great divide between the "north" and the "south", if not also the "east" and the "west".

The need to overcome this Eurocentric perspective in research is, for sociologist Immanuel Wallerstein of utmost importance: *"Social science has been Eurocentric throughout its institutional history ... today, and for the last thirty years, this "Eurocentricism" has been increasingly under attack .. if social science is to make any progress in the twenty-first century it must overcome that Eurocentric heritage which has distorted its capacity to deal with the problems of the contemporary world."* (21)

For us, the integral resolution of such a Eurocentrism involves the coming together of the diverse research, learning and knowledge perspectives that come from our four worlds.

2.4 Conclusion

Are we really living in a Knowledge Society?

Today we claim to live in the so-called knowledge era, but is that really true?

From Singapore (knowledge creating island) to Malaysia, from China to South Korea, from the US and EU (who defined in its Lisbon Strategy an ambitious strategy to create a knowledge creating society) to Dubai's "knowledge village" and Qatar's "education city", to, overall, the organisational buzzword of the knowledge creating organisation and company – there seems to be a universal understanding that this is the way to go.

We have tried to demonstrate that all these ambitions fall short, if we purely focus on technological and lose out on social innovation.

So, if we claim to live in a knowledge era, we need to actually specify that we live in the era of Western and Northern knowledge management. We do not live in the era of all round knowledge creation, that includes social as well as technological innovation; and it is the knowledge of natural science (and the resulting technologies) that predominate.

It is agonizing to witness how the supposed driver of knowledge creation, the academic world, has, while making an enormous impact in the natural sciences (medical science, engineering, communications technology and so on), patently not been in evidence in the social sciences. Indeed the social sciences in that knowledge creating respect are stuck. For example, most of the doctoral research generated, leads, once finalised, a lonely life on some library shelf. And that is, as a counterbalance, where our integral research comes in.

Again, what's wrong with the Social Sciences?

Methodology as Obligation: The current process of social research then does not work. One of the reasons, as we have been intimating, is that the research (or knowledge generating) process utilised simply does not lead to Social Innovation. Most of the researchers in the Social Sciences do not deeply understand research methodologies and the philosophical roots on which such methodologies stand, nor do they work purposefully evolve the social sciences on which they draw. The roots of all research methodologies in the social sciences, however, are comprised of (r)evolutionary philosophical thinking, which emerged out of a deep critique of society, albeit mainly European society, at the time. The innovative and evolutionary impulse of such philosophies however gets completely lost, if the resulting research methodologies are not understood in their specific cultural and historic context when they emerged and were taken developmentally forward to the present time.

Building on such philosophies and research methodologies and re-animating the Social Innovation cycle is our objective and the only way, we believe, to generate socially innovative knowledge. If one critically reflects on the majority of doctoral research work today, in the social sciences, one can see that most postgraduate researchers regard the knowledge and application of "research methodologies" as an unpleasant, if nor merely obligatory, prerequisite of their doctorate, or indeed masters studies. In most cases, the research methodology is inserted in one isolated chapter of the research in order do comply with the regulations. Hence, research methodologies and the innovative power they are potentially carrying is not further evolved; there is no connection anymore between the methodology to generate knowledge and the generated knowledge itself. It is obvious to us, that such knowledge can hardly be innovative.

Eurocentrism: However, it is not only a question of understanding a particular research methodology in its depth. Reviewing the research methodology landscape, we became aware that this landscape is highly Eurocentric. Most of the research methodologies applied have their roots in Western Europe, from hermeneutics to phenomenology, from critical theory to postmodernism. Researchers from all over the world follow these methodologies. In other words, they are trying to build new social knowledge on philosophies and methodologies that have nothing do with the "social soil" they are coming from and – in many cases – in which they are looking to implant their research results. This is the second major dilemma, which we intend to overcome with our integral research design. Such an integral design pays specific and explicit attention to four research worlds.

Mechanical Research Routines: Many universities have established arduous routines for their research processes, ranging from power laden, often wayward supervisors, to an over-emphasis on empirically based "data gathering". While it is important to put a strong emphasis on academic rigour, one needs to question what kind of true benefit comes out of most research work in the social sciences, with their due emphasis on analysis, data gathering, and a mechanical approach to research method or methodology (all too often undistinguishable) in post-graduate programmes all over the world.

The belief that technology can solve it: The strong emphasis on a pragmatic and rational approach towards knowledge generation leads us to the belief, that the modern, analytical mind and modern technology can ultimately solve all our problems. We are hence willing to invest heavily in all kinds of technological innovations, and indeed computerised methods of data gathering, to ensure a happy, wealthy and safe life, or research regime, but do not equally value and promote genuine social innovation.

These issues are interconnected and lead to a total deadlock in the social sciences. The inability of such social sciences, indeed divorced from the humanities (which are much more overtly culture specific), to generate true social innovation confirms – from the perspective of the North-Western mind – that it is only technology and economy (free markets) that can solve the problems within our societies and on a global level.

Our overall argument is that we have got things, research-and-innovation wise, the wrong way around. In other words, the "west", embodying what George Soros has recently called the "feel good" (22) society – for us doing well! – is riding roughshod over the "south" – for us the source of doing good – rather than building accumulatively upon it.

Finally, we express the core message of this chapter in organic terms. The following illustration of our Social Innovation tree underlines why Social Innovation got stuck:

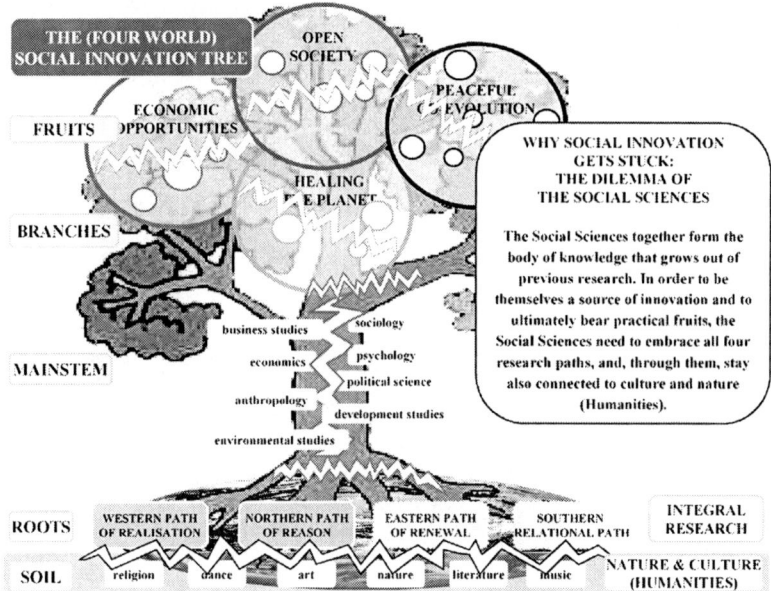

The (Four World) Social Innovation Tree figure contains the following labels:

THE (FOUR WORLD) SOCIAL INNOVATION TREE — OPEN SOCIETY — PEACEFUL CO-EVOLUTION

FRUITS — ECONOMIC OPPORTUNITIES — HEALING THE PLANET

BRANCHES

MAINSTEM — business studies — sociology — economics — psychology — political science — anthropology — development studies — environmental studies

WHY SOCIAL INNOVATION GETS STUCK: THE DILEMMA OF THE SOCIAL SCIENCES

The Social Sciences together form the body of knowledge that grows out of previous research. In order to be themselves a source of innovation and to ultimately bear practical fruits, the Social Sciences need to embrace all four research paths, and, through them, stay also connected to culture and nature (Humanities).

ROOTS — WESTERN PATH OF REALISATION — NORTHERN PATH OF REASON — EASTERN PATH OF RENEWAL — SOUTHERN RELATIONAL PATH — INTEGRAL RESEARCH

SOIL — religion — dance — art — nature — literature — music — NATURE & CULTURE (HUMANITIES)

Figure 2.2: Why Social Innovation got stuck

We are closing this chapter by citing, once again, Wallerstein, one of the most prolific contemporary advocates of a new approach to knowledge creation, an approach that allows for reuniting the social sciences with the humanities:

"Can we tear down the old structure of social science while simultaneously constructing new pillars for some kind of roof? And will the roof be limited to just social science or rather encompass a reunited single world of knowledge that knows no division between humans and nature, no divorce between philosophy and science, no separation of the search for the true and the search for the good. Can we unthink social science while reconstructing the structure of knowledge?" (23)

By introducing Integral Research, we echo Wallerstein's claim. In the next chapter we lay out the structure for this book, which is a direct response to the question at hand, that is how to alleviate the gap between technological and social innovation.

Bibliography

1) **Fukuyama**, F. (2002). *The End of History and the Last Man.* New York: Free Press.

2) **Chua**, A. (2003). *The World on Fire.* London: Heinemann.

3) **Revans**, R. (1999). *ABC of Action Learning.* Rochester: Mike Pedlar Library.

4) **Lessem**, R. (1987). *Global Business.* New York: Prentice Hall.

5) **Lessem**, R. (1999). *Global Management Principles.* New York: Prentice Hall.

6) **Lessem**, R. et al (1993a). *African Management.* Johannesburg: Knowledge Resources.

7) **Lessem**, R. & **Neubauer**, F. (1993). *European Management Systems.* London: McGraw Hill.

8) **Lessem**, R. & **Neubauer**, F. (1993). *European Management Systems.* London: McGraw Hill.

9) **Fals Borda**, O. & **Rahman**, M. (1991). *Knowledge and Action.* New York & London: Apex Press.

10) **Fals Borda**, O. & **Rahman**, M. (1991). *Knowledge and Action.* New York & London: Apex Press.

11) **Lessem**, R. & **Neubauer**, F. (1993). *European Management Systems.* London: McGraw Hill.

12) **Kalthoff**, O. et al (1997). *The Light and the Shadow: How Breakthrough Innovation is shaping European Business.* Oxford: Capstone.

13) **Lessem**, R. & **Palsule**, S. (1997). *Managing in Four Worlds.* Cambridge, Mass: Blackwell.

14) **Kolb**, D. (1991). *Experiential Learning.* New York: Prentice Hall.

15) **Smith**, M. (2002). *Social Science in Question.* London, Thousand Oaks and New Delhi: Open University Press.

16) **Heron**, J. (1993). *Co-operative Inquiry.* London: Sage.

17) **Bloom**, A. (1988). *Closing of the American Mind.* Chicago: University of Chicago Press.

18) **Wallerstein**, I. (1999): *The End of the World as we know it: Social Science for the Twenty-First Century.* Minneapolis: University of Minnesota Press.

19) **Van der Post**, L. (1958). *The Dark eye of Africa*. Cape Town: Lowery Press.

20) **Husserl**, E. (1970). *Crisis in the European Sciences*. Chicago: North Western University.

21) **Wallerstein**, I. (1999): *The End of the World as we know it: Social Science for the Twenty-First Century*. Minneapolis: University of Minnesota Press.

22) **Soros**, G. (2006). *The Age of Fallibility*. London: Weidenfeld & Nicolson.

23) **Wallerstein**, I. (1999): *The End of the World as we know it: Social Science for the Twenty-First Century*. Minneapolis: University of Minnesota Press.

CHAPTER 3

THE DESIGN OF INTEGRAL RESEARCH

"GETTING READY FO(U)R SOCIAL INNOVATION"

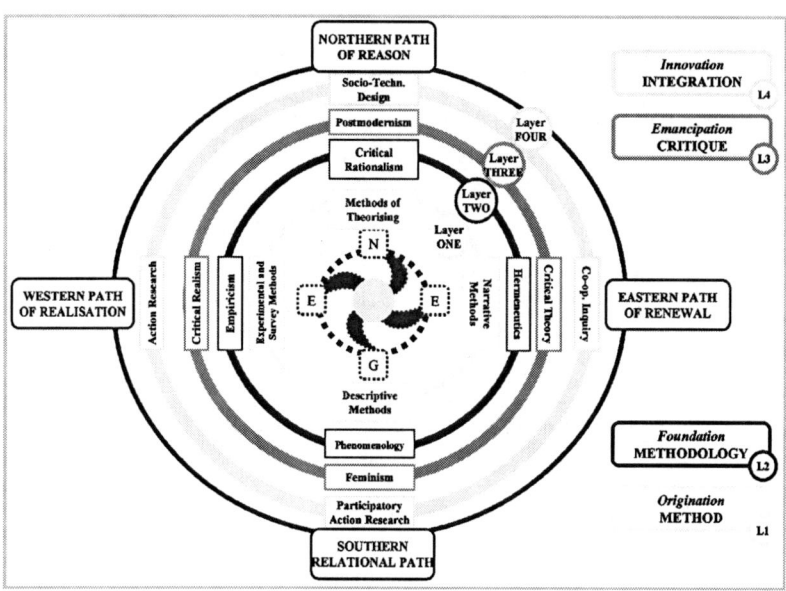

Figure 3.1: Overview Chapter 3 – Integral Research (Full Architecture)

Summary: The Design of Integral Research

- In this chapter we set out the four research paths that you are able to follow: the "southern" and humanistic Relational path; the "eastern" and holistic path of Renewal; the "northern" and rational path of Reason; and the "western" and pragmatic path of Realisation.

- These four discrete paths serve to make up the Integral Research the GENE, a term we have created in previous work. The GENE stands for Grounding, Emerging, Navigation and Effecting, and is the generic driver that releases the full GENEius of a person, a community or a society. In this case, it is the inner driver that releases the GENEius of your research, turning it into Social Innovation.

- Within Integral Research the GENE can be found twice. First, each research path represents one part of a Four World GENE: Within our architecture the relational South is strongest on Grounding; renewal places the greatest emphasis on Emergence; the northern path of reason is predisposed towards conceptual Navigation, and that of realisation towards practical Effect. We call this GENE the Four World GENE constituting Integral Research.

- Secondly, each path holds its own fourfold Path GENE. This is comprised of the four research layers. Each of the four research paths enables you to move through those four research layers: from formative research to transformative innovation: by starting out 1) with research method (origination of your research), followed by 2) methodology (the foundation of our research), onto 3) critique (your emancipation), culminating with the particular social innovation (your integration) embodied in that specific research path in the fourth layer. The Path GENE complements for each path the overall Four World GENE.

- What does that mean for you. Firstly and most important, once you have identified your specific research path, you immerse yourself into a GENE path. For example, if your research path is the southern relational path, you would move from description (Grounding), to phenomenology (Emerging), feminism (Navigating) and ultimately participatory action research (Effecting). However, from the very beginning, you would see your research in the light of the whole, being fully aware of your particular path, but also of the overall knowledge and value creating process you are ultimately contributing to.

- Each layer is differentiated for each of the four research paths. The first layer, in terms of each respective path, of method (origination) is differentiated into descriptive methods (southern relational path) and narrative methods (path of renewal), methods of theorising (northern path of reason) and experimental and survey methods (western path of realisation)

- The second layer of methodology (Foundation) consists of phenomenology (relational) and hermeneutics (renewal), followed by critical rationalism (reason) and empiricism (realisation). Each of them is building upon the research method that came before.

- The third layer of Critique (emancipation) builds in turn on method and methodology, and is constituted of feminism (relational), critical theory (renewal), postmodernism (reason), and critical realism (realisation). Each of these critiques tends to be relatively more rounded than the methodologies that came before. They thereby serve to connect different research paths.

- The fourth layer of ultimate Innovation (Integration), which is the most integral, thereby serving most concertedly to turn social research into social innovation, is comprised of participatory action research (relational), co-operative inquiry (renewal), socio-technical design (reason) and overall action research (realisation).

- Now you, the researcher, are ready to immerse yourself in the roots of knowledge and value creation, that is your specific and layered Path GENE, whichever of the four research paths you pursue. In each case you move from method (origination) to methodology (foundation), to critique (emancipation) and finally, to action oriented innovation (integration).

3.1 Introduction

Within this chapter we shall lay out in detail the roots of knowledge and value creation, growing out of the particular, underlying soil (culture and nature), and linked with a specific mainstem (social science). We build progressively on the general Four Worlds / Four Research Paths that we developed in chapter 1. In that opening chapter we evolved four different paths to social innovation that have been developed over time in different parts of the world.

These four paths within the four-world framework form our Integral Research (Roots) that leads towards Social Innovation (Fruits), by drawing upon the Social Sciences (Mainstem), and on the underlying Nature and Culture (Soils) of a particular society. Soil, Roots and Mainstem are altogether focused on (Branches) which we describe as the four major areas of contribution for Social Innovation. *Healing the Planet, Peaceful Co-Evolution, and the build up of Open Society and Economic Opportunity.*

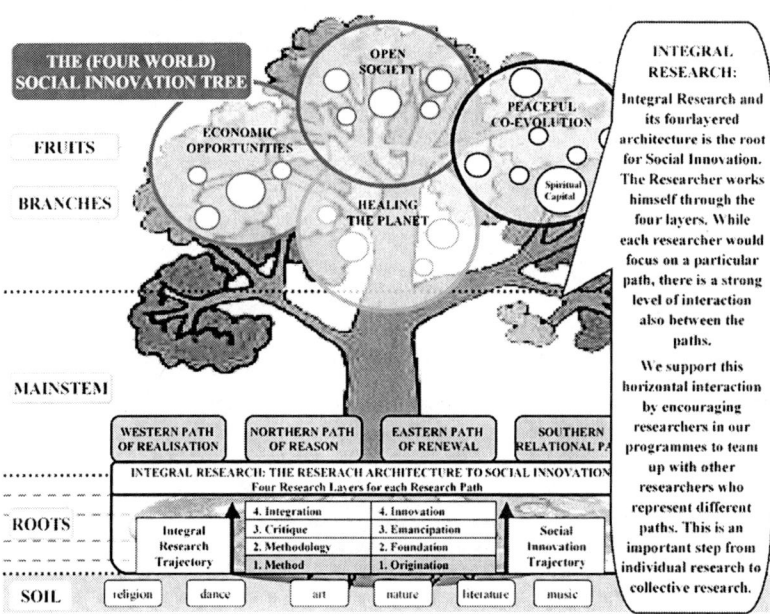

Figure 3.2: The Social Innovation Tree

We will start to build systematically from this basis. While the detailed integral research framework is presented in linear terms, *integral research is quintessentially a back and forth cyclical, spiralling and ultimately original and organic, living process, where the end of "doing well" is created out of the beginning, "doing good".* But let us move forward step by step, or to be more precise, we shall take four steps in each subchapter. So get ready fo(u)r Social Innovation, building upon the social sciences in general, and on the nature and culture of your society.

3.2 Four Research Paths or "The Four World Gene"

The opening integral research design that constitutes the roots of our social innovation tree simultaneously embodies the four worlds and the centre. As an Integral Researcher you start by reconnecting with the creative source of your self, organisation and society, that is your individual, institutional, communal, professional nature and culture. Here, as close as possible to yourself (to home), you find the original seed for your research. You review your own personal and collective centre, before entering a particular research path that is altogether authentic for you, your institution and your society

As we have outlined in chapter 1, it is here, in the natural and cultural "soil" where the "roots" – integral research – of social innovation are lodged, and from which each research path originates.

The process of knowledge and value creation towards social innovation is a highly dynamic one. The paths illustrated here may generate the illusion of a linear movement. But they are nothing else than expressions of archetypal patterns of creation, which serve as an orientation on our way to Social Innovation. You will remember from chapter 1 that the visual social design (like the illustration of the four research paths) is only the outer expression of an inner dynamic process. It is this creative inner process that is a decisive part of your Integral Research, and we shall turn to uncover this innermost "vital force".

3.3 A Fourfold GENEtic Code to Social Innovation: Uncovering the Research Gene

3.3.1 The GENE as a generic form of a transformative process

If you review the examples of dynamically balanced social designs in different civilisations (see chapter 1) and the implicit meaning as well as explicit form of such, you can say, that – without exception – all of them were designed as orientations for knowledge seekers, on a path to social innovation that has emerged in a particular culture and society.

In all cases these designs are invitations to raise consciousness and to engage in a knowledge-creating journey. Many of them refer at some point or another directly to nature itself and build on the wisdom of how nature continuously innovates by developing higher, more suitable forms (outcomes of a "creative synthesis").

We have analysed the knowledge generating (consciousness raising) patterns underlying such diverse social designs. We found that each design has its particular inner process, or vital force, allowing for the "creative synthesis" of and between its parts, also serving to promote a productive interaction with other social organisms (communities or societies). This process is a kind of "vital force or "attractor" that attracts individuals, organisations and societies towards knowledge creation. It is following the course of a particular nature and culture, constituting the very soil or foundations of social innovation.

Distilling our findings in various local natures and cultures, we have distilled a dual rhythm, differentiating and integrating, which we call the Four World GENE and the Path GENE, altogether ensuring dynamic and ongoing interaction between the elements of the Integral Research, as well as between these roots and the fruits.

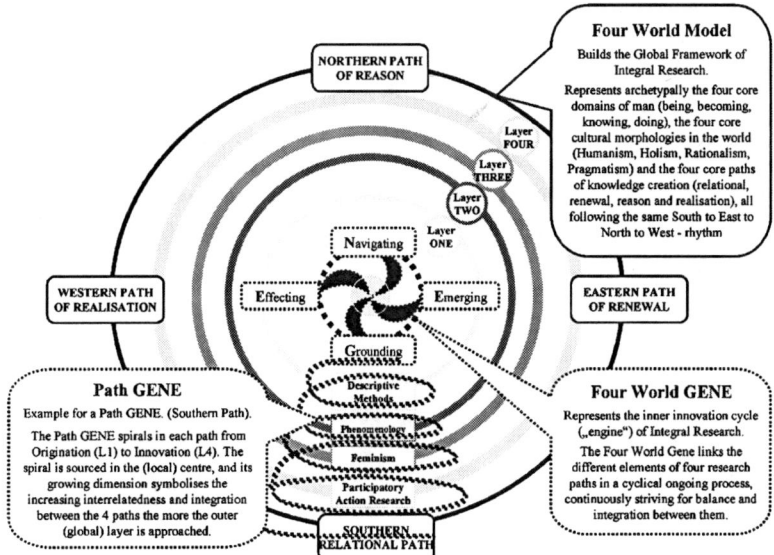

Figure 3.3: The GENES

Based on our argument so far, it is obvious that the Grounding Phase is the first step in the Integral Research. The "effecting" step is the final one, and for once it is the South that leads the process, followed by the East and the North. The archetypal west, so our argument, becomes only truly effective if it builds on the other worlds. In other words, you need to uncover the south, east, north and west, metaphorically, not geographically, of your society, while also, and in the process, drawing from these worlds. The Four World GENE distinguishes between the relational path of research, as well as the research paths of renewal, of reason, and of realisation.

As mentioned hitherto in this chapter, as an Integral Researcher you opt for one of the four specific research paths, one that is authentic to yourself, and your society, while the integral path comprises a synthesis of them all.

3.3.2 The Differentiated Path GENE and the Integral Four World GENE

The two GENEs are the roots of social innovation as shown above. In this next step we align the generic terminology of the Gene with the specific terminology of the Social Researcher-turned-Social Innovator.

Grounding → Research Issue: In grounding yourself in the phenomenon of burning significance to you and in relation to which you want to apply your unique self, you enter into the heart of the general social research, lodged within a particular nature and culture, with which you are engaged. Here you start to envisage, what kind of social innovation you seek to bring about. You also connect with the natural and cultural soils of self, organisation and society.

Emerging → Research Question: The immediate grounds for your research are set within a historical context, out of which your research question emerges. Such a question has individual, organisational and societal origins. In that context it draws upon tradition, while seeking out modernity, and is in that sense original, in serving to fuse the two together. Such a research question then serves to connect past, present and future, through your own interpretation of such. It also sets the overall storyline, which, on the one hand, casts old light on the concrete phenomenon being researched, and, on the other hand, casts new light upon your envisaged innovation through the abstract ideas that will be drawn upon.

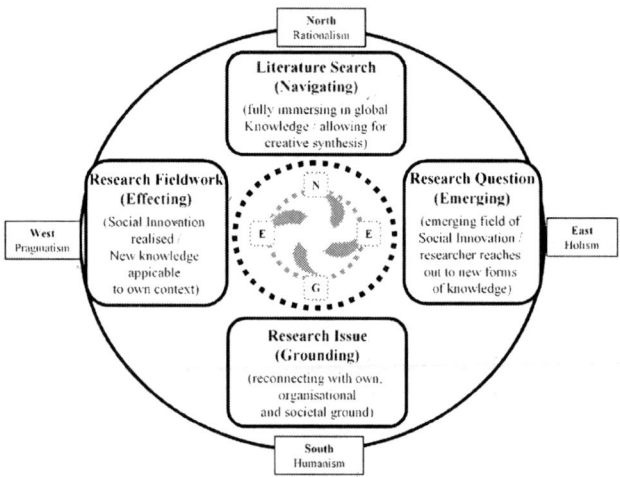

Figure 3.4: The GENE in Research Terms

Navigating → Literature Search: The prior knowledge that you build upon is grounded in your own experience, the indigenous knowledge of your society, as well as emerging out of the historical engagement of both self and society with others. You then build upon the explicit wisdom of the key thinkers, ideologies or paradigms in your field of concern. In consolidating such prior knowledge it is now important to focus on the conventional wisdom in your field. Hence, you are drawing specifically upon one and preferably more of the social sciences, the mainstem of social innovation. This is required in order to formulate hypotheses, or build up scenarios, that combine such with what has come before, based on which you are able to navigate your way into the prospective fieldwork. At such a point, theory and conjecture is about to be tested against fact and observation, so that viable conclusions can be reached.

Effecting → Research Fieldwork bringing about Innovation: The empirical "doing" of research-and-innovation follows upon your being immersed in it in the first place, forming the visible and accessible "knowledge branches", or indeed "know-how" arising out of your research. Becoming original in your progressively emerging interpretation of the research field, you come to know the conceptual foundations within which your interpretations are lodged. Such *doing* of research thereby builds on prior being, becoming and knowing. Such empirically based co-creation is specifically focused now on observation and experimentation.

The Gene uncovers the inner rhythm of knowledge and value generation. We can see how this rhythm of "research to innovation" is deeply connected to the learning rhythm of humans in general. We are tapping indeed into a universal pattern, which in tends to evoke (before logical understanding) immediate intuitive resonance. And it is from this inner rhythm that we can now progressively understand the research that we introduce.

3.4 The Four GENE Constituents: Building accumulatively up towards Social Innovation

3.4.1 Overview: From Origination to Innovation

We shall now move toward the essential elements of the Integral Research. We shall demonstrate here in a first overview, how generations of philosophers and research scientists have developed sophisticated methods and methodologies for the generating of knowledge, and, in the very process became, to a lesser or greater degree, themselves social innovators. They all build in one or other way on the inner rhythm of the GENE, though they may have developed a particular strength in one of its elements, as much as they were "incarnations" of a particular knowledge path. They also, to varying degrees, build explicitly on their underlying soils, and develop visible and accessible know-how,

All such social innovations build on a particular situation and knowledge need within civilisations at different times. They all, as we shall later reveal, react to a specific context and/or herald future developments within societies. In the process, they progressively build the multiple layers or attempts that mankind has developed over time in order to be innovative and to generate new and useful knowledge for a particular time. Our framework shows this development. While we are not saying that our model incorporates each and every systematic contribution towards knowledge generation, we claim, however, to offer a conceptual framework that allows you as an individual or group of researcher/innovators to position the various systems and understand them in their relation to each other. Instead of presenting different research methodologies in an isolated manner, which is done by so many overviews on social science research, we show – within a generic framework – their particular contribution, progressively towards innovation, in an interrelated and accumulative process of knowledge generation.

In order to reconnect with the innermost source of "creative synthesis" the integral researcher needs to understand those various layers, and like an "archaeologist" or a "botanist" not only uncover them, but also make meaning of the progressively more innovative trajectory they are encompassing in its integral entirety. From that deeper understanding of the various layers, you come to understand what your own authentic research path will be and which path (or combination of paths) will lead you from research to social innovation. The first layer is comprised of research methods, serving to originate your research. In most social science research you decide first on a methodology before you select a method or a combination of methods. We, however, do it the other way round, starting with method that is consistent with the overall research-innovation for which you have opted, before you move to a conventional research methodology.

Following the further evolution of social science research you then enter into the second layer of conventional research methodology which serves to establish the research foundation, before evolving further toward the third layer of "postconventional" research, introducing Research Critique through feminism or critical theory. Such a critique or emancipation then serves to connect with the final and fourth layer, which we call Innovation (finally reaching a state of Integration). Researchers who choose a methodology without understanding what evolutionary contribution they are making won't be able to come up with a social innovation that has a true relevance for a particular context.

This chapter only serves as a brief introduction to the four layers in order to give you a first understanding of the entirety of Integral Research. After this we shall introduce the four methods contained in layer 1 in a separate chapter, and then progressively introduce each of the following layers 2, 3 and 4 – all in separate chapters.

Drawing on the same logic that John Heron (1) uses in his approach to action research, that is Co-operative Inquiry (see chapter 10) we argue that origination, foundation, emancipation and integration together form the integral living process. It is for that reason that we take into account all four. We are responding as such to a call of our time, where social innovation, as we have demonstrated in chapter 2, has come to a virtual dead end. We have particularly emphasized, that this deadlock has much to do with a domination of western and northern ways of knowledge generation, on the one hand, and the overtly analytical (as opposed to action centred and transformative) approach to the social sciences, on the other. We therefore need to ultimately come to an integral perspective of the different ways, illustrating the specific contributions which each world or research-to-innovation path represents, each of which is needed in order to enable creative synthesis, resulting out of the constructive interaction within and between the various worlds.

As all truly innovative social scientists have done, we as well try to make a contribution to the particular context we are currently living in – a world, where social innovations are too rare to significantly improve the world in which we live. So let us start to uncover now the various layers of integral research, with which, when understood and acted upon, will enable you to build a solid foundation for future social innovation.

Layer 1 is divided between four kinds of basic research methods, which constitute the origination of one path or another. We shall be only briefly concerned with them in this book, as there have been literally hundreds of volumes already published on such. However, the latter two groups of methods, as we shall see – experimental and survey methods and methods of theorising – have received more emphasis than the former. That having been said, as initial building blocks, these research methods are vital to integral research.

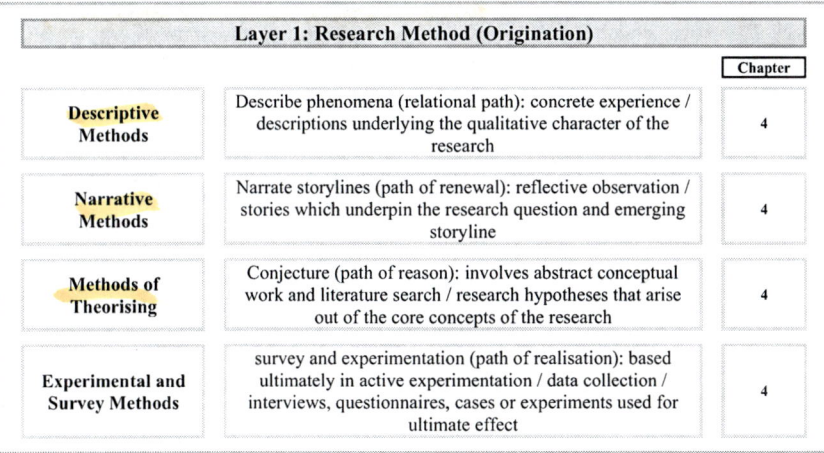

Layer 1: Research Method (Origination)		
		Chapter
Descriptive Methods	Describe phenomena (relational path): concrete experience / descriptions underlying the qualitative character of the research	4
Narrative Methods	Narrate storylines (path of renewal): reflective observation / stories which underpin the research question and emerging storyline	4
Methods of Theorising	Conjecture (path of reason): involves abstract conceptual work and literature search / research hypotheses that arise out of the core concepts of the research	4
Experimental and Survey Methods	survey and experimentation (path of realisation): based ultimately in active experimentation / data collection / interviews, questionnaires, cases or experiments used for ultimate effect	4

Layer 2 is comprised of the more sophisticated but still conventional wisdom on qualitative research methodology, serving to locate yourself in one or other of four respectively phenomenological or hermeneutic (interpretive), rational and empirical (positivist) paradigms:

Layer 2: Research Methodology (Foundation)		
		Chapter
Phenomenology	The research phenomenon in which you are phenomenologically immersed; development of descriptive methods	5
Hermeneutics / Interpretivism	The research question in relation to which you interpretively pursue a development of narrative methods	8
Critical Rationalism	The research hypotheses you pursue and theories you draw upon, as a development of methods of theorising	11
Empiricism	The analysis you undertake through and towards your research through your empirically based fieldwork, as a development of your initial experimental and survey methods	14

Layer 3 encompasses the more contemporary, unconventional wisdom, spanning so-called "critical emancipatory" methodologies, which serve to provide an overtly transformative and socio-political outlook upon your research, involving:

Layer 3: Critique (Emancipation)		
		Chapter
Feminism	Feminism as an experiential and relational development of the descriptive and phenomenological	6
Critical Theory	Critical theory as a reflective and dialectical evolution of the narrative and interpretive	9
Postmodernism	Postmodernism as a conceptual and discursive development of hypothetic-deductive and critical-rational	12
Critical Realism	Critical realism as an active and stratified development of the experimental and empirical	15

Layer 4 serves to ultimately bring about social innovation through a combined process of action and reflection:

Layer 4: Integration (Innovation)		
		Chapter
Participatory Action Research	emerging out of descriptive methods, phenomenology and feminism	7
Co-operative Inquiry	emerging out of narrative methods, hermeneutics and critical theory	10
Social-Technical Design	emerging out of methods of theorising, rationalism and postmodernism	13
Action Research	emerging out of experimental and survey methods, empiricism and critical realism	16

At this ultimately integral point, the individual and the communal need to be mutually aligned to promote social innovation. For integral research is immediately communal, in that you as an individual researcher need to align your activities with the group. Formally speaking, the process of "research supervision" needs to be a simultaneously personal and collective process.

This is realised by an interactive and dialogical approach, which continually invites a comparing and contrasting between the research issue, research question, research hypothesis and research fieldwork, as well as critique of the individual's research, vis-à-vis the group, always and ultimately with a view to social innovation.

We now turn briefly to each method, methodology, critique and integration of your path, bearing in mind, that these are integral to your research-and-innovation as a whole. Subsequently we shall have much more to say on each one through our four-stage process. Each step along the way is involved with particular research methods and methodologies, critiques and ultimately innovations.

3.4.2 Layer 1: Research Methods (Origination)

The first research layer serves to orient your social research, with a view to social innovation. Characteristically such research orientation is heavily biased, as we shall see toward the west. For when we refer in an everyday sense to such typical "research", we have in mind opinion surveys, questionnaires, interviews, experiments and other such commonplace research methods. Moreover, when undergraduates around the world refer to such, they also have in mind such questionnaires or focus groups, to which innumerable academic books and papers have been dedicated. Finally, when an organisation issues questionnaires or conducts sample surveys, this is also the first layer of a "western" research orientation. Lots of this kind of "research" remains at that basic, formative level. We shall not be covering it extensively in this book, but need at least to allude to here, because, while it has been done so many times before, this is from where you need to start.

Even in this initial regard to preconventional wisdom, we can immediately see that there is a "north-western" bias. In other words, there is a bias towards empirically based survey and experimental methods. Such an orientation toward (what we term) practical realisation, preclude, for example, phenomenologically oriented descriptions of people's life worlds and interpretively based life stories. Overall, it is survey and experiment (active experimentation – doing) and hypothesis (conceptual abstraction – thinking) that dominate over narrative (reflective observation – becoming) and description (concrete experience – being).

As we can see below, the research methods in themselves, devoid of subsequently reflective methodology and critique together with the action oriented innovatory phase, will never lead to innovation. Such a formative starting point is nevertheless required as part of an integral whole, covering foundational descriptions, stories, hypotheses and surveys as well as experiments.

At this level of origination, you become attached to an issue, you read a couple of prescribed articles on it, probably on the internet, and you get on with the data collection you reckon you require, usually through questionnaires or interviews, case studies or experiments. As such you may be a social researcher, or indeed a market researcher, if not also researching into "organisational climate", but you are a long way from being a social innovator!

3.4.3 Layer 2: Research Methodologies (Foundation)

On Method and Methodology

As you move on, you engage much more purposefully, and indeed academically, with research methodology. Your method is now further evolved and you develop your integral methodology, not only philosophically and methodologically, but also socio-politically. We now consider each method and methodology in turn. We are starting with phenomenology, which serves to most richly describe your research issue. Such phenomenology, alongside interpretevism, rationalism and empiricism, constitute the four fundamental, differentiated research paradigms or worldviews – for us respectively "southern", "eastern, "northern" and "western" – that underlie our integral approach. Phenomenology, as we shall now see, evolved as a reaction to the all-pervasive empirical paradigm prevailing at the time.

Descriptive Methods to Phenomenology: The Research Issue – Who Are We?

At the turn of the last century, Edmund Husserl, the inventor of phenomenology (a Moravian and Central European by birth and a mathematician by training) wrote his seminal work on "The Crisis of the European Sciences". For Husserl, writing in the 1930's:

"The exclusiveness with which the total world-view of modern man, in the second half of the nineteenth century, let itself be determined by the positive sciences and be blinded by the "prosperity" they produced, meant an indifferent turning away from questions which are decisive for a genuine humanity. Merely fact-minded sciences make merely fact-minded people. Science excludes in principle precisely the questions which man, given over in our unhappy times to the most portentous upheavals, finds the most burning: questions of the meaning or meaninglessness of the whole of human existence. In the final analysis they concern man as a free, self-determining being in his behaviour towards the world around him, that is "free" in rationally shaping himself and his surrounding world. The mere science of bodies has nothing to say about this: it abstracts itself from anything subjective." (2)

All objective consideration of the world, Husserl laments, involves consideration of the exterior and grasps only externals, objective entities. The radical consideration of the world that he advocates is the systematic and purely internal consideration of the subjectivity, which "expresses" itself in the exterior. That, in our integral research context, underlies its essentially qualitative character. Husserl did not reject the worlds of Locke's empiricism, nor that of Descartes' rationalism, as well as of Kant's idealism. In fact, those philosophers, for Husserl, who are most significant for the modern period, are Hume (empiricist), Descartes (rationalist) and Kant (idealist). In conclusion Husserl has this to say:

"Personal life means living communalized as "I" and "we" within a community horizon, and this in communities of various forms – family, nation, supra-national

community. It involves purposeful life, the term life in this context not having a physiological sense, but in the broadest sense creating culture in the unity of a historical development. All this is the subject matter of numerous humanistic developments. Now clearly there exists the distinction between energetic striving and atrophy, between health and sickness, even in communities and states. How is it, then, that no "scientific medicine" has developed in this sphere? The European nations are sick. Europe itself is in crisis." (3)

We now turn from phenomenology to its close "relative" hermeneutics, which represents a shift from a humanistic to a holistic – interpretive – worldview.

From Narrative Methods to Interpretivism / Hermeneutics: The Research Question – What are we Becoming?

We have already noted that Locke, in his seventeenth century time, was a radical critic of theological and political dogma, as were the Vienna Circle in their Nazi ridden times. Yet today, such "positivists" would be seen as a conservative force in the research establishment. The "interpretive" reaction to such is lodged in "hermeneutics". A good example is the contemporary work of American psychotherapist Peter Cushman who has the following to say:

"Hermeneutics' dialectical vision is of we humans as swimming in a sea of culture that is both given to us and continually reconstituted by us ... we can make use of alternative traditions that are available to us in our everyday lives, develop ways of shifting the parameters of our vision, and in the process make more moral ground, and thus more behavioural possibilities open to us. By adjusting our cultural horizon we can allow room for alternative traditions to show up, and then we can use these traditions to create a dialogue with the dominant tradition. We can then, armed with an enriched perspective, fight against the forces that oppress us." (4)

For our research purposes, as we move from phenomenology to hermeneutics, so we move from descriptive to narrative, from immersion in the issue at hand to the essential meaning of the response, to our research question. This is – after "doing good" – the point of "undoing", when our originality begins to make itself felt. Interpretivism, which is rooted in German historicism, is opposed to both empiricism and rationalism, the latter being championed by Anglo-Austrian Karl Popper.

From Methods of Theorising to Critical Rationalism: Literature Search – What Do We Know?

Though hermeneutics is not normally overtly political, it certainly has moral overtones, e.g. in terms of respect for other cultures. Next to empiricism, phenomenology and hermeneutics, in order of prevalence as research methodologies, is "hypothetico-deductivism", as a research paradigm. Renowned in research circles for his deductive orientation towards hypothesis formation and falsification, Karl Popper is well known in philosophical circles for championing "Open Society". In fact both Popper and his contemporary disciple, George Soros, were Jewish emigrants from respectively Nazi and communist oppression. For Popper then:

"The Enlightenment thinker, the true rationalist, never wants to talk anyone into anything. He does not even want to convince: all the time he is aware that he may be wrong. Above all, he values the intellectual independence of others too highly to want to convince them in important matters. He seeks not to convince but to arouse. Free opinion formation is precious to him: not only because this brings us closer to the truth but also because he respects free opinion formation as such." (5)

Popper was of the view that western democracies were exemplars of such "open societies", as they certainly are in comparison with totalitarian regimes, or overtly despotic governments. George Soros has taken Popper's work further and established his "Open Society Foundation". Moreover, and in the same way as an individual researcher is supposed to conduct an exhaustive "literature search", so an "open society" needs to be an open to a wide range of philosophies and ideologies as alternative worldviews.

As we can see, from Popper and Soros, rationally based conceptualisation can be aligned with openness to different arguments, as opposed to a particular dogma or fundamentalism. Soros is describing empirically based "market fundamentalism" as an example of such, by stating: "It would thereby be a mistake to equate the market values that guide individual participants with the social values that ought to guide the setting of rules. Market values can be measured in monetary terms but social values are more problematic." (6)

We finally turn from south, east and north to west, from a rational and deductive to an empirical and inductive research worldview.

From Experimental and Survey Methods to Empiricism: Applied Fieldwork – What Can We Do?

Of course, such market "fundamentalism" originally had impeccably democratic rather than dogmatic credentials. For the emergence of a liberal political and economic philosophy – from Hobbes and Locke through to J.S. Mill and Adam Smith, in Britain during the seventeenth, eighteenth and nineteenth centuries – heralded a subsequent era of political democracy and free markets. Aligned with both of such was a "positivist" approach to scientific method, whereby the investigator was to ensure that he or she stuck positively to the empirical facts, in testing out their scientific conclusions. Such a practical comprehension of the specific results of any hypothesis testing, through experimentation and observation, is the nub of the empirical method. In our Integral Research Architecture, it is the fourth step in the second layer of our conventional research. These are the methodological constructions of your integral research.

As you evolve from method to methodology so:

- being a researcher, generally evolves into deliberately pursuing *qualitative methodology*
- becoming involved in an issue evolves into a dynamically *evolving storyline*
- knowing the odd article turns into a *comparative analysis of the literature*, and
- busy doing data collection turns into *systematic fieldwork*.

We come now to the third layer, which serves to turn social research through socio-political as well as philosophical emancipation towards innovation.

3.4.4 Layer 3: Critique (Emancipation)

Descriptive Methods and Phenomenology to Feminism – Continuing the Relational Path

Whereas layers 1 and 2 are well recognized in the research community, layer 3, embodying the Critical Emancipation is less commonplace. They are, however, quintessential to our approach, serving to build up an analytically based social research trajectory towards a transformative one. We are starting here with the relational path:

- to be originated within descriptive methods
- evolves towards a phenomenological research foundation
- then onto a feminist critique as emancipation
- culminates in Social Innovation through a process of participatory action research

In his "Passion of the Western Mind", the American social historian Richard Tarnas, who is also an exponent of postmodernism, concluded his philosophical journey from the ancient Greeks to the present day: *Western intellectual tradition has been produced and canonized almost entirely by men, and informed mainly by male perspectives.*

The "man" of the Western tradition has been a questing masculine hero, a Promethean biological and metaphysical rebel who has constantly sought freedom and progress for himself, and who has constantly striven to control the matrix out of which he emerged. This masculine proposition in the evolution of the Western mind, though largely unconscious, has been not only characteristic of that evolution, but essential to it.

For the evolution of the Western mind has been driven by a heroic impulse to forge an autonomous rational human self by separating it from the primordial unity of nature. But to do this the masculine mind has repressed the feminine. Moreover, this separation calls forth a longing for a reunion with that which has been lost – especially after the masculine heroic quest has been pressed to its utmost one-sided extreme in the consciousness of the modern mind. As such:

" ... *that is the great challenge of our time, the evolutionary imperative for the masculine to see through and overcome its hubris and one-sidedness, to own its unconscious shadow, to choose to enter into a fundamentally different relationship of mutuality with the feminine.*" (7)

We now turn from feminism to critical theory.

From Narrative Methods and Interpretivism to Critical Theory – Continuing the Path of Renewal

The research methodology and underlying philosophy, which is historically most strongly identified with a socio-political critique is the critical theory, which emerged in Germany during the 1920's and 1930s, until its Jewish originators – Adorno and

Horkheimer, Marcuse and Fromm – all had to flee from Nazi Germany to the United States in the thirties. "Critical theory", which essentially took on from where Marx left off, was both supportive and critical of his basic position. Strangely enough, while their influence on research methodology continues to be strong to this day, as political philosophers they have become virtually extinct. This is particularly ironic, given that at a time when Marxism has been eclipsed, while the flaws of capitalism have become increasingly apparent we have not returned for inspiration to these critical realists. Horkheimer laments:

"The refusal of science to handle in an appropriate way the problems connected with the social process has led to superficiality in method and content, and this superficiality, in turn, has found expression in the neglect of dynamic relationships between the various areas in which science deals. Since the end of the last century scientists and philosophers have pointed out the insufficiencies and unsuitability of purely mechanistic methods. This criticism has led to discussion of the principles involved in the main foundations in which research exists, so that today we may speak of a crisis in science. The inner crisis is now added to the external dissatisfaction with science as a means of production which has not been able to meet expectations in alleviating the general need." (8)

There are ominous signs, that with the energy, time and money going today into fighting "global terrorism", that Horkheimer, writing half a century ago, had a contemporary point. However, conventional students of research methodology are only concerned with the research point that the critical theorists make. While we readily reckon that the natural science of meteorology, or of geology, must be taken into account in verifying the state of "climate change", we are less likely to turn to social science to verify the state of our "social and economic welfare". In layer 3:

- to be originated within narrative methods,
- evolves towards a hermeneutic or interpretive foundation
- and now onto critical theory in an emancipatory transformation
- culminates in social innovation through a process of co-operative inquiry.

We now turn to postmodernism.

From Methods of Theorising and Critical Rationalism as Methodology to Postmodernism – Continuing the Path of Reason

Probably the most poignant discursive critique of contemporary society, and as such antithetical even to Popper's Open Society, is that of the "postmodernists", who are not only powerful philosophers – predominantly French by nationality – but also have made a seminal contribution to research methodology. Next to the empiricists they have been the most explicit and systematic in transforming their overall methodology into a specific method, of so-called "discourse analysis". The most famous, and arguably the most brilliant of the postmodernists has been the Frenchman Michel Foucault, who in his seminal work on "The Archaeology of Knowledge" says:

"If one recognises in science only the linear accumulation of truth, and fails to recognise in it a discursive practice that has its own thresholds, its own various ruptures, one can describe only a single historical division, a division between what is

definitively scientific or otherwise. All the density of disconnections, the dispersion of the ruptures, the shifts in their effects, the play of their interdependencies are reduced to the monotonous act of an endlessly repeated foundation." (9)

In other words, *for the postmodernists, reality and truth is relative to the person and the situation,* so that the notion of the "meta-narrative, be it capitalism or communism, or an open society is a non-starter. *Postmodernists resist the idea of absolute truth, which, inevitably for them, will be promoted by that segment of society, or particular culture, which happens to be in a dominant position,* such as, today, the United States generally, and the business world specifically. For them, *the world is better understood, and negotiated, through multiple discourses,* and in that context research method and methodology lend themselves to a "bricolage" or mix of general perspectives and media.

In layer 3, the thoughtful, abstract, and conceptual navigation:

- to originate within methods of theorising
- evolves towards modernist methodology, that is a critical rationalist foundation
- and now onto postmodernism as an emancipatory transformation
- culminating in social innovation via socio-technical design.

We finally turn to critical realism, the most recent of the critical methodologies to be developed, and the most transcultural of them.

Experimental and Survey Methods to Empirical Methodology onto Critical Realism – Continuing the Path of Realisation

The final critical contemporary methodology that we cite is that of the Anglo-Indian Roy Bhaskar's critical realism. (10) In fact, he is critical of both modernism and postmodernism. What he terms "modern" rationally based formalism results in a glorification of the formal, analytical, abstract, quantitative modes of reasoning and modes of being. All the relations the modernists, like Popper, discussed are mechanical and external, as opposed to organic and internal. They tended to undervalue the role of ideas, consciousness, of intentionality in human life. Everything is done in a calculative way. The ego stands apart from other egos, and relationships are contractual. Moreover, the hallmark of modernity is the isolated ego; a sense of identity which is separated from the rest of the world. Similarly, critical realists criticize postmodernists for denying any form of objective reality, and ending up with a sense of overwhelming despair, in the face of no possible sense of completeness.

From the standpoint of critical realism, what happens in science is that you have "incompleteness". You leave out some aspect of reality; that incompleteness generates a contradiction, which necessitates a move to a greater totality, explained by a new transcending concept. That is the fundamental process of development in science, towards greater completeness. This development is underpinned by a "stratified" ontology, whereby generative underlying forces constitute the "reality", at a deep level, determining what goes on in events, and indeed what is observed and experienced of these, at the surface.

In layer 3, the active, abstract, and practical navigation:

- to begin with is originated in experimental and survey methods
- evolves towards empiricism as a methodological foundation
- and now onto critical realism as an emancipatory transformation
- culminating in social innovation via action research in general.

So what kind of development has occurred?

From Origination to Foundation to Emancipation

As we have seen, in entering fully into the *emancipatory*, so

- gut feel approaches, and thereafter richly descriptive phenomenological methods, turn into critical methodologies interweaving subject and object, self and society: who should we be?
- a specific research issue and developing storyline evolves, from not only a psychological and cultural, but also a political and economic perspective: what are we becoming?
- a scanty literature search, developing into a more considered approach to analysing the comparative literature, evolves further into appreciating multiple discourses, what wide range of perspectives should we come to know?
- finally, superficial data collection and more purposefully applied fieldwork, now turns into acts of practical discovery, arising out of plumbing the investigative depths, and ultimately doing something new about the situation.

We are now ready to consider the fourth layer, where emancipatory thoughts and feelings (as critiques) of the individual researcher are turned into co-creation, leading to practical Social Innovation

3.4.5 Layer 4: Integration (Innovation)

We now turn from the differential to the integral: in other words, co-creation, transformation and social innovation, need to build on all that has come before. Whereas Richard Tarnas (feminism), Herbert Marcuse (critical theory), Michel Foucault (postmodernism) and the early Bhaskar (critical realism), would all have seen themselves as profound critics of their societies, and even as agents of transformation, none of them offered a methodology to practically promote such individual as well as communal transformation. They were more in the way of social critics if not also social activists, and proponents of emancipation, than practitioners who offered a practical methodology for such. Interestingly enough, all were based in Europe and America. The fourth culminating layer brings to bear fully-fledged social innovation, operating at a societal, intrapersonal, organisational and individual level.

- societally, in the South, aligned with feminism we find Columbia's Orlando Fals Borda's societal approach to "participatory action research"

- intrapersonally, in the East, aligned with critical theory, we find John Heron's transpersonal approach to co-operative inquiry and participative spirituality

- **organisationally and communal**ly, in the North, aligned with postmodernism, we find Kurt Lewin's and John Dewey's approach to socio-technical design; and

- **individually and interpersonal**ly, in the West, we find Peter Reason's and Kurt **Lewin's action** research, aligned with critical realism

What started out formatively on layer 1 has now transformed from:

- everyday techniques into an overall process of *participatory action research*
- a basic issue individually researched to a process of evoking *co-operative inquiry*
- an ad hoc literature search to a process of *socio-technical design*
- limited data gathering to an active and reflective process of *action research*

3.5 A Fourfold Reflection on the Four World GENE

3.5.1 Retracing Steps through the Research Jungle

Now you have a **bird's eye view of t**he four layers, almost as if you had cast your eyes upon all of them, in the course of a picturesque journey. As we have mentioned before the research-and-innovation process is a non-linear one, and you are likely to move back and forth between layers, while cycling and re-cycling across each of the elements within each layer, as well as connecting such roots of your research with the underlying soils, the mainstem of your research-and-innovation tree, the branches and ultimate fruits: healing the planet, promoting peaceful co-evolution, building up an open **society, and creating economic opportu**nity.

Before we move on we invite you to undertake a brief reflection on the four research layers just presented to you. Review, for a moment, the overall "landscape of qualitative research", at least as seen by those doyens of qualitative research, Denzyn and Lincoln. We shall then retrace our own steps through the methodological jungle, which hopefully will serve to give you fresh insight into your own journey, so that you can trace a path of your own.

This book is being written for "social innovators" around the world. As researchers, educators and practitioners in the social sciences, conventionally on masters and doctoral programmes, many of you want to find a **way of transforming public, private** or **civic organisations in your socie**ty. (11) As such you are required to become philosophers as well as practitioners, individual social scientists as well as co-operative inquirers, and, most importantly, social innovators as well as social researchers. While this has opened up the "qualitative" research field, it has simultaneously filled us with booming, buzzing confusion, as American psychologist William James used to say!

Faced with such a daunting prospect, researchers and practitioners alike, as we have seen from our own experience, all too often retreat into a self-protective shell. Therein a rigid pursuit of method-laden form (research method) overtakes the supposed emphasis on original, substantive form-and-content (social innovation). At the same time, because of the linear pursuit of an analytically based research project, devoid as such of origination, and lacking the iterative approach we are recommending here, what results is paralysis through analysis. How many research projects then, most particularly doctoral theses have we seen, where, at the end of the day, the research has nothing original to say, and certainly has not made any active contribution to social innovation. The fault, as is so often the case with any science or religion, lies not with the research methodologies themselves, but with the way in which they have been interpreted and disseminated, by the "research powers" that be to you "lesser mortals". Moreover, those integral approaches to research, which serve to ultimately and actively promote social innovation, those related to action research, have typically stood out on a limb, rather than serving as means of innovation.

In addition, in our own case as aspiring citizens of the globe, we have been alarmed by the narrowness of the cultural context of conventional research activity. How then, as academics, researchers, management consultants and aspiring social innovators, have we come to these conclusions, and what specific implications do they have for the twenty first century? For having previously dedicated our thoughts and actions to culture and management, we are now embarking with you on a combined integral "research to social innovation" path. What then, in a mainstream context, is the qualitative research tradition on which we stand? How does our own evolving work relate to the establishment view of qualitative research?

3.5.2 Four Research Moments

Norman Denzin and Yvonne Lincoln (12,13), based at the Universities of Illinois and Texas in the United States, are probably the pre-eminent authorities on "qualitative research" in the world. For them there have been, historically speaking, seven critical moments in the recent development of such. However, the last three of these moments appear so recent, and thereby tenuous, that they hardly seem worth taking seriously. It is the first four such moments, which are critical for our purposes:

① **Positivist-Quantitative Paradigm:** The traditional quantitative period (our first layer) is associated with the foundational "positivist" paradigm, which still exercises a strong empirical influence to this day, and in which basic research methods, quantitative and qualitative, still predominate.

② **Modernist Quantitative-Qualitative Era:** The modernist quantitative-qualitative conventional era comes second (our layer 2): the quantitative "positivist" orientation is now split between the former empirical and the latter rational approach, the one being inductive and the other deductive; at the same time the newly "interpretevist" approach becomes clearly distinguishable in its own right. It is at this point that Husserl heralds the phenomenological "Crisis in European Sciences", and joins hands with the prior hermeneutic influence to make their qualitative stand on research methodology.

③ **Interpretative Qualitative Perspectives:** In the "blurred genres" contemporary era (our layer 3), new, interpretative and qualitative perspectives are vigorously taken up. Such includes, for Denzin and Lincoln, not only hermeneutics and phenomenology, but also structuralism, semiotics, cultural studies, and for us feminism, critical theory, postmodernism (discursive) and critical realism (stratified), as duly reformative.

④ **Crisis of Representation:** In the fourth era (our layer 4), the so-called *crisis of representation emerges.* It becomes apparent that only a very small part of the world, geographically and philosophically, is represented in the overall methodological story.

Transcending this crisis of representation, our Integral Research evolves a co-creative approach that is ultimately transformative, thereby resolving the crisis through its cultural spread.

We now turn to our conclusion, which we would hope would set you in the road to your research path.

3.6 Conclusion: Which path is for you?

The Four World GENE from Grounding to Effect and from South to West involves four research paths, each one starting in the local inner core of self, organisation and society and moving progressively through the four research layers toward the outer periphery, which is representing the global perspective. As such, the integral researcher generates social innovation, which is rooted in a local context but contributes to the global perspective. Let us sum up the core elements of our Integral Research Architecture:

- **Starting from the Research Origin:** As an integral researcher you start with your own life world, thereby reviewing the history of your own self and society to uncover what structures and processes the society had previously developed, which allowed to become a dynamic civilisation. From there you take this story forward and work yourself through the integral research process (represented by the general Four World GENE and the specific Path GENE, progressively leading towards social innovation so that you can ultimately have a truly creative impact on your society.

- **Attracted by the Gene – a Vital Force of Integral Research:** We introduced the vital force behind knowledge generation and called it in its generic form the GENE, which stands for the process of Grounding, Emerging, Navigation, and Effecting. In research terms, it stands for the essential elements of any innovative knowledge generation process, which contain the Research Issue (which you learn about while you are doing your grounding), the Research Question (which emerges out of a deep understanding of your own context and the need for social innovation in relation to such), the Research Hypothesis (which you subsequently build while you are navigating through knowledge relevant to your research question) and ultimately your Research Fieldwork (where you effectively engage in some form of action research to bring about social innovation)

- **Evolving as a cumulative process towards Social Innovation:** We distinguish four research layers: method (origination), methodology (foundation), critique (emancipation) and ultimately integration (innovation). The Integral Researcher moves on his research path towards social innovation through these layers, in the process evolving from research to innovation, through method (grounding), methodology (emerging), critique (navigating) and integral action (effect), interconnected with the underlying soils, and the overarching mainstem, branches, and ultimate fruits. You stay connected with its core, understand the evolutionary process that the layers represent, and through understanding them, transcend and further evolve the landscape.

- **Finding a Research Path:** In contrast to the traditional research approach, our integral one requires you to take account of the full range of methods and methodologies, critiques and integrations, to some degree or another, though you will inevitably specialize. The choice for a particular GENE (research path) is made based on the individual and societal background and context of the researcher. It is important that the research path is authentic to yourself and your cultural context. Each path ultimately reaches into the fourth integral layer, and the strong co-creative nature and scope of it (just listen to the rhythm of terms like e.g. participatory action research and cooperative inquiry) enables each researcher who decided for one of the paths to ultimately embrace them all. However, you approach the integral layer from your particular perspective, represented by one of the paths: relational (southern), renewal (eastern), reason (northern), realisation (western).

- **Being truly integral – Including contributions from all four worlds:** We mentioned that the paths are ultimately archetypal constructions, which represent a particular way of doing research, a particular way of knowledge generation, a particular approach to social innovation. We demonstrated earlier that – archetypally – each of the four worlds (South, East, North and West) has developed over time a particular preference for one way. In our Integral Research framework we are building on these preferences and particular strengths to enable each of you to contribute your strength to the whole.

- **Engaging in Collective Research and Innovation Processes:** In our doctoral programme, for example, different people naturally choose different paths. Due to the growing collective emphasis we ensure that through interaction with other research colleagues, participants continuously reflect their own path and reach out to others. That is practically how we reinforce the principle of creative synthesis in our groups.

- **Releasing your Gene-ius – The Gene and your Path:** While you are choosing one particular path, the cycling Four World GENE is "pulling" you to engage with your "inner four worlds" by guiding you continuously through your own south, east, north, and west. Following such rhythm – our four R's – you avoid getting stuck in a particular world. We have demonstrated in chapter 2 the danger of such stuckness.

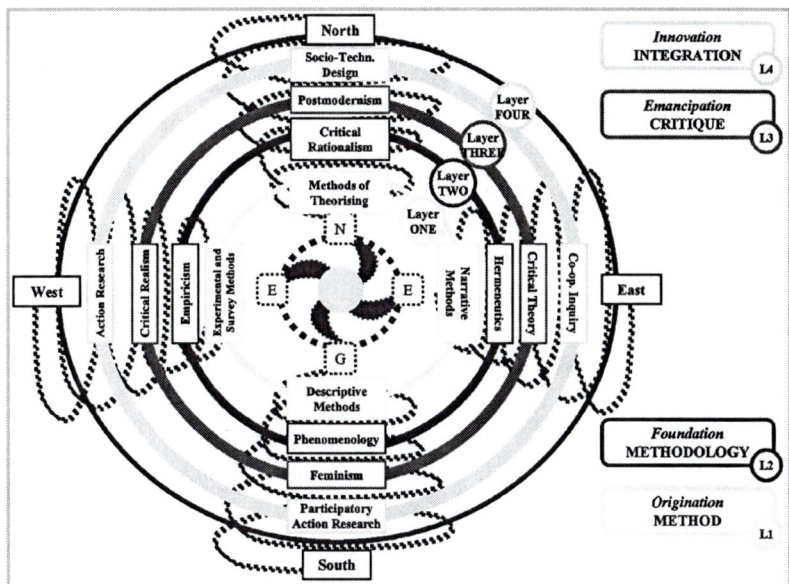

Figure 3.5: Integral Research (Evolving through the four Paths)

- **"Know thou path":** Integral Research starts with reflection: firstly, reflection on your own self/organisation and society/culture in order to reconnect with the innermost strengths of both in relation to knowledge generation and social innovation; secondly, reflection on yourself in relation to your society and your own research preferences and strengths; and, thirdly, reflection on the integral research landscape designed to provide orientation for your own research-and-innovation.

- **From Underlying Soil to Overhanging Fruits:** In the final analysis there is a need to link context and content, form, field and outcome. The context, that is the underlying soils, or humanities, is made up of the particular culture and nature of self, organisation and society. The content, or roots in our case, is constituted of the research paths. The form, or mainstem of our integral organism, is social science. The field of contribution, or branches, is the tangible know-how that is created, and the fruits range from healing the planet to opening up economic opportunity. Finally, the outcome of your particular thesis (that is the fruits) grows out of all that has come before.

In the next chapter we enter the first layer of research method. It is a chapter on method, particularly crafted to enhance your reflection and to help you to identify the research path, which is truly authentic to you. But in addition, the following chapter is a "wake up call", to alert us to the historic and conventional blindfolds that conventional research method has put upon us. "Method" – the first layer – will tell you more about yourself then you had thought before – and indeed, the entire integral research process introduced in this book is ultimately a journey to progressively heightened energy and consciousness – and by far more exciting then the traditional "dry and boring reputation" of research in the social sciences has ever promised.

Bibliography

1) **Heron**, J. (1994). *Co-Operative Inquiry*. London: Sage.

2) **Husserl**, E. (1970). *The Crisis of the European Sciences*. Evanston: Northwestern University.

3) **Husserl**, E. (1970). *The Crisis of the European Sciences*. Evanston: Northwestern University.

4) **Cushman**, P. (1995). *Constructing Self, Reconstructing America*. New York: Da Capo Press.

5) **Popper**, K. (1999). *All Life is Problem Solving*. London: Routledge.

6) **Soros**, G. (1999). *The Crisis of Global Capitalism*. Boston: Little Brown.

7) **Tarnas**, R. (1991). *The Passion of the Western Mind*. New York: Ballantyne Books.

8) **Horkheimer**, M. (1968). *Critical Theory*. New York: Herder and Herder.

9) **Foucault**, M. (1989). *The Archaeology of Knowledge*. London: Routledge.

10) **Bhaskar**, R. (2002). *Meta-Reality*. London: Sage.

11) **Lessem**, R., **Schieffer**, A. & **Palsule**, S. (2008). *The Practice of Transformation*. Forthcoming.

12) **Denzin**, N. & **Lincoln**, Y. (1994). *Handbook of Qualitative Research*. London: Sage.

13) **Denzin**, N. et al. (2003). *Landscape of Qualitative Research*. London: Sage.

CHAPTER 4

THE GROUNDS OF INTEGRAL RESEARCH

"STARTING THE RESEARCH JOURNEY:
METHOD MATTERS!"

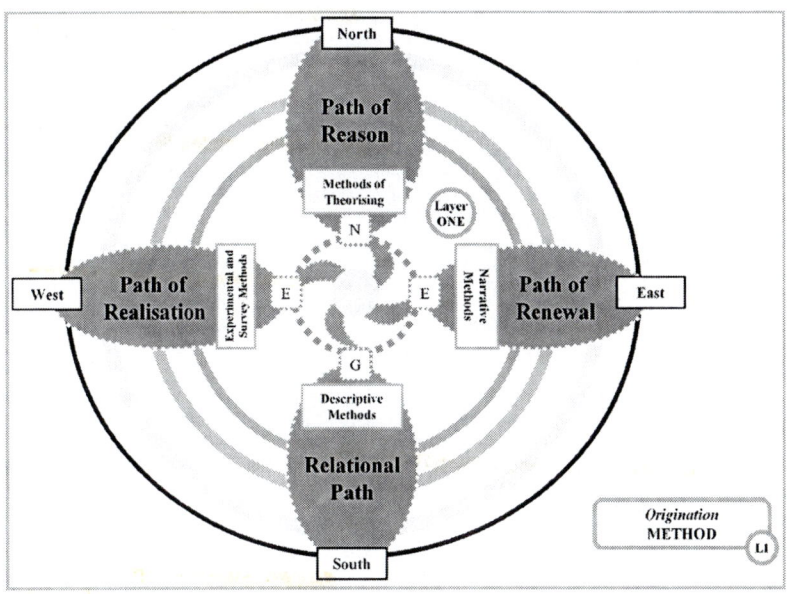

Figure 4.1: Overview Chapter 4 – Method

Summary: The Grounds of Integral Research

- **3 Wake Up Calls for the Social Scientist:** In this fourth chapter, we *originate* our integral research; in parallel, we introduce the specific research methods that go with it. As such we describe what we see to be the basic building blocks of our Integral Research. We start with three wake up calls for the Social Researcher: 1) social science research can lead to social innovation; 2) method and methodology are disconnected and 3) method matters!

- **Wake Up Call No 1:** Many of the key thinkers behind methodology had been profound critics of the societal status quo. The founding fathers of research methodologies were not only philosophers but also innovators, often revolutionaries in their own right. What is stopping us from seeing this all too apparent truth is the fact that we are locked into an analytically based "research" paradigm.

- **Wake Up Call No 2:** There is a vast gulf between methodology (philosophy) and method (technique). Reference to method and methodology tends to be intertwined rather than clearly differentiated. Philosophy remains disconnected from method or practicality, and hence innovation is curbed.

- **Wake Up Call 3:** In the same way as technological innovation is dependent upon both "scientific method" and natural science content, we conclude that social innovation is dependent on its own equivalent "method" and its social science content. We discovered, that the basic orientations to social science research were not the erudite methodologies, but the basic methods. That's why "method matters" and why our Integral Research starts with "method".

- **Four Methods:** There are four general human modes (being, becoming, knowing, doing) and, directly linked to them, four groups of methods, that form the source of origination for our four research paths: Descriptive methods for the southern relational path, narrative methods for the eastern path of renewal, methods of theorising for the northern path of reason and experimental and survey methods for the western path of realisation.

- **Descriptive Methods:** Description is not merely an off the cuff record of what the researchers see going on. Rather it requires you to immerse yourself in a phenomenon similar to the way in which an artist, or an empathetic counsellor might do. Being "scientific" in that descriptive sense involves opening oneself up to a phenomenon, without pride or prejudice, premise or preconception. The method or technique of empirical phenomenology involves opening the door to a fresh start into research in the social sciences.

- **Narrative Methods:** Whereas description is overwhelmingly concerned with locational space and place, in narrative methods we are more concerned with historical time. Here the researcher becomes a "Narrator" of the "stories we are", drawing upon the specific technique of "storytelling".

- **Methods of Theorising:** From narrative methods we enter the human mode of knowing. This – in research terms – is the world of theory building. Here we draw on Karl Popper's method of Hypothesis Building (the method of the formulation of hypotheses), and on Glazer, Strauss and Corbin's grounded theory. For Popper, the emphasis in hypothesizing is on critical discussion. In a rationally based context, we draw on diverse concepts from others, in order to compare and contrast these critically with our own.

- **Experimental and Survey Methods:** We finally introduce the fourth and by far the most prolific of the research building blocks: experimental and survey methods. The specific technique we are focussing on is the case study. Case studies have a particular richness, serving as a bridge between the more passive "survey" and more active "experimentation", and thereby naturally close the "method cycle" of describing, narrating and theorising, and ultimately surveying or experimenting.

4.1 Introduction: Three wake up calls for the Social Scientist

4.1.1 The First Wake Up Call: Social Research can lead to Social Innovation

Forty Years in the Research Desert

In this fourth chapter on the four general research methods or modes, and specific research techniques to go with each one, we shall briefly describe what we now see to be the basic building blocks to our Integral Research. As a prelude we shall illustrate our own protracted route to re-discovering the functioning of such research as an accumulative path to social innovation.

For one of the authors, Ronnie Lessem often says, it had taken him some forty odd years of wandering, like Moses, in the research desert as a management academic, before he saw the Promised Land. This became an integral perspective on research (leading to social innovation), out of which research method was only a small part. For he had been absolutely put off for those four long decades by an initially tedious undergraduate course on "statistical research methods". While the other author, Alexander Schieffer, had developed the same aversion during a doctoral seminar on research methodologies at the University of St. Gallen in Switzerland, he was fortunate to have met Ronnie at an earlier stage of his life to be able to reconnect to this matter.

Ronnie laments, that it took him those long years of travelling through such an educational, managerial and research desert, across four continents, to ultimately transform, with the help of the oases of leading lights he periodically discovered, such prosaic methods into formative grounds for social innovation. *The key that opened such a transformative door was his discovery that* differentiated research paths could not only be horizontally aligned with the four worlds, but that each of them led from research to innovation.

Ronnie had been supervising doctoral and masters students as an academic, within his trans-cultural field, for some twenty-five years, that is since the 1980's, and Alexander since 2002. While the topics of doctoral research that we have supervised had been wide-ranging, the research methods had remained pretty standard, and duly isolated from any developing whole. While the use of case studies has recently predominated, historically speaking survey methodologies generally, and questionnaires and interviews, specifically, have been the order of the undergraduate and postgraduate day. The approach has been invariably pragmatic (realisation) and rational (reason), bereft of humanity (relational) and holism (renewal), invariably combining the use of questionnaires with a statistical analysis of the results.

As far as our practical and project based masters programme in transformation management had been concerned, which had been developed before our doctoral programme, first at City University in London and subsequently at the University of Buckingham, we had fought shy of incorporating research method or methodology, because, for all that we were aware, it would take the managers involved straight down a classically analytically, and thus exclusively rational, research track, rather than furthering the practice of transformation. In fact, for the first time in 2007, after our project based masters had been running for almost two decades, we felt ready to incorpor̲a̲t̲e̲ ̲r̲e̲s̲e̲a̲r̲c̲h̲ ̲m̲e̲t̲h̲o̲d̲o̲l̲o̲g̲y̲,̲ ̲b̲e̲c̲a̲u̲s̲e̲ ̲n̲o̲w̲ ̲o̲f̲ ̲i̲t̲s̲ ̲t̲r̲a̲n̲s̲f̲o̲r̲m̲a̲t̲i̲v̲e̲,̲ action centred orientation, building upon the informative methods, methodologies and critiques that come before.

The Impoverished Conventional Wisdom

As far as the doctoral students were concerned, each research project would include an overarching methodological chapter, which would differentiate between "positivist" and "interpretivist" approaches. Due heed would be paid to inductively oriented Bacon and Mill, and to deductively oriented Popper if not also Hempel. Robert Yin was invariably referred to for his case study method, and, on occasion, Glazer and Strauss for their "g̲r̲o̲u̲n̲d̲e̲d̲ ̲t̲h̲e̲o̲r̲y̲". Ultimately, there would be an extensive reliance on i̲n̲t̲e̲r̲v̲i̲e̲w̲s̲,̲ ̲q̲u̲e̲s̲t̲i̲o̲n̲n̲a̲i̲r̲e̲s̲,̲ ̲a̲n̲d̲ ̲s̲t̲a̲t̲i̲s̲t̲i̲c̲a̲l̲ ̲a̲n̲a̲l̲y̲sis of results. Above all, what would characterize the vast majority of the research, altogether at undergraduate and postgraduate – masters and doctoral – levels, was the *extraordinary lack of originality*.

To be honest, the terms "method" and "methodology" were used interchangeably, both by ourselves and by the students. There was no sense, that *method* constituted the "preconventional" building blocks for a subsequently "conventional" *methodology*, to be followed by a "postconventional" *critique*, and an ultimately action centred *integral* research. Moreover, such a fourfold trajectory, or research-and-innovation path, followed four respective research orientations.

Because of the predominance of survey methods, with or without prior hypotheses, there was simply no awareness of the fact that such evidence of knowing (hypotheses and theories) and doing (surveys and experiments) needed to be underpinned by being (descriptions) and becoming (narrative), to be integral. At no point, for Ronnie, were either the post-graduate students or himself aware that such methods or methodologies had anything to do with something as grand as such "integral research", or indeed – even more distant from our conventional research horizons – social innovation. They were merely required to, in our terms, follow the paths of reason and realisation, that is pursuing a̲c̲a̲d̲e̲m̲i̲c̲a̲l̲l̲y̲ ̲r̲e̲s̲p̲e̲c̲t̲a̲b̲l̲e̲,̲ ̲r̲a̲t̲i̲o̲n̲a̲l̲ ̲a̲n̲d̲ ̲e̲m̲p̲i̲r̲i̲c̲a̲l̲ ̲r̲e̲s̲e̲a̲r̲c̲h, whether in Belgium or Bermuda, Switzerland or Senegal, England or Ecuador. There was no reference, in southern Africa for example, to any possible difference between the basic influence of a "black" or "white" consciousness, vital force or "élan vitale" on the research and development horizons.

Connecting Methodology with Innovation

Then Ronnie' first a̲w̲a̲k̲e̲n̲i̲n̲g̲ ̲c̲a̲m̲e̲,̲ ̲a̲n̲d̲ ̲t̲h̲e̲ ̲r̲e̲s̲e̲a̲r̲c̲h world, for him at least, would never be the same again. In 2003, at the University of Buckingham in the UK, where Ronnie is based, we establishe̅d̅ the T̲r̲a̲n̲s̲-̲c̲u̲l̲t̲u̲r̲a̲l̲ ̲C̲e̲n̲t̲r̲e̲ to focus r̲e̲s̲e̲a̲r̲c̲h̲ ̲a̲c̲t̲i̲v̲i̲t̲i̲e̲s̲ on ̲"̲c̲u̲l̲t̲u̲r̲e̲ ̲a̲n̲d̲ ̲m̲a̲n̲a̲g̲e̲m̲e̲n̲t̲"̲. All too quickly Ronnie was faced with a group of half a dozen part-time doctoral students from the four corners of the globe. While their research topics were fascinating, ranging from sustainable quality management in the Middle East, to evolving a new form of banking in China, the research methodologies to be deployed were of little interest to Ronnie. Whether they were to use case studies or semi-structured interviews mattered little to him; it was the wide-ranging research topics, the depth and breadth of literature to go with it, and above all what they might originate through their research that were of real interest.

It did not dawn on him at this stage, that methodology was an actual precondition for the social innovation he so passionately sought: to heal the planet, to promote peaceful co-evolution between peoples, to build up an open society, and enhance economic opportunity.

So Ronnie asked a close colleague at the University of Buckingham, Mike Lucas, who happened to be completing his own PhD at the time, whether Mike would take over the methodological side of things, once he had completed his own thesis, as Ronnie himself had no interest in such. In one of the research conversations Mike mentioned that he was using "critical realism" as his methodological approach. "Critical what", Ronnie asked Mike? He acknowledged that he had never heard of it. Then Ronnie had another shock. While Mike, as a management accountant, was using so-called critical realism, another colleague of his, who was a tax specialist, had adopted a "postmodern" approach with a particular emphasis on Foucault.

Ronnie had certainly heard of Michel Foucault, but in a completely different light. After all Ronnie was a child of the sixties, and somewhat revolutionary in his ideas, which led him of course to this famed French philosopher and political activist. However, he was unaware that such a notable social innovator as Foucault was connected with "dry" research methodology, and could not see what on earth the radical French philosopher had to do with tax management! Nor indeed, as he began to discover, did the abovementioned tax specialist have anything to do with the real substance of Foucault's post-modern ideas. So Ronnie decided, that it was time for him to wake up to what was happening around him. There was obviously more to research method, or more particularly research methodology than he had ever dreamed of.

Research Methodology to Emancipatation

It was a strange situation, unnerving in fact. There was a new group of six doctoral and now also five full-time masters students doing their research projects, both groups focusing on social and economic transformation, and Ronnie felt – as far as methodology was concerned – nearly as ignorant as they were. Needless to say, in pursuing his own doctorate, Ronnie had flown, methodologically, by the seat of his pants, and got away with it, because his examiners – Reg Revans and John Morris at the time in the early eighties – were world authorities in the field of action learning, on which his thesis was based. They were patently not interested in the niceties of research methodologies. In Alexander's case, at the University of St. Gallen in 1996, a number of general questions on research methodology were asked in a written exam related to his doctorate, but during the oral viva, the focus was purely on the research results. Moreover, at Buckingham, where Ronnie had originally decided to rely on his colleague Mike, he soon realised that it was time to wake up to research methodology, having now received an indirect wake up call from the late Michel Foucault – as opposed to research method with which Ronnie was already somewhat disinterested and familiar.

Ronnie had by then delved into Roy Bhaskar's work on "critical realism", that had been continually referred to in the standard research texts, and he found it absolutely spell-binding. Bhaskar was not only a brilliant philosopher, but was also a profound critic of the status quo, not only as a research scientist, but also as a concerned citizen of the globe, whose doctorate had been in the field of development economics. In short, Bhaskar abhorred the gap between the rich and the poor, the developed and developing world (he is half Indian himself), and saw his "critical realism" as an emancipatory project, or indeed as a social innovation in its own right. Foucault of course was even more radical in his social and political orientation than Bhaskar. We were both gradually discovering that *many of the key thinkers behind methodology, as opposed to method, had been profound critics of the societal status quo, and as innovative, in their social context, as the Einstein's and Heisenberg's of the natural scientific world.* Indeed, many of these research philosophers, from Bhaskar to Foucault, from Adorno to Marcuse, were actually called "critical emancipatory" in their philosophical and methodological orientation.

Social Research and Innovation

In other words, the first new discovery, along the road to methodological Damascus, was that the *people like Bhaskar and Foucault, were not only philosophers but also revolutionaries in their own right.* We developed our methodological (as opposed to method) repertoire, from Hume to Popper, from Husserl to Derrida, we discovered that they were all philosophers, revolutionaries, inventors if not also innovators. What was stopping us from seeing this all too apparent truth was the fact that *we, in the social sciences and in management, were locked into an analytically based "research" paradigm.*

So we had managed to miss this *incredibly obvious fact, that method was one thing, that methodology was totally another, and that the former provided the building blocks for the construction of the latter. As such one provided the initial orientation, or language, for research and the other the fuller scope, ultimately, – for social innovation.* Of course, we could not remember reading one doctoral thesis over the past twenty years that had adopted, or even referred to, such a radical, philosophical-epistemological and also socio-political orientation. Our own doctoral theses were no exception. Ironically, *while research in the physical sciences is intimately connected with innovation, in the social sciences research and innovation are worlds apart.*

4.1.2 The Second Wake Up Call: Method and Methodology don't meet

Research Method and Methodology Fail to Meet

Now we come to the second overwhelming discovery. There was a *vast gulf between methodology (incorporating philosophy) and method (incorporating technique)* of which only the enlightened few had become aware. We had discovered that, amongst colleagues and students alike, *reference to method and methodology tended to be intertwined rather than clearly differentiated.* This mix of terms was replicated in much of the literature. We had found it virtually impossible to discover any research texts that dealt, sequentially and complementarily, with methodology-philosophy and method-technique. Critical realism for example, which had recently become ever more credible as a methodology, prided itself on its pluralism of "method". That for us seemed to be a bit of a cop out!

Such pluralism may appear to welcome flexibility, but it all too often leaves researchers confused. *Methodology, or philosophy, remains disconnected from method or practicality, not to mention the fact that action research is all too often left out of the picture altogether, and hence innovation is curbed.* As such the corrosive gap between the research ivory tower (methodology and philosophy) and the research muck and brass (method and action) is reinforced. Research methodologies were often profound in scope, but they were all too often very difficult to follow, or indeed apply. However, while methods may have been easier to comprehend, it was difficult to decide what method applied to which methodology.

In summary, there were virtually no attempts to bridge the gap between methodology and method, *research philosophy and activity, as between analytically based and action research. Each stood in splendid isolation from the other, so that ultimately social innovation, which needed methodology and critique (philosophy) and method as well as action research (activity), was inhibited.*

Colonization in a Newly Refined Guise

As our journey of discovery accelerated, moreover, Ronnie came to the next revealing realisation that, whereas *methodology was predominantly European* in origin, and *method was more likely to be American,* the *rest of the world virtually did not get a look in at all.* In other words, whether our research students came from South Africa or the Middle East, China or India, as well as Europe and the U.S., their methodological orientation would invariably be European or American. Somehow that did not make sense to us. No wonder the world was on fire! Furthermore, the very fact that the philosophical "northern" Europeans predominated methodologically, and the practical "western" Americans prevailed where method was concerned, meant that there was bound to be gap in the mid Atlantic!

Four Into One Won't Go

Furthermore, we found ourselves confused in between two knowledge domains with very different "rules of the game". For on the one hand, there was the field of business administration where knowledge management, or indeed knowledge creation, had recently become the order of the day. Therein, as was the case for the "knowledge creating company", popularised by the two Japanese organisational sociologists, Nonaka and Takeuchi, it was the *norm to integrate diverse knowledge perspectives.*

This, for example, involved – in the case of their well known "knowledge spiral" – the linking of the so-called "socialization" (our southern and relational) and "externalisation" (our eastern and developmental), "combination" (our northern and reason-able) and "internalisation" (our western and realisable) of knowledge. However, and on the other hand, *when it came to academic research in the social sciences, the norm was to specialize in one knowledge domain or research methodology.* So it seemed, as least in Nonaka's knowledge creating terms that four into one won't go.

Moreover, while Nonaka's approach to knowledge creation was exclusively organisational, no such approach, which we in fact had come to identify as social innovation, existed at the societal level. In fact where there is, increasingly, reference to such entrepreneurship and innovation, there is no connection with academically based research in the social sciences. Unlike the case, as we indicated in chapter one, in the natural sciences, social research and social – as opposed to technological – innovation, are completely split apart.

Grounding Research in Methodology

In the same way as technological innovation was dependent upon "scientific method", as conceived in the natural sciences, we now concluded that social innovation is dependent upon the full social scientific equivalent, that is both content and "method" (including methodology). So in Ronnie's naiveté, hitherto, he had got things completely wrong, that is in believing that originality was to be pursued, in a doctoral programme, through content alone. As such method, methodology, critique and ultimately integrated action research all had their part to play in social innovation. What a turnaround from where we had been some three years before!

But we had one more fundamental discovery to make before finally putting together our thoughts on Integral Research. In fact, with the third wake-up call we would come back full circle to where we had started as undergraduates in Switzerland and what was then Rhodesia, at the University of St. Gallen in the 1980's, and the then University of Rhodesia and Nyasaland, in the 1960's, with research methods.

4.1.3 The Third Wake Up Call: Method Matters!

The Building Blocks of Research Matter

In the autumn 2005 we established our Transformation Programme on the African continent, in conjunction with CIDA (Community and Individual Development Association), South Africa's newest and seemingly most innovative university. Several of the participants from CIDA on our masters programme were tutors at the university, many of them recent graduates. What astounded us was that in their "research proposal" for their first transformation project on our part-time masters, every student followed the same basic "western" approach to research method, which we call *the path of realisation,* including data collection, questionnaires, and the like. After Ronnie's initial dismay, he thereafter began to see the light, indeed three lights.

First, the very fact that these otherwise highly creative students who were doing amazing things in their local communities, started with such an arid approach to research, to which they were obviously paying mere lip service, meant that we had to try all the more to help them evolve their own approach by building on their home African grounds, albeit with a view to pursuing an ultimately integral approach. It then dawned upon Ronnie, moreover, that *such basic foundations of research matter were not the erudite methodologies, but the formative methods, which are deeply connected with the grounds of human being and becoming, knowing and doing.*

The trouble was, that the students focused on using exclusively survey (and partly experimental) methods, while totally ignoring theory formation, descriptive and narrative approaches; further, they were totally oblivious, in this research context, to the grounds of their own "southern" (relational) being. In other words, they were all focused on "western" doing, largely to the exclusion of "northern" knowing, "eastern" becoming and their ultimately "southern" being. As such, they were aiming to be effective (doing well), while lacking appropriate grounding (doing good), emergence (undoing) and, to a large extent, navigation (doing it right) (compare figure 2.1).

We realised that, whether we were dealing with undergraduates or doctoral students, we had to start with their underlying human mode. The equivalent to what we term a "western" (predominantly American) "survey" or "experimental" method, which our students at CIDA had reacted to mechanically, is the "descriptive" or ultimately more southern, relational research path. Such is rooted in the human mode of being. In the same way, as empirical methodology builds upon such original survey and experimental methods, so phenomenology, is a further evolution of such descriptive ones. Ironically, our African students were psychologically much closer to such a descriptive life world, and yet academically totally disconnected from such.

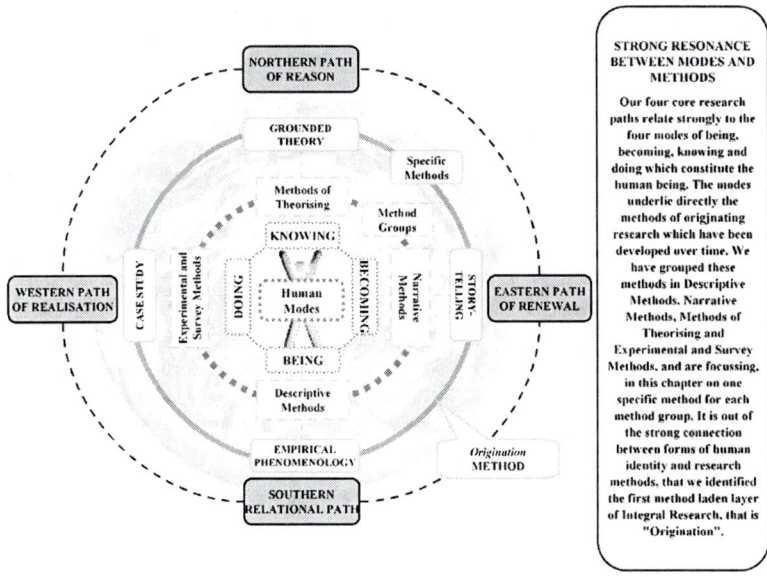

Figure 4.2: Human and Research Foundations – Following the same rhythm

We now go into such descriptive methods and empirical phenomenology as a technique in a little more depth, before working through the other three general method groups as well. Each of the four specific methods/techniques that we shall outline in this chapter for each method group provides the grounds for each of the research paths. That having been said, each of such "grounds" are laden with their respective worldly overtones, that is description with southern "being", narrative with eastern "becoming", theorising with northern "knowing", and both survey and experimentation with western "doing".

4.2 Descriptive Methods and Empirical Phenomenology: Origins of the Southern Relational Path

4.2.1 Descriptive Methods and "Being" in General

We now turn to each of the four research modes in turn, in each case also relating them to the learning and knowledge creating approaches that generally apply to each one, before subsequently focusing on a specific method (technique).

Starting out with such richly descriptive, generally "southern" origination, we find that identity, to begin with, is generically rooted in the "life world" of a local people, as much for the Bedouin or the Bantu as for the Belgians or the Burmese. Such an indigenous world is lodged in nature and religion (from "re-ligere" meaning linking back). We refer to this grounded world as southern though it is to be found all over the world, because of its deep roots in mankind's place of origin, where nature and religion continue to exercise a major influence.

The Spell of the Sensuous – David Abram
Example of rich description

The living world – this ambiguous realm that we experience in anger and joy, in grief and in love – is both the soil in which all our sciences are rooted and the rich humus into which their results ultimately return, whether as nutrients or poisons. Phenomenology, by thus returning to the taken-for-granted realm of subjective experience, not to explain it but simply to pay attention to its rhythms and textures, not to capture or control it but simply to become familiar with its diverse modes of appearance – an ultimately to give voice to its shifting and enigmatic patterns – would articulate the grounds of the other sciences.

The human mind, then, is not some otherworldly essence that comes to house itself inside our physiology. Rather, it is instilled and provoked by the sensorial field itself, induced by the tensions and participations between the human body and the animate earth. By acknowledging such links between the inner, psychological world and the perceptual terrain that surrounds us, we begin to turn inside-out, loosening the psyche from its confinement within a strictly human sphere. Intelligence is no longer ours alone but is a property of the earth; we are in it, immersed in its depths. And indeed each terrain, each ecology, seems to have its own particular intelligence, its unique vernacular of soil and leaf and sky. Each place has its own mind, its own psyche, a place-specific intelligence shared by all the humans that dwell within, in fact by all beings in that zone. Each place is its own psyche. Language, for oral peoples, is not a human invention but the gift of the land itself. By denying that birds and animals have their own form of language, we cut ourselves off from such deep meanings, severing language from that which supports it. We then wonder why we are unable to communicate even amongst ourselves.

In contrast to the apparently unlimited, global character of the technologically mediated world, the sensuous world – the world of our direct, unmediated interactions – is always local. The sensuous world is the particular ground on which we walk, the air we breathe. Human persons, too, are shaped by the places they inhabit, both individually and collectively. Our bodily rhythms, our cycles of creativity and stillness, and even our thoughts are influenced by shifting patterns of the land. It is surely not a matter of "going back" but of coming full circle, uniting our capacity for cool reason with those more sensorial and mimetic ways of knowing, letting the vision of a common world root itself in our direct participatory engagement with the local. Sooner or later, technological civilization must accept the invitation of gravity and settle back into the land, its political and economic structures diversifying into the varied contours and rhythms of a more-than-human-earth. Our task is that of taking up the written word, with all its potency, and writing language back into the land. Our craft is that of releasing the budded, earthly intelligence of our words, freeing them to respond to the green uttering-forth of leaves from the spring branches. It is the practice of spinning stories that have the rhythm and lilt of the local sound-scape, slipping off the lettered page to inhabit coastal forests or desert canyons, letting language, once again, take root in the earthen silence of leaf and shadow and bone. (1)

In knowledge creating terms, this is the realm of socialisation, and indeed of origination. It is identified functionally with community building, and formatively with the animate and with environmentalism. Therein lie the very grounds of our being. This is the home or "oikos" of our vital, individual, organisational and societal force. In terms of research method, this is a richly descriptive arena.

4.2.2 Engage in Experiential Learning

Experiential reality is the indigenous lived experience or the mutual co-determination of person and world. Positioned in a learning or development cycle this provides firstly, a strong emotional base – in the individual case, confidence, fulfilment and positive arousal; in the societal case a well developed, positively functional, open and formative indigenous "local identity". This yields the hypothesis that emotional confidence, fulfilment and positive arousal are the most important for effective individual learning; while a strong local identity, a richly imaginative national culture, an intellectual and institutional capacity to deal with complexity, and an altogether open society constitute its formative, societal potential.

Individual people and whole societies, learn and develop more effectively when they are enjoying themselves and what they are doing; when they are satisfying some felt need or interest, and are emotionally involved in what has personal and societal relevance to them; when they feel good about the whole idea of learning and development as well as the exercise of their learning competence; when they feel confident, secure and in a low threat, co-operative, non-competitive position. We now turn from learning to research, and from the descriptive method (and orientation to learning and knowledge creation) to the descriptive technique: empirical phenomenology.

4.2.3 Focus on the Research Issue

The aim of so-called "empirical phenomenology" is to *produce an exhaustive description of the phenomena of everyday experience.* Typically in phenomenological investigation, the long interview is the method of fieldwork.

Phenomenological Investigation

- What dimensions, incidents and people stand out for you in your proposed research?
- How did the experience of initially engaging in such research affect you?
- How did the experience affect a significant other in your life?
- What feelings were generated by the experience?
- What thoughts stood out with a view to the research with which you prospectively will engage?

Within our integral research framework, *such a descriptive immersion of subject in object also provides the formative grounds for a normative Phenomenological methodology and subsequently reformative Feminist critique, using a relational perspective with a view to human emancipation.*

4.2.4 Empirical Phenomenology

The challenge you face in preparing to *ground* such a descriptive investigation, is to focus on a research issue *that has both social meaning and personal significance. The topic grows out of an intense interest in a particular area.* But what exactly means "immersion" for you as a social researcher?

The Meaning of Immersion

- You seek to reveal more fully the essences and meanings of human experience
- You seek to uncover qualitative and quantitative factors in such experience
- You engage your total self as participant, in passionate involvement with the phenomenon
- You do not seek to predict or to determine causal relationships
- You are illuminated through careful, comprehensive descriptions, vivid and accurate renderings of experience, rather than measurements or ratings.

The people who have done most to uncover this so called empirical-phenomenological approach as a specific descriptive method are the Duquesne School of empirical phenomenology in the United States. The most prominent representative of that School is the phenomenological psychologist Clark Moustakas. (2) As he sees it, *Husserl's descriptive method incorporated three major elements:*

1) starting with epoche,
2) moving onto reduction and
3) imaginative variation.

Starting with Epoche

You set aside predilections, prejudices, predispositions, and allow things, events and people to enter anew into consciousness, and to look and see them again, as if for the first time.

Moving onto Reduction

Describe in textual language what you see, not only in terms of the external object but also in relation to your internal consciousness, that is the rhythm and relationship between phenomenon and self: referring to qualities like fearful and courageous, angry and calm.

Imaginative Variation

Seek possible meanings through the use of imagination, varying the frames of reference, employing possibilities and reversals, and approaching the phenomenon from divergent perspectives, different positions, roles or functions. There is not a single road to truth, but countless possibilities emerge intimately connected with experience.

We now conclude our orientation to descriptive mode and to its technique, empirical phenomenology. You have become aware of its link to the methodology of phenomenology. If you choose to engage fully in the southern relational path, a deep understanding of phenomenology would be the next step. Typical for the relational path is a thorough understanding of the life world and the inclusion of the multiple relations existing within this life world, and you ultimate social innovation will build be lodged within this relational context. Our symbol for the relational path is the network. Before we move from descriptive method to narrative method, we shall lay out once more the relational path before you:

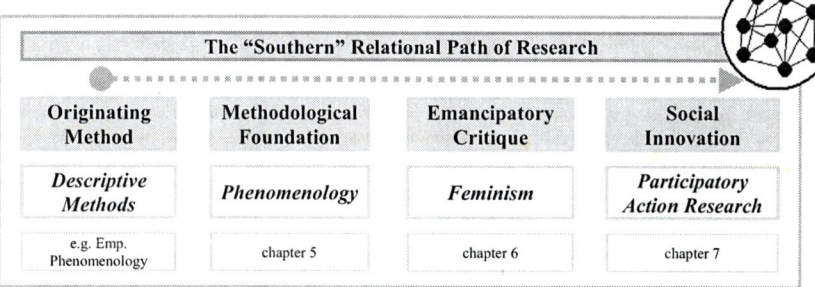

4.3 Narrative Methods and Storytelling: Origins of the Eastern Path of Renewal

4.3.1 Narrative Methods and "Becoming" in General

Becoming is a necessarily aspect of transformation whereby we enter, individually and/or collectively into that no-man's land between the familiar (self) and the other. This is initiated through the unfolding of narrative, through the pursuit of meaning, referred to as the "fusion of horizons". In that emergent world, of loss of identity, of letting go of the old with a view to becoming the new, the power of imagination becomes all-important. Such an aesthetic sensitivity is necessary to make the strange "other" familiar and the familiar "self" strange.

In knowledge creating terms, this is the realm of externalisation, when the tacit knowledge evolves toward the explicit knowledge. Therein lies the narrative for our becoming. In terms of research method and technique, respectively, this is the realm of narrative, aligned with becoming and imaginal learning (method), and of storying and re-storying (technique).

Banker for the Poor – Muhammad Yunus
Example of narrative

The Grameen Bank based in Bangladesh has come a long way in twenty five years, when it was founded by a Bangladeshi professor of economics, Muhammad Yunus, now world famous as the latest laureate of the Peace Nobel Price. From $27 lent to fifty-two people in 1976 to $2.3 billion lent to 2.3 million families in 1998. Grameen programmes now stretch around the world, from Equador to Eritrea, from the Norwegian Artic Circle to Papua New Guinea, from Chicago's inner city ghettos to remote mountain communities in Nepal – by the new millenium fifty-eight countries had become Grameen clones. Unlike other banking establishments, the object of the financial exercise is not, primarily, to earn a good commercial return but, rather as an instrument of cultural production, to enhance people's liberty, their equality and their fraternity. For Muhammad Yunus, the objective is to enable people to make the most of their lives, so that they become authors of their own destiny.

For Yunus then: "when the borrower finally receives her loan, she is literally trembling, shaking. The money is burning in her fingers. Tears roll down her eyes because she has never received so much money in her life. She carries it as she would a delicate bird, until someone tells her to put it away in a safe place. She cannot believe such a treasure has been put in her hands. All of her life she has been told that she was no good, that, being a woman, she only brought misery to her family, because they now had to pay for a dowry, which they could not afford. But today, for the first time, an institution had trusted her with all this money. She is stunned. She promises herself she will never let down this institution, which has trusted her so much. She will struggle to make sure every penny is paid back. And she does it". Grameen then is a self-help organisation. It wants to liberate the genius of individuals to create a better life for themselves. For Yunus, there was never a doubt about their commitment to break away from poverty, which leads us to tell one more of the many Grameen-Stories, that of Jorimon (in Yunus' words):

"Jorimon was born around 1952, suffered a terrible skin rash that almost killed her at the age of 6 and which still scars her today; as a child she also suffered terribly from ringworm. At the age of 10, she was married off to a poorhouse worker twelve years her elder. She had two sons and a daughter. During the famine of 1974 she and her children spent the year in near starvation. Her husband used to beat her up on the slightest pretext and he was always threatening to divorce her. In spite of working non-stop she and her husband knew nothing but suffering, hunger and sorrow. On December 29th, 1979, she and four other women joined the Grameen bank project and in January, her group received its first loan for 600 taka. With the paddy-husking business that she started Jorimon was able to repay her first loan by January, 1981. During this first year she and her family never went hungry thanks to the earnings generated by the Grameen loan. She also had enough money to buy clothes for her family, and had some profit left over. At first her husband was very worried about her joining the group, but once it worked out without problems, he accepted. She went on to buy a cow and to build a house with her profits. In her words "previously we went hungry for days on end; I worked like a slave in other people's houses; I walked from village to village with a heavy load of firewood on my head, trying to get some money in return. We had no home of our own. People used to ignore us all the time. No one ever looked. But today God has shown us the path to happiness through a bank loan". (3)

4.3.2 Engage in Imaginal Learning

Here the material to be learnt is presented so that its pre-conceptual form can be directly grasped by the imaginal mind prior to explicit verbal and intellectual understanding. The material can also be presented in visual paradigms incorporating colours and graphic designs that relate to the meaning of the images portrayed, as well as in a "colourful" form of rich, and textured, metaphorically laden narrative. It can be shown in mobile and dramatic form. It can be elaborated through the imaginative use of metaphor and analogy. Where possible and relevant, the material in all these presentations tells a story, also giving a coherent, global overview of the subject matter, so that the basic "patterning" of its central concepts and principles stand out.

4.3.3 The Unfolding Story: Uncover your Research Question

As we turn from the research issue you address to your unfolding research question, so you move from being to becoming, from empirical phenomenology to "the stories we are". It is in that evolving context, that the character of your research assumes developmental, emergent proportions. Such a narrative then spans the emergence of yourself, your organisation or profession and your society, over the course of research time. In other words, starting out with your research question, the investigation and ultimate creation continually unfolds.

Your storyline underpins both your action and reflection on such. (4) As such a storyline is transplanted from individual to organisation and to society, so the interpretive and the hermeneutic as well as critical theory, as we shall see later in this chapter, come into play. In the latter case, the dialectical interplay between plot and counter-plot, the conflict and tension between one force and another, exercise their dynamic influence. For us, the best guide to such a research method is that of William Randall, a Canadian Professor of English Literature, who has developed a particular method of uncovering "The Stories we Are". (5)

4.3.4 Storying and Re-storying

For Randall, the object of the research exercise is not to survey (through interviews or questionnaires) or experiment, to hypothesize or to theorise. Rather, your aim is to uncover "the stories we are", individually, organisationally and societally. That obviously does not preclude immersing yourself in a phenomenon, from the outset, but rather underlies the ways and means whereby you develop what you become: before, during and after the research. The "Stories We Are" imply that your personal, institutional and societal stories are incomplete: that your individual and collective lives are still unfolding, mysteries yet unresolved, open books for whose endings you can but wait and see. This implies that each one of you, personally and collectively, whether as Simphiwe Thembe, as the Truth and Reconciliation Commission or as South Africa altogether, in your or its own way and in your own time, is legend-ary. In fact, Judeo-Christian tradition, as well as Islam, Hinduism and many indigenous religions are founded on the conviction that *reality itself – at least human reality – is inherently storied, that all events constitute one grand, unfolding story.* This is the story between the world and its Creator, understood as a "cosmic artist". Each event in your individual and institutional lives is therefore emergent and novel, charged actually or potentially with significance.

Strictly speaking, neither you nor your research author your lives and your work. You do not arbitrarily design its plot from beginning to end; you seldom consciously decide what sort of character or culture to construct ourselves into. Yet neither do you merely narrate your lives. Your author-ity, with respect to your unfolding story, lies somewhere in between you and it. *You co-author your story in partnership with some authoritative agent, whether nature, society, fate, God, ultimate reality, or whatever your philosophical propensities lead you to call it.* You are in a position to reconstruct – not so much the events or idea within your research and development story – but the plots whereby you make them into your own. A new plot means a new story, and a new story leads to a new construction.

Thus, over the course of your research project, you critique the old plots by which your story has previously been lived and told, and experiment with new ones, and you thereby assume authority over your work and your life, together with a cast of co-creators. Naturally people and communities vary in that respect. Some are passive in the matter of self-creation; others active. Some are less inclined to compose their own life-plot than to adopt one of the packaged ones proffered them by their family or clan, profession or culture, religion or cult, industry or society. Others reject such patterns passionately, preferring to do it their way, in stages.

Stage 1 = Narrating: According to Randall, the first stage within your research, is that of a research protagonist; in this stage you are narrating the "origin story" of your individual, professional or societal life with a new intensity and honesty to your research colleagues. At this stage the guiding question is simply what is your individual and collective story, at a particular point of time, and how do both serve to address your research question, or the grounds of your prospective innovation? The research supervisor's role, together with that of the research community as a whole, is primarily that of a listener, affirming your emerging novelty.

Stage 2 = Re-Storying: The second stage in re-storying is that of reading the story, that is studying, evaluating and critiquing it as it unfolds. Here the key question is what kind of story is the story – its themes, conflicts, characters, author-ity, plot line, genre? It can also mean inquiring into the themes and characters of the larger stories that envelop your individual, and organisational life – impersonal, institutional, ideological – whereby the personal and institutional can lead to the political and societal. The research supervisor's and research community's role is to expand and deepen your story, thus releasing the energy bound within it.

Stage 3 = "Re-genre-ate" / Re-author: Through both the narrating and the reading, another key question comes – how can we "re-genre-ate", re-author the story – how can you find a research story big enough to accommodate the whole of an individual/organisational/societal life as a coherent whole, with a view to ultimately actualising social innovation? We now turn from the specific "Stories We Are" to the narrative method in general.

We now conclude the narrative methods and "the stories we are". You have become aware of their link to the methodology of hermeneutics. If you choose to engage fully in the eastern relational path, a deep understanding of hermeneutics and interpretivism would be the next step. Typical for the path of renewal is a thorough understanding of the "stories we are", and the capacity to engage in dialogical ongoing process of revealing or "unfolding" the meaning. Hence, our symbol for the path of renewal is the Spiral. A continuous (spiralling) reflective process will lead you from hermeneutics to critical theory, and ultimately to co-operative inquiry. It is here where your Social Innovation would become effective. Before we move from narrative method to the theoretical method of hypothesis building, we shall lay out once more the path of renewal before you:

The "Eastern" Research Path of Renewal			
Originating Method	**Methodological Foundation**	**Emancipatory Critique**	**Social Innovation**
Narrative Methods	*Hermeneutics / Interpretivism*	*Critical Theory*	*Co-operative Inquiry*
e.g. Storytelling	chapter 8	chapter 9	chapter 10

4.4 Methods of Theorising and Grounded Theory: Origins of the Northern Path of Reason

4.4.1 Methods of Theorising and "Knowing" in General

The purposeful navigation of the "renewed" self, organisation or society that we are seeking to establish, represents the knowing consolidation of the prior process of becoming. As such the fully-fledged new concept, as a product or entity, is established out of the prior fusion of horizons. In fact the success of the "north-west" in business, in Europe and America, is born out of just such a "global" fusion. This has recently been the case "east-west" for Japan, and perhaps also now is becoming so, though to a lesser "global" as opposed to "globalising" effect for China. Moreover, the emerging "network society", born out of the critical rationalism embedded into an open society (see chapter 11) is reflected here.

In all these cases, there is a genuine combination between *being* and *becoming*, of different cultures and societies, though it is only in the Japanese case, in business interestingly enough, that this has been made explicit. In fact the Japanese "knowledge creating company" – explicitly builds in such an "east-west" linkage. Conversely, in many a developing society, one local identity dominates or distorts the other, rather than serving to establish a trans-national entity. We now turn, from becoming and imaginal, to knowing and conceptual, learning. Thereafter, we shall focus on the specific research method "grounded theory".

4.4.2 Engage in Conceptual Learning

In knowledge creating terms, this is the realm of combination, that is of explicit knowledge. Therein lies the process of theorising underlying knowing. In terms of research method, this is the realm of such theorising, and of hypothesis formation.

This, for you as a learner, is the conceptual realm of *statements, made in words or numbers, theories or mental models, which yield the explicit intellectual, conceptual content of the material to be learnt*. Hitherto this has been regarded as the central and only medium of learning, and the policy base for development. In this scheme it is only third in importance and order, and tends to become alienated and desiccated if made the sole medium.

We now turn from learning to research, in this case to theorising.

4.4.3 From Learning to Research: Theorise and Build Hypotheses

When the Anglo-Austrian philosopher Karl Popper (6), and originator of critical rationalism speaks of theory building, *as a rationalist you value the intellectual independence of others too highly to want to convince them in important matters.* You seek not to convince but to arouse. *Free opinion formation is precious to you*: not only because this brings you closer to the truth but also because you respect free opinion formation as such. We now turn specifically to what Popper called *"hypothetico-deductivism", the formulation of hypotheses,* after hearing from Paulin Hountondji.

Endogenous Knowledge – Paulin Hountondji
Example of theorising

A standard feature of economic activity in colonial territories was the practical absence of industry. An equally standard feature of scientific activity was a howling absence of theoretical work. Just as there were no colonial factories, there were no colonial laboratories or think-tanks. Now generally speaking advances in all branches of knowledge, whether they belong to the natural sciences, the social sciences or the humanities, necessarily begin in laboratories, broadly defined as venues for the systematic processing of intellectual and scientific knowledge. In fact, the two forms of extraction – material and intellectual – are not discrete realities but two sides of the same coin. The name of that coin is accumulation on a grand scale.

It was altogether natural, given such a perspective, for the physical, geographical annexation of the Third World and its integration into the world capitalist system through the slave trade and colonialism to go hand in hand with the intellectual annexation and integration. The vocation of neo-colonial industry, meanwhile, is to turn out luxury consumer items for privileged minorities. It does not care about producing consumer goods for the masses. It is therefore incapable of serving the social advancement of the majority of the population. Yet that service is the core of real development. Hountondji then refers to Third World countries as typically extraverted:

- *Scientific work depends largely on the use of apparatus imported from the centre.*
- *Intellectual work is to a large extent dependent on journals, libraries, archives, publishing houses and other support facilities in the North.*
- *Scholars and intellectuals are better known and read in the North than in the South*
- *Research in the peripheral countries is trapped in particularistic details, unable and unambitious to break through to the levels of the universal.*
- *The much discussed brain drain that takes Southern intellectuals northwards is a specific expression of the extroversion of intellectual life.*
- *European or American scientists go to Zaire or the Sahara not in search of paradigms or methodological and theoretical models; rather, they go hunting for information and new facts that are likely to enrich their paradigms.*

To break that logic at source, to recover individual and collective initiative, to become ourselves again, as societies in transition, is one of the major tasks prescribed by history. That task, within the specific field of knowledge, amounts to taking an informed enough view of current practices in order to work out other possible modalities of producing knowledge, other possible forms of technological and scientific production relationships, first between the South and North, but also in the South itself, and inside each and every country. (7)

For Popper, theories can only be tentative conjectures about the world, which are ultimately unverifiable by empirical evidence. Their discovery involves imaginative leaps, which are the forerunners of scientific activity. The process whereby predictive and thereby testable hypotheses are deduced from theoretical conjectures and subjected to confrontation with an intellectually accessible world is the distinctive attribute of a critically rational science, subject to falsification rather than verification. According to him, science advances through the detection and elimination of error as falsified theories fall away leaving a core of theory not yet disproved. So such science can only ever be piecemeal and incomplete. Social engineering as a result should involve "piecemeal tinkering", which, combined with critical analysis is the way to achieve practical results in the social as well as natural sciences.

In essence, Popper's *falsification leads to a situation where the strong theories drive out the weak. Empirical data are not the final arbiter of the truth of theory. Finding theories, which are better approximations to the truth, is what the scientist aims at.* This involves the growth of the content of our theories for the development of our knowledge of the world. You learn, in Popper's view, *only through trial and error. Your trials, however, are always your hypotheses.* They stem from you and the concepts that you have inherited, not from your external empirical world. All you learn from the external world is that some of your efforts are mistaken. You are active; you are constantly testing things out, constantly working with the method of trial and error. In this research world you are guided by the following attitude:

- We know nothing – that is the first point.
- Therefore we should be very modest – that is the second.
- We should not claim to know when we do not know – that is the third.

The following assumptions are guiding, according to Popper, the research method of "hypothesis building" (hypothetico-deductivism):

Hypothesis Formation and the Development of Theory
• Nature & social life are regarded as consisting of essential uniformities – patterns of events.
• It is the aim of science to discover these uniformities, to find universal statements, which are true because they correspond to the forces of nature; however sensory experience is rejected as a secure foundation for scientific theories.
• Observations do not make much sense until they have been organised by some "conception", an organising idea, supplied by the researcher; in other words, hypotheses must be applied to bring some order to data.
• We must jump to conclusions, although these may be discarded if observations subsequently show they are wrong; it is a process of conjecture and refutation.
• It is a search for truths about the world, but we can never hope to actually establish such a truth, we can only eliminate those theories, which are false.

We now turn from theorising, and the process of hypothesis formation associated with it to the more specific technique of "grounded theory".

4.4.4 Grounded Theory

Comparative Method

We now turn to grounded theory, as perhaps the best-known approach to systematically developing theory, from the bottom up as it were. *Grounded theory is a comparative method*, as is our own approach to "managing in four worlds". For the constant comparison of many groups draws attention to their many similarities and differences. Considering such leads to the generation of abstract categories and their properties, which, since they emerge from the data, will be an important part of an explanatory theory.

Lower level categories emerge rather quickly during the early phases of data collection. Higher level, overriding and integrating conceptualisations – and the properties that elaborate them – tend to come later during coding and analysis. Although categories can be borrowed from existing theory, generating theory does put a premium on emergent conceptualisations. As they are emerging, their fullest possible generality and meaning are continually being developed and checked for relevance. Conversely, *forcing data to apply to pre-existing theories is sure to arouse the disbelief* of colleagues and laymen from the start. Similarities and convergences with the literature can be established after the analytical core of categories has emerged.

Integration of the theory is best when it emerges, like the concepts. In other words, Glazer and Strauss have a similar notion of experiential Grounding, imaginative Emergence and conceptual Navigation to ours, except for the fact that their experiential ground is empirically, rather than phenomenologically formed. It is thereby *rooted in externally observable data, rather than in the internal life world of an individual or community*. The theory, for them as for us, should never just be put together, abstracted from the underlying grounds, nor should a formal theory be applied unless we are sure it will fit the data (them), and the context (us). The possible use of a formal model of integration can be determined only after a substantive model has sufficiently emerged. The *truly emergent integrating framework, which encompasses the fullest possible diversity of categories and properties, becomes an open-ended scheme.* In working towards such it is critical that collection, coding and analysis of data are done together. (8)

Strauss and Corbin then turn in great detail to what they term "coding". The particular focus of grounded theory, and its real strength (albeit that such *coding* imposes enormous demands on you as a researcher) is such "coding procedures". There are *three types of coding procedures: open, axial and selective. Coding represents the operations by which data are broken down, conceptualised, and put back together in new ways.* It is the central process from which theories are built from data. (9)

Open Coding

Open coding pertains to the naming and categorising of phenomena. During open coding the data are broken down into discrete parts, closely examined, compared for similarities and dissimilarities. Through this process one's own assumptions about phenomena are questioned or explored, leading to new discoveries. In our own case, for example, early in our qualitative research, we established the codes "southern" and "northern", "eastern" and "western", to describe different societal and managerial orientations. More recently we have identified the GENE, in terms of Grounding, Emergence, Navigation and Effect.

Grounded Theory: 1st Coding Procedure

Open Coding

- During open coding the data are broken down into discrete parts, closely examined, compared for similarities and dissimilarities, given a name and a category.
- Open coding is the analytical process by which concepts are identified and developed in terms of their properties and dimensions.
- Two analytical procedures are basic: making comparisons and asking questions.

Axial Coding

Open coding fractures the data and allows you to identify some categories, their properties and dimensional locations. So, for example, "westerners" were identified by us as practical, empirical, individualistic and pragmatic. *Axial coding puts those data back together in new ways by making connections between a category and its subcategories.* Individualism, to take our example further, incorporates masculinity, atomisation, competitiveness and assertiveness.

In axial coding, our focus is on specifying a category – phenomenon – in terms of the conditions that gave rise to it, the context in which it is embedded, the action/interactional strategies by which it is handled, managed, carried out; and, finally, the consequences of these strategies.

Strauss and Corbin term these *specifying features of a category subcategories.* In grounded theory subcategories are linked to a category in a set of relationships denoting:

Grounded Theory: 2nd Coding Procedure

Axial Coding
(specifying categories and subcategories)

- Identify causal conditions – events or incidents that led to the occurrence/development.
- Recognize the central idea, theme, event, happening.
- Focus on location, duration, intensity.
- Identify intervening conditions – the broad and general constraining and enabling conditions.
- Focus on action/interactional strategies directed at responding to a phenomenon.
- Recognize consequences – outcomes of actions/interactions.

Selective Coding

In axial coding you develop the basis for selective coding. You now have categories worked out in terms of their salient properties, dimensions and associated relationships, giving the categories richness and density. You should also have begun to note possible relationships between major categories along the lines of their properties and dimensions. Furthermore, you have probably begun to formulate some conception of what your research is about. The question is how do you take that – which is in a rough form, in your diagrams and memos – systematically forward and turn it into a picture of reality that is conceptual, comprehensible and above all grounded?

For Strauss and Corbin there are ten steps, which we have distilled down to seven, through which such "selective coding" is accomplished:

Grounded Theory: 3rd Coding Procedure

Steps towards Selective Coding

- **Step 1:** A storyline – a descriptive story about the central phenomenon under study – can be aligned with both the phenomenological and interpretive approaches we have seen.
- **Step 2:** From description to conceptualisation – telling the story analytically. The central phenomenon has to be given a name: this becomes the core category.
- **Step 3:** If you tell the story properly, in addition to revealing the core category, the story should also reveal its properties.
- **Step 4:** Relate subsidiary categories around the core category.
- **Step 5:** The relating of the core to the subsidiary categories is through the conditions that lead to phenomenon, lead to context, lead to strategies (action/inter-action), lead to consequences.
- **Step 6:** Revisit the story, arranging and re-arranging the categories and subcategories accordingly.
- **Step 7:** Satisfied that the theoretical framework holds up to scrutiny you can go back to the categories and fill in the missing detail.

We now conclude the methods of theorising. You have become aware of its link to the methodology of rationalism, particularly of Popper's critical rationalism. If you choose to engage fully in the northern path of reason, a deep understanding of that methodology would be the next step. Typical for the path of reason is a thorough understanding of the positivist facts of life; it requires the ability to reason and to build strong hypothesis, which are able to drive out formerly existing weaker ones. You strive to uncover patterns and to codify knowledge. The symbol for the systematic path of reason is the Matrix. From critical rationalism you will move on to postmodernism, where you uncover the matrix of different discourses and learn to engage in them. Ultimately, out of this third critical stage you emerge towards socio-technical design where you engage in the systematic evolution of democratic processes. Before we move from the methods of theorising to experimental and survey methods, we shall lay out once more the path of reason before you:

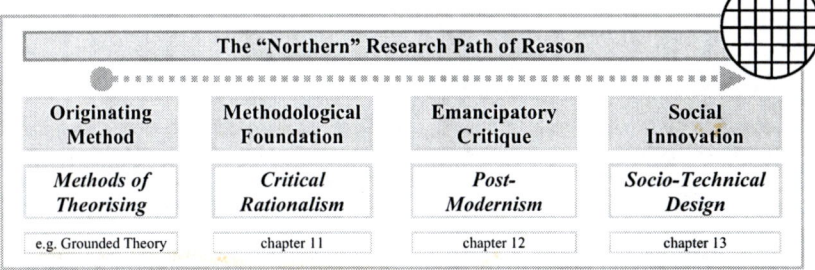

The "Northern" Research Path of Reason			
Originating Method	Methodological Foundation	Emancipatory Critique	Social Innovation
Methods of Theorising	*Critical Rationalism*	*Post-Modernism*	*Socio-Technical Design*
e.g. Grounded Theory	chapter 11	chapter 12	chapter 13

4.5 Experimental and Survey Methods and Case Study: Origination of the Western Path of Realisation

4.5.1 Experimental und Survey Methods and "Doing" in General

The realm of doing represents the practical culmination of our research journey. The term "excellence" has evolved from the Greek "arête", which originally stood for virtue. Such "excellence" involves purposefully incorporating all three other worlds into your own. Ideally, this would mean standing at the centre of all of them. Such a practical and empirically based realisation of a global perspective, as you enter into a unique world of your own, makes for a kind of "global integrity" which is still connected with your local ground. In addition, we need to recognise that:

- each world is incomplete and imbalanced in itself and needs the other three to become fully operational.
- each of the four worlds has its under-developed or dysfunctional manifestation, and its developed, or functional, one.
- each world is divided into topographical layers, from surface inclinations to depth images. Global Integrity in one world is potentially a condition reached when one world is able to engage with the other three worlds and with its own depths – inclinations, institutions, ideologies, and images.

4.5.2 Engage in Practical Learning

Practice, ultimately, can be written, graphic, spoken, or alternatively sung, physically active, interpersonal, as we see today in southern Africa. It can involve extensive collaboration in peer groups, in which much co-operative and self-directed learning goes on. As such the principle overall working hypothesis remains learning through activity, based on prior conceptual discrimination within material which is first of all presented in imaginal form, the whole being grounded on a positive emotional foundation. Whereas what we have indicated, so far, applies to specific learning situations, individually or collectively, how more generally does it apply to the development of a society as a whole? We now turn to such.

In knowledge creating terms, this is the realm of internalisation, that is moving from explicit to tacit knowledge. In terms of research method this is the realm of such survey methods, and of experimentation.

The End of Poverty – Jeffrey Sachs
Survey Example

For Jeffrey Sachs, the Columbia University academic economist closely involved with both the World Bank and also the U.N. Millenium Development Goals, cites empirically identifiable reasons why some countries fail to materially thrive. Of the world's population of 6.3 billion, roughly 5 billion have reached at least the first rung of economic development. In actual economies, for Sachs, a rise in gross domestic product is typically the result of four factors simultaneously at work: saving and capital accumulation, increasing specialization and trade, technological advance and greater natural resources. (10)

The key problem for the poorest countries is that poverty itself can be a trap. When poverty is very extreme, the poor do not have the ability – by themselves – to get out of the mess. Even if such a notion of a "poverty trap" is the right diagnosis, it does not explain why some countries are trapped and others not. The answer, for Sachs, lies in the frequently overlooked, and easily visible, problems of physical geography. Governments, moreover, are critical to investing in public goods and services, like primary health care, power grids, roads and the like. The government may lack the financial means to provide these public goods, however, for at least three reasons. First, the population itself may be impoverished, so taxation is not feasible. Second, the government may be inept, corrupt, or incapacitated, and thereby unable to collect tax revenue. Third, the government may already be carrying a tremendous load of debt. What then are the measurable goals that the world community has set to alleviate poverty and suffering around the "developing" world?

① *Eradicate extreme hunger and poverty: Halve, between 1990 and 2015, the proportion of people on one dollar a day; and halve the people that suffer from hunger*

② *Achieve universal primary education: Ensure that by 2015 children everywhere will be able to complete a full course of primary schooling*

③ *Promote gender equality and empower women: Eliminate gender inequality in primary and secondary education by 2005, and for all levels of education, by 2015*

④ *Reduce child mortality: Reduce by two thirds, between 1990 and 2015*

⑤ *Improve maternal health: Reduce by three quarters between 1990 and 2015, maternal mortality*

⑥ *Combat HIV/AIDS, malaria & other diseases: Begin to reverse, by 2015, the spread of HIV/AIDS, as well as malaria and other diseases*

⑦ *Ensure environmental Sustainability: Integrate the principles sustainable development into country policies; halve proportion of people without access to drinking water by 2015*

⑧ *Develop a global partnership for development: Commit to good governance, development and poverty reduction; address special needs of developing countries; deal comprehensively with debt problems; provide access to essential drugs, in co-operation with drug companies in co-operation with private sector, make available benefits of new technologies.*

4.5.3 The Mode of Survey and Experimentation

We now consider the final one, and by far the most prolific of the functional research building blocks: that of experimental and survey method. For unlike descriptive, narrative and theorising methods, each of which has gained relatively scarce attention in the social sciences (with psychology being to some extent an exception) hundreds of books and billions of dollars have been devoted to such experimental and survey methods of research. Not only that every minute in the day and all over the world undergraduate and postgraduate students will be attending classes on survey methods, ranging from interview methods and questionnaire design to focus groups and to statistical methods. For that reason, we are going to omit such from this particular book, while we recommend, for example, Martin Denscombe's (11) excellent recent work on "The Good Research Guide", to cover such conventional ground.

What we want to focus on here is the case study, as a specific technique that provides a source of origination for the research path of realisation. Such a case study method has in fact only secured intensive coverage from one researcher, inevitably an American, Robert Yin. (12)

4.5.4 Experimentation and Case Study

We first turn briefly to experimentation, and then more specifically to the case study. When researchers around the world, particularly in developing societies, engage in social "research", they tend to focus on the more passive aspect of empirical method, that is survey method, questionnaire design and distribution and statistical analysis. What is left out of account is the more active elements, which we discuss here.

Experimentation, of course, is in the purist sense difficult to achieve within the social sciences. Yet the basic approach underlying *experimentation,* is very much in tune with an inductive, positivist methodology, and also with liberal-empiricist ontology. *Experimentation then involves the manipulation of circumstances.* You need to identify factors, which are significant and then introduce them or exclude them from the situation so their affect can be observed. *The introduction or exclusion of factors to or from the situation enables you as a researcher to pinpoint which factor actually causes the observed outcome to occur.*

Experiments rely on precise and detailed observation of outcomes and changes that occur following the introduction or exclusion of potentially relevant factors. In experiments, you attempt to control the situation in a way that manipulates the range of variables that might have an impact, so that it will be possible to ultimately eliminate interference in the cause-effect chain by any other factor. The aim is to control variables, all at once or in a sequence of experiments, so that only the one factor at the end remains a viable cause of the observed change. As such a factor may be deliberately excluded, or may be held constant, the use of control groups is the most established way of exercising control over significant variables: introducing two matched groups, adding a new factor to one group and not the other, and watching for the difference over time.

The *focus in the experiment is on discovering the dependent and independent variables.* The size, number, structure or volume of the independent variable is autonomous, owing nothing to any other – a change in the independent variable affects the dependent. Experiments normally take place in laboratories because they are purpose built for research. Such experiments are normally relatively short in duration, are on site rather than in the field, involving close control of variables to isolate causal factors with meticulous observation. The use of tests to measure things like knowledge and ability is commonplace – used as diagnostic tools. They do have a place in research through first the application of a uniform procedure, second an emphasis on measuring a specific unit, and third a comparison with some universal standard, through "standardised" tests.

Closely aligned with such experimentation in the social sciences is systematic observation. This has its origins in social psychology – particularly studies of classroom interaction – and is normally quantitative and statistical. *It needs to involve overt measurable behaviour, that are obvious, requiring minimum interpretation, which are not context dependent, while being relevant to what is studied, complete as a category, precise as well as easy to record.*

Such a "closed" laboratory based approach is very difficult to align with the descriptive and narrative methods that have come before. So we need to exercise some artistic licence as integral researchers. The case study method, then, is a more feasible, and versatile means of conducting empirically based, qualitative research. Of course, such a method is likely to incorporate survey elements, like interviewing, as part of a more integral empirical whole.

For Robert Yin, the doyen of case study based approach to empirical research, such a *study is an empirical inquiry that investigates a contemporary phenomenon within its real life context, especially when the boundaries between phenomenon and context are not clearly evident.* In other words, you would use the case study method because you deliberately wanted to cover contextual conditions, believing that they might be highly pertinent to your phenomenon of study. An experiment, by way of contrast, deliberately divorces a phenomenon from its context, so that attention can be focussed on a few "controlled" variables. A history, in comparison, does deal with the entangled situation between phenomenon and context, but usually with non-contemporary events.

For case study analysis *three components of research design are important*:

- *Study Questions:* in terms of "who, what, where, how and why"
- *Study Propositions:* each proposition directs attention to something that should be examined in the scope of a study e.g. "organisations collaborate because they derive mutual benefits". At the same time, in the context of an exploratory case

study, there may be no such definitive propositions, but, in their stead, an overall statement of purpose – like "I want to uncover the constituents of "quality control" that can be identified with Islamic principles and practices" – together with criteria for success.

- *Unit of Analysis:* once the general definition of the case has been established, clarifications regarding the unit of analysis become important. If the unit is a small group, for example, those within must be distinguished from those without (the context). Moreover, boundaries of time and place are all important.

For Robert Yin, the *demands of a case study on a person's intellect, ego and emotions are far greater than those of any other research strategy. This is because the data collection procedures are not routine.* So what are the desired skills?

The Case Study Researcher: Desired Investigative Skills
<ul><li>able to ask good questions – and to interpret the answers</li><li>a good listener – not be trapped by your own ideologies and preconceptions</li><li>adaptable so that newly encountered situations can be seen as opportunities</li><li>having a firm grasp of issues being studied, theoretical or policy oriented</li><li>unbiased by preconceived notions, responsive to contradictory evidence</li></ul>

Intentional action then is at the apex of the supportive pyramid of fourfold being, becoming, knowing, and doing, actualises all of these dimensions and brings it to an integrated focal point. Undertaken by a learning or knowledge creating community, for us embodied in the "four worlds", it becomes a concerted and congruent set of behaviours that is honed through cyclical integration of all four modes, and includes a centred integration, as a necessary condition of its continuing practice. Practice as such, then, as the outcome of an inquiry, fulfils all other modes. It fulfils them because it involves them all, integrates them, gives them human purpose, imbuing them with intentionality, and completes them by manifesting them. Furthermore, it *celebrates* them by showing the reality that they articulate manifests an ultimate effect. It is a declaration by concerted doing.

We are now ready to conclude the experimental and survey methods. You have become aware of its link to the methodology of pragmatic empiricism. If you choose to engage fully in the western path of realisation, you would need to be equipped with strong investigative skills and an open experimental mind, driven by systematic observation and committed to analytically uncover within an experiment the variables and their relationship towards each other. In order to move out of the originally narrow frame of empiricism, which you would need to understand at a following step, you would engage with the critical emancipatory position of critical realism. Here you gain a widened perspective, which allows you then to finally enter in action research where you are supposed to realise your social innovation. The symbol of this path is the arrow pointing to centre, underscoring your commitment to social innovation through action. Before we now conclude this chapter, and for you, before you now move on to fully engage with the various paths or research, we shall lay out, once more, the path of realisation, before you:

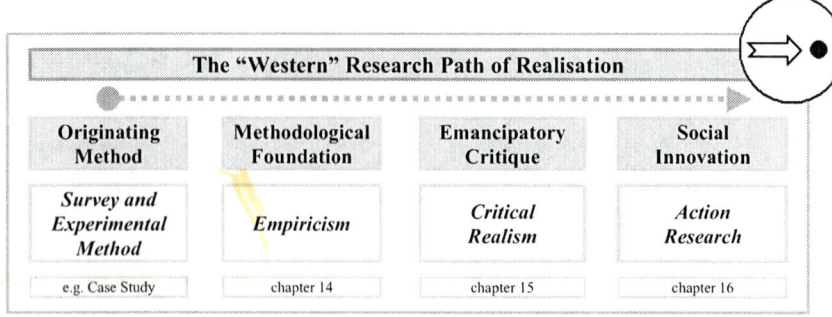

The "Western" Research Path of Realisation			
Originating Method	**Methodological Foundation**	**Emancipatory Critique**	**Social Innovation**
Survey and Experimental Method	*Empiricism*	*Critical Realism*	*Action Research*
e.g. Case Study	chapter 14	chapter 15	chapter 16

4.6 Conclusion: From Wake Up Calls for the Social Scientist to the Overture of the Symphony of Social Innovation

Three Wake Up Calls have changed our perspective on research in the social sciences completely. These calls led us to explore how social science research can be reunderstood in order to evoke social innovation.

⌂ 1st Wake up call: Social Science Research can lead to Social Innovation

- Many of the key thinkers behind methodology, as opposed to method, had been profound critics of the societal status quo, and as innovative in their social context, as the Einstein's and Heisenberg's of the natural scientific world.
- The founding fathers of research methodologies (from Hume to Popper, from Husserl, Bhaskar, Foucault and Derrida) were not only philosophers but also innovators, often revolutionaries in their own right.
- What is stopping us from seeing this all too apparent truth is the fact that we, in the social sciences and in management, are locked into an analytically based "research" paradigm.

⌂ 2nd Wake up call: Method and Methodology don't meet

- There is a vast gulf between methodology (philosophy) and method (technique).
- Reference to method and methodology tends to be intertwined rather than clearly differentiated.
- Philosophy remains disconnected from method or practicality, and hence innovation is curbed.
- Whereas methodology was predominantly European in origin, and method was more likely to be American, the rest of the world virtually did not get a look in at all.

⌂ 3rd Wake up call: Method Matters!

- In the same way as technological innovation is dependent upon "scientific method" (also incorporating basic and applied research as well as product engineering and commercialisation) as conceived in the natural sciences, we conclude that social innovation is dependent on social scientific method and methodology, emancipatory critique and action research, aligned with the social sciences.

- We discovered, that the building blocks of research matter were not the erudite methodologies, but the formative methods, deeply connected with the grounds of human being and becoming, knowing and doing, and even to the four life stages of humans. That's why "method matters" and why our original layer is rooted in human modes and based on general "method groups", and the accompanying specific methods or techniques.

The following figure distils the core relationships between research methods and techniques, our GENE and core human modes, emphasizing once more the importance of going back to the origins of social science research. You, as the Integral Researcher, are now about to choose, according to your path, with which specific method or technique you are engaging yourself. Within this book we highlight one specific technique for each method group.

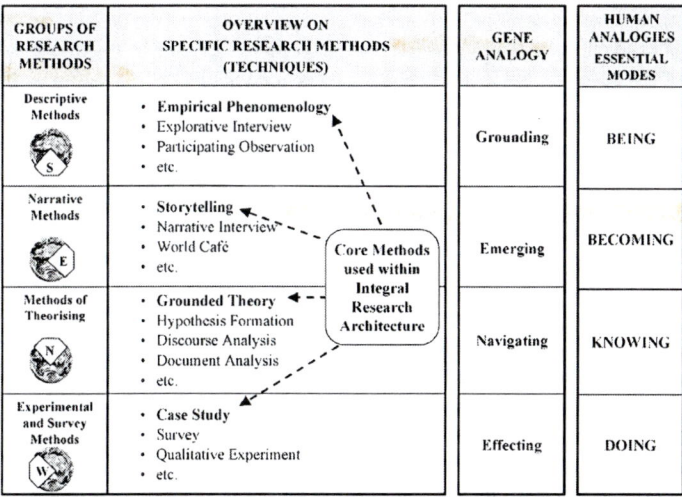

Figure 4.3: Research Methods – Human Modes

We conclude by distilling each of the four research method groups, which serve, in their turn, as building blocks for the four research paths: the relational path (describe), the path of renewal (narrate), the path of reason (theorise) and the path of realisation (experiment/survey). As illustrated, for us, a research method is more than a technique. It is a formative building block for a particular research path. It is like the "overture to a symphony", or the Foreword to a book. It sets the tone for what is still to come.

4.6.1 Descriptive Methods and Empirical Phenomenology

Description, as opposed to an interpretation, analysis, or survey, is not merely an off the cuff record of what the researchers see going on. Rather it requires you to immerse yourself in a phenomenon similar to the way in which an artist, or an empathetic counsellor might do. Being "scientific" in that descriptive sense involves opening yourself up to a phenomenon, without pride or prejudice, premise or preconception. A descriptive phenomenological investigation is, hence, open door to a fresh start into research in social science.

Descriptive Methods: Key Tenets

① Seek to reveal more fully the essences and meanings of human experience
② Seek to uncover qualitative and quantitative factors in such experience
③ Engage your total self, in passionate involvement with the phenomenon
④ You do not seek to predict or to determine causal relationships
⑤ Undertake careful, comprehensive descriptions, vivid and accurate renderings of experience, rather than measurements or ratings

---

4.6.2 Narrative Methods and Storytelling

As we turn from the descriptive to the narrative, so we move from being to becoming, from phenomenon to storyline. Whereas description is overwhelmingly concerned with locational space and place, here we are more concerned with historical time. For Randall, in summary, such "stories we are":

- tell how to do things
- give flesh and blood to abstract ideas
- provide role models to guide yourself and others
- help you identify with their unfolding stories
- confer order on a chaos of circumstances
- help to anticipate unexpected possibilities
- confirm or reconstitutes hitherto unconfirmed thoughts
- focus on a particular field of creative tension
- thereby taking you outside of yourselves, while
- serve to stimulate new levels of self-understanding
- pass on values
- help to uncover an underlying moral
- let you and the reader feel part of a wider group
- help you to reconstruct your worldview in a healthy way

Narrative Methods: Key Tenets

① Your personal, institutional and societal stories are still unfolding.
② Each one of you, personally and collectively, is legendary.
③ Each event in your individual and communal lives is therefore novel.
④ The narrative mode leads to gripping drama, creative origination.
⑤ Tieing together potentials and possibilities of your respective beginnings.
⑥ No struggle, no story; no trouble, no tale; no ill, no thrill!
⑦ A plot shaped by many of the larger strategy-stories in which it is set.

4.6.3 Methods of Theorising and Grounded Theory

From the narrative methods we entered the realm of knowing, of theory building and of hypothesis formation. In terms of research method, we drew here on Karl Popper's approach to hypothesis building and on Glazer, Strauss and Corbin's grounded theory.

For Popper, the emphasis in hypothesizing is on critical discussion. In a rationally based context, we draw on diverse concepts from others, in order to compare and contrast these critically with our own.

What is called theoretical sampling, for Glazer and Strauss, is the process of data collection for generating theory whereby you as a researcher jointly collect, code and analyse data and decide what to collect when, where and from whom to develop his or her theory as it emerges. This process of data collection is controlled by the emerging theory. The initial decisions are not based on a preconceived theoretical model but on the general subject or problem area, for us the phenomenon in which you are immersed, together with your emerging storyline.

As a researcher, you may begin with a partial framework of "local" concepts, designating a few principal or gross features of the structures and processes in the field of study. For example, you know before studying a university that there will be academics, students, administrative staff, specific disciplines and course outlines. These notions give the person a beginning foothold on the research. The categories and concepts that subsequently emerge will be related to the investigated problem (for us the life world) rather than to these pre-formed categories. You may also discover such "local" concepts like teaching as opposed to research, pure and applied research.

You as a researcher also need to be sufficiently *theoretically sensitive* that you can conceptualise and formulate a theory as it emerges from the data. Once started, theoretical sensitivity is forever in continual development. So the researcher needs to be continually asking "what does the theory do"; "how is it conceived"; "what kinds of model does it use"? Such theoretical sensitivity requires not only a personally reflective bent, but also the ability to exercise theoretical insight and to make something of this.

A discovered grounded theory will tend to combine concepts and hypotheses that have emerged from the data (our life world) with some existing ones (our navigation) that are clearly useful. However, an exclusive commitment to a preconceived theory, that is prior conceptualisation, inhibits theoretical sensitivity, for you then become doctrinaire and cannot "see around" a pet theory. You become insensitive to the kinds of questions, which cast doubt on a "pre-packaged" theory, being predisposed to testing, modifying and seeing everything from one angle. The emerging theory then, as far as data collection is concerned, points to the next steps guided by gaps arising in the theory. The basic question in theoretical sampling is what groups or subgroups does one turn to next in data collection? And for what theoretical purpose? In short what comparison groups need to be selected. Glazer and Strauss' criteria are those of theoretical purpose and relevance. The main purpose is to generate theory.

Methods of Theorising: Key Tenets
① You regard nature and social life as consisting of essential uniformities.
② It is your aim to discover these uniformities, to find universal statements.
③ Observations you undertake make sense when organised by some "conception", an organising idea; you apply hypotheses (theories) to bring some order to data.
④ You come to conclusions, engaging in a process of conjecture and refutation.
⑤ In your search for the truth, you cannot establish it, only eliminate what is false.

4.6.4 Experimental and Survey Methods and Case Study

We finally introduced the fourth and by far the most prolific of the research building blocks: survey and experiment. When researchers around the world, particularly in developing societies, engage in social "research", they tend to focus on the more passive source of empirical origination, that is the survey, incorporating "data collection" through the distribution of questionnaires and through statistical analysis. What is left out of account is the more active elements incorporating experimentation, or, as we shall see later, action research. Case Studies, though, have a particular richness, compared with questionnaire-based designs, serving therefore as a bridge between the more passive "survey" and more active "experimentation", and thereby naturally close the "method cycle" of describing, narrating and hypothesizing.

Experimental and Survey Methods: Key Tenets
① You are able to ask good questions – and to interpret the answers.
② You are a good listener – not trapped by your own ideologies and preconceptions.
③ You are adaptable so that newly encountered situations can be seen as opportunities.
④ You are having a firm grasp of issues being studied, theoretical or policy oriented.
⑤ You are unbiased by preconceived notions, responsive to contradictory evidence.

We now turn from research origination to foundation, from research method to methodology, starting out on the relational path, with phenomenology.

We shall then be working our way through each of the research paths, subsequent to the prior originations to which you have now been exposed, in each case in turn.

Bibliography

1) **Abram**, D. (1997). *The Spell of the Sensuous*. New York: Vintage Books.

2) **Moustakas,** C. (1994). *Phenomenological Research Methods*. London: Sage.

3) **Yunus**, M. (1999). *Banker for the Poor*. London: Aurum Press.

4) **Polkinghorne**, D. (1988). *Narrative Knowing and the Human Sciences*. New York: State University of New York.

5) **Randall**, W. (1995). *The Stories We Are*. Toronto: Toronto University Press.

6) **Popper**, K. (1999). *On Problem Solving*. London: Routledge Classics.

7) **Hountondji**, P.(ed) (1997). *Endogenous Knowledge.* Dakar, Senegal: Codesria.

8) **Glazer**, B. & **Strauss**, A. (1967). *The Discovery of Grounded Theory: Strategies for Qualitative Research*. New York: De Gruyter.

9) **Strauss**, A. & **Corbin**, J. (1990). *Basics of Qualitative Research: Grounded Theory Procedures and Techniques*. London: Sage.

10) **Sachs**, J. (2005). *The End of Poverty*. Essex, UK: Penguin Books Ltd.

11) **Denscombe**, M. (2002). The *Good Research Guide*. London: Sage.

12) **Yin**, R. (1989). *Case study research: Design and methods*. London: Sage.

INTEGRAL RESEARCH

PART B:

The Paths to Social Innovation

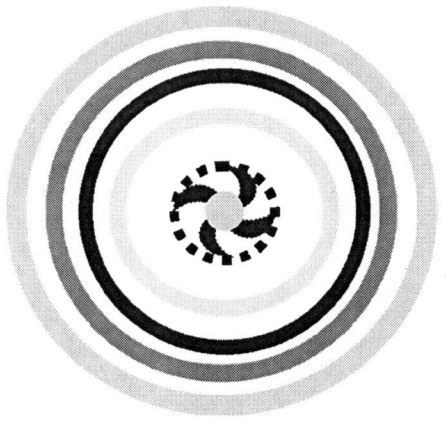

CHAPTER 5

FROM DESCRIPTIVE METHODS
TO PHENOMENOLOGY

"ENGAGE WITH YOUR LIFE WORLD"

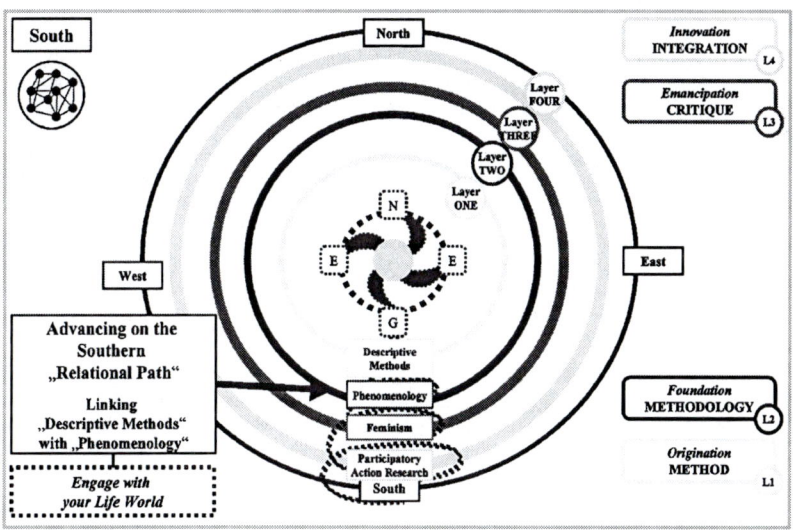

Figure 5.1: Overview Chapter 5 –Layer 1 / South

Summary: Phenomenology

- Advancing firstly on the southern relational path, we now turn from method to methodology. In other words, we turn from descriptive methods and the origination of your research to phenomenology, where you lay the methodological foundation of your work.

- A core claim of phenomenology is that explanations are not to be imposed before the phenomena have been understood from within. Hence, Husserl, the "father of phenomenology" sees this methodology also as putting the study of culture or "spirit" on a proper scientific footing.

- He saw the life world ("Lebenswelt") as the universal framework of human endeavour. For him, there is not one single life world, but a set of overlapping worlds, beginning from the world, which is the "home-world", and extending to other world farther away, the worlds of other cultures.

- He criticizes traditional empiricism for naively dictating that all judgments be legitimised by "experience", instead of realising that many different forms of intuition underlie our judgments and our reasoning process. We overcome the subject-object divide only by finding a deeper meaning within subjectivity itself. This constitutes the "qualitative" character of research.

- For Heidegger, who profoundly altered Husserl's phenomenology, the great threat to human existence is that thinking has become a kind of technical information processing. This leads to a fundamental homelessness and rootlessness (and in such a case to inauthentic research).

- To be authentic – for existentialist (an evolution of phenomenology) Sartre – is to grasp one's freedom and recognize it. Being inauthentic means being in flight from one's freedom, attempting to cover it by clinging to a persona, or indeed adopting one research methodology or another, because that is "what you are supposed to do". Social innovation, in such terms, is a process of authentic engagement with the world, grasping one's freedom by enabling others to realise theirs.

- Rudolph Steiner's anthroposophy is also closely aligned with the emerging phenomenology. Steiner's idea of philosophy was as liberation from limiting forms of thought, rather than as a wagging moral finger or an intellectual programme. Instead of a desperate search for objective foundations, knowledge might emerge from the growing and changing being of man, in a continually developing society.

- From this perspective knowledge ceases to be a mirroring, passive affair and becomes a process whereby we insert ourselves actively in the given setting of our lives. Hence, we need to accept the responsibility that as knowers we change the potential and actual course of the world. In other words, research and innovation are the two sides of the same coin.

- Finally we turn from philosophical thought to socio-political practice, from Husserl's phenomenological "life world" to the Czech Republic's Velvet Revolution and Havel's "living in truth". Here we demonstrate that phenomenology also constitutes a basis for socio-political and economic transformation.

5.1 Orientation to Phenomenology

We now turn on our relational southern research path from method to methodology, in this case from descriptive methods to phenomenology. For each of the methodologies, critiques and action research orientations that follow, within each one of the four respective paths, we shall incorporate, systematically:

- an overall orientation to phenomenology (5.1)
- the key tenets of phenomenology (5.2)
- an orientation to phenomenology in depth (5.3)
- a re-orientation: a global expression of Husserl's methodology (5.4)
- a practical and socio-political example of phenomenology being applied (5.5)

From a phenomenological perspective, all too often in the social sciences, when a researcher refers to him or herself conducting themselves "scientifically", they have in mind an exclusively empirical model of research. It is worth noting, that Edmund Husserl, the father of phenomenology, as will be the case for innumerable others cited in this book, radically parted company from such in the 1930's.

Origins: A Total Transformation of the Task of Knowledge

Phenomenology was initially developed by Edmund Husserl, a mathematician and philosopher, known as the "*father of phenomenology*". His work broke away from the purely positivist orientation of the science and philosophy of his day, giving weight to subjective experience as the source of all of our knowledge of objective phenomena.

Husserl was born 1859 into a Jewish family in Prostějov (Prossnitz), Moravia, Czech Republic (then part of the Austrian Empire). He was a disciple of the Czech philosopher and psychologist Franz Brentano, who influenced him greatly, and Carl Stumpf.

Husserl felt that the objectivism of science precluded an adequate apprehension of the world. (1) He presented various philosophical conceptualizations and techniques designed to locate the sources or essences of reality in the human consciousness.

Husserl proposed a radical new phenomenological way of looking at objects by examining how we, in our many ways of being intentionally directed toward them, actually "constitute" them. In order to better understand the world of appearances and objects, phenomenology attempts to identify the invariant features of how objects are perceived and pushes attributions of reality into their role as an attribution about the things we perceive (or an assumption underlying how we perceive objects).

Franz Brentano	*Edmund G.A. Husserl*	*Martin Heidegger*
(1838 to 1917)	(1859 to 1938)	(1889 to 1976)

Figure 5.2: Phenomenology – Core Thinkers

In a later period, Husserl began to wrestle with the complicated issues of intersubjectivity (specifically, how communication about an object can be assumed to refer to the same ideal entity) and tried new methods of bringing his readers to understand the importance of phenomenology to scientific inquiry (and specifically to Psychology). "The Crisis of the European Sciences" (2) is Husserl's unfinished work that deals most directly with these issues. In it, Husserl for the first time attempts a historical overview of the development of Western philosophy and science, emphasizing the challenges presented by their increasingly empirical and naturalistic orientation. Husserl declares that mental and spiritual reality possess their own reality independent of any physical basis, and that a science of the spirit ("Geisteswissenschaft") must be established on as scientific a foundation as the natural sciences have managed: "It is my conviction that intentional phenomenology has for the first time made spirit as spirit the field of systematic scientific experience, thus effecting a total transformation of the task of knowledge."

How Phenomenology operates

Phenomenology operates rather differently from the former way social science was conducted. While it is a theoretical orientation, it does not generate deductions from propositions that can be empirically tested. It operates more on a meta-sociological level, demonstrating its premises through descriptive analyses of the procedures of self, situational, and social constitution. Through its demonstrations, audiences apprehend the means by which phenomena, originating in human consciousness, come to be experienced as features of the world.

Phenomenological tools include the use of introspective and understanding ("Verstehen") laden methods to offer a detailed description of how consciousness itself operates. (3) Introspection requires the phenomenologist to use his or her own subjective process as a resource for study, while "Verstehen" requires an empathic effort to move into the mind of the other. (4) (5) Not only are introspection and "Verstehen" tools of phenomenological analysis, but they are procedures used by ordinary individuals to carry out their projects. Thus, the phenomenologist as analyst might study himself or herself as an ordinary subject dissecting his or her own self-consciousness and action schemes. (6) In this technique, an analytic attitude toward the role of consciousness in designing everyday life is developed. Phenomenologists use the term „reflexivity" to characterize the way in which constituent dimensions serve as both foundation and consequence of all human projects. The task of phenomenology is to make manifest the incessant tangle or reflexivity of action, situation, and reality in the various modes of being in the world.

What does this suggest regarding humanity and sociology? Phenomenology advances the notion that humans are creative agents in the construction of social worlds. (7) It is from their consciousness that all being emerges. The alternative to their creative work is meaninglessness and chaos: a world of dumb puppets, in which each is disconnected from the other, and where life is formless. (8) This is the nightmare of phenomenology. Its practitioners fear that positivist sociologists actually theorize about such a world. (9)

Phenomenology itself is politically neutral. Inherently, it promotes neither transformative projects nor stabilization. In the work of a conservatively inclined practitioner, the legitimation process might be supported, while the liberative and transformative practitioner might seek to puncture or debunk the legitimations. (10)

Example for Phenomenological Research

Phenomenological work with young children examines how both family interactions and the practices of everyday life are related to the construction of childhood. It is revealed how the children's illustration of family life and common sense are actualized through ordinary interaction. Penetrating the inner world of children requires that the phenomenological practitioner view the subjects in their own terms, from the level and viewpoints of children. Such investigation shuns adult authoritative and particularly scientific perspectives and seeks to give voice to the children's experience of their own worlds. Infants' and children's communicative and interactive competencies are respected and are not diminished by the drive toward higher level functioning. (11)

Heidegger's Critique

While the Moravian Husserl thought philosophy to be a scientific discipline that had to be founded on a phenomenology understood as epistemology, the German Heidegger, however, held a radically different view. According to him philosophy was not at all a scientific discipline, but more fundamental than science itself. He saw science as only one way of knowing the world with no specialized access to truth. Furthermore, the scientific mindset itself is built on a much more "primordial" foundation of practical, everyday knowledge. Martin Heidegger believed that Husserl's approach overlooked basic structural features of both the subject and object of experience – what he called their "being". He expanded phenomenological enquiry to encompass our understanding and experience of Being itself, thus making phenomenology the method (in the first phase of his career at least) of the study of being: ontology. Husserl was sceptical of this approach, which he regarded as quasi-mystical, and it contributed to the divergence between their thinking.

Influence of Phenomenology on Social Sciences

Phenomenology is an influential and complex philosophic tradition that has given rise to various related philosophical movements such as existentialism, poststructuralism, postmodernism, feminism, culture critique, and various forms of analytical and new theory. Major contemporary figures such as the Frenchmen Foucault and Derrida, and America's Rorty, find the impetus and sources of their writings in earlier phenomenological works by Husserl, Heidegger, and the French philosophers Blanchot, Levinas and others.

The phenomenological influence upon contemporary sociology can be seen in the increased humanization of theoretical works, research methods, educational assessment procedures, and instructional modes. (12) Phenomenological thought has influenced the work of postmodernism, poststructuralism, critical theory and constructionism.

Hence, phenomenology, while remaining an identifiable movement within the discipline of sociology, has influenced mainstream research a lot. Inclusion of qualitative research approaches in conventional research generally expresses this accommodation. (13) The greater acceptance of intensive interviewing, participant observation and focus groups reflect the willingness of non-phenomenological sociologists to integrate subjectivist approaches into their work.

Further Influence

Phenomenology also influenced the arts, for example contemporary architecture. Here, phenomenology is seen as a philosophical design and refers to the physical and haptic experience of building materials and their sensory properties. Phenomenology in architecture favored an approach to design that was highly personal and inward looking. (14) (15)

We now turn from our overall orientation to the key tenets of phenomenology.

5.2 Phenomenology – Key Tenets

There are six key tenets of phenomenology, laying out as such the conventional grounds for a relational path to research. These are the following:

Phenomenology – Key Tenets
① Engage in a process of radical inquiry.
② Immerse yourself in a life world of immediately lived experiences.
③ Concentrate on illuminating the nature of the "inner self".
④ Focus on the subjective view of experience.
⑤ Locate every unique cultural history as an episode in the larger story.
⑥ Go beyond reductive positivism and naïve empiricism.

① **Engage in a process of radical inquiry**

Most of the founding figures of phenomenology emphasized the need for a renewal of philosophy as a process of radical enquiry. Above all else, phenomenology must pay attention to the nature of consciousness as actually experienced, not as pictured by commonsense or philosophical tradition; it must make a fresh interpretation of phenomena, "bracketed off" from customary outlooks and conventional assumptions. In our view, such a research approach paves the way for social innovation.

② **Immerse yourself in a life world of immediately lived experiences**

Phenomenology, for Husserl, has as its exclusive concern experiences intuitively seizable in their essence, not empirically perceived and treated as empirical facts. Further, it seeks to avoid all impositions placed on experience in advance, whether these are drawn from religious or cultural traditions, from everyday commonsense, or indeed from science itself. Explanations are not to be imposed before the phenomena have been understood from within.

③ **Concentrate on illuminating the nature of the "inner self"**

The immediate inspiration for the term "phenomenology" was, in 1889, the Czech Franz Brentano. Husserl's phenomenology, has its first anticipation in Brentano's attempt to rethink the nature of psychology as a science. He proposed a form of descriptive psychology, which would concentrate on illuminating the nature of the inner self. Husserl went on to develop this descriptive psychology into the most general version of a science of consciousness, underlying now all forms of scientific knowledge.

④ **Focus on the subjective view of experience**

Despite its initial open antipathy towards history, phenomenology, like all philosophical movements, was shaped by the particular historical and cultural circumstances of its time. In its time, when the advance of "outer directed", objectively cast science and technology was rampant, it steadfastly protected the subjective view of experience as a necessary part of any full understanding of the nature of knowledge. In its profound critique of naturalism as a philosophical programme, Husserl and his followers saw such as self-defeating because it consciously excluded consciousness, the very source of all knowledge and value of all creativity and innovation.

⑤ **Locate every unique cultural history as an episode in the larger story**

Husserl became more urgently aware that the condition of the natural attitude and indeed the scientific attitude were not merely static universal states of humankind, but were historically constituted. He interpreted the threat of National Socialism as part of a larger deformation of our perception of the world, brought about by the one-sided nature of our understanding of the modern world. "The Crisis of the European Sciences" (16) is an attempt to alert the world to the increasing danger of the collapse of a genuinely scientific and philosophical outlook, which had marked out the progress of the West since the time of the Greeks.

⑥ **Go beyond reductive positivism and naïve empiricism**

Husserl was here diagnosing and opposing what he considered being the disastrous social consequences of a science, which espoused reductive positivism and naïve empiricism. He also opposed what he regarded as the misguided, deformed rationalism as a consequence of the Enlightenment, which settled for a naïve objectivism, and did not notice the very subjectivity, which made genuine rational objectivity and creativity possible. For him, science comes from a very special theoretical attitude, one of detached playfulness and curiosity. Galileo had displaced our immediate forms of lived experience with forms of objects as dictated by such curiosity and playfulness. If the objects produced in this play are then uncritically asserted to be the real objects of our experience in the life world, then serious problems will arise. Such was the case with Galileo and this is what happened in modernity; the positivistic world-view predominated.

We now turn from these key tenets of phenomenology to its deeper and broader connotations, starting out with the insights of American cultural anthropologist David Abram.

5.3 Phenomenological Methodology in Depth

5.3.1 The More than Human World

The *crisis in the sciences was mirrored by a crisis in the social and natural world*. One of the most eloquent contemporary exponents of such is the American anthropologist and phenomenologist David Abram, who has spent much of his life in Asia and Africa. We shall now consider Abram's current phenomenological perspective, before returning to Husserl.

Our "life world", for Abram, is both the soil in which all our sciences and institutions are rooted and the rich humus into which their results ultimately return, whether as nutrients or poisons. Our spontaneous experience of the world, charged with subjective, emotional and intuitive content, remains the vital and dark ground of our objectivity. *"Phenomenology" returns to the taken-for-granted realm of subjective experience, not to explain it but simply to pay attention to its rhythms and textures.* For Abram, such a phenomenal "life world" has various layers: underneath the surface layer of a cultural-world there reposes a deeper, more unitary life world. It is always already there beneath all our cultural acquisitions: a vast and continually overlooked dimension of experience that nevertheless supports and sustains all our diverse and discontinuous worldviews. (17)

The true task of phenomenology then lies in its careful demonstration of the way in which every theoretical and scientific practice grows out of, and remains supported by, the forgotten ground of our directly felt and lived experience, and has value and meaning only in reference to this primordial and open realm. European civilisation's neglect of the natural world and its needs, as Afrikaaner novelist and adventurer Van der Post (18) has highlighted in an African context, has clearly been encouraged by a style of awareness that disparages sensorial reality. For it denigrates the visible and tangible order of things on behalf of some absolute source assumed to exist entirely beyond or outside of the bodily world. The Jewish and Christian traditions have followed in the footsteps of Plato's philosophical derogation of sensible and changing forms. Indeed both traditions, for Abram, made use of the strange and potent technology we call "the alphabet".

These letters printed across the page are hardly different from the footprints of prey left in the snow. We read these traces with organs honed over millennia by our tribal ancestors. In fact, the Chinese word for writing "wen" signifies a conglomeration of marks. It applies to the veins in stones and wood, to constellations, to the tracks of birds. The term "wen" has designated, by extension, literature. With the advent of the Hebrew "aleph-beth", a new distance is opened between human culture and the rest of nature. The larger, more-than-human world is no longer a part of the system. But not quite. For example, the Hebrew word for aleph comes from "ox" – an ox head with horns became our letter A. As the Hebrew "aleph" became the Greek "alpha" the sensorial reference to the concrete phenomenon was completely lost.

To members of a non-writing culture, places are never just passive settings. In oral cultures the human eyes and ears have not yet shifted their participation from the animate surroundings, or the beating rhythm of the drums to the written word. Particular mountains, canyons, streams, or grove trees have not yet lost the expressive potency and dynamism with which they spontaneously present themselves to the senses. Indeed, by virtue of its underlying and enveloping presence, the place may even be felt to be the source, the primary power that expresses itself through the various events that unfold there. *To an oral culture, experiences and events remain rooted in the particular soils, the particular ecologies, the particular places, and the particular life rhythms that give rise to them.* This brings us to Husserl's life world.

5.3.2 Husserl's Life World: "Lebenswelt"

The Primacy of Intentionality

Every act of knowledge, for Husserl, is to be legitimised by "ordinary intuition", which lies at the core of his philosophy. *He criticizes traditional empiricism for naively dictating that all judgments be legitimised by "experience", instead of realising that many different forms of intuition underlie our judgments and our reasoning process.* "Given-ness" sums up his view that *all experience is experience to someone, according to a particular manner of experiencing.* In that context, you will need to attend through your research to your particular approach to experiencing the world. It is also critical in that respect that you are aware of what kind of individual and essential "intentionality" you bring to it.

Husserl sees phenomenology as putting the study of culture or "spirit" on a proper scientific footing. In that context your "life world" underlies your intentional experiences. He saw such a *life world as the universal framework of human endeavour* – including our scientific endeavours. It is the ultimate horizon of all human achievement. As conscious human beings, we always inhabit the life world. It is pre-given in advance and experienced as a unity. The life world is the general structure, which allows objectivity and thing-hood to emerge in the different ways in which they do emerge in different cultures. *There is not one single life world, for Husserl, but a set of overlapping worlds: This set is beginning from the world, which is the "home-world", and extending to other world farther away, the worlds of other cultures.*

Practical concerns, culturally laden assumptions and smatterings of scientific knowledge, however, all get in the way of a pure consideration of experience. What Husserl termed *"bracketing" meant that all scientific, philosophical, cultural and everyday assumptions had to be put aside.* Returning to examine this pre-given world is a return to the so-called "Lebenswelt" (life world). Phenomenology has to interrogate the supposedly objective view of the sciences, what has been termed the "God's eye perspective", or the "view from nowhere". *Husserlian phenomenology did not dispute the possibility of our gaining a "view from nowhere" understood as the "objective" view of things.* This indeed accorded with Popper's rationalist perspective. Husserl was anxious to give full credit to this view, but he saw it as an idealisation, one remote from everyday experience.

Besides rejecting such supposedly rationalist and idealist accounts of reality (see chapter 11) *phenomenologists were also critical of the narrow reductionist models of human experience found in various nineteenth century versions of empiricism* (see chapter 14). *Phenomenology claimed to have overcome the basis of the opposition between rationalism and empiricism and indeed to have rejected the subject-object distinction altogether.* Husserl saw intentionality as a way of reviving the central discovery of Descartes' cogito ergo sum. ("I think therefore I am"). *We overcome the subject-object divide only by finding a deeper meaning within subjectivity itself. This constitutes the "qualitative" character of your research.*

Subjectivity and Consciousness

In common with many researchers working at the end of the nineteenth century, such as America's William James and France's Henri Bergson, *Husserl was fascinated both by the ever-changing stream of conscious experience and by its apparent seamless unity.* For Husserl, objectivity was always a particular achievement of such consciousness. Furthermore, consciousness was always particularised as someone's consciousness. Husserl's central concern then, in his "Logical Investigations" was how such objective knowledge can be possible for a knowing subject? His investigations are concerned with analysing the most basic elements, which were required for any form of knowledge. These experiences were to be studied not as factually occurring psychological entities, but in terms of their necessary structure as acts of their kind. In other words, Husserl was asking the question, what is the essence of an act of perception, an act of thinking, and so on. Essences, for him, are the web of ideal possibilities and relationships that constitute a particular domain of experience.

Hence, *phenomenology is a science of pure essences. It must abstract from the purely contingent, factual features of your experience in order to isolate what is essential to all experiences of that kind. And it must overcome contingency, factuality, or factualness.* In that context, phenomenology is stripped of all empirical content, thereby providing essential knowledge, irrespective of what goes on in the actual world. Husserl believed in what he termed *"eidetic seeing", that it was possible to have an insight into the essential nature of things, that these could be "seen" in a manner analogous to the perceptual seeing of a physical object.* Such essential seeing was then "eidetic". For him, *traditional empiricism had allowed itself to be blinded by its faith in a narrow empiricism that ignored the fact that the sciences operated with such essences. Hence the importance of moving from a merely factual to the level of essential truths.*

In contrast to the positivistic outlook of naturalism, Husserl believed that all knowledge, all science, all rationality depended on conscious acts, acts which cannot be properly understood from within the "natural" scientific outlook at all. Consciousness should not be viewed naturalistically as part of the world, since consciousness is precisely the reason there was a world there for us in the first place. *For Husserl it is not that consciousness creates the world – this would be subjective idealism – but rather that the world is opened up or disclosed through consciousness.* Our genuinely natural life, he maintained, is in community, living in a world of shared objects, shared environment, shared meanings, shared language. His treatment of "inter-subjectivity" employed a conception of empathy with others.

We now turn to Martin Heidegger, who, unlike his teacher Husserl, believed that it was necessary to link phenomenology with hermeneutics, the subject of the next chapter.

Linking Phenomenology with Hermeneutics

Phenomenology, for Germany's Martin Heidegger, is transformed into hermeneutical or existential phenomenology. For him the phenomena of existence always require interpretation, and hermeneutics is the art of interpretation. So an interpretation of human existence cannot be a neutral, dispassionate, theoretical contemplation, but must take into account the *involvement* of the enquirer. *Heidegger's ultimate aim is to understand the meaning of being in relation to time* (see also chapter 8). For this purpose he draws heavily on the German historical tradition of Hegel and Dilthey.

According to Heidegger's analysis, the basic structure of "factical" life is "caring" which involves "circumspection". Mostly humans are drawn into the world in a way he characterises as "falling". In falling, humans live their concrete lives as "bogged down in inauthentic tradition and habituation". Heidegger profoundly alters Husserl's phenomenology. He does not refer to natural attitude. He remains more faithful to the *historical, lived,* practical nature of human experience. *"Dasein" ("being"), is not an entity that stands on its own, like a stone or chair; it is always caught up in a world.* "World" here means a context, an environment, a set of references and assignments within which any meaning is located. All neutral understanding of things, for example scientific understanding, presupposes our "existential" encounter (Heidegger is actually an early existentialist) with things and our original interpretation of them in the light of our concerns and dealings with the world.

The Existential Nature of "Dasein"

Your life, for Heidegger, presents itself in terms of the set of possibilities that you are. Of course, a lot of the way your life presents itself is given by the culture you have grown up in, or is simply carried along by a kind of unquestioned horizon of acceptance. But, as Heidegger indicates, *you can choose certain possibilities for yourself.* This part of his analysis was seized on by the existentialists, especially by the French twentieth century existentialist Jean Paul *Sartre, who took from Heidegger*

the view that humans can make themselves who they are by seizing their possibilities.
Sartre's account, however, is much more action oriented than that of Heidegger, who
is really giving a phenomenological description of how we encounter ourselves in our
lives.

For Heidegger *"authentic moments" are those in which we are most at home with
ourselves, at one with ourselves.* You may initiate or take up possibilities as your
own; you have a deep, concrete experience of what is "yours". This "authentic"
orientation can be compared and contrasted with your more usual, normal, everyday
moments, where you do not treat things as affecting you deeply in your "own-most"
being. Heidegger therefore thinks we live in an inauthentic way most of the time.
Anxiety is the recognition of a certain nothingness, a groundlessness in our existence.
As Sartre was to describe it, anxiety leads us into a kind of vertigo where we literally
have no ground beneath our feet. Fear is always fear of *something,* and for the sake of
something. Anxiety, on the other hand, is a rather shapeless mood, which does not
have a precise object. Anxiety reveals to us a certain homelessness – we are not at
home in the world. The world faces us as something weird.

Thrown into Inauthenticity

In our ordinary everydayness, we simply pass information along, not getting wrapped
up in it, and our speech (if not also our research) is merely "idle talk" or "passive
information gathering". This is for Heidegger an inauthentic state. In our everyday
mood we are absorbed in the world, caught up in our tasks; we don't reflect on who
we are, we are "thrown". We are also peculiarly constructed so that we actually run
away from facing up to aspects of our existence. This structural feature of running
away Heidegger calls "falling". *Falling means getting caught up in the public self, so
that we no longer have proper access to our authentic sense of our lives. We are
thrown into history and can experience this as a kind of fateful acceptance, repeating
what is handed down through tradition, or we can try and achieve a moment of
resoluteness, in your case through your research, projecting yourselves into
possibilities.*

*For Heidegger, the great threat to human existence (and specifically here in our
research programme) is that thinking has become a kind of technical information
processing.* This leads to a fundamental homelessness and rootlessness (and in such a
case to inauthentic research). *Against this account of transcendental homelessness
stands genuine philosophy as a kind of homecoming, a thinking back from our current
displaced sense back to finding our place and preserving what we have found.*
Heidegger's later writings develop his thinking on the nature of genuine dwelling and
the global homelessness of humanity. His account of the technological framework
bounding the modern world expands to such a degree that even the early Greeks are
seen as having cast the metaphysical fate of the West to be technological. This is
through the Greeks' earliest thinking about *techne* and *episteme,* skill and knowledge.
Technology is a form of revealing. However, it is a form, which also uses up the
material, which it is setting forth. It turns nature into a mere stockpile of coal, iron,
water etc. For Heidegger, the nature of this technological revealing is such that it
obscures and does not reveal its own essence. Furthermore, it transforms the humans
involved in technology. Human beings have been caught up in this mode of revealing.

The influence of Heidegger on twentieth-century philosophy has been huge. The Canadian philosopher Charles Taylor has said that Heidegger's importance lies in the fact that he is one of the few contemporary philosophers who has helped to free us from the grip of rationalism. Among his own students were Gadamer (hermeneutics), and Marcuse (critical theorist). In Germany he influenced the Frankfurt School of Social Research, from whence came critical theory. Adorno, as a founder of the Frankfurt School juxtaposed the young Marx's view of human alienation and domination by ideology against Heidegger's account of man and the domination of technicity. For Marcuse, Heidegger had articulated the principles of human historicity, a necessary part of the Marxist attempt to explain man with reference to historical movement. Finally, his philosophy was absorbed by French existentialism and by Derrida's deconstruction and Foucault's anti-Enlightenment humanism (see chapter 12 on postmodernism).

Being and Nothingness

Jean Paul Sartre, in the middle of the last century, embraced phenomenology as a way of overcoming "idealism". *For him,* idealism is the view that reality is apprehended only indirectly through mental representations of ideas. *There was now a way to discuss the manner in which* consciousness was immediately in the presence of things. *The real merit of "Being and Nothingness", his most famous philosophical work, is the manner in which it provides close descriptions of various human situations, which are rich in phenomenological and philosophical insight. Chief amongst these are descriptions of what it is to be "in bad faith", to adopt a "persona". In such bad faith a person is denied their true choice.*

Human consciousness, for Sartre, is truly free in this existential and phenomenological context. It can be anything. It is pure possibility, and hence ripe for innovation. *Yet, on the other hand, at every moment we are embedded in the historical situation.* Human nature is caught up in facticity, in what Sartre calls "the situation". *Authenticity is how we respond to the situation in a manner, which acknowledges and preserves our freedom. Husserl had characterized the situation as "mine-ness", which Heidegger had analysed in terms of the basis of possibility that may appropriate one's life either in an "authentic" or an "inauthentic" way. "Being and Nothingness" is an extended meditation on these notions.* To be authentic is to grasp one's freedom and recognize it. Being inauthentic means being in flight from one's freedom, attempting to cover it by clinging to a persona, or indeed adopting one research methodology or another, because that is "what you are supposed to do". Social innovation, in such terms, is a process of authentic engagement with the world, grasping one's freedom by enabling others to realise theirs.

We now turn from phenomenology's most well known heritage (with Husserl, Heidegger and Sartre being amongst its best known representatives) to some of its globally dispersed representatives, starting with Rudolph Steiner in Austria.

5.4 Global Variations of Phenomenology

5.4.1 From Phenomenology to Anthroposophy

The Philosophy of Freedom

Rudolph Steiner, an Austrian who lived at the turn of the last century, was a philosopher and educator, architect and agronomist, historian and musician, economist and political scientist, amongst other things. Because of the esoteric nature of some of his "anthroposophical" work he became disconnected from the philosophical and methodological mainstream. Andrew Welburn, a Fellow of New College, Oxford, has done us a real service by linking Rudolph Steiner's work into the phenomenological establishment. (19)

Actually, Steiner was a leading exemplar of researcher and innovator in the social realm. For not only did he conceive of "anthroposophy" as a philosophical movement, but, through it, he pioneered innovative approaches to art and architecture, medicine and agriculture, education and economics, some of which – particularly in education (Waldorf Schools) and agriculture (biodynamic farming) – have spread throughout the world.

Steiner's idea of philosophy was as liberation from limiting forms of thought, rather than as a wagging moral finger or an intellectual programme. Such liberation enables us to grasp other possibilities, taking place in the thick of life, and coinciding with the freedom to see things anew. Such a concept of freedom is precisely one that may be embodied in the form of a building or a room, in a gesture or in a painting, or in a new approach to economics, for him based on fraternity rather than liberty. Scientific knowing is the way in which we can relate to the world through developing our inner activity. Scientific activity does not reveal our passivity before fixed facts of nature, but our own living process of knowledge, the free development of the self. For example, his concept of "associative" economics was based on what he reckoned to be the phenomenological and concrete "reality" of economic life, rather than the liberal and abstract "ideal" of it embodied in the "free market" approach.

In view of the recent reforms taking place in Eastern Europe then, Steiner's recognition of the need for these to be based on an absolute respect for freethinking individuals is highly germane. For him the individual was a creative force in society, an agent of necessary change, and a constant test of the validity of social forms. Now that, for Steiner, the myths of West and East have played out their extraordinary history on the capitalist-communist stage of the twentieth century, it may be that the signs of a more balanced reappraisal of their respective values may also draw inspiration from Steiner's proposals. Steiner suggested a more dynamically conceived "threefold social order" than capitalism versus communism, designed to obviate the unproductive dualistic tensions built into such assumptions of individual-versus-state. Such an order was comprised of the political, economic and cultural spheres. Steiner saw them as the respective homes of political equality, economic fraternity and cultural liberty – or indeed freedom.

Phenomenology as the Bridge between East and West

The polarizations of the modern world, according to Steiner, were rooted in assumptions that reach back to the beginnings of the nineteenth century and indeed before then. The one side of the polarity, an idealistic philosophy, traced its origin back to Immanuel Kant. The other, an embodiment of a materialistic world-view, had come down from Jeremy Bentham and was influenced by J.S. Mill. There was apparently no middle way. Their clash in the nineteenth century pre-figures some of the terrible struggles subsequently enacted in the twentieth. The struggles above all were concerned with the value of the individual. For Steiner, neither dominant tradition assigns value to the individual as such. Idealist Kant held that moral imperatives come to us with blinding force as "categorical imperatives". The knowing individual has only the function of recognizing the necessary laws of existence. The realist Bentham felt that fulfilment lies in the value of the whole society, tribe or race.

Steiner, in contrast with realism and idealism, is closely aligned with the emerging phenomenology. Instead of a desperate search for objective foundations, knowledge might emerge from the growing and changing being of man, in a continually developing society. That would mean abandoning the notion of the impassive onlooker, and including the seeking, striving human self in the picture we form of the cognitive process. *As such we arrive at a picture, which is neither the blank sheet of empiricism, nor the mind locked up in its own categories as for Kant.* What we know of the world depends on the fact that we are part of the world and have been shaped by it, so that from the beginning our nature and organisation become not a limit, but the actual key to the nature of the universe to which we belong and which brought us into being.

From this perspective knowledge ceases to be a mirroring, passive affair and becomes a process whereby we insert ourselves actively in the given setting of our lives, which therefore always caries a moral significance *(for ourselves and, of course, for our research). Steiner's view is that* we need to accept the responsibility that as knowers we change the potential and actual course of the world. In other words, research and innovation are the two sides of the same coin. His view of knowledge as relationship stresses our own need to be transformed, to learn and grow through cognitive encounter and allow reality to reveal itself in ever-new aspects. *The task of knowledge is not to recapitulate in the form of concepts what is given to us in some other way. It is rather to create an entirely new domain which, when taken together with the world presented through sense perception, yields for the first time full reality.* The human being is not an idle onlooker before the pageant of the world; he is an active participant in a cosmic creative process. That, for us, is the essence of social research and its counterpart social innovation.

We now turn from European phenomenological ontology and epistemology to its more widely dispersed (but still relational) global expressions.

5.4.2 Dispersed Phenomenology: From Locke and Hume to Buddha and Biko via Iqbal

Locke's and Hume's Radical Empiricism and Radical Doubt

We already mentioned in our second chapter that Husserl, through his focus on individual freedom and intentionality, had something in common with "western" Locke and Hume, even though he rejected Locke's exclusive focus on objective reality. He also shared with the Anglo-Saxon empiricists an orientation towards the concrete and "real", as opposed to the ideal. This he termed the "life world", albeit that such was full of subjectivity as well as objectivity. At the same time Husserl was a rationalist, who drew inspiration from "northerner" Descartes, through the latter's sense of "radical doubt", although he disagreed with Descartes' separation of body and mind. In Husserl's words:

"... the European world was born out of reason, that is, out of the spirit of philosophy. The European crisis should therefore not be interpreted as the failure of rationalism ... an impoverished rationalism has become entangled in "naturalism" and "objectivism" (20)

Buddha's Radical Detachment

Even more interesting is the resonance between phenomenology and Buddhism, that is involving self-detachment, alongside of self-interest (intentionality) and self-knowledge (rationality). Caroline Brazier, in her book on "Buddhist Psychology", makes the point that Buddhist psychology is sometimes described as a "non-self" psychology. The self is a defensive structure built in response to affliction. This is what is referred to in Buddhism as ignorance or "avidya". (21) We ignore much that is going on around us and limit our behaviour and interest to things that relate to our self-view. In the process, we initially grasp for something we can hold on to that seems permanent; we call this "me" or self. The self is the fortress we create to protect ourselves from experiencing loss and impermanence. It is our greatest defence mechanism. It is also our prison. Keeping the fortress in place becomes our life project, and consumes large amounts of energy. This constituted, for the Buddha, greed and attachment.

So what has this all got to do with phenomenology? *If Buddhist psychology is a psychology of addiction, then it is also a psychology of encounter.* Encounter is the antidote to those addictive patterns that holds us trapped. *By encountering the world beyond the walls of self, we break through to freedom. The path to health is in encountering that which is not self. In other words, we need to encounter that which is other. To break out of self-absorption we have to allow ourselves to be touched by something beyond ourselves.*

Biko's Radical Consciousness

Interestingly enough, such self-detachment with its characteristically "eastern" self-effacing connotations, is expressed in both similar and different terms within the self-expressive "southern" context of "Ubuntu". The attitude of seeing people not as themselves but as agents for some particular function either to one's advantage or disadvantage is, for the late Steve Biko (a key figure in South Africa's "Black Consciousness" movement), foreign to the African. We are not, he says, a suspicious race:

"We believe in the inherent goodness of man. We enjoy man for himself. We regard our living together not as an unfortunate mishap warranting endless competition amongst us but as a deliberate act of God to make us a community of brothers and sisters jointly involved in the quest for a composite answer to the varied problems of life. Hence in all we do we always place man first and therefore all our action is usually joint and community oriented." (22)

Nothing then dramatises the eagerness of the African to communicate with each other more than their love for song and rhythm. Music in the African culture features in all emotional states, for South Africa's Steve Biko as for Senegal's former philosopher-president Leopold Senghor:

"When we go to work we share the burdens and pleasures of the work we are doing through music. In other words, for Africans, music and rhythm are not luxuries but part and parcel of our way of communicating. Any suffering we experienced was made more real by song and rhythm. There is no doubt that the so-called "Negro spirituals" sung by black slaves in the States as they toiled under oppression were indicative of the African heritage. The major thing to note about our songs is that they were never songs for individuals. All African songs are group songs." (23)

Biko adds that Africans, being a pre-scientific people, do not recognise any conceptual cleavage between the natural and the supernatural. They experience a situation rather than face a problem. By this is meant that they allow both the rational and the non-rational elements to make an impact upon them. Hence, any action they may take could be described more as a response of the total personality to the situation than the result of some mental exercise. As such Africans would obviously find it artificial to create special occasions for worship. Neither did they see it as logical to have a particular building in which all worship would be conducted.

"We believed that God was always in communication with us and therefore merited attention everywhere and anywhere. In rejecting western values, therefore, we are rejecting those things that are not only foreign to us but that seek to destroy the most cherished of our beliefs – that the cornerstone of society is man himself – not just his welfare, not his material being, but just man himself with all his ramifications. We reject the power-based society of the Westerner that seems to be ever concerned with perfecting their technological know-how while losing out on their spiritual dimension. We believe that in the long run the special contribution from Africa will be in the field of human relationships. *The great powers of the world may have done wonders in giving the world an industrial and military look. But the great gift still has to come from Africa – giving the world a human face."* (24)

That is not a million miles away from where Edmund Husserl was coming from, philosophically in entering wholeheartedly into the "life world" of self and other, even though he and Biko were far apart in place and time. Husserl states in such "ubuntu-like" terms:

"Personal life means living communalised as "I" and "we", within a community horizon, and this in communities of various forms – family, nation, supra-national community. It involves purposeful life, the term life in this context not having a physiological sense, but in the broadest sense creating culture in the unity of a historical development." (25)

Most ubuntu thinkers in an African philosophical context formulate their views in terms of "a person is a person through other persons", or, "I am because you are". In this way human dignity gains a central place and seems to be related to both morality and nationality. There is no dualism in this position because rationality and morality are required from community life and do not follow from so-called universal categories or fixed ideologies.

Sharing, for Zimbabwe's management philosopher and consultant Lovemore Mbigi (26), means participation in the context of business management. In the final analysis, he bases his ubuntu model on four principles: "morality", which involves trust and credibility; "interdependence", which concerns the sharing and caring aspect of relationships, that is cooperation and participation; "spirit of man", which refers to human dignity and mutual respect, implying that activities should be person-driven and humanness should be central; and lastly "totality", which pertains to the continuous improvement of everything in the organisation by every member of it.

Reconstructing Islam

We finally turn to the phenomenology of religion. In this case, we do so via the twentieth century Pakistani poet-philosopher, Muhammad Iqbal and his "Reconstruction of the Islamic Religion".

Interestingly enough, Iqbal positions Islam, as does Husserl phenomenology, in between the ideal and the real, emphasizing the relatively concrete nature of Islam vis-à-vis classical Greek philosophy:

"The failure of Cartesian ontological and teleological arguments is that they look upon "thought" as an agency working on things from without. This creates an unbridgeable gap between the real and the ideal. It is, however, possible to take thought not as a principle that organises its material from the outside, but as a potency, which is formative of the very being of its material. Thus regarded thought or idea is not akin to the original nature of things; it is their ultimate ground and constitutes the essence of their beings, inspiring their onward march to a self-determined end. But our present situation necessitates the dualism between thought and being." (27)

Iqbal argues that the radical doubt, that Husserl evolved from Descartes, was anticipated by an Islamic eleventh century philosopher. Iqbal sees Islam as a bridge between the ancient and modern worlds. As such, he also sees Islam as the origin of empirically based scientific method, as we know it today:

"The Prophet of Islam seems to stand between the ancient and modern worlds. In so far as the source of his revelation is concerned, he belongs to the ancient world. At the same time the birth of Islam is the birth of the modern, inductive intellect. In

Islam, prophecy reaches its perfection in discovering the need of its own abolition – in order to achieve full self-consciousness man must be thrown inductively back on his own resources. The abolition of the kingship and hereditary priesthood in Islam, the constant appeal to reason and experience in the Qur'an, and the emphasis that it lays on Nature and History as sources of human knowledge, are all different aspects of the same idea of finality. As such the Qur'an regards both "Anfus" (self) and "Afaq" (world) as sources of knowledge. Inner experience is one source of human knowledge; the external sources are Nature and History." (28)

Ultimately, for Iqbal and for many Islamic scholars, *Islam is rooted not only in concreteness, as opposed to abstraction, but also in a concept of "inner freedom" that anticipates not only phenomenology as a whole, but also and particularly existential phenomenology*, as reflected in the work of Heidegger and Sartre:

"The Qur'an has no liking for abstract universals. It always fixes its gaze on the concrete, which the theory of relativity has only recently taught science to do. Omniscience, abstractly conceived, is merely a blind, capricious power without limits. The Qur'anic legend of the Fall has, in fact, nothing to do with the first appearance of man on the planet. Its purpose is rather to indicate man's rise from a primitive, instinctive state to the conscious possession of a free self, capable of doubt and disobedience. The Fall does not mean moral depravity; it is man's transition from simple consciousness to the first flash of self-consciousness, a kind of awakening from the dream of nature to a throb of causality in one's own being. Man's first act of disobedience was his first act of free choice. Freedom is thus a condition of goodness. But to permit the emergence of a finite ego who has the power to choose, after considering the relative values of several actions open to him, is really to take a great risk. For the freedom to choose good also involves its opposite. (29)

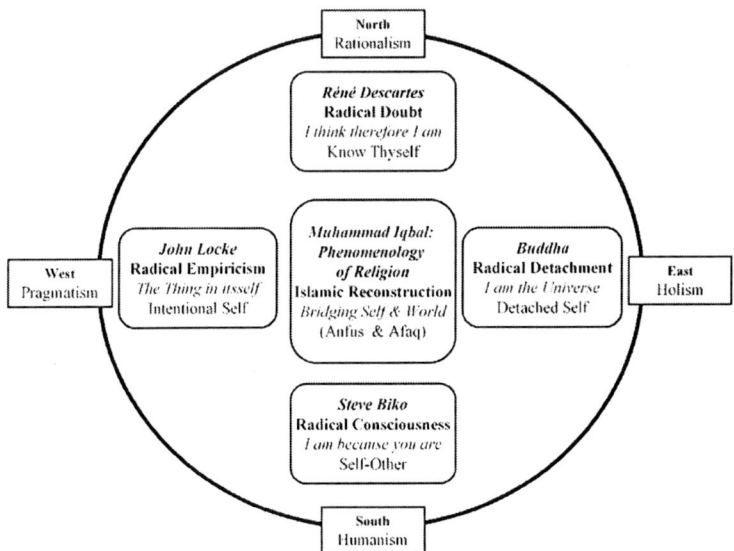

Figure 5.3: A phenomenal field of force

We now turn from theory to practice, from methodology to application. We now return to Europe, in fact to the Czech Republic where Husserl himself was born. Thereby we turn from philosophical (and religious) thought to socio-political practice, from Husserl's phenomenological "life world" to Havel's "living in truth".

5.5 Phenomenology in Practice: The "Czechoslovakia-Case"

From Scientific to Velvet Revolution: Social Science to Social Activism

Phenomenology also constitutes a basis for socio-political and economic transformation, as has been illustrated over the past few decades in the former Czechoslovakia. Unlike Locke and Adam Smith, Rousseau and Marx, *Husserl was not conventionally seen to exercise direct social and political influence. Yet his philosophical revolution, transforming a "free world" into a "life world", unbeknown to most of us, preceded the "velvet revolution"* in which the ex Czech President Vaclav Havel played a central role.

It all started at the turn of the last century, though antecedents date back six hundred years. A prominent background presence for Havel is Thomas Masaryk, a philosopher who served for fifteen years as a member of the Austrian Parliament at the turn of last century. Opposed to Germany's nationalism in Austria and Austria's adventurous policies in the Balkans, Masaryk became convinced that Austro-Hungary could no longer serve as the common homeland for the small nations of Central Europe. Thus, following the outbreak of World War I, Masaryk became the champion of an independent Czechoslovakia, leading troops who fought successfully alongside Allied forces. At the end of the war, Masaryk became president of the first Czechoslovakian Republic, from 1919 to 1938.

Primarily a philosopher, Masaryk had come under the influence of Franz von Brentano during his studies in Vienna. Subsequently, Masaryk developed a friendship with Husserl and was instrumental in convincing him to switch from the study of mathematics to philosophy. And from Masaryk, Husserl acquired a heightened sense of the crisis of the European sciences. *Alarmed that increased scientific sophistication did not bring moral progress, he feared that modern reason had become detached from the world of good and evil, which for him was the foundation of lived reality.* In addition, Masaryk affirmed that Czech national consciousness had been grounded and shaped by the Hussite movement. Through Masaryk's testimony, the national martyr, Jan Hus (1370–1415), gained fresh place in contemporary Czech thinking. So when Jan Palach burned himself after the Soviets invaded Czechoslovakia, it was appropriate for Czech patriots to assign Hussite martyr symbolism to the event. We must also cite the strong influence of the philosopher Jan Patocka, who studied under Husserl, taught Vaclav Havel and subsequently was instrumental in publishing Charter 77. In this statement of resistance to Soviet occupation and communist ideology, Patocka drew upon the thought of his significant predecessors. He studied under Husserl, and he also devoted a good portion of his graduate work to a systematic study of Masaryk's thought.

Charter 77

Patocka initially drew up the so-called "Charter 77" texts, prompted by the 1977 Helsinki Agreement on human rights. These rights affirmed that human beings are obliged to discover and protect a valid moral foundation, since there can be no rightful expectation that salvation will be provided by the state, or that it can be effected by any combination of social powers and forces. In a message to the Czech people, Patocka explained Charter 77 as follows: *a moral system does not exist in order to help society function but simply so that man can be human. It is not man who defines a moral order according to the arbitrary nature of his needs, wishes, tendencies, and desires, but morality defines man.* (30)

Havel himself was arrested and jailed for four months for his part in Charter 77 activities. In 1979 he was convicted again, this time sentenced to four-and-a-half years in prison, but received a suspended sentence because of poor health and an international protest campaign.

Already in the fifties, while the Czech Communist Party was terrorizing the Czechoslovak people, the young Havel drew together a remarkable circle of friends and acquaintances who were all 36, and whom he soon began to call the Thirty-Sixers. His circle was preoccupied with literature, and they learned as teenagers the art of criticising and being criticised in turn – to concede that it was finally necessary to disclose, to reveal oneself, and to look at oneself as well through the eyes of others.

By the early 1960's, it is estimated that nearly half a million men and women of the communist "nomenklatura" occupied key decision-making positions, particularly in the management of enterprises, for which they were formally unqualified. The combined consequences of these various structural problems of the socialist state – unqualified leadership, administrative bottlenecks, economic stagnation, the absence of social "shock-absorbers" – was to encourage a faction of the ruling oligarchy, headed by Dubcek, to go on a dangerous journey called liberalisation. He therefore enabled the growth out from underneath the edifices of state power, of the first tender shoots of social life. In the end though, Dubcek proved a poor match for the political and social forces that he helped to unleash; and in August 1968, when the Soviets invaded, he fell victim to his own success.

Living in Truth

Almost a decade later dissident intellectuals, including Havel himself, signed the famed Charter 77. The centre of gravity of potential resistance is what he called "the existential dimension of the world". That's what Husserl, as we have seen, coined "Lebenswelt": here a different life – what Havel called "living in truth" – can be lived. This system serves people only to the extent that people will serve it.

Havel's thesis necessarily involved something of a Copernican Revolution – following from where Husserl left off – in the way power was conceived. The powerless, then, have within themselves the power to obstruct normality, to embarrass the authorities, to point to the possibility of living life differently – according to values like trust, openness, responsibility, solidarity and love.

"Living in truth requires the cultivation of individuation, self-protection and co-operation. The empowerment of the powerless first and foremost requires individuals to build open, flexible structures of resistance that run parallel to and underneath the late socialist state. There is a fundamental contrast for me and my philosophical predecessors between the world that can be constructed out of some presumed ideological viewpoint and the world that is rooted in trustworthy lived-experience; impersonal, mechanistic, manipulative force can be effectively resisted only by the one true power that all persons have at their disposal, their humanity. (31)

System, ideology and apparat – for Havel as for Husserl – have deprived human beings of rulers, as well as the ruled of their conscience, of their commonsense and natural speech and thereby also of their actual humanity. States grow ever more machine-like and totalitarian; men are transformed into statistical choruses of voters, producers, consumers, patients, tourists or soldiers. In politics, good and evil, categories of the natural world and therefore obsolete remnants of the past, lose all absolute meaning; the sole method of politics is quantifiable success. This absolute power achieved its most complete expression in the totalitarian systems. And *these systems, for Havel, are none other than a convex mirror of all modern civilization.*

The question about capitalism and socialism in the context of such modernization seems to emerge from the depths of the last century. It seems to Havel that these highly ideological and semantically confused categories (isms) have since long been beside the point. *The question for him is wholly other, deeper and equally relevant to all; whether we shall, by whatever means, succeed in reconstituting the natural and human world, phenomenologically, as the true terrain of politics, rehabilitating the personal experience of human beings as the initial measure of all things, placing morality above politics and responsibility above our desires.*

The task therefore is that of resisting vigilantly, thoughtfully and attentively, but at the same time with total dedication, the irrational momentum of anonymous, impersonal and inhuman power: the power of ideology, systems, bureaucracy, artificial languages and political slogans. *We must trust the voice of our conscience more than that of all abstract speculations and not invent other responsibilities than the one to which the voice calls us. We must not be ashamed that we are capable of love, friendship, solidarity, sympathy and tolerance, but just the opposite; we must set these fundamental dimensions of our humanity free from their private exile and accept them as the only genuine starting point of meaningful human community. We must be guided by our own reason and serve the truth under all circumstances as our own essential experience.*

How then, in the wider context of the Velvet Revolution and its aftermath did phenomenology become a socio-political force?

Unleashing Velvet Power – Releasing the "Life World"

The velvet revolution flung everybody temporarily into an everyday world marked by flux, ambiguity, and contingency. On board the revolution roller coaster, Havel worked hard through what had now become known as the Civic Forum, both to ensure its survival and to guarantee its role as the beating heart of the emerging opposition body. With his support the Civic Forum dispatched delegates all over the country with the aim of establishing brother and sister chapters. Meanwhile the revolution itself was proving to be a great spectacle. It enchanted observers and participants alike, and Havel, a master dramatist and compulsive planner of his and others' moves, climbed eagerly onto a stage already clotted with other actors. His public quest to confirm his leadership began at the famous Prague Theatre Laterna Magica. Havel chose that as the site to base the headquarters of the Civic Forum, whose inner circles began to function quickly as a government in waiting.

From the first day of assuming his presidency, Havel began experimenting with his new role as "King of the Castle" – the presidential home was in Prague castle! He tried to transform the Castle into a giant stage. From there he tried to direct a new performance – the biggest so far in his life. The play served as the supreme expression of the revolution. It displayed the newfound sense of collective awareness and solidarity, a blending of the self with the other. There was a cast of thousands of people, some famous and others previously unknown, whose performances would for a time win the hearts of the country's citizenry and attract the attention of the whole world.

Havel therefore emphasised the need to cultivate a tolerant and open civil society, in the process doing battle with the free marketer Vaclav Klaus. The latter was to significantly inhibit phenomenal transformation. So, on the one hand, Havel began to develop a brilliant modern idea: that economic actors always and everywhere go about their business and do their work only insofar as they tap into and cultivate sources of "social capital". A *market economy, he insisted, can only function if its members are "embedded" in a wider civil society that harbours social interaction based on such norms as trust, reliability, punctuality, honesty, friendship, resolution, the capacity for group commitment, humility and mutual recognition.* Yet, on the other hand, there was no dialectical force to ultimately transcend the Havel-Klaus divide. Havel was also opposing the Klausite uncivil effects of the obsession with state-backed privatisation. He criticized it especially for its blindness towards the way markets tend to "fail", in the process weakening or destroying the structures of civil society upon which they otherwise depend for their survival and growth. Meanwhile in 1992, the peaceful co-existence of two close nations, Czech and Slovak, ended. Czecho-Slovakia is now the name of a country from the distant past.

Thesis and Antithesis without Synthesis

Not only then were Havel's hopes dashed, as far as keeping Czechoslovakia together was concerned, but he was also to face stiff opposition within the Czech Republic, to "living in the truth" in the face of global market forces. These forces were welcomed in by that other Vaclav, Vaclav Klaus, a Thatcherite, neoliberal economist who became Prime Minister in the nineteen nineties. At the end of the day, the philosophical and socio-political impulse provided first by Husserl and Masaryk, and subsequently by Patocka and Havel, fell upon the free market economic sword. The conventionally liberal powers that be, and the overarching influence of the west, served to overpower this force from the centre.

We are now ready to conclude.

5.6 Conclusion

The philosophy of phenomenology emerged out of the "crisis of the European sciences" early in the twentieth century. When it began to be reduced to a discrete method by the Duquesne School in America, almost a century later, it inevitably lost some of its radical socio-political character. What Husserl, Heidegger and Steiner were talking about ontologically and epistemologically has only been somewhat digested. In fact, when we come to participatory action research (see chapter 7), we shall find a more thoroughgoing attempt to position phenomenology in the context of social innovation.

In grounding your research, you identify and immerse yourselves into a questioned phenomenon. It is one with which you want to engage because it disturbs you, moves you, calls upon you, and ultimately motivates you to both investigate it further; one that stimulates you to think, feel and act upon it.

Entering into a Life World

As a conscious human being, you always inhabit a life world; it is pre-given in advance and experienced as a unity. The life world is the general structure, which allows objectivity and thing-hood to emerge in the different ways in which they do emerge in different cultures. There is not one single life world, but a set of overlapping worlds, beginning from the world, which is the "home-world", and extending to other world farther away, the worlds of other cultures.

What does that mean for you as researcher? At the outset of your research you enter into your own problematic life world. You have chosen such, because you feel impelled to, because you feel called to, because the world around you, is incomplete without which your research will offer.

Engaging with Reality

The task of pursuing knowledge is not to recapitulate in the form of concepts what is given to you in some other way. It is rather to create an entirely new domain, which yields for the first time full reality. The human being is not an idle onlooker, before the pageant of the world; he is an active participant in a cosmic creative process.

As a researcher and innovator, you not only want to uncover and engage with what is really going on, beneath the surface – internally within yourself and externally in the world around you – but you want to transform it. You have come to recognize your real intentions. At this opening point in your thesis, you are called upon to describe such intentions, richly and intricately, qualitatively and poignantly, in relation to the field into which those intentions are implanted. In other words, you are called upon to lay aside your prejudices, your preconceptions and your analytical frameworks; then you enter into that world and immerse yourself in the phenomenon.

Overlaid With Personal Meaning and Social Significance

For you as a researcher, the challenge you ultimately face is to conduct such a phenomenological investigation in a way that has both social meaning and personal significance. The topic grows out of an intense interest in a particular area, close to your nature and culture, while also reaching out to others. That interest is provoked, outside in, by the unfilled needs that you see around you; it is also provoked inside out, by your own will and intent at this particular point of time.

To the extent, that such an interest is situated in a particular time and place, as well as within you and your profession or institution, so the relational path of research takes us on to feminism.

Bibliography

1) **Husserl**, E. (1931). *Ideas: General Introduction* to *Pure Phenomenology*. W. R. Boyce Gibson, trans. New York: Humanities Press.

2) **Husserl**, E. (1970). *The Crisis of the European Sciences*. Evanston: Northwestern University.

3) **Hitzler**, R. & **Keller**, R. (1989). *On Sociological and Common-Sense Verstehen*. London: Current Sociology, 37: 91-101.

4) **Helle**, H. J. ed. (1991). *Verstehen and Pragmatism: Essays in Interpretative Sociology*. Frankfurt: Peter Lang.

5) **Truzzi**, M. (1974). *Verstehen: Subjective Understanding in the Social Sciences*. Reading: Addison-Wesley.

6) **Bleicher**, J. (1982). *The Hermeneutic Imagination: Outline of a Positive Critique of Scientism and Sociology*. London: Routledge and Kegan Paul.

7) **Ainlay**, S. C. (1986). The Encounter with Phenomenology. In Hunter, J. D. & Ainlay, S. C., (eds.). *Making Sense of Modern Times: Peter L. Berger and the Vision of Interpretive Sociology*. London: Routledge and Kegan Paul.

8) **Abercrombie**, N. (1980). *Class, Structure and Knowledge*. New York: New York University Press.

9) **Phillipson**, M. (1972). *"Phenomenological Philosophy and Sociology."* In Filmer, P., Phillipson, M., Silverman, D. & Walsh, D. (eds.). *New Directions in Sociological Theory*. Cambridge, Mass.: MIT Press.

10) **Morris**, M. B. (1975). *"Creative Sociology: Conservative or Revolutionary?"* American Sociologist 10: 168-178.

11) **Sheets-Johnstone**, M. (1996). *An Empirical-Phenomenological Critique of the Social Construction of Infancy*. Human Studies, 19: 1-16.

12) **Darroch**, V. & **Silvers**, R. J. (eds.) (1982). *Interpretive Human Studies: An Introduction to Phenomenological Research*. Washington: University Press.

13) **Bentz**, V. M. & **Shapiro**, J. J. (1998). *Mindful Inquiry in Social Research*. London: Sage.

14) **Norberg-Schulz**, C. (1980). *Genius Loci: Towards a Phenomenology of Architecture*. New York: Rizzoli.

15) **Norberg-Schulz**, C. (1963). *Intentions in Architecture*. New York: Rizzoli.

16) **Husserl**, E. (1970). *The Crisis of the European Sciences*. Chicago: Northwestern University.

17) **Abram**, D. (1966). *The Spell of the Sensuous*. New York: Random.

18) **Van der Post**, L. (1954). *The Dark Eye of Africa*. Cape Town: Lowery Press.

19) **Welburn**, A. (2004). *Rudolph Steiner's Philosophy and the Crisis of Contemporary Thought*. Edinburgh: Floris.

20) **Husserl**, E. (1970). *The Crisis of the European Sciences*. Chicago: Northwestern University.

21) **Brazier**, C. (2003). *Buddhist Psychology*. London: Constable and Robinson.

22) **Biko**, S. (2004). *On Steve Biko*. Cape Town: Picador.

23) **Senghor**, L. (1964). *African Socialism*. London: Pall Mall Press.

24) **Biko**, S. (2004). *On Steve Biko*. South Africa: Picador.

25) **Husserl**, E. (1970). *The Crisis of the European Sciences*. Chicago: Northwestern University.

26) **Mbigi**, L. (2000). *Ubuntu*. Johannesburg: Knowledge Resources.

27) **Iqbal**, M. (2000). *The Reconstruction of Religious Thought in Islam*. New Delhi: Kitab Bhavan.

28) **Iqbal**, M. (2000). *The Reconstruction of Religious Thought in Islam*. New Delhi: Kitab Bhavan.

29) **Iqbal**, M. (2000). *The Reconstruction of Religious Thought in Islam*. New Delhi: Kitab Bhavan.

30) **Keane**, R. (1999). *Vaclav Havel*. London: Bloomsbury.

31) **Havel**, V. (1987). *Living in Truth*. London/Boston: Faber and Faber.

CHAPTER 6

FROM PHENOMENOLOGY TO
FEMINISM

"UNCOVER INDIGENOUS KNOWLEDGE"

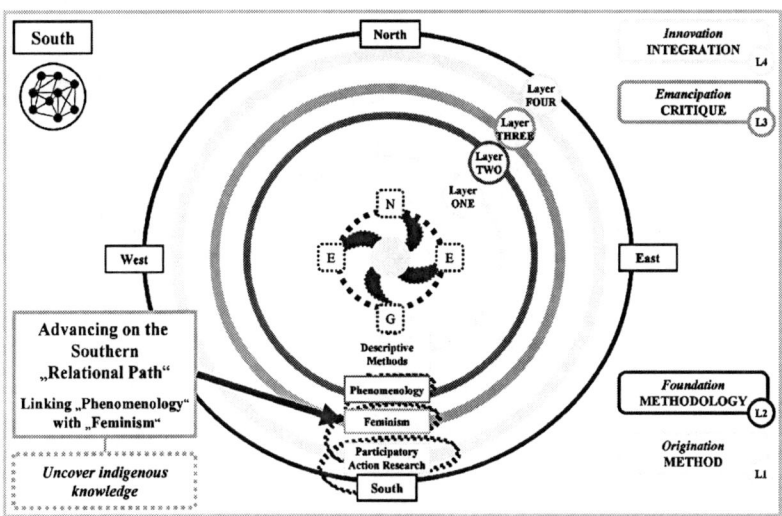

Figure 6.1: Overview Chapter 6 – Layer 3 / South

- Advancing the southern path, we are now entering its critical emancipatory realm (layer 3), where we meet feminism. Feminism, originating in Europe and America in the 1950's and 1960's, could be considered as a further development of Husserl's phenomenology. Both methodologies take "personal experience" as a starting point. However, some researchers claim that feminism takes a more realistic position towards the researched "life world".

- Feminism emerged as an organised movement of social theories, moral philosophies, economic and political thought, all focused on the liberation of women from a perceived subordination to men. With an increasingly broadening focus, feminism can now be regarded as a grassroots movement that does not only focus on gender issues, but seeks to cross boundaries based on social class, race, culture and religion, recently championing the cause of indigenous peoples.

- Feminist epistemology and philosophy of science studies the ways in which gender does and ought to influence our conceptions of knowledge, the knowing subject, and practices of inquiry and justification. It identifies ways in which dominant conceptions and practices of knowledge systematically disadvantage women and other subordinated groups, and strives to reform these conceptions and practices so that they serve the interests of these groups.

- The central concept of feminist epistemology is that of a situated knower, and hence of situated knowledge: knowledge that reflects the particular perspectives of the subject. Further key tenets of feminist research are that it aims to create social change, that it sees knowledge as a tool for liberation (not domination), that it strives to represent human diversity and sees itself as complementary to an androcentric perspective.

- The ontological claims of feminism are that both the natural and social worlds are socially constructed, and that these worlds are constructed differently by people who, in different locations, have different life experiences, for example men and women. Conventional dualisms such as fact/value, objective/subjective, reason/emotion and the separation of the knower and the known are rejected as part of androcentric epistemology.

- Introducing global variations of feminism, we focus in this chapter on Catherine Hoppers' "Indigenous Knowledge Systems". For Hoppers, any dynamic knowledge system has to evolve through the continuance of traditional knowledge and contemporary innovations, and this should be pursued by individuals as well as communities. The present knowledge framework, however, lets knowledge flow in one direction only and excludes indigenous knowledge.

- Hoppers' proposal that we legitimise diverse, and especially indigenous knowledge systems and the one we connect with in the feminist case, which will be introduced at the end of this chapter, is the story of the Australian aborigines. Often termed as "the oldest people of the world", they managed to build the world's longest lasting sustainable society, even while, in modern times, they were persecuted by immigrant white populations. Anthropologists and contemporary investigators on indigenous knowledge systems acknowledge their ability to keep knowledge alive through a strong network of relationships (within their community, among communities, to ancestors, nature and animals) and a simultanous focus on the outer, material (masculine) and the inner, immaterial (feminine) world.

6.1 Orientation to Feminism

Entering the third layer of the Southern Relational Path

We now turn from the first and second to the third layer of our Integral Research framework, from desriptive *methods and methodology ("phenomenology") to critique ("feminism").* As we thereby progressively broaden our research base, so our research points ever more towards social innovation. What exactly happens in this process?

If you engage in feminism, you build on prior foundations. As such you have (in the first layer) grounded your research in a descriptive approach to a problematic life world. There, you have described a qualitative phenomenon with which you have chosen to engage, including your relationship with it.

Subsequently (in layer two), you drew on phenomenology as a distinct methodology. You deepened and broadened your involvement with the questioned phenomenon, now more purposefully articulating the qualitative character of your research. As such you have covered the first two layers of the southern relational path of your research project.

However, as a "would be social innovator", you will need to span the third layer, and you now move into critical terrain. The major critical methodologies, representing together the field of emancipation, are:

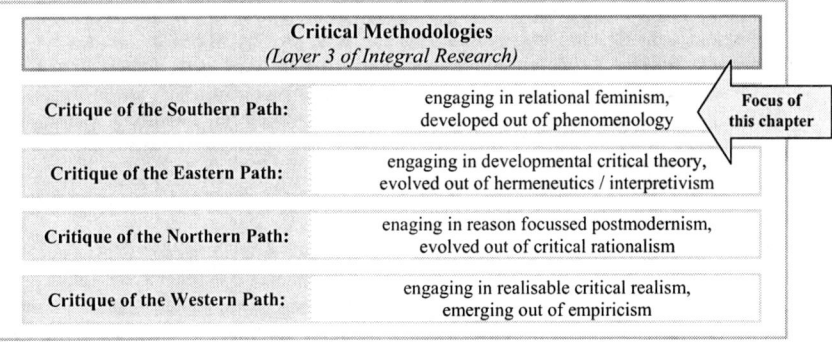

Critical Methodologies *(Layer 3 of Integral Research)*		
Critique of the Southern Path:	engaging in relational feminism, developed out of phenomenology	Focus of this chapter
Critique of the Eastern Path:	engaging in developmental critical theory, evolved out of hermeneutics / interpretivism	
Critique of the Northern Path:	enaging in reason focussed postmodernism, evolved out of critical rationalism	
Critique of the Western Path:	engaging in realisable critical realism, emerging out of empiricism	

The path of this chapter is the southern one; hence we are now engaging with feminism. Let us first retrace steps what feminism is all about.

Origins of Feminism

Josephine Donovan identifies early "Liberal Feminism" as a daughter of the Enlightenment. Thinkers like Mary Wollstonecraft and Sarah Grimké provided an "image of a woman as a rational, responsible agent; one who is able, if given a chance to take care of herself, to further her own possibilities." (1)

These early thinkers shared a belief in a combination of relationality and rationality; a belief that both genders are ontologically the same; the belief that critical thinking is an effective way to transform society; the view that an individual is an isolated entity who operates as a rational independent agent. (2)

Those were the early thinkers. Feminism can now be described as an organised movement of social theories, moral philosophies, economic and political thought, all focused on the liberation of women from a perceived subordination to men. Many feminists are concerned with practices and social, political, economic inequalities that discriminate against women. Some have argued that gendered and sexed identities, even "man" and "woman", are socially constructed.

Feminists may disagree over the sources of inequality, how to attain equality, and the extent to which gender and gender-based identities should be questioned and critiqued; some of this disagreement may stem from continuing pressure to conform to masculine norms. Liberal feminists believe the women's liberation movement revolves around the equality of sexes, and that biological sex should not be the only factor in shaping a person's social identity, socio-political or economic rights. Radical feminists would also argue that feminism is about ending domination or elitism in society. Modern feminist political activists commonly campaign for women's human right to bodily integrity and autonomy on matters such as reproductive rights, including the right to abortion, access to contraception and quality prenatal care; for protection from violence within a domestic partnership.

Many feminists today regard feminism as a grassroots movement that seeks to cross boundaries based on social class, race, culture and religion. They also argue that an effective feminist movement should address both universal issues, such as rape, incest, and prostitution, and culturally specific issues relevant to the women of the society in question, such as female genital cutting in some parts of Africa and the Middle East and "glass ceiling" practices that impede women's advancement in developed economies. Feminism also explores subjects including patriarchy, stereotyping, sexual objectification and oppression.

Feminism's Many Forms

Several subtypes of feminist ideology have developed over the years. Early feminists and primary feminist movements are often called the first-wave feminists, and feminists after about 1960 the second-wave feminists. More recently, some younger feminists have identified themselves as third-wave feminists, although the second-wave feminists are still active.

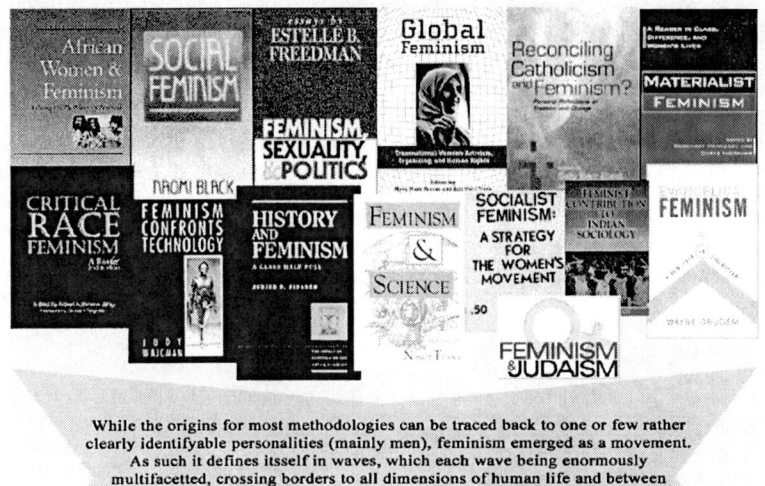

While the origins for most methodologies can be traced back to one or few rather
clearly identifyable personalities (mainly men), feminism emerged as a movement.
As such it defines itsself in waves, which each wave being enormously
multifacetted, crossing borders to all dimensions of human life and between
the sciences. The "movement dimension" underlines not only its "relational
character", it also shows its dedication to bring about social change.
Such can be also seen in feminism as a research methodology.

Figure 6.2: Multifacetted Feminism

The influence of gender on knowledge and knowledge creation

Feminist epistemology and philosophy of science studies the ways in which gender
does and ought to influence our conceptions of knowledge, the knowing subject, and
practices of inquiry and justification. It identifies ways in which dominant
conceptions and practices of knowledge attribution, acquisition, and justification
systematically disadvantage women and other subordinated groups, and strives to
reform these conceptions and practices so that they serve the interests of these groups.
Various practitioners of feminist epistemology and philosophy of science argue that
dominant knowledge practices disadvantage women in the following ways:

- by excluding them from inquiry
- by denying them epistemic authority
- by denigrating their "feminine" cognitive styles and modes of knowledge
- by producing theories of women that represent them as inferior, deviant, or
  significant only in the ways they serve male interests
- by producing theories of social phenomena that render women's activities and
  interests, or gendered power relations, invisible
- by producing knowledge that is not useful for people in subordinate positions, or
  that reinforces gender and other social hierarchies.

Feminist epistemologists trace these failures to flawed conceptions of knowledge,
knowers, objectivity, and scientific methodology. They offer diverse accounts of how
to overcome these failures. They also aim to explain why the entry of women and

feminist scholars into different academic disciplines, especially in biology and the social sciences, has generated new questions, theories, and methods, show how gender has played a causal role in these transformations, and defend these changes as cognitive, not just social, advances.

In summary, the central concept of feminist epistemology is that of a situated knower, and hence of situated knowledge: knowledge that reflects the particular perspectives of the subject. Feminist philosophers are interested in how gender situates knowing subjects.

Based on that introduction, let us look at the key tenets of feminism.

6.2 Feminism – Key Tenets

Feminism – Key Tenets
① You aim to create social change.
② You see knowledge as a tool for liberation not domination.
③ Feminist research strives to represent human diversity.
④ Feminist research complements the androcentric (masculine) perspective.
⑤ As a researcher you as a person are included …
⑥ … and so is nature.

① You aim to create social change

At the heart of much feminist research is the goal, even the obligation, of bringing about change in the condition of women. Even those feminists who don't directly speak of change in the condition of women have social change at the foundation of their goals as researchers. By and large, the international feminist community is committed to the dual vision of research as firstly benefiting the welfare of women and secondly furthering social science knowledge. For example, in delving into the life of an African-American female teacher, feminist researcher Maenette Nee Benham advocates a researcher's role in "giving voice" to ethnic minority women through narrative, or a retelling of their stories, both to empower them and to learn from their experiences. Whether a researcher recommends explicit policy recommendations or less overtly offers social implications of his or her findings, this focus on creating social change appears to be a theme across much of feminist thought.

② You see knowledge as a tool for liberation not domination

Feminism takes a close look at language, gender and power. Language is the medium in which we conduct our social lives and create our symbolic existence; gender is the fundamental dichotomous figure of thought characterising our public as well as private lives; power entangles all of us in its constantly reinvented ruses and snares, which some scientists regard as the fine-grained structure that holds society together. The feminists add the gender dimension to considering the impact of power relations. They regard gender relations as problematic since they are associated with conditions of dominance, inequality, stress and conflict and argue that gender relations are socially constructed, which means they are not given by nature, nor are they inevitable; rather they are the result of socio-cultural and historical conditions and can be radically altered by human action.

③ Feminist research strives to represent human diversity

Feminism offers new ways of viewing human values, decision-making, and the very nature of human experience – beginning with fundamental differences between men and women. For instance, Frances K. Stage, professor of higher education from the University of New York, asserts that scholars have noted that women's judgment and orientation to work differ from those of men. For example, research on gender differences that contrasts the male and female normative ways of "seeing" and "knowing" has come (e.g. in the case of research professor Mary Field Belenky from the University of Vermont) to the following conclusion:

- *Men*: the individual is positioned in a hierarchical social order, seeking power and accomplishment (status); independence is a priority value; the male perspective on self and others is: "we are separate and different"

- *Women*: the individual situated in a network of connections, seeking friendship; intimacy and interdependence are priority values; central to the female perspective is the idea that "we're close and the same"

Another feminist criticism of mainstream androcentric research is that, when it does attempt to include women as important and unique from men, they are viewed as a homogeneous group. Across the works of many researchers, feminism focuses on differences within the community of women. Within the feminist paradigm, there exists a broad diversity of points of view, based on individual and group experiences in society as members of different racial, cultural, and economic groups.

In struggling with this goal of representing human diversity, some contemporary feminist researchers have come to view diversity as a "new criterion for feminist research excellence" and advocate for the inclusion of diversified samples (by race, economic class, sexual preference) in all studies. Others assert that feminist researchers can neither ethically nor successfully study women whose racial, cultural, or social background is different from their own.

④ Feminist research complements the androcentric (masculine) perspective

Something that sets feminist research apart from other approaches to social inquiry is its ontological claim that the reality depicted by much of social science knowledge is incomplete and fundamentally distorted. The world described by many studies of human and organisational behavior is dominated by an androcentric worldview: that means that it communicates the male experience and is based on male assumptions and perspectives. Females – their experience, assumptions, and perspectives – often have been excluded as subjects of study, as researchers, and as interpreters of results.

The androcentric perspective in and of itself is not a problem when the researcher acknowledges that women are missing in the study and, thus, in the interpretation of results. The problem is significant, however, when androcentric research is described as representative of the universe under study and when findings are presented as universally true. Many feminist researchers propose that social science dominated by theories and concepts emerging solely from a male consciousness may be irrelevant for the female experience and inadequate for explaining female behavior.

At the most basic level, then, feminist research simply attempts to incorporate into social reality the female perspective. Further, feminist criticism of established research often stems from a distrust of the power and perspective of androcentrism in research and society, not from a rejection of traditional methods of inquiry. As such, some argue that feminism is rather a perspective than a method in itself.

⑤ **As a researcher you as a person are included ...**

Feminism is seen as a science in which no rigid boundary separates the subject of knowledge (the knower) and the natural object of that knowledge. In contrast to much of mainstream research, which generally seeks to attain value neutrality, femism proposes often a "metabolism of subject and field", seeing researcher and researched as one organism. Feminist researchers will often integrate personal experiences into their research. Personal experiences are not perceived as tainting the methods and results of research. Rather, many feminists, such as Shulamit Reinharz, professor of sociology and founder of the Women's Studies Research Centre at the University of Brandeis University in the US, view it as serving to validate their research. Reinharz quotes her colleague Marie Mies: "Feminist women must deliberately...integrate their repressed, unconscious female subjectivity, i.e. their own experience of oppression and discrimination into the research process." (3)

For example, one of America's leading black feminists, sociology professor Patricia Hill Collins describes her position in her research as very personal: "I often use the pronoun "our" instead of "their" when referring to African-American women, a choice that embeds me in the group I am studying instead of distancing me from it. In addition, I occasionally place my own concrete experiences in the text." (4)

Feminist researchers may use these personal experiences to inform their research questions, to guide their involvement in the research process. However, while the subjective-objective relational character of the research becomes more distinct, the close relationship this establishes between the researcher and the subject of the research has also led to ongoing discussion in the feminist research community about how to walk that fine line and work out the tension between objectivity and subjectivity.

⑥ **...and so is nature**

Feminism can finally be understood as a science where the subject/object split is not used to legitimise the domination of nature. Nature itself is conceptualised as active rather than passive, a dynamic complex totality requiring human cooperation and understanding rather than a dead mechanism, requiring only manipulation and control.

That links with US Cultural Anthropologist Riane Eisler's latest work on "The Real Wealth of Nations" (5), where she proposes a new caring economics that takes into account the full spectrum of economic activities – from the life sustainaing activities of the household to the life enriching activities of carers and communities, to the life supporting processs of nature. Eisler demonstrates how our values are distorted by the economic double standard that devalues anything stereotypically associated with women and feminity; reveals how current economic models are based on a deep-seated culture of domination; and shows how human needs would be better served by economic models based on caring.

For American developmental economist and social activist David Korten the defining choice we have is between two contrasting models of organising human affairs: empire and earth community. (6) Empire features "organisation by domination", which has been a feature of male dominated societies for some 5000 years. Racism, sexism and classicism, for him, have been characteristics of such empire. Earth community, which features "organisation by partnership", a more feminine approach, unleashes the potential for human cooperation and allocates the productive surplus of society to growing the generative potential of the whole.

We now turn to feminist methodology in depth.

6.3 Feminist Methodology in Depth

6.3.1 Phenomenological to Feminist Ontology and Epistemology

As we start to have a closer look at feminism as a research methodology, we remain aware of its close alignment with phenomenology. This is generally true, when we look at feminism from a historical perspective, and particularly when we see how this historical dimension has been reanimated within our integral research framework.

You may recall, that for Husserl, phenomenology was born out of a "Crisis of the European Sciences". He saw in the 1930's that the positivist approach to science could be linked to the totalitarianism that he saw breaking out around him. Husserl was diagnosing what he considered to be the disastrous social consequences of a science, which espoused reductive positivism and naïve empiricism. He also opposed what he regarded as the misguided, deformed rationalism as a consequence of the Enlightenment, which settled for a naïve objectivism, and did not notice the very subjectivity, which made genuine rational objectivity and creativity.

Feminism then, emerging in Europe and America in the 1950's and 1960's, could be considered as a further, reformative development of Husserl's phenomenology. Both methodologies take "personal experience" as a starting point. However, some researchers claim, that in phenomenology, the experience is more important than the external happening that is experienced. A phenomenologist gets therefore sometimes critized as idealist, where the internal experience is the matter of contemplation. Feminism, on the other hand, focuses on what happens external to the impacted entity: it can hence be called a more realistic position than phenomenology. (7)

Feminism also gained power and influence by being more closely aligned with the environmental movement, as David Abram's "eco-feminism" (see chapter 5) has indicated. As described by the social philosopher Richard Tarnas, in his "Passion of the Western Mind", *feminism heralds a complete ground-shift in our societal consciousness.* For Tarnas, feminism is the most important movement of our times.

"The Western intellectual tradition has been produced and canonized almost entirely by men, and informed mainly by male perspectives. The "man" of the Western tradition has been a questing masculine hero, a Promethean biological and metaphysical rebel who has constantly sought freedom and progress for himself, and who has constantly striven to differentiate himself from and control the matrix out of which he emerged. This masculine proposition in the evolution of the Western mind, though largely unconscious, has been not only characteristic of that evolution, but essential to it. For the evolution of the Western mind has been driven by a heroic impulse to forge an autonomous rational human self by separating it from the primordial unity of nature. The fundamental religious, scientific, and philosophical perspectives of Western culture have all been affected by this decisive masculinity – beginning four millenia ago with the great patriarchal nomadic conquests in Greece and the Levant over the ancient matriarchal structures, and visible in the West's patriarchal religion from Judaism, its rationalist philosophy from Greece, its objectivist science from modern Europe. All of these have served the cause of evolving the autonomous human will and intellect; the transcendent self, the independent individual ego, the self-determining human being in its uniqueness, separateness, and freedom. But to do this the masculine mind has repressed the feminine."

This separation calls forth a longing for a reunion with that which has been lost – especially after the masculine heroic quest has been pressed to its utmost one-sided extreme in the consciousness of the modern mind.

"Man now faces the existential crisis of being a solitary ego thrown into an ultimately unknowable universe. And he faces the psychological and biological crisis of living in a world that has come to be shaped in such a way that it precisely matches his world view – in a man made environment that is increasingly mechanistic, atomized, soulless, and self destructive. The crisis of modern man is an essentially masculine crisis, and I believe that the resolution is already now occurring in the tremendous emergence of the feminine in our culture: visible not only in the rise of feminism, the growing empowerment of women, and the widespread opening up to feminine values by both men and women, but also in the increasing sense of unity with the planet and all forms of nature on it, in the increasing awareness of the ecological, in the growing embrace of the human community, in the accelerating collapse of long standing ideological and political barriers separating the world's peoples, in the deepening recognition of the value and necessity of partnership, pluralism and the interplay of many perspectives." (8)

As Carl-Gustav Jung (9) prophesised, an epochal shift is taking place in the contemporary psyche. This shift is about a *reconciliation between the two great polarities, between the long-dominant but now alienated masculine and the long-suppressed but now ascending feminine.* And this dramatic development is not just compensation, not just a return of the repressed. The driving impulse of the West's masculine consciousness has been its dialectic quest not only to realise itself, to forge its own autonomy, but also finally to recover its connection with the whole, to come to terms with the great feminine principle in life, with the mystery of life, of nature, of soul. But *to achieve this reintegration of the repressed feminine, the masculine must undergo a sacrifice, an ego death. The Western mind must be willing to open itself to a reality, the nature of which could shatter its more established beliefs about itself and the world.* This is where the real act of heroism is going to be. A threshold must now be crossed, a threshold demanding a courageous act of faith, of imagination, of trust in a larger and more complex reality; a threshold, moreover, demanding an act of unflinching self-discernment. And this is the great challenge of our time, *the evolutionary imperative for the masculine to see through and overcome its hubris and one-sidedness, to own its unconscious shadow, to choose to enter into a fundamentally different relationship of mutuality with the feminine.*

We seem to be witnessing the labor pains of a new reality being born, a new form of human existence, a "child" that would be the fruit of this great archetypal marriage, and that would bear within itself all its antecedents in a new form. Tarnas therefore would affirm those indispensable ideals expressed by the supporters of the feminist, ecological, archaic and other countercultural and multicultural perspectives. But he would also wish to *affirm all those who have valued and sustained the central Western tradition, for he believes that this tradition – the entire trajectory from the Greek epic poets and Hebrew prophets on, the long and intellectual struggle from Socrates and Plato and Paul and Augustine to Galileo and Descartes and Kant and Feud – that this stupendous Western project should be seen as a necessary and noble part of a great dialectic, and not simply rejected as an imperialist-chauvinist plot.* Not only has this tradition achieved that fundamental differentiation and autonomy of the human which alone could allow the possibility of a larger synthesis, it has also painstakingly prepared the way for its own self-transcendence. Perhaps the end of "man" himself is at hand. But man is not a goal. Man is something that must be overcome – and fulfilled, in the embrace of the feminine.

We now turn to the more specific attributes of feminism as a research methodology.

6.3.2 Feminist Research Epistemology and Methodology

The Natural and Social Worlds are Socially Reconstructed

The ontological claims of feminism are that both the natural and social worlds are socially constructed, and that these worlds are constructed differently by people who, in different locations, have different life experiences, for example men and women. *Feminist epistemology, moreover, substitutes women's experiences for men's. Conventional dualisms such as fact/value, objective/subjective, reason/emotion, and the separation of the knower and the known are rejected as part of androcentric epistemology.*

Many feminist theorists have argued that women have different conceptions of the basic constituents of reality, different assumptions about their own relationships to the natural world, and different views of the importance and connectedness of other people. They are generally more ready to access their own emotions and feelings, and have distinct ways of assessing moral responsibility, based on a context of human relationships rather than abstract rights of isolated individuals.

It has been suggested (10) that the preconditions of a feminist science would be:

Feminist Science: Preconditions
Feminism as a science in which no rigid boundary separates the subject of knowledge (the knower) and the natural object of that knowledge
Feminism as a science where the subject/object split is not used to legitimise the domination of nature
Feminism as a science where nature itself is conceptualised as active rather than passive, a dynamic complex totality requiring human cooperation and understanding rather than a dead mechanism, requiring only manipulation and control

In such feminist imaginings, *the scientist is not seen as an impersonal authority outside and above nature and human concerns, but simply as a person whose thoughts and feelings, logical capacities and intuitions are all relevant and involved in the process of discovery. Such scientists would actively seek ways of negotiating the distances now established between knowledge and its uses, between thought and feeling, between objectivity and subjectivity, between expert and expert, and would seek to use knowledge as a tool of liberation rather than domination. As such, two types of objectivity have been distinguished.*

Dynamic objectivity aims at a form of knowledge that grants to the world around us its independent integrity but does so in a way that remains cognizant of, and indeed relies on, our connectivity with that world. This dynamic objectivity is – not unlike empathy – a form of knowledge of other persons that draws explicitly on the commonality of feelings and experiences in order to enrich one's understanding of another in his or her own right. By contrast, static objectivity is the pursuit of knowledge that begins with the severance of subject from object rather than aiming at the disentanglement of one from the other.

What is Wrong with Conventional Science?

Feminism has provided a collection of themes about what is wrong with conventional science, and what kind of social science will overcome these difficulties, that can be summed up in the following way:

Feminism – Core Themes	
Metabolism of subject and field	deals with the problem of objectivity, proposing the notion of "dynamic objectivity" or of the "metabolism of subject and field" as if they are one organism
New materialism	deals with the "new materialism" in which knowledge is to be grounded in personal experience
Socio-historical location	deals with the problem of the socio-historical location of the researcher
Reflexive nature of social enquiry	deals with the reflexive nature of social enquiry, whereby the researcher needs to reflect, continually, on him or herself
Social sciences as new paradigm	proposes that the social sciences, not physics, should be the paradigm for all sciences
Nature is active and complex	deals with the recognition that nature is active and complex, adopting an ecological or open systems approach
Knowledge for liberation	knowledge should be used as a tool for liberation not domination

As we can see, all these themes are couched in critical-emancipatory language, albeit that the particular focus on nature leads to a close affinity between feminism and the environmental movement. Moreover, the focus on gender, sometime alongside of race and class, is particular to feminism, afro-centricism, and cultural studies, as radical discourses.

Language, Gender and Power

Three dimensions, which are fundamental to all of the above, are language, gender and power. Language is the medium in which we conduct our social lives and create our symbolic existence; gender is the fundamental dichotomous figure of thought characterising our public as well as private lives; power entangles all of us in its constantly reinvented ruses and snares, which some scientists (for example Max Weber) regard as the fine-grained structure that holds society together. The feminists add the gender dimension to considering the impact of power relations that is also of central concern to the critical theorists and the postmodernists. Allowing for considerable variations and conflicts within the feminist movement as a whole, three central elements can be said to prevail:

- First, *gender represents an essential theme in the attempt to understand virtually all social relations*, institutions and processes
- Secondly, *gender relations are seen as problematic since they are associated with conditions of dominance, inequality, stress and conflict*
- Thirdly, *gender relations are regarded as socially constructed, which means they are not given by nature, nor are they inevitable*; rather they are the result of socio-cultural and historical conditions and can be radically altered by human action.

It is felt, that *feminism could make a contribution to social science in the shape of a critique and reevaluation of existing theories, most of which contain gender bias.*

Another of feminism's contributions has been to indicate neglected areas such as sexual harassment in the workplace, or to show how elusive conditions, such as practices of birth control, can contribute to a great variety of social structures. A third contribution of a more general theoretical kind concerns the development of new ways of theorising. In Richard Tarnas' words:

"A new feminist paradigm would place women and their lives, and gender, in a central place in understanding social relations as a whole. Such a paradigm would not only pose new questions about women and gender but also help to create a more complex and adequate account of industrial, capitalist society. A feminist paradigm would also contain a methodology that produces knowledge for, rather than of, women in their many varieties and situations." (11)

6.3.3 Feminist Research Methodology and Method

Relations between Researcher and Researched

Feminism involves above all a close and mutual relationship between yourself as researcher and the research subject. That relationship is seen as critically important, and is evoked within research through descriptive methods. Unless a relationship of trust is developed, between self and other, you can have no confidence that your research on people's lives and consciousness accurately represents what is significant to them in their everyday life worlds, and thus has validity in that sense. Procedures and formal methods are toned down. The research is characterised by an emancipatory knowledge interest, and is often oriented toward everyday life, where there is a pronounced interests in ethics and solidarity.

Emotion, in feminist methodology, is the inevitable and important part of the researcher's motivation and choice of orientation, and of the specific way in which your research is handled.

"Just as observation directs, shapes, and partially defines emotion, so too emotion shapes, directs and even partially defines observation. Observation is not simply a passive process of absorbing impressions or recording stimuli: it is an activity of selection and interpretation. What is selected and how it is interpreted are influenced by emotional attitudes. On the level of individual observation, this influence has always been apparent to commonsense, which notes that we remark very different features of the world when we are happy, depressed, fearful, or confident." (12)

It follows that self-reflection and the critical self-analysis of feelings are an important art of your research process. It does not mean that emotions should be given a more central position than observation, reason or action; nor should they be second to each of these. Martin Heidegger strongly emphasized the inseperability of reason and emotion. Theodor Adorno, the critical theorist, wrote that the highest objectification of the mind is nurtured by human urges and without these no insight would be produced. Even Karl Popper acknowledged that "without passion we can achieve nothing – certainly not in science". What does this imply for a feminist research method?

Descriptive Method to Discourse Analysis

An important research method, which has emerged in recent years, is discourse analysis (DA). As we shall see even more explicitly in chapter 12 for postmodernism it puts great emphasis on modes of expression. *DA is interested in the discursive level – all forms of writing and speech – as well as the relational, and emphasises diversity rather than seeking to reduce variations.* Consequently DA, a variation on basic descriptive method, which is as applicable to feminism as to postmodernism, pays less attention to the "underlying reality" to which critical realism pays so much attention, and pays more *attention to describing modes of expression, and indeed discourse,* that present themselves to you. To that extent, *feminism is influenced not only by phenomenology but also by postmodernism.*

Discourse analysis claims that through language people engage in constructing the social world that is establishing a relationship, as subjects, with it, as an object. There are three aspects to this. Firstly, people actively create accounts on a basis of previously existing linguistic resources. Secondly, they are continually and actively involving some of the infinite words and meaning constructions available, and in rejecting others. Thirdly, the chosen construction has its consequences: the mode of expression has an effect, it influences ideas, generates responses. DA starts from the following assumptions then:

Discourse Analysis: Core Assumptions
Language is used for a variety of functions.
Language is both constructive and destructive.
The same phenomenon can be described in different ways.
Consequently there will be considerable variations in accounts.
There is no foolproof way of determining which is accurate.
The constructive and flexible ways in which language is used should be a central object of study.

In the final analysis, interview statements, written documents and spontaneous talk can be described and interpreted at three levels:

① Discursive level: whereby different people, including yourself, in different contexts express themselves

② Ideational level: at which you speak of your conceptions, values, beliefs, ideas, meanings and fantasies

③ Level of action and social conditions: where your research aims to say something solid about relations, behaviours, social patterns, structures "out there".

As you can see, such a feminist, discourse oriented approach, pays much more attention to the subjectivity and inter-subjectivity of your approach to, and interpretation of, say, an interview or case study, than an empirical approach would involve.

We now turn to a global variation of feminism, in this case focussing on indigenous knowledge systems.

6.4 Global Variations of Feminism: The Example of "Indigenous Knowledge Systems"

For Ugandan born Swedish bred Catherine Hoppers, an international educational expert and visiting professor at Stockholm University, any dynamic knowledge system has to evolve through the continuance of traditional knowledge and contemporary innovations, and this should be pursued by individuals as well as communities. The aim is to connect creative people engaged in generating local solutions that are authentic and accountable, thus facilitating people-to-people learning. (13)

Knowledge then is a universal heritage and a universal resource. It is diverse and varied. The acquisition of Western knowledge has been and still is invaluable to all, but, on its own, it has been, for Hoppers, incapable of responding adequately in the face of massive and intensifying disparities, and rapid depletion of the earth's natural resources. In that context a return to indigenous knowledge, albeit cast in contemporary light, is all-important.

By way of definition, the word indigenous refers to the root, something natural or innate. It is an integral part of culture. The ideal of knowledge as espoused within this framework, for instance, is not just about woven baskets, handicraft for tourists or traditional dances. Rather it is about excavating the technologies behind these practices and artefacts, recasting the potentialities they represent in a context of democratic, equitable participation for community, national and global development in real time.

The issue of indigenous knowledge systems posits profound challenges to contemporary practice, including:

- knowledge generation and legitimation processes, such as the type of knowledge being generated in scientific institutions, as well as in corporate research laboratories
- the social and economic survival of "resource rich but economically poor" local communities
- the need to explore deeper the interface between epistemology, diversity and democracy
- the need to facilitate the active re-appropriation and authentication of IKSs into current, living research work
- subjecting to direct interrogation the discourses behind the semantic shift that turned the illiterate from someone ignorant of the alphabet to an absolute illiterate

- realising the fundamental intolerance of modern science towards the legitimacy of folk or ethnic knowledge, coupled with our inability to develop an ecologically coded society
- moving the frontiers of discourse and understanding in the sciences as a whole, opening new moral and cognitive spaces within which constructive dialogue and engagement for sustainable development can take place
- finally developing a clearer sense of the ethical and judicial domain within which science works, and to begin to understand the political economy of "othering".

Indigenous knowledge systems are characterized by their embeddedness in the cultural web and history of a people, consisting of tangible and intangible aspects that:

- have exchange value and that, with support, can be transformed into enterprises or industries
- perpetuate social, cultural, scientific, philosophical and technological knowledge that can provide the basis for an integrated and inclusive knowledge framework
- It is in turn the re-appropriation of this heritage that may provide new clues and directions as to the visions of human society, human relations, sustainable development, poverty reduction and scientific development, all of which cannot be resolved using the existing ethos of the Western framework alone.

The focus on IKSs then aims at fostering understanding of the interface between culture and science, culture and technology, sustainable human development, and the comprehensive development of human, material and scientific resources, in a manner that gives cognisance to the wisdom and authenticity of traditional practices, institutions and knowledges.

Moreover, it will provide a new basis for the generation of knowledge and a new consciousness in protecting intellectual property and other rights of those who have been ignored or taken for granted for so long.

Towards a Holistic Knowledge Framework

Hoppers goes in her work beyond the gender issue of feminism. By proposing a holistic knowledge framework, builds strongly on the female dimension of relating, integrating, caring and love. For her, the challenge of creating an integrated and holistic knowledge framework for societal progress and development is not only real but also urgent, seeking to make whole that which was partial, incomplete, in large measure stunted and therefore also stunting. A dialogic search for integration is incompatible with legacies in which one group consistently deposits ideas into others. Dialogue cannot exist in the absence of profound love of the world and of people. The search therefore is for a framework that will affirm, not deny, the integrity of all human beings; a framework that by underscoring the notion of "agential citizenry" can posit people not as perpetual victims or pawns, but as knowing subjects, irrespective of the knowledge frameworks within which they are located.

As governments seek to transform their societies and empower local communities, the challenge becomes one of how to "operationalise empowerment" itself in a context where diverse knowledges are barely tolerated and exist only in sufferance and subjective deference to a mainstream, essentially Western form of knowledge. All in all, for Hoppers, a profound cultural imbalance has resulted in the systems of academic, political and economic institutions we see around us.

Instead the contingence of the social and the historical, as well as the affirmation of the multiplicity of worlds and forms of life, need to be recognised and affirmed. De-centred understanding of knowledge systems and other forms of universal conscience are emerging outside the exclusivist frameworks of Western modernity. The total effect of these trends is to bring to bear a forceful return of philosophy to the social sciences, and to the evolution of emergent "open" non-linear and flowing spaces of information. Such is the strength of the new demands that it would appear that the legitimacy of the social sciences no longer rests in the obligation to produce objective knowledge alone, but also in the identification of a nexus between the development of knowledge and the transformation of societies.

Rural people's knowledge and modern scientific knowledge can be seen complementary in their strengths and weaknesses. Combined they can achieve what neither would alone. But for this complementarity to occur, outside professionals have to step in humility down off their pedastels, and sit down, listen and learn. The present framework in which knowledge flows in one direction only – downwards – is not only disempowering but also demeaning.

Hopper's focus on indigenous knowledge, and the marginalised status of indigebous peoples, and their respective knowledge systems, brings us directly to the following case: the hitherto downtrodden, and knowledge-wise unrecognized Australian aborigines. Often coined as "the world's oldest people", their concept of relationality included their own and other communities, the ancestors, the landscape and animals. Their story – though commonly not very well known – is a remarkable proof for the significance of the relational, feminine dimension for the building of a sustainable community and society, in tune with human nature and with nature in large, and offering a new-old sustainable route for mainstream "western" society to follow.

6.5 Feminism in Practice: The World's Oldest People

Recognize Intangible Value

Sveiby and Skuthorpe have recently teamed up to explore the potential for modern-day knowledge creation and new found sustainability of "the world's oldest people". For Tex Skuthorpe, an indigenous aborigine: "Our land is our knowledge, we walk on the knowledge, we dwell in the knowledge, we live in our thesaurus, we walk in our bible every day of our lives. Everything is knowledge. So we don't need a word for it". In fact, for his colleague, the Swede Karl Sveiby, the *Australian Aboriginal society's model for sustainability has the longest proven track record on earth.* (14)

The most striking feature of the particular Nhunggabarra aboriginal society to which Tex belongs, is its *knowledge-based economy.* Because food and handmade tools were the only production scientists and economists have recognized, and have been able to measure, they have long dismissed the Aboriginal economy of producing very little of value. What they have dismissed is more than half of the Aboriginal economy: the very high production of *intangible value,* such as education, knowledge, art, law, entertainment, medicine, spiritual ceremonies, peacekeeping and social welfare. The Aboriginal people created *the world's first systematic approach to eco-farming, and indeed intangible trade.*

The Nhunggabarra did not worship any gods – not even nature spirits. Instead, for them every plant and every landform, every plants and every animal had its own consciousness, just as people did. Everything was alive. Spiritual life was much more significant than material life for the Australian Aboriginal people. Instead of putting their surplus energy into squeezing more food out of the land, Aborigines expended it on *intangibles*: spiritual, intellectual and artistic activities. They carried their palaces on their backs, their cathedrals were built in their minds and they felt no need to glorify human heroes. It is in the mind and the creativity of the spirit – in the intangible rather than the tangible artifacts – that Aboriginal society stands out.

The Nhunggabarra and other Aboriginal peoples conceived time not as a movement from past to future, but as a continuous channeling of consciousness from an intangible and tacit to a tangible and explicit expression. The rock in the landscape was the ongoing tangible expression of the rock's consciousness in the sky world, as it had been since the time of creation. It was the same with people, animals and vegetation. The Nhunggabarra also did not make a distinction between time and space in their language. The suffix – *baa* means both space of and time of. Today of course time is regarded by quantum physicists as part of a space-time continuum, a concept that the West required an Einstein to discover.

Sustaining the Earth

The mission of the Nhunggabarra people was to sustain the earth, to keep totems alive and to keep themselves alive. The Australian landscape was to a large degree an Aboriginal artifact created by thousands of years of sustaining the earth. In that context people and animals were the same. In particular, a person felt responsible for his or her own totem animal. In a hunting ceremony, the Aboriginal men internalized the animal so that they became the animal in spirit. In this way the spirit life of the animal was extended in the men in exchange for the animal's physical death.

Children learnt not by formal education, but by participating in life itself, by doing. Stories, songs and dances had a physical connection to the country, animals and vegetation. Aboriginal children were educated, for example, in how to develop awareness during sleep and how to enter meditative states. They learnt the tricks they could use in hunting, and parents encouraged their children to learn all about the behavior of their totem animals as a way to learn about themselves. Children were taught what was edible and how to locate water. Gradually the person learnt everything there was to learn about the land, so that adults became self sufficient in terms of food all year round. Learners, meanwhile, were never given a test question or a quiz. It was their own learning journey that they undertook – no one imposed an opinion and the old people never gave him a "right" or "wrong" mark.

Journeying toward the Other

At the age of about twelve, the young Nhuggabarra man would embark on a journey, together with his contemporaries, to other communities in his area, and would not return to his community for fourteen to sixteen years. During this initiation period he visited all the communities in his area and learnt from them, and when he eventually returned he would perform three more ceremonies, lasting altogether six months, before he was considered a man. The girls learnt the neighboring habits from the women in the community, who came from all the surrounding areas. One of the ceremonies for the girls was to be taken to a neighboring water hole, where they stayed for three months to observe the "red fly", from whom they learnt the cycle of life. They also learnt many languages from the women.

The so-called coroborees were organised events and performances, involving traditional songs and dances, where the young learnt to regulate social harmony and to connect with the spirit world. Depending on the person's age and experience they would learn at different levels. Trade and trust were similarly interconnected. Characteristically, the Nhunggabarra selected items from their country they had a surplus of and brought it to a designated trading place, placing a message stick therein. Trading parties had to accept all items, even if they did not need them; to leave anything would have shown disrespect. What they did not need they would trade with people further away. In this way a vast trading network was established all across Aboriginal Australia. The trade was entirely based on trust. In the 1930's anthropologist McCarthy identified seven different trunk trade routes traversing the whole continent, based on physical exchange – no money was involved. Trade was community to community rather than individual to individual.

The central element was the enjoyment inherent in the process of giving. The preparation for a visit to relatives, the journey, the ritual, the formalities to be observed, were all enjoyable elements of life. The fact that some artifacts were exchanged was the tangible proof that the process had taken place with mutual appreciation, but it was not the main reason for the "trade". The Nhunggabarra were keen to exchange dances, songs and ceremonies and probably invested considerable time in this kind of trade. Production primarily fulfilled an intangible demand.

The Aboriginal approach to farming was to learn how nature worked and then "help it on the way" with minimum energy and effort. They knew, for example, that fruit trees grow from the seeds of fruits, so they deliberately spat out fruit tree seeds into the debris of fish remains in refuse heaps at the edge of the camp, which were ideal environments for tree growth. The model was "knowledge-based eco-farming" – to learn and adapt but not to change. Fire was the most important eco-farming tool, being used to expose or capture a harvest and to generate and regenerate pastures for grazing animals. Fish traps, moreover, constituted an ecological system for catching the maximum number of fish with the minimum effort, while at the same time sustaining the stock. Meanwhile the Aborigine's physical fitness was due to their active lifestyle and diet, which consisted mainly of natural and unprocessed food. Their methods secured food species available in the field all year round, which enabled more or less immediate consumption of foods and required only limited storage. And when they needed storage, they preferred storing their food live. They knew what we know today, that fresh food tastes best and contains the most nutrients.

A Leader Role for Everyone

The image that emerges through stories of the ideal Nhunggabarra was someone who shared generously, who was an active provider of care for children, and for the old; a person who fulfilled kinship obligations; and who showed compassion for others and respected integrity, taking responsibility for both one's own people and for other communities. Crimes against the law were recognized as offences; however, the offender would not receive a penalty until he or she felt guilt, understood what they had done, and owned up to that error. A recurring theme of Nhunggabarra law stories is respect: for diversity, for other people and countries, as well as for life itself. At the core of such is respect for knowledge itself. The respect for knowledge gave all knowledgeable people a leadership role. But they had to lead without imposing themselves on others, and without giving outright orders. The ideal leaders respected all people, and encouraged people to learn from different perspectives and from different communities.

Everybody had at least one major role to fill on behalf of the community. And because there were no kings or even chieftains there was no army, nor people who were exclusively warriors or soldiers. Everyone had direct access to the spiritual world so there was no need for intermediaries. The roles they did have were: teachers, child minders, story custodians, storytellers, dancers, painters, hunters and gatherers, net and basket makers, spear makers and fishermen, grain grinders and totem minders, medicine men and cooks.

Moreover, these roles evolved. For example, the primary "carer" was to devote more and more time in service to the community as a whole as she matured. Old people generally functioned as teachers and mentors, knowledge repositories and conflict mediators. The ideal that applies to all larger scale organised activities is that everyone should know their role and work should be done with as few directives as possible. The law added support and authority to a multiplicity of such roles because there was a need for respect for the person fulfilling the role. A leader was safe in a role – as long as he or she showed respect for the followers. Finally, the stories provided a means of critical self-reflection among the leaders.

Nhunggabrra women, meanwhile, were the principle contributors to the community's economy, responsible for up to 80% of production. They were expected to undergo a full training, including extensive training in pediatrics, medicine as nursing, as well as ecology, biology and spirituality. Women would build up over time an enormous knowledge of the medicinal plants and herbs of their country, and their usage. They were also the teachers of all children until puberty; they conducted their own sacred ceremonies and greeted newcomers to the community. Finally land was inherited via the women. The European immigrants saw none of this, failing to see that women functioned on equal terms to men in Aboriginal society. What then, overall, was the recipe that the Nhungabarra people had for sustainability?

The Nhunggabarra Recipe for Sustainability

① Mission

- Keep all alive

② Core Belief: All Are Connected

- All are connected – ancestors, people, animals, plants, sky and earth
- Eternal life and reward (when one's mission is accomplished on earth)
- Individual spiritual relationship with ancestors – no formal religion, or gods

③ Core Value: Respect

- For knowledge diversity (learn from foreigners)
- For the rights of foreign people and countries (no conquests)
- For the leadership role of other individuals (do not usurp the role of another)

④ Economy: Intangible

- Tools and equipment made of natural materials – recyclable
- Tightly coupled teams (families) are core production units
- Intangible processes to keep all alive (stories, ceremonies, dances)

⑤ Ecosystem: Core

- Ecological farming methods
- Natural medicine
- Nomadic life (to reduce human pressure on the ecosystem)

⑥ Primary Resource: Knowledge

- Life-long learner driven education
- Eighteen year knowledge journey
- Status from knowledge – not from material wealth

⑦ Leadership: All Have a Role

- Context-specific leadership – all have a leadership role to play
- Knowledge based organising (creating, sharing and maintaining knowledge)
- Consensus decision making

⑧ Society: Build Community

- Fuzzy-country borders – country ends where story ends
- Networking processes for keeping peace (knowledge journeys, marriage rules)
- Individual career (responsibility for functionality of community)
- Generosity and sharing (reinforced by kinship rules)
- Custodianship of land and knowledge – no individual ownership
- Collaborative methods for increasing productivity
- Widows, orphans and elderly cared for by community

Sveiby and Skuthorpe end with a quote from none other than the English explorer James Cooke, from his visit to Australia in 1770:

"From what I have said of the Natives of New Holland they may appear to some to be the most wretched people on Earth, but in reality they are far happier than the Europeans. They live in tranquility, which is not disturbed by the Inequality of Condition. They think themselves provided with all the necessaries of life and they have no superfluities."

We do not know whether the Nhunggabarra built the first sustainable society, but we are reasonably sure that they built the longest lasting one.

6.6 Conclusion

In summary, there are three different versions of feminism, the final one being of broadest relevance in our relational, critical emancipatory context:

- **A first approach covers any understanding of economic, social, or psychological phenomena:** ranging from the division of labour, class conditions, and wage setting to recruitment and selection as well as political and social mores – must *first* start from the recognition that (among much else) there are possible *differences between men and women* in terms of situation, experiences etc. which must be taken into account.

- **A second approach emphasizes the importance of acquiring a broader and deeper descriptive picture of women's conditions and experiences:** Here the ideal is to study various phenomena from the perspective of women or from a feminist point of view. This so-called "standpoint" research strongly emphasizes political and practical relevance. It is not only a question of looking for the truth in an abstract sense; even more important is to *stimulate social change and emancipation.*

- **A third approach calls into question the gender categories that the other two approaches regard as given and unproblematic:** The meaning of concepts such as men and women, male and female, is considered uncertain. Such feminists *emphasize the temporary and fragile nature of social constructions.* Genders as labels and clues to identities are regarded as transient and contradictory. This brand of feminism *shifts the emphasis from gender to an emphasis of diversity.*

The first of the above is strongly influenced by phenomenology, the second by critical theory and the third by postmodernism. In fact, *a strong characteristic of the critical emancipatory approaches is their mutual interdependence on each other, as well as their prior dependence on one or other method and methodology.* So whereas methods are clearly distinct from one another, and conventional methodologies somewhat so, the *postconventional methodologies* (as Denzyn and Lincoln have intimated – see chapter 2) are "blurred genres". Why? First, they overlap with each other, and, second, they are as much socio-political philosophies as they are research methodologies.

We now turn from feminism to participatory action research, as its next evolutionary step. It is also the final step in the southern relational path.

Bibliography

1) **Donovan**, J. (2000). *Feminist Theory: The Intellectual Traditions*. London: Continuum.

2) **Michael**, K. (forthcoming). *Economics as if South Africans Mattered*. Buckingham: Dissertation, Buckingham University.

3) **Reinharz**, S. (1992). *Feminist Method in Social Research*. Oxford: Oxford University Press.

4) **Collins**, P.H. (1990). *Black Feminist Thought: Knowledge, Consciousness and the Politics of Empowerment*. London: Routledge.

5) **Eisler**, R. (2007). *The Real Wealth of Nations*. San Francisco: Berrett Koehler.

6) **Korten**, D. (2006). *The Great Turning – from Empire to Earth Community*. San Francisco: Berrett Koehler.

7) **Michael**, K. (forthcoming). *Economics as if South Africans Mattered*. Buckingham: Dissertation, Buckingham University.

8) **Acker**, J. (1994), in: Blaikie, N. (1994). *Approaches to Social Inquiry*. Cambridge: Polity Press.

9) **Jagger**, A. (2005). *Feminist Ethics*. London: Taylor and Francis.

10) **Blaikie**, N. (1994). *Approaches to Social Enquiry*. London: Pluto Press.

11) **Tarnas**, R. (1991). *The Passion of the Western Mind*. New York: Ballantyne Books.

12) **Van der Post**, L. (1984). *Jung and the Story of our Time*. Harmondsworth: Penguin.

13) **Hoppers**, C. (2002). *Indigenous Knowledge Systems*. Cape Town: New Africa Books.

14) **Sveiby**, K. & **Skuthorpe**, T. (2006). *Treading lightly: The hidden wisdom of the world's oldest people*. Sydney: Allen & Unwin.

CHAPTER 7

FROM FEMINISM TO
PARTICIPATORY ACTION RESEARCH

"LIBERATE THE OPPRESSED"

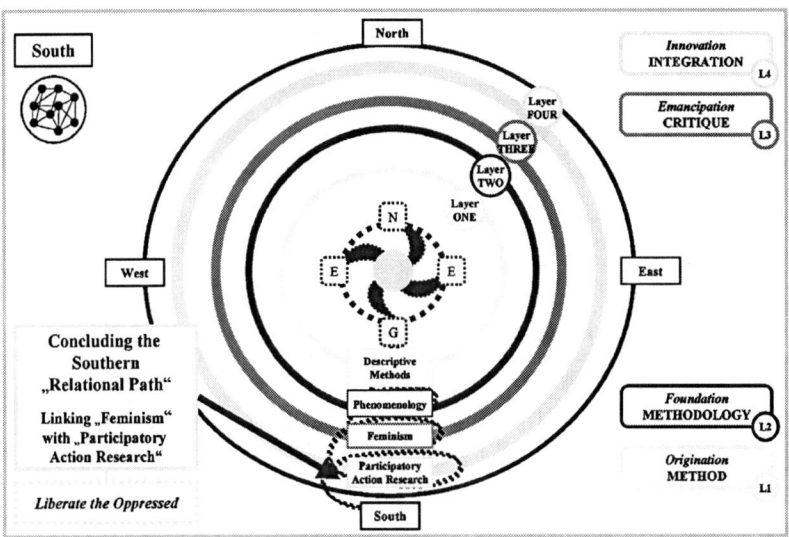

Figure 7.1: Overview Chapter 7 – Layer 4 / South

Summary: Participatory Action Research

- Integration – the fourth layer of our Integral Research framework – starts out with the community, through so-called participatory action research. As a researcher you now enter, finally, fully fledged Social Innovation – following upon the orginal description, phenomenological foundation, and feminist emancipation.

- Such participatory research takes integrally on from where descriptive methods, phenomenological methodology and feminist critique, leave off, following the southern relational path.

- Participatory research, as a branch of action research, is unique in its "southern" origins, most specifically in Latin America, Africa and the Indian sub-continent, with Columbia's Fals Borda, Ecuador's Daniel Selener, and Bangladesh's MD Rahman being its leading lights.

- In place of the phenomenological life world or the Germanic "Lebenswelt", Fals Borda cites the Spanish "vivencia", as a focal point for dialogic research and innovation, oriented toward such questions as "Why is there poverty?" or "Why is there oppression and dependence?".

- Grassroots representatives participate as a reference group in the action-research process, thereby "popularising science", transforming the researcher/researched relationship, and pursuing autonomy and identity in the course of exercising people's own countervailing power.

- The action centered journey for Bangaldeshi academic and social activist M.D. Rahman brings out the dynamic interrelationship between the development of people's consciousness, on the one hand, and the necessary control over the society's resources, and social, economic and political institutions, on the other.

- For Selener, such participatory research is intended to empower the powerless groups in society. Practitioners therefore tend to apply conflict-oriented paradigms, seeking after the transformation of oppressive social, economic and political structures in society.

- Finally, specific examples of PAR are introduced: ranging from the monumental efforts of the Six S movement in Burkina Faso to the significant achievements of the fisherfolk communities in Tanzania.

7.1 Orientation to Participatory Action Research (PAR)

7.1.1 The Cultural Turn

As we have already indicated, *all of the methods and methodologies that prevail originate from either America (method) or Europe (methodology).* The rest of the world hardly gets a look in. In fact, while we have drawn on African philosophers to provide a non-European developmental context, the underlying methods, methodologies and philosophies, have been basically "western" or "northern". That has to be problematic, if we are talking of "integral" research.

At this ultimate stage of the southern relational path of such Integral Research, we retrace steps to Denzin and Lincoln and their "Landscape of Research". (1) There they refer to the "crisis of representation, currently taking place. For them a "fourth" research moment arising out of a "cultural turn". These moments can be described as follows:

Retracing: Four Research Moments According to Denzin and Lincoln
① The first turn, early on in the 20th century, is quantitative in orientation.
② The second turn, toward the middle of the 20th century, is qualitative, but still with a quantitative edge to it.
③ The third turn, in the latter part of the century, is characterised by "blurred genres", that is a mix of qualitative approaches.
④ In the fourth turn, as the 21st century approaches, there is the "crisis of representation", when a cross-cultural orientation first becomes apparent.

Interestingly enough, the point at which the rest of the world begins to exert an influence, is when we move toward the ultimately transformative approaches. For, as has already been indicated by our African philosophers, most particularly Serequeberhan, *nothing short of transformation will enable such societies in transition to authentically research and develop themselves.* Moreover, the "south" and the "east" (culturally and philosophically speaking) are generally less rationally and empirically inclined than the "north" and "west", but have a collective and cultural edge (phenomenologically and interpretively). In other words and in general terms, the north and the west are rational and pragmatic, the south and the east humanistic and holistic.

7.1.2 Origination to Integration

We now have entered into our fourth layer from origination onto foundation, and thereafter onto emancipation and finally, now, innovation. This, in effect, is the complete *integral rhythm,* which cultimates in effect social innovation. For us, the term "action research", which underlies the participatory approach at this stage, does not carry the full impetus that social innovation does. In the table below we summarise the "southern" journey so far, in the context of the other three "eastern", "northern" and "western" journies to come. Then we turn to action research in general before introducing PAR specifically.

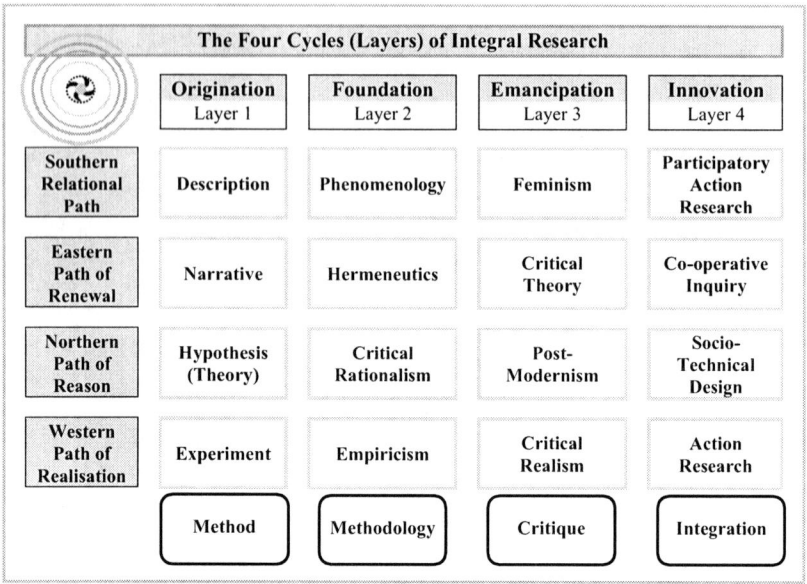

Figure7.2: The Four Cycles of Integral Research

7.1.3 Introducing Action Research as a whole

The founding fathers of "action research" are the American pragmatic philosopher and educator, John Dewey, and the Jewish refugee from Nazi Germany, the social psychologist Kurt Lewin – in the middle of the last century. Action research – for one of its contemporary co-creators Peter Reason at the University of Bath in England, together with a follower of his, Hilary Bradbury based in California – is:

"...a participatory, democratic process concerned with developing practical knowing in the pursuit of worthwhile human purposes, grounded in a participatory worldview which is believed to be emerging at this historical moment. It seeks to bring together action and reflection, theory and practice, in participation with others, in the pursuit of practical solutions to issues of pressing concern to people, and more generally the flourishing of individual persons and their communities." (2)

The following figure illustrates action research's core components:

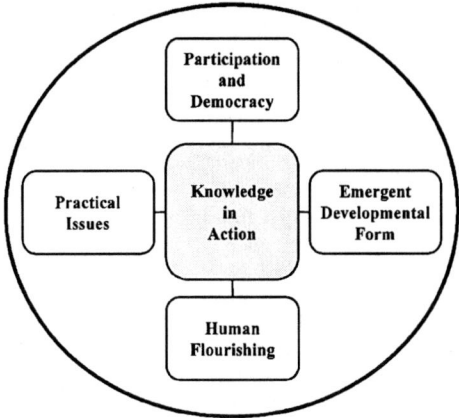

Figure7.3: Knowledge in Action

We now turn specifically to participative action research and to three of its primary instigators.

7.1.4 Participatory Orientation along the Relational Path

Preconventional to Integral: Research Method to Social Innovation

We now set the stage for the ultimately transformative and thereby innovatory effect of the humanistic, relational path to individuation, or indeed social innovation, that of participatory action research.

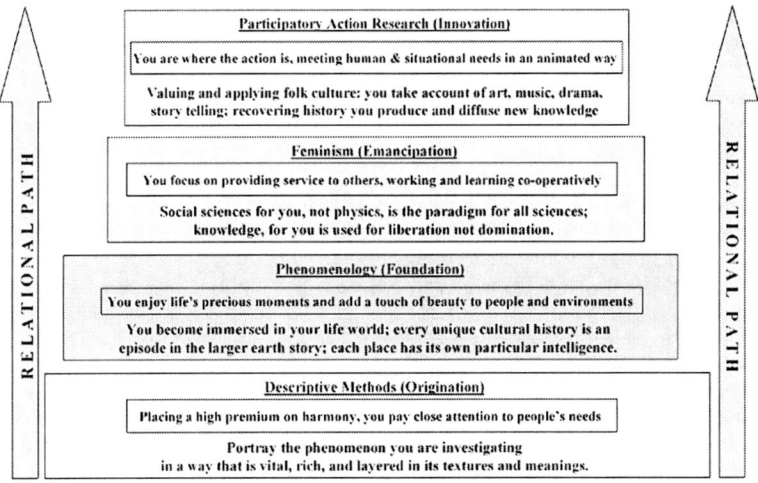

Figure 7.4: Towards Participatory Research

While the overall orientation for particpative research is humanistic, there is, to some extent at least, an orientation toward all four paths of development. It is for this reason that action research is the most fully integral of our research approaches. So, as we shall see with PAR, while the phenomenological orientation toward a community's life world is pre-eminent, there is reference to other critical emancipatory antececedents, most especially to feminism. However, what stands out about PAR is its strong rootedness in the development world, with its founding fathers being a Columbian, Fals Borda and a Bangladeshi MD Rahman, who originally drew their inspiration from Julius Nyerere, the first Tanzanian President.

Founding Mothers and Fathers of PAR

In 1975, a young Canadian adult educator named Budd Hall, at that time temporarily based in Sussex, U.K., compiled a special issue of the journal Convergence on the topic of participatory research. Beyond Hall's expectations, this issue sparked an international network of educators, academics and activists interested in this area, the "International Participatory Research Network", which would grow stronger and larger over the next decades.

The beginning of this story can be traced to Tanzania, where Hall worked from 1970 to 1974. At that time, under the leadership of President Julius Nyerere, Tanzania had launched an experiment in what is known as "ujamaa socialism". In Tanzania, Hall (who would later become Chair of Adult Education and Community Development at OISE/University of Toronto and Dean of Education at the University of Victoria) had the fortune of learning from many inspiring adult educators. Among them were Finland's Marja Liisa Swantz, Brazil's Paulo Freire, and the Tanzanian President himself Julius Nyerere, probably the only adult educator in the world who became president of a country.

Through these experiences, Hall became acquainted with approaches to education based on the principles of self-reliance, active participation, and dialogue. He also became interested in the potential of research to promote transformative learning, local development and progressive social change, and in research models that departed from the traditional positivist approach to social research based on the natural sciences. In 1974/1975 Budd Hall was a visiting fellow at the Institute of Development Studies at the University of Sussex, where he met people from many other countries who were thinking along similar lines to him and his Tanzanian colleagues, seeking a connection between education, research, politics and action. Among them were Francisco Vio Grossi from Chile and Rajesh Tandon form India.

From his experiences in Tanzania and England, Hall noticed that many educators, researchers and activists from different countries were exploring similar paths through independent avenues, in most cases without being aware of related work done by others. At that time they did not constitute yet a community or even a loose network. Moreover, their approaches did not have yet an encompassing name that would capture its essence. The major impetus for the development of a network (and later an international community) came from that special journal of "Convergence" edited by Hall in 1975. In naming the theme of the issue, Hall labelled this approach "participatory research".

That term was used because it seemed to be the best common description of the various approaches that were described within the issue. While Hall had begun to learn about the long traditions in Europe of action research, and Maria Liisa Swantz had been using "participant research" to describe this approach for several years, the choice of the term "participatory research" was simply made as a descriptive term for a collection of varied approaches which shared a participatory ethos.

The topic of participatory research struck a cord among adult educators and community development practitioners around the world, and soon after its publication, all the copies of the issue were sold out, a first in the history of Convergence. Moreover, requests for copies were sent from all regions of the world, and a comment in Hall's article inviting people to exchange information on the topic provided the needed driving force to create a community of practice. This massive response made Hall realise that many people in the world were actively pursuing alternative research avenues that were ignored by most universities, and that these people needed some spaces to establish connections among them in order to share their experiences. That issue of "Convergence", and the active networking of Hall, helped to generate those spaces, which in turn helped to consolidate a vibrant tradition in the field of adult education that would grow year after year for the decades to come. It seems that the time was ripe for an international network on participatory research, but a catalyst was needed.

A few months later, another important catalyst for the development of an international participatory research network came forth when the First World Assembly of the International Council for Adult Education, was held in Dar es Salaam, Tanzania, in 1976. Again, Hall played a key role, acting as Conference Secretary. One of the recommendations of the Dar es Salaam conference was that "adult educators should be given the opportunity to learn about and share their experiences in participatory research." The following year, a conference on action research took place in Cartagena, Colombia. Interestingly enough, the coordinator of this conference, was the Colombian sociologist Orlando Fals Borda, who has since become a leading light in the PAR movement. He was working on the same alternative approach to social research but without being aware of the international initiatives that took place in the previous years. Thanks to Paz Buttedahl, the Latin American programme officer for the International Council of Adult Education (ICAE), a connection was made between the Colombian group and the international network spearheaded by Hall during the planning stages of the conference. Hence, the April 1977 Cartagena Conference provided a third key moment for the expansion the participatory research network, building on the 1975 issue of Convergence and the 1976 Conference in Dar Es Salaam.

Orlando Fals Borda and his colleagues were using the term "action research", a concept that had been used in the 1940s by Kurt Lewin (see chapter 16). Lewin argued that research that produced nothing but books was not sufficient, and that a new type of research for social practice was needed. Thus, he called for "a type of action research on the conditions and effects of various forms of social action, and research leading to social action". At the 1977 Cartagena conference the concept of "action research" used by Fals Borda met the concept of "participatory research" coined by Hall, and the concept of *"participatory action research" was later born. The term was used for the first time by Orlando Fals Borda to name a new paradigm in social research.* Several decades later, the concept became popularized and known by its initials PAR.

We now turn to its key tenets.

7.2 Participatory Action Research – Key Tenets

Participatory Action Research (PAR) – Key Tenets
① The problem is defined, analyzed and solved by the community.
② As a scientific methodology, PAR facilitates an authentic analysis of social reality.
③ PAR involves the full and active participation of the community.
④ PAR is aimed at the exploited, the poor, the oppressed, the marginal.
⑤ PAR creates awareness of the people's own resources, mobilizing for self-reliant development.
⑥ The ultimate goal of the research-and-innovation is the radical transformation of social reality.
⑦ You as researcher/innovator are a committed participant, facilitator and learner in such.

① The problem is defined, analyzed and solved by the community

For Columbia's renegade academic, Fals Borda (3), learning to interact and organise with PAR is based on the existential concept of experience proposed by the Spanish philosopher Jose Ortega y Gasset. Through the actual experience of something we intuitively apprehend its essence; we feel, enjoy and understand it as a reality, and we thereby place our own being in a wider, more fulfilling context. In PAR such an experience, called "vivencia" (akin to life world and aligned to learning with head and heart) in Spanish, is complemented by another idea, that of authentic commitment. In that context both internal and external animators, or agents of change, have the shared goals of social transformation.

These "animators" contribute their own knowledge, techniques and experience to the transformation process. A dialectical tension is created between a Cartesian and academic orientation combined with an experiential and practical one, combining academic and popular knowledge. Through participation a subject/subject relationship replaces the hitherto asymmetrical subject/object researcher/researched relationships; thereby it is attuned to feminism. The general concept of authentic participation as defined here is rooted in cultural traditions of the common people and in their real history referring to core values that have survived the destructive impact of foreign invasions. Such resistant values are based on mutual aid, the communal use of the land, forest and water, the extended family and other old social practices, the endogenous experiences of the common people.

② As a scientific methodology, PAR facilitates an authentic analysis of social reality

For Fals Borda action and knowledge go hand in hand. Historical experience calls for rethinking the meaning of social transformation for people's liberation. The dominant view of such liberation has been preoccupied with the need for changing the oppressive structures of relations in material production – certainly a necessary task. But, and this is the distinctive view of PAR, domination of elites is also rooted in control over social power to determine what is useful knowledge. In fact, existence of the gap in knowledge relations can offset the advantages of reducing the gap in relations of physical production.

People then cannot be liberated by a consciousness and knowledge other than their own. It is therefore essential that people develop their own indigenous consciousness-raising and knowledge generation, and this requires the social power to assert this vis-à-vis elite consciousness and knowledge. The scientific character or objectivity of knowledge rests on its social verifiability, and this depends on consensus as to the method of verification. All scientific knowledge is relative to the paradigm to which it belongs, and the verification system to which it is submitted. An immediate objective of PAR is to return to the people the control over their own verification systems.

③ PAR involves the full and active participation of the community

Bangladesh's MD Rahman provides a good example for grounding PAR: one NGO that he visited in the nineteen eighties pursued self-reliance in Bangaldesh, and was using the Paulo Freirean pedagogy of literacy to develop self-reflected awareness (conscientisation) of the landless. A three month course was the starting point of external intervention to give literacy through words chosen from the people's daily vocabulary, around which discussion on daily reality and ways of transforming it are generated. Through the course the landless developed organisational consciousness and formed their own institution at a village level, starting a savings programme, and (in collaboration with the NGO) launched a succession of social and economic activities.

Work in the particular part of Bangladesh that Rahman visited started five years before, and the organisations of the landless were engaged in various economic enterprises with their own funds and with loans from the intervening NGO. They showed a self-reliance not commonly seen. Stimulated by the quality of the responses Rahman received from some hundred leaders of about thirty landless organisations in as many adjacent villages, he probed deeper. Did they have a position on the land question? Yes they replied. They had been discussing this question for the past five years, and had concluded that the land must be collectively owned and tilled. Were they themselves practicing this? Yes, wherever they were able to lease land they held and tilled it collectively; and they had worked out their own system of collective management. What was their position on the existing political parties? There was absolutely no political party that represented their interests, and only when there would be organisations of the landless like theirs throughout the country would there emerge the relevant political party.

④ **PAR is aimed at the exploited, the poor, the oppressed, the marginal**

Nur Muhammad Momtajuddin, a government agricultural officer and former freedom fighter, initiated a "self reliance" movement in 1973 in the district of Rangpur in Bangladesh, which spread to 60 villages in a year and a half. Under this initiative, villages met in mass meetings to take an oath to reject any form of grant or relief from outside. Rahman took pride from this demonstration of the highest in human spirit, and spent long hours with Momtajjuddin discussing his views of how to reverse the "basket case" image of the nation.

The validity of self-reliance, as a primary human urge, was further confirmed by Bhoomi Sena, an area of landless people, whose leaders in India told that "no outsider will tell us what to do". This suggested to Rahman that there was *a role for carefully conceptualized methodological work, whether by outsiders or insiders, designed to stimulate people's collective self-inquiry without teaching them; such work would be highly sensitive and culture dependent, hence not "trainable" by any blueprint.* They also recognized that their pursuit reflected a sharp contrast to the orthodox left conception of revolutionary intellectuals "indoctrinating" the working class and training "cadres" for this purpose with a doctrinaire approach. This tradition disturbed them deeply. Dutta Sevli then, an educational activist at Bhoomi Sena, had the same conceptual basis as Paulo Freire's (the Brazilian social activist and action researcher): "conscientisation", although separately developed. The participatory development movement had been profoundly influenced by such self-reflected learning as opposed to teaching although methodological approaches to conscientisation vary.

After starting his work in the ILO he linked up with another trend in the participatory development movement: the so-called PAR movement. Here he entered into a continual intellectual collaboration with Fals Borda. *In helping people to develop their collective self-knowledge the concept of "animation" emerged.* At the same time, it was sad to see that some of the great experiments in socialism were swinging from socialist to market fundamentalism, rather than questioning how socialism was misunderstood; also that the leaders who are dismantling socialism seem incapable of inviting the people to participate for once in an intellectual search for an answer to articulate their known vision of the kind of society they want beyond a mere ballot-box democracy. Such is the strength of hierarchical thinking and institutions, which are at the root of the "consciousness gap". This calls for a paradigm shift in development thinking: The assertion of people's development culture and the use of its positive elements as a development force are salient features of African grassroots mobilization. Rahman's work has entered into the realisation that culture is in a sense the central tool for domination and must be resisted with an alternative culture.

⑤ **PAR creates awareness of the people's own resources, mobilizing for self-reliant development**

Work of another NGO in Bangladesh had come to a crossroads. Its earlier work had emphasized conscientisation, not by the Freirean method but by stimulating direct social analysis by the landless. In many places this had led to intense and sustained pressure-group action to confront social injustice and oppression by rural elites. In another area, confrontational activity to resist social oppression by rural elites had been particularly intense for several years and had led to many forms of harassment, both of the landless leaders and NGO workers. After several years of such activity "village development associations" were formed. Rahman, when meeting them, told them that he had come to them hearing about their struggles of several years, wanting to learn from their experience.

- What was their experience?
- What did they learn themselves from this?
- What would they, with their past experience, advise the landless in other villages who might want to get organised?
- What was the relation of their present activities with past ones?

After a dead silence they opened up, one after another, getting stimulated as they narrated stories of their past struggles, their high and low points, after which Rahman asked:

- Would they like to document their story, draw its lessons more systematically after thorough discussion in the base of the organisation, and
- Disseminate them so that fellow landless in other villages would not need to start from zero and could benefit from their experience
- As this was the area of the country's most outstanding *kabial* (village poet-debater), they could document their story through *kabigans* (songs of such poets), and dramas

⑥ **The ultimate goal of the research-and-innovation is the radical transformation of social reality**

For Orlando Fals Borda, those involved in PAR start with the thesis that science does not have absolute or pure value, but is simply a useful form of knowledge for specific purposes and based on relative truths. *Any science as a cultural product carries those biases and values, which scientists hold as a group. It therefore favors those who produce and control it. A people's science may hence serve as a corrective.*

Ingredients and Techniques of a People's Science	
Collective research	obtained from groups through dialogue, discussion, argument and consensus in the investigation of social realities
Critical recovery of history	to discover, selectively through collective memory, those elements of the past which have proved useful in the increase of conscientization, using popular stories and oral traditions "fleshed out"
Valuing and applying folk culture	account is taken of art, music, drama, sports, story-telling and other expressions related to human sentiment and imagination
Production and diffusion of new knowledge	different levels of communication are developed for people ranging from pre-literate to intellectual, using image, sound, painting, mime, photograph, theatre, poetry, music, puppetry and exhibitions. The groups involved include cooperatives, trade unions, cultural centers and so on

Ideally, in the process, the grassroots are able to participate in the research process from the beginning: that is from the moment it is decided what the subject of the research should be, to the time it is completed. Its essence is the proposition that more is to be gained by using the affective logic of the heart than the cold-headed analyses that come from laboratories.

⑦ **You as researcher / innovator are a committed participant, facilitator and learner in such**

Finally, at the micro level, PAR is a philosophy and style of work with the people to promote their empowerment for changing their immediate environment, through socioeconomic initiatives. These often confront state bureaucracies and technocracies that seek to impose their ideas of "development" or modernization. The people's own initiatives seek to promote their authentic self development which takes off from their traditional culture and seeks to preserve the physical environment with which they have an organic association. Two elements, which have PAR priority, are, first, democratic people's organisations and second, the restoration of the status of popular knowledge and its promotion. Both are fostered by a process of awareness raising through a series of social inquiries. These range from dialogue sessions to full-scale historical and socioeconomic investigations. Transforming the relations of knowledge, overall then, has centrality.

The term "conscientization", popularized by Paulo Freire, is widely used to refer to raising such awareness. It is not easy to establish a subject-subject relation to people who are traditionally victims of a dominating structure. To overcome this it may be necessary to make the people the subject, defining the research process as an independent inquiry by the people concerned, with the outsiders to be consulted at the initiative of the people. Thus made autonomous, they experience the power to produce knowledge themselves. Such scales of activity are being attained through two processes of "multiplication": people engaged in one village animating and assisting another; specific stimulation of such by an animating agency. In effect PAR at this stage may be seen as a cultural, rather than a political movement. In the context of such, consciousness is an organic part of one's social existence, which generates its own paradigm for the discovery of the truth. The two truths, between professionals and the people, may only dialogue with each other, and none may claim to be the greater of the two.

PAR induces the creation of its own field in order to extend itself in time and space, in communities and regions. It moves from the micro to the macro as if in a spiral, and thus acquires a political dimension, the applied criterion of the methodology. Catalytic external agents play a crucial role in linking up the local dimension to the regional, and ultimately the national and international, altogether inspired by cultural values based on a truly democratic and human ideal, seeking a return to the human scale. People can be mobilized with PAR techniques from the periphery to the center, so as to form social movements, which struggle for participation, justice and equity.

We now turn from these key tenets of PAR to a more in depth investigation of the work of its two key proponents, Columbia's Fals Borda and Bangladesh's MD Rahman, the one a radical academic, latterly at the University of British Columbia, and the other a longstanding senior representative of the ILO International Labor Organisation based in Geneva, now back in his home country, Bangladesh.

7.3 Participative Action Research in Depth

7.3.1 Action and Knowledge: Orlando Fals Borda

Remaking Knowledge

Doing Research With and For People: Building up people's self-awareness, for Fals Borda, has been an ever-present preoccupation of participatory action researchers – an extremely important task in order for their actions to be effective if they want to avoid the betrayal of ideals. For this purpose Fals Borda places the interplay between explicit and implicit science – or between Cartesian and popular knowledge – as a fact, which has to be taken into account since it involves dialectical encounters, which are inevitably part of day-to-day living. His central concern has been to direct this interplay to allow the common people to have sufficient control over the generation of new knowledge, thereby "remaking science" for the benefit of the masses victimized by power.

The developed world, he says, of course, is too small for this tremendous task: the victims of poverty constitute the majority of the earth's inhabitants and the effort has many detractors. But a hopeful methodological start has been made with participatory action research. In adopting a marginal and even subversive role, following the likes of Ghandi, Luther King and Mandela, PAR is not denying the merits of science; without the scientific bearings they would have felt as if moving in a void. Ways of building connections between different scientific traditions are then sought while doing research with and for people, and not on them, duly combining the role of activist and researcher.

Fals Borda asserts, at the same time, that PAR applies rigor and responsibility in observation-inference or in carefully handling data just as positivists do. But it has had to remake other aspects of their scholarship so as to relate it to ordinary people's way of interpreting reality. In a similar manner it had to discover and apply its half hidden science – "people's knowledge – for the people's benefit. For this purpose, a series of procedures have been developed in which theory and practice, conventional learning and implicit knowledge could be combined in special *vivencias*.

From Life World to Vicencia: The reconstruction of knowledge for the purpose of furthering social progress and increasing people's self awareness with PAR *vivencias* takes dialogue as its point of insertion in the social process. It is dialogic research, oriented to the social situation in which people live. PAR starts by asking such questions as "Why is there poverty?" or "Why is there oppression and dependence?". As such the grassroots representatives should be able to participate as reference group in the action research process from the very beginning that is from the moment it is decided what the subject of research will be. And they should be involved at every step in the process.

Autonomy and Collective Research: Popular knowledge does not come as isolated facts known by specific individuals, but as packets of cultural data generated by social groups. PAR as an autonomous collective investigation is quite different from the detached individual observer undertaking his or her doctoral thesis, advancing science or gaining personal prestige or financial gain. The task now becomes a communal one in which social validation of knowledge is obtained not only by confronting previous ideas but also through the people's own processes of verification.

Three theoretical elements – not usually included in dominant paradigms, are included:

- the ontological possibility of *a real popular science*
- the existential possibility of *transforming the researcher/researched relationship*
- the need of autonomy and identity in *exercising people's own countervailing power*.

People's science does have its own endogenous processes; it is formally constructed on its own terms, with its own practical rationality and empirical systematization and its own way of institutionalizing, accumulating and transmitting knowledge. As such, the wisdom of the sage and the know-how of the scientist converge and intermingle, as recognized during the lifetimes of Descartes, Kant and Galileo themselves. By giving importance to both, a more useful and complete knowledge for social change can be produced. *Emancipatory collective knowledge and popular science become tools then in the quest for justice, and this is the answer to the perennial question "knowledge for what?".*

The second element, transformation of the researcher/researched liaison leads to an interpretation of participation that is indeed demanding, whereby both parties seek the mutual goal of advancing knowledge in pursuit of justice. They interact, collaborate, reflect and report in collectivities on an equal footing, each one offering in the relationship what he or she knows best. In other words, a meeting of diverse scientific traditions takes place, resulting in an enriched overall knowledge, which is more effective in the struggle for justice and the achievement of social progress and peace. The third element – autonomy and identity in collective research – rests on the observation that progressive social movements cherish and fight for their culture and personality to the last, for their lives depend on it. Stimulating autonomous movements and defending the articulation of local life is a worthy goal for PAR researchers, involving both stripping down the oppressor's power and understanding how to internalize one's own. It also includes the power to speak in the context of establishing a "knowledge democracy".

If the eighteenth century in Europe, then, has been called "the Enlightenment" for its collective efforts to revamp science and philosophy, the twenty first century may be expected to be the "Century of Awakening". The common peoples are already awakening to their rights and possibilities for action. They are also responding to the call of their own voices – hitherto half muted – to honor their dignity and the meaning of their own history.

Ways of Stimulating People: Stimulation of the poor and deprived to undertake self-reliant initiatives requires two essential steps. The first is the development of an awareness about the reality in which they live. In particular, they need to understand that poverty and deprivation are the result of specific social forces rather than an outcome of some inherent deficiency on their part or even "fate". Second, based on such critical awareness, they need to gain confidence in their collective abilities to bring about positive changes in their life situations and organise themselves for that purpose.

A stimulation of this sort implies a specific mode of interaction with the people, the essence of which could be summarized as the break-up of the classical dichotomy between "subject" and "object" (manipulation and dominance) and its replacement by a humanistic mode of equal relation between two subjects (animation and facilitation). The essential difference between the latter approach and that typically undertaken by a political party or conventional development practitioner is:

- *Starting from where people are* – their perceptions, knowledge, experiences and rhythm of work and thoughts, as opposed to preconceived agendas
- *Stimulating people (animation) to undertake self-analysis of their life situations*, and helping them to derive from such self inquiry into the political-economic-cultural environment an intellectual base for initiating changes
- *Assisting people to organise themselves* into People's Organisations (PO's) which are non-hierarchical in structure and democratic in operations
- *Facilitating the actions for change,* with the external catalyst paving the way for internal self-reliance
- Stimulating the People's Organisations to *carry out regular self-reviews*, to assess and learn from success and failure

Creation of Sensitized Agents: A cadre of such sensitized agents will have undergone a process of rigorous learning based on exposure to concrete experience and self-reflection rather than formal training. Potential such persons have generally originated from:

- *socially conscious and active segments of the middle class* who have had practical experience in such social activities
- those who had begin to critically reflect on their earlier roles and were *looking for more relevant or fulfilling roles for society*

Specifically then:

- the starting point is a *collective reflection* on the experiences such people already have in working with communities, including self criticism and unlearning
- *exposure to concrete field experiences*, living among selected communities to gather socio-economic information through informal discussions
- through interaction with groups in the community, the learner seeks to stimulate them to *identify issues of common concern*, collect and analyze information on such, to enrich their understanding of their life situations

- while engaged in such fieldwork, meeting regularly as a group amongst themselves as a *collective learning* exercise
- *identify* those individuals within a community who possess potential *skills in animation*, and assist them in improving their skills.

We now turn from action and knowledge to people's self-development.

7.3.2 People's Self Development: M.D. Rahman

Integrating Education with Life Processes

Like many other of his compatriots, MD Rahman (4) had been inspired by popular mobilizations for social reconstruction and development in Bangladesh after its independence in 1971. He saw a breakthrough in the development status of the country to be possible only through a national mobilization for popular initiatives; on smaller scale, such initiatives were demonstrating their potential for solving people's problems and for creating a spirit of personal sacrifice for collective outcomes, challenging the premises of received economics and development thinking which were pushing the country towards humiliating dependence on external assistance rather than indicating a viable path for social progress.

As a teacher, Rahman had been stimulated by demands from sections of Bangladesh's student community for radical reform to integrate educational processes with processes of life. Yet most of the popular initiatives in the country faded, died or were repressed as reactionary forces gradually consolidated their hold on society's commanding structures. Joining the ILO (International Labour Organisation) in 1977, Rahman was able to pursue the same interest, linking up with significant trends in the grassroots movements in several countries and jointly reflecting on their approaches, experiences and visions; initiating methodological experiments in field "animation" work (see below) and in the sensitization of animators; linking with intellectual trends; working with popular movements; and in synthesizing and conceptualizing from the ongoing experiences. In his contribution to the faculty seminars, he raised as a basic problem in the transition to socialism the question of a "consciousness gap" between revolutionary intellectuals who generally provide leadership in socialist transition, and the masses. Socialism would be alienating of this consciousness gap could not be closed. This problem remained one if his central concerns throughout his explorations of participatory or people's self-development, and in his prolific enagement with the NGO movement.

Organising the Rural Poor

According to Rahman, organising the rural poor, for an NGO, can have several different objectives:

Economic Uplift: This means raising the incomes of the poor, giving them greater stability of income, and some social security or insurance against unforeseen situations, old age, and so on. If this is the only or the principal objective, external delivery of such can be in the form of credit, technology and expertise. But emphasis on external delivery contradicts with the other objectives.

Human Development: Creativity is the distinctive human quality, for Rahman, and the human development objective aims to develop creative people. Creation is the product of thinking and action that is *participation.* This consists of investigation, reflection, decision-making and application of decision: reflection upon action gives men and women the sense of creation, of having developed as human beings. Human development is a process of *self*-development – outsiders cannot develop the rural poor. Outsiders can have a role, however, in stimulating and assisting development.

Achieving social and economic rights: The means of elimination of economic and social oppression, and achieving equity in the use of public resources, implies the exercise of collective power of the poor, and often implies *struggle.* The role of outsiders is to help develop a consciousness amongst the poor of short-run failures as a learning process upon which subsequent strategy is to be built.

The above three objectives, moreover, become complementary if they are pursued together. This implies care to pursue the economic uplift objective through primary reliance on the people's own resources and creativity, and channeling their organised efforts towards obtaining their rightful share of normal public resources. In all this, the emphasis must always be on stimulating people's reflection and analysis, assisted but not dominated by external knowledge and intervention. In this way, people's consciousness will keep advancing.

Macro-social transformation: The above three objectives can be considered to be "locally progressive" if they are pursued together, that is progressive at a micro level. Their contribution to macro social transformation can be positive, if such micro work spreads on a broad enough scale. Since the great bulk of the flow of external resources is controlled by external forces, interested (according to Rahman) in dominating and exploiting the country rather than in its self-determination and development, a self-reliant development effort is an absolutely necessary element for the country to shape its own destiny and stand up with pride. Self-reliance at the national level cannot be achieved without self-reliance at the grassroots levels – in fact at all levels. This by itself requires primary reliance on people's own effort and creativity rather than on external deliveries.

However, *successful social transformation, which includes social reconstruction, is much more than the mere act of formal transfer of political power: it requires a social psychology, culture and capability of self-reliant economic and social effort.* A corollary of self-reliant people's effort is reliance on people's own knowledge. *There is no self-reliant way of development without primary reliance on people's resources including their own knowledge, and professional knowledge has to play a complementary but not dominating role in such development.* With this perspective in view, work with the poor which seeks to develop their creativity primarily through their own collective effort, giving *emphasis to both the people's self reliant thinking and acting through which collective action and consciousness both keep advancing,* would be creating positive assets for the task of social transformation.

Overall then, from an NGO perspective:

- The chosen objectives and their rationale should be discussed with the target groups; they should be asked to *reflect why development effort in the country has been a failure,* notwithstanding so-called "learned" men being in charge
- The people should be asked to deliberate *what they want to do in this overall context,* and how the NGO can help them
- The people should have the opportunity to discuss all of such, and *take action in small groups*
- The *people must periodically evaluate their own experience* and review their progress collectively, draw lessons from success and failure, formulate a future course of action based on past experience, and formulate advice on how to achieve agreed objectives. They should be encouraged to document, store, and disseminate their ongoing experience for progressive advancement of their collective knowledge based on their collective effort.
- In areas where there is a past history of collective effort by the poor, this *history should be collected and discussed, and lessons drawn* from them as a guide to current effort.

We now turn from our in depth analysis of PAR, through the eyes of Fals Bordan and Rahman, to its more global expression. "Global", for us in this case, does not refer to the geographical spread of PAR, which has been most prolifically evolved in Africa, Latin America and South-East Asia, but do its broader conceptual base. For such we turn to the recent work of Daniel Selener, starting by positioning PAR in its wider, consciousness raising context, and then continuing by positioning it in a wider conceptual framework.

7.4 Global Variations of PAR

7.4.1 Consciousness Raising: PAR in Community Development

For the most recent of PAR's exponents, Ecuador's Daniel Selener (5), now based at Cornell University in the U.S.A, Paulo Freire is again a major source of inspiration. Freire has been a fundamental influence on the development of participatory research. In his seminal "Pedagogy of the Oppressed" he introduced the concepts of conscientization and critical reflection (chapter 9). The former means the identification and critical analysis of the social, political and economic contradictions leading to organised action to solve immediate problems and to counter the oppressive aspects of society. As a research approach, Freire proposes thematic investigation through which people identify and analyse their own problems in order to solve them. This implies a change in the traditional role of researcher from that of "objective" external researcher to "committed" co-investigator, together with those who are the subjects of the research.

The philosophical origins of participatory research, aside from those already cited, can be traced back to both pragmatism and also historical materialism. Students of pragmatism maintain that knowledge arises from human action. In the view of historical materialists, participatory research is structured by democratic interaction between researcher and the oppressed classes, and takes the form of a dialectical relationship between theory and practice.

The professional origins of participatory research focus on the inability of the dominant, classical positivist paradigm to promote social change. The emphasis on quantitative analysis, critics maintain, reduces the complexity, meaning and richness of social systems. Because survey research oversimplifies social reality, it produces results which are inaccurate in three ways: extracting information from individuals in isolation from one another, diminishing the richness of human feelings and experience; the respondent may be obliged to select a pre-structured response which does not reflect his or her perceptions; survey instruments are a-historical and lack context, a static snapshot of individuals with no past nor future.

Critics further charge that survey research is oppressive and alienating in nature. To maximize objectivity and control over the research process, questionnaires and interview schedules are designed by researchers, and analyzed by them. This approach does not allow the people being studied to participate in the decision making stage. People are regarded as mere objects to be studied rather than active participants. In fact the research conducted may be irrelevant to the problems that the subjects perceive to be a priority. *The distinctive feature of participatory research is that the group researched participates in the whole research process, and such research is directly related to transformative actions*:

7.4.2 A General Framework for PAR Analysis: Equilibrium versus Conflict Paradigms

Theories of Social Change

Daniel Selener, interestingly enough now based in the USA, that is in the developed "north-western" world, has taken the most analytical and conceptual approach, to PAR, of the three philosophers of research that we have cited. As such he has located the relevant theories of social change, of which partipative research is one, below:

Theories of Social Change	
A. **Equilibrium Paradigm**	Evolutionary / Neo-evolutionary Theory Structural-functional Theory Systems Theory
B. **Conflict Paradigm**	Marxist / Neo-Marxist Theory Cultural Revitalization Theory Anarchist-Utopian Theory Participatory Research

He then goes on to describe the characteristics of each.

Equilibrium based Paradigms

Evolutionary and Neo-Evolutionary Theory: *Classical evolutionary theories, influenced by Darwin's work on biological evolution, offer sociological analogues to the living organisms.* They are based on notions of progress involving stages of development from lower to higher forms. Society, according to evolutionary theorists, is an organism with specialized structures facilitating survival. The purpose of social change is the maintenance of equilibrium in society. *As societies progress or become increasingly differentiated, social change efforts should aid individuals in specializing and adapting, altogether leading to "modernizing" the social, technological and educational sectors of society, modeled on developed societies. Overall then for Selener, people embracing evolutionary theories focus on adaptation, specialization and experimentation.*

Structural-Functional Theory: Structural-functional theory is a 20th century version of evolutionary theory, the main difference being that the latter focuses on linked stages of socio-economic and cultural development, whereas the former is concerned with balancing mechanisms whereby societies maintain a "uniform state". Theorists in both camps conceive society as complex and differentiated, but essentially balanced. They are therefore in favor of adaptive and incremental adjustments, which will restore balance to the system. They view forces for change as external to the system, and major conflicts as a sign of system breakdown. *Structural-functionalists view inequality as necessary and inevitable, leading to the rise of the most capable to important roles. Change requires fitting into the existing system, as required by the needs of society as a whole. Those constituencies embracing structural-functionalist theory identify disruptions, or weak links in the system, whereby corrective actions ensue.*

Systems Theory: From a systems theory perspective, the need for reform arises when the system malfunctions, thus jeopardizing efficiency and endangering "equilibrium". Reforms are implemented through innovative problem-solving techniques within existing systems. Inequities and inefficiencies are the result of dysfunctional organisations or ignorant individuals rather than as a consequence of self-interested elites. *Those using systems theory focus on system breakdowns and malfunctions, identifying subsystems requiring change.* Conflict based paradigms are different.

Conflict based Paradigms

Marxist and Neo-Marxist Theory: Marxist and Neo-Marxist theoreticians focus on issues of power, exploitation and contradictions in society. They view change as structural, taking place at economic, political and social levels. While structural-functionalists attribute problems to malfunctions in the system, Marxists trace them to struggles for power, control and status among powerful elites. Changes that occur in institutions or groups are the result of major structural changes in society as a whole. *For advocates of Marxist theory, the focus is on identifying power relations and subsequently transforming such in favor of the powerless.*

Cultural Revival and Social Movement Theory: Unlike Marxist theory, cultural revitalization theory does not focus on social classes, but, rather, on deliberate, organised, conscious efforts by members of society to construct a more satisfying culture. Such revitalization may be based on mass, ethnic, charismatic or revolutionary movements. *For people embracing cultural revival theory, the research agenda may focus on the unique contributions of different people, that is elements in their knowledge, values, ideologies and experiences that promote social justice.*

Anarchistic and Utopian Theory: Anarchistic and utopian theorists of social change share the goals of radical transformation with Marxists, as well as concerns for cultural revival and for individual renewal. Although their ideas are seldom put into practice, they open up debate. *Utopian theorists, finally, may seek to identify a common vision of what the "good society" may look like. Change may be oriented to building such a society.*

He then turns specifically to the participatory research that is our main concern in this chapter.

Participative versus Action Research: Selener finally compares and contrasts, from his perspective, "participative", with more conventional "action" research. *Participatory research* is intended to empower the powerless groups in society. Practitioners therefore tend to apply conflict-oriented paradigms, seeking after the transformation of oppressive social, economic and political structures in society. *Action researchers* work at making organisations more efficient and effective for the purpose of achieving organisational goals. As such they work within the system, making incremental changes and minor reforms.

We are now ready to illustrate the application PAR, with remarkable case stories from Burkina Faso and Tanzania.

7.5 PAR in Practice: Cases from Burkina Faso and Tanzania

7.5.1 Six S in Burkina Faso

PAR as a Cultural Movement

What, then, is the significance of PAR as a macro-level social transformation? Possibly the largest such movement, at least in the early nineties, was the so-called Six S movement in Burkino Faso, which covered about two-thirds of the country's villages. (6)

Bernard Lédéa Ouédraogo, a core initiator of the Six S movement, was born in Upper Volta (now Burkina Faso) in 1930. He completed his secondary education there and gained numerous diplomas before studying in France, where he obtained a doctorate from the Sorbonne in 1977. After finishing school in 1950, Ouédraogo became a teacher and school director and then turned to agriculture, where his talents as a trainer led him to the top echelons of the civil service. But he found he was unable to help the farmers and village groups whom he was supposed to be training, so he left to find out why.

His first question was whether anything existed in the traditional society of the Mossi (Burkina's largest ethnic group) that resembled village groups. "We undertook a thorough study of village social organisation – the people's thinking and their social and economic structures – and we discovered that the Naam group, a traditional village body composed of young people, had the most highly developed cooperative characteristics. We decided we would attempt to work with the Naam structures." The result was an initiative unique in Africa. Despite a lot of problems, the Naam groups prospered. By 1978 there were over 2,500 groups in Yatenga province with 160,000 members. Twenty years later this had risen to 6,480 groups all over Burkina Faso –

almost half of them women's groups – with a membership of 300,000. The transformation of the traditional Naam groups into modern social structures was a brilliant piece of practical sociology by Ouédraogo.

He gives four reasons for their success: dynamic local leadership and activity; maintenance of traditional values; proscription of any sort of social, ethnic, political or religious discrimination; and training and motivation generated from within the group. The activities of the Naam groups are as broad as life itself. They grow, build, manufacture, trade. As of 1999, they had created 235 cereal banks, 115 mills, 22 dams and about 300 wells. In addition they have established 17 credit banks and constructed six cellars in Yatenga for preserving the 1,000 tons of potatoes they grow each year. The Naam groups are helped with aid funds from French, Swiss, Dutch and German agencies, but they generate their own incomes as well. In 1976 Ouédraogo founded, with the French development expert Bernard Lecomte, the Association Six S (Se Servir de la Saison Sèche en Savane et au Sahel), becoming its Executive Director two years later. While Naam is a people's movement, Six S is a non-governmental organisation. It was dedicated to removing three obstacles to peasant mobilisation: the lack of technical know-how for coping with drought and desertification; the lack of negotiating skills to deal with government and aid agencies, and the lack of funds to implement small projects.

Six S became a federation of peasant organisations like (and including) the Naam from nine countries in the Sahelian zone. By the late 1980s, Six S was reckoned to serve over 2 million people, on the basis of a direct membership of 245,000 farmers. More recently, Six S has undergone some restructuring. In the mid-1990s, Ouédraogo was elected Mayor of his hometown, Ouahigouya. Beside the success of Six S, he is doubtful of the future: "The danger for many Africans is that the erosion of our ways by the aggressive ways of others, our own values by foreign values, will destroy our sense of responsibility for solving our communities' problems."

Animating Agency

The enormous scales of activity, described above, are being attained through two processes of "multiplication": people engaged in one village animating and assisting another; and specific stimulation of such by an animating agency. In effect PAR at this stage may be seen as a cultural, rather than political, movement. In the context of such, for MD Rahman, consciousness is an organic part of one's social existence, which generates its own paradigm for the discovery of the truth. The two truths, between professionals and the people, may only dialogue with each other, and none may claim to be the greater of the two.

There is no assured method of transferring commitment to succeeding generations who have not lived through the struggles from which commitment is socio-historically born. Such a pursuit becomes a happy hunting ground for self-seekers. And genuine accountability to the people is not merely a matter of formal institutional structures, but also, and critically, of people's self-awareness and the confidence to assert such in the affairs of society. The crisis of the left – and for that matter of the right as well – ultimately boils down to this dissociation between the productive forces and the leadership of concerned societies. With such dissociation prevailing, the need is to generate social processes, which would promote the possibility of organic leadership. PAR attempts, as has been demonstrated in the Burkina Faso case, just that.

We now turn from Burkina Faso to Tanzania.

7.5.2 Tanzania: A story to tell – 'hili li mama' meaning 'this mama...'

Another compelling example of working with PAR is the story of Mwajamah Masaiganah who worked originally with fisherfolk communites in rural Tanzania.

"My (Mwajamah Masaiganah) journey takes you back to 1985 when, for the first time, I involved myself in participatory action research (PAR) with fisherfolk communities in Tanzania, focusing specifically on women. Back then, I used to do things the way I was told by higher authorities, taking directions or sending messages to communities, be they right or wrong, no questioning! Using PAR and video as a way of communicating changed my way of looking at things, doing things; created a special interest in me for women and community issues, developed in me a respect for communities and in totality, changed my entire life.

During my work with the communities in Mtwara and Lindi regions as a Rural Development Advisor and then as a Facilitator with the fisherfolk communities, we managed to learn from one another, create awareness in communities, create allies (even with politicians). This helped us to integrate with higher government authorities and lobby for policy changes. Our aim was to stop dynamite and other illegal fishing methods, which claimed lives, left people maimed and threatened people's livelihoods. Nobody thought that we were doing the right thing because, to some people, banning dynamite fishing and taking measures to stop it was interfering with their trade. The dynamite traders and illegal fishermen could lose money by stopping the illegal deal.

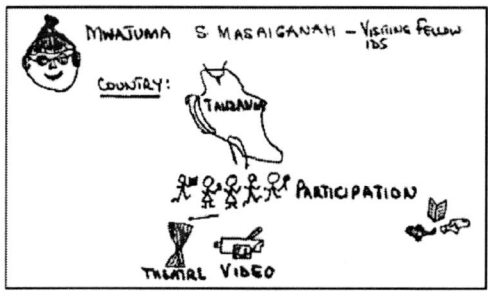

Figure 7.5: Mwajuma's "drawing in action"

I will give just part of my life history working with bureaucrats and within bureaucratic systems, the hustles I encountered and how they helped shape my life. I will narrate my story starting in December 1996, when I facilitated a five-day evaluation workshop with a group of fishermen in Sudi, Lindi district, as part of the RIPS1 marine environment project. Our first meeting in Sudi village led to the Sudi declaration, which was made by fishermen and women from 12 coastal villages of Mtwara, Lindi and Kilwa districts. During this meeting they agreed to form a committee, called the Sudi Committee, to oversee the whole issue of marine environment protection in the area and raise awareness in all people in the area and at regional and national levels. This was to be done through mass meetings, leaders' (villagers') meetings, but using video as a medium of communication.

This idea of using a video was just to start filming when we started the meeting and show back the video every evening of the day's workshop proceedings. This seemed to work, as people, villagers, came forward and volunteered to talk freely in front of the camera and expressed their concerns on the issue of dynamite fishing. This was because, first, video was new in these areas so it was a proud moment for the people to see themselves talking on film. Secondly, people had built trust in us and they knew that it would help us show their leaders what 'they', the people, say. Previously their fears were that whilst many researchers had been talking to them during the many meetings in their villages, all reports from such discussions were just put on shelves and nothing was done. The people were tired because these meetings benefited researchers and their bosses alone, leaving them with nothing.

So, using this kind of media, we assured them that their leaders would see exactly what they said without filtering the information. Therefore, we agreed with them that the Sudi Committee would use the video in their organised tours to create awareness. When we went back to the office, I happened to come across a report or a personal note written by my Chief Technical Advisor, Lars Johanson. It read '...I have never seen in my life such great facilitation skills as displayed by Mwajuma in this exercise ...'

From this, you can imagine how unbelievable it was for me and at the same time how good I felt. I developed and grew even stronger. But, this strength did not take more than four years before landing me into problems and friction with the Regional Authorities.

In January 1997, things started to turn really sour. After an evaluation workshop, the Sudi Committee, formed from the strengthened fisherfolk who had been at the workshop, agreed to meet and draft a constitution to start an NGO called 'Shirikisho' so that they could be independent to do things that concern their lives. In that meeting, one member reported that the situation in the neighbouring region of Kilwa was bad and had reached the extent that illegal fishermen had raised a flag on one of the islands stating, 'Kilwa Hakuna Serikali' meaning 'There is no Government in Kilwa'.

As we were also using media to put pressure on the government to change the policy, I told this story about Kilwa to a newsreader on Radio One. The next morning it was like a hot cake, repeated in the headline news for about a day and a half. After looking for me the whole morning, the Kilwa police left a message that I should report to them. I reported but took along with me the Secretary of Shirikisho. In case something happened to me, then they should know and act quickly.

The police wanted to know why I had made such statements. I said yes, that I had and the reason was that the police were not doing their job. I said that this was highlighted in the evaluation workshop and that in ranking, the police were given zero in efficiency. I explained that I was only telling what people say. After long discussions, they agreed that they are having problems. In a way, it was getting difficult for them to perform their duties because the dynamite problem was an inside job. Then they said that it was the Police Commander that had instructed them to bring me to the police station. I said "Yes, here I am and if only you put me in now, try it, you'll see what happens. The people will retaliate to your actions". I told them we knew much more of what was happening than the police knew and if they wanted to get anywhere, they had to work closely with us. The first agony was over, but I knew I was being monitored.

We decided to record the whole process by video, even the follow up of what happened six months after the evaluation workshop. We made a video documentary and organised trips to visit the Regional Commissioners of Lindi and Mtwara; the Ministers of Communication and Works, Natural Resources and Tourism, the Environment (both in the mainland and in the Isles); the Attorney General and Agricultural and Industries Supplies Company Ltd.; and other companies which are directly or indirectly related to the sale or keeping of dynamite and natural resources. During all these trips, we took video as a means of documenting the process. Many trips of the same kind were made to meet leaders like the then Prime Minister and Vice President who visited the area. In both incidences it was hard for us to get a chance to show them our video or talk to them, as nobody took us seriously. But in all occasions we did actually manage to provide these leaders with a video documentary called Bahari Yetu Hatutaki – meaning 'Not in Our Ocean'.

In February 1997, during the parliamentary session, four Sudi members, plus myself, traveled to Dodoma to meet the Prime Minister, together with Members of Parliament (MPs) from the southern coastal area. To our amazement, they had talked to other members of parliament from the south and they had agreed that the problem did not concern only the coastal constituencies but the entire southern region, because that was their only source of protein – fish from the sea. So, the MPs received us as a team, and made plans to meet the Prime Minister (PM), Mr. Sumaye, the next day. In the morning we attended the parliament session as guests and in the afternoon, we had a very fruitful meeting. I went with the group from Sudi, not as a member, but to document the process. One of our aims was to document and make a video for the purpose of training and educating the masses and policy makers.

So, our meeting started with the current Minister of Regional Administration and Local Government, an MP from Kilwa, introducing the team to the Prime Minister. He said, "Mr. PM, in front of you is a team of four members of the Sudi committee and a group of southern MPs who have come to see you on this issue. Seeing us here as a team, you should understand that we are fed up with the situation…". The PM asked, "You have said four members, but I can see there is one other person. Who is she?". I introduced myself as a facilitator of the process and that I was only there to document what was going on using video and audio on behalf of the communities. During this meeting, the Sudi committee members gave the Prime Minister their video with documentation of the whole process and argued for him to take action, which he did! During this process we also asked for permission to film the meeting session and he permitted us to do so. We explained to him that it was important for the Association to document and that our final video would provide documentation of the whole process.

As facilitator of the process, I never contributed to the discussion in any way. I only documented the process. This group was empowered so much that they needed no outsider to speak for them. Generally the video had a big impact on people to come out and speak because holding the microphone was a way of empowering them and giving them a voice. It draws people nearer as they tend to believe more in what they say, rather than in what we say for them. With the experiences above and the many others which I did not give here, I was moved to look critically at the issue of empowerment, participation, rights and what are the processes of government; laws, policies, acts put in place for us (its people). We need to look critically at whether these processes are benefiting the people of Tanzania in a way that protects their livelihoods and empowers them socially and economically. We need to analyse how and whether the current systems have offered women and the poor what they are supposed to offer, according to what is stipulated in government policies and regulations, for the benefit of the people and the country's benefit at large. And we need to always look at whether the voices of the people are heard in the democratic process."

It is now time to conclude this chapter on participatory action research and people's self-development.

7.6 Conclusion

7.6.1 Reflecting on "What is Development?"

People's collective self-development initiatives, for Fals Borda, not only point to a way out of the development impasse. They also suggest the need for reflection on the very notion of "development". For a long time, development has been associated with the mechanistic notion of the development of physical assets and increasing the flow of economic and social goods and services. Much of the activities articulated here are developmental, but questions remain as to whether the process of people mobilizing themselves is a means of "development" or an end in itself.

Africa in particular, for a Fals Borda writing in the 1990's, is indeed showing evidence of vibrant and assertive people's self development efforts in rural areas, which are in the frontier of such efforts anywhere and from which inspiration can be gleaned and much learned. Genuine people-oriented activists seldom come from the professional classes. However people with a powerful societal vision, conception, intellectual ability and methodological skill for translating conception into practice are needed to provide some guidance and perspective for such initiatives, and for these to spread widely with some coherence. People seem to be ready to respond to such "animation".

Must this be left to spontaneous historical emergence, or can some method of "schooling" be devised to promote a greater concern among a nation's potential intellectual leaders to work *with* and not *upon* the people, so that the "other Africa" could develop faster?

7.6.2 Praxis and the Recovery of History and Culture

Participative action research, in conclusion, has demonstrated in concrete cases its ability to further the progress of the grassroots rather then the vested interests of dominant groups. As such, the rediscovery of cultural roots is an essential element in any effort to improve depressed communities. Recent analysis, moreover, has pointed to the need to distinguish three movements in cultural-historical praxis: investigative, ideological and political. PAR researchers attempt to connect all three in an action-reflection cycle, spiraling towards successively more complex stages of theory and practice. The flavor and ambiance of science, then, has changed dramatically in recent times, as witnessed by the seminal work of such scholars as Capra (Tao of Physics), and the "chaos" theorists, each of whom emphasize the holistic philosophy, relativist knowledge and inter-disciplinary methods. Following Foucault, moreover, the PAR movement may see itself developing hitherto "subjugated knowledges".

The more important practical challenge PAR faces, for Fals Borda, is the need of common people to articulate in social movements, along with new knowledge, the necessary political struggles for justice and progress. As such we are discovering once more the pertinence of participatory action research to the transformation of our societies into a more satisfactory and less violent world.

7.6.3 Spell of the Sensuous to Six S

We have travelled a long way along the relational path, leading towards "healing the planet", both in human and "more-than-human" terms. In terms of practical cases in point we have journeyed descriptively from David Abram's "Spell of the Sensuous" towards, participatively, Bernard Ouedraogo's Six S's in Burkino Faso. In such a journey from the formative to the transformative, from origination to innovation, we moved from the descriptive to the phenomenological, onto feminism and participatory research. In doing so, we moved progressively through being and becoming, knowing and doing. While Abram's primary concern is with a mode of being, Ouedraogo is primarily motivated by doing, Havel with a process of becoming, and Karl Sveiby and Tex Scuthorpe with the mode of knowing.

We now turn from the relational path to the research "path of renewal", starting out with conventional hermeneutics, an interpretive methodology that follows from narrative methods.

Bibliography

1) **Denzin**, N. & **Lincoln**, Y. (2004). *Landscape of Qualitative Research*. London: Sage.

2) **Reason**, P. & **Bradbury**, H. (2004). *Handbook of Action Research*. London: Sage.

3) **Fals Borda,** O. (ed). (1991). *Action and Knowledge*. New York: Apex Publishing.

4) **Rahman**, M.D. (1993). *Peoples' Self Development*. London: Zed Books.

5) **Selener**, D. (1997). *Participative Action Research for Social Change*. Ithaca: University of Cornell.

6) **Pradervand**, P. (1990). *Listening to Africa – Developing Africa from the Grassroots*. New York: Praeger.

7) **Masaiganah**, M. (2004). *A story to tell*. Tanzania: Self-Published Document.

CHAPTER 8

FROM NARRATIVE METHODS TO
HERMENEUTICS

"FUSE HORIZONS"

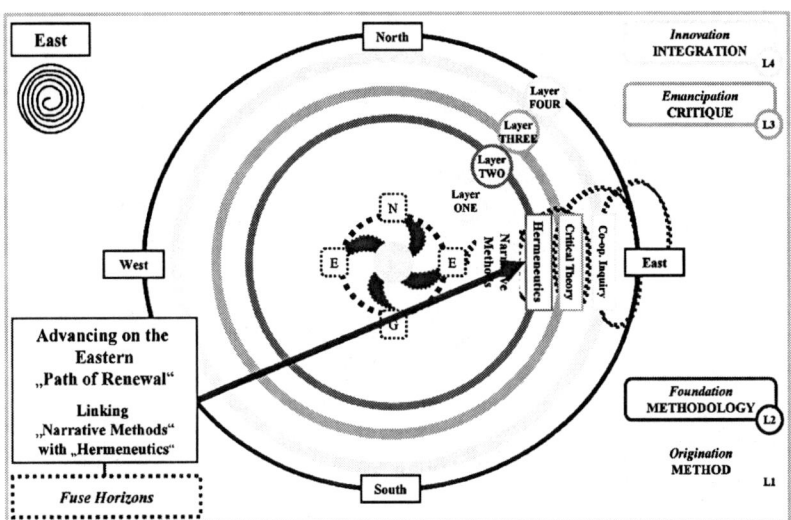

Figure 8.1: Overview Chapter 8 – Layer 2 / East

Summary: Hermeneutics

- We now immerse you in the eastern path of renewal, building on the narrative methods that were introduced in chapter 4. There you were engaged in narrating your own story and that of your life world and society. What then in your research is the emerging storyline that underlies your individual, institutional and societal explorations?

- To discover that, we turn to interpretive hermeneutics: From the hermeneutic perspective, the primary aim of qualitative research is to develop an understanding of how the world is "constructed". The notion of a "constructed" world implies that it is complex, layered, and can be viewed from different perspectives. Interpretevism, hence, gives the other a voice, allows their experiences and stories to be documented. This brings us to cultures and to "multiculturalism".

- Multiculturalism refers to something crucial in the contemporary world: that people importantly differ from one another, are in contact with and must deal with each other. All multi-culturalists focus on understanding and living with cultural and social difference. But such multiculturalism poses an epistemic problem: if others live within their own framework and we live within ours, how can we understand them. That is where hermeneutics comes in.

- Context plays a crucial role: People and things exist only within a certain political and moral context, and they are not understandable outside of it. This is where hermeneutics differs from phenomenology. Individuals and their context form a dialogical, interpenetrating unit. By studying one, the researcher inevitably studies the other. Also, in undertaking a research project, the researcher brings his or her own cultural frame of reference into the picture, which continually and unavoidably frames and shapes the process.

- This chapter distinguishes between the traditional hermeneutic position, originating from Europe and new forms of hermeneutics emerged in transition countries; in this case we focus on Africa.

- European (interpretive) hermeneutics: In the twentieth century hermeneutics came to be seen as perhaps *the* methodology of the social sciences. It is an interpretive social science, taking as its goal the achievement of understanding, backed by rich description and unfolding narrative. The aim is not to conform and extend universalised experiences to attain knowledge of a law but to understand how this man, this people, or this state is what it has become.

- African (transformative) hermeneutics: African and Afro-American philosophers lend a somewhat more transformative edge to "narrative" interpretive method and to "hermeneutic" constructivist methodology than their more purely interpretive European counterparts. The fruitful tension between esteem and criticism, tradition and modernity, when properly cultivated, constitutes the critical edge of transformative hermeneutics. Hermeneutics, here, has also the role of reconnecting a people with its own source. Such a "return" is not a return to tradition or stasis. We as researchers are not engaged in an antiquarian quest for an already existing authentic past tradition. Rather, we are engaged in the affirmation of the historicity of the rural indigenous people.

- In interpretive-hermeneutic terms then, the originating of your research question involves uncovering an original story in each case, a return to source, underlying your research phenomenon.

- In concluding this chapter, we introduce Zahra Al Zeera, an Islamic researcher who discovered hermeneutics as a means of going beyond the positivist and reductionist paradigm in which most education in the Islamic World, in her view, is lodged, to achieve "wholeness and holiness in education". After hermeneutics (foundation) we will turn to critical theory (emancipation).

8.1 Orientation to Hermeneutics

Pursuing a research path of renewal, you move from your narrative origination onto an interpretive foundation, before advancing toward emancipatory critique (in this "eastern" case that of critical theory), culminating in co-operative inquiry, as your ultimate means of social innovation.

You have now the questionable issue that you feel called upon (by your own will and intent) to investigate. Such a question could be, for example: "What are the constraints and opportunities of banking in and for China, from a cultural as well as economic perspective?", or "What are the specific needs and opportunities facing social entrepreneurship in South Africa, as a society and economy in transition?" For you as a researcher one or other of these issues is a burning one, of great significance for you and your society. In addition, getting immersed in a particular subjective way, needs to fit with your unfolding story.

What then becomes your research question? How might it be arising out of that subjective/objective relationship between you as a researcher, and the emergent phenomenon you are researching? What then will constitute your original storyline, one that aligns your own originality with the uniqueness of the particular phenomenon? What in your research is the emerging storyline that underlies your individual, institutional and societal explorations?

We turn now to the interpretive and hermeneutic methodology, which provides the methodological wisdom to build upon the narrative methods that formed an integral part of our flow of innovation in chapter 4. But let us first retrace steps and understand hermeneutics' own story.

Origins of Hermeneutics

Hermeneutics may be described as the development and study of theories of the interpretation and understanding of texts. Essentially, it involves cultivating the ability to understand things from somebody else's point of view, and to appreciate the cultural and social forces that may have influenced their outlook.

In contemporary usage, hermeneutics often refers to study of the interpretation of biblical texts. In fact, it was Rabbi Ishmael Ben Elisha (90 to 135 AD) of the Amoraic era of Judaism who interpreted laws from the Torah through 13 hermeneutic principles. This was the first known appearance of hermeneutics in the world.

In the last two centuries of the modern era, the scope of hermeneutics has expanded to include the investigation and interpretation not only of textual and artistic works, but of human behaviour generally, including language and patterns of speech, social institutions, and ritual behaviours (such as religious ceremonies, political rallies, football matches, rock concerts, etc.). Hermeneutics interprets or inquires into the meaning and import of these phenomena, through understanding the point of view and "inner life" of the researcher, or of the first-person perspective of an engaged participant in these phenomena.

The word "hermeneutics" is a term derived from 'Ερμηνεύς', the Greek word for interpreter. This is related to the name of the Greek god Hermes in his role as the interpreter of the messages of the gods. Hermes was believed to play tricks on those he was supposed to give messages to, often changing the messages and influencing the interpretation thereof. The Greek word thus has the basic meaning of one who makes the meaning clear.

Figure 8.2: Origins of the hermeneutic term

History of Hermeneutics

Hermeneutics in the Western world, as a general science of text interpretation, can be traced back to two sources. One source was the ancient Greek rhetoricians' study of literature, which came to fruition in Alexandria. The other source has been the Midrashic and Patristic traditions of biblical exegesis, which were contemporary with Hellenistic culture. It was actually Aristotle who struck a chord in his treatise "De Interpretatione" that reverberates through the intervening ages and supplies the key note for many contemporary theories of interpretation.

The early Jewish Rabbis and the early Church Fathers deployed similar philological (language based) tools; their biblical interpretations stressed allegorical readings, frequently at the expense of the texts' literal meaning. They sought deeper meanings below the outward appearance of the text. Examples of such interpretations include the writings of Philo of Alexandria, Origen, and the Talmud. Interestingly enough, before the studies of the bible that explicitly gave rise to hermeneutics, innumerable Islamic scholars, from the ninth century onwards, came to study the Qur'an in the same interpretive light.

During the European Renaissance of the 15th century, the discipline of hermeneutics emerged through the new humanist education as a historical and critical methodolgoy for analyzing texts. In a triumph of early modern hermeneutics, the Italian humanist Lorenzo Valla proved in 1440 that the "Donation of Constantine" was a forgery, through intrinsic evidence of the text itself. Thus hermeneutics expanded from its medieval role in purely explaining the correct analysis of the bible. However, biblical hermeneutics did not die off at the time. For example, the protestant reformation brought about a renewed interest in the interpretation of the bible, which took a step away from the interpretive tradition developed during the middle ages back to the texts themselves.

Modern Hermeneutics: From Schleiermacher to Dilthey ...

Modern hermeneutics started with the German philosopher Friedrich Schleiermacher. He explored the nature of understanding in relation not just to the problem of deciphering sacred texts, but to all human texts and modes of communication. Schleiermacher said that every problem of interpretation is a problem of understanding. He even defined hermeneutics as the art of avoiding misunderstanding. He also provided a solution to the avoidance of misunderstanding: knowledge of grammatical and psychological laws in trying to understand the text and the writer.

There arose in his time a fundamental shift from understanding not only the exact words and their objective meaning to understanding the individuality of the speaker or author.

With Schleiermacher, hermeneutics begins to stress the importance of the interpreter and his understanding of the text in the process of interpretation. Understanding, for Schleiermacher, does not simply come from reading the text, but involves knowledge of the historical context of the text and the psychology of the author.

The German nineteenth century philosopher Wilhelm Dilthey broadened hermeneutics even more by relating interpretation to all historical descriptions. Understanding thereby moves from the outer manifestations of human action and productivity to explore their inner meaning. In his last important essay "The Understanding of Others and their Manifestations of Life" (1), Dilthey makes it clear that this move from outer to inner, from expression to what is expressed, is not based on empathy. Empathy involves a direct identification with the other. Interpretation involves an indirect or mediated understanding that can only be attained by placing human expressions in their historical context. For Dilthey, understanding is not a process of reconstructing the state of mind of the author, but one of articulating what is expressed in the work, that is specifically by placing it in its historical context.

... to Heidegger and Gadamer

Since Dilthey, the discipline of hermeneutics has detached itself from this central task and broadened its spectrum to all texts, including multimedia and to understanding the bases of meaning. In the 20th century, Martin Heidegger's philosophical hermeneutics shifted the focus from interpretation to so-called "existential" understanding, which was treated more as a direct, non-mediated, thus in a sense more authentic, way of being in the world than simply as a way of knowing.

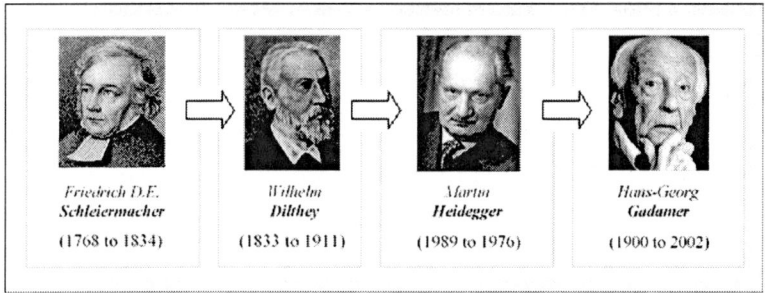

Figure 8.3: Hermeneutics – Core Thinkers

Hans-Georg Gadamer's hermeneutics is a development of the hermeneutics of his teacher, Heidegger. He describes the process of interpreting a text as the fusion of one's own horizon with the horizon of the text. He defines "horizon" as "the totality of all that can be realised or thought about by a person at a given time in history and in a particular culture."

Gadamer's philosophical project, as explained in his opus magnum "Truth and Method", was to elaborate on the concept of "philosophical hermeneutics", which Heidegger initiated but never dealt with at length. Gadamer's goal was to uncover the nature of human understanding. In the book Gadamer argued that "truth" and "method" were at odds with one another. He was critical of two approaches to the human sciences. On the one hand, he was critical of modern approaches to humanities that modeled themselves on the natural sciences (and thus on rigorous scientific methods). On the other hand, he took issue with the traditional German approach to the humanities, represented for instance by Friedrich Schleiermacher and Wilhelm Dilthey, which believed that correctly interpreting a text meant recovering the original intention of the author who wrote it.

In contrast to both of these positions, Gadamer argued that people have a "historically effected consciousness" ("wirkungsgeschichtliches Bewußtsein") and that they are embedded in the particular history and culture that shaped them. *"In fact history does not belong to us; but we belong to it. Long before we understand ourselves through the process of self-examination, we understand ourselves in a self-evident way in the family, society and state in which we live. The focus of subjectivity is a distorting mirror. The self-awareness of the individual is only a flickering in the closed circuits of historical life. That is why the prejudices of the individual, far more than his judgments, constitute the historical reality of his being."* (2)

Thus interpreting a text involves a "fusion of horizons" where the scholar finds the ways that the text's history articulates with their own background. "Truth and Method" is not meant to be a programmatic statement about a new "hermeneutic" method of interpreting texts. Gadamer intended "Truth and Method" to be a description of what we always do when we interpret things (even if we do not know it): "My real concern was and is philosophic: not what we do or what we ought to do, but what happens to us over and above our wanting and doing." (3)

We now turn from an overview of hermeneutics to its key tenets.

8.2 Hermeneutics – Key Tenets

Hermeneutics – Key Tenets
① Understand how the world is "constructed".
② Give "the other" a voice.
③ Interpret reality indirectly.
④ Reconstruct self and society.
⑤ Move from spectator to active agent.
⑥ Evolve from interpretive to transformative.
⑦ Reconnect with the source.

① **Understand how the world is "constructed"**

Hermeneutics is perhaps the most pre-eminent, conventionally "interpretive" qualitative methodology. Qualitative research is a process of a careful inquiry into the social world, and indeed worlds, serving to newly understand them, and thereby produce knowledge that becomes practically useful.

The primary aim of such an interpretive approach is to develop an understanding of how the world is "constructed". The notion of the world being constructed implies that it is complex, layered, and can be viewed from different perspectives. We construct the world through talk, action, systems of meaning, rituals and institutions that have been created, as well as through the ways in which the world is physically and materially shaped. In particular, hermeneutic research seeks to uncover historical and cultural horizons of meaning, that is, if you like, story lines, through which a world is experienced.

② **Give "the other" a voice**

This giving voice to the other is seen as invaluable to the human conduct. Hermeneutic research, hence, serves to expand a practitioner's awareness of the process of management, social work, therapy, social and economic transformation, or whatever, within particular contexts. Such research may cover the historical development of a field, or serve to establish a bridge between one field and another, either in terms of disciplines or in terms of cultures. Hermeneutics is hence "tradition-informed understanding". As such, it is especially suited for a transcultural orientation, and for a grounding of self and organisation in a particular place and time.

Multi-culturalists focus on understanding and living with cultural and social difference. But such multi-culturalism poses an epistemic (knowledge based) problem: if others live within their own framework and we live within ours, how can we understand them? That is where hermeneutics comes in. Hence, the basic question of the philosophy of social science today ought not to be whether social science is "scientific". Rather, it ought to be whether understanding others – particularly others who are different – is possible, and if so, what does such understanding involve?

③ **Interpret reality indirectly**

According to so-called "perspectivism", as an offshoot of hermeneutics, knowers rather approach reality from their own slant, with their own assumptions and preconceptions. Hence, facts are also rooted in such perspectives. In other words, description requires a scheme consisting of terms by means of which facts will be constituted. This is exactly what perspectivism claims: without an organising conceptual scheme, or overall perspective, no intellectual activity can occur. For a blank slate is incapable of learning anything. Knowers have to bring to their experience, their culture and society, a rich assortment of ideas and conceptual commitments to bear upon people and things, in order even to describe what they see, that is in order to have something about which to theorize. Without basic propositions, knowledge itself would be impossible. All knowledge is therefore a constructive activity in which knowers are active contributors.

④ **Reconstruct self and society**

People and things exist only within a certain political and moral context, and they are not understandable outside of it. This is where hermeneutics, as Heidegger pointed out, differs from phenomenology. Individuals and their context form a dialogical, interpenetrating unit. By studying one, you as researcher inevitably study the other. Also, in undertaking a research project, you bring your own individual (self) as well as cultural (society) frame of reference into the picture, which continually and unavoidably frames and shapes the process. Finally, by reconnecting with your own source, you, as a researcher, fully contextualise your research and become an active participant in a creative process of reconstructing self and society.

⑤ **Move from spectator to active agent**

Philosophical schemas, or indeed personal or cultural "self constructed" perspectives, serve as important devices for making a world intelligible at a particular period in time, and for one set of people in relation to another, rather than the whole world for all time. As languages of understanding are developed and disseminated, you as research scientist cross the threshold from passive responder or reactor to active constructer of meaning, and enter not as a spectator of the inevitable, but as an active agent. To communicate your understanding, is to make a small investment in the creation of the future, and, in the process, to participate in social innovation.

⑥ **Evolve from interpretive to transformative**

African and Afro-American philosophers lend a somewhat more transformative edge to "narrative" interpretive method and to "hermeneutic" constructivist methodology than their more purely interpretive European counterparts. Such a different notion is deeply linked to African History. For Serequeberhan, Africa's core hermeneutic philosopher, it is in the painful gap between ideality and actuality that the African hermeneutic philosophy finds its source and the locus of its concerns. As such, Africa and other societies in transition including the ex communist countries of Eastern Europe, China and India need to re-invent themselves to transform themselves, rather than "be developed" by others. In so doing, the review of an individual's, an institution's or a society's own narrative and destiny, is matched by hermeneutical re-invention or re-construction.

⑦ **Reconnect with the source**

Humans do not have a pure, fundamental human nature that is trans-historical and trans-cultural; you are incomplete and therefore unable to adequately function unless embedded in a specific cultural matrix. Hence, the cultural matrix "completes" humans. The material objects we create, the ideas we hold, and actions we take are shaped in a fundamental way by the social framework in which we are raised. These cultural artefacts are not only the reflection or expression of an era, they are the immediate stuff of daily life. Your research task is to interpret the multitudinous and conflicting ways in which various worlds are constructed and human meanings developed.

Finally, as a hermeneutic researcher with a view to social innovation, you should not passively adhere to what is given by tradition. Rather the relation to the tradition is an open-ended encounter, between self and other, past and present, in which what is explicitly preserved and implicitly betrayed by tradition is revealed. Historically – a person, organisation or community – always becomes what it is by projecting itself out of its past, its lived inheritance. Its "destiny" is thus always what comes out of itself, its "has been" out of the prospects of its history and the possibilities of its generation. Hence, in many countries, such a "return" to its history is a cultural and political recovery of the oppressed historic possibilities in the existence of the colonised. However, the "return" is not meant to be a return to tradition or stasis. We as researchers-and-innovators are not engaged in an antiquarian quest for an already existing authentic past tradition. Rather, we are engaged in the affirmation of the historicity of the rural indigenous people.

We now turn from the philosophy to the psychology of hermeneutics, and from a Germanic to a more Anglo-Saxon perspective.

8.3 Hermeneutic Methodology in Depth

8.3.1 Reflexive Knowing

We now consider hermeneutics in more depth, moving from the original German founding fathers – Schleiermacher, Dilthey, Heidegger, Gadamer – to the more contemporary (mostly) Anglo-Saxon interpreters of such a research orientation. In fact, the Scottish researcher, John McLeod, and the American researchers, Fay, Gergen and Cushman, all take a psychological as well as a philosophical approach.

The primary aim of qualitative research is to develop an understanding of how the world is "constructed". This at least is what the Scottish researcher and psychologist John McLeod (4) believes, arguing from a constructivist hermeneutic perspective. *The notion of the world being constructed implies that it is complex, layered, and can be viewed from different perspectives.* We construct the world through talk, action, systems of meaning, rituals and institutions that have been created, as well as through the ways in which the world is physically and materially shaped. In particular, hermeneutic research seeks to uncover historical and cultural horizons of meaning, that is, if you like, story lines, through which a world is experienced. Why then pursue such qualitative inquiry?

McLeod divides his response, both in relation to phenomenology and also to hermeneutics, between one of knowing and that of becoming a knower. Everyday common-sense knowledge, firstly then, is far from being coherent and consistent. There may have been times in the past when people lived according to fixed rules and axioms, but these days are well gone. New elements of common sense become re-worked, appropriated by different groups, and ultimately outmoded. *Qualitative research is a process of careful inquiry into the social world, and indeed worlds, serving to newly understand them, and thereby produce knowledge that becomes practically useful.* McLeod divides such careful inquiry into three areas:

- knowledge of phenomena
- knowledge of the other
- reflexive knowing

Interpretevism gives the other a voice, allows their experiences and life stories to be documented, this being seen as invaluable to the human running. Such research, for McLeod, serves to expand a practitioner's awareness of the process of management, social work, therapy, social and economic transformation, or whatever, within particular contexts. Reflexive knowing occurs when you deliberately turn your attention to your own processes of constructing a world, with the goal of saying something new about that personal (or shared) world that you indeed construct. Such research may cover the historical development of a field, or serve to establish a bridge between one field and another, either in terms of disciplines or in terms of cultures. We start with such cultures in particular, then move onto social constructivism in general, ultimately moving onto hermeneutics per se, both in Europe (as a developed society) and also Africa (reflecting societies in transition).

8.3.2 From Interpretivism to Perspectivism

Beyond Self versus Other

Multiculturalism, for the American social philosopher Brian Fay, refers to something crucial in the contemporary world: that people importantly differ from one another, are in contact with and must deal with each other. All multiculturalists focus on understanding and living with cultural and social difference. But such multiculturalism poses an epistemic problem: if others live within their own framework and we live within ours, how can we understand them? That is where hermeneutics comes in. For Fay, *the basic question of the philosophy of social science today ought not to be whether social science is "scientific". Rather, it ought to be whether understanding others – particularly others who are different – is possible, and if so, what does such understanding involve?*

Prevailing conceptions of multiculturalism emphasize difference, cultural integrity and resistance to cultural domination. They think in rigidly dualistic categories of "self" versus "other"; of "us" versus "them"; of "sameness" versus "difference"; of "assimilation" versus "separatism"; and of "insider" versus "outsider". In place of difference Fay emphasizes interchange; in place of integrity, openness and interaction; in place of resistance he emphasizes learning. Throughout he replaces a dualistic mode of thought with a dialectical one, rooted in a so-called "perspectivism" aligned with "interpretevism".

From Interpretivism to Perspectivism

According to perspectivism, knowers never view reality directly as it is in itself, rather they approach it from their own slant, with their own assumptions and preconceptions. Facts are not just states of affairs, which present themselves immediately sorted out and identified. Without a prior vocabulary, which a describer brings to a situation, there would be no facts whatsoever. Where does this vocabulary come from? Describers must possess some scheme of terms to provide the basic building blocks for their factual descriptions. Put succinctly: facts are rooted in conceptual schemes.

So description requires a scheme consisting of terms by means of which facts will be constituted. *This is exactly what perspectivism claims: without an organising conceptual scheme no intellectual activity can occur.*

Just as descriptive statements are rooted in theories, theories themselves are nested in larger conceptual structures. Science aspires to link individual theories together to form a network of theories. The theories of the unconscious, of dreams, of psycho-social development, and repression are all linked together, for example, to form the Freudian theory of the psyche. Science seeks to explain a divergent and extensive range of phenomena in terms of a few basic principles. Theories are also themselves explained by higher level, more general theories. For example, the theory of consumer behaviour in neo-classical economic theory is itself explained by the more abstract theory of consumer preference. All theories, then, presuppose some basic commitments as to the fundamental core of a subject, to the basic concepts by which to identify and describe such, and to basic claims as to the nature of this core.

This is the way perspectivism portrays science. Human knowers cannot look at reality directly in some unmediated manner, no matter how much they try to purge their minds of prior ideas and concepts. It is a good thing that they cannot: for a blank slate is incapable of learning anything. *Without basic propositions, knowledge itself would be impossible. All knowledge is a constructive activity in which knowers are active contributors.*

8.3.3 Hermeneutics and Social Constructivism

Philosophical schemas, for a constructivist-interpretevist like American philosopher and psychologist Kenneth Gergen (5), serve as important devices for making a world intelligible at a particular period in time, and for one set of people in relation to another, rather than the whole world for all time. *As languages of understanding are developed and disseminated, the scientist crosses the threshold and enters not as a spectator of the inevitable, but as an active agent. To communicate one's understanding is to make a small investment in the creation of the future.*

A theorist is engaged in a form of "ontological education", like you, who creates a compelling theory. Such generative theory challenges the guiding assumption of a culture, raises fundamental questions regarding contemporary life, fosters reconsideration of existing constructions of reality, and, by so doing, furnishes new alternatives of action. *When used generatively, theory may increase the adaptive potential of an individual, institution or society, starting indeed for you as a person.* However, and in our context here, there is more to social innovation than the construction of theory.

America's Philip Cushman (6), based at the School of Professional Psychology in California, has acknowledged, that our dedication to the philosophical frame of reference of the physical sciences has helped us to develop the power to manipulate the physical world in undreamed of ways. But that same frame of reference has within it a built-in paradox. By conceiving of a world that irrevocably separates "inner" from "outer", body from mind, the objectively oriented physical science framework makes it nearly impossible to use traditional ideas, philosophical thinking and a sense of moral authority – and thus to make a subjective moral stand. A society wide consensus, a shared sense of right and good and true, arising out of the interrelatedness of culture, simply does not exist in our time.

To grasp the remarkable interrelatedness of a culture – to sense for an instance how the disparate pieces of the social fabric are woven into a whole, how they politically reinforce, reproduce, collude with, resist, and reshape one another, to understand the innocence, the cynicism, the terror, and the brave fiction of it all – that is the task of interpretive, hermeneutic, cultural history. *People and things exist only within a certain political and moral context, and they are not understandable outside of it.* This is where hermeneutics, as Heidegger pointed out, differs from phenomenology.

Studying humans by abstracting them from their cultural context and observing them in a dispassionate, objective manner in a psychological laboratory is more akin, for Cushman, to removing a fish from water than to picking up a rock from its resting place. Studying people in a "positivistic" way, as we do in chapter 14, renders them lifeless. *Individuals and their context form a dialogical, interpenetrating unit. By studying one, the researcher inevitably studies the other. Also, in undertaking a research project, the researcher brings his or her own cultural frame of reference into the picture, which continually and unavoidably frames and shapes the process.*

According to Cushman, the overall social constructionist argument, inclusive of hermeneutics, as initially proposed by Gergen, can be distilled in eight propositions:

① *Humans do not have a pure, fundamental human nature* that is trans-historical and trans-cultural; we are incomplete and therefore unable to adequately function unless embedded in a specific cultural matrix composed of language, symbols, moral understandings, rituals, rules, institutional arrangements of power and privilege, origin myths and explanatory stories.

② *The cultural matrix "completes" humans,* whereby culture infuses individuals through the social practices of the everyday world, shaping and forming in the most fundamental ways how humans conceive of the world and their place in it, how they see others, and how they engage in a moral framework of mutual obligations and responsibilities.

③ The material objects we create, the ideas we hold, and actions we take are *shaped in a fundamental way by the social framework in which we are raised;* they have been created out of a particular perspective of a specific historical and cultural situation and therefore they express that perspective.

④ These cultural artefacts are not only the reflection or expression of an era, they are *the immediate stuff of daily life,* pertaining to language, clothing, the marking of time, and the concept of self, as well as to monetary exchange and eating utensils.

⑤ Owing to the dual nature of artefacts, whereby they both reflect and produce an era, one task of human science is to discuss the artefact in such a way as to interpret the particular social construction of the era and culture in which it was produced; seen in this way *the research task is to interpret the multitudinous and conflicting ways in which various worlds are constructed* and human meanings developed.

⑥ Because *cultural artefacts* express aspects of the society from which they were created, they also *reinforce and reproduce the constellations of power*, the wealth and powers that dominate in that society; artefacts are not benign, apolitical coincidences, but are part of the subtle and effective social contrivances that keep human communities surviving and functioning. This is something that will be picked up later by Eritrean philosopher Serequeberhan, in an African context.

⑦ *The researcher's task is to define in each culture what constitutes the broad cultural framework*, the institutional structures, and finally the everyday artefacts that instruct, influence and shape the individual's moment-by-moment perspective and experiences.

⑧ Because the West's concept of a bounded autonomous self is an expression of the current historical era, that concept *reinforces and reproduces that era*, serving whatever forces may benefit from the current configuration of power and wealth; because the dominant dynamic of our era is consumerism, the pre-eminence of the isolated, autonomous self is both a consequence of that dynamic and means of reproducing it.

We now compare and contrast the European and the African perspective on hermeneutics, to illustrate how culture and context influence methodology. In this case it is about turning hermeneutics from an informative (European) to a transformative (African) orientation. However, what is clearly common to the two approaches, is the overtly *developmental* orientation that both adopt. In other words, it is now narratively oriented *becoming* rather than descriptively oriented *being* that occupies pride of place.

8.4 Global Variations of Hermeneutics: The Cases of European and African Hermeneutics

8.4.1 Informative and Developmental: European Hermeneutics

Original Imagination

What differentiates objective "methodological sterility" from genuine "inter-subjective" understanding is original imagination. This is how one of the seminal figures in philosophical hermeneutics, Germany's twentieth century philosopher Hans-Georg Gadamer (7), sees things. In fact the origins of hermeneutics, reaching back to Schleiermacher and his biblical interpretations in the late nineteenth century, were entirely German. *Such subjectively imaginative (as opposed to objectively analytical) ability, involves seeing what is questionable in any subject and formulating questions to explore the subject further.* The precondition of this capacity is that, firstly, one is open to be questioned by the other and willing to be provoked to risk involvement in a dialogue that carries you imaginatively beyond the present position. The real meaning of a research context you are seeking to understand, secondly, is always co-determined by the historical situation of yourself as an original interpreter. Thus understanding is not an objective, analytical, reproductive procedure, but rather always a subjective-objective, imaginative and productive one.

Hermeneutics, as we have seen, was originally concerned in the nineteenth century with the interpretation of texts, primarily religious scripts. *Established in the nineteenth century context of scriptural interpretation, in the twentieth century it came to be seen as perhaps the quintessential methodology of the social sciences. It is an interpretive social science, taking as its goal the achievement of understanding, backed by rich description and unfolding narrative.* This use of interpretivism is compared and contrasted with the positivistic scientific orientation of the natural sciences, duly oriented towards explanation, backed by observation, experimentation and survey.

Whereas interpretive social scientists develop understandings of richly textured phenomena, and of "the stories we are", natural scientists carry out experiments and test hypotheses that are derived from explanatory models or theories. It can be argued, though, that what is properly meant by hermeneutics goes far beyond interpretation. The argument, for Gadamer, is that any text is created in one cultural-historical context and then interpreted in another. *It is the dislocation in time and place that makes interpretation necessary.* Our attempt to understand the text is framed by what Gadamer has called "historical consciousness". The act of understanding involves the coming together of the historical understanding of the world, of the interpreter, and the text. This fusion of horizons of each may represent a moment of insight, but, more crucially, it sig*nifies an act of continuing and deepening cultural-historical tradition of which the interpreter is a member.* Understanding is to be thought of as less a subjective act than as participation in an event of tradition, or indeed in a process of origination.

The Enlightenment promoted rationality and empiricism as antidotes to tradition, constructing a modern world in which social life could be re-invented on rational grounds. But this is impossible if we live in history, and in cultures and communities that perpetuate traditions. As such, hermeneutics is tradition-informed understanding, which is especially suited for a trans-cultural orientation, and for a grounding of self and organisation in a particular place and time. For Gadamer, the experience of the socio-historic world in which your research is lodged, cannot be raised to a science by the inductive procedure of the natural sciences. The aim is not to conform and extend universalised experiences to attain knowledge of a law – for example how men, people and states evolve – but to understand how this man, this people, or this state is what it has become, or, more generally, how it happened that this is so.

Self-Formation and "Bildung"

This perspective builds on the prior grounds established by German philosopher Herder covering the historical concept of *self-formation, education, or cultivation* that is *"Bildung".* As we can see, such an approach is very much concerned with both origination and with understanding as well as with contextualisation within a particular individual, institution, society.

We now turn from a European and American perspective on social constructivism, interpretevism and narrative method, to what has been identified as "African Hermeneutics". It is at this juncture (in this chapter and in the next two on methodology that follow) that we bring in the perspective of societies in transition, or what has been termed "developing" societies. As we will see, that developing perspective has more of a socio-political tone to it than its culturally and historically laden "northern" and "western" counterparts, and therefore is more resonant with societies in transition, as in China or the Middle East, Eastern Europe and South-East Asia.

8.4.2 Transformative and Developmental: African Hermeneutics

Dialogical Knowing and Human Becoming

African and Afro-American philosophers lend a somewhat more transformative edge to "narrative" interpretive method and to "hermeneutic" constructivist methodology than their more purely interpretive European counterparts. For Afro-American philosopher Richard Bell, to begin with, in his "Understanding African Philosophy":

" ... we share in forming and expressing our particular life worlds through stories or narratives. It is through such narratives that we see both the uses and the abuses of power and human identity ... Out of our liberation struggles come the poetry, the stories, the telling of Africa's suffering and indignity. From the cries of injustice, the memory and narration, come a new and broader sense of justice and the hope of the transformation of communal values to engage modernity." (8)

We immediately see the different "critical emancipatory" tone when compared, for example, with that of Germany's Gadamer. This "telling" from these "texts" is part of the narrative enterprise that is a diary of philosophy. *Such "interpretative" philosophy takes account of the contexts in which the conversations of human life take place.* It is the narrative aspect of philosophy that is to a culture and gives it its existential texture. It is also this aspect, emerging from the local ground, which preserves it from a globalised abstraction. For Bell, this is what is involved in approaching the nature and scope of our understanding from an aesthetic and thereby also hermeneutic point of view. *It is through our aesthetic consciousness that we see the reflexivity of our human being and the dialogical nature of our knowing and understanding of the world, however "strange' it may seem to us.* In this context, the "Nzonzi" is a most interesting African figure. For the Congolese philosopher Ernest Wamba-di-Wamba, as cited by Bell, the "Nzonzi" was a special kind of leader with an aesthetically laden "mastery of the clarification of speech", whereby he or she:

" ... must know how to listen attentively and tirelessly; to pick up the essence of each spoken word, to observe every look, every gesture, every silence, to grasp their respective significance, and to counter unjust positions, while reinforcing just ones ..."

We now turn from Afro-American Bell to Africa's Eritrean born philosopher Tsenay Serequeberhan (9) and his own African interpretation of hermeneutics.

Local Tradition and Destiny

The Congolese philosopher Okonda Okolo proposes a hermeneutical interpretation of two notions of fundamental importance in Africa – tradition and destiny. In Western anthropology a culture based on tradition is frequently portrayed as one devoid of change. Destiny is portrayed as encouraging determinism, and thereby inhibiting the development of individual initiative. *For Okolo, tradition in Africa is constantly interpreted and reinterpreted – and therefore always changing – by different individuals in different historical contexts. Tradition therefore does not inhibit invention or change, creation or transformation. Destiny, from the vantage point of African hermeneutics, is not a symbol of determinism, but involves a people's "vision of the world".* For Sekem's Ibrahim Abouleish in Egypt:

"I carry a vision deep within myself: in the midst of sand and desert I see myself standing as a well drawing water. Carefully I plant trees, herbs and flowers and wet their roots with the precious drops. The cool well water attracts human beings and animals to refresh and quicken themselves. Trees give shade, the land turns green, fragrant flowers bloom, insects, birds and butterflies show their devotion to God, the creator, as if they were citing the first Sura of the Koran. The human, perceiving the hidden praise of God, care for and see all that is created as a reflection of paradise on earth. For me this idea of an oasis in the middle of a hostile environment is like an image of the resurrection at dawn, after a long journey through the nightly desert. I saw it in front of me like a model before the actual work in the desert started. And yet in reality I desired even more: I wanted the whole world to develop." (10)

As such it represents the history of a people – and of Ibrahim Abouleish himself – their past, present and future and whatever sense of identity they can create and recreate for themselves.

Transformative Hermeneutics – Tradition and Modernity

In his book on the "Hermeneutics of African Philosophy", Serequeberhan is, on the one hand, radically open to that which is preserved in his own Eritrean cultural heritage. On the other hand, he is critical of tradition to the extent that the cultural elements, which have been preserved in it, have ossified and are a concrete hindrance to the requirements of contemporary, or modern existence. *This fruitful tension between esteem and criticism, tradition and modernity, when properly cultivated, constitutes the critical edge of his transformative hermeneutics.*

Emergent transformation is thus a grasping and exploring of grounding concerns, aimed at the enhancement, emergence, and ultimate transformation of its own lived actuality. In Africa's specific political and historical context (this could equally apply to Latin America, and parts of Asia and the Middle East), the concerns of contemporary philosophy are focused on the possibility of overcoming the misery and political impotence of the continent's post-colonial situation. Hermeneutics in such a context has more of a critical, emancipatory and transformative edge to it than it does in the reflectively European one. Postcolonial Africa then poses the challenge of self-transformation and the concrete actualisation of its alleged "independence". It does so in view of the suffering millions that have been victimized by the lived actuality as opposed to the hoped for ideality of an "independent" Africa. This is indeed the case for much of Latin America and the Arab world as well.

For Serequeberhan, *it is in this painful gap between ideality and actuality that the hermeneutic philosophy finds its source and the locus of its concerns*, engaged, in the words of the late Franz Fanon – the extraordinary Martiniquan psychiatrist and philosopher – in *"turning over a new leaf and working out new concepts"*. As such,

Africa and other societies in transition including the former communist countries of Eastern Europe, China and India needs to re-invent themselves to transform themselves, rather than "be developed" by others. In so doing, the review of an individual's, an institution's or a society's own narrative and destiny, is matched by hermeneutical re-invention. In fact this is patently not what is happening in China and Eastern Europe today, neither of which is actually drawing on their combined tradition and destiny, in this sense that Okolo talks about it.

In other words, the philosopher/interpreter should not passively adhere to what is given by that tradition. Rather the relation to the tradition is an open-ended encounter, between self and other, past and present, in which what is explicitly preserved and implicitly betrayed by tradition is revealed. For example, China would engage with its Taoist, Confucian and Buddhist past, with a view to renewing it, in a purposeful and open-ended way. Historically "being there" – a person, organisation or community – always becomes what it is by projecting itself out of its past, its lived inheritance. Its "destiny" is thus always what comes out of itself, out of the prospects of its history and the possibilities of its generation. For contemporary Africans, what impels them to such is precisely the estranged actuality of the continent's present deriving from the colonial experience, the specific particularity of Africa's history. As Okolo points out:

"Our hermeneutical situation is that of the formerly colonized, the oppressed, that of the underdeveloped, struggling for more justice and equality. Here we affirm the methodological pre-eminence of praxis on hermeneutics, praxis understood in the sense of an action tending toward the qualitative transformation of life."

This applies as much for Ibrahim Abouleish (11) in Egypt, as it does for Okolo in the Congo or for Serequeberhan in Eritrea, as it did for Havel in Czechoslovakia.

Fractured Split and Fusion of Horizons

Insofar, as the anti-colonial struggle, for Serequerberhan, is aimed at overcoming colonialism and neo-colonialism, it is an attempt to end the fissure in African existence between exogenous dominance and indigenous tradition. It is in the hope of overcoming this split through a positive union that the counter-force of the colonised acquires a political form and becomes a project for a possible freedom.

In fact, *liberation movements in Africa or in Latin America, in Asia as in the Middle East, are born out of the "fusion of horizons" of two broad segments of society, the urban and the rural.* Each manifests in itself what the other does not have and is estranged from. The Westernised urbanised native is acquainted with the "global" world beyond the colony or neo-colony and the struggles of other peoples. The rural non-Westernised native, on the other hand, is steeped in the broken "local" heritage of his own particular past. In the fusion of these two fractured urban and rural "worlds" the possibility of African, or indeed of Brazilian or Indonesian freedom is concretized or made tangible in the form of specific historical movements. In like manner, in a neo-colonial context, it is when the globalised native puts at the local people's disposal the intellectual and technical capital that he or she snatched, that the dialectic force and counter-force is transcended in the reconstitution of a new ethos. This is the process – for Serequeberhan as for us – that appropriates the global possibilities of a specific local tradition from within the lived confines and concrete possibilities of that tradition itself. Again for Abouleish, as he reflected on himself as a young Egyptian doing his doctoral studies in Austria:

"During my studies, I noticed inner changes taking place within me. I became thoroughly involved with European culture, getting to know its music, studying its poetry and philosophy. Somebody looking into my soul would have seen anything "Egyptian" left completely behind, so I could absorb everything new. Because of my childhood and adolescent grounding in Egyptian culture, I could not leave such entirely behind. I now existed in two worlds, both of which were essentially different: the oriental, spiritual stream I was born into and the European, which I felt was my chosen course. But I was neither Egyptian nor European. I realised this particularly when I was experiencing art. For example I started hearing Händel's Messiah with Muslim ears as praise to Allah. The two differing worlds within me gradually began to dissolve and merge into a third entity, so I was neither completely one nor the other. What I experienced was not a cheap compromise, but an elevation, a real uniting of the two cultures within me." (11)

This lived self-formative ethos of the liberation struggle becomes the practice of freedom. This is the hermeneutical response to the emergent question: what are the people of Africa, or the Middle or Far East, trying to free themselves from and what are they trying to become? This brings us from Serequeberhan onto the work of the French postmodernist Foucault, about whom we shall hear much more in chapter 12.

The Liberation Struggle: Existence and Historicity

Michel Foucault (12), in characterising the focus of his philosophical thought, refers to liberty and liberation as being constituted by the reformative "practice of the self" on the self:

"When a colonial people tries to free itself from the coloniser, that is truly an act of liberation, in the strict sense of the world. But this act is not sufficient to establish the practices of liberty; later on it will be necessary for the people, this society and these individuals to decide upon receivable and acceptable forms of their existence or political society. That is why I insist on the "practice" of freedom."

As Foucault pointedly observes, *the struggle for freedom is indispensable for the practice of freedom, but it is not sufficient.* The question then is, how can one establish the practice or ethos of freedom in the process of liberating one's existence from external, direct or indirect, domination? The "practice of freedom" or liberty is grounded on and arises out of the reformative ethos of a people. This presupposes the liberation struggle as it unfolds within the context of specific and particular histories, and with it the concrete implementation, the practice, of liberty, which is the proclaimed raison d'être of the struggle in its very inception.

In his "Africa in Modern History" (13) the eminent historian on Africa, Basil Davidson, notes that the African countries that achieved independence in the late 1950's and early 1960's were, paradoxically, wedded to colonial attitudes and values. Old inequalities from the precolonial heritage were enlarged by the new inequalities of the colonial heritage. In contradistinction to the above, starting from the 1970's, a more radically democratic conception of liberation took root. In concrete and practical terms, the new liberation movements emerged out of the contrast between the miserable situation of post-colonial Africa and the empty status of "political" independence. They were grounded on the lived and stark comparison between unfulfilled ideals and unforgiving realities. In so emerging, in differing ways and out of the lived exigencies of differing African histories and specific contexts, such becoming served to articulate a notion of liberation as a process of reclaiming history. Such a dialectical notion draws as much on critical theory (chapter 9) as it does on hermeneutics.

Davidson points in this context to the theoretical perspective of Guinea-Bissau's Amilcar Cabral. The political parties initially formed in that country after independence were of and for the urban centre. Their point of reference was European theory and practice. Their basic objective was to transfer power from Europeans to Africans. In the process they were susceptible to the rationality of the coloniser. So, on the one hand, they were the mediating link between colonialism and neo-colonialism; on the other, they abstractly formulated the possibility of African freedom. In the process they suspected indigenous culture as being worthless. It was those who were closest to Europe who became leaders of the pack, and the political parties formed totally disregarded the rural native or indeed the "Lumpenproletariat", that is the coolie labour that inhabited the shantytowns.

The Urban-Rural Dynamic Fusion

The urban parties were not inserted in the lived needs and concerns that move and define the life of the rural native. And yet, in the meeting between those who come from the towns as globalised natives and local country dwellers as peasant or nomads, is the dynamic locus, out of which unfolds self-emancipation.

This approach is instead of a situation where the cities remain the centres of European mimicry and the interior is frozen, mummified and held back in stasis as the enclave of "ethnic cultures", that is as wildlife preserves, and ethnic "cultural" exhibitions yielding foreign exchange. The politics and economics that emanate from the centre are then geared towards Europe, cash crops complemented by Parliamentary "procedures" or socialist edicts of a one-party state.

Even the old colonial policy of divide and rule remains in place, for the Guinea Bissau philosopher and revolutionary Amilcar Cabral, in the 1960's the transfer of power " ...does not take place at the level of structures ... since that caste, the westernised African bourgeois has done nothing more than take over unchanged the legacy of the economy, the thought and the institutions left by the colonialists..."

Return to Source

Therefore, for Cabral, there is a need to return to source. Only when a rooting in history becomes a lived actuality at the grassroots level, through the establishment of local mass political institutions of people's power – peoples' assemblies, village associations and so forth – in which popular democracy is implemented, only in such a context is "the practice of freedom" possible. The struggle secures the support of the mass to the extent that it concretely involves the common folk at all levels, and in doing so helps them metamorphose themselves from inert, a-historical beings absent from history into active and emergent protagonists of their own existence. For Fanon:

"Their ears hear the true voice of the country, and their eyes take in the great and infinite poverty of their people."

This process of becoming does not come out of formal proclamations. It occurs out of cohabiting the same historical, political, and existential space. It occurs by osmosis and diffusion. It is in this concrete sense that the struggle at a fundamental level necessitates the radical reformation of traditional society. Colonialism "globally" petrifies the subjugated culture. This is the "local" state of affairs that needs to be overcome. To date the African liberation struggle has failed in its promise, for Serequeberhan, to reclaim the historicity of African existence.

Such a "return" is a cultural and political recovery of the oppressed historic possibilities in the existence of the colonised. The turning toward the "native mass" is the first moment in the fusion of the rural and the urban. The Westernised urban natives who join the anti-colonial eruption do so by rejecting their assimilation and successfully indigenise themselves into the historicity of their people. It is the moment of a historical and existential decision, at which point the *assimilado* begins the cultural and historical metamorphosis that will positively re-immerse him or herself into the local historicity of the indigenous folk. *The "return" is not a return to tradition or stasis. We are not engaged in an antiquarian quest for an already existing authentic past tradition. Rather, we are engaged in the affirmation by the exogenised native of the historicity of the rural indigenous mass.* For Cabral:

"Urban working classes discover at the grassroots the richness of their cultural values – philosophical, political, artistic, social and moral – and realise, not without astonishment, the richness of spirit, the capacity for reasoned discussion, the facility for understanding, on the part of population groups who were yesterday forgotten."

European values and skills are thus absorbed, in management as in agriculture, in development as in ecology, into a new synthesis, through this hermeneutic fusion of horizons, of self and other, of tradition and modernity, of indigenous and exogenous. This is possible because in embracing indigenous historicity the Westernized native purges himself of the Eurocentric frame that structures his consciousness. The "return" is thus a two-way process of cultural filtration and fertilisation. In this dialectic, European culture/history is recognized as a particular and specific disclosure of existence, aspects of which are retained or rejected in terms of the lived historicity and practical requirements of the history being reclaimed. The ossified African past – embodied in the rural native – is thus not preserved intact, but is cut and cast to fit the historic requirements of the struggle:

" ... the practice of democracy, of criticism and self-criticism, the increasing responsibility of peoples for the direction of their lives, literacy work, creation of schools and health services, training of cadres from peasant and worker backgrounds, and many other achievements ... "

Overall then, for Cabral, " ... the objectives must be at least the following: development of a popular culture and of all positive indigenous values; development of a national culture based on the history and achievements of the struggle itself; constant promotion of the political and moral awareness of the people to the cause of independence, justice, progress; *development of a scientific and technological culture based on a critical assimilation of man's achievement in science, art and literature ...*"

Ironically then, for Cabral and for Serequeberhan, a return to phenomenological origins (in Abram's terms) is called for, in the same way as, for your research question, you need to return to your source.

We finally now turn to an example of the deployment of hermeneutics, in this case the example of Zahra Al Zeera, a Muslim scholar.

8.5 Hermeneutics in Practice: Wholeness and Holiness in Education

8.5.1 Wholeness and Holiness in Education: An Islamic Perspective

Zahra Al Zeera, an educator and researcher based in Bahrain, who pursued her doctoral studies in Canada, introduces in her book on "Wholeness and Holiness in Education" (15) an approach to "transformative inquiry" as an alternative research method that emerges from the Islamic paradigm and leads, for her, to the creation of Islamic science on the one hand and inner self transformation on the other.

Owing to the positivist indoctrination at most universities, Muslim students she argues, like their non-Muslim counterparts, are following the mainstream as an easy and safe passage to their graduation. By doing so they waste the most precious years of their life doing research that neither advances Islamic knowledge nor increases self-awareness and the awakening of the soul. So Muslims are torn between the development of mind and soul. They are indirectly made to choose between the sacred that lies inside of them – invisible, silent and profound – and the secular demands of the modern mind. The more they feel fragmented the more they feel the pain of separation from their inner selves. Both positivist (reductionist) and constructivist (relativist) views are fragmentary.

The concept of transformation is not new; what is new for Al Zeera is the role of the sacred and the spiritual in research and inquiry. For her "social constructivism" is the back door leading to transformative inquiry. Hermeneutics, phenomenology and narrative inquiry can be characterized as such. The transformational perspective, is holistic and relational, viewing the world from a complementary perspective that accepts extremes. Reality, as such, is subjective and objective, real and ideal, material and spiritual. Transformation, or indeed renewal, occurs when a system is open and has dissipative structures where ideas, thoughts and feelings flow freely.

8.5.2 Renewal and Transformation

Instability is the key to transformation. The dissipation of energy creates the potential for sudden reordering. The greater the instability and variation in the society the more interactions occur. If the research methodologies we use allow for free and open interaction between ourselves and other researchers, as well as the situation we are studying, then transformation is more likely to happen. It embraces individual and society. It touches individual and collective consciousness.

A controlled and manipulative system allows energy to only flow hierarchically and in one direction; this consciously blocks all other directions and prevents a natural flow of energy. Thus transformation is prevented. So transformation is not acknowledged in a positivist paradigm because it causes instability and disturbance. Transformation occurs when elements, ideas, thoughts and feelings flow freely. Relationships suffer when there is fragmentation of knowledge since variables are controlled. However constructivism, for Al Zeera, is too open, allowing for a flow of energy in all directions.

Open systems accept a flow of energy in all directions and at all levels by the interaction between the inquirer and the situation, combining wholeness and relationships. A flow of conversation and open interviews promotes transformation. In constructivism the knower and the known are interactive and inseparable. There are no cause-effect laws but all entities are in a state of mutual simultaneous shaping. Elements interact dialectically. To have a transformative relationship you must be open and vulnerable. Although, for Al Zeera, the constructivist paradigm and interpretive research methods promote transformation at certain levels, the Islamic paradigm and transformational research methods have the capacity for a more coherent and comprehensive transformation. A holistic worldview must, in the end, draw all levels – personal, social, spiritual – into a coherent whole. This Islamic worldview transcends the dichotomy between mind and body, inner and outer, the creative dialogue ensuing thereby becoming a basis for creativity. She illustrates such through her own case story.

For Al Zeera, narrative inquiry, if practiced within the Islamic perspective, can illuminate the soul and awaken the inner self, giving us the courage to create and reconstruct our personal experiences, to go beyond the pain and the hurt, and transform such into higher qualities of acceptance, understanding, and submission to God's will. Narrative inquiry can be the first step on the long, spiritual journey, where we are in continual dialogue with our inner self, God and the "other". Any inquiry, regarded from an Islamic perspective, ought to be multileveled and multi-dimensional. Researchers have to be open and flexible, therefore, to operate within different inquiry methods so as to be able to capture the complexity of the phenomena. Whereas phenomenology deals with personal, subjective experiences, hermeneutics interprets the larger social context in which individual meaning is embedded. Here is Zahra's story.

8.5.3 Zahra's Self Transformation

The Starting Point

"Being a graduate student in the Department of Measurement, Evaluation and Computer Applications at the University of Toronto located me at the heart of the empire of figures and numbers. I have always been impressed by Western efficiency, so here I was. Yet what began to trouble me was the paradox in the superficiality of knowledge and the prevailing arrogance of computerized, pre-packaged designs. It is confining rather then liberating thinking."

The Stirring Point

"What troubled my soul, therefore, was the lack of appreciation for intellectuality, for genuine knowledge. The domination and control of hard data and computerized packages are a reflection of the predominant rule of economics and finance over cultural and liberal education. Educators changed their direction to accommodate the financial, industrial world instead of trying to affect change to make the outside world more humane. The paradoxical effect of disempowerment led me to seek an answer to this confusion. The result was an intellectual crisis and a rebellious researcher. I was led to understand Islamic theories and to try to bring them down from the ivory tower to meet practical educational needs. The first result was a term paper "The collapse of Westernized Universities in Islamic Societies". It was a turning point in my life, and I got to know many great Muslim philosophers. I was like a wanderer in a desert who, after a long search for a sip of water, found an oasis in the middle of the desert. For the first time I felt united with myself. The enjoyment came not only from reading the work of those great minds but also from enjoying the richness of the Arabic language.

The paper cited the causes of the decline of education in Muslim-Arab countries in recent times for external and internal reasons. External factors were colonization and modernization. Internal factors were the incongruity and lack of harmony between the original Islamic philosophies and the political, social and educational practice in Islamic countries. The result has been the disempowerment of countries that are dependent economically, intellectually, and even psychologically on their former colonizers. The West has become the standard against which everything is measured. During the summer of 1988 there was great pressure on the volcano inside of me. I was boiling with new ideas and old feelings. After intense reflection I found three landmarks that enriched me then and still now: 1) alternative research paradigms and interpretive research methods; 2) personal practical methods and narrative inquiry; 3) social knowledge and the Frankfurt school."

The Turning Point

"First, I was exposed to new research paradigms, rather than mere methods, and to the overall democratisation of research and learning. Second, I was introduced to personal practical knowledge, which mirrored my emerging ideas of wholeness, democracy, humanity and morality. Third, I did a course on language, power and learning which introduced me to Foucault, Habermas and others. What I came to realise was that my education in the Middle East and then in the West had caused a split in consciousness. Gradually the idea of wholeness began to take shape. In a letter I wrote to my thesis committee I said:

Since I was 17 I have been wandering the world, between the Middle East, Europe and North America, trying to understand myself and the world around me. Different value systems, different lifestyles, different languages … During my journey I suffered severely, from intellectual and spiritual shocks. Between one world and another something was missing, but I was not sure what. At last I came to realise, after a wide range of educational and work experiences, that the whole was missing. Reconciliation between the mind and the soul. Propositional knowledge – explicit – in mind, spiritual knowledge – tacit – in soul.

My thesis proposal, then, was about reconciliation between mind and soul. The journey for reconciliation started inside out. Reconciliation on a personal level was the first step. Personal development goes hand in hand with social development. In February, 1999, I wrote, again to the committee:

The dilemma of Islamic societies lies partly in the fact they imported secular educational systems and planted them into the heart of Islamic traditional societies. To me it is like planting a palm tree in Alaska and expecting it to grow naturally. The lack of harmony between peoples lives inside the university and out, and the conflict between the two extremes, the secular and the religious, confuses everybody. The materialism of the West pushed spirituality out of the curricula; the denial of freedom of speech in the East was a barrier to intellectual development.

Going back and forth between the two caused me immense pain. But from pain new branches grow; the confusion of pain caused me to search for the causes."

Answering Crucial Questions

"In the West I felt my spiritual freedom endangered. In the East my intellectual freedom. Did I have to give one up for the other? Why not keep both? Do we, as a non-Western society have to give up our culture and religion for the sake of economic development?

Eventually peace and harmony might come through communication, interaction, reflection and understanding. A breakthrough came when I saw myself as microcosm and Bahrain as macrocosm.

My life world is not my private world, but rather it is inter-subjective.

Many Muslim students I talked to equated Islamic with religious education. I realised I had to find a balance between scientific and religious education. I sought reconciliation rather than compromise, at a deeper level of understanding. Writing a paper in 1989, for the World Congress of Comparative Education, I said:

The goal of locating my study in hermeneutics is to increase the understanding of how the East and the West came to misunderstand each other. Being the child of East and West I had learnt to compare languages and cultures, histories and personalities. My two selves were in continuous dialogue, even conflict. Since hermeneutics involved dialogue, and dialectical interchange, I came to realise that my own dialectic would involve love rather than hate. I realised that my longstanding struggle was rooted in my feelings of insecurity that I might lose my Arabic/Eastern identity in the West .. hermeneutics is concerned with the interpretation of human products and experiences. The goal of such is understanding.

When the choice is made between two parts of one's being, soul and mind, the spiritual and the intellectual, the struggle is great."

Creating the Framework

"It was only after reading Balleche's 'Dialectical Thinking and Adult Development' that I was able to create a framework for my thesis. I was then able to find a secure home for my dispersed ideas. It was a relief to know that the pain, the conflict, the struggle, were stages in the dialectical thinker's development. The assurance came from Riegel: "Such conflicts and crises are not to be regarded as negative. The discordance and contradiction generated provide the sources of individual and societal change. The synchronous leaps of development are of seminal importance to both." (16) The concept of wholeness itself is dialectical."

Dialectical Thinking, Multidimensionality and Wholeness

Three factors contributed to my dialectical thinking: my bicultural upbringing (Arabic and Persian), diverse educational experiences in the East and West, and the interpretive methods of inquiry to which I had been exposed. I discovered gradually that I had an obsession with the idea of multi-dimensionality. I discovered that the pain of unfulfilment, intellectually and spiritually, was caused by the unidimensional approach to education and to measurement. Overall, moreover, I came to realise that the unidimensional imposition of intellectual and scientific imperialism, as well as political imperialism, imposed on the Middle East, had caused an explosion in my own psyche, as well as in the Muslim world at large. Freedom from intellectual imperialism was the empowerment I had sought and gained. As the Martiniquan poet and statesman Aime Cesaire said: "There are two ways of losing yourself: through fragmentation in the particular, or dilution in the universal".

We are now ready to conclude this chapter on interpretive research methodology.

8.6 Conclusion

Entering the Path of Renewal

You have now engaged in the second stage of your path of renewal that is following an interpretive course that unfolds out of your prior narrative. Your research question and the original storyline that follows emerge out of your questioned life world, and that of the other people and things in which you have chosen to immerse yourself through your research. Your own narrative, that of the profession or institution with which you are engaged, and that of your community or society, forms the developmental backdrop for this "eastern" journey or research path. Moreover, it is "eastern", not in the literal sense of being lodged in an Asian, or even Middle Eastern worldview, but that it lies on the eastern edge (German) of the western European world from both of which most conventionally research methodologies arise.

In other words, whereas Britain and France, and indeed Austria, have played a major part, as we shall see in later chapters, in the "western" and "northern" research paths, it is Germany which has played a leading role from both a northern and indeed also an "eastern" perspective. For both hermeneutics, and as will soon become apparent, critical theory, have been strongly influenced by Germany. For it is in Germany that historicism and holism have had a major part to play, in contrast with the empiricism and pragmatism of the "west". The fact that Germany also has a strong northern and rational side to it, not to mention the recent pragmatic influence from the west, does not preclude this otherwise eastern orientation.

Engaging with Reality

The task of the knowledge you pursue is not to recapitulate in the form of concepts that are given to you by the powers that be. It is rather to create an entirely new domain which, when taken together with the world presented through sense perception, yields for the first time full reality. Hence, you are not an idle onlooker before the pageant of the world; you are an active participant in a creative process.

In other words, you not only want to describe and thereby uncover what is really going on, beneath the surface, internally within yourself and externally in the world around you in the interactive field of your concern, but you want to transform it. You have come to recognize (phenomenologically so to speak) your real intentions. At this opening point, in your proposed research activity, you are called upon to describe such intentions, richly and intricately, qualitatively and poignantly, in relation to the field in which those intentions apply, for real. In other words, you are called upon to lay aside your prejudices, your preconceptions, you analytical frameworks, and enter into that world, immerse yourself in the phenomenon.

Overlaid with Personal Meaning and Social Significance

The challenge you ultimately face, is to conduct such an interpretive investigation in a way that has both social and cultural meaning as well as personal and spiritual significance. The topic grows out of an intense interest in a particular area, close to your nature and culture, while also reaching out to others. That interest is provoked, outside in, by the unfilled needs that you see around you, related to yourself, your profession and your society; it is also provoked inside out, by your own will, and intent, at this particular point of time. How then does such narrative "grounding" relate to what interpretively emerges from it?

Returning to your Original Storyline: As a Researcher-and-Innovator

In interpretive-hermeneutic terms, the originating of your research question involves uncovering an original story in each case, a return to source. Such a story will necessarily be authorised not only by yourself, as researcher, and by the research community around you, including you research supervisor, but also by one or more authoritative agencies – a business, a community, a professional body – with which you are engaging.

To reiterate in Gadamer's philosophical terms: what differentiates objective "methodological sterility" from genuine "inter-subjective" understanding, is your original imagination. Such imaginative, as opposed to merely analytical ability, involves seeing what is questionable and significant, in the state of yourself, your profession, your society, even the world, and formulating questions to pursue, to take the story on to an ultimately satisfactory conclusion. The precondition for such is that you are open to be questioned by the very field with which you are engaged, to be provoked to risk involvement in a dialogue that carries you imaginatively beyond the present position, towards a more desirable one that your research serves to instigate.

Transforming the Plot – As an Original Interpreter

The real meaning of a context you are seeking to evolve is always co-determined by the historical situation of yourself as a shared "original interpreter". Thus understanding is not an objective, analytical, reproductive procedure, but rather always a subjective-objective, imaginative and transformative one.

Further, and in the practical terms set by William Randall, you are in a position to re-construct not so much the events of your story, but rather the plots that underlie them. A new plot means a new story, and a new story leads to a new construction.

Thus, you critique the old plots by which your story has previously been lived and told, and experiment with new ones, and you thereby assume authority over your work and your life. As such, the originating of your research question, and the grounding of your prospective innovation, is the same thing as uncovering the plot. To begin with, you start out as a narrative researcher ... once upon a time ... returning to source.

Making effective History – As a would be Social Innovator

Finally, having then immersed yourself in a significant phenomenon, and having recognized the unfolding plot surrounding it, with a view to changing it, in Serequeberhan's terms:

" ... *the horizon of the past in the form of tradition, that is heritage, is always in motion. It is not historical consciousness that first sets the surrounding horizon in motion. But in this motion it becomes aware of itself. In its lived existence, each generation sees for itself its own-most possibilities out of the concerns of its own horizon. For the "motion" of a heritage becomes aware of itself only in concrete individuals and out of the horizon of their lives' self-awareness. For it is in the living and thinking of those who embrace it that a heritage – an "effective history" becomes aware of itself."* (16)

You, your organisation and your society embody that "effective history". To make history, though, you need to move from uncovering the plot, that is your plot and that of such an institution, and the surrounding community, in narrative terms.

We shall now turn from hermeneutics to critical theory, advancing further on the developmental and dialogical eastern path. For Habermas, the core exponent of critical theory still alive, hermeneutics is only one dimension of critical social theory. He criticized the conservatism of previous hermeneutics, especially Gadamer, because the focus on tradition seemed to undermine possibilities for social criticism and transformation.

Habermas and Gadamer, actually engaged in the 1960s in a famous debate over the possibility of transcending history and culture in order to find a truly objective position from which to criticize society. The debate was inconclusive, but marked the beginning of warm relations between the two men. It was Gadamer who secured

Habermas's first professorship in Heidelberg. Another attempt to engage the French Jacques Derrida to whom we shall turn later (chapter 12) proved less enlightening because the two thinkers had so little in common. After Gadamer's death, Derrida called their failure to find common ground one of the worst debacles of his life. Perhaps, our Integral Research framework serves to make this "common ground" more visible. We now turn from hermeneutis to critical theory, along the research path of renewal.

Bibliography

1) **Dilthey**, W. (1910). *The Understanding of Others and Their Manifestations of Life.*

2) **Gadamer**, H.-G. (1989). *Truth and Method.* London: Sheed and Ward.

3) **Gadamer**, H.-G. (1989). *Truth and Method.* London: Sheed and Ward.

4) **McLeod**, J. (2000). *Qualitative Research in Counselling and Psychotherapy.* London: Sage.

5) **Gergen**, K. (1994). *Toward Transformation in Social Knowledge.* London: Sage.

6) **Cushman**, P. (1995). *Reconstructing Self, Reconstructing America.* New York: Da Capo.

7) **Gadamer**, H. (1976). *Philosophical Hermeneutics.* Berkeley: University of California Press.

8) **Bell**, R. (2002). *Understanding African Philosophy.* London: Routledge.

9) **Serequeberhan**, T. (1999). *African Hermeneutics.* London: Routledge.

10) **Abouleish**, I. (2005). *Sekem – A Sustainable Community in the Desert.* Edinburgh: Floris.

11) **Abouleish**, I. (2005). *Sekem – A Sustainable Community in the Desert.* Edinburgh: Floris.

12) **Foucault**, M. (2002). *The Archaeology of Knowledge.* London: Routledge.

13) **Davidson**, B. (2001). *Africa in History.* London: Weidenfeld & Nicolson.

14) **Trompenaars**, F. & **Hampden-Turner**, C. (1998). *Riding the waves of culture.* 2nd Edition. New York: McGraw-Hill.

15) **Al Zeera**, Z. (2001). *Wholeness and Holiness in Education.* Leicester, UK: International Institute of Islamic Thought.

16) **Al Zeera**, Z. (2001). *Wholeness and Holiness in Education.* Leicester, UK: International Institute of Islamic Thought.

17) **Serequeberhan**, T. (2000). *Our Heritage.* Lanham: Rowan & Littlefield.

CHAPTER 9

FROM HERMENEUTICS TO
CRITICAL THEORY

"DEVELOP A DIALECTICAL ARGUMENT"

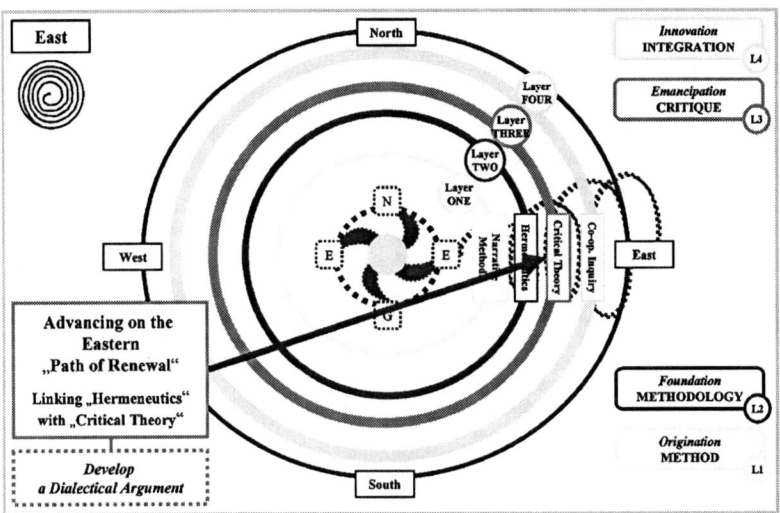

Figure 9.1: Overview Chapter 9 – Layer 3 / East

Summary: Critical Theory

- We shall now introduce critical theory, as we advance on the eastern path from foundation (methodology) to emancipation (critique). Criticial theory, in sociology and philosophy, was a label used by the Frankfurt School. As a term "critical theory" describes their collective work oriented toward radical social change.

- For the core thinkers of critical theory three aspects of their approach stand out: Firstly critical social theory should be directed at society in its historical specificity. Secondly, critical theory should improve understanding of society by integrating all the major social sciences, including economics, sociology, history, political science, anthropology, and psychology. Thirdly, it anticipated "postmodernity" in its orientation toward a post-capitalist, post-industrial, but non-communist world.

- Engaging in critical theory related research includes the rooting of the researcher in concrete experience, that the research issue arises out of problems of everyday life. Further such research needs to be strongly critical in orientation, uncover power relations, analyse the suffering of people, and focusing on promoting "liberation".

- The ways, in which we analyse and interpret information, for critical theorists, are conditioned both by the way our research is theoretically framed and also by your ideological assumptions as a researcher. Therefore research in the critical tradition takes the form of "self conscious criticism" in the sense that you try to become aware of the ideological presuppositions that inform your sense making.

- Further, facts never stand alone in social contexts; the objects of social science rather express precisely that they are part of such a context and need to be interpreted as such. In order to do so, according to Swedish social researchers Alvesson and Skoldberg, critical research methodology demands at least three sorts of theory, which need, to some extent at least, to be taken into account, which they term a "triple hermeneutcs", that is a) a hermeneutic understanding of history, language and meaning, b) a social theory of society as a totality, and c) a theory of the unconscious.

- As a result, critical theory should be simultaneously a critical engagement with the contemporary social world, a critical account of the historical and cultural conditions and a continuous critical re-examination of the constitutive categories and conceptual frameworks of your understanding.

- Whereas philosophers and researchers from the developed world, like Jürgen Habermas, tend to be transformative in words, those like Paulo Freire from the developing world tend to be so also in action.

- Freire is also the most prominent thinker within the tradition of critical theory who also applied the approach towards his immediate life world, based on personal experiences. Hence, as a case for this chapter, we introduce the astonishing case of Freire's activism in promoting literacy in Brazil.

- Critical theory provides the grounds for emancipation and thereby paves the way for the final more action oriented step in this Eastern path of renewal: democratically laden, transformatively oriented co-operative inquiry.

9.1 Orientation to Critical Theory

Origins and Meaning

Critical theory, historically, has taken on from where hermeneutics left off. Both born and bred in Germany, hermeneutics, through Schleiermacher, originated in the late nineteenth century, and critical theory in the early twentieth. Whereas the former emerged out of tradition, that is through the interpretation of religious texts, the latter heralded, at one and the same time, modernity and postmodernity.

Critical theory was a label used by the Frankfurt School. The "school" consisted of members of the Institute for Social Research of the University of Frankfurt in Germany, including their intellectual and social network. As a term "critical theory" describes their collective work oriented toward radical social change.

"Critical theory" was for the first time introduced by one of the Frankfurt School's founding members, Max Horkheimer. He defines it as *a social theory oriented toward critiquing and changing society as a whole, in contrast to traditional theory oriented only to understanding or explaining it.* Horkheimer characterized critical theory as a radical, emancipatory form of Marxian theory. As such he critiqued both the model of science put forward by logical positivism and what he and his colleagues saw as the covert positivism and authoritarianism of orthodox Marxism and communism.

The Term "Critique": Routed in Kant and Marx

The choice of the term "critical theory" was also partly influenced by its wanting to sound less politically controversial than "Marxism". However, in an intellectual context defined by dogmatic positivism on the one hand and "scientific socialism" on the other, critical theory meant to rehabilitate both, through its philosophically critical approach and revolutionary orientation.

Furthermore, critical theorists were explicitly connecting with the 18th century "critical philosophy" ("Critique of Pure Reason") of Immanuel Kant. For Kant the term "critique" meant philosophical reflection on the limits of claims made for certain kinds of knowledge. a direct connection between such critique and the emphasis on moral autonomy. We now turn to the core critical thinkers.

Core Thinkers – Core Concepts

Max Horkheimer, Theodor Adorno and Herbert Marcuse, all of them German and Jewish, became the most prominent thinkers of the Frankfurt School at its early stage, with Jürgen Habermas being the best known representative of the second generation. However, there are many other notable, first generation figures in critical theory, who are globally acclaimed, among them Erich Fromm, Paulo Freire and Walter Benjamin.

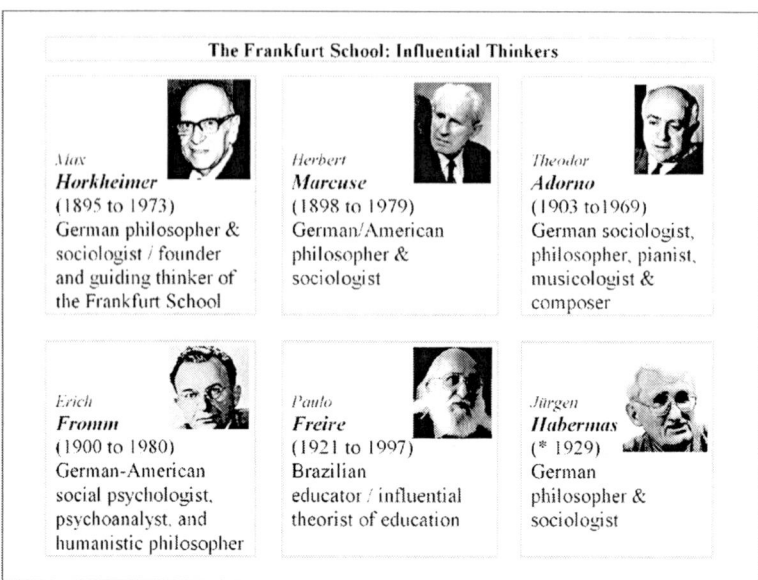

The Frankfurt School: Influential Thinkers

Max
Horkheimer
(1895 to 1973)
German philosopher &
sociologist / founder
and guiding thinker of
the Frankfurt School

Herbert
Marcuse
(1898 to 1979)
German/American
philosopher &
sociologist

Theodor
Adorno
(1903 to1969)
German sociologist,
philosopher, pianist,
musicologist &
composer

Erich
Fromm
(1900 to 1980)
German-American
social psychologist,
psychoanalyst, and
humanistic philosopher

Paulo
Freire
(1921 to 1997)
Brazilian
educator / influential
theorist of education

Jürgen
Habermas
(* 1929)
German
philosopher &
sociologist

Figure 9.2: Critical Theory – Core Thinkers

For all of these critical thinkers three aspects of their approach stand out. *Firstly* critical social theory should be directed at *society in its historical specificity* (that is how it came to be configured at a specific point in time). *Secondly*, critical theory should improve understanding of society by *integrating all the major social sciences*, including economics, sociology, history, political science, anthropology, and psychology. *Thirdly*, it anticipated "postmodernity" in its *orientation toward a post-capitalist, post-industrial, but non-communist world*. Interestingly enough, virtually all of the critical theorists were Jewish, and victims – hence their familiarity with what it means to be oppressed – from Nazi Germany. The one of the critical theorists, who is not Jewish and is still alive today, is Jürgen Habermas. The other, who recently died, and from whom we shall hear much more, is Brazil's Paulo Freire. That leads to the activist side of critical theory.

Political Activism: Marcuse and Habermas

Herbert Marcuse, in escaping from Nazi Germany, emigrated to the United States of America. Marcuse's critiques of capitalist society there (especially his 1955 synthesis of Marx and Freud, "Eros and Civilization", and his 1964 published "One-Dimensional Man") resonated with the concerns of the leftist student movement in the 1960s. Because of his willingness to speak at student protests, Marcuse soon became known as "the father of the New Left", a term he disliked and rejected.

Many radical scholars and activists, however, were influenced by him. Marcuse's 1965 essay "Repressive Tolerance", in which he claimed capitalist democracies can have totalitarian tendencies, has been strongly criticized by conservatives. Marcuse argues that *genuine tolerance does not tolerate support for repression,* since doing so ensures that marginalized voices will remain unheard. He characterizes tolerance of repressive speech as "inauthentic". Instead, he advocates a discriminating tolerance that does not allow repressive intolerance to be voiced.

In the 1960's, Habermas's critical theory conceptualized knowledge in terms that enabled human beings to emancipate themselves from forms of domination through self-reflection. As such he considered "psychoanalysis", including the psychology of the unconscious mind, as the paradigm of critical knowledge. This expanded considerably the scope of what counted as critical theory within the social sciences. Nowadays, the term "critical theory", in the sociological sense, is also used to loosely group all sorts of radical thought, including Michel Foucault, feminist theory and so on, that has in common the critique of domination.

Critical Theory and Literary Criticism

It is worth noting, finally, that in literature, literary criticism and so-called cultural studies, "critical theory" means something quite different. To use an epistemological distinction introduced by Jürgen Habermas in 1968 in his "Erkenntnis und Interesse" ("Knowledge and Human Interests"), critical theory in literary studies is ultimately a form of hermeneutics, with a view to understanding the meaning of human texts and symbolic expressions. Critical social theory in the social sciences is, in contrast, a form of self-reflective knowledge involving both understanding and theoretical explanation to reduce the chance of our being trapped in systems of domination or dependence.

From the 1960s and 1970s onward, language, symbolism, text, and meaning became foundational to theory in the humanities and social sciences, through the influences of such leading philosophical lights as Ludwig Wittgenstein, Ferdinand de Saussure, George Herbert Mead, Noam Chomsky, Hans-Georg Gadamer, Jacques Derrida. These also linked up with other thinkers in such emerging displines as linguistic and analytic philosophy, structural linguistics, symbolic interactionism, hermeneutics, semiology, linguistically oriented psychoanalysis and deconstruction. When, in the 1970s and 1980s, Jürgen Habermas also redefined critical social theory as a theory of communication, the two versions of critical theory began to overlap or intertwine to a much greater degree than before.

We now introduce, more systematically, seven key tenets of critical theory.

9.2 Critical Theory – Key Tenets

Critical Theory – Key Tenets
① As a critical theorist, your research is rooted in concrete experience.
② It arises out of the problems of everyday life.
③ Critical theory is strongly emancipatory in orientation.
④ Critical theory uncovers power relations.
⑤ You analyse specifically the suffering of people.
⑥ Reality is regarded as socially constructed and multiple interconnections exist.
⑦ Critical theory is explicitly focused on promoting "liberation".

① As a critical theorist, your research is rooted in concrete experience

Critical theory is clearly rooted in concrete experience, explicitly conceived with the practical intention of overcoming felt dissatisfaction.

② It arises out of the problems of everyday life

Critical theory arises out of the problems of everyday life, and is constructed with an eye towards solving them; it offers a way out of an untenable situation

③ Critical theory is strongly emancipatory in orientation

Critical theory is ultimately based on an emancipatory interest in achieving rational autonomy of action freed from domination. This orientation includes the conviction that the search for the truth must be tolerant of ambiguity and pluralism.

④ Critical theory uncovers power relations

Uncovering hidden power relations, critical theory engages in the critical interpretation of unconscious processes, ideologies, power relations, and other expressions of dominance of one group of interests over others.

⑤ You analyse specifically the suffering of people

Critical theory names the people for whom it is directed; it analyses their suffering; it offers enlightenment to them about what their real needs and wants are.

⑥ Reality is regarded as socially constructed and multiple interconnections exist

Critical theory assumes, that social and cultural reality are constructed and already pre-interpreted by the participants, and can be changed over time. The process for understanding this socially constructed reality is dialogic; it allows individuals to communicate about their experience within a shared framework of cultural meanings.

As such, critical theory is also a critical and dialectical account of underlying historical and cultural conditions.

⑦ **Critical theory is explicitly focused on promoting "liberation"**

Critical theory is partially determined by whether those for whom it is written recognize it as a way out and act on those principles

Such a critical methodology is initially formed by narrative methods, is ultimately co-operative, and in between is oriented towards historical emergence, and, hence, to consciousness raising and to liberation. We can immediately see, retrospectively, that Sereqeberhan's African Hermeneutics combines interpretevism with critical theory (compare with chapter 8). Critical theory is concerned with the analysis of the current situation, which enables us to understand how it has developed; such analysis *liberates us from seeing the current order as the natural order of things.*

We turn now from these key tenets to a more in depth study of critical theory. We start with critical cooperation and participation, which serves to illustrate how critical methodologies, like critical theory, ultimately serve to connect our separate research paths.

9.3 Critical Theory in Depth

9.3.1 Leading to Cooperation and Participation

Two approaches towards ultimately cooperative and participative research, are highlighted by critical theorists: co-operative inquiry and participatory action research.

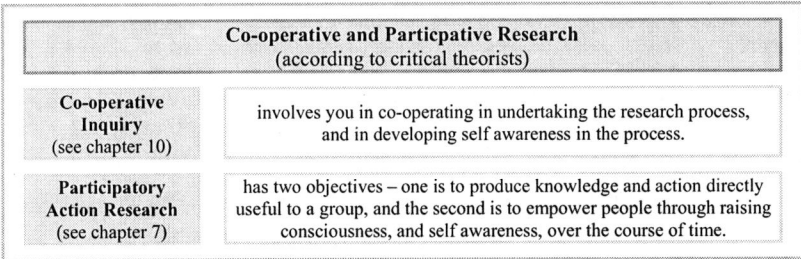

Co-operative and Particpative Research (according to critical theorists)	
Co-operative Inquiry (see chapter 10)	involves you in co-operating in undertaking the research process, and in developing self awareness in the process.
Participatory Action Research (see chapter 7)	has two objectives – one is to produce knowledge and action directly useful to a group, and the second is to empower people through raising consciousness, and self awareness, over the course of time.

Fundamental to these approaches is that the research makes a difference to individuals' experience and that those who are being researched play an active role in the evolving process, rather than being passive subjects. Critical theory is also explicitly value laden in its approach, and geared towards "surfacing" such underlying values and ideologies.

9.3.2 Affirming an Emancipatory Orientation

The ways, in which we analyse and interpret information, for critical theorists, are conditioned both by the way our research is theoretically framed and also by your ideological assumptions as a researcher. Therefore *research in the critical tradition takes the form of "self conscious criticism"* in the sense that you try to become aware of the ideological presuppositions that inform your sense making. Such developing self-awareness emerges interpretively with a narrative identification of your unfolding storyline, alongside that of your society. Validity, in the context of critical theory is associated with:

- The credibility of *portrayals of constructed realities* whereby constructions are deemed plausible to those who constructed them
- *Anticipatory accommodation* serving to accommodate the unique aspects of what you perceive in new contexts
- *Catalytic validity* involving the degree to which research moves those you study to understand the world and the way it is shaped so as to transform it.

Critical theory counteracts empirical research. As a critical theorist you reject the idea of theory-neutral observational language, showing instead that values and interests underpin your knowledge. This will be picked up when we consider co-operative inquiry (chapter 10) later.

9.3.3 Counteracting Empirical Research

Critical theory inspires consideration of a broader context than the more singular, conventional approaches to research methodology, such as empiricism. *The relation between the specific object of cultural critique,* for example the role of capital in business and society, *and the whole historical and social context, is the key issue for critical theory.* It then becomes natural to adopt a freer range in which imagination, creativity and your own evolving insights, together with your analytical and interpretive capabilities, can be called upon.

The focus shifts away from empirical research towards the interpretation and reasoned appraisal of such empirical material. In that respect critical theory is similar to hermeneutics, but it is also further complemented by critical emancipatory observations, as we saw with Serequeberhan, and interpretations of the surrounding societal context. In other words, the storyline that you uncover and evolve has much stronger socio-political overtones than in the purely interpretive case.

If the respondents in an in-depth interview on leadership, maintain, for instance, that: "leadership is important in the workplace", how do you interpret such a response? Do you infer that leadership is necessarily important, or is it merely important for these respondents? In other words, have they have adopted the "leadership ideology", that is of the heroic individual leader or entrepreneur, propounded in prodigious amounts of recent popular literature? It may seem interesting enough that people hold this view, but it might be more important to find out what this view means, where it comes from and what the consequences may be? Perhaps it is just a "semi-deep" notion that could easily change under different circumstances, or is it so deeply rooted in that it has the effect of a quasi-natural position for the people concerned? Perhaps there is a natural law that states that most people are dependent on their leaders?

Facts never stand alone in social contexts researched by critical theorists; the objects of social science rather express precisely that they are part of such a context and need to be interpreted as such. (4)

How then do we probe beneath the surface of such things?

9.3.4 Self Reflection: Towards a Triple Hermeneutics

Critical research methodology, for the Swedish social researchers Alvesson and Skoldberg (5), demands at least three sorts of theory, which need, to some extent at least, to be taken into account, altogether drawing upon an in depth, self reflexive interpretive orientation, which they term a "triple hermeneutcs", that is:

- a hermeneutic understanding of *history, language and meaning*,
- a social theory of *society as a totality*, and
- a theory of *the unconscious*.

In fact, Eritrea's Serequeberhan, as we have seen, quotes extensively from Franz Fanon – the Martiniquan born activist in Algeria during its liberation war – who was a psychiatrist and thereby active interpreter of the coloniser's unconscious, not to mention that of the colonised. To this may be added an anthropological theory or form of understanding, pointing at the relativity of cultural meanings, something that the Senegalese poet-statesman Leopold Senghor often highlighted.

All of these do not replace the need for specific theories associated with the areas to be researched. Some critical researchers, like the critical realists as we shall see in chapter 15, distinguish between surface and deep structures. Surface structure is where individuals lead their conscious lives, where things are natural and existence is (or can be made to be) rational and comprehensible. Deep structure is here taken to refer to those unquestioned beliefs and values upon which the taken-for-granted surface structure rests.

The aim for the critical emancipatory researcher is to be able to identify this deep structure, and in particular such beliefs and values as give rise to "frozen" social institutions and "locked" thought and action. It is in that specific sense, for Alvesson, that critical theory can be described as a kind of "triple hermeneutics":

Critical Theory as Triple Hermeneutics	
Single hermeneutics	Single hermeneutics concerns individuals' interpretations of themselves and their own inter-subjective (cultural) reality, and *the meaning they assign* to this.
Double hermeneutics	Double hermeneutics is what interpretive social scientists are engaged in, when they attempt to *understand and develop knowledge about this reality.*
Triple hermeneutics	Triple hermeneutics of critical theory includes a third element. This encompasses the critical *interpretation of unconscious processes, ideologies, power relations*, and other expressions of dominance of one group of interests over others, within the forms of understanding that appear to be spontaneously generated.

Four broad themes are then integral to critical theory (6):

- *social construction*: an emphasis, as is the case for hermeneutics and phenomenology, on the social construction of reality
- *power and ideology*: a focus on issues of power and ideology, whereby there is an awareness that social constructions are influenced by these
- *multiple interconnections*: the need to understand any social or organisational phenomenon in interdisciplinary terms, that is of its multiple interconnections and location within holistic historical contexts
- *social praxis*: the importance of praxis, that is the ongoing construction of social arrangements that are conducive to the flourishing of the human condition.

As a result, *critical theory should be seen as an interpenetrating body of work*, which demands and produces three particular things:

- *a critical engagement with your contemporary social world*, recognising that the existing state of affairs does not exhaust all possibilities and offering positive implications for social action
- *a critical account of the historical and cultural conditions* on which your own intellectual activity depends
- *a continuous critical re-examination of the constitutive categories and conceptual frameworks* of your understanding, including your historical and dialectical construction of these as a critical confrontation with other works of social explanation.

Where then, in conclusion, does critical theory fit, overall, in our path of renewal?

9.3.5 A Dialectical and Cognitive Approach to Interdisciplinary Development

The ontology (7) adopted by critical theory has much in common with phenomenology and interpretevism – in that both natural and social realities are seen to be socially constructed. However, *it places its pre-emphasis on cognitive interests*. Specifically established in Germany in the 1930's, it *builds epistemologically on European intellectual traditions*. This involves the idea that reason is the highest potentiality of human beings and that, through its use, it is possible to criticise and challenge the nature of existing societies.

Knowledge stemming from sociology, psychoanalysis, philosophy, economics and aesthetics has been combined here in a unique social science environment. The early critical theorists who emigrated from Germany to America in the Nazi period *regarded capitalist society as fundamentally irrational in that it failed to satisfy existing wants, from a humanist perspective, and produced false wants and needs*. As such, the critical theorists departed radically from the liberal market perspective of Locke and Mill, and were also more anti-establishment – in their views – than Popper, with his market based, democratic "open society".

The idea for the critical theorists, is that *social phenomena are best described as changeable elements in a dialectical social development, and are to be understood as an emergent process of becoming*. Statements about society cannot be impartial. Rather they tend to confirm or challenge existing social institutions and establish modes of thought. According to the Frankfurt School, *social science should strive to develop an independent and critical stance vis-a-vis these institutions and modes of thought,* and should call attention to the contradictions in the way society functions. The inherent restrictions and irrationalities that inform modern capitalist societies should be among the major subjects of research. From this perspective, the social sciences are doing the business world, today, a disservice by helping it to enhance its "bottom line" performance.

Whereas social scientists like Elton Mayo and Chris Argyris in the U.S., in the forties and fifties, adopted a critical-emancipatory line, their counterparts today tend to tow the conventional party line. Important sources of inspiration for critical theory, meanwhile, had been Germany's Marx, Weber, Kant, Hegel and Austria's Sigmund Freud. At the same time the school was also powerfully affected by the current political climate in Germany, in the 1920's and 1930's, and the development of authoritarian Stalinism in the Soviet Union. The critical theorist and social psychologist Erich Fromm, for example, emphasized that people's desire to subordinate themselves in authoritarian relationships and ideologies was a mechanism for avoiding the anxiety that freedom and independence can engender.

Now we turn to the overall significance of critical theory in our current day and age, not only in Europe and America (north-west) but also in developing societies (south-east)?

9.4 Global Variations: Critical Theory as Transformative Social Change

9.4.1 Communicative Foundations by Jürgen Habermas

From Monologic to Dialogic ...

Critical theory's two leading contemporary exponents are Germany's academic and social philosopher Jürgen Habermas (developed world), and Brazil's pedagogue and policy maker, the late Paulo Freire (developing world). Whereas philosophers and researchers from the developed world, like Habermas, tend to be transformative in words, those like Freire from the developed world tend to be so also in action. Habermas' intellectual roots were in hermeneutics, and like Gadamer, he claimed that the respective subject matters of the natural and social sciences were completely different. He described *the natural sciences as using "sense experience" and the social and cultural or hermeneutic sciences as using "communicative experience"*. Following Husserl, Habermas today accepts the same two central premises as those adopted by phenomenology and hermeneutics:

- Social and cultural reality is already pre-interpreted by the participants as a cultural symbolic meaning system, which can be changed over time.
- The process for understanding this socially constructed reality is dialogic; it allows individuals to communicate about their experience within a shared framework of cultural meanings.

... and from Empirical-Analytical to Critical-Emancipatory

Alternatively, in the natural sciences and in management science, the process is "monologic"; involving the technical manipulation by the researcher of some aspect of physical or human nature. One of the central concepts in Habermas' understanding of knowledge, is in relation to what he terms *"knowledge-constitutive interests"*. These interests, he argued, *determine what counts as the objects of knowledge.* Habermas therefore classified the processes of scientific enquiry into three categories (8), the first two, in our terms being normative, and the third transformative in orientation:

Process of Scientifc Inquiry Categories according to Habermas	
① The **empirical-analytical sciences**, including the natural sciences, economics, sociology and political science, are interested in *technically exploitable knowledge, in prediction and control*, increasing the possibility of human domination over nature and social relations.	⇨ **Focus on work**
② The **historical-hermeneutical sciences** are based on the practical interest in promoting communicative *understanding between individuals and within and between social groups*, including language and art.	⇨ **Focus on interaction**
③ **Critical Theory** involves self-reflection, and is ultimately based on an emancipatory interest in *achieving rational autonomy of action freed from domination.*	⇨ **Focus on the exercise and abuses of power**

9.4.2 From Germany's Jürgen Habermas to Brazil's Paulo Freire

The Practice of Freedom: Conscientisation

We now turn from the European Habermas to the prominent Latin American critical theorist of our day and age: Paulo Freire. A Brazilian by birth, he spent much of his adult life as an exile from his native land in Chile, and also as Fellow and Visiting Professor at Harvard. Freire was one of the twentieth century's greatest thinkers on education. Overtly transformational in his approach, he operated on one basic assumption:

"... man's ontological vocation is to be a subject who acts upon and transforms the world, and in so doing moves toward ever newer possibilities of fuller and richer life individually and collectively. This "world" to which he relates is not a static and closed order, a given reality which man must accept and to which he must adjust; rather, it is a problem to be worked on and solved. It is material used by man to create history, a task which he performs as he overcomes that which is dehumanizing at any particular time and place and dares to create the qualitatively new." (9)

For Freire, the resources for that task at the present time are provided by the advanced technology of the western world, but the social vision, which impels us to negate the present order and demonstrate that history has not ended, comes primarily from the suffering and struggle of the people of the Third World. Education either functions as an instrument, which is used to facilitate the integration of the younger generation into the logic of the present system and bring about conformity to it, or to become "the practice of freedom", the means by which men and women deal critically and creatively with reality and discover how to participate in the transformation of their world.

Freire's pedagogical theory and practice – for North and South American educators Morrow and Torres (10) – presupposes something like Habermas' threefold account of knowledge interests, but expresses them in more actively transformational terms:

Core Implications of Freire's Pedagogy (according to Morrow and Torres)
Technology, as a form of empirical-analytical knowledge is indispensable for the purpose of fulfilling basic human needs.
Hermeneutic-historical interpretation is the basis for discovering cultural themes necessary for establishing subject-object communication.
Critical insight is required for the movement toward critical consciousness – conscientization – that transforms reality.

Freire's epistemology, like that of Habermas, is also based on a *distinction between two rationalities of action*: first, "manipulative strategies" that treat people as objects to be technically controlled; and second, "dialogical relations" in which there is subject-subject co-participation and mutual learning. In Habermas' work this is elaborated in terms of two forms of rationality: "strategic rationality and communicative action".

For Freire and Habermas, human history reveals a constant struggle for democratisation and the realisation of individual autonomy that is linked to the dialogical and developmental nature of the human subject. For both, however, there is a *problematic relationship between instrumental rationalisation, understood as one sided economic modernisation, and social rationalisation as manifest in authentic democratisation and individuation.* For Freire there is the assumption that within the "culture of silence" there are accumulated experiences, which potentially can take the form of critical knowledge through processes of dialogical learning.

Four types of anti-dialogical actions are identified as mechanisms of hegemony that form a culture of silence:

① "conquest", involving relations of domination and subordination;

② "divide and rule", based on a "focalised" view of problems, rather than seeing the totality;

③ "manipulation" through communicative distortions;

④ "cultural invasion" by directly penetrating the cultural contexts of groups, imposing a view of the world that deprives subordinate groups of any sense of alternative possibilities.

Conscientizacao and Dialogic Praxis

How then can learners escape the "culture of silence", take steps towards critical consciousness, and enter into authentic dialogue? The Portuguese word "conscientizacao", popularised by Freire for educational environments, has been translated into "conscientization" in English. It is a way of reading how society works. This deeper reading of reality is revealed through praxis, identified with cultural action for freedom, whereby the subject finds the ability to grasp, in critical terms, the dialectical unity between self and object. The crucial psychological process required is that of using new forms of language to get "distance" from taken-for-granted realities of everyday life. The revelatory processes unleashed through conscientization are not only cognitive, but also ethical, in evaluating the consequences of domination:

"When we live our lives with the authenticity demanded by the practice of teaching that is also learning, and learning that is also teaching, we are participating in a total experience that is simultaneously directive, political, ideological, gnostic, pedagogical, aesthetic, and ethical. In this experience the beautiful, the decent, and the serious form a circle with hands joined. At the same time, in the context of true learning, the learners will be engaged in a continuous transformation through which they become authentic subjects of the construction and reconstruction of what is taught, side by side with the teacher, who is equally subject to the same process ... I believe that all educational practice requires the existence of "subjects" who, while teaching, learn. And who in learning also teach. The reciprocal learning between teachers and students is what gives educational practice its gnostic character. It is a practice that involves the use of methods, techniques, materials; in its directive character, it implies dreams, utopias, ideas, objectives. Hence we have the political nature of education." (11)

We shall see, later in chapter 10, the similarities and differences between Brazil's Paulo Freire and U.K.'s John Heron, both inspired by critical theory in their educational and political orientations. We end with Freire's five principles of moral philosophy:

A Transformative Approach to Research and Education (based on Freire's Five Principles of Moral Philosophy)	
①	People ought to pursue their ontological vocation of becoming more fully human, through engaging in critical, dialogical praxis.
②	No person or group of people ought to knowingly constrain or prevent another person or group from pursuing their vocation.
③	We ought – collectively and dialogically – to consider what kind of world, including social structures, processes and relationships, would be necessary for all to pursue their humanization.
④	All people ought to act to transform existing structures where critical reflection reveals that these structures serve as impediments.
⑤	Educators and others who assume positions of responsibility in the social sphere ought to side with the oppressed in seeking to promote a better world through their activities.

We now turn, finally, to the practice of critical theory, as illustrated by Paulo Freire.

9.5 Critical Theory in Practice: Paolo Freire's Reflective Activism

Paulo Freire is certainly the most prominent thinker within the tradition of critical theory who also applied the approach towards his immediate life world. In order to understand Freire's work it is important to see him in his own context.

Freire's Context: Pedagogy of the Opressed

Born in 1921 to middle class parents in Recife, Brazil, Freire knew poverty and hunger during the 1929 Great Depression, an experience that would shape his concerns for the poor and would help to construct his particular educational viewpoint.

Freire entered the University of Recife in 1943, enrolling in the Faculty of Law, but also studying philosophy and the psychology of language. Following his entrance into the legal bar, he never actually practised law and instead worked as a teacher in secondary schools teaching Portuguese. In 1944, he married Elza Maia Costa de Oliveira, a fellow teacher. The two had five children and worked together for the rest of her life. In 1946, Freire was appointed Director of the Department of Education and Culture of the Social Service in the State of Pernambuco, the Brazilian state of which Recife is the capital. Working primarily among the illiterate poor, Freire began to embrace a non-orthodox form of what could be considered liberation theology. In Brazil at that time, literacy was a requirement for voting in presidential elections.

In 1961, he was appointed director of the Department of Cultural Extension of Recife University, and in 1962 he had the first opportunity for significant application of his theories, when 300 sugarcane workers were taught to read and write in just 45 days. In response to this experiment, the Brazilian government approved the creation of thousands of cultural circles across the country. In 1964, a military coup put an end to that effort, Freire was imprisoned as a traitor for 70 days. After a brief exile in Bolivia, Freire worked in Chile for five years for the Christian Democratic Agrarian Reform Movement and the Food and Agriculture Organisation of the United Nations.

In 1967, Freire published his first book, "Education as the Practice of Freedom". The book was well received, and Freire was offered a visiting professorship at Harvard University in 1969. The previous year, he wrote his most famous book, "Pedagogy of the Oppressed", which was published also in Spanish and English in 1970. Because of the political feud between the successive authoritarian military dictatorships and the Christian socialist Freire, it wasn't published in Brazil until 1974, when General Ernesto Geisel took control of Brazil and began his process of cultural liberalisation. After a year in Cambridge, USA, Freire moved to Geneva, Switzerland to work as a special education adviser to the World Council of Churches. During this time Freire acted as an advisor on education reform in former Portuguese colonies in Africa, particularly Guinea Bissau and Mozambique.

In 1979, he was able to return to Brazil, and moved back in 1980. Freire joined the Workers' Party (PT) in the city of São Paulo, and acted as a supervisor for its adult literacy project from 1980 to 1986. When the PT prevailed in the municipal elections in 1988, Freire was appointed Secretary of Education for São Paulo. Freire died of heart failure in 1997.

The following case describing Freire's work is taken from "Literacy: Reading the Word and the World" by Paulo Freire and Donaldo Macedo. (12)

Imagining a Changed World

A dialectical exchange: Language for Freire, is not merely a means to a literate end, but it assures the power of envisaging things: because we can name the world and thus hold it in mind, we can reflect on its meaning and imagine a changed world. Language is the means to critical consciousness, which, in turn, is the means of conceiving change and of making choices to bring about further transformations. Thus, naming the world transforms reality from "things" in the present moment to activities in response to situations, processes, to becoming. Liberation comes only when people reclaim their language and, with it, the power to envision their future, the imagination of a different world to be brought into being.

Instead then of education as extension – a reaching out to students with valuable ideas we want to share – there must be a dialogue, a dialectical exchange in which ideas take shape and change as the learners in the Culture Circle think about their thinking and interpret their interpretations. The dichotomy of the "affective" and the "cognitive" plays no part in Freire's pedagogy, important as it is in American educational theory. He sees thinking and feeling, along with action, as aspects of all that we do in making sense of the world. In summary, the basic themes of Freire's ongoing literacy campaign, over the course of his life, were:

- comprehension of the work process and the productive act in its complexity
- ways to organise and develop production
- the need for technical training, though not reduced to narrow specialization
- comprehension of culture and its role, not only in the process of liberation, but also in national reconstruction
- problems of cultural identity, whose defense should not mean the ingenious rejection of other cultures' contributions

What if … the power to dream?: Criticism for Freire always means interpreting one's interpretations, reconsidering contexts, tolerating ambiguities so that we can learn from the attempt to resolve them. By thus representing the power to envisage – "What if … How could it be if … – language provides the model of social transformation. Dreams are formed by a critical and inventive imagination, exercised in dialogue, in the naming and renaming of the world, which guides its remaking. The lecture, in that context, is a late medieval invention instituted because books were scarce. In its stead Freire is saying: "there is no way to transformation, transformation is the way".

The Pedagogy of Political Empowerment

Language and transformation: Central to Freire's approach to literacy, is a dialectical relationship between human beings and the world, on the one hand, and language and transformative agency, on the other. Within this perspective, literacy is not merely approached as a technical skill to be acquired, but as a necessary foundation for cultural action for freedom, a central aspect of what it means to be a self and a socially constituted agent. In this sense, literacy is fundamental to aggressively constructing one's voice as part of a wider project of possibility and empowerment.

To be able to name one's experience is part of what it means to "read" the world and to begin to understand the political nature of the limits and possibilities that make up the larger society. Language is the "real stuff" of culture, and constitutes both a terrain of domination and a field of possibility. Critical literacy is both a narrative for agency as well as a referent for critique. As a narrative for agency, literacy becomes synonymous with an attempt to rescue history, experience and envision from conventional discourse and dominant social relations. It means developing the theoretical and practical conditions through which human beings can locate themselves in their own histories, and in doing so make themselves present as agents in the struggle to expand the possibilities of human life and freedom.

To be literate is not merely to be free, it is to be present and active in the struggle for reclaiming one's voice, history and future. That includes a view of human agency in which the production of meaning takes place in the dialogue and interaction that mutually constitute the dialectical relationship between human subjectivities and the objective world. Such a pedagogy of empowerment needs to be centered in a social project aimed at the enhancement of human possibility.

Production of knowledge as a developmental and relational act: Hence, the production of knowledge is both a developmental and a relational act. For teachers this means being sensitive to the actual historical, social and cultural conditions that contribute to the forms of knowledge and meaning the students bring to school. In its more radical sense critical literacy means making one's self present as part of a moral and political project that links the production of meaning to the possibility for human agency, democratic community, and transformative social action. As used here, history means recognizing the traces of untapped potentialities as well as sources of suffering that constitute one's past. To define literacy in the Freirean sense as a critical reading of the world and the word is to lay the theoretical groundwork for more fully analyzing how knowledge is produced and subjectivities constructed within relations of interaction. As such teachers and students attempt to make themselves present as active authors of their own worlds.

A curriculum itself represents a narrative or voice, one that is multilayered and often contradictory but also situated within relations of power that more often than not favor white, male, middle class, English-speaking students. What this suggests for a theory of critical literacy is that curriculum in the most fundamental sense is a battleground over whose form of knowledge, history, vision, culture, language and authority will prevail as a legitimate object of learning and analysis.

The importance of the act of reading: Language and reality are, for Freire, dynamically interconnected. The understanding attained by critical reading of a text implies perceiving the relationships between text and context. Freire describes his birthplace in Recife, Brazil. The trees that surrounded him felt like persons, such was the intimacy established. Animals were equally part of that context – the way the family cats rubbed against his legs, their mewing of entreaty or anger. Part of the context of his immediate world was also the language universe of his elders, expressing their beliefs, tastes, fears and values, which linked his world to a wider one whose existence he could not even suspect. Hence, reading a word, a phrase, a sentence never entailed a break with reading the world. Reading the word meant reading the word-world.

Freire always saw teaching adults to read and write as a political act, an act of knowledge, and therefore a creative act. The student then becomes the subject of a process of learning to read and write, as an act of knowing and creating. Reading the world always precedes reading the word, and reading the word implies continually reading the world. However, we can go further and say that reading the word is not preceded merely by reading the world, but by a certain way of writing or rewriting it, that is of transforming it by means of conscious, practical work.

Words, for Freire, should be laden with the meaning of the people's existential experience, and not of the teacher's experience. Surveying the word universe thus gives us the people's words, pregnant with the world, words from the people's reading of the world. We then give the words back to the people inserted in what Freire calls "codifications", pictures representing real situations. Decodifying or reading the situations pictured leads them to a critical perception of the meaning of culture by leading them to understand how human practice or work transforms the world. To sum up, reading always involves critical perception, interpretation, and rewriting of what is read.

Education models souls and re-creates hearts as a fulcrum for change: To impose on people one's own understanding in the name of their liberation is to accept authoritarian solutions as ways of freedom. But to assume the naiveté of those becoming educated demands from educators a most necessary humility to assume also their ability to criticize, thus overcoming, our naiveté as well.

The neutrality of education, which results in being understood as a pure task, to serve in the formation of an ideal type of human being, disembodied from what is real, virtuous and good, is one of the most fundamental connotations of the naïve visions of education. From the point of view of such a vision, the world is reborn in the intimacy of consciences, moved by the goodness of hearts. And since education models souls and re-creates hearts, it is the fulcrum of social change. Conversely from the authoritarian, elitist, reactionary point of view, the people's incompetence is almost natural. The people need to be defended because they are incapable of thinking clearly, of abstracting, knowing and creating; they are eternally "of lesser value" and their ideas are permanently labeled exotic. Popular knowledge does not exist. The notion of emancipatory literacy, for Freire, suggests two dimensions. On the one hand, students have to become literate about their histories, experiences, and the culture of their immediate environments. On the other hand, they must also appropriate those codes and cultures of the dominant spheres so they can transcend their own environments. There is often an enormous tension between those two dimensions of literacy.

For Freire, the consciousness of the world is constituted in relation to the world. The world enables you to constitute the self in relation to it. The transformation of objective reality, in other words the "writing of reality", represents precisely the starting point where the animal that became human began to write history. It started when these animals began to use their hands differently. As this transformation was taking place, the consciousness of the "touched" world was constituting itself. It is precisely this consciousness, touched and transformed, that bred the consciousness of the self.

For a long time these beings, who were making themselves, wrote the world much more than they spoke it. They directly touched and affected the world before they talked about it. Sometime later, these beings began to speak about their transformed world. After another long period of time they began to register graphically the talk about the transformation. Before learners attempt to learn how to read and write, therefore, they need to read and write the world. They need to comprehend the world that involves talk about the world. The reinvention of power that passes through the reinvention of production, therefore, would entail the reinvention of culture, within which environments would be created to incorporate, in a participatory way, all those discourses that are presently suffocated by the dominant discourse. The legitimation of these different discourses would authenticate the plurality of voices in the reconstruction of a truly democratic society. Human agency, finally, makes sense and flourishes only when subjectivity is understood in its dialectical, contradictory, dynamic relationship with objectivity, from which its derives.

9.6 Conclusion

In concluding this chapter on critical theory, from a dialectical and also developmental perspective, *we can see, that the perspectives from the developed and the developing worlds are somewhat different. While both have strongly socio-political overtones, they are more overtly so in the latter case.* While Habermas is an academic with strong political views as well as epistemological perspectives, the late Paulo Freire was much more of a political and social activist, his medium for such being education. In that light, we conclude with an appropriate quote from Freire:

"One of the first kinds of knowledge indispensable to the person who arrives in a ghetto, or in a place marked by our betrayal of the right "to be" is the kind of knowledge that becomes solidarity, becomes a "being with". In that context, the future is seen as something not inexorable but as something that is constructed by people engaged together in life, in history. It is knowledge that sees history as possibility, not as determined. The world is not finished. It is always in the process of becoming. The subjectivity with which I dialectically relate to the world, my role in the world, is not restricted to a process of only observing what happens, but it also involves my intervention as a subject of what happens in the world. My role in the world is not simply that of someone who registers what occurs but of someone who has an input into what happens. I am equally subject and object in the historical process. In the context of history, culture and politics I register events not so as to adapt myself to them but so as to change them." (13)

We now turn, along the eastern path of renewal, from narrative methods, hermeneutics and now critical theory, to co-operative inquiry. John Heron, as we shall see in the next chapter, takes on – politically and epistemically – from where the critical theorists left off.

Bibliography

1) **Johnson**, P. & **Duberley**, J. (2000). *Understanding Management Research*. London: Sage.

2) **Blaikie**, N. (1994). *Approaches to Social Inquiry*. London: Pluto Press.

3) **Alvesson**, M. & **Skoldberg**, K. (2000). *Reflexive Methodology*. London: Sage.

4) **Held**, M. (1980). *Introduction to Critical Theory*. London: Routledge.

5) **Held**, M. (1980). *Introduction to Critical Theory*. London: Routledge.

6) **Held**, M. (1980). *Introduction to Critical Theory*. London: Routledge.

7) **Held**, M. (1980). *Introduction to Critical Theory*. London: Routledge.

8) **Held**, M. (1980). *Introduction to Critical Theory*. London: Routledge.

9) **Freire**, P. (1972). *Pedagogy of the Oppressed*. Harmondsworth: Penguin.

10) **Morrow**, R. & **Torres**, C. (2002). *Reading Freire and Habermas: Critical Pedagogy and Transformative Social Change*. New York: Teachers College Press.

11) **Freire,** P. (1972). *Pedagogy of the Oppressed*. Harmondsworth: Penguin.

12) **Freire**, P. & **Macedo**, D. (1987). *Literacy: Reading The Word And The World*. South Hadley, Mass.: Bergin & Garvey.

13) **Freire**, P. (1972). *Pedagogy of the Oppressed*. Harmondsworth: Penguin.

CHAPTER 10

FROM CRITICAL THEORY TO
CO-OPERATIVE INQUIRY

"UNCOVER SHARED POTENTIAL"

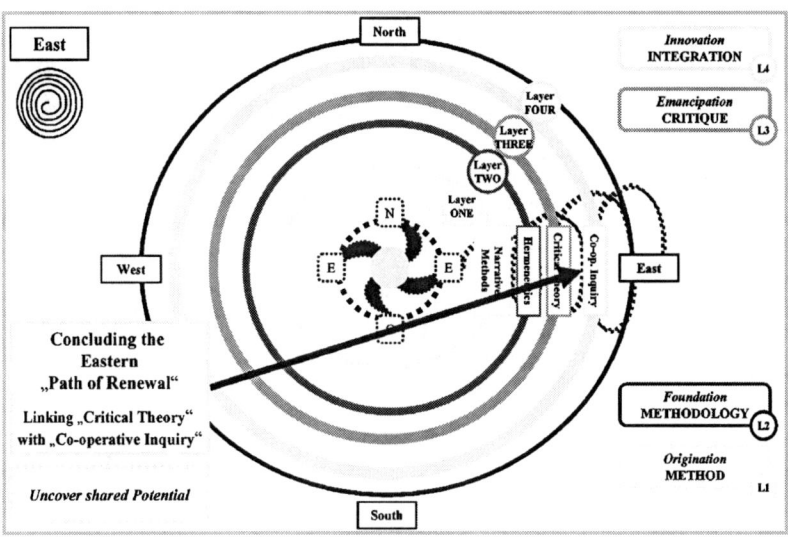

Figure 10.1: Overview Chapter 10 – Layer 4 / East

Summary: Co-operative Inquiry

- The cultmination of your research path of renewal lies in co-operative inquiry, which most explicitly addresses social innovation in this context.

- Co-operative inquiry, invented mainly by UK action researchers John Heron and Peter Reason, takes on from where narrative methods, interpretive methodology (hermeneutics), and critical theory leave off, giving rise to an ultimately transformative and integral approach.

- Such an approach to co-operative research is both politically integral and transformative, in that it involves co-researchers working together, as fellow subjects rather than as researcher/subject and researched/object, and encompasses experiential, imaginative, conceptual and practical ways of knowing.

- These four ways of knowing or modes of consciousness include altogether the southern humanistic (experiential) and the eastern holistic (imaginative), the northern rational (conceptual) and the western pragmatic (practical) dimension, albeit that the holistic path to renewal and innovation holds pride of place.

- Overall, the guiding objectives of co-operative inquiry are: political flourishing in individual and social life which includes a process of social participation where there is a balance between autonomy, co-operation and hierarchy; epistemic flourishing in individual and social life which includes a growing participative awareness of social contexts; and a conscious indwelling and resonsonance with the cultural life of the planet.

- In concluding this chapter with a practical application, we introduce the Japanese concept of Ba. This eastern concept, adopted by Japan's knowledge management icon, Ikijiro Nonaka, offers remarkable analogies to co-operative inquiry. Ba and its application demonstrate the relevance of Heron's developmental and spiralling rhythm (from the experiential to the practical) in today's organisational practice, particularly for the area of knowledge creation.

10.1 Orientation to Co-operative Inquiry

10.1.1 PAR to CI

As in the previous case of "southern" innovation through participatory action research (PAR), so in this "eastern" case, co-operative inquiry is integral, in that it draws to some extent on the three other research paths (or espistemologies), albeit being most firmly lodged within the path of renewal. This is what gives John Heron's work its "worldly-ness". However, while participatory research has strongly "southern" and relational overtones, co-operative inquiry has more "eastern" developmental ones. While participatory research is aligned with rich description, phenomenology, and feminism and also with the human mode of "being", co-operative inquiry is dialectical and spiritual in orientation. It is therefore more closely aligned with narrative methods, interpretevism, and critical theory, and with a process of "becoming". This, altogether, constitutes the holistic path, starting with and unfolding through "the stories we are".

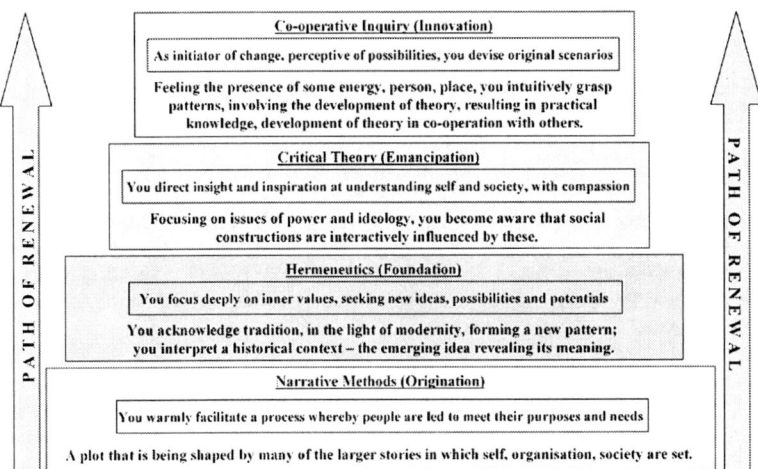

Figure 10.2: Towards Co-operative Inquiry

Co-operative inquiry is explicitly transformative as well as informative in its approach. Moreover, it deals with such issues as research validity and quality, which adds an orthodox flavour to it. Finally, as was the case for participative research, *while co-operative inquiry has a distinctively holistic feel to it, it also has shades of humanism, rationalism and empiricism.*

10.1.2 Co-operative Inquiry in an Action Research Context

A Changing East-West Paradigm

John Heron, while an educator and psychologist at the University of Surrey, together with his close colleague Peter Reason at the University of Bath, were the two leading co-creators of action research in Britain. Later, Reason and Bradbury, in their

"Handbook of Action Research" (1), took on, where Heron and Reason had left off. For them, the idea of a paradigm in science can be transferred to the worldview of a whole culture, and to the notion that the Western worldview may be in evolutionary transition. Research in the West, hitherto, has been associated with a so-called "positivist" worldview, a view that sees science as separate from everyday life and the researcher as a subject within a world of separate objects. This is part of a worldview based on the metaphor of linear progress, absolute truth and rational planning. Seeking objective truth, this modern worldview makes no connection between knowledge and power.

John Heron
(*1928)
South Pacific Centre for Human Inquiry
New Zealand

Peter Reason
(*1944)
Centre of Action Research
University of Bath, UK

Figure 10.3: Cooperative-Inquiry – Core Thinkers

For Reason, Bradbury and Heron, such a positivist view has outlived its usefulness. For the contemporary German philosopher and critical theorist Habermas, such western "modernism is dead". Against such a historical backdrop, what does action research stand for today, set in the trans-personal and even spiritual "eastern" context of this chapter?

Contemporary Action Research: Towards a Participatory Worldview

The emergent worldview that action research espouses can be described as systemic, holistic, relational, feminine, and experiential, but *its defining characteristic is that it is participatory and developmental*; our world does not consists of separate things but of *relationships which we co-author.*

John Heron, who is now in his late seventies, was a pioneer in the creation of participatory research methodologies in the social sciences. As such, he was the founder and director of the Human Potential Research Project at the University of Surrey in England from 1970 to 1977, the first university-based centre for humanistic and so-called "transpersonal" psychology and education in Europe. He was Assistant Director of the British Postgraduate Medical Federation at the University of London from 1977 to 1985, in charge of an innovative programme of personal and professional development for hospital doctors and GPs, including a co-operative inquiry into whole-person medicine, out of which the British Holistic Medical Association was formed. Later, from 1990 to 2000, he became the director of the International Centre for Co-operative Inquiry in Tuscany in Italy, where radical forms of spiritual inquiry were developed. Currently, he is co-director of the South Pacific Centre for Human Inquiry in Auckland, New Zealand.

Within the context of co-operative inquiry, human persons are linked in a generative web of communion with other humans and the rest of creation. *Human persons do not stand separate from the cosmos; we evolved with it and are an expression of its intelligent and creative force.* As we are part of the whole we are necessarily actors within it, which leads us to consider the fundamental importance of the practical. All ways of knowing, then, support our skillful being-in-the-world from moment to moment, our ability to act intelligently in support of worthwhile purposes. Hence, human inquiry is necessarily practical, and any participatory form of inquiry is, for Reason, Bradbury and Heron a "sacred science". It is a kind of knowledge, moreover, that one has only from within a social and (in this "trans-personal" case) within a spiritual situation.

Such a participatory worldview is at the same time a political statement as well as a theory of knowledge. Just as the classical Cartesian worldview emerged out of the political situation of the time, and found its expression in science and technology, so a participatory worldview implies democratic, peer relationships as the political form of inquiry. The political dimension affirms people's right to have a say in decisions that affect them and which claim to generate knowledge about them. It asserts the importance of liberating the muted voices of those held down by class structure and neo-colonialism, by poverty, sexism, racism and homophobia. To paraphrase the eighteenth century American revolutionary Tom Paine, the democratic activist in the late eighteenth century:

"It is for people themselves, in their own right, to enter into agreements with each other to discover and create knowledge, and this is the only principle on which research and inquiry has a right to exist."

Healing and Whole Making

A participative worldview invites us to inquire into what we mean by flourishing and into the meaning and purpose of our endeavors. As the contemporary philosopher and priest Thomas Berry has written: "What is the 'great work' of humanity in our time, and how are our individual human projects aligned with it?" For him, sacred experience, like sacred science, is based on reverence, in awe and love for creation.

Given the condition of our times, a primary purpose of human inquiry is not so much to search for the truth but to heal. For Reason and Bradbury then:

"To heal means to make whole: we can only understand our world as a whole if we are part of it; as soon as we attempt to stand outside, we divide and separate. In contrast, making whole necessarily implies participation: the individual is restored to a circle or community and the human community to the context of the wider natural world. To make whole also means to make holy: a participatory worldview restores meaning and mystery to human experience, so that the world is experienced as a sacred place." (2)

As we have seen, co-operative inquiry and its creator John Heron have been born and bred in the "west". However, Heron is certainly an unusual "westerner", in that he has been heavily exposed to the "north", "south", and, most particularly, the "east". (3)

In the latter respect he has been influenced by critical theory in the overtly political and critical emancipatory stance he takes towards both research and also education. The self-generating culture he has sought to promote is a research community whose members are in a continuous process of co-operative participation, learning and development. Its forms are consciously adopted, periodically reviewed and altered in the light of experience, reflection and ever-deepening vision. Its participants continually recreate themselves and their work through cycles of collaborative inquiry in living and working together. At the same time co-operative inquiry has affinities with the more conventionally recognized approach to action research as well as experiential learning, that arose originally from the work of the social scientist Kurt Lewin, and was duly espoused by the critical theorists, whereby:

"In action research, all actors involved in the research process are equal participants, and must be involved in every stage of the research process ... Collaborative participation in theoretical, practical and political discourse is a hallmark of action research and the action researcher." *(4)*

We now turn to the key tenets of co-operative inquiry.

10.2 Co-operative Inquiry – Key Tenets

Co-operative Inquiry – Key Tenets
①   You engage in a politically oriented process, in a participative form of inquiry.
②   You are involved in a knowledge-oriented process – epistemic in nature and scope.
③   You engage in an alternating current of informative and transformative inquiry.
④   You undertake your research in successive action-reflection cycles.
⑤   The validity you seek for your research is goodness, trustworthiness and authenticity.

① You engage in a politically oriented process, in a participative form of inquiry

Oriented to Being Values

The co-operative paradigm has two wings, that is political (value based and transformation oriented) and epistemic (knowledge based and informative). *Co-operative inquiry, distinctively speaking, does research with other people, who are invited to be full co-inquirers with the initiating researcher.* They become involved in operational decision-making, and are then committed to this kind of research design in principle, both politically and epistemologically. We can see already the resonance with critical theory, if not also with feminism.

The political wing of the participative paradigm is formed by a theory of value, oriented for Heron to being values, which holds that:

- *human flourishing is intrinsically worthwhile;* it is construed as a process of social participation in which there is a mutually enabling balance within and between people, of autonomy, hierarchy and co-operation, and is conceived as inter-dependent with the flourishing of the planetary system.

- *what is valuable as a means to this end is participative decision making,* through which people speak on behalf of the wider ecosystem of which they are a part, including the way that integral research is conducted within our research community.

Political Participation

The reasons for political participation are:

- persons have *a right to participate in research* – or educational – *design,* the purpose of which is to formulate knowledge about, and through them
- this gives them the opportunity to *identify and express their own preferences and values in the design,* in association with the other members of their research community
- it *empowers them to flourish* as fully human persons in the reseach, and to be represented in its conclusion
- it *avoids their being disempowered,* oppressed and misrepresented by the researcher's implicit values in any unilateral research design.

② **You are involved in a knowledge-oriented process – epistemic in nature and scope**

Focusing on Truth Values

The epistemic wing, formed by truth-values, is:

- *an ontology that affirms a mind-shaped reality which is subjective-objective*: it is subjective because it is only known through the form that the mind gives it; and it is objective because the mind interpenetrates the given cosmos it shapes

- *an epistemology that asserts the participative relation between the knower and the known,* and where the known is also a knower

- *a methodology that commands the validation of outcomes through the congruence of practical, conceptual, imaginal and empathetic forms of knowing* amongst co-operative knowers, and the cultivation of skills that deepen these forms.

Multiple Ways of Knowing

Co-operative inquiry is ultimately geared towards social innovation, insofar as it evolves from the experiential to the practical. Four ways of knowing are distinguished:

- **Practical knowledge**, evident in exercising skill, and closely aligned with the empirical, and with the path of realisation, builds upon the experimental, and the real

- **Propositional or conceptual knowledge**, closely linked with theory, and closely aligned with critical rationalism, builds on hypothesis formation, and upon multiple discourses

- **Presentational or imaginal knowledge**, which can be identified with interpretive approaches, evident in the intuitive grasp of the significance of patterns, builds upon the narrative and dialectical

- **Experiential (empathetic) knowledge**, closely aligned with phenomenology, and evident in meeting and feeling the presence of some energy, person, place, process or thing

As a result, for Heron:

- *experiential* knowing lies at the base of a "knowledge pyramid", comprising the direct, lived "being-in-the-world", aligned with your research *grounds*
- *imaginal* knowing, underlying your interpretive research as it *emerges,* which
- supports *propositional* or conceptual knowledge, your concepts or *navigation*
- upholds *practical* knowing, the exercise of your practical research-and-innovation effect.

At the same time, what is above consummates what lies below. Practical knowing, know-how, research method, is the consummation of the knowledge quest. It is grounded in and empowered by all the prior forms of knowing, and is immediately supported by propositional knowing which it celebrates and affirms at a higher level in its own relatively autonomous way. It affirms what is intrinsically worthwhile, by manifesting it in action.

③ **You engage in an alternating current of informative and transformative inquiry**

Uniquely in co-operative inquiry – when compared and contrasted with other research methodologies – there are two distinct forms of inquiry, the first being "informative":

Informative Inquiry

- participation in nature: molecules to galactic clusters
- participation in art: sculpture to song
- participation in intra-psychic life: sensations to ecstasies
- participation in interpersonal relations: one to one to large groups
- participation in forms of culture: environment, economics, politics, education
- participation in altered states of consciousness: ESP to cosmic consciousness

The second form covers transformative inquiries or research that have a practical or skill based outcome. This form is more in line with action research generally, and also with our kind of integral research project.

Transformative Inquiry

- transformation of the social and economic structure, organisation development, economic and political transformation, liberation of the disempowered
- transformation of the environment: ecology to architecture
- transformation of education: birth to death, self directed learning
- transformation of professionalism: creating a culture of competence, or even de-professionalisation
- transformation of personhood: personal growth skills, interpersonal skills
- transformation of lifestyle: from intimacy and domicile to occupation and recreation

④ **You undertake your research in successive action-reflection cycles**

There are four specific stages of inquiry:

Inquiry Stage 1: The First Reflection Phase

- the focus or topic of inquiry
- a launching statement of the inquiry topic
- a plan of action for the first action phase to explore some aspect
- a method of recording experiences in the first phase

Inquiry Stage 2: The First Action Phase

- exploring in action and experience some aspect of the inquiry topic
- applying an integrated range of inquiry skills
- keeping records of the experiential data gathered

Inquiry Stage 3: Break through into new Awareness

- loose your way
- transcend the inquiry format

Inquiry Stage 4: The Second Reflection Stage

- review and modify the inquiry topic in the light of making sense of the data
- choose a plan to explore a different aspect of the inquiry topic
- review and amend the systems of recording data

Figure 10.4: Stages of Inquiry

After the first four stages are completed, the inquiry continues through several more reflection-action-reflection cycles. Positively, such research cycling refines, clarifies, extends and deepens the focus. Negatively, such cycling checks, corrects, amends.

⑤ The validity you seek for your research is goodness, trustworthiness and authenticity

Qualitative researchers include all those methods, which have in common the study of people in in their own social setting, and the understanding of them in terms of their own categories and constructs. Generally, these methods accept an interpretevist or constructivist view of reality as mind-dependent, especially applied to people's view of their own social situation and context. Validity, for Heron, becomes a matter of quality or goodness or trustworthiness. He further proposes some of such "authenticity criteria":

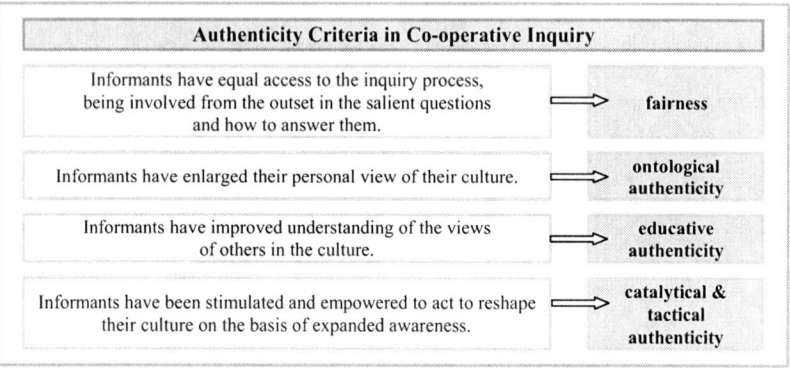

The change of criteria, for Heron, is a move from a concern with truth to a concern with goodness, from whether the outcomes are credible to whether they are desirable, from epistemology to axiology. The new criteria are all to do with values, with what states of human affairs are intrinsically worthwhile. We now turn from the five key tenets of co-operative inquiry, to an in depth investigation of those tenets which are most critical, that is the political/participative, the epistemic/knowledge oriented, and finally Heron's unique perspective on research validity from a qualitative perspective.

10.3 Co-operative Inquiry in Depth

10.3.1 The Political Perspective: Participation "with" People

Beyond the Academic Status Quo

Research in the human sciences is very much an academic pursuit, based in and originating from the kind of universities Alan Bloom has described in chapter 2. They are committed to the intellect as the controlling force in individual and social life, and to the pre-eminence of propositional knowledge, a set of intellectual statements published in systematic form. Faculty, as such, unilaterally make decisions on behalf of students. They decide what the students should learn, how and when, and assess such according to their own criteria. Academics, as has also been our experience in the various institutions with which we have been involved, do not need to acquire the kind of emotional and interpersonal competence to empower students to learn more holistically, and participate in educational decisions to enable them to become progressively more self-determining.

For Heron, this model of authoritarian control is transferred from teaching to research. The same kind of authority is exercised over the research subjects, as has taken place amongst teaching their students. While we consider, then, that the 18 year old has the right to vote, he or she has no right to participate in educational decision-making. We consider that a person has the choice whether to take part in a research programme, but has no right to have a say in what it is about. As such, people are surveyed, but not enabled, case studies are drawn up, but the cases in point are not emancipated as a result. As well as universities sustaining a model of seemingly authoritarian intellectual control of students, in education and as subjects in research, they are also, as Heron has said, biased in favour of propositional knowledge. Such involves intellectual statements, verbal and numeric, that can be suitably examined, and conceptually organised, so as not to infringe on rules of logic and evidence. This one dimensional approach to "knowing" offends a fundamental principle of systemic logic, that the conceptual part is interdependent with the experiential, imaginal and practical whole.

Beyond Research "on" People

Co-operative inquiry, hence, favours, as we do, research "with" over research "for" people. It is a form of participative, person-centred inquiry, which does research with people and not on them or about them. What then are the defining features of such?

Research with people – Defining Features
All the subjects are involved in decisions about content and method of research.
There is an intentional interplay between reflection and making sense, on the one hand, and experience and action on the other.
There is shared explicit attention to the validity of the inquiry.
It is both informative about and transformative of the issues at hand.

What does this imply, epistemologically and politically?

Research with people – Core Implications
Propositions about human experience that are the outcome of the research are of questionable validity if they are not grounded in your experience as a researcher.
The most rigorous way to do this is for you to ground the statements directly in your experience as a co-subject: this involves a deep kind of participative knowing.
The human condition is one of shared and dialogic embodiment; you can only operate through the full range of your sensibilities, in a relation of reciprocal dialogue.
This enables you as a researcher to come to know not only the external forms (individual and collective) but also the inner apprehension of these.

We now turn from the political to Heron's epistemic perspective, whereby we go into more depth in relation to his distinctive "ways of knowing".

10.3.2 The Epistemic Perspective: Ways of Knowing

Four Inquiry Outcomes: Experiential to Practical

For Heron, there are at least four main kinds of inquiry outcomes, corresponding to the four modes of inquiry:

① Transformations of personal being, for you as a researcher, through engagement with the focus and process of the inquiry

② Presentations of insight about the research inquiry, through expressive modes such as your drawing or participation in drama, providing significant patterns in our realities

③ Propositional reports which are informative about your research inquiry domain, describing and explaining what has been researched, through your research activity

④ Practical skills you exercise, which are connected with transformative action within the inquiry domain, on the one hand, or are connected with various kinds of participative knowing and collaboration on the other

Inquiry Outcomes as an Up-Hierarchy

There are two important features of this fourfold epistemology. (3) Firstly, there is a pyramid of support or grounding. Experience of a presence is the ground of having presentational knowledge of significant patterns of imagery. Both these together are the ground of propositions about it. *Experiential knowing is the ground of fourfold knowledge, intentional action the consummation of it, and presentational as well as propositional knowing mediates between them.* Because of their relatively autonomous form, each of these can function in a limited way without the other three, except for practical knowing.

There is a fundamental asymmetry in the epistemological pyramid. Thus you can experience a phenomenon with little or no presentational (perceptual) data about it, as with audio-visual images, in the absence of the people being filmed, without propositional information about them, and without acting in relation to them. However, you cannot take intentional action in direct relation to something without having some conceptual information about it, without some presentational data, and without meeting it.

Intentional action, at the apex of the supportive pyramid of fourfold knowing, consummates it and brings it to an integrated focal point. Undertaken by a group of co-inquirers, it becomes a concerted and congruent set of behaviors that is honed through cyclical integration of all four modes, and includes that integration as a necessary condition of its continuing practice. "Practice as consummation", in that context, is a way of saying two things.

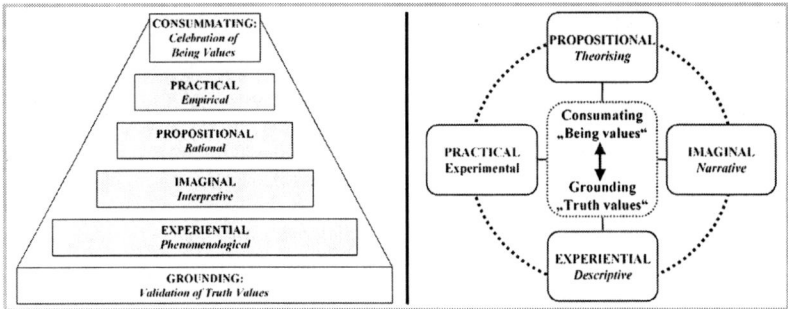

Figure 10.5: Bipolar convergence (pyramid) and
bipolar congruence as a dialectical process (cycle)

Grounding and Consummation

What is below, then, grounds and validates what is above, and what is above consummates, celebrates and shows forth what is below. Whether it is illustrated as a pyramid form or a four worldly circular process form (see figure), the following is important: At one pole it is the congruence between the four modes of knowing as their grounding in each other, and ultimately in experiential knowing, unrestricted and integral lived experience that makes their expressions valid. At the other pole is their congruence as being consummated in and through excellent and concerted practice, the apex of the pyramid that fulfils them and shows them forth. This crowns their world with the value of human flourishing. Valid outcomes alone are not enough. They need to be self-transcending and metamorphose into exuberant outcomes.

10.3.3 Validity and Co-operative Inquiry

Validity in General

For Heron, the outcomes of co-operative inquiry are valid only if they are well grounded in all four modes – practical, propositional, imaginal, experiential. While practice is the primary outcome, it is validated by being grounded on criteria of sound practice: so-called "executive", "technical", "psycho-social" and "value" criteria. This can be compared and contrasted with the more narrowly circumscribed validity criteria in quantitative research, as indicated below.

Validity in Quantitative Research

Traditional positivist research assumes there is one objective reality; hence, the world is empirically perceived by the senses, which is the same for all observers and independent of what they think about it. Research findings are sound if they are accurate, if they match this reality and measure it correctly. This is so-called internal validity and it appeals to a simple correspondence, or dictionary theory of truth. This holds that truth is in conformity with the facts, as if facts are out there, empirically, quite independent of us and waiting to be confirmed.

This in turn dictates criteria for an acceptable methodology. The research must be designed so that its findings are generalizable – so-called external validity – hence, for example, the importance of randomised sampling. It must be designed so that it can be replicated by others with similar results thus establishing the reliability of its findings, their consistency or stability. And it must be designed so that it is free of your bias and distortion, thus ensuring the objectivity of the findings. The collapse of such overt positivism, with the advent of phenomenological, interpretive, and critical emancipatory orientations, has led to the collapse of the necessarily objective fact. *The well-established counter-positivist view is that every statement of fact is theory, or perspective, laden.* It is, for Heron, an interpretation of reality.

Participative Reality

Rejecting outright positivism, *Heron's transactional or participative view of reality is seen as subjective-objective, an intermarriage between the creative, construing human mind and what is externally given.* Participative reality is neither wholly subjective nor objective, neither wholly dependent on your mind nor independent of it. It is always subjective-objective, inseparable from the creative, participative, engaged activity of your mind but never reducible to it, always transcending it.

Truth and Reality

"Valid" then becomes a perfectly healthy word, and in a generic overall sense – applied to the expression of the diverse modes of being, becoming, knowing and doing – simply means sound, well founded, well grounded. "True" is a closely related, and also healthy word as long as it is stripped of any necessary association with objective fact. What is important about it, once the notion of independent fact is taken out of it, is that it implies some validating relationship with reality, other than the mistaken notion of correspondence. Heron uses it then in the generic sense of "articulating reality", meaning a combination of revealing and shaping. Further he proposes that "true" is applied not just to propositions but also to the forms of expression of the other three modes. We can hence speak of four "types" of validity:

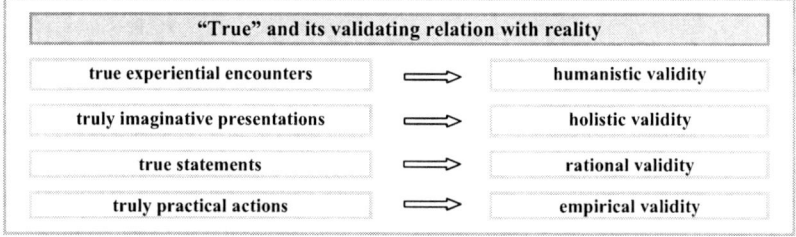

So we can say that:

- interpersonal encounter (experiential being) involves a true meeting of minds;
- a piece of music (imaginal becoming) is true to heartfelt experience; and
- your knowledge of a text (propositional knowing) is accurate
- a person's action (practical doing) is true to his or her principles.

What makes a subjective-objective reality a reality, for Heron, is a congruence between the four modes. By means of cycles of inquiry, the four ways are brought successively and repeatedly to bear upon each other. Ultimately, though, and this is where Heron remains true to his Anglo-Saxon heritage, the outcome of practical knowing, albeit built upon the other three, is the most critical.

Reality, in terms of each of the four modes, can then be understood as follows:

- experiential: reality is the lived experience of the mutual co-determination of person and world.
- imaginal: reality is significant form and pattern, in perceptual and other imaging, that interconnects analogically and metaphorically the whole network of other significant forms and patterns
- prepositional: reality is the combined sense and reference of concepts
- practical: reality is excellent practice and its affects.

The Validation of Practice

Practice as the culminating mode has a self-validating criterion internal to it, which is the knack of knowing how to perform it, according to:

Executive Criteria
- Can you execute the practice?
- Can you do it elegantly, with style and grace?

Technical Criteria
- Does the practice have the effects claimed for it?
- Is this form of practice the most effective?

Psycho-Social Criteria
- Is the practice relatively free of social pathology – free of distortions caused by personal distress?
- Is the practice relatively free of organisational pathology – the distortion of restrictive and rigid norms and values?

Intentional Criteria
- Is the practice intentional, not merely ad hoc or reactive?
- Do the inquirers give evidence of creatively sustaining congruence among the components of their practice – its motives, guiding purpose and values, strategy and norms, actual behavior and effects?

Value Criteria
- Does the practice contribute to personal and social transformation as to your view of an intrinsically worthwhile way of life for human beings?
- Does the practice support your view of basic human rights?

For any given practice some will be more relevant than others. The value criteria, though, are indispensable for any transformative inquiry. We now turn to the more global expression of what Heron now terms "participative spirituality". For it is in relation to such that Heron makes a strong turn toward the "east", by focussing on what he terms "sacred" science.

10.4 A Global Variation of Co-operative Inquiry

10.4.1 Sacred Science Defined

Heron in his "Participative Spirtuality" (5) defines the "sacred" as:

- the all inclusive illimitable presence of *what there is*
- that which calls human beings to *comprehensive flourishing*

"Science", for him, is an activity, which exercises critical rigor in articulating human experience of what there is. The twin pillars of such are:

① Sacred Science – Pillar 1: discriminating judgment both individually and collectively, involving:
  o personal apprehension and reflection
  o shared debate and dialogue
  o apprehending the significance of patterns
  o understanding the validity of propositions

② Sacred Science – Pillar 2: being engaged with what there is has a subjective and objective component:
  o in terms of our own sensitivities
  o relating to what is there, what is cosmically given
  o meeting what there is
  o taking action in relation to what there is

10.4.2 Participative Ontology: A View of Present Reality

For Heron, present reality is *subjective-intersubjective-objective.* In the very process of meeting what there is, we know there is a cosmic given, which at the same time is given shape by our enacting it, our forming and shaping it, in terms of our own sensitivities. Present reality can then be desribed as:

- *participative*: we are conjoined with it
- *incomplete*: it is transient, and contextual
- *distinctive*: each has its own potential
- *seamless*: there is no gap between subject and object

Epistemology: Ways of Knowing

Sacred science involves four ways of knowing which are mutually supportive and correlative with each other. Each of them has a strong resonance with one of the four worlds:

The 4 Ways of Knowing of Sacred Science		
Sacred Science is practical	= western =	engaged with the active transformation of the human experience of being, in the interest of comprehensive flourishing
Sacred Science is conceptual	= northern =	generating language, mental models and maps which symbolize the human experience
Sacred Science is aesthetic	= eastern =	evokes human experience through visual, auditory and kinesthetic patterns of vital significance
Sacred Science is experiential	= southern =	inclusive of the whole range of sensitivities whereby human beings engage with other humans and life forms

In relating to each other, there are two kinds of congruence:

- *groundedness*: the lower forms validate the higher
- *consummation*: the higher forms serve to fulfill the lower

altogether leading to a *cycle of accumulative flourishing.*

10.4.3 Participative Axiology: A View on Value

Sacred science presupposes a view that what is intrinsically valuable is comprehensive human flourishing, set within, firstly, individual and social life, and, secondly, within a planetary and cosmic context. With regard to each there is a political and cosmic dimension:

- **Political flourishing in individual and social life:** a process of social participation where there is a balance between autonomy, co-operation and hierarchy

  Autonomy (fulfill own true needs) is about deciding for yourself, *co-operation* (mutual aid and support) about deciding with others, and *hierarchy* (taking appropriate responsibility) about deciding for others. Hierarchy therefore has value when it is:

  o manifested by a person well grounded in their own autonomy and co-operation, both rooted in a deeply participative relationship with others
  o exercised to empower the emergence of autonomy and co-operation with others
  o reduced as that emergence occurs
  o abandoned when that emergence has occurred; otherwise it is oppressive.

- **Epistemic flourishing in individual and social life:** a growing participative awareness of social contexts, from face-to-face to global associations, a conscious indwelling, and resonance with, the cultural life of the planet

- **Political flourishing in a planetary and cosmic context:** a process of eco-participation, locally and globally

- **Epistemic flourishing in a planetary and cosmic context:** a growing participative awareness of, and felt resonance with, the biosphere, solar systems and galaxy.

We now turn, finally, from the sacred depths of Heron's "global" reach to the equally spiritual, but at the same time practical, effects of his co-operative inquiry, now linking it to the seminal work on knowledge creation of Japan's Ikijiro Nonaka. In fact, what Nonaka and his colleague at Hitotsubashi Universty in Japan have done, is to take not only Heron's co-operative approach a step further, into an organisation as a whole, but also to turn his modes of knowing, from a linear pyramid into a "knowledge spiral", thereby making it even more authentically "eastern". In combination, the Japanese "knowledge creating company" becomes an enriched expression of "co-operative inquiry", now placing its pre-emphasis on active "creation", as opposed to more purely reflective "inquiry".

10.5 Co-operative Inquiry in Practice: BA

From Ba to Co-Existence

For Ikijiro Nonaka, renowned for his research into the "Knowledge Creating Company" (6), his eastern evolutionary spiral is a continuous, self-transcending process through which one transcends the boundary of the old self into a new self by acquiring a new context, a new view of the world. In short, it is a journey "from being to becoming", and in John Heron's terms from the experiential to the imaginal, onto the conceptual and the practical, via four version of Japanese *Ba* (which signifies a physical or spiritual place). One also transcends the boundary between self and other, through the interactions amongst individuals or between individuals and their environment.

It is important to note that the movement through such modes of development forms a spiral, not a circle or a straight line, as Westerner Heron had depicted. In such a developmental spiral, the knowing interaction between tacit (subjective knower) and explicit (objective known) is amplified through these four levels of meaning. The spiral becomes larger in scale as it moves up and through these levels, expanding horizontally and vertically across organisations, such as those researched in Japan, as Sharp and Sony, Honda and Toyota.

It is a dynamic process, starting at the individual level and expanding as it moves through communities of interaction that transcend sectional, departmental, divisional and even organisational boundaries. Development is a never-ending process that upgrades itself continuously. This interactive spiral process takes place both intra- and inter-organisationally, transferred beyond organisational boundaries. Through dynamic interaction, one organisation's development can trigger that of outside constituents such as consumers, affiliated companies, universities or distributors. For example, an innovative new manufacturing process may bring about changes in the suppliers' manufacturing process, which in turn triggers a new round of product and process innovation within the organisation. It should be also noted that *development is a self-transcending process, in which one reaches out beyond the boundaries of one's own existence, transcending the boundary between self and other, inside and outside, past and present.* (7)

Ba: Shared Context in Motion

'Ba' in General: Based on the philosophy originally developed by Nishida, and subsequently further developed by Shimizu (8), *'ba' is here defined as a shared context in which being and becoming, and thereafter knowing and doing are communicated, created and utilised.* In such generation and regeneration Ba is the key, as Ba provides the energy, quality and place to perform the individual conversions, and to move along the evolutionary spiral. Social, cultural and historical contexts are important for individuals; as such contexts provide the basis for them to create meanings. Ba then does not necessarily mean a physical place. The Japanese word means not just a physical space, but a specific time and space. Ba therefore is a time-space nexus, or as Heidegger expressed it, a "locationality" that simultaneously includes space and time. It is a concept that unifies physical space, virtual space such as e-mail, and mental space such as shared ideals. *The key concept in understanding Ba is interaction. Development then is a dynamic and indeed dialectical human process.*

Ba can be described as "shared context in motion". Ba is the context shared by those who interact with each other, and through such interactions, those who participate in Ba and the context itself, evolve through self-transcendence to evolve. Participants of Ba cannot be mere onlookers, as is so often the case on the objectively oriented, analytical north and west. Instead, *such co-evolvers are committed to socially constructing Ba through action and interaction.*

Ba has a complex and ever-changing nature. It sets a boundary for interactions amongst individuals, and yet its boundary is open. As there are endless possibilities to one's own contexts, a certain boundary is required for a meaningful shared context to emerge. Yet Ba is still an open place where participants with their own contexts can come and go, and the shared context (Ba) can continuously evolve. By providing a shared context in motion, Ba sets binding conditions for the participants by placing certain limits on the way in which the participants view the world. And yet it provides participants with higher viewpoints than their own. Ba lets participants share time and space, and yet it transcends time and space.

Four Types of Ba: There are four types of Ba. In our four world terms, those are: originating Ba (southern – experiential), dialoguing Ba (eastern – imginal), systemising Ba (northern – conceptual), and exercising Ba (western – practical). These, altogether, are defined by two dimensions of interaction. One dimension is the type of interaction; whether the interaction takes place individually or collectively. The other dimension is the media used in such interactions; whether the interaction is through face-to-face contact or virtual media such as books, manuals, memos, e-mails or teleconferences. Each Ba offers a context for a specific step in the evolutionary process, though the respective relationships between each single Ba and conversion modes are by no means exclusive. For us (encompassing the four worlds), building, maintaining and utilising Ba is important to facilitate conscious organisational evolution. Hence, one has to understand the different characteristics of Ba and how they interact with each other. The following paragraphs describe the characteristics of each kind of Ba:

- *Originating Ba is defined by individual and face-to-face interactions.* It is a place where individuals share experiences, feelings, emotions and mental models. Originating Ba then is an existential place in the sense that it is the world where an individual transcends the boundary between self and others, by sympathising or empathising with others. From such originating Ba emerges care, love, trust and commitment (for us characteristics of the archetypal south), the ground for evolution within and among individuals and organisations.

- *Dialoguing Ba is defined by evolving and interactive dialogue.* It is the place where individuals' mental models and skills are shared, converted into common terms, and articulated as concepts. What is articulated is also brought back into each individual, and further articulation occurs through "eastern" style self-reflection, and contemplation. Dialoguing Ba is more consciously constructed than originating Ba. It involves the conscious use of metaphor and analogy, as well as negation and affirmation, transforming eastern non-being into being, to make the tacit explicit.

- *Systemising Ba is defined by "northern" style depersonalised and virtual interactions.* Information technology, through on-line networks, groupware, documentation and databanks, offers a virtual collaborative environment for the creation of systemising Ba. Today, many organisations use electronic mailing lists and news groups through which participants can exchange necessary information or answer each other's questions.

- *Exercising Ba is defined by personalised, individual as well as virtual "western" style interactions.* Here, individuals embody explicit facts and concepts communicated through virtual media, such as written manuals or simulation programmes. Exercising Ba synthesises transcendence and reflection through action, while dialoguing Ba achieves this through thought.

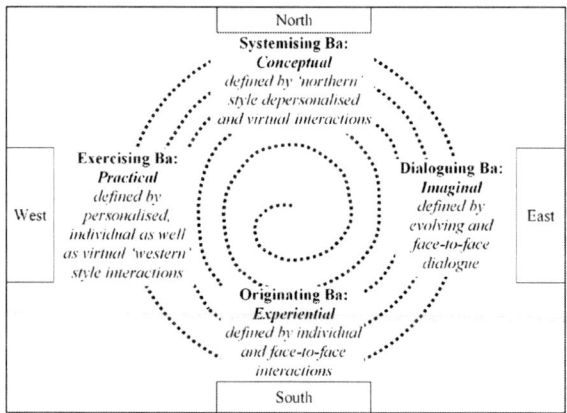

Figure 10.6: Four Types of Ba (Japan)

The emergent, Japanese style evolutionary spiral, is arising out of an eastern, consciousness-based perspective; it mirrors, in its modes of becoming, the process of co-operative inquiry.

We are now ready to conclude this chapter on co-operative inquiry.

10.6 Conclusion

10.6.1 Research with People

In our integral research context, co-operative inquiry sets the expectation that such research is an egalitarian group and inter-personal, rather than an expert laden, individual and personal process. Interestingly enough, though most of the underlying methodologies that we have considered would be philosophically in sympathy with such, none of the research methods has focused on co-operative inquiry. However, with a view to operationalise co-operative inquiry, Heron has developed a very detailed "Complete Facilitator's Handbook" (9), of which we will give a brief overview here, before reaching our final conclusions.

10.6.2 Co-operative Facilitation

Heron divides facilitation, as he does co-operative inquiry, into a processal and a political orientation. As we see, the two are aligned with one another.

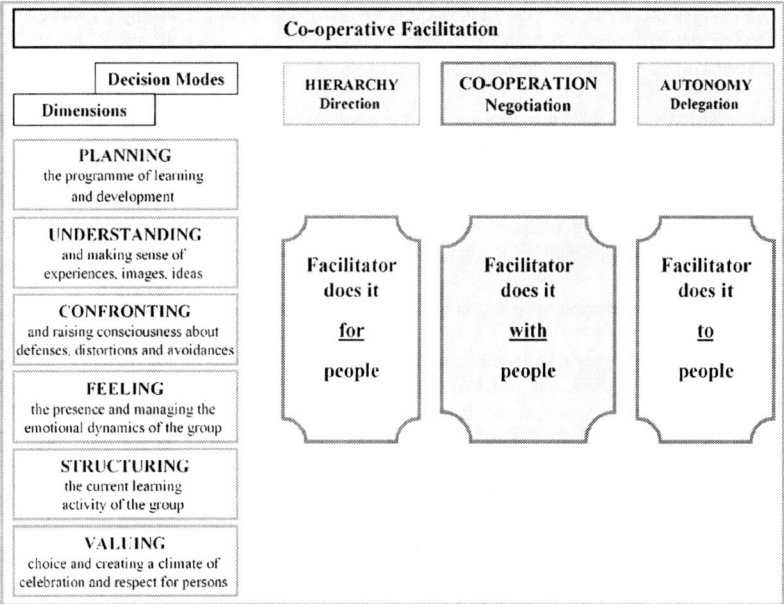

Figure 10.7: The Role of the Facilitator

Core Dimensions of Co-operative Facilitation: Planning to Valuing

The planning dimension: this is the goal oriented ends and means aspect of facilitation, to do with the aims of the group

The meaning dimension: this is the cognitive aspect, to do with the participants' understanding of what is going on

The confronting dimension: the is the challenge aspect, to do with raising consciousness about the group's resistances and avoidances of things

The feeling dimension: this is the sensitive aspect of facilitation; to do with the management of feeling and emotion in the group

The structuring dimension: this is the formal aspect, concerned with the methods of learning undertaken by the group

The valuing dimension: this is the integrity aspect, to do with creating a supportive climate and celebrating the personhood of group members

Core Decision Modes of Facilitation: The Politics of Learning

The hierarchical mode: here you as facilitator direct the learning process, leading from the front by thinking on behalf of the group

The co-operative mode: here you share your power over the learning process and manage the different dimensions together with the group, enabling and guiding the group

The autonomous mode: here you respect the total autonomy of the group, giving them the freedom to find their own way.

The role of facilitation is a crucial one in the context of co-operative inquiry, that is in promoting an overall process of co-creation, both in socio-political and in epistemic-knowledge creating terms.

10.6.3 Co-operative Inquiry to Socio-Technical Design

In conclusion, co-operative inquiry, as well as participative action research, are humanistic and holistic approaches to research-and-innovation, albeit that they are generally integral in nature and scope. Co-operative inquiry is actually a half way house between social research and innovation, information and transformation. For whereas Heron does focus on both, he is still recognized as part of the academic research community. In fact Denzin and Lincoln, in their "Landscape of Research", are great supporters of his approach. Although Heron was influenced by the East, he remains true to his Anglo-Saxon pragmatic colors, with practicality as his hallmark.

We have now journied, altogether via the path of renewal, through narrative methods and hermeneutics, critical theory and co-operative inquiry, through a process of co-evolution. We now turn from the path of renewal to the path of reason, and from peaceful co-evolution to the building up of an open society. We are starting out with critical rationalism.

Bibliography

1) **Reason**, P. & Bradbury, H. (2004). *Handbook of Action Research*. London: Sage.

2) **Heron**, J. (1994). *Co-operative Inquiry*. London: Sage.

3) **Heron**, J. (1994). *Co-operative Inquiry*. London: Sage.

4) **Heron**, J. (1997). *Feeling and Personhood*. London: Sage.

5) **Heron**, J. (2006). *Participative Spirituality*. North Carolina: Lulu Press

6) **Nonaka**, I. & **Takeuchi**, H. (1995). *Knowledge Creating Company*. Oxford: Oxford University Press.

7) **Nonaka**, I. (2000). *SECI, Ba and Leadership*. Long Range Planning: International Journal of Strategic Management, 33.

8) **Shimizu**, H. (1995). *Ba-principle: new logic for the real-time emergence of information*. Holonics, 5 (1).

9) **Heron**, J. (2005). *The Complete Facilitator's Handbook*. London: Kogan Page.

CHAPTER 11

FROM METHODS OF THEORISING TO
CRITICAL RATIONALISM

"BUILD UP A THEORETICAL PERSPECTIVE"

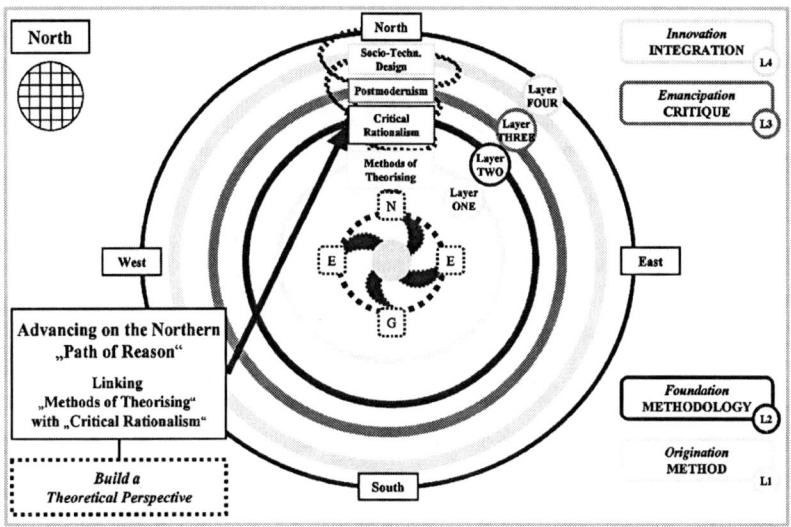

Figure 11.1: Overview Chapter 11 – Layer 2 / North

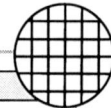

Summary: Critical Rationalism

- Having built up your capacity to theorise, and to thereby develop theories from the data you have gathered, we now turn to critical rationalism as a means of consolidating upon such theoretical ground, drawing primarily on the work of Karl Popper.

- In Popper's theory of knowledge, hypotheses, theories or conjectures precede all observation. Analytically based concepts, emerging out of your experience and imagination, serve to evolve your original research question into a set of testable hypotheses.

- Popper was also the leading advocate of an "open society". For him and for George Soros, an open society is one in which critical thinking and discussion can flourish; the society is open to improvement. The key to progress towards such is the recognition of your fallibility.

- From Popper we turn to Paulin Hountondji, who is considered to be the pre-eminent rationalist amongst African "professional" (as opposed to "ethno") philosophers. In turning from Europe to Africa, we take particular account, again, of the research needs of societies in transition.

- There are two currents of "critical rational" philosophy in the African context: the universalist approach of Kwasi Wiredu, and the dialectical current of Paulin Hountondji. For Hountondji, the universalist approach risks African philosophy being overtaken by a Western bias; a dialectical current is more in tune with the political struggles and recent history of Africa.

- Whereas Africa was for him phenomenologically and interpretively richly endowed, it lacked critical rational thought where "professional philosophy" came in. This is not "scientism": science is not valued for itself, but for its human significance and meaning for life.

- Modern science, hitherto, was introduced by the coloniser in the overseas territories in the form of an impoverished science, deprived of the theory-building activity that makes integral science. This, in fact, was a side-affect of the same colonisers' launch of so-called "modern", rational and pragmatic economies in these territories, devoid of holistic and humanistic underpinnings.

- What is needed in Africa today is not just to apply traditional knowledge, while continuing to import from the West technologies that are poorly understood and mastered by the local users. What is needed, instead, is to help their people and their educated elite, to capitalise and master the existing indigenous knowledge, and develop new knowledge in a continual process of uninterrupted creativity, while applying the findings in a systematic and responsible way to improve their own quality of life.

- For the same reason the notion of philosophy (and research) has to be re-examined. Hountondji deplores Africa's exclusion from science, as is the case for most of the developing world, and their remaining on the margins of the global production of knowledge, and he argues for constructing a new space of theoretical construction.

11.1 Orientation to Critical Rationalism

Theory Building to Critical Rationalism

We now turn from the process of theory building generally, and grounded theory specifically, along the northern path of reason upon which you have embarked here, to fully-fledged critical rationalism. In other words, whereas grounded theory is a very elaborate method or technique for processing data, so as to build up theory, from the ground up, critical rationalism is a fully-fledged epistemology.

The doyen of such rationality is the late Anglo-Austrian philosopher and leading advocate of "open society", Karl Popper (1), in fact a central European neighbour of Moravia's Husserl. After exploring Popper's rich European heritage we shall turn again to an African counterpart of his, the "professional philosopher" from the Centre for Advanced African Studies in Benin, Paulin Hountondji, for his reformative version of such rationalism in the context of a developing society. As is the case for Eritrean born philosopher Tsenay Serequeberhan (see chapter 8), such a developmental orientation tends to be lead towards a new version of, in this case, critical rationalism. Interestingly enough, Hountondji was a student of Husserl's, but deliberately put phenomenology on the "back burner" until he had pursued the rational and professional philosophical course he felt his continent required of him.

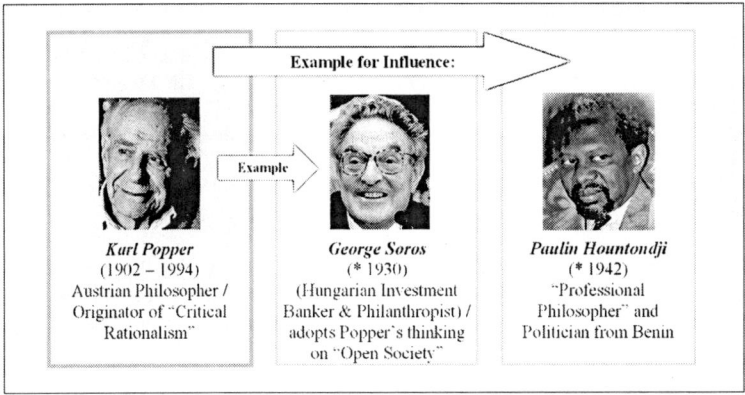

Figure 11.2: Critical Rationalism – Core Thinkers

Karl Popper was born in Vienna (then in Austria-Hungary) in 1902 to middle-class parents of Jewish origins, who had both converted to Christianity. Popper received a Lutheran upbringing and was educated at the University of Vienna. His father was a bibliophile who was rumored to have 10,000 volumes in his library at home. He took a PhD in philosophy in 1928. In 1934 Popper published his first book, "The Logic of Scientific Discovery", in which he criticized the inductive approach to scientific method, and the logical positivism that underlay it. At the same time he put forth his theory of potential falsifiability being the criterion for what should be considered science.

In 1937, the rise of Nazism led Popper to emigrate to New Zealand, where he became lecturer in philosophy at Canterbury University College New Zealand (at Christchurch). In 1946, he moved to England to become reader in logic and scientific method at the London School of Economics, where he was appointed professor in 1949. He was president of the Aristotelian Society from 1958 to 1959. He was knighted by Queen Elizabeth II in 1965, and was elected a Fellow of the Royal Society in 1976. He retired from academic life in 1969, though he remained intellectually active until his death in 1994. Popper was a member of the Academy of Humanism and described himself as an agnostic, showing respect for the moral teachings of Judaism and Christianity.

Popper's Philosophy of Science

Popper coined the term "critical rationalism" to describe his philosophy. The term indicates his rejection of classical empiricism. Popper was holding that scientific theories are universal in nature, and can be tested only indirectly, by reference to their implications. He also held that scientific theory, and human knowledge generally, is irreducibly conjectural or hypothetical, and is generated by the creative imagination in order to solve problems that have arisen in specific historico-cultural settings.

Popper's account of the logical asymmetry between verification and falsifiability lies at the heart of his philosophy of science. It also inspired him to take falsifiability as his criterion of demarcation between what is and is not genuinely scientific: a theory should be considered scientific if and only if it is falsifiable. This led him to attack the claims of both psychoanalysis and contemporary Marxism to scientific status, on the basis that the theories enshrined by them are not falsifiable. For Popper, it is in the interplay between the tentative theories (conjectures) and error elimination (refutation) that scientific knowledge advances toward greater and greater problems; in a process very much akin to the interplay between genetic variation and natural selection. Where does "truth" fit into all this? As early as 1934 Popper wrote of the search for truth as *"one of the strongest motives for scientific discovery"*.

We now turn to the key tenets of critical rationalism, starting with Popper's attack on logical positivism, which, as we shall see from chapter 14, was in fact the Anglo-Austrian school of empirical thinking that came before him.

11.2 Critical Rationalism – Key Tenets

Critical Rationalism – Key Tenets
① Empirical science has nothing absolute about it.
② Derive theories from tentative conjectures.
③ Falsify rather than verify.
④ Strong theory drives out the weak.
⑤ Natural and social science are value neutral.
⑥ You ultimately formulate an overall deductive strategy.

① Empirical science has nothing absolute about it

The empirical basis of science has nothing absolute about it. (1) Science does not rest on solid bedrock. The bold structure of its theories rise above a swamp. It is like a building erected on piles. The piles are driven down onto the swamp, but not down to any natural or given base; and if we stop driving the piles deeper, it is not because we have reached solid ground. We simply stop when we think that the piles are firm enough to carry the structure at last for the time being.

② Derive theories from tentative conjectures

So Popper's skepticism led him to reject the absolute certainty of Descartes' rationalism and yet preserve the view that knowledge as an external reality is possible – albeit that it is uncertain and fallible. Theories can only be tentative conjectures about the world, which are ultimately unverifiable by empirical evidence. Their discovery involves imaginative leaps, which are the forerunners of scientific activity. The process whereby predictive and thereby testable hypotheses are deduced from theoretical conjectures and subjected to confrontation with a cognitively accessible world is the distinctive attribute of a critically rational science, subject to falsification rather than verification. In effect, science advances through the detection and elimination of error as falsified theories fall away leaving a core of theory, which has not yet been disproved.

③ Falsify rather than verify

Basically Popper attacks the inductive base of logical positivism "because it excluded as sheer gibberish metaphysical ideas which were often the predecessors for scientific cones". The key outcome was the replacement of inductivist and verificationist principles with those of education and falsification – the hypothetico/deductive method. Inductivists look for evidence to confirm their generalisations, sometimes referred to as justification. Deductivists try to refute their hypotheses, to falsify them, thereby referred to as falsification.

④ Strong theory drives out the weak

Science can only ever be piecemeal and incomplete. Social engineering, as a result, should involve "piecemeal tinkering", which, combined with critical analysis is the main way to achieve practical results in the social as well as natural sciences. In essence, Popper's falsification leads to *epistemological Darwinism* where the strong theories drive out the weak. As such, he still shares with the logical positivists the epistemological commitment that empirical data are the final arbiter of the truth of theory.

"... finding theories, which are better approximations to the truth is what the scientist aims at ... This involves the growth of the content of our theories, the growth of our knowledge of the world."

⑤ **Natural and social science are value neutral**

At the same time Popper preserved the unity of the natural and social sciences, only arguing that, in the latter, causality was contingent whereas in the former it was invariable. Popper revitalizes key aspects of logical positivism; specifically the possibility of a theory-neutral observational language; a modified correspondence theory of truth; skeptical anti-metaphysics; the methodological unity of the sciences; and the utility of science for enabling human intervention into the social and natural worlds.

⑥ **You ultimately formulate an overall deductive strategy**

Popper's deductive strategy can be summarised as:

- Begin by putting forward a tentative idea, a conjecture, a hypothesis or set of hypotheses that form a theory.
- With the help of other previously accepted hypotheses, or by specifying conditions under which the hypotheses are expected to hold, deduce a conclusion, or a number of conclusions.
- Examine the conclusions and the logic behind them; compare this argument with existing theories to see if it constitutes an advance in understanding; if so
- Test the conclusion by gathering appropriate data; make the necessary observations or conduct the necessary experiments.
- If the test fails – if the data are not consistent with the conclusion – the "theory" must be false; the original conjecture must be rejected.
- If the conclusion passes the test, because the data are consistent with it, the "theory" is temporarily supported; it is corroborated, not proved to be true.

A deductive theory consists of a set of hypotheses or propositions, which are arranged in such a way that from some of the propositions all other propositions follow. Such a theory has the form of a logical argument that leads to certain conclusions.

11.3 Critical Rationalism in Depth

11.3.1 Towards an Open Society

For Anglo-Austrian Karl Popper (2) as for Anglo-Hungarian George Soros (3), an *open society is one in which critical thinking and discussion can flourish.* To be free to hypothesize or conjecture is to be free to construct your own thoughts and to debate these with others. Whereas Popper was a victim of the Nazi regime in Austria, and, as a Jew, had to flee from his country, Soros, who is also Jewish, had to flee from a communist and anti-semitic Soviet Union. They had therefore experienced in their own life worlds (being) the evils of closed societies first hand, so that their evolving stories (becoming) were infused with such.

Both Popper and Soros became avid opponents of "closed societies", this forming the backdrop to their rational "knowing". For Soros, open society falls short of perfection, but it has the great merit of assuring freedom of thought and of speech, giving ample scope to experimentation and creativity. In partaking of such you must content yourself with a form of social organisation that falls short of perfection but holds itself open to improvement. *This is the concept of an open society – a society open to improvement.* Therein lies its superiority over closed society, which seeks to deny its own imperfection even as the world around it changes. *Recognition of your fallibility is the key to progress towards an open society*, in the latter case truly embracing a "rainbow society", for which Mandela's South Africa aspires.

As had originally been the case for the Anglo-Saxon liberal thinkers in the eighteenth and nineteenth centuries, Popper and Soros have also been political radicals in their own right. Critical rationalism, as Popper conceived it in a "modern" moment, has more to it than first meets the conventional rational eye. Hypothesis setting, he argues, is not entirely the rational-empirical exercise that it is conventionally set up to be. Why is that?

11.3.2 Rational Methodology and Beyond

Worlds within Worlds

Popper was not the "pure rationalist" he is claimed to be. For he describes three worlds:

- the *physical cosmos* – World 1;
- the world of *conscious human processes* – World 2; and
- the world of the *objective creations of the human mind* – World 3.

The worlds of physical and mental events, for Popper, are relatively straightforward. The difficulty begins with "World 3". In the broadest sense it is the world of products of the human mind; in the narrow sense it is the world of theories. Moreover, he conjectured, literary and artistic works such as Mozart's operas might even belong to a "World 4".

Creative World 3 usually has an indirect effect on physical World 1, via the mental World 2. If a skyscraper or bridge collapses this is sometimes attributable to a World 2 error in thought, or else to a false objective theory or error in World 3. The existence of World 3, and the fact that we can grasp World 3 objects through thought processes in World 2, play a critical role in accounting for human self-consciousness, for self-awareness, and for the human mind, as distinct from the animal mind. Let us return to these rational and deductive as opposed to inductive thought processes.

Underlying Critical Rationalism

The underlying idea of Popper's theory of knowledge is that problems and attempts to solve them through hypotheses, theories or conjectures precede all observation. Logically as well as historically, theories come first in our experience of the world, first both in our personal history and in the history of humanity. What correspond to theories at a pre-human level are dispositions and expectations. Magic and ritual probably have close antecedents in the animal realm. What we humans have in addition is the speech form of story telling. The novelty in human language is that it can describe and argue. With the problem of whether an account is true or merely wishful boasting, the decisively important problem of truth makes its appearance. At the same time, the telling of fairy tales or stories becomes possible.

Such tales or stories or myths are also the original theoretical explanations: the beginnings of science among the Greeks go back to Homer and Hesiod; the beginnings of art, the prehistoric cave paintings of hunting and animals are magical stories; Egyptian and Assyrian art largely comprise illustration of contemporary stories and events. This is how World 3 began to develop. Our humanity, for Popper, is rooted in the existence of World 3, if not also a World 4, in the world of creation myths as well as of objective truth. So critical rationalism (or knowing as such) was built on the prior grounds of being and becoming.

For example, as Popper saw it, the reality (World 1) that Kepler sought behind appearances was inspired by the Pythagoreans and Kepler's own interest in music (World 3 or 4). The great astronomer thought that the world was filled with melodious sound, conducted and held together by harmony and resonance, but also by dissonances and their eventual resolution. The world, for him, was a divine symphony, architecture of the divine, and a heavenly beauty. This idea made him a relentless seeker after the truth. The truth, for Popper, must be beautiful; it must reveal a heavenly beauty. *Popper's whole methodology consists in the acknowledgement that the natural sciences try to find a reality hidden behind appearances.* To that extent, his conceptual world, aside from seeking empirically based falsification, is founded upon a prior experiential and imaginal world (see John Heron and co-operative inquiry in chapter 10).

Whenever we know nothing we must guess, just as Kepler did. If we want to subject our testable hypotheses to the strict test of experience, these are no longer metaphysical but scientific ones that enable us to learn from our mistakes. Kepler, like every scientist, was guided by intuition, by trial (hypothesis) and error (empirical refutation). Without intuition and imagination, Popper asserts, we get nowhere, even though most of our intuitions turn out wrong. We need intuitions, ideas, if possible competing ideas; and we need ideas about how those ideas can be criticized, improved, and critically tested. So Popper and Husserl had their subjectively intuited similarities as well as their objectively empirical differences.

We now turn to Paulin Hountondji, who is considered to be the pre-eminent rationalist, amongst African "professional" (as opposed to "ethno") philosophers. In turning from Europe to Africa, we take particular account of the needs of a society in transition, and one, like most societies in Africa, Asia and Latin America, that have experienced colonisation.

11.4 Global Variations of Rationalism

11.4.1 Professional Philosophy in an African Context

Critical Rationalism to Professional Philosophy

Like Popper, the Ghanean philosophers Wiredu and Gyekye, and Benin's Hountondji, are committed to an open society. At the same time, Hountondji does not entirely part company from the interpretative and phenomenological approaches, which we have investigated so far. There are, then, for Afro American philosopher Barry Hallen in his "Short History of African Philosophy" (4), *two currents of "critical rational" philosophy in the African context. These are the universalist approach of Kwasi Wiredu, and the dialectical current of Paulin Hountondji.* For the universalist, African philosophy must be opposed to traditional cultural beliefs. For Wiredu, the African philosopher must combine insights from the East and West with his own indigenous philosophical resources. The point is to lift the philosophical enterprise to a universal level of discussion, and then turn to the specific existential conditions and priorities of the African social and political context, combining these to seek a truth.

Wiredu rejects an "objectivist" theory of truth; whatever is called truth is always someone's truth. "What I mean by opinion is a firm rather than an uncertain thought. I mean what is called a considered opinion". Moreover, several "traditional" practices should be carried over into contemporary African politics. Wiredu is sceptical of the "western" multi-party system, which serves to heighten social and ethnic tensions in Africa. Affirming and reformulating the traditional consensus based approach would be preferable. Wiredu's most illustrious philosophical compatriot in this respect is the Ghanean Kwame Gyekye, whose work on tradition and modernity will be reviewed by us later.

Kwame Gyekye (5) also considers how philosophical inferences can be derived from traditional (in his case Akan) cultures. Gyekye criticizes the notion of ethnicity (tribalism) in Africa as a dangerous invention and tool of political ideologies and argues that it must be supplanted by notions of group identity comparable with those found in multi-cultural societies. His vision of modern African society becomes one which incorporates and interrelates the best elements of other cultures in the "world" with those aspects of Africa's cultural heritage which deserve to be valued. The transcendent and universal criterion on the basis of which the positive contribution of any of these elements can be rated is humanistic: "bringing about the kinds of progressive changes in the entire aspects of human culture necessary for the enhancement and fulfilment of human life".

We now turn to Hountondji, the best known of the African professional philosophers. For those of you in China or India, the Middle East or Latin America, it is instructive to note how strong the contemporary African philosophical orientation is, and to perhaps use it as a counter-force to the dominant, European philosophical discourse, so as to develop a healthy dialectic between them.

Hountondji's Pluralism

For Hountondji (6), the universalist approach risks African philosophy being overtaken by a Western bias. He believes that a dialectical current of critical philosophy would be more in tune with the political struggles and intellectual history of contemporary Africa. As we can see immediately, there is a critical emancipatory, prior foundation to his rationalism. In that sense ethno-philosophy and negritude are philosophies of an earlier age – texts to be taken up dialectically into a new stage of ongoing dialogue.

The present debate on the question of African philosophy, for Hountondji therefore, can be seen to form part of a comprehensive process of reflection by the African intelligentsia upon its historical being: it represents a significant moment in the intellectual response of Africans to the challenge of Western civilisation. In the same vein, such ontology provides for a reformation of Eurocentric research methodology, and we invite the other transitional societies amongst us to take the story on from here.

Hegel's philosophy of history, Houtondji asserts, remains the most exalted statement of European self-affirmation in opposition to other races, the most elaborate rationalisation of European ethno-centrism. It provided a powerful philosophical base for the chorus of denigration of the non-white races, which buoyed up the European colonial adventure. The high point of such denigration was attained in the work of French anthropologist Lévi-Bruhl, who devoted his career to demonstrating the "primitive mentality" of the non-Western peoples. On the one hand, for him, there were the Western societies that had emerged from the Mediterranean civilisation, within which developed rationalist philosophy and positive science, and on the other hand, "primitive" societies ruled by a mentality to which the Western mode of thought was alien. Such societies, he argued, were "pre-logical". It is worth noting that Lévi-Bruhl rescinded before he died, declaring himself to have been wrong.

What then about African philosophy in taking the story on from there?

To gain our African Soul we must lose it

African philosophical literature sometimes rests on a confusion between the popular (ideological) and strict (theoretical) use of the word philosophy. According to the first meaning, philosophy is any kind of wisdom, intended to govern the daily practices of a people; in the second sense philosophy is a discipline, like mathematics, with its own exigencies and rules – Hountondji of course favours the latter. As such, he reckons that ethno-philosophers, like Senegalese poet-statesman Leopold Senghor, have wasted their time with ready-constituted thought – whether Dogon, Yoruba or Rwandais – to justify themselves in European eyes. Instead, African philosophers should have thrown themselves into the fray in order to confront today's and tomorrow's problems.

In a completely sterile withdrawal, Hountondji laments, Africa goes on vindicating its cultures instead of transforming them. He who must gain his soul must lose it, which harks of our reformative process of emergence, prior to a newly normative navigation. *By dint of trying to defend African cultures, they have been mummified. Africa has betrayed its original cultures by showing them off for external consumption. Such is the theoretical impasse into which such thinkers as Leopold Senghor, for Hountondji, have stumbled.* Since then Africa's philosophical thinking has marked time, serving merely to re-construct an African world-view as "a mad and hopeless enterprise". Such (phenomenologically based) "ethno-philosophy" has got bogged down in an ideological discipline without recognizable status in the world of theory. People forget that "African Studies" was invented in Europe.

Motivated by the genuine need for an African philosophy, ethno-philosophical predecessors have wrongly believed that it lies in the past, needing only to be exhumed and then brandished like a miraculous weapon in the astonished face of the colonialist European. They have not seen that African philosophy, like science or culture in general, lies before you and me, and must be created, albeit embracing the heritage of the past. Philosophy needs to be active, not passive, and, as for Popper and Soros an open system rather than a closed one:

"... we want the relentless questioning, the untiring dialectic that accidentally produces systems and then projects them towards horizons of fresh truths. African philosophers who think in terms of Plato and Marx and then transcend such are producing authentic African work." (7)

The real problem is not to talk about Africa but to talk amongst Africans, or for that matter amongst Latin Americans, amongst Arabs, or amongst Chinese, Japanese or Indians, all of the latter being influenced by their Buddhist – amongst others – heritage. Europe is what she is today because she transformed the heritage of other peoples, including the ancient Egyptians, and conducted innumerable conversations across her diverse nationalities and peoples. Africa must liberate its thoughts from a previous ghetto, open up a breach in its closed space of its collectivist fantasies, so that theoretical issues will surge in, to be shared first of all with our immediate brothers, thus to steep them in the melting pot of African science.

The real problem is to liberate the theoretical creativity of African peoples, or indeed in our programmes, of Arabs, or Muslims, or Chinese, or indeed Americans, which is the transformative orientation of our integral research. Everything else, including science, and in our terms social innovation, will come afterwards.

African Philosophy: Myth and Reality

Most African "philosophers" in the first half of the nineteenth century have been men of the church, including Father Temples from Belgium, Alexis Kagame in Rwanda, and Kenyan pastor John Mbiti. *All have been preoccupied with finding a psychological and cultural basis for rooting the Christian message in the African's mind, without betraying either.* Such philosophy is perceived as a stable system of beliefs. Other lay thinkers, such as Senghor in the Senegal, and, for Hountondji, even Nkrumah in Ghana, were trying to identify a solid bedrock of African beliefs, a passionate search for the identity denied them by the colonisers. The idea was that every culture rests on a metaphysical substratum. Such "philosophy" becomes a collective worldview, a collectively indigenous unanimity, rather than a specific discipline.

Such African philosophy, Hountondji asserts, does exist, but as a literature produced by Africans, dealing with philosophical problems. In other words, it exists as a body of literature, rather than as one prescribed text. This body of literature is written by Africans, thereby excluding Europeans like Placide Temples. Some of these African philosophers, including Hountondji himself, reject the exclusively ethno-philosophical approach, others like Wiredu, wrote about subjects other than African ones. It is impossible to debate amongst the comparative merits of these approaches without freedom of expression and discussion. What then is the nature and scope of such a critical, written philosophy?

Philosophy and its Successive Revolutions

Philosophy is firstly a history and not merely a system. As such it is an open process, a restless unfinished quest, for us an ongoing research project, not closed knowledge. Second, this *history does not move forward by continuous evolution but by leaps and bounds, by successive revolutions and consequently follows a dialectical path.* Thirdly, *African philosophy may be going through a decisive mutation, its outcome depending on contemporary philosophers today.* Similarly, the same could apply for other transitional societies in that context. Czechoslovakia, as we saw in chapter 5, could be seen as one such, until global market forces got in the way of "living in truth"-doctrine.

No philosophical doctrine, notwithstanding Havel's "Living in Truth", can be regarded as the truth. The absolute is contained in the relative of an open-ended process, set within the context of an open society. In other words, *truth is the process where we look for propositions, concepts, theories, more adequate than others. Truth lies in a journey that takes into account all prior doctrines and ideologies and then outdoes them.* Traditional African systems of thought, but also traditional Islam or indeed Hinduism, limited for Hountondji as such, are not in themselves such a journey. There is no philosophy, that would be an implicit system of propositions or beliefs to which all individuals of a society (past, present and future) would subscribe. The issue then is: why should such an "African" philosophy have been sought after, by a European investigator like Temples, in the first instance. Each – European and African – in their own way needed something definite, that could be taken in at a glance, something they could hold onto, maintain and control. The same could apply today, if we are not careful, to the growing global interest in African "ubuntu" today, and in the "real values" of Islam, rather than seeing both as dynamic, evolving belief systems.

A poem or a novel is valuable in itself. Philosophy, on the other hand, is only intelligible as a moment in a debate that sustains and transcends it. It always refers to antecedent positions, either to refute or to confirm and enrich them. It takes on meaning, only in relation to history, through which one generation questions the other. In the strictest sense, art has no history, though it unfolds in history. Every great philosophy, moreover, is a rebirth, a radical questioning, as Christianity and Islam both were at their formative stages. But the break occurs after the event, through a kind of recursion that is essential to all philosophy, as a necessary moment in the history of philosophy, a turning, a renascence, a revolution, a mutation taking place within history and not a suppression coming in from the outside. Every great philosophy, to establish itself, must ravage the existing theoretical space. The same applies to a great piece of research, which serves to make it a social innovation, as hopefully this integral research text may be!

True and False Pluralism

For Hountondji, European civilisation is not a closed system of values, but a set of irreducible cultural products, which have appeared on that great continent. Actually, our integral research approach is the same. At a deeper level, it is the set of these products and of the creative tensions which underlie them, the necessary infinite act of these products and tensions, in the forms they have assumed in the past and the yet unpredictable forms they will assume, that emerge out of that little strip of the world called Europe. Nor is African civilisation, Arab civilisation, Indian or Chinese – even American – civilisation, a closed system. It is the unfinished history of a similarly contradictory debate.

We now retrace steps and re-visit phenomenology through "professional" philosophical eyes.

11.4.2 The Struggle for Meaning

The Phenomenology of Science

For Husserl – whom Hountondji actually studied under – science occupied the highest rung in the hierarchy of cultural practices. To him, no other form of thought, way of life, vocation, art or religion, appears nobler. This is not, Hountondji emphasizes, "scientism": *science is not valued for itself, but for its human significance and meaning for life. It is subordinated, like any other cultural production, to ethics; its exceptional value – far from its technical accomplishments – is that it is the bearer of norms and generative values.* In our terms, and for Hountondji's (8), it emerges out of a particular and formative "life world", African or Arab, Indian or Chinese, French or Japanese, subsequently reformed through exposure to other such worlds, and thereafter bears new norms and values.

Science, for Husserl, can either be defined pragmatically, as an experimental montage, a body of regulated material practices, or psychologically, as a linkage of acts of cognition. The term "scientific rigour", usually associated with rigorous empiricism, is a total misnoma. Husserl mentions the "science" only to annex it immediately to the "acts of cognition"; instruments and apparatuses will never be anything but extrinsic tools linked to a unity of acts of thought. Hountondji's doctoral research, when he was based in France, was based on Husserl's philosophy. Interestingly, he deliberately held his research back until he had deepened and extended his critical and dialectical analysis, believing that such was required first, as a prelude to rationally based, scientific research. *Whereas Africa was for him phenomenologically and interpretively richly endowed, it lacked critical rational thought where "professional philosophy" came in.*

Impoverished Science and Detached Philosophy

For philosophy and research methodology, for Hountondji as for us, must bring about the transformation of the world. *In Africa, as everywhere else, theory has meaning only if it is organised and subordinated to practice, where it derives its legitimacy in relation to other practices.* The myth of white supremacy, in that respect, cannot be dealt with by attachment to a counter myth of "black supremacy" or "yellow supremacy". A simplistic comparison between a stereotyped "north" and "south" (or indeed "east") will not do without due consideration of the interactions between them (also including the "west").

The problem for Africa and many other transition countries today – which is all too evident in their business schools and universities – is that they have to a large extent internalised the discourse of their former masters in their research and educational activities, including their denigrating views on African (or Arab or Latino) ways of life and thought. At the same time Hountondji warns against the opposite danger, that of closing off Africa's or Islam's heritage without any critical approach, without any attempt to update and renew the intellectual legacy, in a way that allows a higher degree of rationality, and a steadier march towards efficiency and self-reliance. Things have to be considered afresh, at an equal distance from cultural alienation, which takes up the colonial masters' prejudices and any self-denigration, both of which results in a kind of intellectual self-imprisonment. Most transitional societies cultures are caught in between such closed traditions and a westernised modernity.

Hence, in the process of scientific investigation in today's social sciences, the decisive stage is neither the collection of data, as fieldwork that so often starts the whole process off, nor the application of theoretical findings to practical issues, which is all too often the final stage. The decisive stage is what comes between them – the interpretation of raw information, the theoretical processing of the data collected, and the production of those particular utterances which we call scientific statements, or indeed theory building. For Hountondji, *the one essential shortcoming of scientific activity in the colonies was the lack of the intermediate stage. He claims, that the former colonies missed the central operation of theory building, then as now.* They only had, and still have, the first and the third stages of the process:

- Stage 1: the data collection, the feverish gathering of all supposedly useful information, and
- Stage 2: the intermediate theory building then took place in the so called "mother country"
- Stage 3: the partial, occasional and limited application of the research outcomes to local issues

Thus science in the former colonies was, and indeed still is, characterised by a theoretical vacuum – the lack of those intellectual and experimental procedures that, being at the heart of the entire enterprise, depended on infrastructure that existed only in the ruling countries. This theoretical vacuum (stage 2) was substantially the same as the industrial vacuum that used to, and still does, characterise economic activity. Universities today fall into the same trap, where the west and north lead, and the south and east follow; however, we are determined, with you, to get out of there.

Deprived of Theory Building

Modern science was introduced by the coloniser in the overseas territories in the form of an impoverished science, deprived of the theory-building activity that makes integral science. This was a side-affect of the same colonisers' launch of so-called "modern", rational and pragmatic economies in these territories, devoid of holistic and humanistic underpinnings. The theoretical emptiness of scientific activity in the colony derives from the very nature of peripheral capitalism. For Hountondji, it is a mode of production based on the search for surplus, as in Europe, but deprived of the industrial activism. Such activism involves the will to transform, rather than "collect data", that is the creativity and inventiveness, the sense of initiative and propensity to risk, that makes capitalism productive in the coloniser's own country.

As a consequence of what Hountondji terms "extroversion", local scholars tend to address issues that are primarily of interest to the Western public. The problem, however, is that this orientation indulges too often in some kind of imprisonment into the particular. In order to give a proper account of the local peculiarities of our culture, we first need to be aware of what is universal about them. You need to take that minimum theoretical distance that allows you to put things into perspective.

What is needed in Africa today is not just to apply traditional knowledge in agriculture or medicine, economics or management, while continuing to import from the West technologies that are poorly understood and mastered by the local users. What is needed, instead, is to help their people and their educated elite, to capitalise and master the existing indigenous knowledge, and develop new knowledge in a continual process of uninterrupted creativity, while applying the findings in a systematic and responsible way to improve their own quality of life. Instead, for Hountondji, indigenous people have been serving as learned informants, for a theory-building activity located overseas and entirely controlled by the people there. Africa needs to invent ways in which knowledge can be better shared by the North, West and East, as well as the South, in all its phases, be it the phase of production, accumulation and capitalisation, or of application. It needs to develop an ambitious strategy of knowledge appropriation that will allow Africans to freely and critically take up anything that can be useful for them in the intellectual heritage now available in the world.

The Liberation of the Future

The illusion of timelessness that is associated with any reductive reading of African civilizations, the tendency to mummify them, to empty them of their history, evolution, diversity, and of their creative tensions, is therefore questioned by Hountondji. *What is demanded instead, is the internal dynamism of African cultures, the pluralism of beliefs transmitted by them. Individual speech must be liberated, and a multiplicity of speeches must be released and related to each other. African thought must be released from its local confines, and related for instance, as Nkrumah has done at least in part, to Plato or Aristotle, Plato or Marx. The great issue at stake, therefore, in Hountondji's critique of ethno-philosophy, is the liberation of the future.* For the African intellectual, the burden of having to conform to a system of thought that had been worked out in advance, had to be lifted. It had to be demonstrated that the freedom of the individual could not be restricted in advance. The horizon of possibilities had to be opened. In short, the over-determination of the concept of Africa is an obstacle to the freedom of Africans.

For the same reason *the notion of philosophy (and research) has to be re-examined, to describe a history not a system, a discipline in which results matter more than reasoning, whose goals is to go beyond the results to achieve better ones.* To liberate the future requires disentanglement from the collective "us". *To liberate the future, the past has first to be liberated by restoring movement, contradiction and dynamism to it,* in the same sense as Nkrumah (10) conceived of, but did not apply. Real pluralism does not only consist in affirming – against the West's cultural hegemony – a plurality of cultures, but recognizing the complexity, diversity, tensions, contradictions, internal dynamics of each world, and seeing in that a source of richness.

The African philosopher should not be required to reflect on Africa alone. Hountondji's critique of ethno-centricism leads to a de-territorialisation of cultural values. At a stroke this approach makes it possible for African science to claim to be universal. He deplores *Africa's exclusion from science, as is the case for most of the developing world, and their remaining on the margins of the global production of knowledge, and he argues for constructing a new space of theoretical construction.* He seeks to de-marginalise Africa, to place it firmly at the centre of its own history in a pluralized world, whose unity needs to be periodically re-negotiated. The reinsertion of thought in the real movement of history should enhance both a recognition of the specificity of works of speculative thought and their relationship to the social, political and economic context of different periods. It should find a pluralist vision of philosophy and African culture by sweeping away unanimist prejudice. It should see such critical rationalism in an integral research light. This brings us on to the practice of an open society.

11.5 Critical Rationalism in Practice: George Soros and the Open Society Foundation

The Meaning of Open Society

Open society is not an easy idea. (11) It resembles the concept of liberal democracy but there is an important difference: it is an epistemological concept, not a political one. It is based on the recognition of our imperfect understanding, not on a political theory.

Popper's book "The Open Society and its Enemies" (12) made a great impact on Soros in his youth. It threw a new light on the ideologies that had such a decisive influence on his life: Fascism, National Socialism and Communism. Each asserted they were in possession of one valid interpretation of reality. But the ultimate truth is beyond reach; therefore these ideologies could only be imposed on society, and repression serves to bring about a closed society. In Popper's open society people of different views and interests live together in peace. Tribal morality, according to French philosopher Henri Bergson (who coined the term "open society"), gave rise to closed society, whereas universal morality leads to an open one, which recognized fundamental human rights, irrespective of tribal, ethnic or religious affiliation.

For Soros, a traditional mode of thinking has only one task: to accept things as they are. This supreme simplicity extracts a heavy price; it generates beliefs that may be completely divorced from reality. Soros calls this the "organic" society, a society in which individuals are organs of a social body. In a changing world, on the other hand, people are confronted by an infinite range of possibilities. The great merit of the critical process is that it can provide a better understanding of reality; its major drawback is that it does not satisfy the quest for certainty. The dogmatic mode, conversely, gives the illusion of certainty.

Free markets do offer economic choice, but they are not perfect, as market participants do not have perfect knowledge. Moreover, they are not designed to take care of social needs – such as the maintenance of law and order, social justice, and stable markets – as distinct from the needs of individual participants. The satisfaction of social needs is the domain of politics. On their own, individuals provide an uncertain foundation for values sufficient to sustain a structure that will outlast them. Yet such a value system is needed to sustain society.

The conceptual model outlined above was developed in "The Burden of Consciousness", which Soros completed at the age of 33, in 1963, and which he sent to Popper. Despite receiving some encouragement from him, Soros proceeded to get lost in philosophical abstractions, so he quit philosophy and decided to devote himself to making money. His success in the financial markets exceeded expectations, and by the time he was fifty the size of his hedge fund was approaching $100 billion. So he started wondering what to do with the money, and that process of reflection took him back to his framework of open and closed societies, and to the set up of his Open Society Foundation.

The Open Society Foundation: Operating in Far-From-Equilibrium Situations

Soros' first major engagement was in South Africa, where he gave scholarships to African students attending the University of Cape Town. He was trying to use the system to undermine apartheid society from the inside, as the university involved proclaimed its commitment to the ideal of an open society. Unfortunately, the black students remained alienated and resentful, and Soros abandoned the scheme. He started supporting Charter 77 in Czechoslovakia, Solidarity in Poland, the Jewish Refuseniks in the Soviet Union. In Hungary, he supported experimental schools and libraries, artistic and cultural projects. Open Society Foundations were then set up in Hungary and in the Soviet Union. By 1991, there were Foundations in twenty countries, throughout Eastern Europe and the ex Soviet Union, in South Africa and in America.

Soros, by then, considered himself a specialist in far-from-equilibrium situations, having learnt from his father that, at the height of a revolution, almost anything is possible. He had political convictions, financial means, and an understanding of the importance of the moment. The Central European University was established in Budapest, as an intellectual resource centre for the foundation network. Annual expenditures jumped from $3 million to 300 million.

Applying the Framework

During all this time Soros was guided by the conceptual framework outlined, and in his book on "Opening the Soviet System" (13) he combined static models of open and closed societies with his theory of reflexivity to interpret the rise and fall of the Soviet system, his contention being that changelessness can initially be self-reinforcing, but is ultimately self defeating. In fact, reform accelerates the process of disintegration.

In an open society, every citizen is required to form his or her own view of the world, and society needs institutions that allow people with different views and interests to live together in peace. The task is so immense that it is impossible to make the transition form closed to open society without a helping hand from outside. Regrettable, in the former Soviet Union, the West never rose to that occasion. Open society constitutes near-equilibrium conditions precariously poised between the static disequilibrium of closed society and the dynamic disequilibrium of chaos and disorientation.

The Next Challenge

The challenge that now preoccupies Soros is that of the U.S. Who would have thought that the most powerful open society in the world could pose a threat not only to open society at home but to the peace and stability of the world? The Bush agenda that has been set is the wrong agenda, Soros asserts, for the world. The survival of the fittest is a major theme and competition, rather than cooperation, is supposed to determine who is fittest. Yet our globalised world is not a jungle ruled by naked power. In fact, globalisation has made the world increasingly interdependent, and the challenges that mankind faces can be met only through increased cooperation. Little can be achieved without the U.S.'s leadership. Now that the United States has become an imperial power, it bears a unique responsibility for the future of the world.

In concluding, we retrace original steps, before distilling the rational ground we have now additionally covered, starting by reviewing Popper's contribution.

11.6 Conclusion

11.6.1 From Life World to Open Society

The "swamp" that Popper has referred to is that prior phenomenological and interpretive ground. It is necessary, but all too blurred – though not the case for Hountondji – in the vision of the critical rationalist. Yet as conscious human beings, phenomenologically speaking, we always inhabit the life world; it is pre-given in advance and experienced as a unity, as was the case for Popper himself, as a Jew, in Nazi infested Austria. The life world is the general and indeed questionable structure, which allows objectivity and thing-hood to emerge potentially as concepts, in Africa or in Europe, in the U.S. or in the Middle East, in China or in India, in the different ways in which they do emerge in different cultures. In Popper's own case, his actual and horrific experience of fascism, mediated by the force of his own and others' imagination (Frances Bergson – another Jew – first coined the term "open society"), ultimately gave rise to his philosophy of an "open society". There is not one single life world, but a set of overlapping worlds, beginning from the world, which is the indigenous "home-world", and extending to other worlds farther away. For Popper, as for Soros, their horizons extended from central to Western Europe, from Austria and Hungary to Britain and America.

11.6.2 From Popper to Hountondji

Rootedness and Freedom

For Hountondji, you have to exist first, to take interpretive root in a tradition, but at the same time, you must be capable of keeping your rational distance from that cultural tradition. You must invent again and again, something with which Karl Popper would have much sympathy. In every society there exists a minimal consensus, a small common denominator, a spiritual cement that ensures the system's cohesion. But it must always be subject to critique. For us, the "south" has always to be re-viewed in terms of the other worlds, but for Hountondji such re-viewing has to always take place through African eyes, in other words, by African philosophers.

The term "extraversion" has been used in contrasting a self-sustaining economy that is capable of counting on its own resources, and of being self reliant by ensuring its own internal coherence, with the underdeveloped economy organised and subordinated to the needs of the ruling classes in the industrial capitals. Such an extraverted economy aims above all to furnish raw materials and outlets for the manufacturing industries located at the centre. Hountondji sees intellectual extraversion in the same light. *One thing missing in each case is transformation, the transformation of raw materials into finished products in the one case, and the theoretical treatment of data in the other, the production of general statements from initial information, in other words an integral science.*

Towards Reappropriation

Science is not reducible to one single methodology, that is the empirically based collection of information, and empirical observation, any more than it can be confused with a technical object that is only its technical by-product. *Science is an activity, for Hountondji, whose goal it is to produce true statements. Such an activity was seriously lacking in the dominated territories. The colonies lacked laboratories as they lacked factories.* Once this theoretical void – the equivalent of an industrial void – is acknowledged, you get a fairer picture of development. Decolonisation did not put an end to this, with the former colonies as huge reservoirs of facts and raw data, and second, as testing fields for the results of metropolitan inventions. The system has quite simply become more refined. The research institutions at the periphery are mere annexes of the mother institutions at the centre.

The theoretical demand like the economic one comes from the centre. In Africa, no effort was made to formulate new and original questions. To answer the questions of others seemed to be the continent's destiny. The international division of scientific labour freed Africa from thinking. To develop it had to apply the inventions of others, still the case today; social innovations like the Truth and Reconciliation Commission in South Africa are a notable exception. The four weaknesses that Hountondji has specifically detected, that prevent African scientific practices from serving its peoples, are:

- financial dependence vis-à-vis the outside world,
- institutional dependence vis-à-vis the research centres of the north,
- primacy of North-South vertical scientific exchanges over South-South ones,
- intellectual subordination to the questions and expectations of the learned public in the West.

What we need, he says as a critical rationalist, is ultimately a "radical appropriation of theory".

Periphery cut off from the Centre

Theory then, from a peripheral perspective, is always physically distant. The best universities, the best business schools, the best businesses, the best laboratories, the greatest libraries, the most credible publishing houses, the best researchers, are massively located in industrialised countries. The result is that the African or Arab or Chinese researcher in search of the sacred fire – the material and intellectual tools of knowledge – must move elsewhere. Just as integration into the world capitalist markets had resulted in the destruction of the equilibrium mechanisms of subsistence economies, without giving rise to industrial development in the periphery, so integration into world scientific research resulted in arresting the development of pre-existing forms of knowledge, all the while pushing the periphery into subaltern roles in relation to the global process of knowledge creation.

Research wise, the periphery is shut off by the local and the particular, which becomes their research domain, at the expense of theory. Abstract universalism of course, as in the natural sciences, is no better, for it eliminates an essential question, that of the collective appropriation of the universal both as project and result. The African historian must be as interested in the process of industrialisation in Japan as in the slave trade. Studying Japan or Finland or Ireland gives one an understanding, through contrast, of one's own society. As soon as it is produced, African knowledge is "stolen" and integrated into the world system of knowledge administered from abroad.

To put an end to extraversion, to break with a marginalisation that constantly siphons the results of their research, peripheral researchers need to be involved in what Thomas Kuhn called "extraordinary" science (14), to maintain a critical relationship with the paradigms in each discipline, and to raise new problems that are linked to the preoccupations of their societies. The researcher at the periphery has to go back to the paradigms themselves, and challenge them, developing his or her own basic research, promoting invention in all its forms. There is a great need for a sociology of science to be developed at the periphery.

Participating in the Construction of the Future

To participate in the construction of our future, in Africa as in the Middle East, in Latin America as in South-East Asia, *we need a double movement, a critical appropriation of the scientific and technological heritage available globally, and, at the same time, a re-appropriation of indigenous local knowledge.* In fact, the knowledge produced in the North has been produced over centuries. Rationality is therefore not appropriated in advance. It is still to be built. Hence the immense responsibility of contemporary generations: that of *contributing together in a spirit of solidarity and sharing to the building of the common edifice, so that the germs of irrationality and progressively of ignorance and poverty will be eliminated* forever from the planet earth.

We now turn from Hountondji, the professional philosopher, and Popper, the original critical rationalist, to the next critical step along the path of reason, from modernism to postmodernism, from rational debate to multiple discourses.

Bibliography

1) **Popper**, K. (1990). *On Problem Solving*. London: Routledge.

2) **Popper**, K. (2002). *Open Society and its Enemies*. London: Routledge.

3) **Soros**, G. (2000). *Open Society*. Boston: Little Brown.

4) **Hallen**, B. (2002). *A Short History of African Philosophy*. Bloomington: Indiana University Press.

5) **Gyekye**, K. (1997). *Tradition and Modernity*. Oxford and New York: Oxford University Press.

6) **Hountondji**, P. (1983). *African Philosophy*. Bloomington: Indiana University Press.

7) **Hountondji**, P. (1983). *African Philosophy*. Bloomington: Indiana University Press.

8) **Hountondji**, P. (2002). *The Struggle for Meaning*. London, Thousand Oaks and New Delhi: Open University Press.

9) **Serequeberhan**, T. (2000). *Our Heritage*. Lanham: Rowan and Littlefield.

10) **Nkrumah**, K. (1970). *Consciencism*. New York: Monthly Review Press.

11) **Soros**, G. (2006). *The Age of Fallibility.* London: Weidenfeld.

12) **Popper**, K. (2002). *Open Society and its Enemies*. London: Routledge.

13) **Soros**, G. (1990). *Opening the Soviet System*. London: Weidenfeld.

14) **Kuhn**, T. S. (1996). *The Structure of Scientific Revolutions*. London, Chicago: University of Chicago Press.

CHAPTER 12

FROM CRITICAL RATIONALISM TO
POSTMODERNISM

"ACCOMMODATE MULTIPLE DISCOURSES"

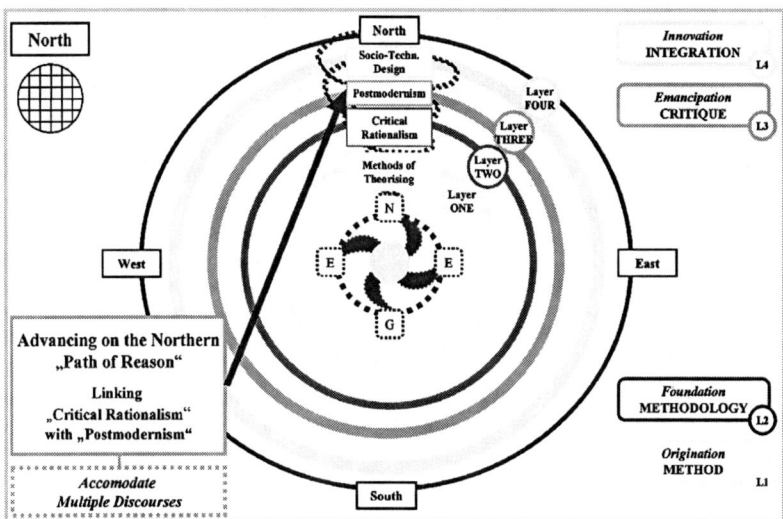

Figure 12.1: Overview Chapter 12 – Layer 3 / North

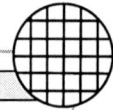

Summary: Postmodernism

- You are now entering the third layer of the northern path of reason. You have started out with the originating methods of theorising (most likely via grounded theory) and have then worked yourself through Karl Popper's modernist approach to critical rationalism. We now turn from modernity to postmodernity.

- While modernist critical rationalism has Anglo-Austrian roots in Europe, and was picked up by the so-called "professional philosophers" in an African context, postmodernism is strongly French in its original orientation.

- While modernism and thereby critical rationalism is oriented towards uncovering an "objective truth", postmodernism argues that there are multiple truths, depending on the time and place, and that discontinuity rather than continuity is the order, or indeed disorder, of the postmodern day.

- The key tenets of postmodernism extend from the nature and scope of such multiple discourses, to the language that underlies such discourses, to the extent that it is subjectively constructed by the reader or interpreter, and cannot be taken as an objective given.

- The originators of postmodernism are primarily French philosophers, including Foucault, Derrida and Saussure, though Foucault remains the most prolific of these originators, and was himself a revolutionary in his own right, joining in with the French students who took to the streets, against the status quo, in the 1960's.

- The postmodernist perspective has spread from France to, in particular, the Muslim world, to the extent that the power of the "other", the marginalized person, has been taken up vigorously by the Islamists, and philosophically by Karen Armstrong and academic, writer and philosopher Ziauddin Sardar. Sardar, one of the leading intellectuals in the Muslim world, is arguing for a trans-modern approach to mutuality.

- It is indeed Sardar's "Islamic Future Studies" that we have chosen as an illustration of a practical application of postmodernism. It shows the potential contribution of Islam, together with Christianity, for the building of an alternative more sustainable future, more precisely, a (global) open society.

- Such a postmodern reality, incorporating the emergence of multiple voices, has been turned, by American social philosopher Richard Tarnas, into the hallmark of our contemporary age. After postmodernism we shall come onto socio-technical design, and with that to the culminating social innovation along this northern research path.

12.1 Orientation to Postmodernism

Modernism to Postmodernism

We now turn, in this chapter, from critical rationalism to postmodernism, its more recent and better-known counterpart. While the former had strong Anglo-Austrian roots, the latter is French in origin. While such a postmodern orientation toward the relativism of multiple discourses is a deliberate reaction against the modern notion of "absolute" truth, both of these "reasonable" research orientations are indeed "rational". Actually, the very fact that such French intellectuals as Foucault and Derrida have taken up the postmodern high ground, is a reflection of such ultra-rationality.

The evolution from so-called modernism to postmodernism, towards (in the late Peter Drucker's terms) the "Age of Discontinuity" (1), and (for UK's management guru Charles Handy's) "The Age of Unreason" (2), is perhaps the most distinctive overall movement of our times. For American social philosopher Richard Tarnas, what we can see in the twenty-first century, and which he anticipated in his "Passion of the Western Mind", was a postmodernity that was reflected:

"... in the widespread call for and practice of open 'conversation' between different understandings, different vocabularies, different cultural paradigms. Not only is the postmodern mind itself a maelstrom of unresolved diversity, but virtually every important element of the Western intellectual past is now present and active in one form or another, contributing to the variety and confusion of the contemporary Zeitgeist. Moreover, these in turn have been joined, and affected by a multitude of cultural perspectives from outside the West, such as the Buddhist and Hindu mystical traditions; by underground cultural streams from within the West itself; and by indigenous and archaic perspectives antedating Western civilization altogether – all gathering now on the intellectual stage as if for some kind of climactic synthesis. The postmodern collapse of meaning has been countered by an emerging awareness of the individual's self-responsibility and capacity for creative innovation and self-transformation in his or her existential and spiritual response to life. In virtually all contemporary disciplines it is recognized that the prestigious complexity, subtlety and multi-valence of reality far transcend the grasp of any one intellectual approach, and that only a committed openness to the interplay of many perspectives can meet the extra-ordinary challenges of the postmodern era." (3)

As we shall see later in this chapter, the Muslim voice has been vocally added to the others that Tarnas mentions. What is unique to postmodernism and which makes it an excellent "navigational vehicle" for our northern research journey, is that it has developed a distinctive method as well as methodology which, while rationally based, is much more discursive than analytically oriented towards building up an overall theory or hypotheses, and then seeking to debate such, with a view to getting closer to a universal truth.

Popper to Foucault

In other words, Michel Foucault like Karl Popper is very much in favour of discussion, but such discussion is not aimed at revealing or falsifying a single truth, but rather at acknowledging a multiplicity of discourses.

Michel Foucault was a French philosopher and historian. He held a chair at the Collège de France, giving it the title "History of Systems of Thought" and taught at the University of California, Berkeley, from 1975 until his death in 1984. He is known for his critical studies of various social institutions, most notably psychiatry, medicine, the human sciences, and the prison system, as well as his work on the history of sexuality. His work concerning power, the relationship between power and knowledge and "discourse" in relation to the history of Western thought, has been widely discussed and applied. His work is often described as postmodernist or post-structuralist by commentators and critics, although he was more often associated with the structuralist movement during the 1960s. He was initially happy with this description, but later vehemently distanced himself from structuralism and he always rejected the "post-structuralist" and even "postmodernist" labels, even though he has been the seminal influence on what has come to be known as "postmodernism".

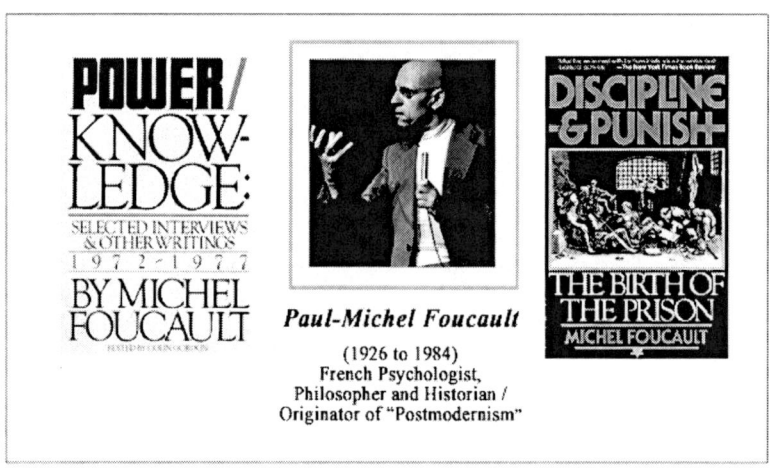

Figure 12.2: Postmodernism's leading thinker – Michael Foucault

Foucault was born in 1926 in Poitiers as Paul-Michel Foucault to a notable provincial family. His father, Paul Foucault, was an eminent surgeon and hoped his son would join him in the profession. His early education was a mix of success and mediocrity until he attended the Jesuit Collège Saint-Stanislas, where he excelled. During this period, Poitiers was part of Vichy France and later came under German occupation. After World War II, Foucault gained entry to the prestigious École Normale Supérieure, the traditional gateway to an academic career in the humanities in France.

Foucault's personal life during the École Normale was difficult – he suffered from acute depression, even attempting suicide, and was subsequently taken to see a psychiatrist. Because of this, or perhaps in spite of it, Foucault became fascinated with psychology. He earned a degree in psychology, a very new qualification in France at the time, in addition to a degree in philosophy. He was involved in the clinical arm of psychology, which exposed him to thinkers such as the German psycho-analyst Ludwig Binswanger. Foucault joined the French Communist Party from 1950 to 1953. He was inducted into the party by his mentor Louis Althusser. He left due to concerns about what was happening in the Soviet Union under Stalin.

Foucault passed his agrégation in 1950. After a brief period lecturing at the École Normale, he took up a position at the University of Lille, where from 1953 to 1954 he taught psychology. In 1954 Foucault published his first book, "Maladie mentale et personnalité", a work which he would later disavow. It soon became apparent that Foucault was not interested in a teaching career, and he undertook a lengthy exile from France. In 1954 Foucault served France as a cultural delegate to the University of Uppsala in Sweden (a position arranged for him by Georges Dumézil, who was to become a friend and mentor). In 1958 Foucault left Uppsala for briefly held positions at Warsaw University and at the University of Hamburg.

Foucault returned to France in 1960 to complete his doctorate and take up a post in philosophy at the University of Clermont-Ferrand. There he met Daniel Defert, with whom he lived in a non-monogamous partnership for the rest of his life. In 1961 he earned his doctorate by submitting two theses (as is customary in France): a "major" thesis entitled "Folie et déraison: Histoire de la folie à l'âge classique" and a "secondary" thesis which involved a translation and commentary on Kant's "Anthropology from a Pragmatic Point of View". "Folie et déraison" (Madness and Insanity; ironically published in English as Madness and Civilization) was extremely well-received.

After Defert was posted to Tunisia for his military service, Foucault moved to a position at the University of Tunis in 1965. In 1966 he published "Les Mots et les Choses" (The Order of Things), which was enormously popular despite its length and difficulty. This was during the height of interest in structuralism and Foucault was quickly grouped with scholars such as Jacques Lacan, Claude Lévi-Strauss, and Roland Barthes as the newest, latest wave of thinkers set to topple the existentialism popularized by Jean-Paul Sartre. Foucault made a number of sceptical comments about Marxism, which outraged a number of Left wing critics, but he quickly tired of being labelled a "structuralist". He was still in Tunis during the May 1968 student rebellions, where he was profoundly affected by a local student revolt earlier in the same year. In the fall of 1968 he returned to France, where he published "L'archéologie du savoir" (The Archaeology of Knowledge) – a methodological response to his critics – in 1969.

In the aftermath of 1968, the French government created a new experimental university at Vincennes. Foucault became the first head of its philosophy department in December of that year and appointed mostly young leftist academics whose radicalism provoked the Ministry of Education to withdraw the department's accreditation. Foucault notoriously also joined students in occupying administration buildings and fighting with police. Foucault's tenure at Vincennes was short-lived, as in 1970 he was elected to France's most prestigious academic body, the Collège de France as Professor of the History of Systems of Thought. His political involvement now increased. Foucault helped found the Prison Information Group to provide a way for prisoners to voice their concerns. This fed into a marked politicization of Foucault's work, with a book, "Discipline and Punish", which "narrates" the micro-power structures that developed in Western societies since the eighteenth century, with a special focus on prisons and schools.

In the late 1970s, political activism in France tailed off with the disillusionment of many left wing militants. A number of young Maoists abandoned their beliefs to become the so-called New Philosophers, often citing Foucault as their major influence, a status about which Foucault had mixed feelings. Foucault in this period embarked on a six volume project on "The History of Sexuality", which he was never to complete.

Foucault began to spend more time in the United States, at University at Buffalo (where he had lectured on his first ever visit to the United States in 1970) and especially at UC Berkeley. In 1979 Foucault made two tours of Iran, undertaking extensive interviews with political protagonists in support of the new interim government established soon after the Iranian Revolution. His many essays on Iran, published in the Italian newspaper "Corriere della Sera", only appeared in French in 1994 and then in English in 2005. These essays caused some controversy, with some commentators arguing that Foucault was insufficiently critical of the new regime.

Foucault died of an AIDS-related illness in Paris in 1984. He was the first high profile French personality who was reported to have had AIDS. His death marks the beginning of the post-AIDS era in France.

We now turn to the key tenets of postmodernism.

12.2 Postmodernism – Key Tenets

Postmodernism – Key Tenets
① Pursue multiple discourses.
② Focus on meanings as multiple and shifting.
③ You socially construct meaning.
④ Every word you use is packed with meaning.
⑤ Use language as cultural representation.
⑥ Focus on transformation.

① Pursue multiple discourses

In our (Ronnie Lessem) own previous work on "Business as a Learning Community" (4), and on "European Management Systems" (5), we not only introduced a multiplicity of worldly truths – pragmatic and rational, holistic and humanistic – but also connected them explicitly with different orientations toward knowledge. Here indeed we have connected each one of these to diverse reaearch paths: pragmatic to *realisable*, rational to *reasonable,* holistic to *renewal*, and humanistic to *relational.* Indeed postmodernism was specifically to herald a newly post-industrial, post-capitalist, knowledge based society, which, for us, was built upon such multiple perspectives. Reality then, from a postmodern perspective, is not a solid, monolithic and self-contained given but a fluid, unfolding discursive process, an "open universe", continually affected and molded by a diversity of actions and beliefs. It is possibility rather than fact. We cannot regard reality as a removed spectator against a fixed object; rather we are always and necessarily engaged in reality, in its multiplicity of forms and perspectives, thereby at once transforming it while being transformed ourselves.

A "modern" approach to deductively or inductively based research sees useful knowledge as a hypothesis shaped (critical rational) or reflection (empirical) of things in the world. An evolved, postmodernist one, in contrast, involves *constructing specific accounts of the world, through language and archive, discourse and culture, that forms complex representations which have cultural significance.* In the last three decades of the twentieth century, all the disciplines of the social sciences have experienced a fundamental reappraisal of their basic assumptions, the most significant of such (following on from phenomenology and most particularly hermeneutics) is the recognition that *"culture" deserves much more serious attention as an object of study in its own right.* Together with such has been *a focus on knowledge, arising out of culture, in the context of a post-industrial, knowledge based society.*

This, altogether, has been described as a *"cultural turn" in the social sciences.* It is equivalent to the "fourth moment", that is the "crisis of representation" to which Denzin and Lincoln have alluded (see chapter 3). As such *we move from an absolute to a relative notion of truth*, parting company here from both positivists and realists, and now focusing on "discourses" rather than either facts (empirical), hypotheses (rational) or indeed dialectical forces (critical theory).

② **Focus on meanings as multiple and shifting**

In their text on "Discourse Analytic Research", UK based psychologists Erica Burman and Ian Parker point to the way in which language organised into discourses, or interpretative repertoires, has an immense power to shape the way that people behave in the world. (6) Specifically, they refer to the fact that, instead of studying the mind as if it were outside language, discourse analysts study spoken and written texts – that is conversations, debates, and discussions – where images of the mind are produced and transformed.

Such a "discourse analysis" offers a social account of subjectivity by attending to the linguistic sources by which the socio-political, and indeed the organisational and managerial, realms, are produced and reproduced. The overall implication is that *meanings are multiple and shifting, rather than unitary and fixed.* For such postmodernism or post-structuralism research involves a commitment to the socially constructed nature of reality; and a good way to examine such is through "discourse analysis".

For leading social constructionists and postmodernists, as Potter and Wethereall (7) in Britain and Elliot Mishler (8) in America, *conventionally "modernist" survey methods are flawed because they do not take into account the true variability of human thought and action, instead concentrating on the uniform, rational and classifiable.* Moreover, for Mishler, a focus on meaning construction requires purposeful interaction between researcher and researched, interviewer and interviewee. Rather then therefore restricting respondents to particular responses, it is seen as important that they can discuss in full their ideas and understandings of the questions being asked. If this is allowed, then variation will emerge due to the complexity of the issues explored. Finally, whereas modern attitudinal research sees language as an essentially colourless, transparent medium, unproblematically describing some underlying "real" entity, *discourse analysis takes language as actively constructing versions of the social world.*

③ You socially construct meaning

For discourse analysts, all forms of social reality have a peculiarly human and socially constructed nature. In other words, they share an assumption that "knowledge of" can never be an objective fact, as all knowledge is produced, bounded and sustained by human beings and their constructions. *This postmodernist constructivist and historicist commitment leads to a heightened emphasis on the means through which human meanings and experience are manufactured, that is through discourses. Such "discourse" refers not only to observable linguistic activities, but also to the world of human signs, symbols, activities, texts that together comprise a particular worldview.*

For environmentalist Philip Macnaghten (9), "nature", as he discovered through discourse analysis, can alternately be conceived of as "wilderness", as "harmony" and in terms of "ecology". The three statements below represent these respective discourses, as revealed in research public reactions to a local government's environmental orientation:

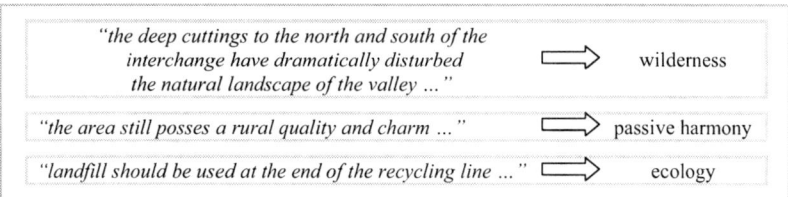

④ Every word you use is packed with meaning

Such "thematic decomposition" attempts to separate a given text (or context) into coherent themes or stories. This approach is informed by the *idea that discourse does not simply express or reflect meanings, but that meanings are constructed through discourse.* These meanings are useful and have "cultural currency" because they are social and enable a shared understanding. They should not, for the social constructionists, be considered the product of any one individual. However, such discourses represent an amalgam of hypotheses, narratives and descriptions, rolled up into one. We use narratives and discourses, so our discourse analysts say, with themes that have already been socially arranged for us. (10) Such stories can be thought of as trans-individual, historically localised, culturally specific formations of language-in-use.

The French linguistic theorist, Ferdinand de Saussure (11) was interested in the meaning of cultural representations, for him embodied in language. For example, take the case of the distinction between "man" and "beast" in Western culture. This distinction clearly separates human beings from other animals. To be a "beast", as is conventionally understood, is to be savage. The concept of "man", conversely, is conceived as civilized. In this way we place values on things through the very words we use in a given language. In turn, these words only make sense on the context of the systems of values we share within social communities.

If we turn from English or French to say, Arabic or Chinese, we will find that we enter into very different language-and-culture worlds. So what does Saussure tell us? In contradiction to the positivist vision of scientific knowledge, his approach suggests there is no simple or neutral act of perception. Every word we use to understand natural things, for example in Sutu or Zulu, as opposed to English or French, is packed with meaning. The way we distinguish human activity from natural relations and processes is a reflection of the values we hold. These types of distinction reveal a lot about the way in which Western societies demarcate culture from biology, masculinity from femininity, and how we see cultural differences.

⑤ **Use language as cultural representation**

Semiology brings the study of language into line with the study of culture. Roland Barthes (12), another French postmodernist, is concerned with the way in which "mythologies" are generated throughout culture. Barthes makes the distinction between how signs operate at the level of denotation and how these are transformed through connotations. To denote something is to identify what is widely accepted as a descriptive and factual account, like "this is an oak tree". However, when we connote meaning to such, we recognize that, for instance in English culture, the "oak tree" is understood as a symbol of cultural strength, of working within a cohesive social order with solid foundations. This is the difference between language (denotation) and meta-language (connotation).

For Michel Foucault and Jacques Derrida, all forms of representation can be rearticulated and transformed. In that context the reader is a "proactive" agent in the production of meaning through the text concerned. The idea of "discourse", Foucault suggests, enables us to think about how language is situated and constructed through the cultural values of a particular historical and cultural context. By looking at the lived experiences of other cultures, their rituals, family structures, transitions through life, gift relationships and so on we can identify what is distinctive about our own culture. *So cultural studies involve the unfinished business of understanding our own social existence. As Derrida suggested, it is only through the construction of otherness that we are able to locate our own identity.* The characterisation of culture as open to universal definition can be described as nomothetic, whereas specific historical-social relations are ideographic. This also serves to differentiate the archive from the document, in a postmodern research context.

⑥ **Focus on transformation**

A fascinating recent example of the use of the "archive", as both a vehicle for research and also a stimulus for transformation, was in the new South Africa, in the 1990's; it was a process in which Jacques Derrida himself participated:

"We have to create new expanses where one is able to reclaim the past, revisit the legacies of suffering and triumph, in ways that will help to transform our present reality. The archive draws us forward in taking us back. Every beginning gathers energies from antecedent endings. All forgetting of the past is also a forgetting of the future. A focus on history as narrative and history writing as a charged political act has made the thinking about archives no longer the pedestrian pre-occupation of flat-footed archivists. The archive is not a library of events but a system of their enunciabilities." (13)

We now turn to a consideration of postmodernism in greater depth, most particularly, to the work of Michel Foucault.

12.3 Postmodern Philosophy and Methodology in Depth

12.3.1 Foucault's New Order of Things: The Force of Discontinuity

The high priest of postmodernism, as we have seen, is the late Michel Foucault. For him, in the history of ideas, that is of thought in general and of the sciences in particular, the same mutation has broken up the long series formed by the progress of consciousness, or the teleology of reason, or the evolution of human thought. It has questioned the themes of convergence and culmination; it has doubted the possibility of creating totalities. It has led to the individualisation of different series juxtaposed upon one another, overlapping and intersecting, without being able to reduce them to a linear schema. (14)

Thus in place of the continuous chronology of reason there have appeared periods that are sometimes very brief, distinct from one another, irreducible to a single law. These periods bear a kind of history peculiar to each one, and thereby cannot be reduced to the general model of a consciousness that acquires, progresses, and remembers. It has now become one of the basic elements of historical analysis. As such *the historian is trying to discover the limits of a process, the point of inflexion of a curve,* the boundaries of an oscillation, the threshold of a function, the instant at which a circular causality breaks down. One of the most essential features of the new postmodern approach to history, for Foucault in his "Archaeology of Knowledge" (15) then, is this *focus on the discontinuous*, and as such:

- its integration into the discourse of the historian where it no longer plays the role of an external condition that must be reduced, but that of a working concept
- and therefore the inversion of signs where it is no longer the negative of the historical reading, but the positive element that determines its object.

Globalisation, in that postmodern light, is such a discontinuous element, a blip on the economic horizon, rather than part of an evolutionary trend. The parallel forces of

Islamicism and environmentalism, therefore, are equally part of such emergent discourses.

The use of concepts of discontinuity, rupture, threshold, limit and transformation presents historical analysis with theoretical problems. These problems are analysed by Foucault in the context of the history of ideas, of science, and of knowledge. There is first the negative work to be carried out: we must rid ourselves, he insists, of a whole mass of notions, each of which, in its own way, reinforces the theme of continuity. There are the notions of development and evolution: they make it possible to group a succession of dispersed events, to link them to one and the same organising principle, to subject them to the exemplary power of life, to discover, already at work, a principle of coherence and the outline of a future unity. There is the notion of "spirit", which enables us to establish between successive phenomena a community of meanings, allowing the sovereignty of collective consciousness to emerge as the principle of unity and explanation. *As soon as one questions that unity, it becomes no longer self evident; it indicates itself, constructs itself, only on the basis of a complex field of discourse.*

12.3.2 Discursive Events

Pre-existing forms of continuity, all these syntheses that are accepted without question, must, for Foucault remain in suspense. They must not be rejected definitively of course, but the tranquillity with which they are accepted must be disturbed; we must show that they do not come about by themselves but are always the result of a construction the rules of which must be known. In short, they require a theory, and this theory cannot be constructed unless the field of the facts of discourse are built up as such. So globalisation, for example in this postmodern context, has been uniformly thrust upon the world, through the force of imposed capitalist circumstances, rather than naturally emerging out of the world's diversity.

In placing yourself in whatever unities are already given, such as psychology or economics, business or management, you need to question by what right they can claim a field that specifies them in space and time; according to what laws they are formed; against the background of what contexts they stand out; and whether or not they are ultimately the surface effect of more firmly grounded unities. You accept the groupings that history suggests only to break them up and then to see whether they can be legitimately reformed.

Once these immediate forms of continuity are suspended, an entire field is set free. One is led therefore to the project of a pure description of discursive events, or a multiplicity of discourses, as the horizon for the search for the unities that form within it. We must grasp the statement in the exact specificity of its occurrence; determine its conditions of existence, fix at least its limits, establish its correlations with another state that may be connected with it. Like every event it is subject to repetition, reactivation, or transformation. By freeing it from pre-existing groupings, such as modernisation and globalisation, new unities can be perceived. It is not therefore an interpretation of the facts that might reveal them, but the analysis of their coexistence, their succession, their mutual functioning, their reciprocal determination, and their independent or correlative transformation. In the final analysis, the chosen field cannot be regarded as definitive or absolutely valid; it is no more than an initial approximation that must allow relations to appear, which may erase the limits of this initial outline: through discursive reality.

12.3.3 Discursive Reality

The term "discourse", according to Foucault's "Archaeology of Knowledge", can hence be defined as the group of statements that belong to a single system of formation, such as clinical discourse, economic discourse, the discourse of natural history, or psychiatric discourse. Discourse in this sense is not an ideal, timeless form. The problem therefore is not to ask oneself how and why it was able to emerge and become embodied at the present point in time. It is, from beginning to end, a fragment of history, a discontinuity in history itself, posing the problem of its own limits, its divisions, its transformations, the specific modes of its temporality. What Foucault has called "discursive practice" is a body of anonymous, historical rules, always determined in time and space that have defined a given period, spanning a given social, economic, geographical or linguistic era. What does this more specifically imply?

Discourse, for Foucault, has not so much a meaning or a truth, but a history, and indeed a specific history: It involves a type of history, a mode of succession, of stability and of reactivation, which belongs to it alone. It is caught up in the very things it connects; and if not modified by history it modifies it, and is transformed by it into certain decisive thresholds. It also ceases to appear as the inert, smooth and neutral element in which they arise, each according to its own movement, or driven by some obscure dynamics or themes, ideas or concepts. We are now dealing with a complex volume, in which heterogeneous regions are differentiated. As such, we are not seeing, in the great mythical book of history, lines of words that translate into visible characters, thoughts that were formed in some other time and place. We have instead, in the density of discursive practices, systems that establish statements as events, with their own conditions and domains of appearance, and things with their own possibility and fields of use. The same is true for management.

12.3.4 Power, Construction and Deconstruction

A postmodernist approach would treat the constituent disciplines of management not as dealing with resources, connected to different aspects of reality, but as discourses, which socially construct and certify particular meaningful versions of reality. *The manager is constituted and reconstituted through historically and socially contingent discourses. Any management discipline would hence be seen as a particular historical and social mode of engagement that restricts what is thinkable, knowable and doable.* For Foucault, so-called "genealogy", is the analysis of the conditions that make it possible for a particular discourse to develop, change and adapt.

In the construction and deconstruction of the taken-for-granteds that underlie a particular discipline, or indeed management in general, a key focus would be to analyse the socio-historical conditions that made it possible for a particular discourse to be developed and through which it might change. Moreover, central to a postmodern analysis, as for critical theory, would be power. Such power is seen to reside not in individuals as conscious agents but in the discourses themselves. For Foucault the exercise of power perpetually creates knowledge and, conversely, knowledge constantly induces effects of power. *The deployment of any discourse is seen as empowering those people with the power to speak while subordinating others who are the object of the knowledge and disciplines produced by the discourse.*

Meanwhile the disempowered collude in the relationship by accepting the authority of discourse speakers to analyse and categorise, thereby empowering them. Likewise those with privileged access to the relevant discourse gain a sense of meaning and identity from the practices it sanctions. In this manner individuals and collectivities become constructed, classified, known and transformed into self-disciplining subjects through the power they don't possess. In this sense postmodernists see power as being everywhere but nowhere – as a relationship between subjects and yet independent of subjects – which in effect suppresses the articulation of alternative possible "truth-effects".

Research methodology is hence part of such a power structure, affecting the relationship between research student and supervisor, not to mention the relationship between the research subject and the people connected with it. Such an underlying power structure, in broader and much more poignant guise, underlies the relationship between fundamentalist Islam and the secular "west" in our day and age.

12.4 Global Variations of Postmodernism

12.4.1 Modernism, Postmodernism and Fundamentalism

Fundamentalism – Jewish, Christian, and Islamic – for ex Catholic nun Karen Armstrong (16), *is a global fact and has surfaced in every major faith in response to the problems of modernity.* At first religious people, for Armstrong, try to reform their traditions and effect a marriage between them and modern culture, as many Islamic reformers in Egypt and Iran attempted (in the fifties) to do. But when these moderate measures are seen to be of no avail, some people resort to more extreme measures, and a fundamentalist movement is born. Of the three monotheistic religions, Islam was the last to develop a fundamentalist strain, when modern culture began to take root in the Muslim world in the 1960's and 1970's.

Such *fundamentalist movements*, for Armstrong in all faiths, share certain characteristics. They *reveal a deep disappointment and disenchantment with the modern experiment*, which has not fulfilled all that was promised. They also *express real fear. Every single fundamentalist movement that she has studied is convinced that the secular establishment is determined to wipe it out. As such, fundamentalism is an essential part of the modern scene. The fundamentalist community can thus be seen as the shadow-side of modernity; it can also highlight some of the darker sides of the modern experiment. It therefore exists in a symbiotic relationship with a coercive secularism.* Fundamentalism therefore reveals a fissure in society, which is polarised between those who enjoy secular culture and those who regard it with dread. Fundamentalists, moreover, have been successful to the extent that they have pushed religion from the sidelines back into centre stage.

Fundamentalism, for Armstrong, *can be seen as a postmodern movement* that rejects some of the tenets and enthusiasms of modernity, such as colonialism. Many Muslim women feel that veiling is a symbolic return to the pre-colonial period, before their society was disrupted and deflected from its true course. Yet they have not simply turned the clock back. A large proportion of veiled women hold progressive views on such matters as gender. They are coming to join the modern world but on their own terms and in an Islamic context that gives it sacred meaning. Uniformity of dress abolishes class differences and stresses the importance of community over Western individualism. Muslims then, Armstrong maintains, want modernity, but not one that has been imposed on them by America, Britain or France. For when Muslims look at Western society, they see no light, no heart, no spirituality. Another contemporary Muslim scholar, Ziauddin Sardar, has a somewhat different perspective.

12.4.2 Islam, Postmodernism and Transmodernism

Sardar, a Professor of Cultural Studies at City University in London, has placed himself on the side of the "Other", the dialectical opposite of the dominant mode of thought and action, whether in the west or internally within Islam. He is always on the side of the marginalized and the oppressed, always arguing for distributive justice, always trying to decentre the centre, always a radical. Islam, for Sardar, is a worldview, a vision of a just and equitable society and civilization, a holistic culture, an invitation to thought for discovering the way out of the current crisis of modernity and postmodernism. To reduce it to a recipe for do's and dont's is a category mistake. For Sardar, Islam as such has to be reinterpreted in every era.

In sharp contrast to many modernists and secularists who believe that there is something culturally lacking in Muslim, Chinese, Indian and African cultures that keeps them in chains and underdeveloped, Sardar believes that cultural authenticity actually contains the seeds for the regeneration of these societies. But for this regeneration to occur, both tradition and culture must be seen in their dynamic forms:

"Traditional pluralism is a mark of common respect we are called on to pay to each tradition in a world of diverse traditions; it is the basic idea that we might just know what is best for ourselves. It is the notion that inventiveness, ingenuity, enterprise and common sense are integral to all traditions; and that every traditions, if given the resources, opportunity, tolerance and freedom, can adapt to change and solve its own problems with their own traditions." (17)

In other words, while Sardar is a great believer, like the postmodernists, in pluralism, for him *traditional* pluralism is of the essence. Trans-modernism, as opposed to both the modern and postmodern, for Sardar (18), is a synthesis between life enhancing tradition, amenable to change and transition, and new forms of modernity shaped by traditional cultures themselves. In other words, it sees tradition as dynamic, and eager to change; and traditional cultures not as pre-modern but as communities with potential to transcend the dominant model of modernity. Transmodernism forces us to see non-western cultures on their own terms, with their own eyes (ideas, concepts, notions), as part of a common future rather than as the past of humanity. A good example of such, according to Sardar, is contemporary Islam. The west has always seen Islam through the lens of modernity and concluded that is a negative, static, closed system. Yet from Morocco to Indonesia, Islam has changed profoundly in the last decade, particularly after the events of September 11, 2001. But to notice this change, Islam has to be seen from the perspective of trans-modernism and understood through its own concepts and categories.

Trans-modernism is all about listening, in the context of *mutually assured diversity,* to what we term diverse "worlds"; and realising that local identity as a cultural context is as much work in progress in traditional societies as in western ones. In our terms, such local identity, in order to progressively actualize itself, needs to enter into dialogue with others such local identities, with a view to assuming a "global integrity". Indeed, this is what took place in the Arab world in the ninth to thirteenth centuries. And it is exactly that what Sardar calls for today, in the Muslim *ummah,* from Mali to Malaysia, from Guyana to the Gulf region, from Amman to America.

Such *mutually assured unity-in-diversity* is founded on the proposition that all identities have futures, and that their futures are most assured in mutual association. That local identity is then the cultural attitude to speak a better future, fashioned out of all the possibilities and predicaments offered by the contemporary times and circumstances, and in the light of histories that shape these circumstances. What is diverse is the means, institutions and social forms of delivering unifying values. To arrive at mutually assured unity-in-diversity requires, for Sardar, learning to see not only the debates, knowledge and distinctness of various different cultures, but to see how within them common values and commensurate ideas are enacted in radically different ways.

Mutually assured diversity, then, makes cultural relations part of the human condition and *opens the way to acculturation,* the multiple ways, or mutual processes of learning from, and exchanging ideas between different local identities. This is precisely where modernity and multiculturalism have failed. Acculturation is an adaptive process that domesticates influences, translates them into indigenous categories and applies them where they are of most benefit. Acculturation is not an imitative process; it is creative, innovative, and endlessly diverse in its outcomes, ultimately building up integrity. We now turn from postmodern philosophy and methodology to one of its effects, represented in Islamic Future Studies.

12.5 Postmodernism in Practice: Postmodernism as a Basis for Open Society

Islamic Future Studies (Christianity and Islam in the Postmodern Age)

Human history has now reached a particularly interesting turning point – which gives Islamic futurist Ziauddin Sardar his main reason for hope. The grand narrative of secularism, as he sees it, has all but failed; under the passions, problems and predicaments of twentieth century, the wishful intellectual structures of a narrow version of rationality, the dreams of the unchecked one-dimensional secular progress of the Enlightenment have collapsed. Philosophy is in disarray and science is in crisis. The changes of mind characteristic of the seventeenth century's turn from religion to rationalism are being reversed: from reduction to synthesis, from parts to whole, from structure to process, from clinical objectivity to epistemology, from building blocks to networks, and we are returning to tradition as the essence of meaning and identity. (18)

Modernity has been stripped naked of its pretensions: deconstructionists like Derrida and Foucault have shown how threadbare is the fabric of modernity. But as modernity self-destructs there is seemingly nothing to take its place. So the role is that of the believers to fill the moral and social vacuum with an ethical system that is both distinctively contemporary and deeply rooted in authentic religious traditions. As the grand narrative of secularism reaches its cul-de-sac, as the project of modernity loses its momentum, there is a dire need for a successor programme, a joint Christian-Muslim ethical enterprise.

For decades the church, Sardar maintains, has turned its back on the fight for real dignity and honor of humanity; the fight against a notion and practice of freedom that is divorced from responsibility, is based on self-indulgence and that tries to resolve moral and political problems with engines of self-enrichment, material expansion and economic manipulation. Muslims have been unwitting participants in this game; and where they have been aware of the true dangers of secular culture they have sought to resolve the problem through isolation, censorship, suppression of freedoms and by political violence. Yet only by making the ethical connections that are the true heritage of the Abrahamic faiths, and working together for the establishment of an objective moral order, can we make genuine progress toward the creation of true Christian and Muslim societies.

Pros and Cons of Postmodernism

The transition from the modern to the postmodern worlds is based on a number of key developments that have jolted modern consciousness in the last two decades: Thomas Kuhn's demystification of "scientific truth"; the emphasis on indeterminacy in quantum physics; Foucault's emphasis on discontinuity and difference in history; Bell's sociology of postindustrialism; and the newly discovered concern for the other in ethics, anthropology and politics. For American postmodern philosopher and guru, Richard Rorty, it is function rather than philosophy, narrative rather than theory that provides a better perspective on human behaviour.

While, for Rorty, anything seemingly goes, he remains wedded to the values of liberalism. At the same time, for Sardar, postmodernism plunders history to render it meaningless. He argues, that the reduction of history to instant consumerism leads to an instant loss of depth. For plurality in postmodernism serves as an end in itself. It is not the contents of other cultures that concern it, but merely the fact that they are different. In fact the new kind of postmodern assimilation of non-western cultures is best seen in the marketplace where all the world's commodities are assembled under one roof for the consumer to experience "different worlds". In this banal plurality, Sardar maintains, with the confusion of the real and the artificial, meaning is sought by the purchase of the image.

The End of Civilization?

European ethnocentricism presents a conflict-ridden view of history, honed and sharpened by the techniques employed to effect change in European consciousness. Its rallying cries are familiar: liberty, individual conscience, equality, democratic freedom, justice, fraternity, liberality, tolerance, freedom of speech. All of these are noble qualities and enduring values. The distortion comes about in understanding them only as they have been defined and delivered within the context of a western history of conflict.

In a world where domination is the rule, as well as the ruler, the distorted imagination has been appropriated within the traditional cultures through the colonization of the mind. The effect is the appearance of those who accept the logic and gratify the west, amplifying its prejudices and repudiating their own cultural heritage. That is not to say that the rest of the world has been an idyll, as the nostalgics today maintain. In fact, there is a growing understanding in the Muslim world, and elsewhere in non-western civilizations, that nostalgics make good slogans but reify (reduce to a "thing") a reductive vision of indigenous history. Both the dominance of the distorted imagination and the more visible opposing ranks of the nostalgics and the apologists, are an impediment to the recovery of a genuine, autonomous history, a realistic perspective on what constitutes tradition and how that tradition can be employed today. Muslims must develop a new language of self-expression, for it is only by this means that they can address their own urgent agenda and continue the long war of attrition on the distorted imagination.

All this means that Islamic culture and other non-western cultures have to be understood on their own terms, by their own inner dynamic, by how they see themselves, by what they think their sacred scriptures are saying – in other words, far above and beyond the distorted imagination, at the level of genuine authenticity. When Muslims look toward the Medina state of the Prophet Muhammad, they are not looking to go back to some medieval history; they are looking forward to capturing that sense of equality, freedom and justice, which it represented.

The Course of Futures Studies

The Western Technological Imperative: For Sardar, the future has already been colonized and its liberation is the most pressing challenge for the peoples of the non-west if they are to inherit a future made in their own likeness. The future, as it stands, is little more than the transformation of society by western technologies. Thus there is an in-built momentum that seems to take us to a single, determined future. Technology is projected as an autonomous and desirable force. Its desirable products generate more desire. This trajectory is indeed an arch-ideology. The future, for Sardar, is thus waiting to explode. The process, which is transforming the world into a "global village", is also shaping the world in the image of a single culture and civilization.

Globalisation can then be identified with two elements. First, the economic wave of liberalisation. Production is being replaced by consumption as the central economic activity, and privatisation is becoming the norm. Secondly, the wide acceptance of liberal democracy is leading to a total embrace of western culture. At the same time there is a total lack of future consciousness in most non-western societies. Such a non-western project should insist on exposing the political dimension of all knowledge related to the future, and cast such as a contested arena of conflictual practices, thereafter revealing the kind of alternative futures that might be shaped by the desires and vision of non-western societies. However, a chasm has opened between the appreciation of tradition and the imaginative capacity to think traditions forward. If the future is a state of awareness then that awareness can only have genuine meaning if it emanates from the indigenous depths of a culture. The plurality of futures has to be reflected in the plurality of cultures.

Newly Contested Terrain: The power that western civilization exercises over other cultures derives not from its military or technological might, nor even from its economic strength and political muscle and stability. The real might of the west resides in its power to define. The west defines everything – and the rest of the world is expected to embrace such. The west defines what is science, rationality, religion, civilization, freedom, democracy, human rights. Other cultures must accept these and the enslavement and cultural subservience that follow.

But definitions of what it means to be human and civilized will be a contested arena in the future. Asian civilizations (China, India, Islam) for example, have their own definitions of what is freedom, participatory governance, human rights, and so on, which differ from the western notions. Western atomism is rejected by Asian civilizations, where communal harmony is preferred over individualism. Already, Asian societies are increasingly repudiating the idea of "human rights" as just another tool of imperialism and have replaced it with their own notion of "human dignity", which incorporates the rights not just to political dissent, but also the right of basic needs and freedom from exploitation and cultural imperialism.

Beyond Development – An Islamic Perspective: The basic assumption of development, no matter how it is defined, are always of a linear teleology vis-à-vis the standard yardstick of measurement: western civilization. The western traditions are thus the model of "developed" states, with their industrial policies, free market economies, technological advancement, political, economic and social institutions. Within the framework of the Islamic way of development, material and spiritual aspects of life are complementary. To be able to live the good life of devotion to God, we have, therefore, to make the best use of the material resources of our world. Talking about development without considering the spiritual side of people is meaningless; development must preserve, for Sardar, the essence of our humanity. As such:

- the Islamic concept of development has a comprehensive character and includes moral, spiritual and material aspects
- the focus for development effort and the heart of the development process is man; development therefore means development of man and his physical and socio-cultural environment
- in an Islamic framework, development is nothing but a multidimensional activity, establishing a balance between different factors and forces
- economic development involves a number of changes, quantitative as well as qualitative
- among the dynamic principles of social life Islam has particularly emphasized two – firstly the optimal utilization of resources that God has endowed to man, and his physical environment; and secondly their equitable use and distribution and the promotion of all human relationships on the basis of rights and justice.

The idea of balance and harmony is deeply embedded in this concept. A development-free multi-civilisational world, then, could generate a more companionable concept of distributive well-being, of new kinds of growth that can be shared, or new alliances of interests and common aspirations that can collaborate across civilisational lines without demanding the denial of anyone's identity either in the non-west or the west. A development-free world of numerous big and small civilizations, each working out its distinctive way of knowing, doing and being, offers the prospect of discovering that the highest human aspirations are shared values, whose expression through difference makes their realisation more attainable for all people – in the non-west as well as the west.

We are now ready to conclude.

12.6 Conclusion: The Postmodern Mind

All is a Matter of Subjective Interpretation

Out of this maelstrom of highly developed and often divergent impulses and tendencies within postmodernism, such as those manifested in today's Muslim world, a few widely shared working principles – according to Richard Tarnas (19) – have emerged.

The quest for knowledge, for you as a postmodernist, must be endlessly self-revising. You must try the new, experiment and explore, test against subjective and objective consequences, learn from your mistakes, take nothing for granted, treat all as provisional, assume no absolutes. The mind is not the passive reflector of an external world and its intrinsic order, but is active and creative in the process of perception and cognition. Reality is in some sense constructed by the mind, not simply perceived by it, and many such constructions are possible, none necessarily sovereign. There is no empirical "fact" that is not already theory-laden, and there is no logical argument or formal principle that is a priori certain. All human understanding is interpretation, and no interpretation is final. Up until this last statement, there was much in common between critical rationalism and postmodernism, though, for the latter there is no objective truth, no universally falsifiable hypothesis. All is a matter of subjective interpretation.

Knowledge is Constituted of Variable Predispositions

All human knowledge is mediated, for postmodernism by signs and symbols of uncertain provenance, constituted by historically and culturally variable predispositions, and influenced by often unconscious human interests. Hence the nature of truth and reality, in science no less than in philosophy, religion or art, is radically ambiguous. The subject can never presume to transcend the manifold predispositions of his or her subjectivity. Postmodern philosophers, then, can compare and contrast, analyse and discuss the many sets of perspectives human beings have expressed, the diverse symbol systems, the various ways of making things hang together, but they cannot pretend to possess an extra-historical point from which to judge whether a given possibility validly represents the "truth". Postmodern thought has encouraged a vigorous rejection of the entire Western "canon" as long defined and privileged by a more or less exclusively male, white, European elite. Received truths concerning "man", "reason", "civilization", and "progress" are indicated as intellectually and morally bankrupt.

Under the cloak of Western values, too many sins have been committed. Any alleged comprehensive, coherent outlook is at best no more than a temporary useful fiction, masking chaos, at worst an oppressive fiction masking relationships of power, violence and subordination. Not only, then, is the postmodern mind itself a maelstrom of unresolved diversity, but virtually every important element of the Western intellectual past is now present and active in one form or another, contributing to the variety and confusion of the contemporary Zeitgeist. Moreover, these in turn have been joined, and affected by a multitude of cultural perspectives from outside the West, such as the Buddhist and Hindu mystical traditions; by underground cultural streams from within the West itself; and by indigenous and archaic perspectives antedating Western civilization altogether – all gathering now on the intellectual stage for some kind of climactic synthesis.

We Are Free to Choose Our World

The human predicament is here regarded as a human "adventure", the challenge of being a radically self-defining entity. Human understanding is not unequivocally compelled by a set of data, to adopt one metaphysical position or another. The irreducible element of human choice intervenes. Hence there enters into the epistemological equation, in addition to intellectual rigor and socio-cultural context, other more open-ended factors such as will, imagination, faith, hope and empathy. The more complexly conscious and ideologically unconstrained the individual or society, the more free is the choice of worlds, the more profound their participation in reality. In the wake of such developments, the original project of Romanticism – the reconciliation of subject and object, human and nature, spirit and matter, conscious and unconscious, intellect and soul – has re-emerged anew.

Epochal Transition

For Tarnas, two antithetical impulses can thus be discerned in the contemporary intellectual situation, one pressing for a radical deconstruction and unmasking – of knowledge, beliefs, worldviews – and the other for a radical integration and reconciliation. The intellectual question, that looms over our time is whether it is indeed the entropic prelude to some kind of apocalyptic denouement of history; or whether it represents an epochal transition to another era altogether, bringing a new form of civilization and a new world view with principles and ideals fundamentally different from those that have impelled the modern world through its dramatic trajectory. Ironically, and at the time of writing in November 2007, the conflict being played out in Pakistan (where Sardar was born), between the secular and Islamist, democratic and militarist, western and middle eastern, forces, is indicative of such.

It is our role, as social researchers and innovators in such a postmodern and also value-laden context, to help promote such an epochal transition. This brings us finally on the concluding step of the research path of reason, to so-called "socio-technical design".

Bibliography

1) **Drucker**, P. (1992). *The Age of Discontinuity*. New York: HarperCollins.

2) **Handy**, C. (1995). *The Age of Unreason*. New York: Random House.

3) **Tarnas**, R. (1991). *The Passion of the Western Mind*. New York: Ballantyne Books.

4) **Lessem**, R. (1993). *Business as a Learning Community*. London: McGraw Hill.

5) **Lessem**, R. et al. (1993). *European Management Systems*. London: McGraw Hill.

6) **Burman** E. (ed) (1993). *Discourse Analytic Research*. London: Routledge.

7) **Potter**, J. & **Wetherell**, M. (1987). *Discourse and Social Psychology*. London: Sage.

8) **Mishler**, E. (1986). *Research Interviewing: Context ad Narrative*. Cambridge, Mass.: Harvard University Press.

9) **Macnaghten** P. (1993). *Discourses of Nature: Argumentation and Power*. In E. Burman and I. Parker (eds.), Discourse Analytic Research: Repertoires and Readings of Texts in Action. London: Routledge.

10) **Culler**, J. (1987). *Ferdinand de Saussure*. Ithaca: University of Cornell.

11) **Barthes**, R. (1993). *Mythologies*. London: Vintage Classic.

12) **Hamilton**, C. (ed) (2002). *Re-figuring the Archive*. Cape Town: David Phillip.

13) **Berger**, P. & Luckman, T. (1967). *The Social Construction of Reality*. Harmondsworth: Penguin.

14) **Foucault**, M. (1989). *The Order of Things*. London: Routledge.

15) **Foucault**, M. (1984). *The Archaeology of Knowledge*. London: Routledge.

16) **Armstrong**, K. (2002). *A Short History of Islam*. London: Phoenix Press.

17) **Inayatullah**, S. & **Boxwell**, G. (2003) *Islam, Postmodernism and other Futures: a Ziauddin Sardar Reader*. London: Pluto Press.

18) **Sardar**, Z. (2006). *How Do You Know?* London: Pluto Press.

19) **Inayatullah**, S. & **Boxwell**, G. (2003) *Islam, Postmodernism and other Futures: a Ziauddin Sardar Reader*. London: Pluto Press.

20) **Tarnas**, R. (1991). *The Passion of the Western Mind*. New York: Ballantyne Books.

CHAPTER 13

FROM POSTMODERNISM TO
SOCIO-TECHNICAL DESIGN

"EVOLVE DEMOCRATIC PROCESSES"

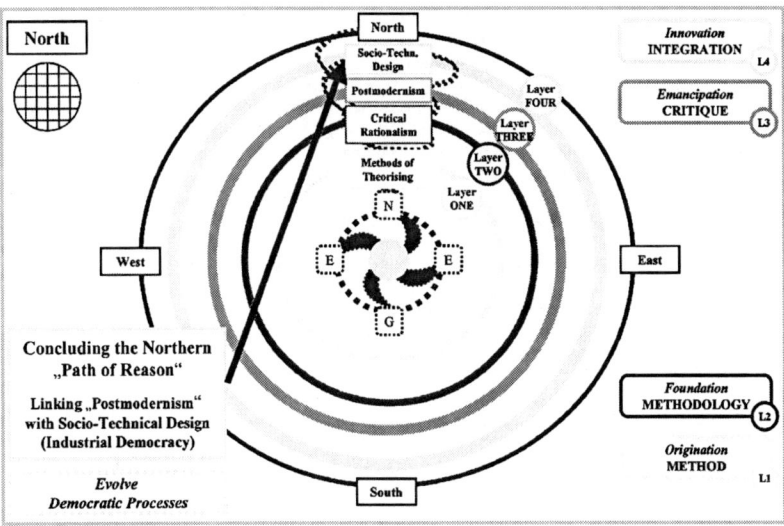

Figure 13.1: Overview Chapter 13 – Layer 4 / North

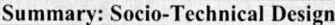

Summary: Socio-Technical Design

- Socio-Technical Design is the culmination of our northern research path of reason. It builds progressively on methods of theorising, critical rationalism and postmodernism. In relation to postmodernism it builds particularly on the impulse of integration (rather than further fragmentation).

- Such integrated designs focus on the development of open socio-technical systems within institutions. In pursuit of organisational freedom, these are strongly rooted in industrial democracy. The close link to Popper's and Soros' shared concept of an open society becomes immediately evident, though the focus here is more strongly on the "open" organisation.

- The originators of such socio-techncal design, from Europe and America, were Kurt Lewin and John Dewey, the one a social scientist and a refugee from Nazi Germany, the other an educator and philosopher, with a passion for democracy in both educational and political institutions, both with an overall leaning toward action oriented research.

- Socio-technical design is indeed an action research approach, which is both socio-politically and techno-economically integral and transformative. Why? Because it involves co-researchers working together, within democratic institutions, as fellow subjects rather than as researcher/subject and researched/object.

- This approach was most prolifically embodied in selective experiments in workplace democracy in the north and east; in the north it were Norway and Sweden that took the lead, in the east it was Japan, where it was combined with the evolving "quality circles".

- In the world at large, subsequent to such experimentation in the latter part of the twentieth century, organisations have regressed, in the face of pressures from globalization and the financial markets, whereby economic fundamentals have superceeded such social and technical experiments in democracy.

- To that extent Habermas' warning is notable that, in the absence of a newly normative theory emerging at a macro level, which could underpin such new formations, they could prove to be short-lived; in our own terms resulting in a lack of thoroughgoing social innovation.

- However, examples of effective socio-technical design can be found. At the end of this chapter we introduce the Mondragon Co-operatives in Spain as a remarkable case in point for an industrial democracy, initiated, decades ago, by a catholic priest, Father Arizmendiarrieta.

13.1 Orientation to Socio-Technical Design

Overview

On the northern research path of reason, you have now progressed through methods of theorising onto the methodology of critical rationalism through emancipatory postmodernism. Altogether, you have progressively evolved toward the knowledge era (in such rational northern terms), culminating in what has been termed "socio-technical design". Such socio-technical design is an overall manifestation of action research, duly incorporating industrial democracy.

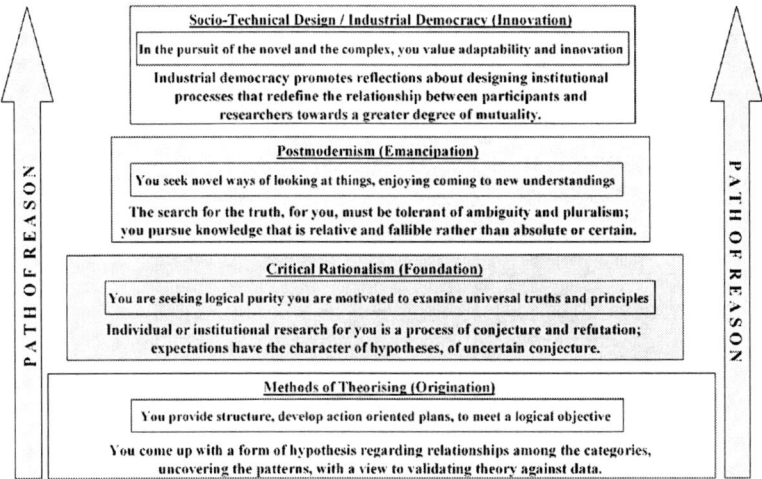

Figure 13.2: Towards Socio-Technical Designs

Industrial democracy promotes reflections about *designing* institutional *processes* that redefine the relationship between participants and researchers towards a *greater degree of mutuality.*

Once again, though, one path overlaps to some extent with the others. In this culminating stage of the research path of reason, there is something of an overlap between realisability (west) and reasonability (north), as well as relationality (south) and renewal (east). In fact the two founding fathers of action research in general and of socio-technical design in particular were such typically rounded characters. Between them, Kurt Lewin and John Dewey spanned philosophy and psychology, biology and education.

The Founding Fathers: Lewin and Dewey

Kurt Lewin's work had a profound impact on social psychology as well as on experiential learning, group dynamics and action research. He was born in 1890 in Prussia (now part of Poland) as one of four children in a middle class Jewish family. In 1909 Kurt Lewin entered the University of Freiburg to study medicine. He then transferred to the University of Munich to study biology. Around this time he became involved in the socialist movement. His particular concerns appear to have been the combating of anti-semitism, the democratization of German institutions, and the need to improve the position of women. Along with other students he organised and taught an adult education programme for working class women and men.

His doctorate was undertaken at the University of Berlin where he developed an interest in the philosophy of science and encountered "gestalt psychology". In 1921 Kurt Lewin joined the Psychological Institute of the University of Berlin – where he was to lecture and offer seminars in both philosophy and psychology. His work became known in America and in 1930 he was invited to spend six months as a visiting professor at Stanford. With the political position worsening in Germany, he and his family settled 1933 in the USA. Kurt Lewin was first to work at the Cornell School of Home Economics, and then at the University of Iowa (this was also the year when his first collection of papers in English "A Dynamic Theory of Personality" was published).

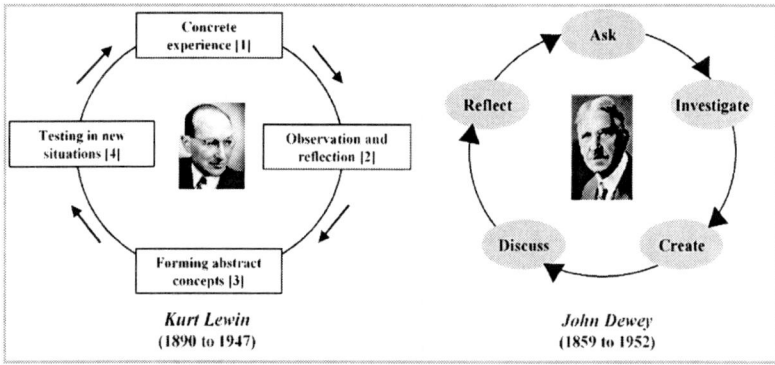

Figure 13.3: Socio-Technical Design – Leading Thinkers

The University of Iowa remained Kurt Lewin's base until 1944. There he continued to develop his interest in social processes. He also became involved in various applied research initiatives linked to the war effort. These included exploring the morale of the fighting troops, psychological warfare, and reorienting food consumption away from foods in short supply. His social commitments were also still strong – and he was much in demand as a speaker on minority and inter-group relations. He wanted to establish a centre to research group dynamics – and in 1944 this dream was realised with the founding of the Research Center for Group Dynamics at MIT. At the same time Kurt Lewin was also engaged in a project for the American Jewish Congress in New York – the Commission of Community Interrelations. It made use of Lewin's model of action research (research directed toward the solving of social problems) in a number of significant studies into religious and racial prejudice. It was also out of some of this work in 1946 with community leaders and group facilitators that the notion of "T" (for sensitivity) groups emerged. He and his associates were able to get funding from the Office of Naval Research to set up the National Training Laboratories in 1947 in Bethel, Maine. However, Lewin died of a heart attack in 1947, before the Laboratories were established.

Lewin is generally accredited with the coining of the term action research: "The research needed for social practice can best be characterized as research for social management or social engineering. It is a type of action research, a comparative research on the conditions and effects of various forms of social action, and research leading to social action. Research that produces nothing but books will not suffice". He was also closely aligned with the views of his compatriot John Dewey, in their belief that democracy had to be continually invented anew. We now turn to John Dewey.

John Dewey, the American philospher on democracy and education, whose long life overlapped with that of Lewin, has made, arguably, the most significant contribution to the development of educational thinking in the twentieth century. Dewey's philosophical pragmatism, concern with interaction, reflection and experience, and interest in community and democracy, were brought together to form a highly suggestive educative form. In many respects his work cannot be easily slotted into any one of the curriculum traditions that have dominated North American and UK schooling traditions over the last century.

John Dewey's significance for informal educators lies in a number of areas. First, his belief that education must engage with and enlarge experience has continued to be a significant strand in informal education practice. Second, and linked to this, Dewey's exploration of thinking and reflection – and the associated role of educators – has continued to be an inspiration. We can see it at work, for example, in the models developed by e.g. Kurt Lewin and the organisational psychologist Donald Schön at MIT. Third, his concern with interaction and environments for learning provides a continuing framework for practice. Last, his passion for democracy, for educating so that all may share in a common life, provides a strong rationale for practice in the associational settings in which informal educators work. We now turn to the key tenets of socio-technical design.

13.2 Socio-Technical Design – Key Tenets

Socio-Technical Design – Key Tenets
① You adopt a problem solving orientation.
② Your research is inevitably linked to action.
③ Your research is geared toward social betterment.
④ You use a co-generative approach to organisation development.
⑤ You act as a "friendly outsider".

① **You adopt a problem solving orientation**

Action research from an organisational perspective focuses on *solving real-life problems*. The focus of such institutionally based action research, for Greenwoord and Levin (1) is *determined by what the organisational participants consider important, what affects their daily lives*. The inquiry process is thus linked to actions taken to provide a solution to the problem being examined.

Institutionally based action research is framed as a democratic process supporting the creation of knowledge that potentially can be liberating. Obviously then, the inquiry process has to aim to solve problems important to the organisational participants, and the knowledge produced by the *inquiry process must increase participants' control over their own situations*. This is consistent with Freire's "conscientization", which identifies the inquiry process as one shaping knowledge relevant to action, as well as being built on a critical understanding of the historical and political contexts within which the participants act. It is also consistent with John Heron's process of democratically based co-operative inquiry, albeit now operating across a larger institutional scale. The participants must be able to use the knowledge that emerges, and this knowledge must support the enhancement of the participant' goals. In that context, it is easy to see the humanistic, as well as rational and pragmatic elements creeping into organisationally based action research.

Local knowledge, historical consciousness, and everyday experiences of the insiders, complements therefore the outsiders' skills in facilitating learning processes, in bringing in technical skills into research procedures.

② **Your research is inevitably linked to action**

Knowledge then emerges institutionally and is evaluated through acting or as a consequence of actions. The discovery process is not purely mental, receding into the intellectual sphere at a distance from human actions. *In such action research insiders and outsiders join in a mutual learning process. The enabling mechanism for this is communication. New understandings are created through discourses between people engaged in the inquiry process*. For this to occur, a mutually understandable discourse is required, and this is achieved through living together over time, sharing experiences and taking actions together (somewhat akin, as we have seen, to Nonaka and Takeuchi's "socialisation" process). (2)

This is the crux of the credibility-validity issue in action research. The conventional social research community believes that credibility is created through generalizing and universalizing propositions (that is what Nonaka has called "combination") whereas *action research believes that only knowledge generated and tested in practice (Nonaka's "internalisation") is credible*. Conventional social research assumes that only a community of similarly trained professionals is competent to decide issues of credibility, while *action research places emphasis on the stakeholders' views on such*.

③ Your research is geared toward social betterment

Kurt Lewin, together with some others of its early proponents, operated with a view of social research as both scientific and socially engaged. For Lewin "nothing is as practical as a good theory", and "the best way to understand something is to try to change it". He articulated these views in the 1930's and 1940's, echoing the earlier ideas of John Dewey. As we can see, such organisationally based action research has strong European and American (in our terms: northwestern) credentials.

The social sciences themselves began as a form of engaged political economy, aimed at social betterment. Only as the social sciences were split out into the various existing conventional disciplines and subjected to harassment and purges because their social activism, for Greenwood and Levin (see chapter 16), offended the rich and powerful, did the social sciences become separated from action. Greenwood and Levin view such *social sciences, today in the twenty first century, as an impoverished derivative, albeit a methodologically and theoretically sophisticated one, of the original social sciences to which they see action as the natural heir.* In fact, the American social scientists who made up the so-called "human relations" school in the middle of the last century, such as Mayo and Rothlesberger at Harvard, were much more radical in their humanistic perspective, than their equivalents – management thinkers like America's Tom Peters and Britain's Charles Handy – today. The so-called "co-generative" model used here, retains its wholesome link to social betterment, as well as to social science.

④ You use a co-generative approach to organisation development

Organisationally instigated action research can be thought of as a process consisting of at least two analytically distinct phases. The first involves the clarification of an initial research question, whereas the second involves the initiation and continuation of a "social change and meaning construction process". Both then have a northwestern problem solving orientation.

Greenwood and Levin view the problem definition process as the first step in a mutual learning process between insiders and outsiders. Central to the co-generative process in action research, is further its *ability to create room for a learning process resulting in interpretations and action designs that participants trust. In arenas, subsequently, communication between insiders and outsiders aims to produce learning and open up a process of reflection for the involved parties. These discussions and reflections are the engine of the ongoing learning cycle. The democratic ideals of action research also mandate a process in which the outsider gradually lets go of control so that the insiders can learn how to control and guide their own developmental processes.*

Thus action research is a strategy for orchestrating a variety of techniques and change-oriented work forms, in an intentionally designed process of co-generative learning. Such an approach examines pressing problems, designs action strategies based on the research of these problems, and then implements and evaluates the liberating forms of action that emerge. While conventional social research is oriented around professional enlightenment, such institutionally based action research is oriented to achieving particular social goals, not just to the generation of knowledge to satisfy curiosity, or to meet some particular professional academic need. *There clearly is a built-in tension here. Action research projects owe their first allegiance to the local stakeholders and their issues.* But for such research to continue to develop and for strategies and learning about effective action research to develop, the processes and results have to also take the form of credible knowledge that can be shared effectively with practitioners, researchers and stakeholders alike.

Levin and Morten emphasize that action research for organisational learning and knowledge creation is not so much a method as a way of collaboratively orchestrating social research processes to enhance liberating social change processes. They assert that action research can use almost any research technique found in the sciences, social sciences, and humanities when such a technique is contextually appropriate to a collaboratively orchestrated research process.

⑤ **You act as a "friendly outsider"**

A professional action researcher must know how to be a "friendly outsider". This role is vital in action research because the external perspective is a key element in opening up local group processes for change. But this outsider is "friendly" in a special sense. He or she must be able to reflect back to the local groups things about them, including criticism of their own perspectives, in a way that is experienced as supportive rather than negatively critical or domineering.

The friendly outsider must also be expert at opening up lines of discussion, a kind of good Socratic teacher. Often local organisations or groups are either stuck in positions that have hardened or they have become pessimistic about the possibilities for change. Flexibility and opportunities for change are pointed out to local people, along with encouragement in the form of moral support, and information from other cases, where similar problems existed but change turned out to be possible.

Another key role of the friendly outsider is to make evident the tacit knowledge that guides local conduct. This can be in the form of critical reflections or supportive comments about local capabilities. The outsider, who is not used to the group and to the local scene, is ideally placed to notice such. Related to this is the role of speaking the unspeakable. Local people, because of their history together, or because of mere decorum, are often unable to express uncomfortable things. However, too much feedback can block a group; too little can prevent the group from moving ahead. At the same time the outsider's links to the outside world – state, nation, international agencies, unions, professional consultants – may be of considerable practical value to the project. It is the link between outsider and insider, which is key to resulting socio-technical design, which we now explore in greater depth, focusing in particular on the process of knowledge generation.

13.3 Socio-Technical Design in Depth

13.3.1 Knowledge Generation in Action Research

The crux of the action research based knowledge generation process is the encounter between local insights and the understanding that the outsider brings to the table and the fusion of these insights into a shared form of understanding that serves as the basis for solving practical problems. An affirmation or proposition from one of the parties (thesis) is brought forward and is met with demanding and challenging questions and counterpropositions (antithesis), and out of this friendly encounter of points of view an understanding (synthesis) will gradually evolve.

Such organisationally based action research is *based on the affirmation that all human beings have detailed, complex and valuable knowledge about their lives, environments and goals.* This knowledge is different from scholarly knowledge because everyday knowledge is embodied in people's actions, long histories in particular positions, and the way they reflect on them. This kind of knowing is different from much conventional scientific knowledge because practical wisdom, practical reasoning and tacit knowledge are its central characteristics. *Action research then centers on a co-generatively structured encounter between the worlds of practical reasoning and those of scientifically constructed knowledge, integrating practitioners and professionals in the same knowledge generating process that it calls "co-generative" learning.*

Furthermore, a local theory is context bound and makes sense in the context of years of local processes matching interpretations with concrete experiences. *In action research, the central intent is to generate knowledge that bridges these knowledge worlds.* Conventional social researchers, who have severed the connection between research and action, rarely know whether they are right or not, as their findings are seldom acted upon and the practical results from their research rarely have direct consequences for them. Local knowledge belongs mainly to insiders, but outsiders can also develop varieties of local knowledge through ethnographic research based on local engagement over the long term. This conception of knowledge can be traced back to Aristotle's "phronesis": the ability to spot the action called for in each situation.

Because action research privileges local knowledge, it necessarily works with the role of narrative in the research process, as well as in writing up the results. For most logical positivists (conventional social researchers), as well as those using formal qualitative techniques, the strong presence of narratives is taken to be hopelessly "unscientific" and incapable of producing valid knowledge. In this respect, the rational-pragmatic bias of action research is combined with a holistic and also humanistic orientation.

13.3.2 The Knowledge Generation Process

In organisationally based action research, *the research process must be democratic in the sense that it is open, participatory, and fair to all the participants.* In addition, the outcome of action research should support the participants' interests, as was also the case for co-operative inquiry and indeed for participative research, so that the knowledge produced increases their ability to control their own situation. Action research, then, is a co-generative process through which professional researchers and interested members of a local organisation, community, or a specially created organisation, collaborate to research, understand and resolve problems of mutual interest. Action research is therefore a social process in which professional knowledge, local knowledge, process skills, research skills, and democratic values are the basis for co-generated knowledge and social change.

Conventional researchers view research techniques as important to the extent that they impart control, distance, and objectivity to the researcher, so that any other similarly motivated researcher can reproduce the same results using the same techniques. Action researchers reject this view on a variety of grounds. They do *not accept that it is possible to separate the research process from its human dimension or to separate the process from the results. Action research therefore seeks to bring the process and the results into the closest possible relationship and builds research upon fundamental respect for and trust in human capacities.* Action research also emphasizes democratic values and processes by co-creating knowledge applicable by the local stakeholders in their efforts to increase control over their own situations.

In addition, action researchers aim to reopen the possibility for change, enhance a sense of responsibility for the direction of the future, and emphasize that human agency, not impartial control systems, is the centerpiece of social change. One consequence of this perspective is that organisationally based action researchers do not "apply" techniques to a situation. Rather they bring knowledge and skills to a group of people who collaboratively open up the possibility for self-managed social change. (3)

The more overtly political as well as rational and humanistic orientation (from an institutional as opposed to societal perspective) is the one to which we now turn, starting out with so-called socio-technical systems and ending up with industrial democracy, altogether born out of the initiating process of action research.

13.3.3 Action Research and Socio-Technical Systems

Coining the term "action research" was an honor that was held jointly by John Collier and the more famous Kurt Lewin. Collier, a commissioner for American Indian Affairs from 1933 to 1945, applied the term to his work in improving race relations, through a participative approach to collaborative research between whites and native Indians. Social scientist Lewin, as a refugee from Nazi Germany to the United States, held strong beliefs in democracy generally, and in action research specifically, as a tool that could advance science while dealing with practical societal concerns.

In Iowa, he worked with social psychologist Alex Bavelas to enhance productivity in a manufacturing company, by inviting workers to participate in experimental changes to work methods. They were encouraged *to experiment, to discuss the results, and to choose the most effective methods*, anticipating the development of the learning organisation today. Together with the American management philosopher Douglas McGregor, he experimented at a later stage with group dynamics, thereafter founding the "Institute for Applied Behavioral Science" in the United States.

Meanwhile psychologist Wilfrid Bion, at the Tavistock Institute in London, took on Lewin's collaborative approach to behavioral change to investigating the performance of small groups of people at work. His concern was to get them to deal with the problems they faced in their workplace, and to help them regain a sense of control over their lives. Democratic processes, in other words, were used to involve people in reconstructing their social arrangements.

After the war, another social psychologist, the Australian Eric Trist took up the action research cause at the Tavistock Institute, focusing his efforts on productivity in the coal mines. Workers in the more highly productive mines, he found, operated as *self-managed groups*. The miners themselves devised systems that allowed them to be *multi-skilled and self-directing*. He was able to *demonstrate that the social and technical systems were interdependent: hence "socio-technical systems"*. In Norway, a series of efforts there became known as the "Norwegian Industrial Democracy Projects", whereby such socio-technical systems were diffused through action research, building upon an egalitarian culture. This "social-democratic" process of progressively greater worker involvement spread from Norway to Sweden and Holland.

13.3.4 Socio-Technical Systems Theory

Trist's colleague, the British social scientist Fred Emory, led the efforts to conceptualize these theories. Emory *argued that because organisations employed whole persons, it was important to pay attention to human needs beyond those required for the regular performance of tasks dictated by technology*. His paradigm, therefore, was directly in conflict with the master/servant relationship that characterized many workplaces.

In fact, Lewin as well as Trust and Emory, were committed to advancing scientific knowledge, particularly knowledge that could address practical problems of the day, and that would enable organisations and societies to better themselves. Each work group with which they were involved, started with the premise that change begins with the involvement of those directly affected. Each believed that the predominant paradigm of the time, based on expert hierarchical control of social systems, would never prove adequate to face the challenges of a modern, post-industrial society. In Norway, as we have already intimated, action research was evolving to accommodate initial moves toward industrial democracy.

13.4 Global Variations of Socio-Technical Design

13.4.1 Towards Industrial Democracy

Greenwood and Levin, drawing now upon Gustavsen's approach to action research in Norway, have documented his experience in arranging discourse "conferences", within and across organisations, between management and unions. The core contribution of such action research in the nineteen sixties and seventies was to create relationships between actors, and arenas where they can meet in democratic dialogue. For Scandinavian Gustavsen, what made enlightenment possible, was not the recognition that "I think therefore I am", but the recognition that *unless people can relate in a democratic way to one another, no new ideas, no just causes, or indeed any science, social or other, are possible*.

Gustavsen argued that a mediator was needed between one party and another, if purposeful thought and action was to be promoted, between them. Interestingly enough, and somewhat in contrast, the renowned German critical theorist, Jürgen Habermas, was of the view that the liberation of the oppressed, from the prevailing powers that be, had to start with new theory, and action, in the interim, was futile. In fact, from a twenty first century perspective, as market fundamentalism seemingly rides rampant over such experiments in industrial democracy, notwithstanding some distinctive exceptions like the Mondragon Co-operatives in northern Spain, the John Lewis Partnership in the UK, and (as we shall see in chapter 16) Cashbuild in South Africa, Habermas may well have had a point.

13.4.2 From Germany to the U.S., from the UK to Norway to Japan

That having been said, the emergence of what came to be called the "industrial democracy" tradition or movement, refers to the first systematic and reasonably large scale action research effort in Western industrialized countries. Its roots trace back to Kurt Lewin's early work in the United States – first at Cornell University and then at MIT. His ideas re-crossed the Atlantic, and he found fertile ground at the Tavistock Institute of Human Relations in London. Though there were a number of action research related activities in Great Britain, most specifically related to the development of socio-technical systems, the major source of large-scale, institutionally oriented action research projects, turned out to be in Norway in its Industrial Democracy project. Many of these ideas were reinvented in the form of industrial management strategies in U.S. and Swedish industrial firms; later, and in fact more prolifically, they reached Japan as well.

Lewin, as we learned earlier on, was trained as a social psychologist and his central interest was in social change, specifically questions about how to conceptualize social change and promote it. In action research, Lewin envisaged a process where one could construct an experiment in a rational and holistic social and material situation with the aim of achieving a certain goal. Lewin's thinking about experimentation in a natural setting became the main strategy for the Norwegian Industrial Democracy project.

Two other strands of Lewin's thinking have an influence on the development of the industrial democracy tradition. First, Lewin conceptualized change as a three-stage process:

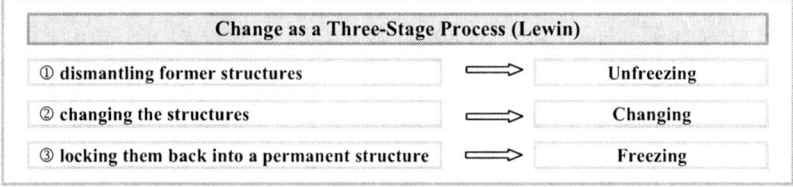

Change as a Three-Stage Process (Lewin)		
① dismantling former structures	⟹	Unfreezing
② changing the structures	⟹	Changing
③ locking them back into a permanent structure	⟹	Freezing

Second, his work on group dynamics, identifying factors and forces important for development, conflict and co-operation in groups, led to the concept of so-called T-groups, or sensitivity training, which have a rich subsequent history. In summary, the new paradigm that he and his colleagues brought to work and organisation is the following:

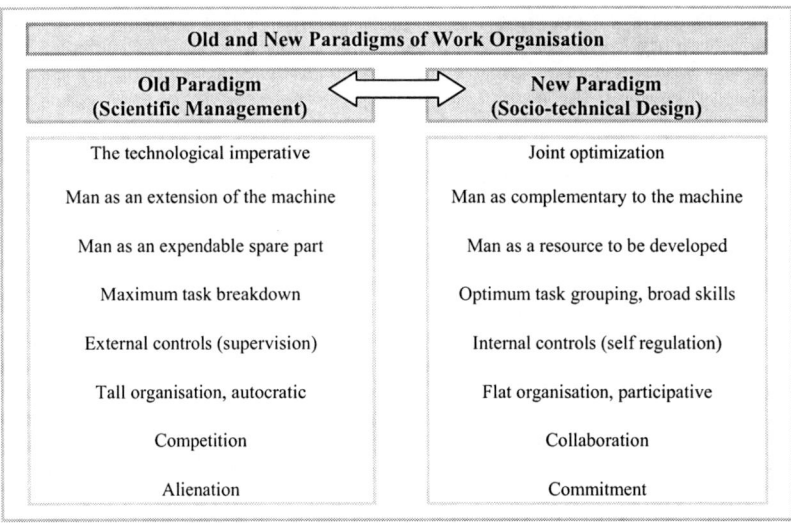

Old and New Paradigms of Work Organisation	
Old Paradigm **(Scientific Management)**	**New Paradigm** **(Socio-technical Design)**
The technological imperative	Joint optimization
Man as an extension of the machine	Man as complementary to the machine
Man as an expendable spare part	Man as a resource to be developed
Maximum task breakdown	Optimum task grouping, broad skills
External controls (supervision)	Internal controls (self regulation)
Tall organisation, autocratic	Flat organisation, participative
Competition	Collaboration
Alienation	Commitment

For Greenwood and Levin though, *Lewin's specific orientation to managing change, related to unfreezing and re-freezing, is limiting. They argue in favor of action research as a continuous and participative learning process, not as a form of short-term intervention. For them, the change process has an open starting point and no absolute ending point.*

However, Lewin's work remains a fundamental building block of what today is called action research oriented towards organisational change. He set the stage for knowledge production based on solving real-life problems. From the outset he created a new role for researchers, and redefined criteria for judging the quality of the inquiry process. It was Lewin who shifted the researcher's role from being a distant observer to involvement in concrete problem solving. The quality criteria he developed for judging a good theory focus on its ability to support practical problem solving in real-life situations.

With a view to such, in Great Britain after World War II, rebuilding the industrial base was a major political goal. During the years of the war, this industrial base had been severely damaged and national efforts were launched immediately to revitalize the economy. The Tavistoc Institute of Human Relations in London was therefore called upon by the British government to support various parts of this effort. No such organisational imperative, in Britain if not elsewhere today, parallels such. In fact, the recently proliferating impact of climate change on organisation, has if anything further reinforced the emphasis upon technological or fiscal-economic fixes, rather than upon overall social innovation.

Yet, in the latter part of the last century, the industrial democracy thinking also inspired other national movements. Japan was looking for ways to organise its industrial production that would secure both high productivity and excellent quality. Two U.S. scholars who specialized in quality control, Juran and Deming, played an important role in the Japanese industrialization process. Their models for obtaining quality production were easily picked up by the Japanese companies. Actually, the Japanese were much more receptive to them than their U.S. counterparts. *The central themes of industrial democracy found fertile ground in Japan because collective work had a strong cultural base in the country. In Japan these activities appeared in the form of quality circles and problem solving groups.* In such an approach action learning emerged from an ongoing process of experimentation and reflection, in which mutual learning is the driving process for sustainable change and knowledge generation.

Industrial democracy in the "west", though more in theory than in practice, also began the first reflections about designing research processes that redefined the relationship between participants and researchers towards a much greater degree of mutuality. Carole Pateman, in her 1975 book on "Participation and Democracy" (4), drew a genealogy from Rousseau's and Mill's thinking to the modern debate on democracy at the shop-floor level. Despite this, the strongly idealistic-democratic content of this first decade of the industrial democracy tradition was gradually replaced by pragmatic arguments. The rhetoric shifted towards empowerment, from participation as the key to democracy to participation as a means to motivate workers to shape a more effective and profitable organisation. For Greenwood and Levin, empowerment with its hierarchical connotations is an inevitable step backward.

13.4.3 Looking Towards the Future

While action research continues to exist and to be widely practiced in organisations and communities today, it remains an alternative paradigm. Human needs continue to be secondary to technical and economic advancement. The new paradigm required would, then as now:

Qualities of a new Research Paradigm
• elevate the quality of the total human experience above measures of economic progress as the primary measure for the advancement of society • devise ways of making expert knowledge readily available to those who need it • place speed of learning and adaptation above costs and efficiencies • elevate environmental and community issues above creation of wealth • restore human dignity as underlying educational, organisational, political systems • enhance diversity in scientific methods and ways of knowing • locate control over systems to users rather than experts or designers • develop ways for people to utilize diversity effectively, working together globally • continue to explore ways for organisations and societies to develop, to realise and utilize the tremendous potential currently trapped in rigid structures.

We now finally turn to a case example of such a socio-technical design, that of Mondragon in Spain.

13.5 Socio-Technical Design in Practice: The Making of Mondragon

For Greenwood and Levin: "Institutionally based action research is framed as a democratic process supporting the creation of knowledge that potentially can be liberating. Obviously then, the inquiry process has to aim to solve problems important to the organisational participants, and the knowledge produced by the inquiry process must increase participants' control over their own situations. This is consistent with Freire's "conscientization", which identifies the inquiry process as one shaping knowledge relevant to action, as well as being built on a critical understanding of the historical and political contexts within which the participants act." (5)

A specific case in point is Mondragon in Spain's Basque country, which was been build as an industrial democracy by the remarkable Father Arizmendiarrieta

Culture and Structure of Mondragon Today: Cognitive and Procedural

The Mondragon Co-operatives Corporation (MCC) in the latter part of the 1990's was worth some $6 billion in sales, and had co-operatives ranging from construction to retailing, semi-conductors to household goods, banking to education. For its founder, the catholic priest Father Don Jose Maria Arizmendiarrieta in the 1940's:

"It is a social monstrosity that a system of social organisation is tolerated in which some can take advantage of the work of others for their exclusive personal profit. The co-operatist distinguishes himself from the capitalist, simply in that the latter utilizes capital in order to make people serve him, while the former uses it to make more gratifying and uplifting the working life of the people." (6)

In Arizmendiarrieta's library we find not only books of the key French Catholic philosophers (Jacques Maritain and Emmanuel Mounier) of his day, but also those of Karl Marx, Herbert Marcuse, Paulo Freire, JK Galbraith and Vanek's Yugoslav "Self Management". Maritain and Mounier in particular – both adherents of the so-called "personalist" school of philosophy – saw capitalism as well as socialism as being incompatible with such personalist values. For Mounier, in his "Personalist Manifesto" of 1938, the point is not to attack capitalist society, but instead to "*implant in the vital organs, at present diseased, of our decadent civilization the seeds and the ferment of a new civilization.*"

To understand Mondragon, we need to understand its organisational, as well as Basque societal, culture, including the support system that maintains that culture and influences its ability to change in adaptive ways. In their book on "Making Mondragon" (7), William and Katherine Whyte think of the culture of the Mondragon cooperatives in terms of two categories of concepts: the cognitive framework and the shaping systems. The cognitive framework is the set of ideas and beliefs about basic values, organisational objectives, and guiding principles that form the foundation of any organisation. *Shaping systems enable an organisation to be maintained or to change.* A culture does not maintain itself but is shaped by forces such as major policies, structures, and instruments of governance and management.

The Cognitive Framework of Mondragon

The following "cognitive framework", for the Whytes, characterizes the Mondagon Co-operatives:

Basic Values

- *Equality:* All human beings, in the Mondragon context, are deemed to have been created equal, with equal rights and obligations.

- *Solidarity:* Members of a given cooperative should rise and fall together; this principle also applies to relationships between cooperatives, and between Mondragon and the Basque community.

- *Dignity of labour:* There should be integrity to any labor, blue or white collar.

- *Participation:* Members have the right and obligation to participate as much as possible in shaping the decisions that affect them.

Objectives

- *Job creation:* The creation of jobs was a primary objective from the very beginning, and the cooperatives retain a strong commitment to it.

- *Employment security:* Every member in good standing should be able to expect continuous employment, but not a particular job, up to the age of retirement.

- *Human and social development:* Making the work itself humane and fostering the social development of the members.

- *Autonomy and self-governance:* Developing autonomous and self-governing organisations that are linked together to help in coping with national and international economic conditions.

- *Economic progress:* The generation of profits is viewed as a limiting condition (not the fundamental purpose) of the organisations.

Guiding Conditions

- *Balance:* Life in a cooperative should not be carried out as a zero-sum game where one gains and the other loses; there must be a balancing of interests and needs; financial needs of the firm must be balanced with the economic needs of members; social and technical balance is also to be pursued.

- *Future orientation*: Planning must be oriented toward a future well beyond the time when the immediate issue has to be resolved.

- *Organisational self-evaluation:* What now exists must never be considered perfect and immutable; it is important to carry out frequent self-critical evaluations.

- *Openness:* Nondiscriminatory in nature, the cooperatives are open to anyone with the requisite skills and training.

- *Pluralistic political orientation:* From the beginning, the leaders of the cooperatives avoided identification with any established political party or political ideology, in contrast, for example, to the situation with cooperatives in Italy, where they are affiliated with the unions or the communists.

- *Freedom of information:* If members are to make intelligent decisions they have to have access to relevant information for decision-making.

- *Intercooperative complementarity:* Individual cooperatives should buy from and sell to one another unless it is disadvantageous to one or the other.

- *Formation of cooperative groups:* To achieve economies of scale and strengthen solidarity with the movement, it is important for individual cooperatives to join together.

- *Size limitation:* This principle is based on the assumption that it is difficult for an organisation to remain flexible, democratic and efficient when it grows beyond a certain size.

We now turn from principles and guidelines to systems and structures. What about the systems that supported this cognitive framework?

Shaping Systems to Maintain or Change the Organisational Culture

The forces shaping the organisational culture at Mondragon fall into three categories: major policies, structures and systems of governance and management. Some of these shaping systems attest to the extraordinary creativity of Mondragon on producing social inventions: new ideas put into place to meet important needs of the cooperatives.

- *Major policies:* Membership is based on labor rather than capital; since 1965 all the surplus allocated to members have gone into their capital accounts rather than being distributed in cash. The policy has contributed enormously to the strength and stability of the cooperatives. Moreover, because the cooperatives are not free simply to lay off surplus workers they are driven to create new cooperatives and expand employment.

- *Structures and systems for governance and management:* Mondragon has created both significant internal structures and a crucially important network of collaborating and supporting organisations. As well as providing for social security and unemployment compensation, the so-called Lagun-Aro plays an important role in placing members in other co-operatives when any one group is unable to provide jobs within its own group. The educational system, beginning with Escuela Politecnia, strengthened by the development of further research and educational institutes, provides members with knowledge and skills essential for Mondragon's future. Distinct social inventions include the financial institution specifically designed to develop cooperatives, and the applied research institute, with its network of mutually supportive relations.

Mondragon also has several instruments of management systems and practices for shaping the work process. Some of these have been borrowed from abroad. For example, Mondragon modelled its initial management programme on the principles of scientific management propagated by F.W. Taylor. As they became increasingly aware of the limitations of these they reached out for guidance as to how to redesign work. They now speak of "participatory management by objectives".

We are now ready to conclude this chapter and thereby the path of reason.

13.6 Conclusion

What are the implications for our integral research, set here in the context of organisationally oriented action research generally, and socio-technical systems accompanied by industrial democracy, specifically?

As we can see, *social innovation is an institutional, as well as a communal and a group process*. Specifically, the academic establishment hosting the research integrates it within its knowledge creating and community building orientation. In the process, a university as a public, private or civic enterprise is refocused on social innovation.

What is becoming ever more apparent, as we move from the humanistic (PAR) towards the more rationally based approaches to building socio-technical systems and industrial democracies, is that one requires the other, if a process of integral research, with a view to social innovation, is to take place. Moreover, the development of such democratic processes in the workplace, to accompany such evolving socio-technical systems, is likely to come to a halt if profounder shifts in the power balance, as the postmodernists would have called it, fail to come about. In other words, the formative build up of new theories, for example ones dealing with enhanced participation, in the absence of a reformative approach to building open systems within and around organisations will fall on stony ground. Further, on a societal level, without the development of new postmodern norms around the power and participation of hitherto marginalised (race, class, and gender based) groups, actions on a group or organisational level are likely to fail. The kind of democratic and participative vision that the likes of Dewey and Lewin held will inevitably fail to materialise, unless horizontal and vertical social innovation takes place.

We have now completed the journey through the path of reason, towards the build up of an open society. To that extent we have purposefully embarked, with the help of Popper and Hountondji, on theorising, which for the latter is "introverting theory", so that it is generated within, rather than imposed upon, a society. On the second research layer, through critical rationalism, we have built up, with the help of George Soros, for an open society. Subsequently, with the support of Ziauddin Sardar, we have served to ensure that it takes on board middle-eastern as well as northwestern perspectives. Finally, mediated through Arizmendi's Mondragon Co-operatives in the Spanish Basque country, as interpreted by William Whyte at Cornell's Institute for

Industrial Relations in the United States, we have come up with a socio-technical design for corporate democracy. We now turn from the path of reason to that of realisation.

Bibliography

1) **Greenwood**, D. & **Levin**, M. (2007). *Introduction to Action Research*. London: Sage.

2) **Nonaka**, I. & **Takeuchi**, H. (1995). The Knowledge Creating Company. Oxford: Oxford University Press.

3) **Reason**, P. & **Bradbury**, H. (2004). *Handbook of Action Research*. London: Sage.

4) **Pateman**, C. (1975). *Participation and Democracy*. Cambridge: Cambridge University Press.

5) **Greenwood**, D. & **Levin**, M. (2007). *Introduction to Action Research*. London: Sage.

6) **Whyte**, W. (1991). *Making Mondragon*. Ithaca, New York: Cornell University Press.

7) **Whyte**, W. (1991). *Making Mondragon*. Ithaca, New York: Cornell University Press.

CHAPTER 14

FROM EXPERIMENTAL AND SURVEY METHODS TO
EMPIRICISM

"GATHER RELEVANT DATA"

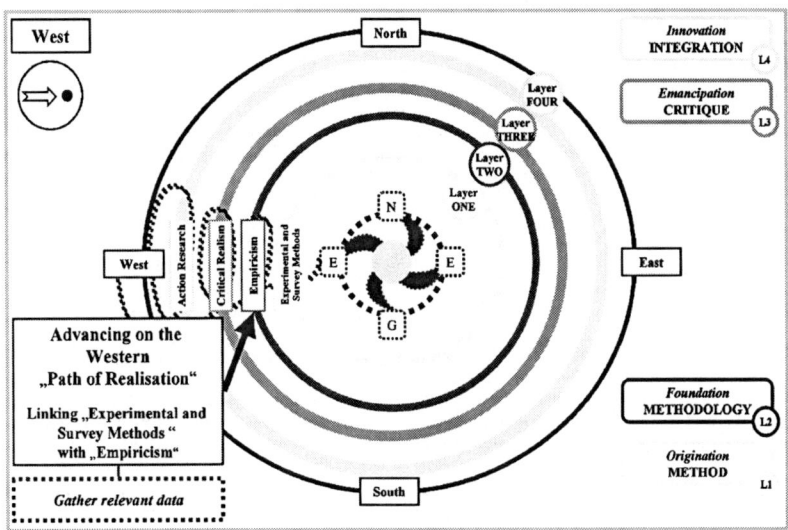

Figure 14.1: Overview Chapter 14 – Layer 2 / West

Summary: Empiricism

- We shall now immerse ourselves in the western research path of realisation. Building on the experimental and survey methods constituting the originating layer one (method) of our Integral Research approach, we are now moving on to the foundational layer 2 (methodology). Here we engage with empiricism.

- Empiricism is a theory of knowledge emphasizing the role of experience in the formation of ideas, while discounting the notion of innate ideas. Empiricism is closely related to positivism, seeking after the "positive" facts, rather than relying on pure faith or indeed dogma.

- Positivism incorporates a "western" ontology of an ordered universe made up of atomistic, discrete and observable events, typified by the economic marketplace. Only that which can be observed, that is experienced by the senses, can be regarded as real. In such an epistemology, knowledge is seen to be derived from sensory experience by means of experimental or comparative analysis.

- Empiricism was spearheaded by such European luminaries as political scientists John Locke and David Hume, political economists Adam Smith and John Stuart Mill, and natural scientists Frances Bacon and Galileo Galilei. All together, these positivists were responsible for three of the major social innovations of the past two to three hundred years: free markets and liberal democracy, and classical scientific method itself, in its classically "western" vein.

- The success of the classical scientific "method" is explained in terms of its ability to reveal the truth. Such a search for truth was assumed to be an intentional activity that reflected the needs of humanity and, as a consequence, secured human progress. In order to achieve progress, the researcher should deploy his capacity for reason within the methodological rules of scientific method.

- As the empiricist employs such "scientific method" he searches for an assumed truth, seeks only for the "positive" facts, distinguishes clearly between facts and values, collects observational data, builds theories and controls the research through "closed systems". The scientific experiment was Newton's way of artificially replicating the idea of a closed system, enabling researchers to isolate the objects they wish to investigate from all other objects, which would confuse the picture.

- Typical of such a "closed" scientific orientation, especially in the twentieth century, was the use of mechanical and experimental metaphors, along with a desire to emulate physics as the purest form of scientific activity. The idea of such "closure" has been an important part of all scientific disciplines, which have sought to establish objective knowledge, including the social sciences.

- This metaphor of the "closed system" become hugely problematic if it is accepted that social objects have an internal complexity and structure as a complex responsive open system. Yet the traditional "quantitative" orientation, historically promoted by the physical sciences in the "west", has reinforced the "closed" nature of much research in the social sciences until this date.

- There is however, hope. We shall illustrate, in the case presented in this chapter, the growing number of empirical economists worldwide, taking empiricist research out of its narrowly positivist perspective. Such empiricist research is then moving from a purely informative into a more reformative realm. Our example here is David McKibben's "Deep Economy", which is providing "empirical proof" of the dysfunctionality of the current economic growth paradigm, also laying the ground for the critical methodology introduced in the then following layer 3: critical realism.

14.1 Orientation to Empiricism

Empiricism has certainly been the single most influential force in modern science. It is not only the core research orientation within the natural sciences, it has – until recently – also been the core research paradigm in the social sciences. We have highlighted various times in this book the danger and consequences of a predominating western empiricist perspective and an isolated focus on such a methodology. However, empiricism, in our Integral Research framework, remains the foundation and an important ingredient of the western path of realisation, thereafter, as we shall see later, transcended by the emancipatory critique, that is critical realism (chapter 15), and ultimately by an ultimately integral action research (chapter 16).

Empiricism itself builds on experimental and survey methods, which have emerged out of the mode of "doing". Such "doing" is not only the culmination of each of our research paths, it is also the particular emphasis of the western path. The "doing" hence is the crucial and ultimate culmination of our research, however, it needs to be an integral part of a whole. The western perspective in isolation from the south, east and north has no sustainable ground to build on (as we can see from the desolate state of today's social sciences); and each path, without moving through its originating method, a foundational methodology, a substantive and emancipating critique has little chance, so we argue, to build a sustainable, integral social innovation. Let us now turn to an overview on empiricism.

Empiricism – A Conceptual Overview

Empiricism is a theory of knowledge emphasizing the role of experience in the formation of ideas, while discounting the notion of innate ideas. In the philosophy of science, empiricism is a theory of knowledge, which emphasizes those aspects of scientific knowledge that are closely related to experience, especially as formed through deliberate experimental arrangements.

Empiricism – The Term

The term "empiricism" has a dual etymology. It comes from the Greek word εμπειρισμός, the Latin translation of which is experientia, from which we derive the word experience. It also derives from a more specific classical Greek and Roman usage of empiric, referring to a physician whose skills derive from practical experience as opposed to instruction in theory. In fact, the term "empirical" was originally used to refer to certain ancient Greek practitioners of medicine who rejected adherence to the dogmatic doctrines of the day, preferring instead to rely on the observation of phenomena as perceived in experience.

Empiricism is closely related to positivism, seeking after the "positive" facts, rather than relying on pure faith or indeed dogma.

Positivism incorporates a "western" ontology of an ordered universe made up of atomistic, discrete and observable events, typified by the economic marketplace. Only that which can be observed, that is experienced by the senses, can be regarded as real. In such an epistemology, knowledge is seen to be derived from sensory experience by means of experimental or comparative analysis. (1) Scientific theories are regarded as law-like statements, specifying simple relations or constant conjunctions between phenomena. Value judgments and normative statements require a separation of "facts" and "values"; furthermore values are denied of having the status of knowledge. The grounds for origination are lodged entirely and objectively in the external world "out there", rather than in the internal and subjective world, in yourself, as researcher and would-be social innovator. As a result, so-called objective based survey methods, including questionnaires and structured interviews, incorporating also statistical controls, constitute the formative base to such.

Such scientific "method" with its conventional procedure of observation, experimentation, and verification, emerged in the 17th century. It was forged out of a "liberal" and reasoned Enlightenment reaction to the perceived dogmatism of religious orthodoxy in Europe. As such it was spearheaded by such European luminaries as political scientists John Locke and David Hume, political economists Adam Smith and John Stuart Mill, and natural scientists Frances Bacon and Galileo Galilei. These kindred spirits were the early advocates of democracy, free markets and the pursuit of the "scientific" truth. In their day, they were all radical thinkers, staking their liberal claims – often risking their lives – against the conservative status quo. All together, these positivists were responsible for three of the major social innovations of the past two to three hundred years: free markets and liberal democracy, and scientific method itself, in its classically "western" vein.

Early forms of Empiricism

Early forms of empiricism include the epistemological works of Buddha (2), Aristotle (3) and church father Thomas Aquinas. The first empiricists in Western philosophy were probably the Sophists (ca. 5th Century BC), who rejected the rationalistic speculations about the nature of the world common among their predecessors, in favour of focusing "on such relatively concrete entities as man and society". The Sophists invoked sceptical semantic arguments, using examples that could be readily seen and observed by others, to undermine the claims of pure reason.

Among the medieval Scholastics, Thomas Aquinas derived from Aristotle the famous axiom: "Nothing is in the intellect which was not first in the senses". Aquinas argued that the existence of God could be proved by reasoning from sense data. (4) He used a variation on the Aristotelian notion of the "active intellect", which he interpreted as the ability to abstract universal meanings from particular empirical data.

Origins of Modern Empiricism: Locke, Hume, Bacon

The doctrine of empiricism was first explicitly formulated by John Locke in the 17th century. Locke argued that the mind is a tabula rasa ("clean slate" or "blank tablet"; Locke used the words "white paper") on which experiences leave their marks. Such empiricism denies that humans have innate ideas or that anything is knowable without reference to experience.

Locke made however an important exception: He, for his part, held that some knowledge (e.g. knowledge of God's existence) could be arrived at through intuition and reasoning alone.

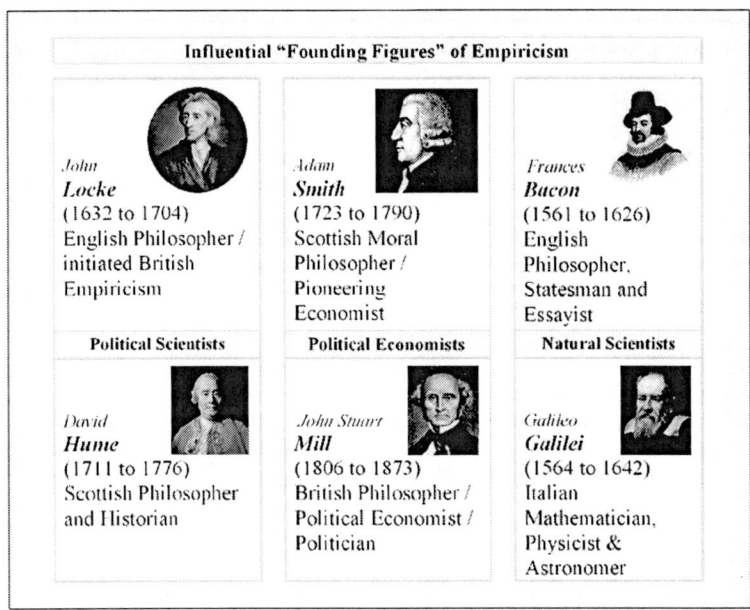

Figure 14.2: Empiricism – Core Thinkers

Earlier concepts of the existence of "innate ideas" were the subject of debate between the Continental rationalists and the British empiricists in the 17th century through the late 18th century. John Locke, David Hume and Frances Bacon were among the primary exponents of empiricism.

Responding to the continental "rationalism" most prominently defended by René Descartes, John Locke, writing in the late 17th century, in his "An Essay Concerning Human Understanding" (1689) proposed a new, and ultimately very influential view wherein the only knowledge humans can have is a posteriori, that is based upon experience.

Locke's ideas had enormous influence on the development of political philosophy, and he is widely regarded as one of the most influential Enlightenment thinkers and contributors to liberal theory. His writings influenced Voltaire and Rousseau, many Scottish Enlightenment thinkers, as well as the American revolutionaries. This influence is reflected in the American Declaration of Independence.

Locke's theory of mind is often cited as the origin for modern conceptions of identity and "the self"; it figured prominently in the works of later philosophers such as David Hume, Jean-Jacques Rousseau and Immanuel Kant. Locke was the first philosopher to define the self through a continuity of "consciousness."

The Scottish philosopher David Hume added to the empiricist viewpoint an extreme scepticism. Via his sceptical arguments he maintained that all knowledge, even the most basic beliefs about the natural world, cannot be conclusively established by reason. Rather, he maintained, our beliefs are more a result of accumulated habits, developed in response to accumulated sense experiences. (5) Among his many arguments Hume also added another important slant to the debate about scientific method – that of the problem of induction. Hume argued that it requires inductive reasoning, that is generating theories from facts or data, rather than the other way around, to arrive at the premises for the principle of inductive reasoning, and therefore the justification for inductive reasoning is a circular argument. Among Hume's conclusions regarding the problem of induction is that there is no certainty that the future will resemble the past. Thus, as a simple instance posed by Hume, we cannot know with certainty by inductive reasoning that the sun will continue to rise in the East, but instead come to expect it to do so because it has repeatedly done so in the past. (6)

Hume concluded that such things as belief in an external world and belief in the existence of the self were not rationally justifiable. According to Hume these beliefs were to be accepted nonetheless because of their profound basis in instinct and custom. Hume's lasting legacy, however, was the doubt that his sceptical arguments cast on the legitimacy of inductive reasoning, allowing many sceptics who followed to cast similar doubt. (7)

Frances Bacon, who is best known as a philosophical advocate and defender of the scientific revolution, established and popularised the inductive methodology for scientific inquiry, often called the Baconian method or simply, the scientific method. In the context of his time such methods were connected with the occult trends of hermeticism and alchemy, against which the empiricist Bacon reacted. His resultant demand for a planned procedure of investigating all things marked a new turn on the framework for science, much of which still surrounds conceptions of proper methodology today. His dedication to experimental science brought him however into a rare historical group of scientists who were killed by their own experiments. (8)

Empiricism and The rise of Economics

Empiricism also gave rise to a new discipline called economics. The Scottish philosopher Adam Smith, who is depicted on the back of today's Bank of England £20 note, was probably the most pioneering thinker in this field. It was Smith's systematic studies of the historical development of industry and commerce in Europe that led to his famous treatises: "The Theory of Moral Sentiments" (1759) (9), and "An Inquiry into the Nature and Causes of the Wealth of Nations" (1776). (10) Smith's work helped to create the modern academic discipline of economics and provided one of the best-known intellectual rationales for free trade, capitalism, and libertarianism. In the empirically laden process, of course, his latter book on the wealth of nations, proceeded to eclipse the former, much less popular work.

Smith libertarian ideas were taken forward by John Stuart Mill whose early economic philosophy was one of free markets. Mill's "Principles of Political Economy" (11), first published in 1848, was one of the most widely read of all books on economics in the period. As Adam Smith's Wealth of Nations had during an earlier period, Mill's Principles dominated economics teaching, in England then, and today in the wider world.

Empiricism and the Rise of a new Natural Science

The Italian physicist, mathematician and astronomer Galileo Galilei is also closely associated with the scientific revolution. His achievements include the first systematic studies of uniformly accelerated motion, improvements to the telescope, a variety of astronomical observations, and support for Copernicanism. Galileo's experiment-based work is a significant break from the abstract approach of Aristotle.

Galileo is often referred to as the "father of modern physics", and as the "father of science". The motion of uniformly accelerated objects, treated in nearly all high school and introductory college physics courses, was studied by Galileo as the subject of kinematics. Galileo pioneered the use of quantitative experiments whose results could be analysed with mathematical precision. He recognized that his experimental data would never agree exactly with any theoretical or mathematical form, because of the imprecision of measurement, irreducible friction, and other factors.

Although he tried to remain loyal to the Catholic Church, Galileo's adherence to experimental results, and their most honest interpretation, led to his rejection of blind allegiance to authority, both philosophical and religious, in matters of science. In broader terms, this helped separate science from philosophy and religion, a major development in human thought. Albert Einstein, in appreciation, called Galileo the "father of modern science". According to Stephen Hawking, Galileo probably contributed more to the creation of the modern natural sciences than anybody else.

We now turn to the key tenets of empiricism.

14.2 Empiricism – Key Tenets

Empiricism – Key Tenets
① Search for truth.
② Seek after the "positive facts".
③ Separate facts and values.
④ Collect observational data and build theories.
⑤ Control the research through "closed systems".

① Search for truth

The search for truth is assumed to be an intentional activity that reflects the needs of humanity and, as a consequence, secures human progress. In order to achieve scientific progress, you should deploy your capacity for reason within the methodological rules of scientific method. Scientific statements are seen as pictures or snapshots of the things they refer to. Reality for the empiricist is made up of atomistic, discrete and observable experiences and events. Hence, one of the core "instruments" of the positivist is the method of induction. Such a method refers to a logical process of constructing knowledge about observed relationships between variables in particular instances.

② Seek after the "positive facts"

The empiricist seeks after the "positive" facts, rather than relying on pure faith or indeed dogma. Only that which can be observed, that is experienced by the senses, can be regarded as real. Knowledge is seen to be derived from sensory experience by means of experimental or comparative analysis.

③ Separate facts and values

Value judgments and normative statements require a separation of "facts" and "values"; furthermore values are denied of having the status of knowledge. The grounds for origination are lodged entirely and objectively in the external world "out there", rather than in the internal and subjective world, in yourself, as researcher and would-be social innovator. As a result, so-called objective based survey methods, including questionnaires and structured interviews, incorporating also statistical controls, constitute the formative base to such.

④ Collect observational data and build theories

The logical positivist uses induction to collect observational data and build theories to explain the observations. The method of induction refers to a logical process of constructing knowledge about observed relationships between variables in particular instances. This can be taken as a basis for making universal generalizations in as yet unobserved, particular instances. As a researcher you identify a limited number of variables and observe their behaviour and changes of one in relation with the other. Therefore, you identify factors, which are significant so their effect can be observed and you pinpoint which factor actually causes the observed outcome to occur.

⑤ Control the research through "closed systems"

Research happens within "closed systems", enabling you as a researcher to isolate the objects you wish to investigate from all other objects, which would confuse the picture. Such a "closed system" research – means in addition to the identification of variables and the observation of their behaviour – that you avoid any interference from unexpected external forces. Exclusion clauses ensure that the mass of possible influences is screened out (ceteris paribus). It is you who controls the situation by manipulating variables.

We shall now have a close look at empiricism, a core expression of the positivist worldview, which has its purer pedigree in the natural sciences.

14.3 Empiricism in Depth

14.3.1 The Nature and Scope of Classical Scientific Method

For Open University based social scientist Mark Smith in the UK, in his "Social Science in Question" (12), the *success of the scientific "method" is specifically explained in terms of its ability to reveal the truth.*

Such a search for truth was assumed to be an intentional activity that reflected the needs of humanity and, as a consequence, secured human progress. Each part of the circuit is defined through its relationship with the others. In order to achieve progress, we should deploy our capacity for reason within the methodological rules of scientific method, in order to establish the truth of a situation and use this as a means of serving the needs of humanity. These were the roots of so-called "positivism", today seen in much more traditional, and now conservative guise in the social sciences than hitherto. However, in more recent years during the twentieth century, the radical nature and scope of such theorists has been dissipated, and they have come to represent the status quo, at least in "western" secular terms. Let us explore further the link between the empirical methods and the positivist philosophy underlying them, drawing upon the even more refined version of such empiricism, that is "logical positivism".

14.3.2 The Inductively based Logical Positivist Approach

Logical positivism placed an exceptional emphasis upon sensory perception and the role of observation in research as the foundation for knowledge. Scientific statements were seen as pictures or snapshots of the things they refer to. The more contemporary origins go back to England's Bertrand Russell and Austria's Ludwig Wittgenstein subsequently promoted by the Vienna Circle from the 1920's. To each object, they maintained, corresponds a definite statement. For Austrian Rudolph Carnap, an influential member of the circle, this approach was identified as "physicalism".

The logical positivist uses induction to collect observational data and build theories o explain the observations. Thus the method of induction involves two movements simultaneously: from the particular to the general, and from observed events to theoretical constructions. Such induction, with its focus on doing, can be compared with deduction (focus on knowing), retroduction (oriented towards becoming) and abduction (linked with being).

To summarize, *the method of induction refers to a logical process of constructing knowledge about observed relationships between variables in particular instances.* This can be taken as a basis for making universal generalizations in as yet unobserved, particular instances. The *strength of induction lies in its appeal to data collected through human senses*, rather than perceived intuitively, or conceived abstractly, as a means of validating propositions. The explanatory power of this approach is said to rest upon its predictive uses. However, such prediction tends to be restricted to "closed" systems.

14.3.3 Closed Systems take Precedence over Open Systems

Typical of such a "closed" scientific orientation, especially in the twentieth century, *was the use of mechanical and experimental metaphors,* along with a desire to emulate physics as the purest form of scientific activity. Indeed, experimental method was correlated with scientific method. Newton (1642 to 1727), for example, in his study of matter, motion and light, was developing the method of induction by using observations of particular conditions – experimenting with light through the use of prisms and pieces of white card – as a foundation for constructing a general theoretical account of light. Within such a closed system it is possible to:

- identify a limited number of variables
- observe their behaviour, the frequency of changes in one in relation to the other
- account for or avoid any interference from unexpected external forces.

The scientific experiment was Newton's way of artificially replicating the idea of a closed system, enabling researchers to isolate the objects they wish to investigate from all other objects, which would confuse the picture. Identifying simple relations between discrete things would enable a scientist to understand and explain events beyond the experimental situation. The idea of such "closure" has been an important part of all scientific disciplines, which have sought to establish objective knowledge, including the social sciences. In psychology, for example, such experimental closure involves the physical separation of human beings from their normal context, and subjecting them to particular stimuli with a view to gauging their response.

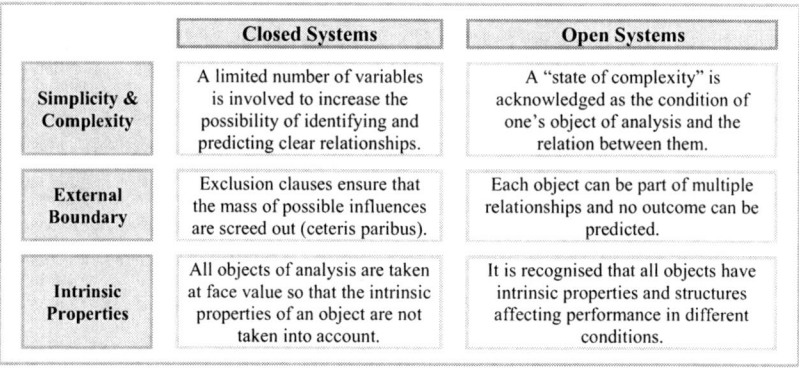

	Closed Systems	**Open Systems**
Simplicity & Complexity	A limited number of variables is involved to increase the possibility of identifying and predicting clear relationships.	A "state of complexity" is acknowledged as the condition of one's object of analysis and the relation between them.
External Boundary	Exclusion clauses ensure that the mass of possible influences are screed out (ceteris paribus).	Each object can be part of multiple relationships and no outcome can be predicted.
Intrinsic Properties	All objects of analysis are taken at face value so that the intrinsic properties of an object are not taken into account.	It is recognised that all objects have intrinsic properties and structures affecting performance in different conditions.

Figure 14.3: Closed and Open Systems

Through theoretical closure, in econometric models for example, the economy is replicated as a series of variables and relationships through a computer programme, including growth measures, the money supply, manufacturing output, employment levels and prices. The relationships between the variables are conceived of in terms of the susceptibility of one variable to changes in the others. No model though, however elaborate, can mirror or replicate the uncertainties or complexities of the real economy. Furthermore, statistical closure involves a situation in which quantitative numerical data sets are processed to identify correlations, as for example with the study of voting behaviour. As soon as the complexity of social life is acknowledged in social research, though, these techniques for simulating closure are problematised and the status of causal laws produced in this way is dramatically altered. *This problem is accentuated if it is accepted that social objects have an internal complexity and structure as a complex responsive open system* (see figure above). Yet the traditional "quantitative" orientation, historically promoted by the physical sciences in the "west", has reinforced the "closed" nature of such a "positivist" epistemology. This applies as much to experimental research method, as it does to positivist research methodology.

14.3.4 Positivist Epistemology in the Social Sciences

Such positivist approaches to the social sciences often exclusively claim the label of "scientific", for they assume things can be studied as hard facts, and the relationship between these facts established as solid, empirically based, scientific laws. For such positivists, these laws have the status of truth as social objects, and can be studied in much the same way as natural objects. Not surprisingly, *classical economics, with its belief in "market mechanisms" is heavily influenced by positivism.*

The most influential early positivist in the social sciences was France's Auguste Comte (1798 to 1857). He brought together the search for the truth with his faith in progress. To replace "divine truths", Comte looked to the natural sciences, calling his approach "social physics". Comte sought to identify the laws of social statics and social dynamics with a view to social engineering. The English utilitarian Jeremy Bentham, following in Comte's footsteps, characterized human beings as pleasure seeking or pain avoiding, based on their making rational choices. This approach treated aggregate bodies as the total of individual actors, with a view to gaining "the greatest good for the greatest number". The economy is thus an aggregate of individuals, firms and households; the political process is an aggregate of voters in elections and parties and pressure groups. We now turn, problematically as we shall see, to global variations.

14.4 Global Variations of Empiricism

14.4.1 The Local-Global Empirical Conundrum

Unlike the other three classical methodologies of Integral Research's layer 2 (that is phenomenology, hermeneutics and critical rationalism), each of which has been evolved and adapted in other parts of the world, empiricism remains a home-grown "western" product. In other words, and because (at least in its pure form) it is alien to the "north", "east" and "south", if not also the "middle east", it has no explicitly global variations. Actually, in our own experience, working in such far-flung placed as in China and India, Africa and South-East Asia, it tends to be misused, rather than evolved, in these places. In other words, research-wise, it became something like a lowest common denominator.

One of us will never forget an experience during the early stages of a doctoral thesis being undertaken by one of our Jordanian participants, Mohammad Al Zoubi, a civil servant and member of a prominent local family, in Jordan and Syria. Working on a topic connected with globalisation, and its economic impact on his society, he asked

Ronnie Lessem, at their first session together, "what do you think are my independent and dependent variables?". Needless to say Ronnie's answer was "I would not start from there".

Although empiricism has not evolved geographically through global variations, over the course of time such an empirical-pragmatic course of evolution has taken place in the Anglo-Saxon world.

14.4.2 Emerging Pragmatism

In the late 19th century and early 20th century several forms of pragmatic philosophy arose out of empiricism. The ideas of pragmatism developed mainly from discussions that took place while Charles Sanders Peirce and William James were both at Harvard in the 1870's. James popularised the term "pragmatism", giving Peirce full credit for its patrimony, but Peirce later demurred from the tangents that the movement was taking, and redubbed what he regarded as the original idea with the name of "pragmaticism". Along with its pragmatic theory of truth, this perspective integrates the basic insights of empirical (experience-based) and rational (concept-based) thinking.

Charles Peirce (1839 to 1914) was highly influential in laying the groundwork for today's empirical scientific method. Although Peirce severely criticized many elements of Descartes' peculiar brand of rationalism, he did not reject rationalism outright. Indeed, he concurred with the main ideas of rationalism, most importantly the idea that rational concepts can be meaningful and the idea that rational concepts necessarily go beyond the data given by empirical observation. In later years he even emphasized the concept-driven side of the then ongoing debate between strict empiricism and strict rationalism, in part to counterbalance the excesses to which some of his cohorts had taken pragmatism under the "data-driven" strict-empiricist view.

Among Peirce's major contributions was to place inductive reasoning (data comes first) and deductive reasoning (theory comes first) in a complementary rather than competitive mode, the latter of which had been the primary trend among the educated since David Hume wrote a century before. To this, Peirce added the concept of abductive reasoning, evoked directly out of peoples' life worlds, which we have identified with our relational research path. The combined three forms of reasoning serve as a primary conceptual foundation for the empirically based scientific method today. Peirce's approach "presupposes that firstly the objects of knowledge are real things, secondly the characters (properties) of real things do not depend on our perceptions of them, and thirdly everyone who has sufficient experience of real things will agree on the truth about them". In his Harvard "Lectures on Pragmatism" (1903), Peirce enumerated what he called the "three contrary propositions of pragmatism", saying that they "put the edge on the maxim of pragmatism". (13)

The renowned US-American Social Philosopher and Educationalist John Dewey (1859 to 1952) who became one of the founding fathers of "action research" (see chapters 13 and 16) built on such theories on pragmatism to form a theory known as instrumentalism. The role of sense experience in Dewey's theory is crucial, in that he saw experience as unified totality of things through which everything else is interrelated. Dewey's basic thought, in accordance with empiricism was that reality is determined by past experience. Therefore, humans adapt their past experiences of things to perform experiments upon and test the pragmatic values of such experience. The value of such experience is measured by scientific instruments, and the results of such measurements generate ideas which serve as instruments for future experimentation. Thus, ideas in Dewey's system retain their empiricist flavour in that they are only known a posteriori. (14)

Finally, we can see today that a broadly based empiricism, and indeed pragmatism, can lead to factual observations that serve to transcend the conventional wisdom on free market economics (see "deep economics" below).

14.5 Empiricism in Practice: The Wealth of Community

14.5.1 Growing Economic Inequality

Though the American economy of late has been striving, income inequality between rich and poor has been growing. The median wage in the U.S. is the same as what it was thirty years ago. More than eighty countries have seen per capita incomes fall in the last decade. Basically almost all of the growing wealth accumulates in a few pockets. The 2006 tax-cuts, for example, delivered 70% of its benefits to the richest 5% of Americans. Alongside the exhilaration of the flattening earth, celebrated by journalist Thomas Friedman, the plane is containing an increasing number of flattened people, flattened by the very forces that are making the few, for McKibben, wildly rich. (15)

When Thomas Newcomen launched the Industrial Revolution, he was using coal to pump water out of a coalmine. The birth of the industrial revolution was all about fossil fuel. We have learnt an enormous amount in the past two centuries through our ever-growing body of scientific knowledge, but coal and oil and natural gas are still at the bottom of it all. Now it is plausible, indeed likely, that if we run short of such; our lives may fundamentally change as scarcity of energy wreaks havoc. Moreover, even before we run short of energy we are running short of planet. If the Chinese, by 2030, are to become as rich as Americans are, they will consume 20 million more barrels of oil per day than the entire world consumption today.

Then there is Global Warming

Then there is global warming. All of those pools of oil and beds of coal beneath our feet are being drilled and dug. For a brief moment the resulting energy burns and does something useful: moves your car, heats you shower. But after that instant of combustion most of the carbon in the coal or oil mixes with oxygen in the air to form the gas carbon dioxide, which drifts into the atmosphere, creating almost a mirror image of the reservoir you drilled it from in the first place. The molecular structure of carbon dioxide than traps heat from the sun that would otherwise radiate back into space. That is what global warming is – the gaseous remains of all fields and coal beds acting like an insulating blanket. The year 2005 in already the warmest on record, and none of the ten hottest years were in the decade that preceded it. Indeed everything frozen on earth is now melting and melting fast. And climate change has only just begun! The WHO expects vast changes in mosquito born diseases, as just one result, warning that climate change could kill 184 million people in Africa alone before the century is out. Humans have never done anything bigger, not even the invention of nuclear weapons.

While American industry may be using less energy per dollar's worth of stuff it produces, as the knowledge based economy takes hold, so much more stuff will be produced per year that the carbon emission totals keep rising. Between 1990 and 2003, for example, annual emissions increased by 16%.

The Advent of Ecological Economics

The creeping recognition that economics, even in its ever growing mathematical sophistication, has become abstracted from the actual planet we inhabit has spurred the steady development of an increasingly impressive new school of ecological economics. As far back as the 1960's economists like Kenneth Boulding were at work on what he termed "the economics of the coming spaceship earth". In the 1970's, a World Bank economist, Herman Daly, published a collection titled "Toward a Steady State Economy" that actually began to nose around the question whether perpetual growth was possible. And by the 1980's Daly, together with Bob Constanza, had formed the Society of Ecological Economics.

At the same time, the last decade has seen one effort after another to replace, or at least supplement, gross national product as the measure of our success. Under the current system, all we do is add together expenditures so that the most "economically productive" citizen is a cancer patient who fills up his car with petrol on the way to meet his divorce lawyer. Instead many have proposed a "green national product" or an "index of sustainable economic welfare".

Towards Happiness and Satisfaction

For McKibben, ideas like happiness and satisfaction have traditionally been waved aside by economists as poetic irrelevancies, when compared with "utility maximization". Such a conventional economic theory holds that every time a person buys something, sells something, quits a job, or invests, he is making a rational decision about what will provide him "maximum utility". In recent years, however, something new has happened. In 2002, Daniel Kahneman, trained as a psychologist, won the Nobel Prize in economics. In his book "Well-Being" he announced the development of a new field called hedonics, defined as "the study of what makes experience and life pleasant or unpleasant".

The idea that there is a state called "happiness", and that we can dependably figure out what it feels like and how to measure it, is extremely subversive. It would allow economists to start thinking about life in far richer terms, allow them to stop asking "What did you buy?", and start asking "Is your life good?" On average, all of us in the West are living lives materially more abundant than most people did a generation ago. What's odd is that is does not seem to have made us happier. In 1946, according to McKibben, the United States was the happiest country amongst four advanced economies; thirty years later it was eighth amongst the eleven most advanced; a decade later it ranked tenth among twenty-three.

In the United Kingdom, for instance, gross national product per capita grew 66% between 1973 and 2001, yet people's satisfaction with their lives changed not at all. Japan saw a fivefold increase between 1958 and 1986 without any reported increase in satisfaction. In one place after another, rates of alcoholism, suicide, and depression have gone up dramatically, even as the amount of stuff has accumulated. If satisfaction was our goal, therefore, the vast expenditure of effort and resources since 1950 have been largely a waste. For the peasant farmer in China, for example and on the other hand, a boost in income brings tangible benefits. Up to a certain point, income-wise, more does certainly mean better. So China's relentless growth – 9% per year for the last couple of decades – has indeed lifted lots of people out of poverty and made their lives happier. McKibben cites researchers as saying that up to $10,000 per annum money does buy happiness, and then the correlation disappears.

Where then did we go wrong? The answer is obvious! We kept doing something past the point where it worked. Since happiness had increased with income in the past we assumed it would continue to do so in the future. At the time of Adam Smith a concern with economic issues was understandably primary. Meeting simple human needs for food, shelter and clothing was not assured, and satisfying these needs moved lockstep with better economics. In 1820 the average American earned the equivalent, in current dollars, to the present African average. In what Richard Layard calls a "cultural lag", market democracies continue to emphasize the themes that have brought them to the current position. As he says in the conclusion to his book on "Happiness": "Utilitarianism is the guiding philosophy of our time, but theories of what produces happiness have changed since Bentham". We need, in short, a new utilitarianism.

14.5.2 The Wealth of Communities

Starting with Energy

Perhaps we should start by thinking about energy in new ways. Instead of something that you buy from far away, energy becomes something you help make and distribute to your neighbours. By their very nature, fuels like solar and wind are diffuse and dispersed: instead of a few people digging them from the ground, a great many of us can harvest energy from the planet's surface. To make localized power generation work you need community. Ask yourself why Japan leads the world in building a decentralized solar-panel energy economy. Because it has so much sun (it does not) or so much fellowship. People in Japan feel they are able to trust each other.

Consolidation or Localization

If our larger society, moreover, is running up against the realisation that "more is not necessarily better", then one of the alternatives is to think on a different scale. And, for McKibben, food may be the place to begin. A Harvard Business School professor recently reported that "fifty per cent of the world's assets and consumer expenditure belong to food system". Half the jobs too. The "food system" in America has been made over in the name of efficiency and growth as much as any other: the average bite of food has travelled 1500 miles before it reaches our lips.

The self-sufficient all round farms with which the colonists covered the country have largely disappeared, at least outside Amish country. But there is now an exception to this trend: the quick spread in the last decade of "community-supported agriculture" or the CSA farm. Consumers pay farmers a few hundred dollars apiece in midwinter and then are supplied with a weekly bin of incredibly diverse vegetables throughout the growing season and deep into autumn. Almost every corner of America now has a CSA nearby.

From America to Cuba – Semi-Sustainable Agriculture

Surprisingly, in Cuba, new farming "technologies" are emerging that are the most exciting inventions of our age, for McKibben perhaps more exciting than even the iPod or the Internet. The unlikely scene for a major such experiment is Havanna. With the sudden collapse of the Soviet Union, Cuba fell off a cliff of its own and became the first place in the world to face peak oil. All those tractors and combines had been products of an insane "economics" underwritten by the Eastern bloc for ideological purposes. Castro spent three decades growing sugar and shipping it to Russia and east Germany, both of which paid a price well above the world level, sending the ships back to Havanna equipped with rice, wheat and oil, and more tractors. When all of that disappeared, virtually overnight, Cuba had nowhere to turn. In other words it became truly an island, not just a real one, but an island outside the international economic system.

During the Soviet era much of what Cubans ate came straight from Eastern Europe, and most of the rest was grown industrial style, on the big state farms. All those combines needed fuel and spare parts, and all those long rows of grain and vegetables needed pesticides and fertilizer, none of which were available any longer. What happened was simple, though unexpected. Cuba learned to stop exporting sugar and instead started raising its own food again, growing it on small private farms and in thousands of pocket-sized urban market gardens. Since the country lacked fertilizers the food became de facto organic. Cubans produce as much food today as they did before the collapse of the Soviet Union. In so doing, they have created what may be the world's largest working model of a semi-sustainable agriculture, which has benefited enormously from Castro's lavish spending on education, organic farming being no simple task. In fact, its new agricultural system is no less of an invention as the tractor farming it replaced. In the interim, back in the United States, the country had 340 farmer's markets in 1970, 1700 in 1994, and 3,700 in 2004. Community supported agricultural farms (CSA's) meanwhile have grown from just one in 1985 to 1500 today.

Changing Course

For McKibben, if the rich countries of the world cannot change course, then the poor countries will not. America's biggest exports are television programmes and movies – modelling its idea of the good life, wildly out of scale with the rest of the world, and what it can deliver. If we continue to idolize the likes of a Donald Trump, the Chinese will create their own versions of him. If America cannot move away from the ideal of the hyper-individual, then much of the world will keep running in the same direction. So first-world countries must become less growth oriented and more locally rooted. What then should development in the future look like? It should look to the local far more than to the global? It should concentrate on creating and sustaining strong communities, not creating a culture of economic individualism. It should worry less about what is ideal from a classical economist's view of markets, and far more about what is ecologically possible. It should aim not at growth but at durability. It should avoid the romantic fantasies offered by the prophets of endless wealth in favour of the blunter realism of people holding out for each other, as they have done over millennia of human existence.

We are now ready to conclude this chapter.

14.6 Conclusion

The Empirical bereft of the Integral

We highlighted in this chapter the limitations of an empircism, which acts in isolation and is bereft of an integral perspective. While the same applies to any one, single method or methodology, the fact that empiricism is the most commonplace, worldwide, makes these limitations more marked. Indeed, it was this isolated and unrelated (to context) perspective that gave rise, in the 19th century, to phenomenology.

That having been said, there are a number of strengths, that empiricism, well used, brings to the table in the Social Sciences. Specifically, it is overtly practical, seemingly evidence based, and coherently argued. It clearly presents a particular perspective, argues its case demonstrably, and incorporates many well-researched facts and figures to back up its overall argument.

However, its weakness often lies in its surface nature, unable to accommodate the depths of a particular nature and culture, as seen "through local eyes". Often, the actual faces or voices that (locally) belong to the researched context are not seen or heard. They remain silent.

Moreover, and historically, there is no acknowledgment, or indeed reporting, on what has come before. Empiricism, in most cases, does not embed the research in its larger historical or societal context. Its mode of comprehension, while full of facts and figures, is bereft of a particular life world; history or philosophy are often left out of empirical account.

Reformative and Transformative left out of Account

In such a narrowly empirical form, there is no attempt to co-create a new world, simultaneous to investigating it. As a result, a purely empirically based research, lacking integral credentials, is unable to pave the way for any form of social innovation, or indeed social and economic transformation.

It is for that reason that we now turn from empiricism to critical realism, from what is observable and measurable to, in addition, the underlying, generative forces. It is hence time, to enter the third layer of "critique". Here on our western path of realisation, critical realism will probe beyond the empirical surface, and take us a step further to innovation.

Bibliography

1) **Markie**, P. (2004). *Rationalism versus Empiricism*. In Edward D. Zalta (ed.), Stanford Encyclopedia of Philosophy.

2) **Kalupahana**, D.J. (January 1969). *A Buddhist Tract on Empiricism*. Honolulu, University of Hawaii Press: Philosophy East and West 19 (1), p. 65-67.

3) **Aristotle** (2007). *Posterior Analytics*. Translated by G. R. G. Mure. Adelaide: University of Adelaide.

4) **Macmillan Encyclopedia of Philosophy** (1969). *Thomas Aquinas*. Subsection on "Theory of Knowledge". Vol. 8, pp. 106-107.

5) **Hume**, D. (1975). *A Treatise of Human Nature*. L.A. Selby-Bigge (ed.). London: Oxford University Press.

6) **Hume**, D. (1902). *An Enquiry Concerning Human Understanding*. In Enquiries Concerning the Human Understanding and Concerning the Principles of Morals, 2nd edition, L.A. Selby-Bigge (ed.). Oxford: Oxford University Press. (Orig. 1748).

7) **Chisolm**, R. (1948). *The Problem of Empiricism*. New York: Journal of Philosophy 45, 512–517.

8) **Achinstein**, P. & **Barker**, S.F. (1969). *The Legacy of Logical Positivism: Studies in the Philosophy of Science*. Baltimore: Johns Hopkins University Press.

9) **Smith**, A. (1759). *The Theory of Moral Sentiments*. Oxford and New York: Oxford University Press.

10) **Smith**, A. (1759). *An Inquiry into the Nature and Causes of the Wealth of Nations*. Oxford and New York: Oxford University Press.

11) **Mill**, J.S. (1848). *Principles of Political Economy*. Oxford and New York: Oxford University Press.

12) **Smith**, M. (2000). *Social Science in Question*. London, Thousand Oaks and New Delhi: Open University Press.

13) **Peirce**, C.S. (March to May 1903). *Lectures on Pragmatism*. Cambridge. Reprinted in part, Collected Papers, CP 5.14–212. Reprinted with Introduction and Commentary: Turisi, P.A. (ed.) (1997). Pragmatism as a Principle and a Method of Right Thinking: The 1903 Harvard "Lectures on Pragmatism". Albany: State University of New York Press. Reprinted, pp. 133–241, Peirce Edition Project (eds.), The Essential Peirce, Selected Philosophical Writings, Volume 2 (1893–1913), Bloomington: Indiana University Press, 1998.

14) **Dewey**, J. (1906). *Studies in Logical Theory*. Chicago: The University of Chicago Press.

15) **McKibben**, B. (2007). *Deep Economy: The Wealth of Communities and the Durable Future*. New York: Times Books.

CHAPTER 15

FROM EMPIRICISM TO
CRITICAL REALISM

"DISCOVER UNDERLYING REALITY"

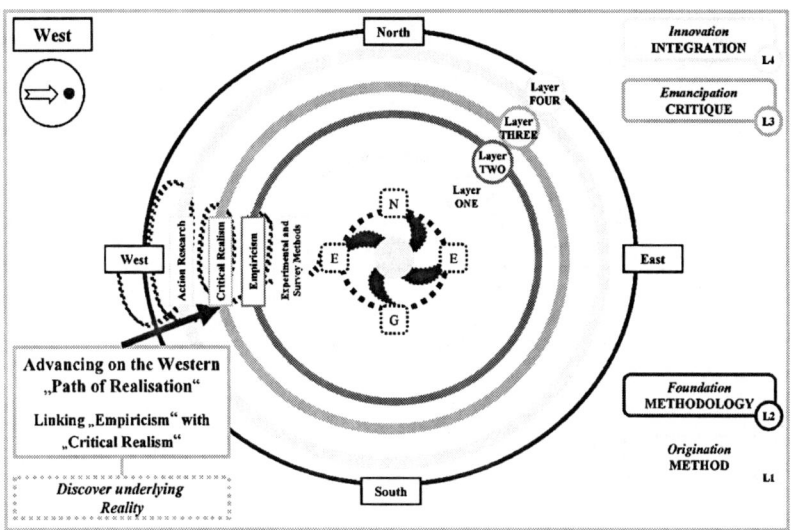

Figure 15.1: Overview Chapter 15 – Layer 3 / West

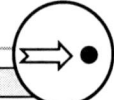

Summary: Critical Realism

- Following the path of realisation we now turn to critical realism (emancipation) as an evolution from experimental and survey methods (origination) and conventional empirical methodology (foundation).

- The originator of critical realism is the Anglo-Indian social philosopher, Roy Bhaskar, who was influenced in turn by the New Zealander Rom Harre, and the Argentine Mario Bunge.

- The key tenets of critical realism are its combined objective and subjective nature, its interpretive as well as explanatory orientation, its stratified nature, its recognition of human fallibility, as well as its critical as well as emancipatory orientation.

- Explored in depth, it is characterised by a pragmatic orientation and a focus on abstraction, by a metaphysical orientation and a focus on different levels of theory, as well as by its explicitly scientific approach.

- In its more global reach it is associated with an "eastern" turn, whereby its focus on "meta-reality" explicitly brings in a spiritual dimension that was previously only implicit, and a dialectical orientation to supplement the pragmatic orientation.

- At the end of the chapter we offer Homer Dixon's work on "The Upside of Down: Catastrophe, Creativity and Renewal" as a practical application of critical realism. While this Canadian peace activist and environmentalist empirically engages with the downside of today's consumerism and growth paradigm, he also uncovers the deeper layers of stress underneath the surface of our societies.

15.1 Orientation to Critical Realism

With critical realism we enter the third layer of the western path of realisation. While we have positioned critical realism on the western path, it is a kind of a "mixed breed". While it has western (realistic) connotations, it also carries a strong eastern flavour, adding to the visible surface of the research object its more invisible ground of origin. In that sense it clearly transcends a purely positivist empiricism. Adding, critically, a deeper (subjective) experiential ground to the outer (objective) empirical surface, it enables the researcher to connect inner subject to outer reality. As such, it paves the way for the final innovatory layer of the western path, an integrated action research, which follows in chapter 16.

15.1.1 The Origins of Critical Realism

Roy Bhaskar is unique in having given birth, almost single-handeldly, to a research philosophy, that is critical realism. Actually, when one of us began to first discover the profound difference between research method and methodology – or philosophy – it was the discovery of critical realism which first enabled Ronnie Lessem to come to such a conclusion. Soon after that, Ronnie met up with Bhaskar, at a seminar in London, and was overwhelmed by his casual, offbeat appearance, a tall, longhaired man, shoddily dressed in jeans and sneakers. Immediately he began to speak, though, the attending participants became enthralled.

Bhaskar was born in London, to an Indian father and English mother, both of whom were theosophists, heavily influenced by eastern philosophies, upon which, in his later years in particular, Roy Bhaskar would draw. As a young man in 1963 he went up to Baliol College, Oxford, on a scholarship to read Philosophy, Politics and Economics. Having graduated with first class honours in 1966, he began to work on a Ph.D thesis dealing with the relevance of economic theory for under-developed countries. This research led him to the philosophy of social science and then the philosophy of science. In the course of this Rom Harre became his supervisor. Harre, of French Huguenot stock, but born and bred in New Zealand, is a philosopher, psychologist and anthropologist who spent much of his adult years teaching philosophy at the University of Punjab in India.

Bhaskar was also influenced in his early thinking by the Argentinian philosopher, Mario Bunge. Bunge set out his thinking systematically in his "Treatise on Basic Philosophy", a monumental work in eight volumes, comprising semantics, ontology, epistemology, philosophy of science and ethics. In 40 books, and some 400 papers, Bunge develops a comprehensive scientific outlook, which he then applies to the various natural and social sciences. Bunge was also a left wing intellectual, and his interdisciplinary approach and political credentials appealed to the young Bhaskar.

Bhaskar's own consideration of the philosophies of science and social science resulted in the development of critical realism, an emancipatory body of thought that aspires to move beyond the Enlightenment, avoiding reductionist rationalism through enhanced historical self-awareness and use of dialectical thought. To achieve this, it draws on pre-modern spiritual traditions as well as on positive aspects of the Enlightenment: its commitment to scientific inquiry and to freedom.

It is interesting to note that Bhaskar has no fixed academic abode. He remains a truly fee spirit, on the edges of academia, though he, with his close colleagues, has developed an International Association for Critical Realism.

In the year 2000, Bhaskar published his "From East to West: The Odyssey of a Soul", in which he first expressed ideas related to spiritual values that came to be seen as the beginning of his so-called spiritual turn. This was initially very controversial, but has since won growing support after the publication in 2002 of his book on the radical development of critical realism which he called "The Philosophy of Meta-Reality"; here he made it clear that this latest phase of his thought applied to people of all faiths and no faith, i.e. was susceptible to a purely secular interpretation.

What he refers to as Meta-Reality, however, may be seen as a different philosophy altogether. In his "Reflections on Meta-Reality", he states:

"This book articulates the difference between critical realism in its development and a new philosophical standpoint which I am in the process of developing, which I have called the philosophy of Meta-Reality."

The main departure, it seems, is a shift away from Western dualism to a non-dual model in which emancipation entails "a breakdown, an overcoming, of the duality and separateness between things." In effect, in his midlife, Bhaskar has turned very explicitly back to his "eastern" roots, and combined such with his "western" realist approach, in a very distinctive way.

15.1.2 From Empiricism to Critical Realism

Like in postmodernism, critical theory and feminism, so also in critical realism knowledge is socially constructed, but only in "transitive" part. For, in critical realism unlike in postmodernism an objectively based reality does exist, "intransitively" so to speak. So reality is partly pre-existent and partly socially constructed. Insofar as reality is pre-existent, such a "realist" approach shares with empiricism its grounding in an objectively definable world. However, for such critical realists, that is not the end of the story.

What is of profound importance for them is that *ontology is stratified, with underlying reality constituting the generative depths. Our emancipation, hence, is preconditioned by our coming to understand and work with such "real" depths.* As a result:

Let us now investigate, more purposefully, the origins and scope of critical realism.

15.1.3 Realism rather than Empiricism

Roy Bhaskar
(* 1944)
British Social Philosopher / Originator of "Critical Realism"

Figure 15.2: Critical Realism's Core Thinker – Roy Bhaskar

Roy Bhaskar's "Realist Theory of Science" (1) was strongly influenced by his doctoral supervisor Rom Harre, who in his book "The Method of Science" (2) had laid early critical-realist foundations with his comprehensive criticism of positivism. Harre argued that *there had to be underlying generative mechanisms in order to analyse the world in terms of cause and effect.* For Mario Bunge (3), moreover, *reality is arranged in levels; something qualitatively new can only emerge from a lower level.*

There is therefore a *distinction between a real world and a conceptual one, and empiricism is criticized for reducing reality to the observable.* Bhaskar then, took the realist story on, from a newly critical-emancipatory perspective, building on the prior ground that his predecessors, from their diverse cultural heritages had established.

15.1.4 From "West" to "East": Realism to Meta-Reality

What then is this stratified, critical-emancipatory perspective? For Roy Bhaskar it seemed in fact, in the late sixties when he was writing his doctoral thesis, that the most important problem facing mankind was that of overcoming world poverty. As such, and not unlike his kindred "critical theory" spirits, he was tapping into his humanistic roots. Specifically then:

"What is required is a revolutionary transformation far more profound than any of us can imagine. Unless capitalism is overturned, by a revolution, which will be at once much more peaceful and deeper than the one that overthrew socialism, that will draw on resources and aspects of our being that are at once spiritual and cultural, set in the context of a feasible transition, and done in a non-violent way – unless capitalism is overturned in that way, I can see very little prospect of humanity surviving much into the 21ˢᵗ century on this planet."

Human freedom, for Bhaskar, depends above all on understanding the truth about reality and acting toward it. The task of social innovation is thereby one, that his transformative approach to "Meta-Reality" (4) would take on, from where analytically based critical realism leaves off, the two together forming the emancipatory platform for such innovation.

So it is essential for the critical realists, that science and philosophy should be explicitly concerned with human liberation. The key to such liberation, though, was to uncover the generative forces, that underlay our economic and social, as well as our physical reality.

The further development of critical realism, what Bhaskar terms Meta-Reality, makes possible a re-evaluation of the old dispute between idealism and materialism. Capitalism at the moment is the dominant world order. It is, however, faced with two pressing contradictions. A rising organic composition of nature threatens to tear the world itself apart with ecological contradictions, while, at the same time, a rising organic composition of ideas makes possible the notion of a new organisation of the social world attuned to universal self realisation and harmony. A new synthesis is what is required between "leftist" politics and "new age" psychology. Such a synthesis, for Bhaskar, will need to be set in a context of a global philosophy, which resonates with themes traceable back to the dawn of the great world civilisations – such as Buddhism and Taoism – rather than only drawing upon modern Euro-centric times.

The philosophy of Meta-Reality describes the way in which this very world nevertheless depends on, is ultimately sustained by, and only exists in virtue of: the free, loving, creative and intelligent energy and activity of states of our "real" being. In becoming aware of this we begin the process of transforming and overthrowing the totality of structures of oppression, alienation and mystification and indeed misery, which we have produced. Such a vision opens up a balanced world, of a society in which the free development and flourishing of each unique human being is understood to be the condition, as it is also the consequence, of the free development and flourishing of all.

In that sense Bhaskar is taking psychologically and spiritually on, from where Marx left economically and socially off. In that context he rubs shoulders with his critical theory oriented counterparts. However, unlike them, there is a strong pragmatic and Anglo-Saxon edge to his argument. Alongside such, we can see the influence of his

Indian heritage, where the notion of "levels of consciousness" (or indeed, for him and his Anglo-Saxon colleagues: the stratified nature of reality or ontology) predominates. We now turn to the key tenets of critical realism, starting with the notion that critical realism is indeed "critical", and ending with the hermeneutic, as well as pragmatic, side to critical realism.

15.2 Critical Realism – Key Tenets

Critical Realism – Key Tenets
① Critical realism is critical of the status quo.
② You become involved with a stratified or layered reality.
③ You view such a layered perspective on reality as fallible.
④ You conceive reality as both transitive (subjective) and intransitive (objective).
⑤ There is a hermeneutic as well as an empirical side to critical realism.

① Critical realism is critical of the status quo

"Transcendental realism" signifies an ontology transcending the empirical level; in this sense relating to a critique of "flat" empiricism. In being critical of the merging of structure and agency, Bhaskar transcends such through his transformational model of social action, culminating in his "meta-reality". Any universalist claims to truth need to be set, in addition to their objectively "intransitive" reality, in the context of a subjectively "transitive" character of science

② You become involved with a stratified or layered reality

The most fundamental enterprise in science is to find the inherent mechanisms that generate events; it is these inherent properties the critical realists call "causal powers". Critical Realists distinguish three domains: the basic one is the domain of the "real" – here we find the generative mechanisms, existing irrespective of whether they produce an event or not. When mechanisms produce a factual event it comes under the domain of the actual, whether we observe it or not; when an event is experienced, it becomes an empirical fact. Insofar as reality is stratified, what is important is that new mechanisms are created in their respective strata, through emergent powers.

③ You view such a layered perspective on reality as fallible

All knowledge is socially produced, but not all is equally valuable; critical realism presents a "third way' between empiricism/objectivism and relativism/idealism. Agreeing with the critique of neutral empirical observations: all knowledge is conceptually mediated and concept-dependent. There is, first, a real world independent of our knowledge of it, and second, it is possible to gain knowledge about this world; however, knowledge is always fallible.

④ You conceive reality as both transitive (subjective) and intransitive (objective)

An external reality exists, independently of our conceptions of it. The purpose of science is to come as close to this reality as possible. It is such theories of reality (e.g. the laws of gravity) that constitute objective knowledge of it, that is its intransitive object – the transitive dimension is socially determined, subjective and changeable. What makes social science special, compared to natural science, is that social scientists seek knowledge about a socially produced reality, not just a socially defined one.

⑤ There is a hermeneutic as well as an empirical side to critical realism

For critical realism, society is made up of thinking and reflective human beings who are capable of continually changing their perception of social reality. Hence, you as a researcher are supposed to study other people's interpretations of the social world – the object of study is therefore socially defined. It is important to note, that social systems are rather open than closed: we cannot just isolate social events in order to manipulate a situation, with the purpose of studying what happens.

We now turn to a consideration of critical realism in greater depth.

15.3 Critical Realism in Depth

15.3.1 Reality is ultimately layered

For Roy Bhaskar, the nature of reality, of "what exists" and the "essence of things", is intrinsically ontological (underlying the nature of reality) and must necessarily form the foundation for everything. This has been clearly spelt our by his fellow critical realists Berth Danemark and her Scandinavian colleagues in "Explaining Society" (5). A distinction can therefore be made between three ontological domains:

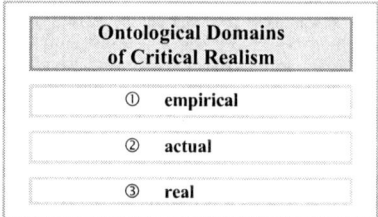

The observation of the "real" domain of stratified reality, the deep dimension of so-called generative mechanisms, is thus what distinguishes critical realism. It is this deep dimension of reality, not immediately observable, the level of the real, that forces us to seek knowledge rather than just accumulate experiences and facts. Since reality is differentiated, structures are stratified, and involve many different and sometimes conflicting practices and interests; there also exist several parallel conceptual frameworks and sometimes-competing interpretations. Knowledge, independently of what it is about, is always a social product. Facts are relative to the conceptions we initially form of the phenomena.

Natural and social science "facts" therefore are theoretically and/or ideologically determined. Critical realists argue however that *the fact that social phenomena are concept-dependent should under no circumstances be seen as if the social world only exists as a mental construction in people's minds.* For the social structures that are reproduced or transformed, when members of society act in accordance with their concepts of reality, are real. They contain powers and mechanisms, which operate independently of the actions here and now.

Natural science, then, explores a basically value-neutral world, where the objects are neither good nor bad; they simply exist. *Social science, on the other hand, investigates an inherently value-charged world of social phenomena, positions, roles, identities and relations.* When social science brings into question and analyses everyday knowledge, it therefore not only risks getting into conflict with alternative experiences and concepts, but also with deeply felt issues and ethical guidelines. Thereby it also challenges vital power and dominance relationships. These relationships are invariably hidden from immediate view. They therefore need to be conceptualised, from a perspective of hidden depth, as they cannot be directly perceived, experientially, from an empirical surface.

15.3.2 Conceptualisation and Abstraction are key

For the critical realists, conceptualisation stands out as the most central social scientific activity. Vital here is the understanding that the critical realists have of the stratification of reality, of emergent powers, and of open and closed systems. *A very common and important route to conceptualisation is through abstraction.* Everyday knowledge tends to oppose abstraction in the same way as theory is opposed to practice. It is associated with vagueness and distance from reality. The concrete, on the other hand, is what "exists". It is tangible, real and observable. Thus *abstract knowledge is considered, by empiricists, to be "out of touch with reality". Critical realists take the opposite view.*

Abstractions, hence, freeze the moment. If we wish *to understand the dynamic dimensions of reality the abstract and structural analyses need to be supplemented by causal analysis*, which deals with explaining why what happens, happens. Understanding such causal relations is central to science, connected to the fact that it is a practical activity we make use of to orient ourselves to life. If we know what underlies a certain course of events we can also intervene and direct future events. *The predominant methods of empiricist social science, the study of empirical regularities or co-variation between standardised variables, cannot answer questions regarding causes.* This is critical realism's fundamental, structure changing departure from positivism, while retaining its practical orientation. To ask what has caused something, for Bhaskar, is to ask what makes it happen, what produces, generates, creates or determines it, enables or leads to it.

From a realist perspective, it is not a matter of a relation between events, separated and demarcated from each other. It is a matter of what causal powers or liabilities there are in a certain object or relation. Thus water has the causal power to quench fire; living creatures have the power to reproduce; human beings also have "work power" and "love power". It is important to observe, moreover, that "powers and liabilities" also include such properties as "weakness" and "vulnerability". Water has the intrinsic liability to evaporate, living creatures have the similar liability to die, human beings to be dependent on others. It is critical therefore to recognize that powers and liabilities exist whether exercised or not. Water can quench fire irrespective of whether anyone uses it thus. People can work even when they are unemployed, and love whether or not they enter a love relation. The Mainland Chinese generally have such a subservient attitude to authority, whether or not it is immediately applied. On the other hand, the existence of causal powers is not an assumption about fixed, unchangeable, eternal essences. Things can and do change. China today is not what it was yesterday.

15.3.3 A Theoretical Continuum from "Meta" to "Descriptive" exists

Such causal powers are underpinned by three different kinds, or indeed levels, of theory: meta-theory, normative theory and descriptive theory. It is these levels of theory, which distinguishes critical realism from critical rationalism, where such stratification is absent.

① *Meta-theory is theory about the foundational assumptions and preconditions of natural or social science* – critical theory, critical realism, feminism and postmodernism as well as phenomenology, hermeneutics, critical rationalism and empiricism – are all examples of such, each building upon alternative ontologies and epistemologies. They indeed provide the underlying foundations, or indeed research *character*, for the activity outlined here.

② *Normative theory refers to the theoretical language and argument*, which examines as well as supports various ideas of how something might be, and is thereby incorporated into much of your mainstream literature search. It can be a theory focusing on moral, political, ideological or managerial issues.

③ *By descriptive theories one means those able to describe and characterize more fundamental properties, structures, internal relations and mechanisms.* Classical economic theory, for example, with its accompanying properties of demand and supply, price equilibrium, and marginal utility, is an illustration of such a "descriptive" theory. Theories demarcated for specific objects of research, like unemployment, drug abuse, consumer debt, and managerial attitudes and behaviors are applicable here.

15.3.4 Pragmatic Realism – the active role of the Human Agent

Realists, and particularly critical realists, for Johnson and Duberley (6), are united by a *rejection of the view, held for example by the postmodernists, that the world is created by the minds of human observers. However, critical realists specifically reject a merely "empirical realism", where the facts of a cognitively accessible reality supposedly speak for themselves.* A central issue in critical realism is the active role of the human agent, particularly with reference to his or her interaction with an independent external reality, which can constrain or facilitate human action. *So while – for the critical realists – so-called "transitive" personalised explanations of events, change according to socio-cultural variations in human understanding, intransitive depersonalised, causal mechanisms located in external reality do not change, unless they are themselves dependent on human agency and intent.*

Thus *science is seen as the result of both social action and also nature's dynamics. Science is therefore construed as a social activity where people intervene and manipulate an "intransitive" reality. As such they confront and change things on the basis of socially constructed "transitive" theory, through practice.* The underlying theoretical schema is principally assessed through evaluating the effectiveness of an intervention in achieving particular ends. *So for critical realism, rather than rejecting experience and observation, in order to delve deeper and beyond the conceptual limitations they impose, any analysis should include both such surface features as well as unobservable structures and subjectively experienced social phenomena.* Whereas management research is currently dominated by a particular form of positivist epistemology, which encourages an exclusive focus upon deductive and often quantitative methodologies, the pragmatic-critical realist position is more qualitatively variegated.

For critical realists, the context-dependence of (in our case) business and management knowledge, necessitates the investigation of the socio-historical development of such social scientific recipes. This needs to involve a focus upon how they enable the interest-laden, but fallible, interaction of humans with their external worlds. Therefore *such knowledge must be conceptualised as a changeable cultural resource that influences, constrains, and legitimises particular social and organisational arrangements, relationships and practices.*

15.3.5 Language, Concepts and Reality

The predominant understanding of the concept of "science" for Roy Bhaskar in conclusion, has, for a long time, been the notion of an activity steadily accumulating general and objective knowledge of its object, by means of systematic and neutral empirical observations. This conventional scientific paradigm, which in its pure form may be called an empiricist/objectivist ideal, is still very influential all around the world as the "traditional movement" in practical research activity. It also corresponds rather well with our everyday understanding of "how we can know".

Criticism of this ideal of science, this "naïve objectivism", has called attention in particular to the complex relation between language/concepts and reality. If our different ways of seeing things, mediated by language, irretrievably determine what we see, for postmodernism for example, what then remains of the scientific project? In their more radical forms such relativists imply that we cannot uphold the existence of any reality. Critical realism, on the other hand, bears the criticism of "naïve objectivism" (empirically based) in mind, while trying to maintain the positive claims to a useful and liberating knowledge, which was the basic motivation for the Enlightenment project. Realism then holds to the view that reality does exist, independently of our knowledge of it.

We now turn to the more "global" reach of critical realism, in fact now heralding its "eastern" turn towards "meta-reality".

15.4 Global Variations of Critical Realism

15.4.1 Adult Anglo to Midlife Indian

Interestingly enough, the birth and growth of critical realism took place during the 1970's and 1980's, when Roy Bhaskar was in his twenties and thirties, during and after his doctoral studies at Oxford, in England. It was as he approached his midlife, and was undergoing such a midlife crisis and resolution, in the 1990's and into the new millennium, that his original philosophy, critical realism, underwent a "west-east" metamorphosis. It newly evolved into his "Meta-Reality". In the same way as commentators refer to the early and late philosophical orientations of the great Austrian philosopher Ludwig Wittgenstein, the same can be said about the adulthood and midlife of Roy Bhaskar.

In his early adult writings on critical realism, Bhaskar remained closely wedded to western pragmatism, though of course arguing against pure positivism and empiricism. While then, even at this initial stage of his philosophical analysis, he opposed a "naïve objectivity", preoccupied with surface analysis, he retained a practical and rational orientation, and one causally oriented towards "generative mechanisms" underlying events and experiences. In other words, while his underlying philosophy was critical of the purely empirically based "western" mainstream, the overall rational-pragmatic language remained true to his Anglo-Saxon and indeed European heritage. Moreover his doctoral supervisor at Oxford, Rom Harre, though New Zealand born and bred, was of "northern" French Huguenot origins.

Bhaskar's two seminal works in the 1970's, at this "adult" stage of his philosophical and psychological development, were a "Realist Theory of Science" (7) aimed at the natural sciences, and "The Possibility of Naturalism" (8) focused on the social sciences. The break then came, explicitly and publically at least, in the early nineties, when he published his "Dialectic – The Pulse of Freedom". (9) At that point he turned from West to East (though still in a European context) serving to link western European "realism" with central and eastern European "idealism". Here he was duly influenced by Germany's Hegel, alongside of the Anglo-French Rom Harre. In the final analysis, though, Bhaskar retained his overwhelmingly realist orientation.

15.4.2 Dialectical Emergence

The first explicitly eastern turn (albeit to begin with in European guise) was towards Hegel. The German 19th century philosopher saw splits, dichotomies, disharmonies and fragmentations as calling for restoration or unity in diversity, in his absolute idealism. Negation, as such, always calls for a new and richer determination. The mutual exclusion of opposites passes over into their reciprocal interdependence. For Hegel then the truth is a whole, and the whole is a process. Error lies in one-sidedness. Its symptom is the contradictions it generates and its remedy involves their incorporation into richer, more inclusive conceptual forms. Either the implicit is made explicit (telemony), or some want or inadequacy is repaired (teleology), both of which correspond with Bhaskar's notion of "negation". This is also picked by Nonaka and Takeuchi, in terms of their knowledge "externalisation". (10)

"Dialectical" then, in contrast with the analytical and reflective, grasps concepts and forms in their systemic interconnections, not just their determinate differences. It considers each development as a product of a previous less developed phase, whose necessary truth or fulfilment it is. So there is always a tension between a latent form and what it is becoming. For Bhaskar this is the power of *emergence,* upon which we have also "genetically" drawn. In short, Hegelian dialectic is the actualised entelechy of the present, comprehended as everything that has led up to it. It involves a transformation of the consciousness of the dialectical observer as well as the expansion of the existing conceptual field.

15.4.3 Meta-Reality to Transformative Agency

The possibility of human emancipation, for the now "easterly" facing Bhaskar depends not on "western" democratic freedoms and free markets, but on expanding the zone of "non-duality" within our lives. That is the level of what Bhaskar calls a being's *"ground-state"*, which is its most essential level. It is the level upon which all other levels depend, which has much in common with a phenomenological "essence". It also serves to depend his prior notion of an underlying, generative reality. Altogether, in this newly "meta-real" case, every human situation, as such, must now be characterised by MELDA:

① **(M)**, an element of potential, which corresponds to the critical realist domain of stratified ontology, grounded in Meta-reality

② **(E)** creativity, that is the Emergence of something new, even if this novelty is a repeat of the old, which would not otherwise have occurred

③ any human situation must be characterised by that form of bonding, solidarity, compassion, care and consideration that Bhaskar calls, altogether, *Love* **(L)**,

④ each agent in the situation needs to be capable of Doing **(D)** something, spontaneously and correctly so that in each situation, creating an effect

⑤ the agent's intentionality will be in some manner fulfilled **(A)**: aah (I see!)

Bhaskar in his midlife then produced such books as "Meta-Reality: Creativity, Love and Freedom" (11), "Reflections on Meta-Reality" (12) as well as "From East to West – Odyssey of a Soul" (13) taking forward this MELDA theme. In this last book, Bhaskar reviews several great world belief systems – including Ancient Greek, Judaic, Essene and Christian, Hindi (Vedic), Buddhist, Confucian, Taoist, Zen, Islam (Sufi) and modern materialist thought. He uses such a retrospective to cast light on the contemporary crises in Western social and philosophical thought. These themselves reflect wider and deeper crises in society, which he relates to a dialectical chain of "avidya" (ignorance), "dualism" (split) and "maya" (illusion) itself grounded in ontological (existential) "insecurity".

While on the one hand, Bhaskar's fellow critical realists (as Anglo-Saxon pragmatists) may consider that their founding father has become ever more "esoteric" of late, for us, overall, the reverse is the case. For, in turning "east", Bhaskar has become more practically transformative, and indeed globally integral, in his orientation. Indeed our own GENE effectively evolved out of Bhaskar's Meta-Reality.

We now turn to our critical reality "case", that of the Canadian peace activist and environmentalist, Thomas Homer Dixon, whose work involved penetrating to the generative depths – so called tectonic stresses – of the issues we face today, and positing theories underlying creativity, catastrophe and renewal.

15.5 Critical Realism in Practice: The Upside of Down

15.5.1 Tectonic Stresses

Stresses and Multipliers

The twenty-first century will be, for Homer Dixon at the Trudeau Center for Peace and Conflict Studies in Toronto, the *age of nature*. (14) We will learn, probably the hard way, that nature matters: we are not separate from it, we are dependent on it, and when there is trouble in nature there is trouble in society.

According to Homer Dixon, the following "tectonic stresses" are accumulating deep underneath the surface of our societies:

- *population stress:* arising out of the differences in growth rates between rich and poor societies, and the spiralling growth of mega-cities in poor countries
- *energy stress:* above all from oil scarcity
- *environmental stress:* from increasing damage to land, water, forests, fisheries
- *climate stress:* from changes in the makeup of our atmosphere
- *economic stress:* from global financial instabilities and growing income gaps, which is our point of focus here, in relation to economic opportunity.

In addition to these five *stresses* are two *multipliers,* which combine with the stresses to make breakdown more likely, widespread and severe. The first is increasing speed and connectivity of activities, technologies and societies. The second is the escalating power of small groups to destroy things and people.

From Management to Catagenesis

Today most experts who take our global problems seriously advocate what Homer Dixon terms a "management" response. While this may be better than denying our problems, it often does not help very much. For any management policies that really address the underlying causes of our hardest problems usually require big changes in the existing political and economic order. After all, that very order is the reason why our problems are so bad. Surprisingly too, there is no term in English for the commonplace occurrence of renewal through breakdown. So Homer Dixon calls it *catagenesis,* from the Greek for "down", that is *cata,* and that for "birth", which is *genesis.* Whether the breakdown in question is psychological, technological, economic, political or ecological – or some combination of these – catagenesis involves the reinvention of our future.

Complex systems adapt to their changing environment by going through a four-stage cycle of growth, breakdown, reorganisation and renewal. Specialists have a term to describe complex systems; they call them *path dependent.* Here the system depends at any time on the tortuous, circuitous route by which it got there.

15.5.2 The Income Gap and the Growth Imperative

What is the way out of constant growth?

For Homer Dixon, never in history have the differences between us, of income and opportunity, been so great. Whereas in 1870 the average income of the world's richest country was about nine times that of the poorest, by 1990 it was forty-five times greater. Meanwhile, within a particular even developed country, if material desires are not satiable, and if significant numbers of workers cannot move smoothly to more high-skill jobs, over time our economy's workforce will tend to polarize between, on the one hand, a shrinking but ever-richer elite of hyper-cognitively-adept workers who own and run the ferociously productive technologies of our economy, but who are unwilling to consume all its products, and on the other, an expanding mass of technologically displaced workers – who cannot generate enough demand to consume the boom.

What is the way out: constant economic growth? Growth creates the new industries and generates the new jobs needed to absorb technologically displaced workers. The American economy, for example, must expand 3 to 5% annually – doubling its size every 15 to 25 years – just to keep unemployment from rising. And to get this growth – operating on the assumption that people can be inculcated with insatiable desires and ever rising expectations – encourage us to become relentless consumers. In essence, the logic of our economic behavior works like this: if we are discontented with what we have, we buy stuff; if we buy enough stuff, the economy grows; if the economy grows enough, technologically displaced workers can find new jobs; and if they find new jobs there will be enough economic demand to keep the economy humming and to prevent wrenching political conflict. Modern capitalism's stability – and increasingly the global economy's stability – requires the cultivation of material discontent, endlessly rising personal consumption, and the steady economic growth this consumption generates. Without this economic growth, rich and poor people would soon confront each other in a fierce zero-sum conflict, and over time the widening gap between rich and poor would tear our societies apart.

Our economic role in this culture of consumerism, for Homer Dixon, is to be little more than walking appetites that serve the function of maintaining our economy's throughput. Our psychological state is analogous to that of drug addicts needing a fix: buying things does not really make us happy, except perhaps for a moment after the purchase. But we do it over and over anyway. Why? There are many reasons. Consumerism helps anaesthetize us against the dread produced by many empty lives. New technologies create constant economic upheaval, which means that an average person in the American economy, for instance, has to change jobs every four years or so. The chronic economic security cranks up stress in our lives, while the churning of our economy atomises society as a whole. Both of these trends shred the social fabric of trust, caring and reciprocity that is essential to our happiness. So in place of vital connections between people that come with strong communities, families and friendships, we substitute the transitory pleasures provided by newly bought things.

The flip side of such economic growth, meanwhile, include rich society's epidemic of eating disorders, like obesity and anorexia. Indeed, the number of overweight people in the world (about 1.2 billion) now matches those that are undernourished. Then there is the related and more general problem of depression, that has become three to ten times – depending on how it is measured – more common in the last fifty years. Explanation for all of such include the erosion of community and family, an economic culture that promotes chronic insecurity and extreme individualism.

Winners and Losers Made Manifest

Today's global capitalism – which has linked the world together and subordinated people everywhere to its relentless energy as never before – is producing a stew of changes and stresses that is almost a perfect recipe for widespread and even violent resentment of the world's rich by the world's poor. Because capitalism cultivates material discontent, because we naturally compare ourselves with each other, and because comparisons are now so easy, through the Web and television, widening gulfs of wealth and opportunity cannot but encourage huge numbers of people to be chronically dissatisfied with their lot. We now live with an inescapable juxtaposition of winners and losers. Everyone knows who is ahead and who is behind.

At the same time, many people in poor societies feel that Western markets and cultures are submerging their local cultures and institutions. Combined, for Homer Dixon, these are astonishingly dangerous trends. If our global society is to be resilient and adaptable – and if it is to be peaceful – it must give its citizens roughly equal opportunities to advance their economic and political interests, and it must give them ways of expressing their diversity within a shared human identity. But instead it is giving people ever more unequal opportunity and ever-starker differences in their daily lives. Compare, for example, the day-to-day experiences of a bond trader in the City of London with those of a slum dweller in Sao Paulo or Karachi. These people have little in common on which to build a shared identity. At the same time capitalism is promoting a relentlessly homogenized, mass culture of consumerism. The question ultimately is, how much more unequal world income distribution can become before the resulting political instabilities and flows of migrants reach the point of directly harming the well-being of the citizens of the rich world and the stability of their states. To survive, let alone prosper, in our new and more dangerous world, however, we need to open our minds to change.

15.5.3 Introducing Panarchy

Ecological Economics

A noted proponent of such change, or indeed transformation, is the ecologist Crawford Holling. For him, during the early phase of growth, the forest ecosystem is steadily accumulating capital. As its total mass grows, so does its quantity of nutrients, along with the amount of information in the genes of its increasingly varied plants and animals. Over time, as the forest matures and passes into the late phase of growth, the mechanisms of self-regulation become highly diverse and finely tuned.

Species and organisms are progressively more specialized and efficient in using energy and nutrients available in their niche. Indeed the whole forest becomes extremely efficient – in a sense it effectively adapts to maximize the production of biomass from the flows of sunlight, water, and nutrients it gets from its environment. This phase cannot go on indefinitely. Its ever-greater connectedness and efficiency reduces its capacity to deal with severe external shocks. Eventually the ecosystem loses resilience, and its high degree of efficiency makes it harder to realise its potential for novelty. Overall it becomes "an accident waiting to happen". Actually, the collapse of the whole ecosystem liberates its potential for creativity and allows for novel and unpredictable recombination of elements. It is as if somebody threw the energy flows and genetic information, the plants and nutrients, into a gigantic mixing bowl and stirred. Once marginal species can now capture and exploit newly released nutrients, and genetic mutations, which were a bane, can now be a boon.

In these ways the forest ecosystem reorganises and regenerates itself, quite possibly in a very new form. Put simply, the catastrophe of collapse allows for the birth of something new. And this cycle of growth, collapse, reorganisation and rebirth allows for the forest to adapt over the long term to a constantly changing environment. The adaptive cycle embraces growth and stability, on the one hand, change and variety on the other. It is at once conserving and creating, a characteristic of adaptive systems. Moreover, no one adaptive cycle exists in isolation: it is usually sandwiched between lower and higher ones. Panarchy theory, then, helps us understand how complex systems of all kinds evolve and adapt. Its core idea – that systems naturally grow, become more brittle, collapse and then renew themselves – repeatedly recurs in literature, history, philosophy, religion, as well as in the natural and social sciences. We are currently in a period of great volatility in the world system. Some kind of systemic breakdown, for Homer Dixon, is inevitable, and we ought to do what we can to avoid deep collapse, and to rather exploit the opportunity.

15.5.4 Beyond Catagenesis

Breakdown tends to be disruptive to parts of the system, but it need not be, for it can produce exactly the conditions required for a burst of creativity, reorganisation and renewal. A long view of human history reveals not regular change but spasmodic, catastrophic disruptions followed by long periods of reinvention and development. Breakdown is something that human social systems must go through to adapt successfully to changing conditions. In our communities, towns, and cities, we can use small-scale experiments to see what kinds of technologies, organisations and procedures work best under different breakdown scenarios. Scientists moreover have found that complex systems that are highly adaptive – like markets and even the immune system of mammals – tend to share certain characteristics. First of all, the individual elements that make up the systems are extraordinarily diverse. Second, the power to make decisions is not centralized in one place. Thirdly and finally, highly adaptive systems are unstable enough to create unexpected innovations but orderly enough to learn from their successes and failures. We are all familiar with just such systems – the Internet, and the Worldwide Web. So far we have only tapped the surface of the potential for such adaptive systems.

We now are ready to conclude this chapter on critical realism.

15.6 Conclusion

Critical realism is the fourth one of our critical emancipatory orientations to research (layer 3). While on the one hand, it follows in the pragmatic footsteps of experimental and survey methods and empiricism, ultimately leading to integral action research, on the other hand, like the three others, it is both critical and emancipatory.

Along the research path of realisation, critical realism has a pragmatic orientation, geared towards an ultimately transformative effect, as well as being grounded in an objective, as well as subjective reality. However, it is more broadly based then experimental method and empirical methodology, in that it deals with an overtly stratified reality, and it values abstraction. In other words, and like the other critical emancipatory approaches, it is more "worldly" than its predecessors.

Secondly, in comparing and contrasting critical realism with the other three emancipatory orientations, we find that the realistic emphasis on stratification compares and contrasts with that of postmodernism (*reason*), critical theory (*renewal)* and feminism (*relational).*

As we evolve via this western path of research towards social innovation, we now turn from critical realism to action research.

Bibliography

1) **Bhaskar**, R. (1977). *The Realist Theory of Science*. London: Verso Press.

2) **Harre**, R. (1970). *The Method of Science*. New York: Crane Russak & Co..

3) **Bunge**, M. (1973). M*ethodological Unity of Science*. Dordrecht-Boston: Kluwer Academic Publishers.

4) **Bhaskar**, R. (2000). *Meta-Reality*. London: Sage.

5) **Danemark**, B. et al. (2002). *Explaining Society*. London: Routledge.

6) **Johnson**, P. & **Duberley**, J. (2000). *Understanding Management Research*. London: Sage.

7) **Bhaskar**, R. (1977). *The Realist Theory of Science*. London: Verso Press.

8) **Bhaskar**, R. (1979). *The Possibility of Naturalism*. New York: Harvester.

9) **Bhaskar**, R. (1993). *Dialectic – The Pulse of Freedom*. London: Verso Press.

10) **Nonaka**, I. & **Takeuchi**, H. (1995). *The Knowledge Creating Company*. Oxford: Oxford University Press.

11) **Bhaskar**, R. (2000). *Meta-Reality: Creativity, Love and Freedom*. London: Sage.

12) **Bhaskar**, R. (2002). *Reflections on Meta-Reality*. London: Sage.

13) **Bhaskar**, R. (2000). *From East to West – Odyssey of a Soul*. London: Sage.

14) **Homer Dixon**, T. (2007). *The Upside of Down: Catastrophe, Creativity and Renewal*. Toronto: Vintage Canada.

CHAPTER 16

FROM CRITICAL REALISM TO
ACTION RESEARCH

"BECOME A SCIENTIST IN ACTION"

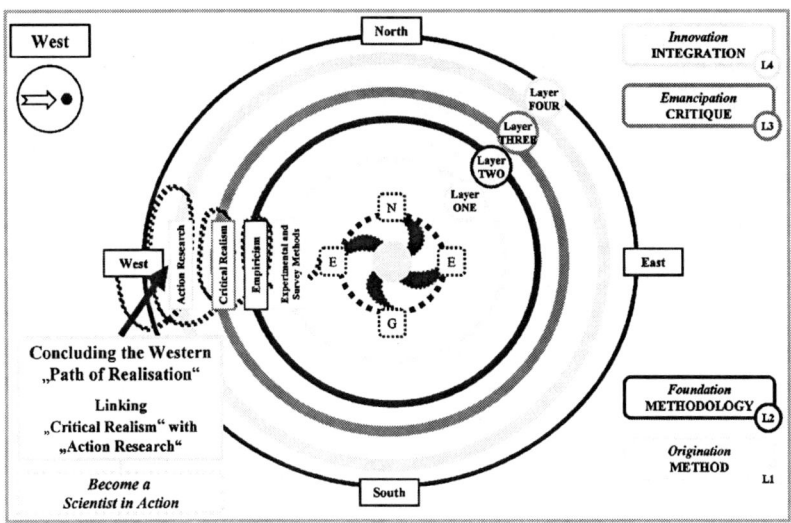

Figure 16.1: Overview Chapter 16 – Layer 4 / West

Summary: Action Research

- Finally we are concluding the western research path of realisation, by entering into its fourth and integral layer: action research.

- Action research was originally developed by Kurt Lewin, in the middle of the twentieth century in the United States, and has been taken forward, in the twenty first century, by Peter Reason in the UK.

- Action research is a form of collective self-reflective enquiry undertaken by participants in social situations in order to improve the rationality and justice of their own social or educational practices, as well as their understanding of those practices and the situations in which the practices are carried out.

- Action research refers to the conjunction of three elements: action, research and participation. AR aims to increase the ability of the involved community or organisation members to control their own destinies more effectively and to keep improving their capacity to do so within a more sustainable and just environment.

- Action research in depth involves a consideration of the management of change, alongside of learning from experience, individually and organisaitonally.

- In its global variations, the participatory dimension in action research takes pride of place, building up its political alongside its individual and organisational reach.

- An effective business case story in point is that of Cashbuild of South Africa, and its social innovator Albert Koopman who, through an ongoing process of action and reflection, theory and practice, progressively turned the company into an industrial democracy.

16.1 Orientation to Action Research

16.1.1 Societal to Individual Orientation

We begin in this culminating chapter on action research by retracing our steps. In the same way as action research, in terms of your research path of realisation, builds upon experimental and survey methods, empirical methodology, and a critical realist approach to emancipation, it is (via layer 4) interconnected with participatory action research (in the south), co-operative inquiry (east) and socio-technical design (north). In the latter respect, it is individually, as opposed to communally (PAR), transpersonally (CI) and organisationally (socio-technical design) oriented.

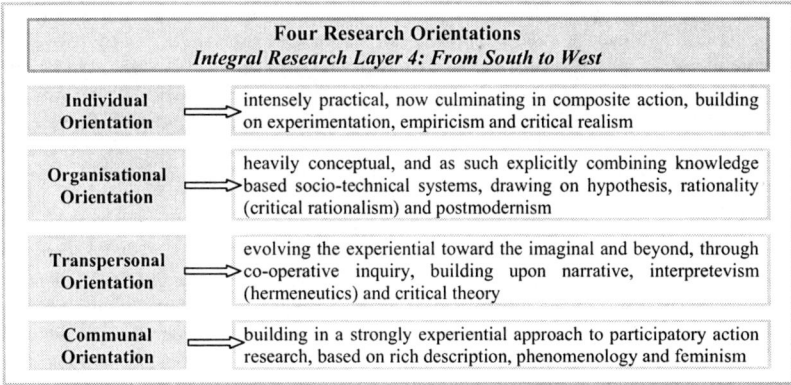

Four Research Orientations *Integral Research Layer 4: From South to West*	
Individual Orientation	intensely practical, now culminating in composite action, building on experimentation, empiricism and critical realism
Organisational Orientation	heavily conceptual, and as such explicitly combining knowledge based socio-technical systems, drawing on hypothesis, rationality (critical rationalism) and postmodernism
Transpersonal Orientation	evolving the experiential toward the imaginal and beyond, through co-operative inquiry, building upon narrative, interpretevism (hermeneutics) and critical theory
Communal Orientation	building in a strongly experiential approach to participatory action research, based on rich description, phenomenology and feminism

16.1.2 Origins of Action Research

Kurt Lewin and the Origins of Action Research

The origins of action research, as we indicated in chapter 7, can be traced back to Kurt Lewin and to John Dewey. In a specifically "action research" context, Lewin's approach can be articulated in terms of a series of steps, each of which is composed of a circle of planning, action and fact-finding about the result of the action.

The first step then is to examine the idea carefully in the light of the means available. Frequently more fact-finding about the situation is required. If this first period of planning is successful, two items emerge: namely, "an overall plan" of how to reach the objective and secondly, a decision in regard to the first step of action. Usually this planning has also somewhat modified the original idea. The next step is composed of a circle of planning, executing, and reconnaissance or fact-finding for the purpose of evaluating the results of the second step, and preparing the rational basis for planning the third step, and for perhaps modifying again the overall plan. What we can see here is an approach to research that is oriented to problem solving in social and organisational settings, and that has a form that parallels, as we shall see, Dewey's conception of learning from experience. The approach does take a fairly sequential form – and it is open to literal interpretation. Following it can lead to practice that is 'correct' rather than 'good'.

Action research, in the United States at least, did suffer a decline in favour during the 1960's because of its association with radical political activism. However, it has subsequently gained a significant foothold both within the realm of community-based, and participatory action research; and as a form of practice oriented to the improvement of educative encounters. The use of action research to deepen and develop classroom practice has grown into a strong tradition of practice. For some there is an insistence that action research must be collaborative and entail groupwork.

Action research is a form of collective self-reflective enquiry undertaken by participants in social situations in order to improve the rationality and justice of their own social or educational practices, as well as their understanding of those practices and the situations in which the practices are carried out. The approach is only action research when it is collaborative, though it is important to realise that action research of the group is achieved through the critically examined action of individual group members. Finally, when set in historical context, while Lewin does talk about action research as a method; he is stressing a contrast between this form of interpretative practice and more traditional empirical-analytic research. The notion of a spiral may be a useful teaching device – but it is all too easily to slip into using it as *the* template for practice.

John Dewey and the Origins of Action Research

John Dewey, to whom we were first introduced in chapter 7, moved to the University of Chicago at the turn of the 19th century to head the department of philosophy, psychology, and pedagogy. It was at this time that Dewey began to consider the philosophy of education in a serious and systematic way. In 1896, he founded the University Laboratory School now better known as the "Dewey School". The Laboratory School was not a model institution; rather, it truly lived up to its name. It was a place for educational experiments in the genuine etymological sense of experiment, that is, to make a trial of something. Theories and practices were developed, tested, criticized, refined, and tried again. Experimentalism became increasingly important as Dewey's philosophy matured. For him, not only were these experiments falsifiable, but in a contingent evolving world, their generalizability was always subject to revision. There is no end of inquiry for Dewey; nonetheless, he believed it the best way to render human experience intelligent.

The Laboratory School was not the only site for educational research in Chicago at that time. Jane Addams and her work at Hull House, for which she eventually received the Nobel Prize, greatly influenced Dewey. Rosalind Rosenberg writes, that for Dewey, Hull House was a laboratory and an example of what he was trying to accomplish in education. Dewey visited Hull House even before moving to Chicago. Upon his arrival there, Dewey actively participated in the life of Hull House. There he met some of the most influential early feminists whose involvement in the political issues of the day caused by massive immigration, the social and economic effects of urbanization, and rapid technological advance exercised considerable influence. He also mixed with workers, trade unionists, and political radicals. Some of his most influential educational works emerged out of these laboratories. These works not only set out Dewey's practical pedagogy, but they also outlined the psychological and philosophical principles upon which it relied. These principles devolved from the trial and error experiments that occurred within and without the walls of the Laboratory School.

16.1.3 From Experimental and Survey Methods to Action Research

As we journey along the research path of realisation, from experimental method to empirical methodology onto critical realism and ultimately action research, so we forge such a path to "western" pragmatically based social innovation, in a way with which John Dewey would have felt very much at home.

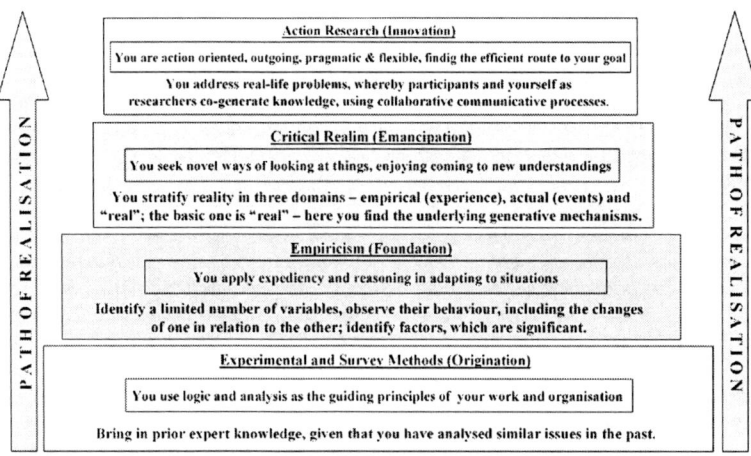

Figure 16.2: Towards Action Research

We now turn to the key tenets of action research.

16.2 Action Research – Key Tenets

Action Research – Key Tenets
① You start out with appreciative inquiry.
② You challenge power relations.
③ You diverge and you converge.
④ You undertake social research for social change.
⑤ Knowing *how* is more important than knowing *that*.
⑥ Action research incorporates action learning.

① You start out with appreciative inquiry

Appreciation rather than Critique

The notable Peter Reason at the University of Bath in England and his colleague Hilary Bradbury based in the United States have played a leading part in articulating (1) the wider reaches of action research. In so doing, for example, they cite David Cooperider's "Appreciative Inquiry", a noted communally based research method in its own right, as for them representative of a participative approach to action research.

In their original formulation of appreciative inquiry Cooperider and Srivastva, twenty years ago, argued that action research, if not also participative action research, had largely failed as instruments for advancing socio-organisational transformation, because of action research's preference for critique as opposed to appreciation. For if we devote our attention to what is wrong with organisations and communities, we lose, according to Cooperider, the ability to sustain and enhance their life-giving potential:

"More than a method or technique, the appreciative mode of inquiry ... engenders a reverence for life that draws the researcher to inquire beyond superficial appearances to deeper levels of the life-generating essentials and potentials of social existence. That is, the action researcher is drawn to affirm, and thereby illuminate, the factors and forces that serve to illuminate the human spirit." (2)

Appreciative inquiry then, as a constructive mode of such action research, can unleash conversation and change in organisations by unseating existing patterns, creating spaces for new voices and new discoveries, and expanding circles of dialogue to provide a community of support for innovative action, premised on the notion that organisations are open books, continuously in the process of being co-authored. Past, present and future are continuously in the process of being co-created. In fact, citing social constructionist Kenneth Gergen, critique is considered, by Cooperider and by Gergen, as detrimental:

Appreciative Inquiry:
Why critique is considered to be counterproductive in transformation processes

- Critique contains conversation: by curtailing the exploration of new knowledge.
- It silences marginal voices: producing a binary argument (either/or).
- It erodes community: those under attack close ranks.
- Critique creates social hierarchy: via vocabularies of deficit; not living up to an ideal.
- It enfeebles: the language of deficit becomes part of the prevailing vocabulary.

Appreciative inquiry distinguishes itself from critical modes of research by its deliberately affirmative assumptions about people, organisations and relationships. It therefore focuses on the *unconditional positive question* to ignite transformative dialogue and action within human systems.

Phases of Appreciative Inquiry

Appreciative Inquiry is undertaken in distinctive phases. The purpose of the *discovery* phase, firstly, is to search for, highlight and illuminate those factors that give life to the organisation, the "best of what is" in any given situation, dislodging the certainty of existing deficit constructions. The second phase is to *dream* about what could be. As alternative voices enter the conversation, new ways of seeing and under-standing the world begin to emerge. The third phase is to *design* the future through dialogue, a process of finding common ground by sharing discoveries and possibilities.

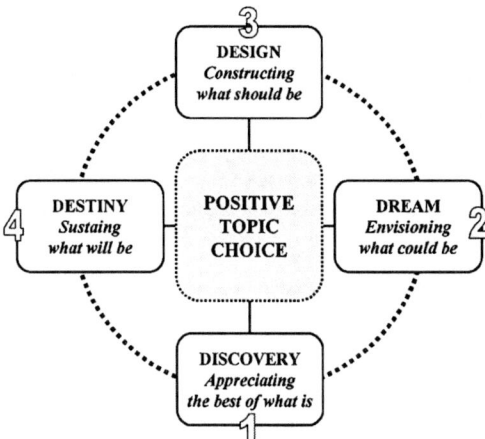

Figure 16.3: Appreciative Inquiry

The key to this phase is to create a deliberately inclusive and supportive context for conversation and interaction. The final phase, *destiny,* is an invitation to construct the future through innovation and action, including ever-broader circles of participants.

Despite its concern for the community and its overall appreciation of such, appreciative inquiry is still oriented towards the individual, or perhaps a group, undertaking it. PAR, as we have already seen, is different.

② You challenge power relations

Action research, from the outset and symbolized by Kurt Lewin's status as a refuge from Nazi Germany, has always had a political dimension to it. Overlapping with both feminism and critical theory, action and participatory research are closely interconnected. For feminist action researcher Patricia Maguire, contesting the voice of authority has always been a keynote of her work. Drawing from renowned Brazilian educator Paulo Freire's work to pierce the culture of silence among marginalized groups, North American sociologist Budd Hall, to whom we referred in chapter 7, maintains that participatory action research is fundamentally about the right to speak, arguing for the articulation of points of view by the dominated or subordinated. Similar to Freire, Israeli feminist sociologist Reinharz observes that, by dealing in voices we are affecting power relations. To listen to people is to empower them. Before you can expect to hear anything worth hearing, you have to examine the power dynamics of the space and the social actors. For practitioner-researcher Susan Noffke:

"... we must see ourselves as part of the process of breaking apart the barriers for speakers and listeners, writers and readers, which are perpetuated through, and act to support our privileged positions. " (3)

③ You diverge and you converge

While on the one hand, action research is building upon appreciative inquiry while challenging power relations, on the other hand, action research has intrapersonal as well as interpersonal connotations.

John Heron compares and contrasts (5) a form of "Apollonian Inquiry", which takes a rational, linear, systematic, controlling and explicit approach to cycling between reflection and action, with a "Dionysian inquiry" that takes a more imaginative, spiraling, diffuse, impromptu and tacit approach. Any effective process of action research requires both.

Specific skills are needed in the kind of action research, which overlaps with co-operative inquiry. They involve:

- *Being present and open: empathy, resonance and attunement*
- *Bracketing and reframing: holding in abeyance the constructs we impose*
- *Radical practice: being aware of one's own underlying values and motives*
- *Non-attachment: not investing one's own identity and security in an action*
- *Emotional competence: ability to identify and manage emotional states*

To ensure the overall validity of the inquiry process, there should be:

- *Research cycling: between action and reflection*
- *Divergence and convergence: looking several times at the same issue in ever more detail; looking at different issues in ever more variety*
- *Reflection and action: balancing between the two*
- *Chaos and order: interdependence of chaos and order*

④ You undertake social research for social change

Davydd Greenwood, as we saw earlier, is an anthropologist, like Daniel Selener based at Cornell University in America, and Morten Levin is a sociologist with a background in engineering, based at the Norwegian University of Science and Technology. (6) For them, *action research is a set of self-consciously collaborative and democratic strategies for generating knowledge and designing action in which trained experts in social and other form of research and local stakeholders work together.* The research focus is chosen collaboratively among the local stakeholders and the action researchers, and relationships amongst the participants are organised as joint learning processes. Action research centers on doing "with" rather than doing "for" stakeholders and credits these with the richness of experience and reflective possibilities that long experience living in complex situations brings with it.

Action, Research and Participation

Action research then is social research carried out by a team that encompasses a professional action researcher and the members of an organisation, community or network, who are seeking to improve the participant's situation. AR promotes broad participation in the research process and supports action leading to a more just, sustainable, or satisfying situation for the stakeholders. Because it is a research practice with a social change agenda, AR involves a critique of conventional academic practices and organisations that assert either the necessity or desirability of studying social problems without trying to resolve them.

Action research refers to the conjunction of three elements: action, research and participation. AR aims to increase the ability of the involved community or organisation members to control their own destinies more effectively and to keep improving their capacity to do so within a more sustainable and just environment. Greenwood and Levin believe that social knowledge can only be derived from practical reasoning engaged in through action. As action researchers, they believe that action is the only sensible way to generate and test new knowledge. The following table shows how action, research and participation interconnect:

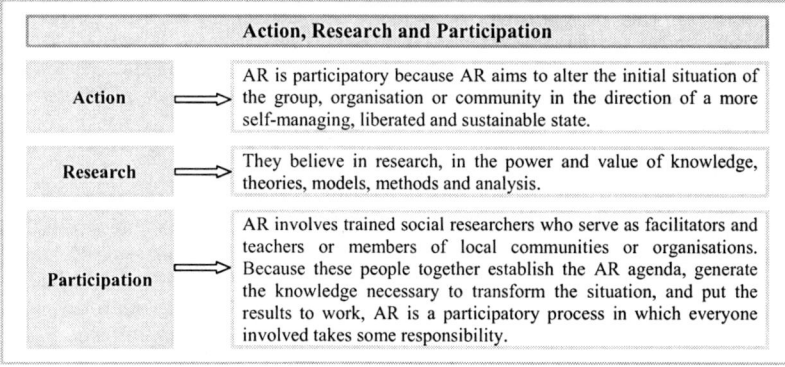

Action, Research and Participation	
Action	AR is participatory because AR aims to alter the initial situation of the group, organisation or community in the direction of a more self-managing, liberated and sustainable state.
Research	They believe in research, in the power and value of knowledge, theories, models, methods and analysis.
Participation	AR involves trained social researchers who serve as facilitators and teachers or members of local communities or organisations. Because these people together establish the AR agenda, generate the knowledge necessary to transform the situation, and put the results to work, AR is a participatory process in which everyone involved takes some responsibility.

We now turn to the most overtly "scientific" element of action research, that is science from a classically analytic perspective.

⑤ Knowing *how* is more important than knowing *that*

Doing Scientific Research

To anchor their discussion, Greenwood and Levin *define scientific research as investigative activity capable of discovering that the world is or is not organised as our preconceptions lead us to expect, and suggesting grounded ways of understanding and acting on it.* Scientific research documents both the investigative processes and conclusions arising from them in sufficient detail for other interested parties to be able to evaluate the information and interpretations offered and examine the consequences of the sequence of actions taken.

Scientific knowledge is not a fixed entity but should be understood as an ongoing discourse among scientists struggling to make sense of the world. Scientific knowledge is in a constant state of transition, searching for the best possible understanding and management of specific phenomena and processes. Doing scientific work is not copying methodological blueprints written up in textbooks, but applying research methods in the complex setting of the social world, an approach that harked back to American pragmatic philosopher and educator, John Dewey.

Pragmatic Philosophy and Research

John Dewey believed that all humans are capable of scientific judgment and that society could be improved to the extent that these capacities are increased among all society's members. Consistent with this, he strongly opposed the division of public education into vocational and academic tracks, seeing this as the preservation of inequality and ultimately the weakening of democracy as a whole. Everyone could be a capable participant in experimental knowledge creation. He believed that limiting the learning of any individual ultimately limited society as a whole.

For Dewey, scientific research was not a process separate from democratic social action. Scientific knowing, like all other forms of knowledge, was a product of continuous cycles of action and reflection. The center of gravity was always the learner's active pursuit of understanding through puzzle-solving activity with the materials at hand. The solution achieved were only the best possible ones at that moment with the material at hand, hence the denomination of his philosophy as pragmatism.

⑥ Action research incorporates action learning

Ironically, for us, the seminal influence on action research, in Britain at least, if not also in Europe, America and the developing world, was someone who is barely recognized in the literature today. Reg Revans, one of Britain's most creative management thinkers, and originator of 'action learning' (7), spent half a century – from the 1940's onward – trying to raise managers' and nations'consciousness of their unique origins and destiny. Revans had long maintained that the salvation of individual countries and their enterprises is not to be found by observers scouring the world in the hope of turning up some miracle there. Their salvation, their *'Kingdom of God', is rather to be found within their own shores, their local source, and within the wills of their own people.* At the level of the individual enterprise, he further argues, it is not unreasonable to suggest that an essential part of any research and development policy is the study of the human effort, out of which the saleable products of the enterprise are largely created. Such a study involved "scientific method" (survey, hypothesis, test, audit and control = the core elements of the action learning cycle).

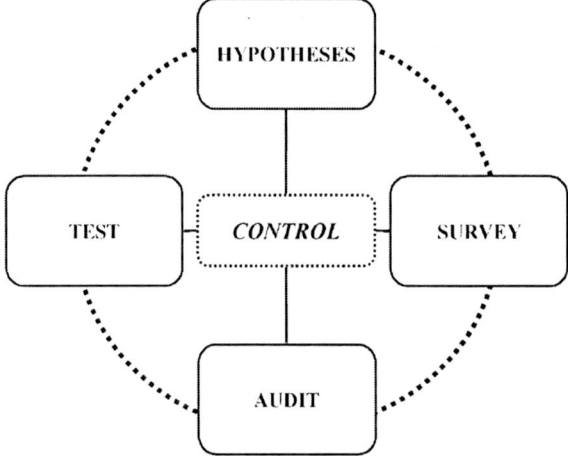

Figure 16.4: Action Learning Cycle

Learning moreover must demand not only research and analysis. It must demand power to get the knowledge needed to see one's part in what is going on. In particular, one needs to know the effect of one' behaviour upon those with whom one works.

For Revans, this is best achieved within small 'action learning' groups. In the Japanese context, he referred particularly to the establishment of small work groups, not only with a high degree of autonomy, but organised in a way that it gave people a continuing opportunity to develop. You learn with and from each other, in small groups or 'learning sets', by supportive attacks upon real and menacing problems, through:

- an exchange of information – ideas, advice, contacts, hunches, concepts
- interaction between set members, offering each other support/challenge
- behavioural change resulting more often from the re-interpretation of past experience than the acquisition of fresh knowledge

If we take a more pragmatic look at group meetings:

- they provide an opportunity for knowledge creators to seek each other's help
- meetings serve as an external source of pressure upon members to move on
- they are a source of progress planning and review
- sessions can lead to the provision of formal inputs
- reflection leads to the gaining of insights
- meetings can provide for mutual encouragement and support, in our case for
- grounding, emerging, navigation and finally effecting transformation.

Finally, if a sponsoring organisation is to engage in action learning seriously, it will need, for Revans, to take a number of key considerations into account. Organisational commitment to learning needs to be developed through engaging with the:

- choice of problems around which to form projects
- roles and responsibilities of agents of transformation as clients
- qualities and selection of participants on the programme
- induction of participants into their projects
- monitoring of projects and transformative groups
- continued role of line management in projects

We now turn from the key tenets of action research to a consideration of action research in depth, focusing on three key issues therein: the dimension of praxis, the dimension of science, and the participatory dimension.

16.3 Action Research in Depth

16.3.1 The Dimension of Praxis

AR focuses on specific contexts, demands that theory and practice are not separated, and is committed to the idea that the test of any theory is its capacity to resolve a problem in a real life situation. This focus on the world of experience, with its complexity, historicity and dynamism, means that AR distances itself from the then purified world of conventional, social research with its friction-free, perfect information and "others being equal" assumptions that make being an academic easier though at the cost of being irrelevant. AR as a form of research has the following core characteristics:

- AR is context bound and addresses real-life problems holistically.
- AR is inquiry through which participants and researchers co-generate knowledge using collaborative communicative processes.
- AR treats the diversity of experiences and capacities within the local group as an opportunity for the enrichment of the research-action process.
- The meanings constructed in the inquiry process lead to social action or these reflections on actions lead to the construction of new meanings.
- The credibility-validity of AF knowledge is measured according to whether actions that arise from it solve problems (workability) and increase participants' control over their own situations.

The focus of the inquiry is determined by what the participants consider important, what affects their daily lives. The inquiry process is thus linked to actions taken to provide a solution to the problem being examined. This leads us onto so-called "action learning" and indeed "action science".

16.3.2 The Scientific Dimension

Action Science and Organisational Learning

The Israeli organisational psychologist Victor Friedman provides three definitions of "action science" (8) at the outset:

Action Science: Three Definitions
"The action scientist is an interventionist who seeks both to promote learning in the client system and to contribute to general knowledge." (Chris Argyris, 1985)
"An action science would concern itself with situations of uniqueness, uncertainty and instability which do not lend themselves to the application of theories and techniques derived fro science in the mode of technical rationality. It would aim at developing themes from which, in these sots of situations, practitioners may construct theories and methods of their own." (Donald Schon, 1988)
"Action science focuses on creating conditions of collaborative inquiry in which people in organisations function as co-researchers rather than as subjects." (Argyris & Schon, 1996)

Action science attempts to address the widening gap between social science theory and research and social science-based professional practice. Technical rationality, and its positivist foundations, in requiring completeness and precision, produces theories that are too complex for practitioners working in real time. Moreover, phenomenological and interpretive research methods offer a useful approach to practitioners who require theories that explain problems in particular settings and systems of meaning.

The principal architects of AS (action science) and OL (organisational learning) are the American organisational psychologists Chris Argyris and Donald Schon. (13) *A key method in action science is confronting, a process whereby social actors are forced to come to terms explicitly with their own defensive reactions to changes and perceived threats by inquiring into the causes of these reactions and analyzing the consequences of giving in to them.*

But the goals of action science are even more ambitious:

- Inquiring into the variable embedded in the status quo that keep it there;
- Inquiring into the variables involved in changing the status quo and moving toward liberating alternatives;
- Inquiring into the variables in a science of intervention that will be required if the previous propositions are ever to be tested;
- Inquiring into the research methodology that would make change possible and simultaneously produce new knowledge.

In the process "espoused theory" refers to the account actors give for their actions. "Theory-in-use" refers to observer-analyst's inferences about the theory that must underlie the observed actions. Secondly, and of particular relevance to Argyris, *single loop learning refers to a situation where people or organisations alter their behavior but do nothing to change the behavioral strategies that gave rise to the problems faced. By contrast, double loop learning results from responding to a problem by stepping back and examining larger frames in which the problems could be put.* The immediate problem is seen to be the result of a context, which needs to be altered. By altering this context a group can now move on to organisational learning. Action science, moreover, generally views the persistence of single-loop learning as the product of defensive reactions.

For Greenwood and Levin then, *action science takes a very narrow cut of the complexities of human psychology*, even though they welcome its analysis of motivation and behavior. They criticize that *human psychology, as relevant to action, is reduced to the production of defense routines leading to single loop outcomes. The richness of human motivations, the complex interactions between cultural ideas and the economics and politics of certain situations, and the complex differences between all participants in a particular situation, are not explored if the analysis focuses only on defensiveness.*

From Action Science to Communities of Inquiry

Action science involves research in practice rather than research on practice. This involves "communities of practice", that is professionals who share a common "language of practice", that is a set of values, knowledge and procedures. Science, as such, represents a "community of inquiry", whose central activity is the creation of knowledge. Action science then assumes that human beings are theory builders who "construct" theories of reality, which they constantly test through action.

Action science addresses the problem of multiple interpretations by requiring both practitioners and researchers to make their own interpretation processes explicit and open to public testing. Such explicit theories of action can be used to predict behavior. Finally, action science takes a particular interest in intractable problems, helping practitioners to change systems and "transform their world". We now turn to Peter Senge's community action research.

For Peter Senge and Claus-OttoScharmer (9) of the "Society for Organisational Learning" (SOL), industrial age institutions face extraordinary challenges to evolve which are unlikely to be met in isolation. Collaboration and joint knowledge building are vital. Competition, which fuelled the industrial era, must be now tempered by co-operation. Indeed the frenzy for optimal return on financial capital today threatens health and sustainability on all levels, not only of individual institutions but also of their members and indeed the larger social and natural systems in which they are embedded.

Community action research, then, represents an approach to collaborative knowledge creation with which Senge and Scharmer have been involved for a decade. Like action research, it confronts the challenges of producing practical knowledge that is useful to people in the everyday conduct of their lives. But unlike the traditional approach to such, it focuses on fostering relationships, creating settings and leveraging progress:

Community Action Research
• **fostering relationships** and collaboration amongst diverse organisations
• **creating settings** for collective reflection that enable people from different organisations to "see themselves in one another"
• **leveraging progress** in individual organisations through cross-institutional links to sustain transformative changes that would otherwise die out

The purpose, building knowledge for institutional and social change, is why the community exists. Understanding the knowledge-creating process, something Nonaka and Takeuchi have investigated in depth (10) enables everyone to see how their efforts fit in a larger system, involving a continual cycle of creating theory, tools and practical know-how. Especially in times of deep change, sustaining adaptive institutional responses requires better theory, method *and* practical know-how. We now turn to the participatory dimension, lodged more specifically in the "southern" as opposed to "western", "northern" or even "eastern" orientations of action research.

16.4 Global Variations of Action Research

In turning toward the "global variations" of action research, we actually revisit the "southern" grounds of "participatory action research". Though this does obviously overlap with our previous chapter 7, this is the nature and scope of action research, in that its different manifestations (see conclusion to this chapter) are strongly interwoven.

16.4.1 Destabilising Power Relations: Feminism to Cultural Studies

Feminist and participative action research, particularly that in the "south", both seek to unsettle and change the power relations, structures, and mechanisms of the social world. Unsettling such is multifaceted, ranging from redefining power to rethinking the very purposes of knowledge creation. Turning the relationship inside out by promoting the approach of co-researchers in an effort to share or flatten power is at the heart of action research. Feminist scholars, at the same time, often disclose their biases, feelings, choices and multiple identities, clearly locating themselves within the research process. There we get glimpses of how we might each further transform ourselves as action researchers engaged in transforming the world. Finally, the research approach developed in the Black Liberation Movement includes:

- moving beyond traditional methods by
- creating knowledge for the sake of economic, political and social change in the Black community, and
- without forsaking rigorous social investigation.

PAR then, as we saw in chapter 7, becomes a tool to dismantle the master's house, and to achieve social justice. It was also to be used as a building block to build "black" social institutions. Under these circumstances, the role of the "black" social scientist was to be both scholar and social activist. This stance of community members being responsible for building knowledge for the purposes of social equality and organisational change is one of the core values of action research. Co-inquiry emphasizes the research process as an elevating learning experience for all those involved in the research endeavor, stimulating dialogue between researcher and participant in the creation of new knowledge.

16.4.2 Promoting a Liberatory Transition: Towards Vivencia

The year 1970 was the first in a series of turning points for those (mostly in sociology, anthropology, education and theology) who were increasingly preoccupied with life conditions, which appeared unbearable in communities surrounding them. Fals Borda and his colleagues took for granted that these conditions were produced by the spread of capitalism and universalistic modernization which were seen to be destroying the cultural and biophysical texture of rich and diverse social structures dear and well known to them. They just could not be blind or silent when witnessing the collapse of positive values and attitudes towards humankind and nature. This seemed to require a radical critique and reorientation of social theory and practice. Conceptions of Cartesian rationality, dualism and "normal" science were challenged, as they could not find answers from the universities that had formed them professionally. Many therefore broke shackles and left the academies. During the course of 1970 some began to formalize *alternative institutions and processes for solving regional problems involving emancipatory educational, cultural and political processes.*

Soon after 1970 it became clear that the P(A)R crowd were looking for a new conceptual element to guide fieldwork. They wanted to go beyond social psychology (Lewin), Marxism (Lukacs), anarchism (Kropotkin), phenomenology (Husserl) and classical theories of participation (Owen, Rousseau, Mill). They also wanted to respect the critical methodology they had inherited from the hermeneutic philosopher Gadamer, and to remain disciplined researchers. At the same time they wanted to link such thoughts with their experiences in the field. Recognizing that knowledge was socially constructed, rather than objective truth, they postulated that the main criterion should be to obtain knowledge that would be useful for dealing with worthy causes. As such, the rebel, the heretic, the indigenous and common folk may prove to be more significant than themselves. Discussing then the evasive problem of purpose in science and knowledge, they went back to Newton's operational rationality and Descartes' instrumental reason, oriented towards controlling nature, since labeled "scientism". On the other hand, Bacon and Galileo were more ready to acknowledge the role of practice and community to explain the functions of everyday life. Indeed popular knowledge has always been a source of formal learning. Overall though, *it was felt that science was in need of a moral conscience, and reason needed to be enriched with sentiment and feeling.*

Rejecting the academic tradition of doing research to promote academic advancement, they had to "de-colonise their minds". Their praxis-inspired commitment sought after role models such as Paulo Freire, Mahatma Ghandi and Julius Nyerere, seeking to theorize and obtain knowledge enriched through direct involvement and social action. Moreover, they followed Francis Bacon's original guidelines (1607): truth is revealed and established more through the testimony of actions than through logic or even observation". They had to consider, then, researcher and researched both as real "thinking-feeling persons" whose diverse views on the shared life experience had to be taken into account. In fact, if applied in earnest, *such a participatory philosophy could produce social/collective transformations* between them. New "reference groups" were formed with grassroots leaders. Hard core data was combined with imaginative, literary and artistic interpretations.

In learning to develop an authentic attitude toward others, which was called *vivencia,* meaning entering into the other's life experience (Husserl's life world), it became easy to listen to discourses coming from diverse origins. Participatory research, at an international conference in 1977, was defined as "vivencia" necessary for the achievement of progress and democracy, thereby becoming not only a research methodology but also a philosophy of life that would convert its practitioners into thinking-feeling-persons.

16.4.3 Liberationist Perspectives and the New Paradigm

The overall objective then was to use the knowledge gained to understand better, change and re-enchant our plural world. For Immanuel Wallerstein – founder of the World Systems group in America – the "two modernities" were those of technology and liberation, Fals Borda's orientation being towards the latter rather than the former. Thus to the Marxist orientation towards praxis is added the Aristotelean "phonesis", that is the pursuit of judgment and wisdom for the achievement of the good life. The two-pronged *commitment to liberation and service* then undergrids PAR lifestyle and practice. *It is not only a quest for knowledge, but also a transformation of individual and communal attitudes and values, personality and culture, an altruistic process:* the construction of a practical and morally satisfying paradigm for the social sciences to make them congruent with the ideal of service, especially in the South of the world, combining ethics and praxis, academic knowledge and popular wisdom, the rational and existential.

For Fals Borda this is the most overarching challenge we face. We have moved together from 18th and 19th century participatory and utopian theories to the threshold of another set of theories on chaos, complexity and postmodern liberation. This has been done with guidance from intellectual and political giants. Now alert philosophers of action, eloquent postmodernists and critical theorists have taken this story on, with a view to liberating peoples who are under the heel of oppressive power systems. *The need now is to construct an altruistic ethos for heterogeneous forms of cultures, times, spaces and peoples; that however implies a worldwide effort to combine political, economic and intellectual resources from North and South, East and West.* For a while, our concern for knowledge, power and justice and their relationships grew independently in our respective regions. In the final analysis, the effect of P(A)R work carries a liberating, political accent world-wide. The rising universal brotherhood of critical intellectuals tends to construct open pluralist societies in which oppressive central powers, the economy of exploitation, monopolies and the unjust distribution of wealth, the reign of terror, the dominance of militarism, and the abuse of the natural environment, as well as racism, is proscribed. As we arrive at a new millennium, it would be great to think, Fals Borda proclaims, that *P(A)R will be able to do its share to find better scientific, technical and social ways for improved living conditions, and for the enrichment of human cultures.* We now turn to power and knowledge.

16.4.4 Power as a Relation of Domination

The role of participatory action research is to empower people through the construction of their own knowledge, in a process of action and reflection, or "conscientization", to use Freire's terms. Lack of empowerment occurs for several reasons. First there is the argument that the positivist methods distances those whose "stuffy reality" (expertise) *is* disconnected from those who experience knowledge through their own lived subjectivity. Second there is the argument that traditional methods of research – especially surveys and questionnaires – may reinforce the passivity of powerless groups, quantitative forms of knowing, moreover, reducing the complexity of human experience. Third, there is the critique that dominant knowledge marginalizes other forms of knowing. PAR on the other hand, recognizing that knowledge is socially constructed, allows for social, collective analysis of life experience. Participative research makes claims to challenge power relations in each of its dimensions through addressing the needs for knowledge, action and consciousness:

Participative Research: Challenging Power Relations in Three Dimensions

Knowledge ⟹ as a resource which affects decisions

Action ⟹ which looks at who is involved in the production of knowledge

Consciousness ⟹ how the production of knowledge changes the worldview of those involved

---

One of the most important contributions of PAR to empowerment and social change is in the knowledge dimension. Through a more open and democratic process, new categories of knowledge, based on local realities, are framed and given voice.

However, relatively powerless groups may merely speak in ways that echo the voices of the powerful. Treating situated representations as facts serves to characterize positivism. Actually, to fulfill its liberating potential, PAR must surface and reinforce alternative forms and categories of knowledge, which may not at first appear. Such knowledge must be embedded, moreover, in cycles of action and reflection. In other words, a process of critical consciousness needs to ensue. Ultimately, developing and using new forms of participatory knowledge on a large scale, as the World Bank has begun to do, thereby promoting and using new forms of participatory democracy, involves ordinary citizens in using their knowledge and experience to construct a more just and equitable society. At a time when inequality between rich and poor is greater then ever before, the challenges of going to broader scale with PAR are enormous, but so also are the risks of failing to do so.

16.4.5 Research of the People, by the People, for the People

PAR then is research of the people, by the people, for the people. The more obvious purpose of such is to bring about changes by improving the material circumstances of affected people. To this end, people engage in different kinds of activity: inquiring into the nature of a problem to solve it by understanding its causes and meanings; getting together by organising themselves as community units; and mobilizing themselves for action by raising their awareness of what should be done on moral and political grounds. For the first of these objectives, the inquiry makes use of conventional methods, additionally facilitated by art and theatre, oral history, music and dance, to reveal the more submerged and difficult-to-articulate aspects of the issues involved. In all cases, however, group processes play an important role. Dialogue, in particular, looms large, whereby participants can share experiences and information, create common meanings, and forge concerted actions together. Overall then, the kind of knowledge that the research generates needs to produce technically useful results while at the same time strengthening community ties and heightening transformational potential through critical consciousness.

To demonstrate the effect of action research, that is a continual cycling between action and reflection, between theory and practice, we introduce here the case story of Cashbuild. We will learn how through a painful and protracted, but ultimately fruitful and proactive, process of action research, Koopman and Cashbuild had been inching their way towards an industrial democracy. While such a focus on industrial democracy, as in the Mondragon case, is a feature of socio-technical design, the pre-emphasis in the Cashbuild case is upon the successive processes of action and reflection, experimentation and observation, deployed "scientifically" by Cashbuild's former CEO Albert Koopman.

16.5 Action Research in Practice: The Cashbuild Case

What happened at Cashbuild in South Africa resonates with the views of action researchers Greenwood and Levin: "Institutionally based action research is framed as a democratic process supporting the creation of knowledge that potentially can be liberating. Obviously then, the inquiry process has to aim to solve problems important to the organisational participants, and the knowledge produced by the inquiry process must increase participants' control over their own situations. This is consistent with Freire's "conscientization", which identifies the inquiry process as one shaping knowledge relevant to action, as well as being built on a critical understanding of the historical and political contexts within which the participants act." (11)

Cashbuild, the South African retailer of building material, was turned – at least for a period of two decades from the mid 1980's to early part of the twenty first century – into an African industrial democracy, as well into a successful business, by the redoubtable Albert Koopman. (12) All this happened in the most turbulent time in South Afria's recent history. We shall present Cashbuild's story in Koopman's own words.

The Cashbuild Story

"I was raised as a street fighter. My mother died when I was 13 and my father lived in Mozambique, 1240 miles from me. Set free at a very early age I had to learn to survive. That meant dealing with people, including people who had hang-ups, and people who wanted to do me in for what I believed. The one thing that I learnt as a result was that I was going to enter my life as a clean, moral fighter, someone who sterilised his bicycle chains before he entered the fight of interpersonal relationships. Unlike the animals with claws and teeth, God gave me his supreme gifts; choice and intellect. Making use of these two gifts, I was able to meaningfully observe, and speculate in different ways, upon my fellow man going about his daily activities. From this I acquired my moral purpose. The story you are about to hear is one of my personal experience in an African context, through my involvement as the Chief Executive of a Cash and Carry Building Material Merchant in South Africa. It is a story of success and many failures, a story of victories and sadnesses in my attempt to create an excellent company, to put it mildly, in a somewhat turbulent society. It is the story of how a white (northern) man in Africa became a White African (southern). It is the story of how I combined the rationality of the First World with the humanity of the Third."

Cashbuild was started as a wholesaler in 1978 and became a very successful business in a short space of time. Situated predominantly in the rural areas of South Africa and focusing on the black housing market, our staff complement consisted of 84% black, 13% white and 3% Indian. However, by mid 1982, with 12 outlets, profits started sliding. Everything "northern" was in place – systems, procedures, technology, combined with a booming market – but something was going wrong and Koopman did not know enough about the south, at that point, to recognise where to start looking.

"We embraced our cardinal principles of giving value to our customers, being innovative, adaptable, and totally committed to the business as well as having efficient organisational structures, but obviously something was changing and we did not know what it was. Our hierarchy was well displayed on the walls of all our outlets, everyone was placed in neat little boxes with prescribed job descriptions and functions, and no one was achieving our objectives as had been laid out! I came to the conclusion that we had a lot of trained men but no actual committed soldiers."

"It was clear that our organisational structure was autocratic, as was my own personal management style. We had to change, but how? What if people started seeing me as soft, when I became more participative and democratic? What about the chaos that might occur during the period of transition? Well there was no other way to do it at the time but by MBFA – Managing by Fumbling Around. There was no alternative but to plunge in at the deep end and to risk my neck and possibly be forced to say "I'm sorry" for my original way of doing things. I immediately commissioned an attitude survey and found that pro-company feelings, to the tune of 89% in 1980, had slipped to 74% in 1982." (13)

Arising out of 3,000 issues that came to Cashbuild's attention through the brainstorming sessions, Koopman drew up a set of cardinal principles emerging out of the interdependent relationships that existed between customer, employee, company, competitor and motivation. He realised, at the same time that the "northern" principles would have to embrace the "southern" spirit of every employee, so they were spelled out as follows:

- "We recognise that the marketing process of getting goods from supplier to customer is the concern of every employee and that we have to liberate him/her to achieve this"

- "We want to strive for quality service through people and keep our system as balanced as possible through on-the-job training, motivation through better supervision, self measurement and statistical control rather than boss control, giving people a say over their workplace"

- "We recognise that quality service and total productivity will only come if we rediscover the spirit of man within the workplace, providing job enrichment by changing the work people do."

- "People need to belong to and identify with the company's cause; customers must be satisfied through committed people."

No stone was left unturned and over a period of one year Koopman listened to why people worked, with whom they preferred to work, and what they saw would be the design of the perfect workplace. After spending extended periods of time living amongst his black employees, experiencing life within their communities, and consulting with them directly, he found he had to review his whole understanding of the people he employed, as well as how they saw their relationship with the business and with its philosophy. The degree to which aspects of indigenous "southern" culture were to become "spiritualised" in the workplace was to depend on the type of "northern" organisation imposed upon the individual, including the degree to which the organisation would allow expression of these elements.

"We had to turn our thinking about people upside down and look at our business totally differently. The perception of capitalist exploitation at Cashbuild had to be changed. This change needed to be achieved not merely through some superficial "western" programme of empowerment, but through an active "northern" restructuring of the hierarchy, to liberate the work ethic. We had to design an organisation that was truly free so that the co-operation between all individuals became its own sustainable social form." (14)

Koopman needed a social form that could accommodate the freedom to be enterprising, as well as harnessing the spiritual consciousness of all the employees. His CARE philosophy was "Cashbuild's Aspirations with Regard to Excellence". In essence the CARE philosophy sought to bring about a balancing of power within the organisation. At that stage, in 1982, authority was vested with management (but no power) and power with the unions (but no authority). Firstly, we built in mechanisms for the protection of individual rights vis-à-vis the organisation, through a "northern" code of conduct. Secondly, CARE groups were formed to give expression to the "southern" spiritual consciousness of individuals, serving as a vehicle for discussion of issues affecting their working life. Groups were formed at five levels – general labourers, semi-skilled personnel, junior, middle and senior managers – each with their own majority elected president. Thirdly, these groups were to engage with the economic process, sharing information about efficiency and productivity, and learning about as well as influencing the company's wealth creating process. A CARE philosophy designed by the people for the people spelled out how our workplace should be regulated, and set out the rules of the business game. Some of the salient points were:

- a commitment to joint decision making at all levels, with everyone playing their part in finding solutions to problems

- an open and free culture with everyone in the organisation having access to any line manager

- a team consisting of different races, sexes and cultural creeds, none of which were to be discriminated against

As such, Cashbuild became a fully-fledged industrial democracy and remained such for some fifteen years, till the first decade of the twenty first century.

"This was our company. It was proposed that a governing body of five people be constituted to each outlet – the VENTURECOM – with each person being democratically elected to hold a portfolio, save for the manager who was appointed to the operations portfolio, based on his or her expertise. This portfolio was concerned with the "hard" variables whereas the Safety, Labour, Merchandise and Quality of Work-Life portfolios were the "soft" ones. Moreover, each of these managers was continually assessed by lower levels in the hierarchy. The subsequent newspaper headlines – "Cashbuild – the company where workers have the right to dismiss their managers" – frightened the hell out of the capitalist fraternity. Yet precisely because that right existed within the workforce we never needed to use it. In fact, this Cashbuild VENTURECOM system was socialistic in that it reinstated distributive justice and offered security against destitution. It was likewise capitalistic to the extent that individual expression was given its due reward, and group development its due recognition. Our system thus gave expression to the work ethic and also to the enterprising spirit of people." (15)

This process of action research took place through several years of trial and error, action and research; it remained in place for several years after Albert Koopman left the company, in the latter part of the 1990's, and when it was run by his own protégé. But when the protégé in turn left, that was the end of the democratic Cashbuild story, and since 2005 it has reverted to classically undemocratic business type. Agency and structure, leadership and organisation, in other words, go hand in hand. We are now ready to conclude.

16.6 Conclusion

We find it remarkable that action research, as a whole, while a strong research movement in its own right, is so often cut off from the mainstream of research method and methodology. Its limiting factor, perhaps, is that this "western" approach to action research retains a somewhat analytic – albeit combined with action – orientation. In other words, it lacks some of the dynamic and transformative elements associated with innovation, and thereby needs to be supported by the origination, foundation and emancipation brought to bear upon the integral nature and scope of each research path. Actually, all too often, action research is considered in isolation of these. With Integral Research we sought to overcome exactly this isolation; indeed we have moved from isolation to integration.

Each of our four research paths, as we have now seen, has ended with its own particular variation of action research, illustrating a particular southern, eastern, northern or western flavour. Invariably though, the four approaches to action research overlap. In some respects, they are not easy to distinguish. Their closeness to each other underlines the "integrated dimension" of layer four of Integral Research. That is one of the reasons why this fourth layer is called "integration". Not only does it serve to integrate the three layers that came before (origination, foundation and emancipation), vertically as it were, it is also horizontally integrative so to speak, in that the four approaches to action research have close links to each other. That is also the reason, why we re-introduced southern PAR as a global variation in this western chapter on action research. The following table gives a concluding overview on the action research territory:

SOCIAL INNOVATION TERRITORY					
Forms of Action Reseach	Core Exponents	Level	Type of Transformation	Contribution to Integal Social Innovation	
Participatory Action Research / Appreciative Inquiry	Fals Borda (Columbia) / Cooperider (USA)	Communal	Social Transformation	Provides Underlying Grounds	SOUTH
Co-operative Inquiry / Participative Spirituality	Heron (UK)	Trans-personal	Spiritual Growth	Source of Emergence	EAST
Knowledge Creation / Socio-Technical Design	Gustavsen (Norway)	Organi-sational	Industrial Democracy	Provides Navigation	NORTH
Action Science	Revans / Argyris / Schon (USA)	Individual	Action Learning	Ultimate Transformative Effect	WEST

Figure 16.5: Social Innovation Territory

As we have seen and in very simplistic terms, action research is a very "broad church". In fact, it may even be considered too broad, as it incorporates:

- participative action research (our southern grounding)
- co-operative inquiry (our eastern emergence)
- socio-technical design (our northern navigation)
- action learning and action science (our western effect)

all under one "action research" roof. However, we have choosen it as our penultimate chapter. Integrally crafted action research has a highly integrative and innovative nature and scope. To the extent that it serves to integrate the research layers that come vertically before and to the extent that it is open to the full span of action research, horizontally, it serves to release the full GENE-ius of Social Innovation. Such is demonstrated by the following concluding graph.

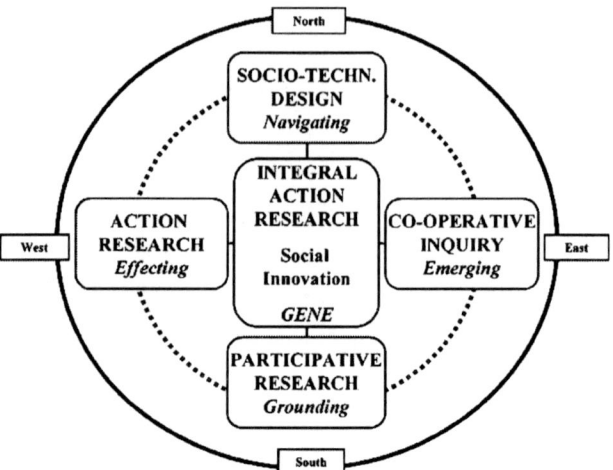

Figure 16.6: Action Research leading to Social Innovation

We are now ready to draw together the threads of our integral research argument. For this, we invite you to a journey into the Middle East, following the (research) paths of Oman's remarkable Sultan Quaboos.

Bibliography

1) **Reason**, P. & **Bradbury**, H. (2004). *Handbook of Action Research*. London: Sage.

2) **Cooperider**, D. & **Whitmore**, D. (2005). *Appreciative Inquiry*. San Francisco: Berrett Koehler.

3) **Reason**, P. & **Bradbury**, H. (2004). *Handbook of Action Research*. London: Sage.

4) **Reason**, P. & **Bradbury**, H. (2004). *Handbook of Action Research*. London: Sage.

5) **Heron**, J. (2006). *Participative Research*. San Francisco: Lulu Press.

6) **Greenwood**, D. et al (2007). *Introduction to Action Researc*. London: Sage.

7) **Revans**, R. (1999). *The ABC of Action Learning*. London: Mike Pedlar Library.

8) **Reason**, P. & **Bradbury**, H. (2004). *Handbook of Action Research*. London: Sage.

9) **Greenwood**, D. et al (2007). *Introduction to Action Researc*. London: Sage.

10) **Nonaka**, I. & **Takeuchi**, H. (1995). *The Knowledge Creating Company*. Oxford: Oxford University Press.

11) **Greenwood**, D. & **Levin**, M. (2007). *Introduction to Action Research*. London: Sage.

12) **Koopman**, A. (1991). *Trans-cultural Management*. Oxford: Blackwell.

13) **Koopman**, A. (1991). *Trans-cultural Management*. Oxford: Blackwell.

14) **Koopman**, A. (1991). *Trans-cultural Management*. Oxford: Blackwell.

15) **Koopman**, A. (1991). *Trans-cultural Management*. Oxford: Blackwell.

INTEGRAL RESEARCH

PART C:

Conclusion: The Social Innovator

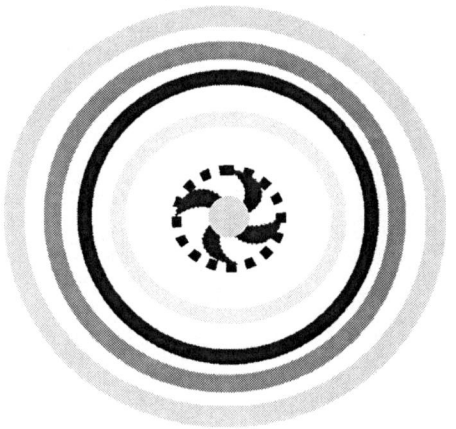

CHAPTER 17

INTEGRAL RESEARCH
TO SOCIAL INNOVATION

"AN INTEGRAL SOCIAL INNOVATION:
THE STORY OF OMAN AND ITS SULTAN QABOOS"

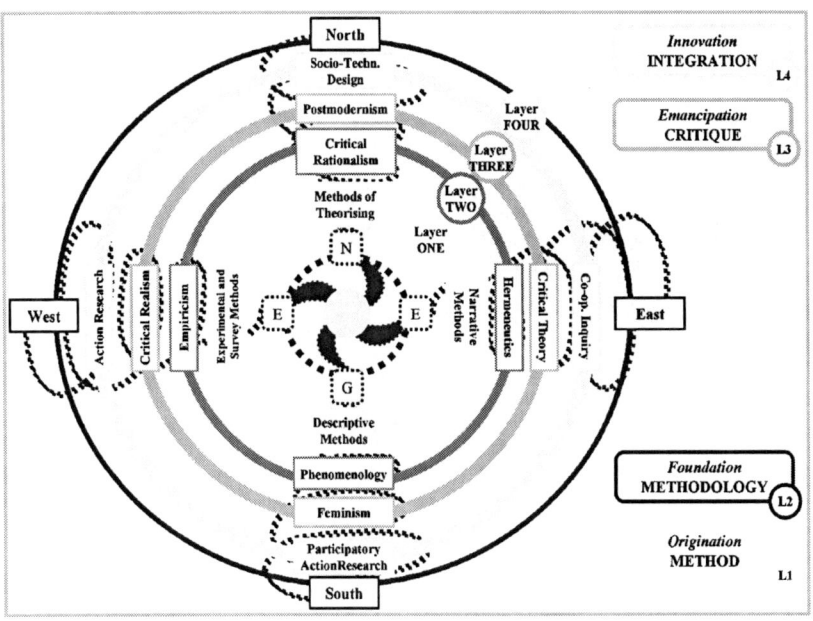

Figure 17.1: Overview Chapter 17– Integral Research (Full Architecture)

17.1 Introduction: The Integral Case of Oman and its Sultan

In this concluding chapter we want to attempt a creative synthesis of all four of our paths to integral research, and, in the process, serve to illustrate what the process of social innovation is like. In fact the very term *integral*, that we have used in this book as the keynote of our research approach, serves to promote a creative synthesis. As we have indicated in the opening chapter, such a synthesis lies, for the African philosopher Ali Mazrui, at the heart of an evolving civilization. For us, such a synthesis embodies social innovation, contextualized within a particular society.

The society we shall be choosing, perhaps surprisingly for illustration, is that of Oman, situated at the geographical crossroads between the Arabian Peninsula, Africa and Asia. Materially and spiritually in close contact with the South and the East, Oman has also drawn on the North and West, most particular on Europe. In fact, over the course of the last 37 years, there has been a veritable social and economic transformation in the whole of Oman, spearheaded by the remarkable Sultan Qaboos bin Said, who ascended to the throne in 1970.

Sayyed Qaboos
bin Sa'id Al Bu Sa'id
(* 1940)
Sultan of Oman

Figure 17.2: Qaboos, Sultan of Oman

Qaboos bin Sa'id Al Bu Sa'id

Social innovation involves following a particular research and development path that is authentic to your self, your institution and your society. Such authenticity, as will be exemplified through Sultan Qaboos of Oman, is born out of:

- *local roots:* being true to your own culture: local identity
- *global reach:* simultaneously reaching out to others: global integrity
- *integral research:* origination, foundation, emancipation, innovation
- *social innovation:* connecting up local roots, global reach and integral research

along a primarily southern relational path, as well as paths of eastern renewal, northern reason and western realisation, culminating in an integral combination of the four paths.

As we will see, Qaboos not only pursued an integral (combined) path, societally, but also remained true to his unique self (Sultan Qaboos) and to his royal dynasty (Said al Said), drawing on the formative influences of those who had come before. In reaching out to others, he has drawn institutionally upon specifically English influences, but he has generally immersed himself in the music of all spheres: Arabic and Asian, African and European. We shall now review how he has pursued an integral research path, thereby fusing together local Qaboosi-Said-Omani roots (one world), global reach (four worlds) and integral research (fourfold trajectory) into social innovation. We invite you as a researcher-and-innovator, simultaneously, to re-view your self, organisation and society, and to chart your own integral research path – south, east, north, west – accordingly. Though your own trajectory may not be as grand as that of Qaboos, he serves as a kind of benchmark.

17.2 Relational Research: Grounding Innovation

17.2.1 Southern (Humanistic): Towards the Relational

Our first relational trajectory extends from a descriptive phase to an ultimately participatory process. When fused with individual and institutional orientation, it ultimately leads to social innovation.

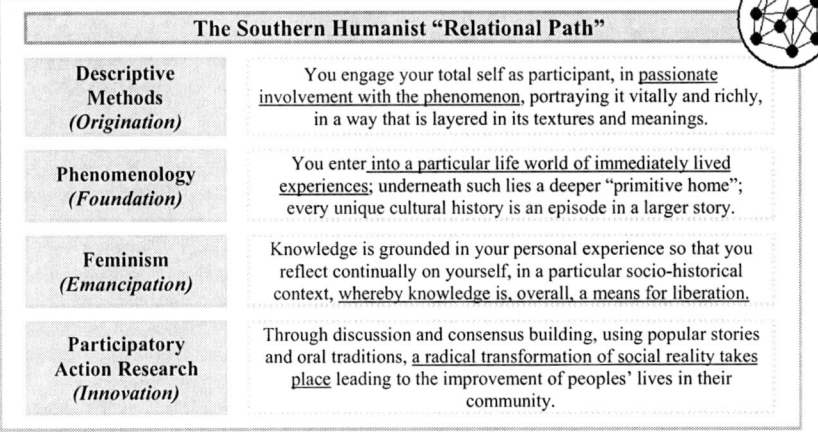

The Southern Humanist "Relational Path"	
Descriptive Methods *(Origination)*	You engage your total self as participant, in passionate involvement with the phenomenon, portraying it vitally and richly, in a way that is layered in its textures and meanings.
Phenomenology *(Foundation)*	You enter into a particular life world of immediately lived experiences; underneath such lies a deeper "primitive home"; every unique cultural history is an episode in a larger story.
Feminism *(Emancipation)*	Knowledge is grounded in your personal experience so that you reflect continually on yourself, in a particular socio-historical context, whereby knowledge is, overall, a means for liberation.
Participatory Action Research *(Innovation)*	Through discussion and consensus building, using popular stories and oral traditions, a radical transformation of social reality takes place leading to the improvement of peoples' lives in their community.

Figure 17.3: The Southern Humanist "Relational Path"

We now turn from humanistically oriented integral research, to the process of social innovation that individually, organisationally and societally ensues, through Sultan Qaboos, the Said dynasty, the nature of Oman and Omani society, drawing altogether on Serghey Plekhanov's marvelous biography of "The Reformer on the Throne" (1). We start from a relational perspective, and then continue with the dialogical, reasonable and realisable perspective, making an appropriate Omani illustration.

17.2.2 Descriptive: Sultan Qaboos of Oman

On 18 November, 1940, the then Omani Sultan's wife, Miyzun bin Ahmed Alma'ashani gave birth to a son Qaboos. As he grew up and learnt to read and write, one of the first questions to arouse the curiosity of the young Sayyid was why his country was named Oman. Arab cultures had long since merged with the black tribes there, creating a strange world that spoke Swahili and danced to torrid African rhythms. Oman also had a large contingent of Balochi peoples. Balochi speakers live mainly in an area now composed of parts of southeastern Iran and southwestern Pakistan that was once the historic region of Balochistan. They also live in Central Asia (near Merv, Turkmenistan) and southwestern Afghanistan.

17.2.3 Phenomenological: Omani Life World – Human and More-than-Human

Qaboos loved exploring the geography of his Oman. One of his chief pleasures was to study books and maps, traveling in his imagination from Omani town to town. Stories about different parts of Oman enthralled him as much as history lessons. He was naturally drawn to the ordinary Omani people. Whilst encounters with those of the royal entourage were predictable and therefore lacking much interest, his encounters with desert dwellers, fishermen and merchants were far more rewarding. He was avid to learn about his people and the country and quickly realised that these were the best teachers. The fragmentary information that Sultan Qaboos received in his first years at school and during his meetings with peoples of different nations and tribes gradually coalesced into an attractive, but incomplete picture of his country. He needed to look at the detail, at the entire sweep of Oman's history and at the nation's place in the world. So the heir began to study his country more thoroughly, supervised by a talented tutor chosen by his father.

Oman is a land that is at once beautiful and mysterious. Its beauty is bound up in a collage of towering mountain ranges, highlands, regions rendered fertile by intricate water systems, and deserts. Oman's coastline is touched by four seas – the Gulf, the Arabia Sea, the Gulf of Oman, and the Indian Ocean. A richly diverse terrain is captured vividly in Oman's mountain ranges with their jagged and angry profiles, rocks that are folded and pleated like some exotic garment, rock faces that are veritable interwoven tapestries of multi-coloured minerals, or cascades of mountains and hills that dissolve into the distant horizon in rhythmic undulation. The changing hue of the mountains as dawn progresses to dusk adds a further dimension to the beauteous vista of Oman. Such beauty is not skin deep because these richly diverse features have profound geological significance to the discerning eye of the geologist. It is here that the sense of mystery lies as the secrets of the earth's formation and subsequent evolution with time are gradually revealed in this singular hub of geological activity. Indeed it is a geological wonder of the world with features that are unparalleled in their composition, formation and accessibility.

Aside from his love of the exploration of nature, Qaboos was also engaged with the spirit of his Omani place, that is with the spirit of Islam.

17.2.4 Feminist: Passionate Engagement – Spiritual Fulcrum

Thoughts about life, about relations between people, and ultimately with God, began to interest the royal child at an early age. Among the many books he read, a collection of Shakespeare's tragedies compiled by an Arab writer impressed him most. He was already reaching out from the local to the global, albeit in this specifically English context. Having learnt to read at five, the future Sultan enjoyed immersing himself in a complex world of human passions. But the most important book that the heir to the throne discovered for himself was the Holy Qur'an. At every stage of his life it has been his spiritual fulcrum. For Qaboos, reaching out to God, and to the people and nature that surrounded him were one and the same thing, a unified field or "tawheed" as it were.

17.2.5 Participatory: Giving People a Voice in their Destiny

Qaboos' great predecessor, Said bin Sultan (1806 to1856), realised that the state could only be strengthened by enlarging the base of political power. He therefore created the Sultan's Council which included representatives of different classes. When he ascended to the throne Sultan Qaboos started his tours around the country, lasting several weeks, inaugurating consultations with local people from all walks of life. The former Said bin Sultan, well aware of the fact that in an autocracy the real power belongs to those who have access to the ruler, decided to make himself as accessible as possible. In the 30 years of his rule, the current Sultan has elaborated his own ceremonious annual "meet the people" tours, making the event a holiday for all concerned. On the outskirts of desert settlements or in the villages of the foothills, camps are organised. At a distance, under the shade of acacia trees, groups of people sit all day in the hope of seeing the Sultan. One by one people approach the ruler. He listens carefully, occasionally asking questions of a minister or an assistant. Many of his decisions or decrees have been formulated after such meetings.

The meetings end with a recital by local poets or tales of the glories of the homeland. Sometimes small festivities follow; the sound of flutes and drums fill the air and men sing songs of battle from long ago. During these trips the Sultan usually visits three of the eight provinces, passing a week or two at each location. Ministers and dignitaries visit the neighboring villages and nomadic encampments, asking people what they need, sometimes remedying complaints on the spot, sometimes initiating more complex solutions through discussions with local officials. Many projects involving both the ministries and Muscat have been the result of such discussions. For Qaboos:

"To fail to give one's people a voice in their destiny, to regard them as automatons for only to be directed and not consulted, is a sure way to disaster. This has never been the Omani way, and I have every intention of ensuring that this popular form of participation is further developed to the benefit of my people and country."

Indeed the call of destiny, if you like the journey from being to becoming, from descriptive to narrative, from the essence of Omani life to its essential meaning and purpose over time, has been all-important to Qaboos. In that respect he needed to turn from a passionate individual immersion in his people and his land, together with the collective and participatory process that accompanied it, to the making of effective history, in the terms used by Tsenay Serequeberhan (see chapter 8). In fact, he was a man marked out by destiny, as we shall see, right from the start.

17.3 The Research Path of Renewal: Emerging Innovation

17.3.1 Eastern (Holistic): Towards Renewal

The second renewal based research trajectory extends from the narrative to the co-operative, from "the stories we are" to a process of co-operative inquiry.

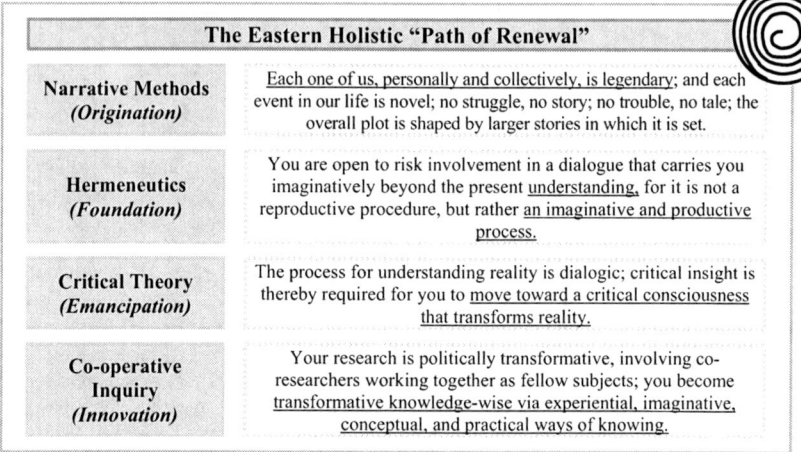

Figure 17.4: The Eastern Holistic "Path of Renewal"

We now turn from theory to practice, and from the research path of renewal to Qaboos' pursuit of his destiny, that of his royal dynasty, and of his Omani society.

17.3.2 Opening Narrative: Local Identity

The Beauty of Calligraphy

The young Sultan to be had been christened "Qaboos", a rare name in the Arab world, and the title of Sayyid (his Highness) indicated his unique destiny as a future ruler of his people. In his early years he was brought up in the green south of the country, in a place called, melodically, Salalah.

The library at the palace in Salalah holds a large collection of books, some of great antiquity. The beauty of the calligraphy in those ancient books is in itself an aid to contemplation, and it would have been natural for the young Sayyid to gaze at the exquisite characters and long to understand their meaning. As his understanding developed, the very first lines of each *"sura"*, or verse from the Qur'an, arranged so carefully, would have captured his attention with their concepts of singular wisdom.

However, he was not only to draw on this longstanding, spiritual and historical tradition, but also on the more immediate dynasty from which he hailed.

The Rise and Fall of a Dynasty

Most modern historians agree on 1744 as the date of the birth of the dynasty from which Qaboos was descended, with the investiture of Ahmed bin Said (1744 to 1784). This was the fifth dynasty since the beginning of the Islamic period, the previous five having faded out, through failing to curb the tribal element in Oman. For the young Qaboos, the figure of his great ancestor was of particular importance. Though separated by two centuries they had much in common. For Ahmed, like Qaboos, came to power after many years of administrative decay. Devastation and misery surrounded both of them.

To restore the dignity of Oman, as Ahmed realised, the people's faith in the possibility of renewal also had to be restored. It was a difficult period that called for a leader with well-developed foresight and the ability to recognize potential allies, while remaining prepared to confront mighty states when necessary. From a country unable to protect itself, over a period of 40 years, Oman during that period of renewal became a powerful state. The one crucial matter that Ahmed overlooked, though, was the matter of succession. So the seven sons of the founder of the dynasty were drawn into internal conflicts, until Said bin Sultan came to power.

Once the young Sayyid Qaboos had learned the fundamentals of the dynasty history, he began to focus on the achievements of his second great ancestor (1806 to 1856), in particular his transformation of Oman into one of the great states of the Indian ocean. He studied all the facets of Said bin Sultan's political life, because, from an early age, he dreamed of matching his 19th century ancestor's great triumphs. As he explored the character and policies of his two great ancestors, he found that both had a capacity to dream, and a passionate desire to realise their dreams, combined with a more than common intelligence and competence. When Said bin Sultan died on board of the *Victoria* en route from Muscat to Zanzibar, which had become his second home, his empire was flourishing. Who could have thought that not many years after his death not even a trace would be left of that glory and that the Omani empire would be once more driven by war and revolt.

We now return to Qaboos' own life story, and to the relentless pursuit of meaning, and understanding, that has characterized it, and the ultimate search for renewal, for both himself and his people, that ultimately has accompanied it. We start out from his youth, with a fusion of horizons, in his case Omani and English.

17.3.3 Hermeneutic – Interpretive: Local-Global Reach

Fusion of Horizons: Suffolk and Salalah

For century after century the sun had shone relentlessly on the Arab land. When Qaboos bin Said arrived in cool and misty London the sensitive young man was overwhelmed by contrasts. Everything aroused a burning interest – the climate, the vegetation, the buildings, the people, the vehicles. His father, Sultan Said bin Taimur, had chosen the county of Suffolk as the place for his son to begin his studies abroad.

Looking through the window of his room at boarding school, seeing the tiled roofs of the ancient town, the gothic needle of the cathedral church rising into the overcast sky, it was difficult to wrest his imagination from this serene little world in contrast to the sun-baked lands of the Middle East.

In his years at Bury St Edmunds Qaboos became accustomed to Western culture. The very atmosphere of the venerable town, named after the shrine if the last king of the east of England, inspired him to plunge into the world of ancient English lore and architectural antiquities. Bury has a glorious history, epitomized in the town's motto: "A king's shrine is the cradle of the law". Qaboos was also fascinated by photography and took his camera everywhere, trying to capture the remarkable places and scenes. As his horizons widened, he grew to realise that to confine his interest to the affairs of the homeland and the Arab world was not only politically naïve, but impossible to one who had grasped the fact that all these events were links of the same chain.

Over the years, the bond between mother and son grew stronger and relations with his father cooled. In fact his father's fear of change made him suspicious and distrustful. The unstable political situation in and around Oman altered Said bin Tamur's character. He felt an outsider in the world, where new leaders were drowning him out. Time after time, Arab countries blocked his attempts to enter international organisations. His reactionary image, indeed, was to a great extent the creation of his opponents, whose condemnation of the Sultan's regime, combined with a refusal to recognize their own deeply reactionary nature, ensured his progressive withdrawal and distrust of intellectuals. Such conditions induced political paralysis.

Sandhurst to Sibelius: Music of the Spheres

In the autumn of 1960, Qaboos was sent to Sandhurst, the UK's pre-eminent military training establishment. After lessons in the classroom and the parade ground, or after several hours in the library, Qaboos liked to sit alone in his room and daydream, listening to music. One of his favorite pieces was Händel's "Water Music".

He felt that Händel's music identified the unchanging essence at the heart of British culture, something sensed by Händel in 1717, and by Qaboos now. Songs and melodies from many native lands found a place at Sandhurst, and commanders and teachers made no class distinctions amongst their cadets, whether British or foreign. When he completed his training at Sandhurst, Quaboos chose to broaden his European exposure by taking up a post with the British army in Germany.

Music of the Different Spheres: Art and Culture

Qaboos was accustomed to learning things thoroughly, so he was not satisfied with a superficial acquaintance with Germany and its culture. He admired the compositions of Bach and Brahms, but although music can communicate the emotions of the soul across cultures and languages, Qaboos recognized the necessity of learning at least elementary German if he was to gain a political understanding of the country.

After his stay in Germany, he proceeded onto a three-month world trip. He was overwhelmed with enthusiasm and reverence for the power and originality of ancient cultures. He photographed ancient monuments and ruins, trying to imagine scenes of modern life against this background. He continued to be attracted by a combination of art and culture. Then it was time to return to Oman.

17.3.4 Critical Theory: Critical Reflection with a View to Liberation

Not Born to Labour over Folios

After his experiences in England and in other progressive countries it was difficult for Sayyid Qaboos to adjust to the confined atmosphere of a huge family ruled by a form of extreme paternalism. The whole of Oman was the family and the Sultan, his father, was the stern paterfamilias. All subjects were considered as children under his personal supervision. Moreover, in December 1963, the independence of Zanzibar was proclaimed, black nationalists ousted the last Sultan there, and an atrocious massacre ensued, resulting in the death of some 20,000 Arabs. Sayyid Qaboos' return to Oman coincided with the Zanzibar tragedy, and he constantly thought about the destiny of monarchy in the modern world: is it capable of resisting extremist forces armed, not only with guns, but also with populist slogans of equality and prosperity.

Said bin Taimur meanwhile expressed the wish that Qaboos studies more thoroughly the history of Oman and Islamic theology. If initially this may have seemed reasonable as a means of familiarizing the heir to the throne with native traditions and culture, after his long years in the West, as the years passed, and as the father yielded no authority to his son, Qaboos became increasingly frustrated. Mulling over various events in the history of Oman, he came to the conclusion that most successful Imams and Sultans did not follow the well-beaten and conservative path, but instead progressively accelerated their country's all round development.

At the same time, laying out on a carpet giant photographs of Qur'anic texts that had been made to his order in the Cambridge University library, the Sayyid studied, the works of ancient calligraphers and assiduously read explanations by Islamic theologians. He was overwhelmed with ideas and it seemed that time was passing away fruitlessly like water running through the fingers. Several hundred miles away, new life in the Gulf was in ferment – new towns were being created, roads were being built, huge aeroplanes were taking off from brand-new airports. But Oman seemed unable to shake off the country's drowsiness.

While the heir venerated the works of Muslim scholars of previous ages, he was not born to labour over folios. He loved his country, and could not understand why his father did not give him at least a minor role in government. Though Qaboos was now 25 years old, he had never seen the capital city, Muscat, and did not really know the country he would probably have to lead. So he spent the long hours available to him, pouring over books on history and theology interspersed with long walks by the ocean.

Music relieved the heir's monotony a little, and he was attracted to the lute. The West learned about the lute from the Arabs in the time of the Crusaders. Sayyid Qaboos not only played famous melodies, he often improvised, trying to express his moods and thoughts. In effect under house arrest, Qaboos was vigilantly watched by palace guards. Had it not been for his mother, who regularly smuggled "The Times", concealed in her clothes, into her son's rooms, the future ruler would have remained ignorant of world events. But times, toward the end of the 1960's, were about to change.

A Time for Change

During his first audience with Brigadier John Graham, appointed at the beginning of 1970 as the commander of the Sultan's Armed Forces, Said bin Taimur spoke apprehensively of the "wicked and dangerous" Dofaris in the south of Oman, who had to be "eliminated". Having learned of the state of the armed forces, the Englishman concluded that they were too weak to subdue the guerillas. In any case, Graham considered Taimur's proposed tactics as uncongenial and counterproductive. He had no desire to conduct a war of extermination, seeing quite clearly that an enemy armed with fanatic devotion to an aggressive ideology can only be defeated by political means. It was in that context that the British played their part in promoting regime change in Oman. And Qaboos, while having spent many years immersed in his country's culture and history, was prepared to take over command from his increasingly disinterested father.

17.3.5 Co-operative Inquiry: Seeking Unity and Brotherhood

Oman rapidly found out about the changes that had taken place on July 23, 1970: the young Sultan's declaration spread through the country at the speed of lightening:

"My first act will be the immediate abolition of all the unnecessary restrictions on your daily lives. My people, I will proceed without delay to transform your life into a prosperous one with a bright future. Every one of you must play your part toward this goal. Our country in the past was famous and strong. If we work in unity and cooperation, we will regenerate that glorious past and we will take our rightful place in the world. We hope that this day will mark the beginning of a new age and a great future for us all. The government and the people are one body. If one of its limbs fails to do its duty, the other parts of the body will suffer. We hope that you will think well of us and at the same time we hope that we shall think well of you."

The sense of brotherhood and unity in those heady days was so unusual that everyone wondered whether this could possibly be true. The Sultan called on expatriate Omanis to return, and an amnesty was proclaimed for all who had taken arms against the old regime.

In the journey the new Sultan took around the interior of Oman, he found a way of addressing his subjects that later, as we have already seen, acquired the importance of a major rite. His annual tours around different provinces would enable the Sultan to renew his acquaintance with practically all of the authoritative people in Oman. His own authoritative stance was born out of the royal dynasty of which he was a part, the historical analysis he had conducted of his most authoritative predecessors, his military training at Sandhurst, and the overall analytical prowess Qaboos had acquired.

Qaboos had spent many years studying the spiritual heritage and history of Oman. He knew his country deeply, but all his knowledge was filtered as though by a screen through which no more than a glimpse of the present actuality could be seen, and through which he was completely invisible to his people. Now his country was lying open before him, and he, too, was no longer hidden from view. The world tour that Qaboos had undertaken before may have broadened his mind, but his tour around his own country tapped deep into his soul. It was that mixture of heart and soul, with body and mind, which would serve to build up the Sultan's creative synthesis, experientially and imaginatively, theoretically and practically, which in turn would serve to re-form Oman, politically and economically, educationally and spiritually. But such dynamic re-formation also required the evolution and establishment of new structures and norms, to provide the country with a enduring stability.

17.4 Research Path of Reason: Navigating Innovation

17.4.1 Northern (Rational): Towards Reason

We now turn from the humanistic and the holistic, that is from the relational and the dialogical, to the rational, or what we call the path of reason. It is at that point that the southern and eastern orientation, which has characterized our phenomenological and interpretive research so far, changes its tune, and becomes more rational and northern in its focus. In fact, and as we will see in Qaboos' case, he turns from his aesthetic and historical inclinations to pursuing a more militaristic and managerial approach to command and control, actively, and to theory and analysis, reflectively.

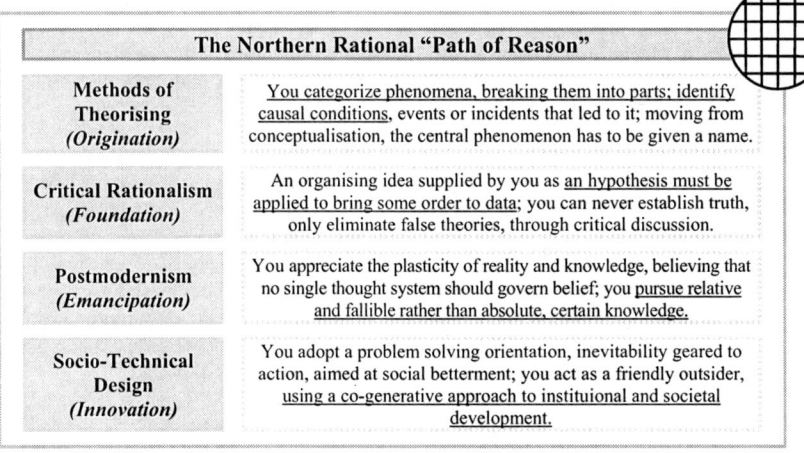

The Northern Rational "Path of Reason"	
Methods of Theorising *(Origination)*	You categorize phenomena, breaking them into parts; identify causal conditions, events or incidents that led to it; moving from conceptualisation, the central phenomenon has to be given a name.
Critical Rationalism *(Foundation)*	An organising idea supplied by you as an hypothesis must be applied to bring some order to data; you can never establish truth, only eliminate false theories, through critical discussion.
Postmodernism *(Emancipation)*	You appreciate the plasticity of reality and knowledge, believing that no single thought system should govern belief; you pursue relative and fallible rather than absolute, certain knowledge.
Socio-Technical Design *(Innovation)*	You adopt a problem solving orientation, inevitability geared to action, aimed at social betterment; you act as a friendly outsider, using a co-generative approach to instituional and societal development.

Figure 17.5: The Northern Rational "Path of Reason"

Indeed, the Omani Sultan is most unusual in being able to combine these diverse attributes, that is the relational, the dialogical and now the reasonable, in his own uniquely creative synthesis, building on his unique individual, institutional and societal attributes, entering centre stage in Oman in 1970.

17.4.2 Theory: The Monarch as Mirror to the People

As quoted by Plekhanov, in his book on the Sultan, for Sultan Qaboos a monarch is a mirror. He stated to a journalist:

"He reflects his people's history and culture. They can understand their collective identity much better through him. He must always understand them, inform himself of their needs. He should do this in their interest before they ask him to. Young people get bored with old kings. They think they know better, so the system cannot stand still. It must improve all the time and you must never allow cracks to develop."

To go about such task, mindfully as well as spiritually, requires inner discipline and outer structure, as well as drawing purposefully upon the "best practices" or relevant others, for all of which Qaboos was well prepared, in order to ultimately get things right.

From the moment he had entered Sandhurst in the 1960's, he had had to forget everything he had been accustomed to since childhood – the deference and privilege – and learn the formative art of submission itself, or indeed self-discipline. Related to such was another important lesson he acquired, that of self-control. After Sandhurst, Qaboos could have left for his homeland right away, but he preferred to put his knowledge into practice, and, like the majority of graduates, received orders for active service in the British army. The only difference between Qaboos and his fellow students is that he was allowed to choose where he would serve. He purposefully chose the Scottish Cameroonian regiment, because of its long standing traditions, and established regimental structures and formalities, as one of the oldest regiments in the British army, then based in Germany.

Back to Oman, in distant if not recent history, it seemed initially strange for the young Qaboos, that Sultan Said made no attempt to seize territories and create a colonial Empire, similar to those of the Europeans. The Arab settlements, which stretched in a loose chain from Oman to Mozambique, had long been centres of Arab culture and trade, magnets for the African interior. Relations between them had been based on mutual advantage, and not on dominance and submission. In fact, the submission with which Qaboos had become acquainted was something different, a submission in the form of inner self-discipline. Outer directed discipline, for Qaboos, was related more to knowledge than to control, in this case knowledge of administration.

In fact, Qaboos had spent a whole year in Hampshire, in England, studying the details of local government administration. He studied government institutions, took a course in management, and visited factories, banks and company boards of directors. He was already forming an idea of what was required to transform Oman into a modern state.

Pride in his native land's history did not blind Sayyid Qaboos to the misery into which Oman had fallen after a century of decay. He was well aware of the dismal statistics, which showed the Sultanate lying near the bottom of the world table in education and public health. By the end of 1964 he had completed the programme of preparation, in England, for state management. This was to come in handy, six years later, once he had returned to Oman, and assumed power as Sultan in a new government.

17.4.3 Critical Rationalism: Building an Omani Style Democracy

Invoking Consensus and Debate

Every day, immediately after he assumed power, Qaboos faced new problems in need of urgent attention. His father had led the state into deep crisis, and it was difficult at times to decide which problem was the most pressing. On top of all the internal problems, the country had to break into the international arena to re-establish itself in the diplomatic field. Qaboos invited representatives of many other countries to come and visit Oman in order to see the country and establish relations on an equal footing. The first attempt to carry out the monarch's overall plans was the creation of a Provisional Consultative Council, born in effect out of the prior research Qaboos had conducted, especially into the life and work of Said bin Sultan.

Many things written about the times of Sayyid Said are strikingly topical. His statecraft, similar to that of most of the leaders of the developed countries in the mid-twentieth century, seemed to Sayyid Qaboos to provide a suitable template for transforming Oman into a significant power once again: what he saw around him seemed backward when compared to the conditions that prevailed during the great epoch of the great Sultan. He admired particularly the Sultan's dedication to the principle of direct and frequent consultation with his people. Despite commanding a rich and powerful state, he appeared to Qaboos to have been neither arrogant nor despotic. Representatives of the population gathered in his palaces on Fridays and Mondays and his espousal of democratic freedoms made him extremely popular with his subjects, as did the interest he took in their personal affairs. At the same time Qaboos had to establish a new administration.

In 1970, heads were appointed for the ministries of Internal Affairs, Justice, Religious Endowments, Health, Education, Labour and Social Insurance, and Information. He reserved for himself the portfolios of defence, oil and finance. An acute shortage of qualified personnel was an obstacle to the creation of new government bodies and to the realisation of large-scale projects. The high rate of illness and disability was evident everywhere, and most people were illiterate. Oman's infant mortality rate was one of the highest in he world. Of the many Omanis that had received their education abroad, almost none had returned. When Qaboos called for their return, the response was enthusiastic. The difficulty of the transformation, though, was that it had to be undertaken with such urgency, and that everything had to be done simultaneously.

Take your Natural Place in Service

Moreover, by the time the change of power had occurred in 1970, pro-communist insurgents has seized most of the southern province and had even set up their own authoritative bodies in some parts. Qaboos set his government the target of defeating the rebels where they were strongest. Literacy, medical services and technical advances had to come to the mountains of Dhofar, from Muscat and Salahlah. It was important to oppose the brainwashing of the tribes with real improvements in their lives.

In November 1970, Qaboos received the first group of "jebali" – people of the mountain – who had defected to the government. When five guerrillas arrived, the

Sultan came out to meet them wearing a simple "dishdasha". They were pleased to see that the ruler, who was their age, was indicating he was just a Dhofari, as they were. In true "*jebali*-style", he had a thick black beard, and he addressed them in their native language. Subsequent meetings between the Sultan and the people were a powerful impulse for altering the psychological climate in Dhofar. Unlike his predecessor, who had confined himself to the palace for the last four years of his reign, the young ruler was keen to hear his subjects' troubles at first hand.

The Sultan's message also sought to warn the *jebalis* against what the communists really stood for. One of the leaflets dropped from aeroplanes in 1971 told the people of Dhofar:

"The communists do not serve your interests. The communists are your worst enemies, do not let them deceive you. Pay heed, my brother, to what the communists have said and done. The communist says, "there is no God, no Creator". The communists do not recognize the Prophet Mohammad and other prophets of God. There is no place for rights among the communists, my brother. You are their fuel and their slaves. Link up with your brothers and take your natural place in service of your government and your country."

Eliminating Poverty and Inequality

The establishment of schools, the building of roads, and the organisation of basic trade on the tribe's own land gradually neutralized the communist propaganda. As the zones controlled by the government troops grew larger, so did the scale of development. That having been said, by 1971, every family in Oman had lost someone in the war. One could not talk of modernizing the country while its lifeblood was draining away. Hence, Qaboos had to search for an immediate settlement to the conflict. The Sultan therefore approached the Shah of Iran for help and a Special Forces battalion arrived in early 1973. By early 1975 they had taken the rebel capital, the port village of Bakhyut, supported by the Sultan's fleet. A ceasefire was declared in December of that year. For the first time in many years there was peace in the Dhofar region.

The Dhofar campaign proved the efficacy of a strategy, which recognized and tackled the underlying causes of all political unrest, thereby pursuing a reasonable or well reasoned, as opposed to a vengeful, course of research and action. The Sultan's emphasis on eliminating the poverty and inequality, which had hitherto allowed revolutionary ideas to gain a foothold, were crucial to the subsequent military successes. His attention to the material and spiritual well-being of his people allied to his comprehensive modernization of the state's infrastructure ensured a loyalty based on appreciation rather than the fear which ideological revolutions are bound to provoke. In other words, Qaboos operated under the assumption, or hypothesis, that the communist insurgence had taken place in a poverty stricken setting, which has called for a desperate response, and he had to therefore remove those endemic sources of conflict. But that was a short-term strategy. The long term called for something else.

17.4.4 Postmodernism: Mutually assured Diversity

Tradition, Modernity and Trans-Modernity

The war in Dhofar was an enormous drain on the country's finances, with military expenditure accounting for more than 40% of the country's budget. The overarching task faced by Sultan Qaboos during the first years of transformation was the social and economic development of the country. From the outset, Sultan Qaboos took the view that the build of the country's infrastructure and knowledge base was of primary importance.

The period that began in Oman in 1970 might be called "nahda" or renaissance. This term describes very accurately the essence of what happened – the country returned to, and built upon, its former flourishing state. And this meant that the political authorities had to overcome the overwhelming stagnation into which the country had sunk not only because of external circumstances, but also because of the century-long conflict between the traditionalist tribes and the enlightened central powers. In other words, there had to be a break with the tribal-laden, traditional past, towards a modern, or even trans-modern future. For given the fact that Oman was made up of Balochis and Swahilis, as well as native Omanis, not to mention the expatriate populations, in terms used by the contemporary Islamic scholar Ziauddin Sardar in his "Islam, Postmodernism and Other Futures":

"Trans-modernism is all about listening, in the context of mutually assured diversity, to diverse worlds; realising that local identity as a cultural context is as much work in progress in traditional societies as in western ones. Such mutually assured unity-in-diversity, then, is founded on the proposition that all identities have futures, and that their futures are most assured in mutual association. That local identity is then the cultural attitude to speak a better future, fashioned out of all the possibilities and predicaments offered by the contemporary times and circumstances, and in the light of histories that shape these circumstances. What is diverse is the means, institutions and social forms of delivering unifying values. To arrive at mutually assured unity-in-diversity requires learning to see not only the debates, knowledge and distinctness of various different cultures but to see how within them common values and commensurate ideas are enacted in radically different ways." (2)

Promoting "Ilm Laden Education"

A great merit of Qaboos bin Said's approach was his respectful attitude toward the customs and culture of all of the peoples in the country. In the absence of a "spiritual infrastructure" the reforms could not have had a solid base. For Qaboos:

"Each country goes through periods of progress and decline. We had to find a way of renewal, but funds from the sale of oil alone could not do that. Education is a key to success. It is not an end in itself; it is a means, first of all to self-knowledge. Without education people cannot distinguish good from evil, cannot take care of themselves."

As such, he was only too aware of the role that knowledge had played in the heyday of Muslim societies, in the ninth to fourteenth centuries. In Islam, the pursuit of knowledge is acknowledged as a basic, God-given, human instinct. It fulfils the person in his/her quest for truth and confers greater insight into the workings of nature, thereby strengthening the relationship between man and God. The much quoted aphorism, "for even knowledge itself is power", first articulated by Frances Bacon, was implicit in the earliest teachings of Islam. It was given practical expression in the establishment of schools, academies, libraries and observatories in the main Islamic centres of learning throughout the world.

Knowledge by its nature, for McBrierty and Al Zubair in their recent book on "Oman: Ancient Civilization, Modern Nation", has always been global with the responsibility for its creation, preservation, and dissemination, ebbing and flowing between nations and cultures over the centuries. In this regard, the universities as creators and interpreters of new knowledge could claim with some justification to be the first global communications network. During Europe's dark ages between the eighth and twelfth centuries the Islamic world carried the torch of knowledge and kept the concept of universities alive, having earlier acquired and subsequently enriched the ancient learning from the Greeks and Romans. As noted by Altbach:

"The wisdom of the Greeks and Romans was saved in the libraries of the Islamic world, used by Arab scholars during the European Dark Ages and later returned to Europe ... These are some of the elements of the international knowledge system as it has evolved over the centuries and as it exists today." (3)

Muslims were equally innovative in the transformation of new knowledge into technology, in medieval times up to about 1500. Thus today, Muslims are actively encouraged to inquire into the world around them, but they are also required to exercise responsibility in the use of new knowledge, to promote the well being of humankind as a whole.

17.4.5 Socio-Technical Design: Design for Evolution

From Technology to Humanity

For Irish academic Vincent McBrierty and the former President of Sultan Qaboos University Mohammad Al Zubair, the emerging knowledge era, in the world at large, can be divided into four eras, Oman being well equipped, under Qaboos' leadership, to enter into the fourth one. For them, the knowledge economy, at the dawn of the twenty first century, has been shaped by a series of transitions from:

- an initial embryonic phase characterized by the unprecedented generation of new knowledge,
- to a phase dominated by information and communications technology
- onto a transformation phase in which virtually every sector of society is affected,
- and currently to a phase in which the wider and humanistic implications of new knowledge are coming ever more sharply into focus.

In other words, there is an ever-increasing realisation that the march of technology cannot continue unabated without a much greater concern for the more social, ecological and humanistic aspects of economic growth. The long-term future of economies depends upon more sophisticated, broad-based strategies that include not only a renewed respect for ethics, but also culture, tradition and preservation of the environment. For Qaboos then, from the 1970's onwards, the literacy programme and the establishment of schools, and ultimately universities, turned out to be not only the basic ingredients of Oman's development, but also important steps toward reforming the country's political system. The monarch was convinced that without education all attempts at liberalization would degenerate into anarchy – only informed subjects can consciously participate in the rebuilding of society. Even before the realisation of the first development projects, schools and centres of adult literacy were created throughout the country. In 1982, by decree of the Sultan, construction began on Oman's first university. In four years, a piece of desert was replaced by a magnificent campus.

Given a new Lease of Life

Another top priority for Oman had been the creation of a modern health service. Omanis have literally and metaphorically been given a new lease of life – the average lifespan in Oman nowadays is 72 years, whereas 30 years ago it was a mere 50 years. Every major facility built in Oman in the first years of Qaboos bin Said's rule caused a revolution in some sphere of life: an international airport in Seeb in 1973; a television station in Muscat in 1974; power stations and desalination plants; modern roads connecting the capital with the other cities. All this swiftly and dramatically changed a lifestyle established over centuries.

Many Third World countries experienced social instability connected with the sudden influx of petro-dollars. Nigeria, Iran and Indonesia, all of whom received colossal revenues from oil, have also received monumental social crises. These, and others, including some Arab countries, have been plagued by leaders whose megalomaniac plans to build gargantuan armies led them to squander the nation's wealth on military adventures. For such leaders the Omani proverb "His name is renowned, but his stomach is hungry" is a fitting epitaph. Only stable political leadership and a clear programme of action can make money work for the benefit of the nation and prevent the unhappy side effects of sudden riches.

The Past brought into the Future

The Sultan thought it necessary to involve the people in the country's reconstruction. But from the beginning he realised that the traditional system of government, with its reliance on the tribal structure, should not be totally demolished. It was his opinion that everything that was valuable from the past ought to be brought into the future. Therefore, Qaboos reassured the tribal sheikhs that they were an essential part of the country's future. As far as the monarchy as a political institution was concerned, he had no doubt that it was absolutely essential – Oman could not survive without it. It was, however, clear to him that flexibility and efficiency must be an integral part of the role he had taken over from his father if Oman was to be protected from the unrest that threatened to envelop it.

Qaboos was very conscious of the fact that the promise of uncompromising progress without any accompanying action poses the danger of stirring up violent political extremism even amongst those engaged in the process of attempting to bring about such a development. The people of Oman had to see, and be involved in, actively implementing change for such a catastrophe to be averted. When Sultan Qaboos took the first steps to create modern management structures, the administrative system, organised into "wilayats", was retained without significant changes. They were headed by "walis", who in turn relied on tribal chiefs. Later, while making modifications to such procedures in forming local authorities, he was careful to preserve their basis. The role of the "walis" was that of working with sheikhs and explaining to them the particulars of governmental plans.

Drawing out the creative Potential of traditional Structures

In contrast to the reformers of many other countries, Qaboos always aimed to draw out the creative potential of the traditional structures, whose roots reach deep into the past. Over the past quarter of a century, numerous laws and codes defining relations in the economic and social spheres have been adopted. And although "shari'a" has remained the foundation of Omani legislation, the promulgation of what has been termed Basic Law has completed the creation of the legislative system. Such a Law bestowed by the Sultan defines the fundamental principles of state policy, and also the system of forming authoritative institutions. For the first time in the nation's history, the Sultan's prerogatives, as well as the mechanisms for the functioning of the monarchy and for the transfer of power are underlined.

The activity of the supreme ruler has therefore become subject to legislative regulation; thus, obligations to the country have been codified. The rights of citizens to privacy, to possess property and to express their opinions are legally established; everyone is guaranteed religious freedom and the right to create organisations or associations and participate in them. It would not be an exaggeration to say that this document is the cornerstone on which Omani society and the Oman state is built. Such a Basic Law therefore plays a consolidating role: it does not weaken the monarchy but reinforces it. It removes the monarchy from the ambit of tradition and the minutiae of law, while keeping it at the centre of the political structure.

Shura: From Consultation to Democracy

In 1982 the Sultan promulgated a decree establishing the State Consultative Council (SCC = "Majalis al-Astishari") made up of 17 members representing the "wilayats", 17 state officials and 11 members from the private sector. In his speech to them he said:

"While we entrust your Council with the duty of giving opinions and advice, it should also be the framework for a joint effort between government and public sectors for studying the aims and dimensions of our development plans, the priorities fixed for their projects and the obstacles which stand in the way of implementing these plans, and suitable solutions for them."

The membership of the SCC was completely replaced every two years. Its members made many tours of the country, meeting the *walis* and other representatives of the people, a strategy, which permitted an objective analysis of the government's actions and an evaluation of the efficiency of the development programme. The Council has also become a kind of school of politics for the subjects of Sultan Qaboos, as television eventually began to broadcast their discussions. In 1991, the SCC was replaced by the Consultative Council ("Majilis al-Shura"). The Islamic principle of "shura" was made the foundation of its activity. The most authoritative people in the Sultanate were permitted to vote for nominees to membership of the Council. Representatives of the government were no longer automatically granted seats on it. Three years later elections for the "Majalis" were held. In a major break with tradition two women entered the chamber of people's representatives for the first time. The Council was enlarged to 80 members.

The third *Majalis al-Dawla* was elected in 1997. For the President of this council:

"The creation of the Majalis al-Dawla is the last phase of building a system of organisation. There was a need for a body that would evaluate the results of the government's activity, that would help the government. Then came the moment for a specialized independent body that would evaluate what had been done over the previous thirty years, to use the positive results for the future and avoid the negative ones. The most prominent, well prepared and well educated representatives of Omani society make up the Council, having worked in all spheres of statecraft: they have been ministers, vice-ministers, ambassadors."

Like the first chamber of the Omani Council, the "Majalis-al-Dawla" has five women members, including a university professor and the editor of a weekly women's magazine, both of whom have considerable experience of working in state and commercial structures and taking part in discussions on political and economic strategy. In no Arab Gulf country to women participate to this extent. The elections of 2000 to "Majalis al-Shura" were conducted by a board of electors, but on the basis of direct voting by the people. Democracy in Oman is based on a long-term strategy, the scope of which is to make the structure of power stable and involve the people in administration. The same kind of partnership approach has applied to Sultan Qaboos' external relations.

Becoming an Integral Part of the Whole World

In the years after Sultan Qaboos came to power he visited most Arab capitals. These visits were the foundation of the Sultanate's transformation from outsider status to that in which it was recognized as being an integral part of the Arab world. In 1973, the country became a member of the non-aligned nations. The Sultan, though at the time in the frontline of the battle against world communism, had a vision of a multi-polar world, which would be based not on rivalry between military-political groups but on multi-lateral partnerships. Already in the 1970's, Arab leaders were experiencing the new ideas and unusual diplomatic style of the ruler of Oman. What may have seemed at first an idiosyncratic style of negotiation turned out to express a sophisticated political view.

The years spent in the southern Omani city of Salalah poring over historical volumes and spiritual treatises had sharpened his perception of history. He saw the need for changes similar to those Said bin Sultan had brought about at the commencement of his rule; the resolve not to be imprisoned by regional conflicts, but to find their resolution within the context of expanding dialogues with partners far and near; the clarity to repudiate stereotypes and the proliferation of empty ceremonies in order to accelerate the processes of rapprochement, reconciliation and collaboration.

Expanding Local-Global Dialogues near and far

The Sultan's longstanding desire to involve the world's leading states in the affairs of the region, reflected his understanding of modern geopolitics as the cultivation of partnership and not rivalry: to link as many countries as possible by common interests meant reducing the possibility of confrontation. The policy of Qaboos regarding the Arab-Israeli settlement has also remained consistent. Oman was one of the first nations to establish economic relations with the Jewish state, and this was where his freedom from ideological blinkers was most apparent. In this sense, the ruler exemplifies the tolerance peculiar to the Omani ruling dynasty founded by the member of a family of merchants, the great Said bin Sultan. Oman moreover, which is a member of the WTO, believes the main trends in the twenty-first century are towards a lessening of the sovereign powers of individual states through economic interdependence.

We now turn, finally, to consider what has been ultimately realised through the process of experimentation in which Qaboos has been engaged over the past thirty-seven years.

17.5 Research Path of Realisation: Effecting Innovation

17.5.1 Western (Pragmatic): Towards Realisation

The experiment that Sultan Qaboos has undertaken has in fact drawn upon prior relational, renewal, and reasoned foundations, so that it has not been realised in a vacuum. In other words, the empirical or indeed "western" orientation is the culmination of what has come humanistically, holistically and rationally before. As such, it represents a creative synthesis of our four worlds. Actually, for contemporary Islamic scholar Ziauddin Sardar the followers of Islam, the Muslims, are designated as the "Middle Community". (4) In Islam, the most significant indicator of man's nobility, besides righteousness, is the use of moderation and balance in his material dealings, reasoned pursuits and spiritual quests. It is by virtue of moderation that *order, proportions, refinement and beauty* are created. These are the aspects that Islam seeks to propagate in its synthesis of three basic aspects of civilization: pragmatism, rationalism, and holism, and we have added to such our fourth category of "southern" holism. By achieving an *organic synthesis* of these aspects, Islam presents a composite picture of what human civilization ought to be. The synthesis of outlooks outlined above produces "a way of knowing" that has access to experience, experiment and observation; rational and intellectual inquiry, as well as meditation and inner reflection. Moreover, it emphasizes diversity *and* interconnectedness.

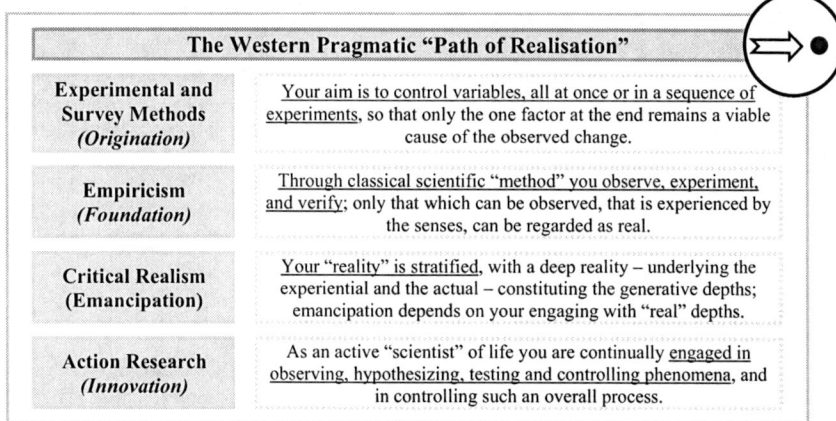

The Western Pragmatic "Path of Realisation"	
Experimental and Survey Methods *(Origination)*	Your aim is to control variables, all at once or in a sequence of experiments, so that only the one factor at the end remains a viable cause of the observed change.
Empiricism *(Foundation)*	Through classical scientific "method" you observe, experiment, and verify; only that which can be observed, that is experienced by the senses, can be regarded as real.
Critical Realism (Emancipation)	Your "reality" is stratified, with a deep reality – underlying the experiential and the actual – constituting the generative depths; emancipation depends on your engaging with "real" depths.
Action Research *(Innovation)*	As an active "scientist" of life you are continually engaged in observing, hypothesizing, testing and controlling phenomena, and in controlling such an overall process.

Figure 17.6: The Western Pragmatic "Path of Realisation"

17.5.2 Experiments: A Process of Experimentation

Husbanding Social, Economic and Natural Resources

Oil has been the basis of economic development in Oman from the very beginning of the Omani renaissance. Having begun in 1967 with average daily production of 300,000 barrels a day, by 2000 the average daily production had risen to over 900,000 barrels. However, in contrast to its neighbours, Oman could never count on massive profits from oil and therefore must husband its resources carefully in order to fulfil its development programme, while promoting a process of continual experimentation, with a view to its economic diversification from its oil and petroleum base. For the time being, the export of oil accounts for about 70% of total revenues. This is a considerable improvement in comparison with the first decade of Oman's renaissance, when dependence on oil was absolute. But before oil runs dry alternative sources of income have to be found. Hopes are high for the gas industry in Oman. One of the world's biggest container ports has been constructed in Salalah, which is situated only 150 miles from the main shipping lanes between the Far East, Europe and America.

Sultan Qaboos, in accordance with his vision of the country's future, aspires to the creation of a true market economy, where the state plays a regulatory role and public citizens become the main agents. The successful launch of a stock exchange in the Muscat Security Market in 1989 shows that conditions in Oman are ripe for the development of financial services. New large-scale projects are being carried out with the support of both domestic and foreign capital. For Qaboos:

"The private sector now, more than at any time in the past, is required to redouble and accelerate its efforts, with confidence, and utilizing all opportunities in promisingly productive avenues ... Consider what happened to certain countries where the citizen depended wholly on the State. These countries collapsed and poverty and instability prevailed. No country in the world can eliminate the role of the individual, nor can the individual depend wholly on the State.

*This is also against the teachings of religion, which recognizes and respects private
ownership and urges the individual to work. When he works, he gains wealth and
gives others a chance to work with him to earn their living. Thus the bounty of God is
well distributed among individuals and societies and thereby increased in their midst.
He who is capable gives a chance to another who is capable, and the latter gets the
opportunity and the means to feed his family so all can benefit."*

Such private initiatives, set within the context of a market economy, albeit embedded
within Oman's public-private-civic orientation, is consistent with an ongoing process
of economic and social experimentation.

The "Omani Velvet Revolution"

Oman, today, is a modern society. And it has avoided the pitfalls of societies, which
have experienced rapid and far-reaching change – especially depersonalisation and
standardization. This is what makes the renaissance initiated by Sultan Qaboos
unique. His personality, his aesthetic inclinations and his loyalty to historic traditions
and religious values have been the most important factors of this velvet revolution. In
the process of renewal, care has been taken not to damage the natural environment.
Hundreds of historic forts, mosques, palaces and public buildings have been
preserved. The modern architecture of Oman also pays the greatest respect to its own
national traditions. However, care for the environment, as Sultan Qaboos has often
stressed, has to be an international, as well as a national concern. In both national and
international cases, the past needed to be brought into the future, via the present.

17.5.3 Empiricism: The Empirical Results

Economic Growth and Economic Development

In a recent publication "Oman Beyond the Oil Horizon: Policies Toward Sustainable
Growth" (4), edited by Ahsan Mansur and Volker Treichel, it has been pointed out
that, with the steady increase in crude oil production and exports and the surge in oil
prices in the mid- and late 1970s, Oman embarked upon an economic development
path that transformed it into a prosperous country. Prudent utilization of oil revenues
to develop social and physical infrastructure, with substantial investments undertaken
in health, transportation, electric power, water supply, and communications,
contributed to a rapid transformation of Oman's economic foundation and structure.
Today Oman boasts an impressive physical infrastructure, much improved socio-
economic conditions, and a high standard of living.

Over the last two decades Oman has recorded one of the highest growth rates in the
Middle Eastern region and in the world. Oman also experienced persistent growth in
non-oil GDP, financial stability, confidence in the economy, and a stable currency,
despite severe external terms-of-trade shocks resulting from sharply lower crude oil
export prices in the 1980s and early 1990s. Real annual growth in the non-oil sector
averaged 7.3% over 1980 to 1997. Domestic inflation, measured in terms of the
consumer price index, averaged 3.8% a year over the same period, supported by the
fixed peg of the Omani Rial to the U.S. dollar, by open trade and payments systems,
and by a prudent stance of monetary policy. Oman's economic gains and growing

private sector confidence and participation in the economy have been reflected in the prosperity and well being of the Omani population in general.

17.5.4 Critical Realism: Underlying Layers

If we look beyond or behind these statistics to uncover the generative forces, which underlie them, we find that, for Sultan Qaboos:

"The observance of our religious and cultural traditions is deeply embedded in the life of our country and our people, and it provides them with a comprehensive reference and guidelines within which to lead their lives – both with respect to religious observance and in their secular activities. Many years ago I told my people that they should be ready to accept what is good from the modern world, but reject those influences from it which are bad; this I feel we have succeeded in doing."

In other words, modernization, including the development of a sound political, economic, educational and communications infrastructure, has been built upon traditional forms, rather than displacing them. This is unique to the Arab world, and with the recent exception of Japan unique in the world generally; it serves to bring about, at least in this specific Omani case, a genuine Arabic renaissance.

17.5.5 Ongoing Action Research

Three decades of the Omani renaissance ("nahdi") have enriched all the elements of society: state structures, the economy, culture, science and education. Every year the health system becomes more comprehensive, the country and its citizens become more closely integrated, with the rest of the world, and all without social unrest. The policy of reconciliation conducted by Sultan Qaboos from the beginning of his reign cut the ground from under the feet of those who dreamt about a violent transformation of the society. Omani society is united, as it never was before. Moreover, the Omani "nahdi" is still work in progress, that is ongoing action research, involving a continual process of hypothesis formation and testing, observation and auditing, through the succession of five years plans that are regularly devised, in consultation with the people.

In the process the historical observations and reflections of the Sultan and his fellow policy makers, leading to the hypotheses Qaboos had formulated, were continually tested in the field, and indeed audited by the consultative assemblies, and open parliaments, that he had constituted. Key to any understanding of the central value of the modern sultanate is recognition of the continuing utility of its age-old traditions, its institutions of power and its cultural manifestations. Oman is one of those rare societies to have accomplished modernization and innovation while maintaining a firm grip on traditional values, built up over an immense period of time.

17.6 Conclusion

17.6.1 The Conductor and his Orchestra

The might of this modern nation is commanded, for Plekhanov, by a man sitting out of sight in his crimson tent. In this austere setting where long ago Imams judged tribal disputes and discussed the finer points of "fikh" (jurisprudence and religious law) with lawmakers, investment projects worth hundreds of millions of dollars are today being considered. They include plans for a large-scale domestic Internet network, the development of modern metallurgical and chemical production, and the laying of a gas pipeline on the bottom of the Indian Ocean.

"Just by seeing and listening to the Sultan in person, you begin to understand the nature of his policies more deeply. He is a personality who brings artistry to everything he touches, from the colourful annual tours around the country to his military and political decisions with their heady combination of swiftness and foresight, their apparent effortlessness reflecting a brilliant analytical mind." For us, such "artistry" is represented in both the humanistic (relational) and the holistic (renewal) approach he adopts to people and to things. Moreover, we would add that Qaboos also has some of the traits of a social scientist, if not also a natural scientist, which come to the fore in the rational (reason) and pragmatic (realisation) approaches that he has taken, over and above the others. In fact, an *integral* approach to the social "sciences" also incorporates the humanities, and hence the arts. In his rare moments of leisure then, Qaboos bin Said reads books on history, politics, science and the art of war, alongside the pursuit of his greatest passion, which is music. He has even established his own classical orchestra in Oman, something unique in the region. Music is almost as important to him as politics:

"I like many European composers, for example Sibelius, Brahms, Bach, Elgar and Olsen. But I also enjoy folk music from different countries and continents – Polish, Rumanian, and Arab melodies. I like the music of Andalucia, Turkish and Iranian music, a lot of Indian and African music. Of course I love music from other African countries, and in particular from the Yemen."

17.6.2 Social Research to Social Innovation

Doctoral and Masters Research of a Transformational Nature

We now come to the conclusion of our book. What we have set out to illustrate is that, just like the build up of a civilization, which requires a creative synthesis between diverse worlds, a mutually assured unity-in-variety, so *integral research*, with a view to social innovation, requires the same of us. That having been said, not all of us is a Sultan Qaboos, so the integral course we have pursued is a more modest one, albeit still modelled on such societal "best practice".

What we have advocated, in your pursuit of doctoral research, is that you select one of the four research paths, and pursue it to the full, that is incorporating method (origination), methodology (foundation), critique (emancipation) and integration (innovation) approaches. In other words, in pursuing such a coherent mix of methods and methodologies across such a trajectory, you do necessarily evolve your approach towards the integral, albeit in relation to a particular worldview.

At the same time, and through our communal approach to research and innovation, we do invite you as individual researchers to cross-fertilize with others, in your research community, each adopting different research paths.

Further, we advocate that each of you chooses one path, but on this occasion focusing on the innovatory end of things – participatory research, co-operative inquiry, socio-technical design or action research. Simultaneously you are taking account of the methods, methodologies and emancipatory critiques that come before. So, for example, in adopting a "western" pragmatic orientation, you would utilize action research, while taking account of experimentation, empiricism and critical realism. We now turn, finally, back to our Omani case in point.

Social Research to Social Innovation

Concluding, it may appear somewhat strange for you as a doctoral or masters "student", that a "success story" in the Arab world, as opposed to one in America or Europe, or even in China or India today, should have been selected as our primary example of social innovation. Some of you might wonder what such a case has to do with your research at a masters, doctoral or post-doctoral level.

Our response to the first question is straightforward. Whereas there are ample examples of technological innovations, most of these coming from the "western" or "northern" worlds, our so-called "social innovations" are very thin on the ground. To the extent that they do exist, in historical form – such as applies for example to the first joint stock company, the first recorded industrial democracy (Robert Owen's Lanark Mills), or the first documented representative parliament – they tend to be institutional forms rather than whole societies. Arguably then, Oman today is one of those very rare instances, in our day and age, of socio-political (societal) innovation.

What then, in our responding to the second question, constitutes such innovation? We would argue, true to our Integral Research, that such innovation involves the relational, renewal, reason and realisation, and the full trajectory from origination to innovation in each case. In the process, we turn research on its head, taking it away from the exclusive realms of the proverbial ivory tower, and bring it, as Sultan Qaboos has done, into the mainstream of society. However, and to the extent that the Sultan has done so, from the point of view of social innovation, it needs to involve the combination of action and reflection, art and science, tradition and modernity, individual and community, that he has deployed.

In the final analysis though, the Omani innovation is still work in progress. Astounding as the Omani example is, there is still room for improvement. Firstly, the family dynamics in the country are still a long way from fusing together tradition and modernity, to the extent that women still remain, all too often despite official policy, second class citizens. Secondly, the economic realm has not received the same transformational treatment as the political one. Thirdly, the much vaunted new Sultan Qaboos University, at least insofar as we are aware, has not embodied in its own research and educational programmes, the overall context to which this chapter has alluded.

That having been said, we find it quite remarkable that this Omani societal innovation has not received more worldly acclaim, in the research community if not amongst the political and economic powers that be. In concluding our own work, we are enormously grateful to be able to incorporate it as an example of social innovation, with its distinctly integral overtones. It is now over to each and all of you, as researchers-and-innovators, to take on from where Qaboos, and the innumerable others examples we have cited, have left off.

Bibliography

1) **Plekhanov**, S. (2004). *The Reformer on the Throne*. London: Trident Press.

2) **Inayatullah**, S. & **Boxwell**, G. (eds.) (2003). *Islam, Postmodernism and Other Futures: A Ziauddin Sardar Reader*. London: Pluto Press.

3) **McBrierty**, V. & **Al Zubair**, M. (2004). *Oman: Ancient Civilization and Modern Nation*. Dublin: Trinity Press.

4) **Sardar**, Z. (1987). *The Future of Muslim Civilization*. London: Mansell.

5) **Mansur**, A. & **Treichel**, V. (eds.) (1999). *Oman Beyond the Oil Horizon: Policies Toward Sustainable Growth*. New York: IMF International Monetary Fond.

EPILOGUE

E U R E K A !

Hiero, when he obtained the regal power in Syracuse, having decreed a crown of gold to be placed in a certain temple to the immortal gods, commanded it to be made of great value, and assigned an appropriate weight of gold to the manufacturer. He, in due time, presented the work to the king, beautifully wrought, and the weight appeared to correspond with that of the gold which had been assigned for it. But a report having been circulated, that some of the gold had been abstracted, and that the deficiency thus caused had been supplied with silver, Hiero was indignant at the fraud, and, unacquainted with the method by which the theft might be detected, requested Archimedes, an ancient Greek mathematician, physicist and engineer, to give it his attention. Charged with this commission, he by chance went to a bath, and perceived that, as his body became immersed, the water ran out of the vessel. Whence, catching at the method to be adopted for the solution of the proposition, he immediately followed it up, leapt out of the vessel in joy, and, returning home naked, cried out with a loud voice that he had found that of which he was in search,
for he continued exclaiming, in Greek, EUREKA! (εὕρηκα)
"I have found it out".

Integral Research in Action

By now you have worked yourself through the full approach to Integral Research, culminating in the astonishing case of Sultan Qaboos of Oman, a true Social Innovator. You are either (hopefully) already pursuing your own social innovation, or feel inspired to follow your (research) path to such.

We, for our part, are working with doctoral researchers from all over the world, engaging with us in Integral Research. The two main applications of Integral Research, which serve as a "test bed for continual transformation" is our masters programme on Social and Economic Transformation, our doctoral programme on Social Innovation, both accredited by the University of Buckingham in the UK, and the Doctor of Ministry Programme of the University of Bethel in St. Paul in Minnesota. While the participants from our masters are based in Southern Africa and the Middle East, those on our own doctoral programme come from all the four worlds. The participants on the US based programme are mainly US Citizens but, true to the American melting pot, embody the four worlds by origination.

In all three cases, the context is exciting, and it is surprising to see how the Integral Research framework and process challenges everybody individually (to fully root his or her social innovation in the very specific life world of the person, its organisation and wider community and society), but also collectively. Embracing the different orientations to research from all over the world, Integral Research is a framework that continuously challenges ones own path and perspective and brings it in creative interaction with others. In the final analysis, it always proved to be fruitful. Referring to Amy Chua, the renowned Chinese Philippine Professor of Law at Yale University in America, who claimed in her famous statement that "the world is on fire". We, together, belief, that Integral Research can contribute to extinguish this fire. It can do so through Social Innovation, which is authentic to specific contexts, and it can do so by bringing the researcher in dialogue with him- or herself and with his or her colleagues. Civilisation, according to Ali Mazrui, the well-known Muslim scholar of African descent, comes out of the creative synthesis between different cultures – and that is exactly what we are trying to foster in our own four-world research community.

Ultimately, in our work, we are seeking to overcome the notion of individual research and enrich it through collective research-and-innovation. What is common practice in the natural sciences, where groups of researchers work together to solve complex problems, is still not common in the world of the social sciences. Still, the ancient prototype of an individual researcher (we are reminded of Faust in his chamber) prevails – a tragedy given the enormous complexity of today's social issues.

From Integral Research to TRANS4M
(From a Framework to an Institution)

One way in which we seek to overcome this "research individualism" is mirrored in how we do research ourselves and in the institution we are building.

This book has not only been developed by the two of us in an intense act of co-creation (and through a synthesis of a south-northern and north-western mind), it has also been tremendously influenced by our colleagues and co-researchers, mainly from the participants of our doctoral programme.

In addition, with TRANS4M we have set up a Four World Center for Social Innovation in Geneva, which is fully dedicated to Social Innovation, determined to lay sound foundations within research and education in the area of Social Innovation. Such foundations shall support masters students, doctoral candidates and post-doctoral researchers to engage in Social Innovation, each of them contributing to an improvement of society, each of them tackling a burning social issue of our time. TRANS4M, however, is not only developing the knowledge base and framework for this to happen; in addition, we are determined to build a community platform that allows researchers to connect and co-create in the most meaningful way.

Learning from Technological Innovation
and inspired by Archimedes

On our way, we learnt from technological innovation and were inspired by Archimedes, one of the great scientist and technological inventors of classical Greece.

What then did we learn from technological innovation? Within the natural sciences, from physics and chemistry to biology and medical science, the practice of innovation is well known. Famous technological innovators like James Watt in England in the 19th century and Thomas Edison in the United States in the 20th are often cited. The Menlo Park Laboratory in New Jersey where Edison and his fellow scientists worked, has gained almost mythical status as a source of prolific innovation. We would be hard pressed, though, to find any such prominent example of a laboratory for social innovation.

Processes of invention and innovation, fundamental research and its application, have not been transferred up to now from the physical to the social arena. Great theorists such as Adam Smith and Karl Marx in economics, Sigmund Freud and Carl-Gustav Jung in psychotherapy, Max Weber and Auguste Comte in sociology, Margaret Mead and Claude Lévi-Strauss in anthropology, not to mention John Locke or Immanuel Kant in philosophy, have not been seen as "inventors" per se. Neither are the more practical innovators, like French engineer Henri Fayol and Austro-American political economist Peter Drucker seen in this light. However, both of them helped to give rise to the practice of management in the last century. To take even more recent examples: a systems theorist like Peter Senge ("The Fifth Discipline") in the US or a sociologist like Ikijiro Nonaka ("The Knowledge Creating Company") in Japan may be seen as highly creative social scientists; however, they are not labelled as social innovators, in the same way as Edison or Watt or, in our case, Archimedes, may have been recognized. Why is that so?

The simple fact is that we do not value social – in the same way as technological – innovation. Could that "undervaluing" be one of the reasons why there are so many intractable social problems in the world? Fact is, that the world's social problems stand in vast contradiction to the impressive technological achievements of our time. Whereas, in the natural sciences, necessity has been identified as "the mother of innovation", the same motto is not applied in the social sciences. The result is that we have all too few social, including economic breakthroughs.

There is a need to rethink the current situation in the social sciences. We need to come up with frameworks and processes that can enhance social innovation. Integral Research aims to contribute to that field. But we also need to build laboratories and ecosystems that provide a nurturing context for social innovations to be bred. With TRANS4M we have set out to build such a laboratory, that provides, together with others, an ecosystemic context for social innovation.

Having learnt, that technological innovation in the natural sciences always follows the full path from fundamental research to application, we asked ourselves, how such a path would look like in the social sciences, pursuing social innovation.

In our search, we were inspired by Archimedes. The accomplished scientist, confronted with a task of high importance, acclaimed in joy "EUREKA" when he finally found the solution. How then could EUREKA be translated into the Social Sciences?

EUREKA!
Walking along the Social Innovation Value Chain

With Archimedes' help (it was indeed a little Eureka for us when we designed this model), we identified a process that is relevant for all true, and fully rooted social innovations. We called this process – surprise, surprise – EUREKA.

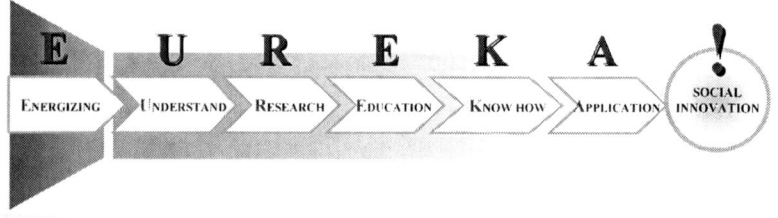

Social Innovation, hence, has six core ingredients:

① **E = Energizing:** A particular issue of concern is "energizing" the Social Innovator-to-be.

② **U = Understanding:** The Researcher reaches deeply into nature and culture to gain a thorough understanding of the true context for social development.

③ **R = Research:** The Researcher now fully recognises and understands the pioneering forces of yesterday and today and is starting to create the new for tomorrow. He or she is now fully immersing in a particular research path, together with co-researchers.

④ **E = Education:** Here, the research findings need to be "processed" so that they can enter the curriculum for education.

⑤ **K = Know How:** At this step a bridge between the theoretical and the practical is built. Applicable know how is created. Here also opportunities to apply a particular Social Innovation are identified.

⑥ **A = Application:** At this step, Social Innovation is brought fully into life. It transforms yourself, organisations and communities.

Integral Research' core domain within the EUREKA Value Chain is the "R". That is where its framework and process are fully applied. However, while our doctoral programmes have a strong focus also on the E and the U as well, the masters Programme, though intimately connected to the E and U and R is by far more application oriented (linking R and E, heading towards A).

All our research focussed programmes start, however, with the E and U. You can only fully immerse in your research and move towards your particular social innovation, once you are deeply in touch with the energizing issue that drives you (E) and with the creative sources of your cultural context (U).

The Social Science Researcher should always have the full value chain in mind. As different steps require different talents, he or she might look for appropriate co-researchers, educators, and practitioners to bring the social innovation fully alive. In that respect the value chain also represents an ecosystem. A social innovation – in order to flourish – needs to be embedded in the six-step value creating ecosystemic process. The notion of the ecosystem brings us finally back to the Social Innovation Tree, which we introduced in chapter 1.

More Fruits to come:
Jointly nurturing the Social Innovation Tree

The Social Innovation Value Chain allows the Integral Researcher to see his or her work in an even larger perspective and to carefully think through, in what way all six steps are taken into account. In that sense, the value chain becomes a quality check for your own research. Indeed, with our masters and doctoral participants we are using the value chain also as a tool for self-reflection and improvement, individually and collectively.

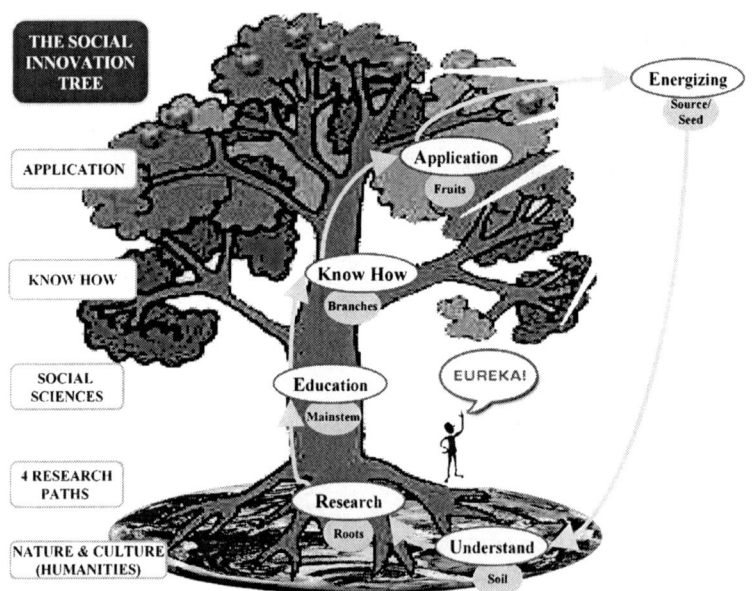

The Social Innovation Tree broadens the perspective once more, in that it shows the positioning of Integral Research as the missing link between the social and cultural context (humanities) and the body of social knowledge of a society (represented by the social sciences). The metaphor of the tree underlines that a social science disconnected from the humanities (its soil) can hardly respond adequately to a specific social context. Further, it is then also unable to contribute to the constant renewal of the society's body of knowledge (the mainstem of the tree), representing the capacity of a society to address its burning social issues.

Integral Research is designed – as roots – to bridge the gap between humanities (soil) and social sciences (mainstem) to further develop applicable know how (branches), resulting in applied social innovations (fruits). However, while establishing an integral research orientation, it seems to us also important to question the traditional perspective on Social Sciences. This is the focus of our current research and we shall soon release a first prototype of a more integral perspective on the social sciences in general.

Looking forward

We are now inviting researchers from all over the world to co-engage with us in Social Innovation. The task is huge, and the journey is long. Integral Research in itself is a process with which you can work, readily and instantly. A separate workbook, to further support your research work, is already available. Through it we will serve to heal the planet, promote peaceful co-evolution, build up open societies, and create economic opportunities, together, locally and globally.

ANNEX

KEY TENETS
OF THE FOUR RESEARCH PATHS

THE SOUTHERN "RELATIONAL PATH" – KEY TENETS

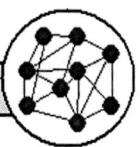

Origination
METHOD — **Descriptive Methods**

- Seek to reveal more fully the essences and meanings of human experience.
- Seek to uncover qualitative and quantitative factors in such experience.
- Engage your total self, in passionate involvement with the phenomenon.
- You do not seek to predict or to determine causal relationships.
- Undertake careful, comprehensive descriptions, vivid and accurate renderings of experience, rather than measurements or ratings.

Foundation
METHODOLOGY — **Phenomenology**

- Engage in a process of radical inquiry.
- Immerse yourself in a life world of immediately lived experiences.
- Concentrate on illuminating the nature of the "inner self".
- Focus on the subjective view of experience.
- Locate every unique cultural history as an episode in the larger story.
- Go beyond reductive positivism and naïve empiricism.

Emancipation
CRITIQUE — **Feminism**

- You aim to create social change.
- You see knowledge as a tool for liberation not domination.
- Feminist research strives to represent human diversity.
- Feminist research complements the androcentric (masculine) perspective.
- As a researcher you as a person are included …
- … and so is nature.

Innovation
INTEGRATION — **Participatory Action Research**

- The problem is defined, analyzed and solved by the community.
- As a scientific methodology, PAR facilitates an authentic analysis of social reality.
- PAR involves the full and active participation of the community.
- PAR is aimed at the exploited, the poor, the oppressed, the marginal.
- PAR creates awareness of the people's own resources, mobilizing for self-reliant development.
- The ultimate goal of the research-and-innovation is the radical transformation of social reality.
- You as researcher/innovator are a committed participant, facilitator and learner in such.

THE EASTERN "PATH OF RENEWAL" – KEY TENETS

Origination
METHOD | **Narrative Methods**

- Your personal, institutional and societal stories are still unfolding.
- Each one of you, personally and collectively, is legendary.
- Each event in your individual and communal lives is therefore novel.
- The narrative mode leads to gripping drama, creative origination.
- Tieing together potentials and possibilities of your respective beginnings.
- No struggle, no story; no trouble, no tale; no ill, no thrill!
- A plot shaped by many of the larger strategy-stories in which it is set.

Foundation
METHODOLOGY | **Hermeneutics**

- Understand how the world is "constructed".
- Give "the other" a voice.
- Interpret reality indirectly.
- Reconstruct self and society.
- Move from spectator to active agent.
- Evolve from interpretive to transformative.
- Reconnect with the source.

Emancipation
CRITIQUE | **Critical Theory**

- As a critical theorist, your research is rooted in concrete experience.
- It arises out of the problems of everyday life.
- Critical theory is strongly emancipatory in orientation.
- Critical theory uncovers power relations.
- You analyse specifically the suffering of people.
- Reality is regarded as socially constructed and multiple interconnections exist.
- Critical theory is explicitly focused on promoting "liberation".

Innovation
INTEGRATION | **Co-operative Inquiry**

- You engage in a politically oriented process, in a participative form of inquiry.
- You are involved in a knowledge-oriented process – epistemic in nature and scope.
- You engage in an alternating current of informative and transformative inquiry.
- You undertake your research in successive action-reflection cycles.
- The validity you seek for your research is goodness, trustworthiness and authenticity.

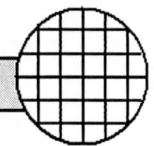

THE NORTHERN "PATH OF REASON" – KEY TENETS

Origination
METHOD

Methods of Theorising

- You regard nature and social life as consisting of essential uniformities.
- It is your aim to discover these uniformities, to find universal statements.
- Observations you undertake make sense when organised by some "conception", an organising idea; you apply hypotheses (theories) to bring some order to data.
- You come to conclusions, engaging in a process of conjecture and refutation.
- In your search for the truth, you cannot establish it, only eliminate what is false.

Foundation
METHODOLOGY

Critical Rationalism

- Empirical science has nothing absolute about it.
- Derive theories from tentative conjectures.
- Falsify rather than verify.
- Strong theory drives out the weak.
- Natural and social science are value neutral.
- You ultimately formulate an overall deductive strategy.

Emancipation
CRITIQUE

Postmodernism

- Pursue multiple discourses.
- Focus on meanings as multiple and shifting.
- You socially construct meaning.
- Every word you use is packed with meaning.
- Use language as cultural representation.
- Focus on transformation.

Innovation
INTEGRATION

Socio-Technical Design

- You adopt a problem solving orientation.
- Your research is inevitably linked to action.
- Your research is geared toward social betterment.
- You use a co-generative approach to organisation development.
- You act as a "friendly outsider".

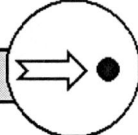

Origination
METHOD — **Experimental and Survey Methods**

- You are able to ask good questions – and to interpret the answers.
- You are a good listener – not trapped by your own ideologies and preconceptions.
- You are adaptable so that newly encountered situations can be seen as opportunities.
- You are having a firm grasp of issues being studied, theoretical or policy oriented.
- You are unbiased by preconceived notions, responsive to contradictory evidence.

Foundation
METHODOLOGY — **Empiricism**

- Search for truth.
- Seek after the "positive facts".
- Separate facts and values.
- Collect observational data and build theories.
- Control the research through "closed systems".

Emancipation
CRITIQUE — **Critical Realism**

- Critical realism is indeed critical of the status quo.
- You become involved with a stratified or layered reality.
- You view such a layered perspective on reality as fallible.
- You conceive reality as both transitive (subjective) and intransitive (objective).
- There is a hermeneutic as well as an empirical side to critical realism.

Innovation
INTEGRATION — **Action Research**

- You start out with appreciative inquiry.
- You challenge power relations.
- You diverge and you converge.
- You undertake social research for social change.
- Knowing *how* is more important than knowing *that*.
- Action research incorporates action learning.

DETAILED CONTENT

Prologue	How can Research be turned into Innovation?

PART A. THE FOUNDATIONS OF SOCIAL INNOVATION

Chapter 1	How to become a Social Innovator?	*Start by connecting to your* *own innovative roots*

| Chapter 4 | The Grounds of Integral Research | *Starting the Research Journey: Method Matters!* |

PART B. THE PATHS TO SOCIAL INNOVATION

The Southern „Relational Path"

Chapter 5	From Descriptive Methods to Phenomenology	*Engage with your Life World*

Chapter 6	From Phenomenology to Feminism	*Uncover Indigenous Knowledge*

The Eastern "Path of Renewal"

Chapter 9	From Hermeneutics to Critical Theory	*Develop a Dialectical Argument*

Chapter 10	From Critical Theory to Co-operative Inquiry	*Uncover Shared Potential*

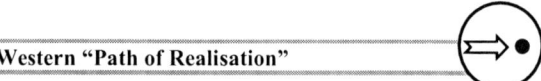

The Western "Path of Realisation"

Chapter 15	From Empiricism to Critical Realism	*Discover Underlying Reality*

Chapter 16	From Critical Realism to Action Research	*Become a Scientist in Action*

PART C. THE SOCIAL INNOVATOR

Chapter 17	Integral Research to Social Innovation	*An integral Social Innovation: The Story of Oman and its Sultan Qaboos*

Epilogue	EUREKA!

ANNEX

Annex	Key Tenets of the Four Research Paths

Printed in the United Kingdom
by Lightning Source UK Ltd.
128744UK00001B/313-342/P